Soldiers
War of the Citizen Soldier

By

Alexander Lopez

PublishAmerica

Baltimore

Softcover 9781462646128
PUBLISHED BY PUBLISHAMERICA, LLLP
www.publishamerica.com
Baltimore

Printed in the United States of America

For

My Parents:
You have always supported me in whatever I've done and have
always been there. If it wasn't for you both, I wouldn't have been
able to do so many great things with my life or be the person I am
today.

Jen:
Difficult, complicated, and forever caring. More patient and
forgiving with me then I could have ever deserved, it was easy to
fall in love with you. You're an amazing person, and one of the few
people who have been there for me. There are no words to describe
how truly wonderful you are or just how lucky I am to be with you.
You gave me inspiration, support, and happiness, and you mean the
world to me.
I love you!

Mrs. Waller:
Through one year of English and another of Creative Writing, you
encouraged me to write to the best of my ability. You've helped
me improve my skills through your hard work and dedication. You
inspired some of my favorite high school memories and have helped
me with my work so many times, and for that, I thank you.

Prologue
Bolger Farm, Pennsylvania Countryside
July, 1930

"Now, you check the breach by lifting the bolt and pull it back until you hear a click," Dad said, in an authoritative tone. My father was teaching me how to clean, assemble, repair, and fire a rifle. "Once you hear the click, you scan the breach for anything that can affect the weapon. Dirt, rust, water, sand, anything like that can cause a jam or even have the weapon explode in your face."

"Yes, dad," I responded, looking in awe at the Springfield bolt action rifle.

"Now," he said handing me the empty rifle, "try loading and firing the rifle, and aim at the bottle I set up on the fence."

Nodding with enthusiasm, I accepted my father's rifle. It was the same rifle my father took to France during the First World War, staying with him through basic training, through the muddied trenches, and then smuggled back home. The rifle was the only thing my father kept from his days as a soldier. Dad's medals and old dress uniform stayed tucked away in a locked case in our attic, never to be seen again, until his death.

Holding the aged rifle, I ran my fingers over the well-kept wood of the stock before moving to the polished steel of the barrel, trigger, and sights. Hands steady from dozen of hours spent practicing on the empty weapon; I expertly loaded a single five round clip. The clip slid cleanly into the breach as I pushed the bolt forward and down, cocking the rifle with a series of metallic clicks. I held the rifle to my shoulder, feeling its weight pulling on my hands.

Steadying the barrel, I lined up the sights on the empty pop bottle sitting on the old, rickety, wooden fence on my grandfather's farm. Both weary soldiers stood behind me and watched as I steadied the weapon. Remembering my father's words, I held my breath and squeezed the trigger, the rifle jumping suddenly. I half expected the violent jump, the rifle pushing back into my shoulder as I heard glass shatter.

"Hell of a shot, kiddo," my grandfather said with a grin. "Just like your father."

"Oh, he'll be better then me one day," my father admitted, taking the rifle from my hands.

"Going to be a soldier like us old fools?" my grandfather asked, smiling at me and my father.

"Yes, sir!" I said with pride, desperately wanting to be a big hero like my father and grandfather.

My father chuckled and handed me the rifle. "While he'll be too smart to be a halfwit ground pounder, he'll be the best shot around," My father said, still laughing at his own comment. Dad set up another half dozen soda pop bottles on top of the fence and said, "Here, knock off the rest of the bottles."

"No problem, dad," I laughed. I took the rifle and returned to my shooting, dreaming about being a big hero soldier with every crack of the rifle.

Part I
The Desert Fox

"It doesn't matter where you came from, just what you do from this point on. Don't fuck up and die and you're fine." –Captain John Hiller, US Army

Chapter 1
HMS *Queen*
Off the Coast of Oran
November 8th, 1942

It was an ungodly hot and humid day aboard the British Troopship *Queen*, the temperature jumping just over ninety-eight. It was only about six in the morning, just an hour or so before the landings at Oran. I was sitting on the starboard side of the ship, resting against one of the crates of supplies that were stacked on deck. Around me, hundreds of other American soldiers of the First Infantry Division were waiting for the order to load into the transports and storm the beaches.

I wasn't looking forward to the invasion, having some pre battle jitters that mixed in with the heat. I took off my helmet off and placed it my lap, while I brushed the sweat from my short, brown hair with a rag. More sweat was dripping down my neck and cheeks, soaking my uniform shirt and dripping onto my M1 Garand Rifle. I shifted under the heat and slipped the heavy rut sack off my back and onto the deck.

"Corr?" someone called my name. I looked up to see Jay Hawkins, a squad mate and friend of mine, squirming through the crowd of soldiers on the deck. I waved him over and he dropped down next to me, resting his rifle against his shoulder.

"How are you doing, Jay?" I asked.

"Hot and sweaty, but fine," he said, wiping some sweat from his forehead with his sleeve. "You?"

"Same, I'm a bit nervous, though," I admitted. Jay shrugged and took out his canteen and said, "Yeah, me too, this is our first fight, but I hear the Vichy on the beach aren't soldiers, just conscripts." I nodded in agreement, but I knew not to underestimate them. In basic training, I was told to expect the enemy to be highly trained and deadly.

"Corporal Bolger, Private Hawkins," called our squad leader, Captain Hiller, from across the deck. Together, we stood up and quickly threw on our gear, running over to him.

"Sir!" we said together with a salute. Captain Hiller returned the salute.

"You boys ready, or what?" The Captain asked as he sized us up.

"Ready and able, sir!" we answered.

"Good, now go get the squad together and meet me back here. We're loading up and shipping out," Captain Hiller barked. We both saluted the Captain and then walked away to find the squad. Even though both the holds and deck were crowded with solders, we were able to find them by one of the life rafts. They were sitting on their rut sacks, playing cards, reading, or smoking.

"Vic, you do know that will kill you," I said to Private Vincent Lenatie, who was leaning over the railing, smoking a cigarette. He flashed a cold smile and took a long inhale before tossing it into the water.

"Well, sure as hell the Germans won't kill me," he said, shouldering his Browning Automatic Rifle, or BAR.

"Yeah," Corporal Don Hicks chimed in. "Just make sure you shoot accurate with that thing." Donny wasn't our squad sniper, Jay was, but Don had a knack for sharp shooting.

"Hey!" Private George Rested yelled, tugging on Donny's arm. "Either raise or call, pal." The two were playing cards with one another, tossing dollars into a helmet that sat between them.

"Relax, I'll take your money, don't worry," Donny said, shuffling the five cards in his hand. "Check."

"Let's see 'em." George demanded. Donny revealed his hand, four nines and a king. A smile crept across his face, but George laughed. "Good hand, but a straight flush to the ace is better." Donny folded his cards together and tossed them at George.

"It's rigged," he mumbled while George collected his winnings.

"If you girls are finished playing, grab your gear. The Captain wants us loaded up, so it's best not to keep him waiting," I said in a joking tone. Everyone began packing up and collected their gear. Then we began walking, in a slow pace, back to the captain.

"How bad do you think it'll be out there?" Private Homer Gusten asked in a shaky voice, as we walked toward the captain.

"Don't know," I admitted to him. "The Germans have been at this fighting since 1939, so they have experience. Then again, this is the first time they faced Americans since the Great War."

"True and we won't be alone, right?" Homer nervously asked. It was apparent that he was afraid, as we all were, but some of us hid it better than others.

"Nope, the Brits are making their attacks along with us. We'll have the Germans on the run before we know it." I told him, trying to seem confident, in truth; I wasn't sure what was going to happen. This was our first time in combat, but we trained hard and the Captain was a veteran soldier.

"Relax, Homer," Vic added. "The Germans will get one look at me and run the other way."

"Yeah, because you're so damn ugly," George snickered. Private Timothy Vates and Lance Corporal Tony Fletcher started laughing, but stopped when Vic gave them a harsh look.

"Vineti," Captain Hiller intervened as we approached him. "Let' em laugh. You can't argue with the truth." The entire squad started laughing at Vic, who pulled his helmet over his eyes. "Let's load up." Captain Hiller ordered.

Over the side of the troop ship was one of several Higgins Landing Boats, held up by a set of pulleys. Slowly, two members of the ship's crew lowered the boat into the water, draping a cargo net over the side once it touched water.

"Clear to go," one of them said. Hiller nodded and climbed over the railing and began climbing down the net. It took some courage, but I climbed over the railing and followed. The net was slippery and swayed back and forth from the water current. The Higgins boat tossed in the water bellow me, soaking me with cold water. The water added weight to me, making it harder to climb down.

Taking it one step at a time, I made it to the Higgins.

The boat rocked unevenly, tossing me back and forth. Slowly, the rest of the squad climbed into the boat. Hiller stood near the side, helping them into the boat. It took several minutes, but soon everyone was aboard. Captain Hiller pushed the cargo net away from the boat and signaled the boat commander to go. With a hard shutter and lurched forward, the boat pulled away from the troop ship.

The Higgins cruised in between the other ships until it was in front of the fleet. Clear of the larger ships, the boat joined into a formation of a dozen or so other landing boats. Under strict orders, we were to sit in the water while the intelligence boys aboard ship were seeing if the French soldiers on shore would surrender to us. A few guys in the squad found this to be stupid idea.

"Why are we warning those Vichy pricks that we're coming? Just gives them a chance to dig in more," Corporal Edward Sanders said, sounding annoyed.

"Doesn't matter either way," Vic said pushing Sanders with his BAR. "When I hit the beach, they'll be no hope for' em."

"Shut it, both of you," Captain Hiller said coldly. "You better hope they give in, or you'll be slogging ashore."

"Yes, sir," they both said meekly. I smiled slightly at the two of them and looked over to my right when Tim bumped into me. He was holding a hand over his mouth, with his face a pale green color. Tony was patting him on the back, but soon faced him over the side of the boat. After a few seconds, he began throwing up into the sea.

"Big meal," Tony said, sneering a little.

"Fun….ny," Tim said, in between throwing up his food.

"Keep it together, Vates," Captain Hiller ordered.

"He'll be fine, sir," Tony answered for him. Captain Hiller rolled his eyes, giving the rest of the men a dirty look. I didn't put too much into it; he always gave dirty looks. Behind us, someone blew a whistle, just barely audible over the sound of the fleet. Once I heard it, I gripped my M1 Garand Rifle tighter in my hands, and the whistle signaled the start of the landings.

"This is it," Captain Hiller shouted, as the landing boat lurched forward. The sudden motion tossed all of us forward, banging into one another. I fell face first into Jay's back, pushing him forward. I regained my balance and held onto the side of the landing craft for stability.

The landing boats crashed through the churning seas, spraying salt water onto us. The water soaked our uniforms and gear. The constant uneven tossing form the water churned the remains of my breakfast in my stomach. I held my mouth shut, closing my eyes to relax.

"Thirty seconds, boys!" the boat operator yelled from behind. Captain Hiller, standing near the ramp, turned to face his squad.

"Listen up! The French ashore have been given a chance to surrender, so when we get to the shore, they are our enemies and you will treat them as such. When we hit the beach, get out of the water and make it to the seawall. We will regroup there and fight our way inland," He screamed.

"Move fast, keep your head down, and don't get shot! If you do everything I've taught you since day one you'll make it off this beach alive!"

"Ten seconds!" Captain Hiller shouted as he braced himself against the ramp and placed his hand on the release. We pressed forward and got ready to run. I rested my right trigger finger over the guard on my rifle and took a deep breath. Inside, I was shaking with fear, but adrenalin surged through my veins, making my heart beat faster, I could hear it in my head, pounding.

There was a hard thud and a shutter as the boat came to a stop.

"Ramp down! Advance!" He ordered. The forward ramp dropped down into the water, sounding like thunder, and making a huge splash. Captain Hiller ran out first, followed by the rest of the squad. I was last out, falling on my face into the shallow water. Quickly, I picked myself up and ran down the beach.

Captain Hiller took half the squad to the left side of the building, while the rest, including myself, followed the Sergeant. He led us down the boardwalk next to the warehouse to an outdoor staircase that led to the top of the warehouse. The door at the top was open, a Nazi flag hung from the doorframe.

"We head up and shoot down on the Nazis," Sergeant Hanes ordered, pointing to the door. He checked the clip in his carbine rifle and darted up the stairs. With a loud clatter, the rest of us chased after him. Our gear bumped against the rusted railings, producing more noise. Luckily, the sounds of gun fire and explosions covered our movement.

Sergeant Hanes hugged the wall next top the door and peered inside, but the flag blocked his view. With a hard yank, he ripped the flag from the door and tossed it into the churning water under the dock. Jay grunted in anguish as the flag flew." That would have been one good souvenir," he said, watching it flutter and fall.

"Get ready. The catwalk wraps around the upper area and comes to a control box that is located over the doors to the dry dock. Corr, take Jay, Homer, Tony, and Phil to the right and take the control box. The rest of you, follow me and shoot at the Krauts below. Ready? Go!" Sergeant Hanes yelled as he ran inside, closely followed by me. As he ran left, I went right with the assigned troopers.

The catwalk was suspended high over the warehouse floor, giving a perfect position to shoot from. Crates and boxes were scattered across the way, providing good cover. Below us, Captain Hiller and the rest of the squad advanced in through the doors at the front. They took the brunt of the enemy fire, since they didn't see us yet, but that changed.

Halfway down the catwalk, a German soldier popped out from behind a crate. He held the German made MP-40 sub-machine gun and aimed it at me. In a second, I fired three rounds into him. The bullets impacted his chest, soaking his chest with his own blood. The force of the impact knocked him back against the handrail and he fell over, and as if in slow motion he continued, tumbling to the floor below. His body made a sickening thump as it hit the ground.

It was the first time I had ever killed a man. At the time, I held my rifle tight and kept running forward. My hands were shaking and my stomach was churning from the sight of his dead body falling to the ground. Keeping to my training, I blocked it from my mind and continued on. As I was told, it was either him or me.

The control box, at the end of the catwalk, held several German and Vichy soldiers, who were setting up a machine gun in the front window, they began firing down on Captain Hiller and the others. I signaled Jay to take out the gunner, but to wait until I took everyone else to the box door. He nodded in understanding and rested his rifle on a crate, aiming for the gunner. I took the rest of the troopers and darted across the rest of the catwalk, ducking behind crates to avoid being seen.

Without being seen, we made it to the control box. The door was closed, so we stacked up on opposite sides of it. Tony stood with me on the right and Homer and Phil on the left. I looked back to Jay and signaled to shoot. He rested his head against his rifle and aimed down the sight. Within a few seconds of aiming, he fired once, ending the clatter of the machine gun fire.

Just then, I kicked the door open and Tony tossed in a grenade. The thing exploded in a few seconds, creating an deafening boom and cloud of black smoke. Once the explosion echoed out, we rushed inside, spraying the room with bullets. The un-aimed rounds pinged off the metal control panels in the room and then everything went quiet inside. The smoke cleared out through the shattered windows, bringing back visibility.

Inside, the room was in ruins. Dead German and Vicky bodies littered the floor. Blood stained the walls and floor, mixing with shattered glass and metal. The MG-42 dangled outside the window for a second or two, before breaking of its mount and tumbling to the floor. I waved Jay back to us and cleared a space to aim out of the window where the MG used to be.

I signaled the others to take up aiming positions in the windows, so we could fire on the Germans below. Standing still, I rested against the blown out window frame. My rifle steady in my hands, aiming down the sights, and remembering everything from training, I lined up the nearest enemy. It was a German firing a rifle from behind some crates. I brought the cross hairs to line up on his back and fired twice, but one round fired, hitting him in the middle of his shoulders. There was a metal ping and the empty clip from my rifle shot out.

"Idiot!," I mumbled to myself for not counting how many rounds I fired. Quickly, I pulled another eight round clip from my belt, slid it into the rifle, and pushed the guard over it.

Loaded, I aimed down and found more targets. Fixing my aim, I fired a burst of three rounds. The Germans dropped under the umbrella of bullets.

"Look at that," Jay said, loading his Springfield rifle.

"What?" Tony asked, still shooting.

"That moron, Vic. He's spraying the area with his BAR! Bastard can't shoot for shit!" Jay sneered.

"As long as he knocks off the Germans," I said to Jay, reloading my rifle after firing five more times.

Below, the Germans could not hold back Captain Hiller and handle the shooting from the catwalks. While the Captain and his part of the squad fired on the Germans, Sergeant Hanes and his men dropped grenades from above, while we picked off stragglers. Eventually, the Germans retreated from the warehouse and took cover in the dry dock. Soon, the shooting inside died down.

Captain Hiller took his men in pursuit, firing from the door of the warehouse facing the dry dock. Hanes regrouped with us and together we formed back up with the Captain.

"Good work inside," Captain Hiller said to us, reloading his Thompson. "Now we just have to clear them from the docks and take that French ship intact."

Within the dry docks were several French destroyers that had been captured by the Vichy. They were sitting in port for repairs and were easy targets for our ships, but our orders were to take them. The ship we were taking was a small scouting ship, one that had been repaired. It sat in the dry docks ready for launch, but the Vicky and Germans would defend it or destroy it.

"We need to grab the two cranes standing over the ship. We take them and we can use our snipper. Hanes, secure the one closest to us and get Jay atop for sniper support. Vic, suppress the Germans from regrouping on the docks, while the rest of us storm the ship. Tony and Jones, stay with him."

"Sir, we can only pin them for so long before they see it's just three of us," Tony pleaded.

"Mack!" Captain Hiller yelled. Corporal Martin 'Mack' Franco ran from his cover to where the Captain was. "Where is the.30 cal?"

"I lost it on the beach, sir. The ammo too," Mack answered, flinching as bullets tore holes in the ground next to him, causing little clouds of dirt to rise.

"What? Damn it, soldier! I gave you one order before we landed and that was to hang onto the.30 and the ammo for it! Hanes, head to the crane and get Jay up there. Vic, do as I said and the rest of you, storm the ship and let's use their deck guns against them." Captain Hiller screamed, as spit sprayed from his mouth.

Vic, Tony, and Jones hunkered down by a stack of crates and set up Vic's BAR. Tony and Jones stood next to him and fired with their rifles while Vic pounded away with the BAR. Sergeant Hanes took a handful of troopers with him and moved to take the crane. The Captain had us wait for Vic to suppress the Germans and then we stormed up the loading ramp to the ship.

Captain Hiller took the lead, with me behind him. The Vichy and Germans aboard were only sailors, armed with Lugers and a rifle or two. Using our Thompson's and Grand's, we tore through the defenders and we made it aboard breaking off into separate groups and spreading out over the ship. Donny and I went with Private Joseph Waters down through a hatch on the deck and into the small cabins below.

Once there, we searched and cleared a radio room and small storage areas. Being a scout ship, this thing was small, so there were very few places to hide. While the others fought above deck, I crept through the cramped rooms and found the door to the engine room. The air was hot and steamy, and smelled like body odor. The door was a small, red, metal blast door that was closed, but not locked. Slowly, I open the water tight door just a crack. Then I took a grenade from my belt, pulled the pin, counted to three and tossed it inside, closing the door.

The grenade detonated with a loud explosion, followed by the muffled cries of the crew inside. I opened the door again and fired several shots before entering. Stepping inside, I did a quick visual of the room. Inside, were several members of the ship crew crumpled over on the floor. All were dead, still clutching the tools they were using to repair the engine. Startled by a muffled moan that crept out from one of the bodies, I jumped back and lost my balance.

Panicked, I slung my rifle over my shoulder and drew my Colt.45 sidearm, as I knelt over the body. Gently, I turned over the sailor, seeing a gaping hole in his chest. His eyes were closed, blood seeped out of his mouth and wound. I reached over to take his pulse and found none. The man was dead. He looked to be my age, and I imagined, for a moment, that it had been me. I holstered my sidearm and un-slung my rifle when someone stepped in behind me.

Out of shock, I whirled around and slammed the man against a bulkhead. Pinning him with my rifle, I struggled with him. Then, he stopped and held his hands up in surrender.

"Easy, Corr, "It's Donny." Donny laughed. Relived, I took my rifle away from his chest and stood back.

"Sorry, you scarred the shit out of me," I admitted to him.

"No harm, no foul, buddy," he looked over the damage inside. "Looks like things are all wrapped up here; I think we're needed topside." He said. I nodded.

We climbed back out of the hatch on deck and found the Germans battling to take the ship. The squad was fighting from the bridge and behind, using anything for cover. Some used the deck mounted machine guns, a Flack 88 cannon, and a 38mm flack gun mounted on the stern. We found a shielded spot behind some stacked steel beams and began shooting back.

I knelt by the edge of the stack and leaned out to shoot. Ducking in to avoid being hit, I fired in quick, three round bursts until the clip ejected after the eighth round. I jerked my head back as more bullets pinged off the metal beams, causing me to flinch and fumble with the new rifle clip. Taking a second to think and steady my nerves, I was able to reload and tilted my body forward to shoot.

As I fired, I pulled back when the ship's 88 fired, letting out an ear shattering explosion. The 88 was close to me and the resonance from the blast thumped in my chest. The explosion shook me so hard I dropped down and clutched my chest.

"Corr, you hit?" Donny asked, bending down.

"Ah, no," I answered, as I tried to catch my breath. "Just lost my footing." Donny reached his arm out and hauled me to my feet. Thanking him, I returned back to the shooting, when a flight of German JU-87 Stukas passed over head. Like a cluster of sharks, the flight of five bombers circled overhead. The dive bombers seemed to be waiting to strike, waiting for the attack orders. Then, like sharks sensing blood in the water, the group stopped circling and began to dive, in a frenzy, towards us. Panic washed over me, and the rush of adrenaline threw my body into action.

I tugged on Donny's shoulder, pointed at the bombers and then the flack gun and 88. He nodded and knew what I was going to do. Donny took his rifle and fired one round into the deck below us, sending the spent clip in his rifle to eject. He slid in a fresh clip and readied to provide cover fire as I gripped my rifle and nodded to him.

Donny stood up and fired his weapon at the Germans, causing a distraction. While he shot, I ran from behind cover and across the deck to the flack 88. The 88 was just a few feet away, mounted just on the port side of the ship.

I ran as fast as I could across the deck, gear webbing and pack slowed me down. Bullets whizzed past me, some hitting the deck and others missing me by inches. As I ran, time seemed to slow and everything went quiet. Even as bullets flew past me and explosions caused the deck below me to vibrate, everything went silent. I didn't realize what was happening until I bumped into Private Jacob Wilson, who was loading the 88.

"Whoa, watch it, Corr," he said, nearly dropping the 88 shell he was holding.

"Stop aiming at the Germans on the ground and hit them!" I yelled, pointing at the bombers. Corporal Mark Jamison, the operator of the gun, rotated the 88 around to face the Stukas, which were closing in.

Jacob loaded the 88, closed the gun breach, and stood back. Mark held his hands on the control wheels of the 88, turning them as he lined the lead bomber up in his sights. He aimed as the lead bomber leveled off for an attack run and readied to fire. His hands dropped to the lanyard, when a volley of bullets peppered the gun. Jacob and I jumped back, throwing up our arms to shield our faces.

When the volley subsided, we turned back to see Mark arched over on the deck next to the gun. Jacob ran to his aid, while I jumped on the weapon. Since I had never used one before, I quickly learned which wheel moved the gun up,, down, left, and right.

Aiming carefully, I quickly lined up the Stuka as he readied to release his deadly bomb. Yanking the lanyard, the wrong thing to do, the 88 erupted in a cloud of black smoke as the shell screamed into the air and exploded on contact with the plane. The bomber burst into flames and over shot the ship, slamming into the beach next to the dry dock.

A wave of relief washed away the fear as the plane crashed, but there were still four other bombers. I looked back and saw them continue on their run toward us. I grabbed Jacob's uniform and tried to get him to help me load and fire again, but he stayed with Mark.

"He's dead, help me!" I yelled, but he didn't move. I looked around and found another shell for the gun. I lifted the heavy thing up and readied to load, but it was too late. The four bombers dropped their payloads right onto us.

Two of the bombs landed onto the warehouse we were just in, blowing the thing to hell. The other two found their marks on the ship. One punched through the deck next to the bridge and erupted below, tossing the ship into the air, while the other exploded on the dock next to us. The blast tore a nasty hole in the side of the ship.

The explosion sent a burst of heated air and debris straight toward me and everyone else on deck. The shockwave picked me up and threw me into the air, flinging me off the deck and back onto the dock. I landed onto the wooden dock with a hard crash and rolled towards the burning warehouse. I came to a stop when I hit a stack of crates that were still standing.

When I landed, my eyes were clenched closed, it felt impossible to open them. A stinging pain shot up from my left arm and a warm liquid rushed down my left arm and into my hand. Another burning pain ebbed from my head, creating a killer headache.

Struggling to stay awake, I opened my eyes and found myself lying on my back, looking up at the sky, which was clogged with black smoke. The smell of burning wood and steel filled the air, mixed with an odor of seared flesh.

Carefully, I propped myself up on my right arm and pulled myself up to lean against the crates. Sitting up, I looked back towards the ship, seeing only a burning hulk and choking, black smoke. The ship was gone, along with a huge section of the dock around it. I could hear groans and cries coming from inside the smoke, but I could hardly see anyone.

Looking to my right, I saw a trooper lying face down on the dock, his pack and gear torn to shreds. Ignoring the pain in my arm and head, I crawled over to the trooper. Knelling over him, I saw a deep gash in his back, his uniform saturated with blood. Using my right arm, I flipped over the trooper, and saw that it was Tony.

His eyes were closed and his face was covered in dirt and ash. He wasn't moving, and his chest was still. I placed my hand to his neck to look for a pulse, but found none. Then, I realized that there was a piece of shrapnel sticking out of his leg, blood still oozing. The chunk of metal opened the main artery in his leg. Tony was gone. Then I heard footsteps and a crashing sound.

I turned to see Vic, limping towards me, holding onto some crates for support. His helmet was missing and he had a shallow gash running under his close cropped black hair. His uniform was ripped and torn, with small blood splotches splattered about, and his left leg was bloody.

"Shit, I'm screwed up," he grunted, dropping down next to me. He looked at Tony's body and sighed. "Tony?"

"Yeah, he's gone," I mumbled, pressing against my wounded arm. "You see anyone else?"

"No, I just staggered over here." He said as he struggled to pull off his pack. "Med pack is in there somewhere."

I fumbled around inside his pack and pulled out his first aid kit, along with a pack of cigarettes. Opening the kit, I pulled out two bandages. First, I leaned over Vic and tied off the nasty cut in his leg. Then, I handed him a cigarette and lit it. He gave a thankful head nod and puffed away. I tied off my arm and held it close to my chest.

"Will you be alright without me?" I asked him.

"Go, just leave the smokes, " he groaned. I tossed the pack into his lap and looked around for my pack, which had been ripped from me. I found it torn to shreds, but salvaged my aid kit. I stuffed the kit in my leg bag, which managed to survive the explosion and then looked around for survivors.

The burning ship left of a huge, choking cloud of black smoke from its burning fuel, making it hard to see. The sounds of battle still echoed across the docks, mixed with the occasional secondary explosion. I could still hear moans and cries from wounded troopers, but I couldn't see any of them.

Stumbling through the smoke, I found Private David Jacobs. He was laid out behind a pile of burning steel, clutching his right leg. I ran over to him as fast as I could, nearly collapsing from the pain in my arm and head. I dropped down next to David and took out my aid kit.

"Hey," David mumbled, blood dripping from his nose and mouth.

"Hang on, bro," I said, looking at his leg.

David was pressing his hands over a nasty shrapnel wound in his right leg, blood flowing from between his fingers. Gently, I pulled his hands away and pressed a bandage in their place. I then placed his hands back on the bandage. "This should do, for now." I said as I took out a pack of cigarettes I kept in my leg bag and handed one to him.

"You're a regular saint, ya know that?" David said and then took the cigarette and lit it by using the burning steel next to him. "Hey, I saw the doc helping the Captain just over there." He pointed towards the warehouse on the opposite side of the docks from the one that was destroyed.

"Thanks," I grunted, packing up and running off.

I ran for the warehouse David pointed out for me, navigating through the smoke. Along the way, I found Donny and George helping Tim with a bad chest wound. I helped them carry Tim back to the warehouse were the Captain was, hoping doc could help him.

The four of us stumbled around a bit, but found the entrance to the warehouse. Captain Hiller was sitting against a German staff car, his Thompson trained on the door. Homer was lying on a makeshift stretcher next to him, with Private Gold, Private McAllen, and Lance Corporal Fitzgerald. Our medic, Lance Corporal Doug 'Doc' Tavin, was dashing back and forth between wounded troopers to help them. He looked up and saw us carrying Tim and pointed to stack of boxes to lay Tim down on. We gently placed him down and doc came running over.

"How's he doing?" he asked, looking at Tim's chest.

"He was shot just before we were bombed. I think there's some shrapnel mixed in too," Jay reported. Doc peeked under the mix of bandages pressed on Tim's chest, giving a grim look.

"Doc?" Donny pressed.

"Shit, he's got some serious wounds and needs a surgeon." Doc sighed.

"Will he live?" Donny asked.

Doc shook his head and looked at Tim, who was now unconscious. "If we don't get him to a medical ship or an aide station, he'll die in less than half an hour."

Donny was taken aback by the news, nearly crying. Tim was his best friend and the two were nearly joined at the hip, brothers through it all. Donny grew frantic from the news, speaking a mile a minute.

"What if we link up with the rest of the landing force and get' em a jeep back to the beach so he can take a Higgins back to a medical ship? Would that work?" he asked.

"Ah, maybe. If you hurry, his chances are still slim." Doc said in a doubtful tone.

"Corr, You, Jay, and I are in the best condition out of all of us. We'll go into town and find the rest of the division and save Tim." Donny ordered.

"You're risking your necks if you do that," Captain Hiller grunted from behind us, shuffling over from the door. "We have no clue if the rest of the division even made it into town or if they are still stuck on the beaches. You could run into the whole German garrison and get killed."

"Sir, I'd take the risk to save a fellow soldier!" Donny defended.

"So would we," I added, Jay nodding his head in agreement.

Captain Hiller sighed and looked over at Tim. "Don't get shot. Hanes!"

Sergeant Hanes ran over to us. "Sir?" Hanes responded.

"Give Bolger your sidearm" Captain Hiller told Hanes. Hanes tossed me his Colt.45 and two ammo magazines. "Good hunting," he said.

After I reported where to find Vic and David, we raced back onto the docks and towards the road leading into town.

Chapter 2

The three of us followed the main road in the port, which lead us to the main gate. We found the gate blown open, the Germans guarding it were all dead. We carefully passed through and began a long walk/jog into town.

The path was a poorly paved dirt road that linked the main city of Oran to the coastal ports. From the amount of damaged trucks and tanks, the Air Forces pounded the hell out the area, destroying any reinforcements heading to the ports. We hoped to find a working truck or car on the road, but the flyboys did too good of a job. Everything on the road was either on fire our burnt to a crisp. It didn't take us that long to reach the town.

The city of Oran was still a hot zone, with heavy fighting going on in the upper areas. We approached from the south western route, while the rest of the First took the direct west route. Chances were good, if the rest of the forces reached here, that we wouldn't run into much trouble.

Sticking close to the buildings, we walked up the winding streets until we found an intersection. When we did, Jay pulled out a map and did his best to get his bearings.

"Okay, if this is the port and the road out, then…..here!" he pointed to a street labeled Corridor Able. "So, if we came from the west and are at this intersection, then the division is advancing through here. If we head north and stay on the road, we'll meet up with them at rally point baker," Jay said.

"Let's get going, then!" Donny yelled, as Jay folded up the map.

Donny was desperate to get Tim help as soon as possible. He ran down the streets as fast as he could, never checking alleys and side streets for Germans. Jay and I followed as close as we could, but we had to slow down and keep alert. After all, it won't matter how fast we run, we can't help anyone if we're dead.

Donny continued to run, not paying attention at all to his surroundings. When we came to a large intersection, Jay and I stopped and ducked behind a destroyed Panzer IV. Both of us wanted to check out the area before crossing, but Donny didn't want to slow down.

"Come on! What are you waiting for?" Donny yelled at us. "Tim's dying!"

"Yeah, well if we die Tim dies," Jay said in a low voice.

"Exactly, so get down and lower your voice," I added.

Donny wouldn't hear it. He looked even more desperate than before and panicked. He cursed at us and decided not to wait. He ran to a house on the edge of the square, looked out and ran. Donny ran across the square, only focused on the other side. Jay and I still hid behind the Panzer. Then, there was a single, loud pop from afar. Donny's back seemed to explode, blood erupted from in between his shoulders. With a low cry, he fell to dirt, unmoving in a pool of growing blood.

"Donny!" Jay tried to climb over the tank to reach him, but I pulled him back. As I did, there was another pop and then a bullet pinged off of the tank, just where Jay was.

"Shit, he spotted us!" I said. Both of us pressed against the tank, trying to not be seen. I dropped into a crouch and slowly peered around the side of the tank, leaning against the treads. I managed to see a tower rising high into the air, just on the opposite side of the square. I pulled back as a bullet bounced against the tank, next to my head.

"See him?" I asked. "I think he might be in the tower on the edge of the square. Maybe top or second to top window."

Jay took a quick glance over the tank and dropped next to me. "I think I got 'em." He made some adjustments to the Springfield's scope and cocked the rifle. "Mind being bait?" Jay joked.

I sighed and shrugged. "Don't miss," I ordered. I slid my leg bag off and held my .45 "Ready?" I asked. Jay nodded, and I crept towards the edge of the tank and readied to run. I looked back to see Jay ready his rifle and he nodded. GO!

I took a deep breath and scurried away. I darted out from behind cover and ran across the square, jumping over debris and weaving back and forth, hoping to avoid getting shot. There was a pop, followed by a thud as a bullet impacted at my feet.

Miss one.

I didn't look back or slow. I kept going as fast as I could and heard another pop and thud.

Miss two.

I could see a building on the other side of the square with a whole in the wall. I planed to run and jump through the hole and wait. As I approached the wall, I aimed myself to jump when there was another pop. I jumped forward and passed through the hole, tumbling inside. I jumped to my feet and hugged the wall. Then, everything went quiet.

"Corr!" Jay yelled, "I got'em!"

Carefully, I crawled out from the building and saw Jay come running towards me. He was pointing to the tower and I looked up. Hanging from the top window was a sniper rifle, dangling by the strap. I nod in approval to Jay and ran to Donny.

He was lying in a pool of his own blood in the middle of the square. He had a baseball size hole in the middle of his shoulders, blood soaking the back of his uniform. Jay dropped to his knees when he saw him, thrown into shock. I gently rolled him over and retrieved his dog tags, watch, and wallet to be sent to his family in New Jersey.

"We better get going," I said to Jay, placing a hand on his shoulder.

"Right," he said, voice dry. I helped him to his feet and we continued to walk when we heard an engine running.

"You hear that?" I asked. Jay nodded yes and we began to look around and find the source.

Across from us, the wall of the building I was just in collapsed into a pile of rubble and dust. Behind the dust cloud, rolled a tan painted Panzer IV, its main gun swiveling to face and fire on us. The ponderous German tank rolled through the cloud of dust, grinding the dirt and rock beneath its treads. The giant rolled to a stop a few feet from us, the main gun turning towards us. Without saying a word, we ran.

Knowing that thing could blow clear through the buildings around us, we ducked, for cover, behind the destroyed Panzer IV. We dove behind it as the tank fired, blasting apart a building behind us. The tank corrected its aim and fired on the tank we were behind. The shell exploded on the armor, setting the tank ablaze.

Fearing for our lives, we ran from behind the tank and to an alley between two houses. The tank fired again, ripping a whole through the two buildings. Debris from the explosion peppered our backs and tossed us forward. We landed on our faces, causing me to get a deep cut on my cheek.

"Hang on, Corr," Jay said, pulling me up.

Dazed, I rose to my feet, my head throbbing with pain and ears ringing. Jay encouraged me on and we ran down the alley only to meet a brick wall too tall to climb. I turned back and heard the tank moving towards us. We were trapped.

"Trapped between a rock and a hard place," I said and then asked if he had any ideas.

I looked around the alley for a window to break in or a hole to climb through, but nothing. Solid wall on both sides, the only way out was leading back to the tank. I considered lifting Jay up the wall, but my left arm was out and if he lifted me, I couldn't pull him up.

The tank rolled to a stop next to the alley. The turret swung around to face us, slamming through a wall. The main gun stopped, aimed directly at us. It was over and I turned to Jay to say goodbye when an explosion tossed dirt onto the tank. The tank turned the turret away from us and drove backwards. Confused, we ran to the alley entrance.

We exited to find the Panzer rolling back through the square as explosions rocked the ground around it. Just then, a pair of M3 Stuart Light Tanks rolled into the square from the opposite end and fired on the German tank.

The weak gun on the Stuart couldn't damage the German tank enough, so the Panzer swung their gun around and blasted one of the Stuart's to a burning hulk. The other Stuart fired again and began a retreat, when an M4 Sherman rolled up from behind us, along with a squad of infantry.

The Sherman blasted away at the Panzer, destroying its treads. Weakened, the Panzer fought to run, but never moved. The infantry with the Sherman loaded a pair of M1 Bazookas and fired on the Panzer, setting it on fire. The infantry began to cheer as the ammo inside the tank cooked off and exploded.

Extremely gratefully to the other troopers and the tankers, we applauded them. We shook hands with them and they thanked us for taking out that sniper. Turns out, he was preventing the tank crews from refueling and repairing their tanks in town. Once we killed him, they were able to move.

"We appreciate the help, gunny," I said to the gunnery sergeant in charge of the tanks.

Jay and I shook hands with him. "No problem, but you helped by taking out that sniper."

"Thank you, gunny." I said.

"Boys, fan out and secure the square. Kegan, move the tank to cover the road leading north and have the Stuart and cover our rear," The gunny ordered his troopers to set up a perimeter and wait for reinforcements. "Zinski, bring up of the jeeps and sent out a patrol to..." he began.

"Excuse me, gunny, but we need a jeep," I said. "We have wounded down at the docks and need to get a man to a field hospital."

"You boys are from the docks? We saw the German bombers gut that place, thought no one survived. Zinski, give them a jeep and get on the radio and tell command to get some medics to the docks," he ordered.

"On it," the private responded. He called up one of the jeeps and gave it to us.

"Take this one, free of charge," the gunny joked.

"Thank you, gunny," Jay and I said, hopping in the jeep. The gunny gave a final wave as Jay started the jeep and pulled away.

Jay drove in reverse, turned into an alley, made a turn and drove off. He kept his foot pressed down on the accelerator and the jeep rocketed down the empty roads and out off town. Going so fast, Jay swerved past debris in the road and nearly crashed into a ditch. Luckily, he managed to keep us on the road and we arrived at the docks to meet doc.

Surprised at our success, he loaded Tim on the back.

"About time, where's Donny?" Jay and I looked at one another and then doc, shaking our heads. "Damn, but we can still save Tim. Corr, I need you to…."

The rest of Doc's words seemed to blur together and I felt dizzy. I rubbed my head and tried to focus, but I couldn't. My head seemed to weigh a ton and I fell to my side, tumbled out of the jeep, and landed on the ground. My vision began to fail and everything went dark.

Chapter 3

"God, you are some new kind of idiot," someone was saying over and over again. The voice was so familiar, yet distant. It was low, but full of anger and annoyance. I know I heard the voice before, but I couldn't see anything.

"He is," a second, more feminine voice said. "A person with so much potential and yet he throws it all away to be a soldier and join up." I knew the voices, my high school home room teacher and my mom. The two were the leading forces behind me not joining the military. They didn't want me in the Army, my older brother to join the Army Air Force, or my younger brother to join the Marines. They saw us throwing away all we achieved in school and what we could do, but the three of us decided together, if we were going to make the best of our lives, we would serve.

"Doctor, he's coming too," a voice echoed.

"Ah, good," another said.

Slowly, all my senses returned to me. My head felt lighter and the pain in my left arm and cheek were gone. My throat was dry, almost arid like a desert. I felt weak and groggy as I opened my eyes. I awoke to see I was in a room full of other wounded troopers, nurses, and doctors, and an aide station.

"Corporal….Bolger, how are you feeling?" asked a strange voice. I turned and saw a nurse standing next to me.

"Where am I?" I asked in a low moan.

"The field hospital in Oran. Do you know what your unit you're in?" she asked.

"Ah, Third Squad, Second Platoon, C Company, U.S. First Infantry Division," I answered.

The nurse wrote something on her clipboard. "Where were you born?" she questioned.

"Bayonne, New Jersey. Why the questions?" I wondered aloud.

"You had a nice size head laceration on your head and a slight concussion. I'm making sure your memory isn't damaged." she answered. A doctor walked over and looked at the nurse's clipboard.

"I see the Corporal is coming along nicely," he said. "I trust you're comfortable?"

I raised myself up on my shoulders. "As can be expected," I assured him. A throbbing headache echoed through my head as memories of the attack flooded back. The landings, the warehouse attack, the ship attack, the explosion, Donny's death, everything came back at once. It made me jump.

"Are you sure you're okay?" The nurse seemed worried.

"Fine, and ready to leave," I said.

"That would be against my advice, but it's…"

I cut him off. "But I can leave if I'm up to it." I told him.

The doctor sighed. "Yes, you can, but you should stay."

"Doctor!" a medic yelled from across the tent. "We have wounded inbound."

"How many?" he asked.

"Too many, sir, the voice answered.

The doctor looked back at me and scribbled something on his clipboard. "Fine, you can leave. I have a fresh uniform for you, but everything else you need to get from supply," he said as he rushed off.

With that, I jumped out of the cot and quickly dressed. As I did, I could feel the bandages on my arm and leg pull against my skin. It was uncomfortable, and would get worse in the heat, but I couldn't sit back while my friends risked their necks at the front.

Tying my boots and grabbing my helmet, I quickly left the tent. Since I was a kid, I always hated hospitals and being there was killing me inside. It felt good to step outside and take a breath of fresh air, even though it was filled with the smell of exhaust, oil, sweat, and blood. To me, it was better then the smell of antiseptic in a hospital.

"I see you're better." I turned to see Jay waiting by a jeep near the medical tent, sniper rifle resting against his leg.

I smiled and walked over to him. "Better is a bit of a stretch, but tired and annoyed is more accurate." The two of us shook hands. "How you holding up?" I asked.

Jay shrugged and slung his rifle over his shoulder. "Good, being on the crane kept me safe." He held up his arm and pointed to the bandage on it. "Just a minor burn," Jay said.

"Do you know where the rest of the squad is?" I asked.

"No, I met the Captain and he said to meet at the troop depot when I got you re-supplied." He reached back into the jeep and pulled out a torn and tattered backpack. "It's yours and I figured you could salvage some things." Jay said with half a smile.

I took the pack and opened it. Inside, I managed to salvage a few things. I found a picture of my two brothers and myself before we shipped out. My older brother Matthew was in his Air Force uniform, proudly pointing to the wings pinned on his shirt. Next to him, my younger brother Frank was in his Marine uniform, everything neat and in order like every other Marine. In the middle was me, in my Army uniform, showing my marksmen medal I earned in training.

With that, I found my Zippo lighter, a letter I was writing home, a pack of cards, and a knife my father gave me. These were all the things I could rescue, everything else was worthless. Being either burned or torn, it was of no value and could be replaced. I slung the bag over my shoulder and thanked Jay.

"Thanks, Jay. So, where's the supply depot?" I asked.

"Just down the road, I'll show you," he said as he pointed. The two of us began walking, and we noticed more and more soldiers had entered the town.

Soldiers and tanks clogged the roads as they came ashore from the fleet. Many of them were being moved up to the front, while others were re-arming. The engineers were fast at work to set up a base in the town. They were clearing out debris from the road and setting up in the abandoned buildings. Many of them were working on bringing in supplies from the ships.

"So, what happened after I blacked out?" I asked.

"Doc jumped to help you and we were loading you into the jeep when the rest of the division arrived. They gave us a med evac to town. They took us to the hospital, but discharged me after they bandaged my arm," Jay explained.

As we walked, a bulldozer tore through a bombed out building next to the road. The building easily collapsed in on itself, throwing up a cloud of dust. Next to us, a small Stuart Light Tank towed an abandoned Panzer IV off the road and to the motor pool. There, the engineers would cut the thing apart for spare parts and reuse the steel.

"Any news on the other landings?" I asked.

"I heard Patton's boys grabbed Casablanca and have established a foothold. I also heard some rumors about Ryder's forces, but nothing for sure. Some say they are stalled out in Algeria and others say he pushed inland too much and has his flanks exposed. Oh, here's the supply depot," Jay said.

The supply depot was a large lot cleared by the engineers with a makeshift hut in the center. The lot was filled with crates and boxes stacked high into the air. At the far end of the lot, trucks brought in more and more supplies, stacking the lot with more boxes and oil drums. The lot itself was fenced off, with MPs standing guard.

Jay and I walked up to the guard shack near the entrance and checked in with the men on patrol. They let us through with no problems and directed us to the hut to get supplies from the Sergeant in charge. We followed the directions, which took us down a twisting path that was lined with walls of crates. The stacks towered over the path, producing some welcome shade from the day's heat.

We continued on the path to the makeshift hut in the center of the lot, finding the sergeant. He sat behind a desk, which consisted of a wooden board resting on a pair of oil drums. The sergeant shuffled papers and wrote on several clipboards piled on another table next to him. He seemed rather frustrated at his work, cursing as he wrote.

"Excuse me, sergeant?" I asked.

He grunted something and looked up from his work. "What?"

"I need new gear and equipment, sergeant." I showed him my torn pack.

"You know, right now I have to categorize, log, and ship out tons and tons of supplies to the dozens of units in this operation. Between the screw ups aboard the supply ships, the dumb supply drivers, and this god damn heat, I'm a little flustered. Forgive me if I don't jump and tumble to help you." He sighed and rubbed the bridge of his nose. "Collins!" he screeched.

A young private ran in from behind the entrance and stood at the sergeant's side. "Sir?" he asked with a salute.

"Take these two to get new equipment and then show them out. Is that clear enough for you?" the sergeant asked in a sarcastic tone.

"Clear, Sergeant Rice. If you two would follow me…" the young private asked.

We followed as the private lead us out of the building and down a row of crates. He took us to a building next to the dump, entering through a hole in the wall. Inside, the room was set up like the sergeant's. A makeshift desk, stacks of crates, several clipboards nailed to the wall, a pair of radios, and a lot of papers. Collin's dropped into a chair behind the desk and took a swing from his canteen.

"How can I help?" he asked.

"I need a new pack, rifle, and gear webbing. All loaded with standard supply loads." I told him.

Collins stretched and walked over to some open crates.

"Ah, here…" He pulled out a new backpack and gear webbing. "Those crates over there have the supplies you need. I'll go and get you a new Garand," he said pleasantly.

As Colin's left, I walked over to the crates he pointed to. They were all closed, but labeled. I picked my way through the crates, opening a few at a time. Inside them, I found a second uniform to store, several pairs of socks, two packs of sealed C rations, four field medical kits, a rolled up blanket, two empty canteens, wire cutters and rope. I packed it all away in my backpack, slipped on my gear webbing and then the pack.

"Why rope?" Jay asked.

"One of my father's rules says if it has a use, it'll be needed," I said, securing the canteens to the webbing.

"Hey, can you help?" Collins asked, entering with several boxes stacked in his hand and a rifle slung over his shoulder. Jay and I grabbed the boxes and placed them on a stack of crates. "Thank you." He swung the rifle off his shoulder and handed it to me. "One M1 Garand Rifle, fresh from the factory," he chimed.

I took the rifle and slid my fingers across, feeling no nicks or cracks. I shouldered the rifle and aimed up at the sky, checking the sighting. Then I opened the breach and checked the barrel. Everything was in place and combat ready.

"Now, where is that…," Collins picked up a crowbar leaning against the wall and broke open a box. He removed the lid and searched inside. "Here," Collins pulled out two handfuls of M1 ammo clips and tossed them to me. I took them and filled the ammo pouches on my belt. Once they were full he gave me three extra, one to load now and two hold on the sling.

"Just need some grenades," I said.

Collins cracked open another box and handed me six fragmentation grenades and two smoke grenades. I placed the smoke grenades in my pack and clipped four on my belt and two on the straps stretching from my shoulders to my belt. "Here, take these." I looked up to see Collins hand me a Colt.45 and an ammo pouch with two extra clips and a holster.

"I'm a rifleman, and riflemen don't get a sidearm," I protested.

"Take it, I literally have thousands." I thanked him, adding the holster and ammo pouch to my belt, sliding the.45 into the holster. "That should do it."

"Thanks, Collins," I said to him, shaking hands.

"No problem. Good hunting out there," said Collins.

Jay and I left the supply depot and proceeded to the motor pool. Along the way, I filled my canteens at a well being used by several other troopers. Once filled, I took a quick drink. The water was cool and refreshing.

"You know," Jay said while were walking, "I wouldn't mind working in supply. Less danger, but I'd never handle a sniper rifle."

"I guess that's a deal breaker, eh?" I joked.

"Safe and quiet is good, but it can drive a man crazy," Jay chuckled.

"My, I mean, our folks would beg to differ on that." I laughed.

"True, but what fun is the Army without some danger," Jay added sarcastically.

"Hey, if you two men be so kind as to hurry up!" Captain Hiller yelled as we approached the troop depot.

The two of us broke into a quick jog and rushed to reach the Captain. The short run stretched and burned my mussels, bringing back the exhaustion from the landings. Being a soldier in combat, I pushed the pain and weariness out of my mind.

"Sorry about that, sir," Jay said as we came to a stop.

"Sorry?" Captain Hiller shook his head. "Never mind, just shut up and listen."

"Guys, sit here," Vic called, gesturing to some crates next to a halftrack.

Captain Hiller drew a piece of paper from his pocket and read over it out loud," Okay, I have a list of names of the men we lost. Resten, Vates, Gusten, Vega, Hicks, Sims, Gold, McAllen, Fitzgerald, and Boyd are gone. The only ones left are you three, the doc, Hanes, and myself. Jones is being sent stateside because of his wounds, so we are being folded together with 2nd and 3rd squad, who also took a beating."

A group of ten soldiers walked out from the depot and stood next to Captain Hiller.

"These men are from the other squads, four from 2nd and six from 3rd. They are now the new members of 1st squad, so get to know each other. Now, I would introduce them, but we don't have time," Captain Hiller said and continued, "Command has given new orders to the Division. It seems our forces in Algiers have moved too fast and have left their flanks exposed with a gap between them and us. We are moving up with the rest of C Company to bridge the gap and cover their left flank by securing several small hamlets in between us and

Algiers. This squad will take a refueling station to allow our tanks to move up quicker."

"The station isn't heavily defended, but we will divert from the main force to capture it. If something goes wrong, we need to bug out quick, because no one is coming to help. So, mount up in the halftracks. Bolger, take Hawkins and these two in the jeep behind mine. Let's go."

Two of the new soldiers from the other squads followed me and Jay as we followed the Captain to our jeep. The rest of the squad, mounted up in two halftracks that were with us, while the Captain took the lead jeep. Jay, the other two troopers, and myself boarded the second jeep.

Jay slid into the driver's seat and started up the engine. I sat next to him in the passenger's seat, and the two troopers sat in back, one mounting the.30 cal machine gun. Captain Hiller sat in his jeep with a driver and pulled out in front of us, waving to follow him.

"He can drive, right?" the troopers sitting asked.

Jay laughed as he drove after Captain Hiller. "Drive, you say? Of course, I got my license from a box of cereal!" Jay snickered.

Chapter 4

The convoy, moving out to secure the gap between Oran and Algiers, was rather larger than I expected. Consisting of halftracks, jeeps, Stuarts, M4 Lee's, and a handful of British Grant's, the convoy snaked across the desert. Over head, British Spitfires circled around, watching for German fighters and bombers. In several halftracks, quad.50 cal AA guns pointed skyward, their crews ever observant. In others, troopers sat ready for battle, fighting off the heat and waiting for combat.

In the convoy, our jeep drove tenth from the lead Stuart tank. Captain Hiller was in front of us and the two halftracks carrying the squad behind. I sat in my seat, rifle resting in my lap, watching the endless sand dunes and sloping hills pass by. The heat of the desert caused me to sweat like crazy, drenching my uniform around my neck and chest. Constantly, I tugged at my bandages, which itched, and rubbing away the sweat collecting on my forehead just under my helmet.

"Hey," one the troopers behind me shouted, tapping my shoulder.

"How can I help?," I asked, just loud enough to be heard over the engine noise.

He stretched out his hand and I shook it. "Private Nathaniel James." he said.

I introduced myself. "Corporal Corrigan Bolger, Corr for short."

"Nice to meet you, Corr. That's Private Adam Sullivan." He pointed to the trooper manning the.30 cal.

"He's Private Jay Hawkins," I gestured to Jay.

"Hi, you'll forgive me if I don't shake hands," Jay said without turning around.

"I'm from New York, the Bronx to be precise," Nathaniel said. "Oh, you can call me Nate."

"Well, Nate, I'm from Jersey," I told him.

"I'm from Maine," Adam said

"Maine, huh? I've been there before, my uncle lives up there. He owns a fishing boat," I said to Adam. "Lot's of good fishing up there."

"Don't I know it," he added cheerfully. "My parents had a small fish canning company. They own several small fishing boats, but they closed down when the war started. Damn kraut U-Boats were sinking ships too close to the fishing grounds, so they closed up shop."

"Is that why you joined?" Jay asked.

Adam shrugged at the question. "Sort of, my mother's brother died at Pearl and I felt I needed to do something, so I enlisted."

Nate jumped in. "I joined because prison wasn't attractive."

"Prison?" I asked, raising an eyebrow.

"Oh, I was arrested for stealing some stuff. It was my third strike and it was either enlist or sit in a cell." Nate bragged.

"What did you steal?" Jay asked.

"Ah, I swiped some…books," Nate said.

Adam laughed. "When we were in training, he told what he stole. They weren't adult books, he stole Shakespeare. The idiot was arrested for stealing Shakespeare, ha!"

Nate hit Adam in his leg with a fist and cursed. "That isn't funny, you can't even read it!"

"So you joined to avoid prison. Not a bad trade off, no jail to be a riflemen." I said.

"Actually, I'm a translator with a rifle. I speak and write German, French, Polish, Russian, and a little Swiss," said Nate.

"Ah, really? I know Gaelic, French, and some German." I said. Jay laughed at the German. "Fine, I barely know German. Besides counting to five, I can say 'put it on my friend's tab' and 'hey good looking," I confessed.

"Well, I speak English and that's it," Adam jumped in. "Now, I ain't special, but I handle the radio." He patted the field radio strapped to his back.

"If you handle the radio, why aren't you up with the Captain?" Jay asked.

Adam shrugged off the question. "Don't know, I guess he prefers the one in the jeep."

Jay tapped my arm. "Hey, looks like the convoy is breaking up."

I looked out ahead and saw the lead group turn down a separate road to the right. Once they broke off, Captain Hiller signaled to turn left, across a small bridge over a ravine. Jay followed close, as the Captain broke away. Jay signaled the two halftracks behind to come along. Once we broke off, the rest of the convoy pulled on ahead, not slowing.

"So, what are we taking again?" Nate asked.

"A refueling point for our tanks," I answered. "It's a right across the bridge and around a low hill."

The jeep jumped a little as it rattled across the wooden bridge. Below, a large, open void loomed. It looked to be a long way down. I silently prayed the bridge wouldn't collapse. I wasn't afraid of heights, but I didn't want to go falling into a pit.

"I dare ya to spit over the edge," Adam said to Nate.

"How 'bout I throw you over, that'll be even better," Nate asked. Adam quickly shut up as we drove along.

"Hey, I just remembered something," Nate said, breaking the silence.

"What is it?" I asked.

"Back when I was a kid, my friends and I used to hang around an old train bridge over a river near our houses. It was linked to an abandoned train station that we used to play around in. One time, we were walking home along the tracks, when one of my friends challenged me to walk across the bridge only staying on one rail."

"Naturally, I did it without complaint. I stopped halfway and gloated about not falling. My friend that challenged me got pissed and followed me out, showing me he could do it too. He walks out, shaking like a frigging' leaf, and stands next to me. He was leaning too far back and lost his balance, and fell backwards and pulled me with 'em! I snagged my clothes on the bridge, while he fell into the water. Bastard's been out to get me for years," Nate declared.

"And so that proves you're a boastful son of a bitch?" Adam joked. Nate just waved off the comment.

"Hey, looks like the Captain wants us to pull over," Jay intervened.

Captain Hiller pulled his jeep over on the side of the road, just at the base of a hill. He waved for us to pull next to him, while the tracks stayed on the road. We wondered what it could be.

Jay pulled the jeep next to him and came too a stop. "There a problem, Captain?" Jay asked.

"No, this is where we stop," he said, pulling out a map. He spread it out over the hood of our jeep and we gathered around him. He waved the rest of the squad to dismount and join around, as well. "All of you, listen up. This is the refueling point, here." He tapped a small circled area on the map.

"The base is basically a grouping of poorly made buildings. They have a large supply of oil and ammo packed away in a cave, here. They also set up several repair stations, as well. The camp is guarded by several towers at the perimeter, just inside the wire fence. They have a Garrison of roughly two dozen armed troopers and a handful of mechanics."

"Roughly, sir?" one of the replacements asked.

"Yeah," Captain Hiller continued, "intel is piss poor on this, so we assume at least three dozen men. The good thing is a recon flight took these pictures." He pulled several photos from his jacket pocket and dropped them on the map. "It shows that the four guard towers are unmanned and security is lax."

"So, what's the plan?" another replacement asked.

"Okay, I want those who road in the tracks to mount up and breach in through the main gate. Use the tracks for cover and draw their attention. Vic, you'll be in charge of them. While you are distracting them, I will take Bolger, Hawkins and these two," he pointed to Nate and Adam. "Up the hill and attack from their flank, creating crossfire. This will let the breach team push in and take the barracks on the west side of the gate and then branch out to secure the rest of the base.

I'll head in and infiltrate through the rear fence, here, as he pointed. Inside, we'll grab as much attention as possible. This should give the impression we are a larger force then we are. Jay will be on the hill for sniper cover and we could mount some of the tower guns to provide fire support. Questions, no? Good, let's get moving," said the Captain.

Captain Hiller folded up the map and placed it in his jacket with the photos. The squad mounted back up in the tracks and readied to move. Jay and I grabbed our rifles from the jeep and walked with Adam and Nate up the hill. Captain Hiller loaded his Thompson and waved the tracks to go forward. As they drove on, Hiller ran, with us, up the hill.

Taking a short run up the hill, we stopped at the top. As soon as we stopped, the Captain ordered us to drop to our stomachs. We did as ordered, dropping to the sandy ground with thuds. When I hit the ground, the bandage on my arm yanked back on my skin, creating a quick shock off pain. Rolling on my back, I rubbed my arm and the pain soon dulled.

"Can you work from here?" Captain Hiller asked Jay.

Jay crawled forward a little and drew his binoculars. He looked through and studied the camp for a few seconds. "This isn't the best spot, sir, but good enough," Jay said as he took his pack off and used it to balance the rifle.

"Where can't you cover us?" Captain Hiller asked.

"Ah, I can see nearly the entire camp from here, expect for the buildings on the far edge. The stacks of supply crates and oil drums are shading them. I can hit a few spots, but most of the area is covered. I could move to another spot, but I won't be able to see the entire camp from anywhere around here, sir," Jay said.

"Stay here and cover us as best as you can. Now, the second the tracks hit the gate, we sneak down and cut the wire to get in. Once we're inside, follow me and do as I do. If I die, link up with the tracks. Hawkins, take out anyone in the towers when the tracks show up," Captain Hiller ordered.

With that, everyone went quiet. We stayed sprawled out on the ground, on our stomachs, watching over the camp. I was trying to see how many troopers were in sight' I spotted the ones that were manning the MG nests. Now and again, I would roll over and rub my bandages as sweat collected under them. The things were made to hold in blood, but they soaked up the sweat just the same.

"Look," Adam whispered, pointing to the gate.

We looked and saw the two tracks charging the gates. The German guards were yelling for the tracks to stop, not knowing they were American not German. As the tracks drew close, the gunners mounted the turret.50cal machine guns and began to fire on the Germans. They scattered under the fire, running for cover instead of firing on the tracks.

"Okay, let's move!" Captain Hiller yelled. Together, we rose from our position and made a run for the fence. The fence was only a few meters down the hill, but it was all open ground the entire way.

Running as fast as I could, I tried to make it across without being seen. The Germans were occupied with fighting off the tracks at the gate, so they weren't watching the wire. The guard towers facing us were empty, and there were no soldiers patrolling on foot. It was easy to reach the wire without being shot, but the boiling sun caused us to sweat profusely and our uniforms were soaked with sweat and drained our energy.

We made it to the wire safely and unharmed. We came upon a section of wire that was next to a supply building, blocking the view of the Germans in camp. Captain Hiller pulled a pair of wire cutters from his belt and began cutting the ties that held the wire to a fence post. Cutting a small section on the bottom, he pulled out a section of wire so we could crawl in.

I crawled through behind Adam, keeping my rifle on my back. Once through, I gripped my rifle in my hands and ducked behind the building for cover. Once everyone was in, Captain Hiller edged over to the side of the building and glanced out into the compound, but pulled back quickly.

"We have a problem," he said, waving Adam over. "We got four Panzers and two flatbed mortars being fueled up just a few yards away. The tanks looked like they were being loaded with more shells and the mortars are gassing up."

"What do we do now, sir?" Nate asked.

"Shouldn't we flank around the tanks and climb on top to drop some grenades in their hatches?" I asked.

"That would be best, but if we're spotted too early, we'll be in some serious trouble," the Captain said as he thought over the plan and finally agreed. "Okay, we follow along these perimeter buildings and sneak behind those supply stacks to get behind the Panzers. Since there are four of us, we each board one tank. On top, pop the hatches, roll a grenade in, close the hatch, and then jump clear."

"Sir," Adam said. "I don't have any grenades."

Captain Hiller sighed. "Bolger, give him some of yours, now let's move."

I handed three grenades to Adam, leaving the rest for myself. I ran behind the Captain as we darted behind the buildings near the wire. We kept close to buildings and checked before running in between them. If we were spotted, the Panzers would swing around and fire on us. If that happened, the troopers at the gate would be slaughtered.

As we ran, the troopers near the flatbeds began shouting to one another. The Captain Took Adam and Nate behind a stack of crates and told me to wait behind one of the buildings. I stayed back and watched the men by the flatbeds. They were shouting orders to one another, but they seemed confused. Well, I thought, I guess they should've taught the Vichy German.

The Vichy troops were poorly trained and didn't know how to properly man the mortars. Either they couldn't understand the Germans or they never trained them on the mortars. Either way, it was funny watching them fumbling with the mortar's controls and trying, but failing, to properly load them.

Across the compound, Captain Hiller, Nate, and Adam were ducking behind the Panzers. They signaled me with a wave, which meant I was to draw the fire of the Germans. When Hiller tapped his Thompson, I was ordered to fire on the enemy and draw there fire while they spiked the tanks. It wasn't a step up or down from the original plan, but I didn't like being the target.

The Captain tapped his SMG and I nodded.

Leaning out from behind the building, I took aim at the Vichy trying to load the mortar. Carefully, I lined him up in the crosshairs. Slowly, I took a breath and let it out, squeezing the trigger back. With a pop, the soldier's chest erupted in a puff of red mist and he tumbled off the flatbed. The other soldiers scrambled for cover and began shooting back. I fired three more rounds and pulled back as bullets whizzed by and crashed against the building.

Then I heard a separate, louder pop over the echo of machine gun fire. It was Jay helping out with sniper cover. I guessed his fire spooked the Germans, but they began firing into the hills. I leaned out and emptied the rest of my clip, killing two more Germans. I pulled back and loaded another clip, when there was a series of three explosions and then a fourth a second or two later.

I peered out and saw the four Panzers, billowing smoke rising from their hatches and main cannons. They were all spiked and were no longer a threat. Captain Hiller and the others used them for cover and began firing on the mortars. I fired again, helping create crossfire between the Captain and myself. The fire was concentrated and we killed the mortar crews along with the Germans guarding them.

As the shooting in the area died down, the echo from the gate also died, I regrouped with the Captain by the flatbeds. He gave an approving head nod as he stepped over the soldier I killed, with a shot to the chest. He handed Nate two grenades and pointed to the mortars. Nate took them and jumped onto the flatbeds, dropping the grenades in the tubes.

"Good work," Captain Hiller said to us. "Now, we need to get to the gate and help the others." The grenades exploded, destroying the mortars. "Ready? Let's move."

The four of us walked down the gate through the center of the camp. The area was made of makeshift buildings and tents, with oil drums stacked everywhere. The area, was also deserted, with no Germans of Vichy around. We found rifles and MP-40's lying on the ground along with ammo pouches and backpacks. Scattered about them, were footprints that led away from camp and to the perimeter fence. Along the wire, I could see a section was cut away. The Germans and Vichy had ran from the fight.

"Son of a bitch cowards," Nate spat. "No fight in them at all. No fun."

Captain Hiller slapped Nate in the back of his head and knocked off his helmet. "You want the real fight of the Nazi's? What kind of idiot are you?"

"Sorry, sir," Nate whispered, picking up his helmet.

"Don't apologize, it makes you look weak," the Captain shot back as he walked on. Once he was far enough ahead, Nate turned to me in confusion.

"Relax," I said, giving a reassuring shove.

"Is there anything else I should watch out for with him?"

"No, I'll sum it up for you. Welcome to the squad," I smirked.

Chapter 5

The good luck, our squad was experiencing, would be short lived. While we took the supply point with little effort and had the enemy running for the hills, things weren't good for the rest of the division. In the days following our landing, we linked the land between Oran and Algiers, uniting with the British and with the rest of the U.S. troops in Casablanca. Soon, our forces began to push eastward and had taken Tunis. Along the way, we ran into the hardened forces of Rommel's Afrika Korps. While clashing with them, U.S. and British services were beaten to shit. It got so bad, I thought our advance might stall and we'd be put on the defense.

By February, our company took six defeats against the Germans. On February 28, 1942 we were stationed at the defensive line in the Kasserine Pass. There, forces from the other infantry divisions linked together, to a staging area, to support the British, in attacking Tunisia and taking Tunis. Unfortunately, General Patton took command of our company before we were transferred to the command of General Terry Allen. That pain in the ass Patton forced the strictest regulations on us, but we were paid to fight Germans, so he was a tolerable pain, for now.

When we arrived in the pass we were stationed in the hills, on the far right of the pass. We overlooked the southern entrance that faced the German forces. The squad settled in the rocky hills and set up mortar and machine gun positions to fire down on the Germans. Below us, other troops built up trenches, tank traps, barbed wire entanglements, mine fields, and artillery stations. One position was O.P. 21, which was far ahead of our lines.

O.P. 21 was a small trench/foxhole two miles ahead of our lines. The trench was covered with a tin tarp to block out the sun and it had a small, well used, field radio. The site was built in the open sun, not in the shade of the hills. With the heat and no real way of getting to the lines in case of attack, it was the worse place to be. We were asked to give two troopers to man it, Vic and I drew the short straw.

"It's damn hot," Vic mumbled as he sat at the bottom of the trench, BAR leaning against the wall.

"Yeah, it was hot ten minutes ago when you first said it," I shot back, leaning on my rifle at the top of the trench.

"You're smart, make it cooler," he grunted, drinking from his canteen.

"Sorry, I can't. Stop thinking about the heat and you'll feel cooler," I offered.

"That's your wisdom? How'd I get stuck with you?" Vic cried. I ignored him and picked up my binoculars. I looked through at the burning desert in front of us, seeing only the ripples of heat rising.

The sun pounded on us as it reached midday. My sweat trickled down my neck and soaked my shirt; pooling by my dog tags and making them stick to my body. I rubbed my chest and pulled my tags out, resting them on the outside of my shirt. Still, more sweat formed under the rim of my helmet and rolled into my eyes. Constantly, I wiped my eyes, but to no avail. I glanced at my watch and slid down next to Vic.

"Your turn on watch, Vic," I said, removing my helmet.

"Perfect," he moaned as he stood up, pulling the BAR with him. I handed him my binoculars and pulled out my canteen.

Taking in a long swing of warm water, I moistened my arid throat. Then I pulled a rag from my belt and wiped away the sweat from my head and neck. It brought some minor relief so, I decided to finish my letter, to my older brother Matthew, who was a fighter pilot in England.

Dear Matt,

Well, bro, I managed to get a minute of relief in under this unforgiving sun. Right now, I sit far ahead of our forces with only one other trooper with me. When Rommel comes knocking, I'm the doorman. What a life, eh? Then again, it is not to ask why, just to do and die.

So, how are things on your end? I'm guessing it's easy to fly and shoot down some Germans and then go home to drink and fraternize with the English women. Man, I wish I could be in your shoes, but I guess they need boots on the ground.

Well, I best get some sleep for the first time in a week while I can. Good luck, Matt, master of the skies.

P.S. If you hear from Frank, let me know. I can't get any mail to him or from him, must be a Marine thing.

The middle child,
Corr, 1st Infantry DIV

After I finished my letter I tucked it into my shirt pocket, for safe keeping. I pulled off my backpack and placed it against the wall of the trench while taking took off my helmet. It was comforting to lay back against my pack, using it as a pillow. I tapped Vic on the boot to get his attention.

"Wake me for my shift," I told him, closing my eyes to the sun.

"Huh? Oh, fine, I'll just sit in the sun" he moaned to me. Slowly, I began to fall asleep, ignoring the heat and bright sun. Eventually, I fell asleep for the first damn time in weeks.

Sometime later, I felt Vic tugging at my leg. I moaned for being woken up and kicked at him to stop. He cursed and kicked me back. That got me to jump up. "What?" I questioned.

"That!" he yelled, pointing out into the desert. I stood up and looked out to where he was pointing. I saw a line of dull sand colored behemoths grinding towards us, with lines of soldiers in between them.

"Rommel's back," I whispered to myself, looking at the line of Panzers and German infantry rolling towards us. The sound of tracks grinding on the packed sand and the thuds of boots echoed through the hills behind us and scarred the hell out of me. I noticed two lightly armed troopers against Rommel's armored corps. "Call command and let them know what's coming, now," I ordered Vic.

"On it," Vic ducked down and fumbled with the radio until it crackled to life. He yelled into the receiver, shouting our position, and that of the Germans, back to command. Judging by his shouts and frustration in his voice, he could not get through. "No good, the things dead, " he said annoyed.

"Perfect," I huffed, grabbing my rifle and placing my helmet back on. "We need to alert command as fast as possible."

"If we run, they'll pick us off before we reach the hills," Vic said.

"Let's head to OP 19, it's the closest to us. Maybe their radio is working," I suggested.

"And if it's not?" Vic asked.

"Then we run to the next post until we find a working radio or until we reach the main line. So, let's get ready to run." I said as I looked over our surroundings and saw mostly flat desert. There were hills to our flanks, but they were too far off. Our only cover was a series of low knolls directly behind us. There was a stretch of open land between them and our foxhole which gave the Germans a chance to kill us. "We head to the knolls."

"That's more open ground then I like," Vic sounded worried, something that rarely happened.

"We'll make it if you don't slow down, big boy," I said as Vic grunted at my response and crawled out of the trench, lying low. Once he was out, I climbed up behind him and dropped low.

Taking a breath, I nodded for him to run. He nodded back and together we rose to our feet and began the dash to the knolls. Juggling the weight of my pack and rifle, I managed to run as fast as possible, with Vic keeping up, clutching his heavy BAR. I had to slow down a bit to make sure he didn't fall behind. Then a section of dirt exploded, sending chunks of sand into the air. The Panzers began to fire on us.

We split apart from one another and stopped running in strait lines to prevent the tanks from getting a beat. Still, they fired with thunderous roars, sending shells screaming overhead and detonating in front of us. Plumes of dirt and sand exploded into the air around us and then rained back down. Chunks of packed dirt pelted my helmet and nearly knocked me off balance, but I managed to reach the knolls and find cover.

I rolled onto my stomach and crawled to the top of the knoll to look for Vic. As I reached the top, he came sprinting over and slammed into me, sending both of us tumbling to the bottom.

"Get off!" I yelled to Vic, over the roar of tank fire. "I'm trying to!" he shouted back as I tried to push his heavy weight off me. He jumped off me and we began to crawl over a second knoll to reach dry riverbed, on the other side. I took the lead in front of Vic and crept over first, landing in the riverbed. Vic followed and dropped next to me as the top of the knoll vanished in an explosion.

"Now what?" Vic asked.

"We follow the riverbed to the OP, so stay close," I answered, checking to see the riverbed was clear.

After deciding which way the OP was, we began down the riverbed, which acted as a natural trench. We ran, staying close to the wall of the river. Tank and artillery shells soared overhead and exploded as they either fell short or over shot our position. Some shells came close and exploded on the edge of the bed next to us or on the opposite side. The explosions kept us ducking for cover as we ran, nearly stopping when the shells landed too close. Then, we heard the sound of artillery, soon combined with the whiz and crack of rifle and machine gun fire.

Bullets whizzed overhead and thudded into the sand and dirt around us. They marked that the advancing Germans were in rifle range. Now arty and tanks shells exploded around us as bullets soared past, narrowly missing us. At one point, a bullet hit the webbing strap on my left shoulder, nearly severing it. The bullet tore half the fabric and embedded itself in my shirt. That was too close for comfort.

Running as fast as we could, we finally spotted the O.P. at the edge of the riverbed, near wear the river used to snake through the hills. The

O.P. was manned by four troopers armed with a.30cal machinegun and one AT rocket launcher, or bazooka. They could buy us some time to contact command with the warning.

Vic and I ran through the riverbed and came upon the O.P. Two of the troopers were manning the.30cal and one was loading the AT launcher. The fourth sat loading his Thompson when he saw us. He alerted the others, who waved us to them. We ran to them and hunkered down behind the machinegun.

"Who are you?" asked the sergeant who was loading the bazooka.

"Corporal Carr Bolger, C Company. We just came from O.P. 21," I answered.

"Why didn't you radio us? Why did you abandoned your post?" He demanded.

"Our radio was broken and we needed to alert you, I hope your radio works," Vic answered for the two of us.

"Well, we radioed ahead already." A tank shell exploded behind us, sending down a shower of dirt. "Leonard, Gates, get that.30 firing when they come into range," he yelled to the two troopers manning the machine gun. "Ellis, take the bazooka and knock the first tank that comes in range."

"We can't hold them off," Vic objected.

"I know, we need to take as many of them down, as we can, before pulling out. You two, get to the hills and get ready to cover us when we pull back. Go!" He yelled. Vic and I ran down the riverbed, into the hills, and climbed. The hills had enough large rocks and boulders to use for cover, not to mention caves. We climbed up a few feet to get a good line of sight on the O.P. Vic lay down on a ledge and propped his BAR on a rock. I kneeled behind a large boulder and pulled out my binoculars. I would watch for the Sergeant to retreat and then cover them.

I observed the troops down below, manning their machine gun, open fire, as the Germans came into range. The.30 cal bullets cut down lines of infantry, but pinged off the tanks. The single bazooka operator fired at the leading panzer as it charged towards them. The rocket slammed into the tanks right tread and broke the tracks, causing the tank to stop. The others remained on task, not slowing as infantry fell. Then I saw a German Hummel take position on a ridge behind the advance.

The Hummel was a German self propelled artillery piece, mounting a 122mm gun. The Hummel hurled heavy shells over long distances and could tear apart a defensive line in seconds. Now three more Hummel's joined the other, on the ridge, and pointed their barrels skyward. Just then there was a volley of loud, low pitched explosions as the Hummel's fired.

It was too late to warn the Sergeant and his men. They were still fighting as the arty shells slammed into the O.P. A series of explosions and consumed the O.P. in a cloud of smoke, dirt, and fire, obliterating the Sergeant and his men in an instant. The cloud slowly disappeared and I saw the blackened crater of the O.P. I felt a twinge of pain at the loss, but I grabbed Vic and we began to move our way through the, to our lines.

We moved slowly and cautiously as we snaked through the hills. The German advance past us and we could hear explosions coming from the direction of our lines. On the horizon, clouds of dark, smoke rose into the air and turned the sky black. Mixed with the dark sky, the dull shadows of German aircraft dipped in and out of the clouds, their engines giving off a whining drone.

"I wonder if our guys still hold the pass," Vic asked aloud as we trekked across the hills.

"I'm guessing we do, since the arty hasn't let up in the last hour of walking," I shot back, adjusting my rifle sling on my shoulder.

"Well, I hope we get back in time to kill some Germans. Hey, look," Vic said. I turned to see another line of tanks advancing in the pass below. The group of panzers and halftracks were making full speed toward our lines. Thankfully, their speed aided us, since they weren't focused on watching the hills.

"That is not good. We need to hurry before they overrun the pass." I huffed out a breath of air and began moving faster in the slopped hills. I climbed over boulders and rocks as fast as I could, nearly falling several times. Vic kept up with me, but grunted every time he had to climb over something. I offered to help carry the ammo clips for his BAR, but he cursed every time I asked. After awhile, I gave up on talking and kept walking.

After hours of walking, it became night. The burning sun disappeared behind the horizon and the cool night emerged. It was a welcome relief, but the temperature could drop extremely low. We continued on in the hills until we found the German base of operations. Their base was nestled in the pass just a half mile out from our lines. They set up tanks to guard their base, but they didn't have many scouts in the hills. We managed to sneak by and reach the hills overlooking our front line.

We carefully climbed down from the hills just a few dozen meters from the trenches and foxholes that made up our frontline. There were only had a handful of MG nests and AT guns set up to defend the line. Mixed with a few Stuart tanks and several AT halftracks, it was a poor example of a defensive line, it was a surprise that the Germans hadn't broken through already.

Slowly, I approached one of the trenches on the edge of the line, keeping Vic in the hills. I drew closer, on my own, so I could let the troopers know I was a friendly and they didn't shoot us. The foxhole I came upon held a pair of troopers armed with a small knee mortar. I had to get their attention, so I hugged the ground near their position and whistled. The soldiers jumped at the sound and drew their weapons, aiming towards my position.

I held my rifle in the air for them to see, but I kept down. "Hold fire, hold fire," I yelled to them. They kept their weapons drawn in alertness. "Bronx, Bronx." I yelled the first half of the clear code I was given in Oran.

"Bombers," the troopers answered, completing the code. "Stand up and keep your hands up.

"Don't' shoot." I kept my rifle raised and slowly stood up. With the low light, I could just make out the two soldiers.

"Stop right there and keep your hands up," one soldier ordered as he stepped out from his foxhole, cautiously walking to me. He stepped in closer and looked me over, slightly lowering his rifle.

"Corporal Corr Bolger, C Company," I shouted, as I kept my rifle above my head and tried not to move.

"What are you doing out here?" A soldier asked.

"I was stationed at a forward O.P. and we had to retreat. My buddy and I pulled back here. He's just up in the hills," I said and pointed to Vic's location and whistled for him to come down. Slowly, he walked down and stopped next to me, hands in plain view.

"You think they're legit?" one soldier asked, rifle aimed at my chest. The other shrugged and stepped closer to us, looking me up and down before shrugging.

"I think they're legit," one said. The troopers lowered their weapons and let us step into their trench. Several other troopers were with them, mounting a bazooka and a.30 cal machinegun. I sat down next to Vic and took off my helmet.

"You said you were stationed at an O.P.?" one trooper asked, cleaning his bazooka with a rag.

"Yeah, a few miles out," Vic answered, resting his BAR in his lap.

"We heard reports that the posts out front were all destroyed. How'd you make it back?" The trooper asked.

"Long story, but I really want to sleep," Vic said. I nodded, and

rubbed my eyes. The troopers glanced at one another and returned to their posts. Vic stretched out and pulled his helmet over his eyes, drifting off to sleep in a few seconds. I drew my knees to my chest and rested my head on my knees. I wanted to sleep, but I just couldn't. Everything that happened since the landings had been bothering me. I'd seen so much death and loss. Eventually, I drifted off to sleep, curled up in a tight ball.

I could never get much sleep during combat. Whenever I seemed to fall asleep, something would wake me up. This time, it was the rolling thunder or German arty. I awoke in a state of surprise and shock as an arty round impacted a few feet from the trench. I shot up and noticed it was still dark. I glanced at my watch and saw it was around five in the morning, just before sunrise. The German artillery barrage was just beginning.

"Not long before they attack again," one of the troopers grunted, cleaning his rifle, paying no heed to the arty fire.

"Just one more hour of sleep, just one!" another trooper yelled. "Fucking Germans."

"Yeah, keep running your mouth, Swanson," a sergeant snorted, changing out the clip on his Thompson sub machinegun.

"Leave junior alone, Joe," another sergeant said calmly, leaning against the wall of the trench.

"Sure, you stop him when he starts foaming at the mouth, Pat," someone called out.

I sat up as the thunder of arty fie grew louder and closer. Placing my helmet on, and getting my rifle ready, I stood up to see out of the trench and watched as the arty shells exploded in the open desert.

"They may seem to be wasting ammo," the corporal with the bazooka informed us. "But, they're just bracketing us. The next two volleys or so will bring it right over us."

"How do you know, Mr. Genius?" Swanson asked, watching the barrage through a pair of field glasses.

"I'm an arty man," he said proudly. "I should be back there readying a counter barrage for the Krauts, but no, they stick a bazooka into my hands and put me up here."

"That's the Army way," Pat shot back, grinning slightly.

"Fucking A!" Vic grunted loudly, clicking the safety on his BAR. There was another round of explosions that kept creeping closer and closer to us. Then, it stopped, as if the Germans ran out of ammo.

"You were saying?" Swanson said to the corporal, words dripping with uncontrolled humor. Before the corporal could answer, the barrage landed right on top of us. Explosions shook the ground as the arty landed spot onto our position. Everyone dropped down, trying to get as low as possible. I held my helmet on my head and squeezed my eyes shut. Vic was lying next to me, BAR clamped tightly in his fists. Up above, the arty shells exploded everywhere. Deadly white hot shrapnel whizzed everywhere, slicing up anyone or thing above ground. We could her soldiers screaming in pain of the explosions mixed with the noise of crunching steel and dirt as chunks of sand and rock rained down on us.

"Just stay down!" Sergeant Patrick yelled to all of us. "Keep low and you will survive."

I silently prayed to myself, promising God I would give anything to live another day. I prayed that the one arty shell that might land in our trench was a dud or missed by an inch or two.

"Isn't this fun?" Vic shouted over the roar of the artillery fires. I kept my head down and covered my ears, trying to muffle the ear shattering explosions, but the barrage soon tapered off. Within a few minutes of the start, the barrage ceased. It was quiet afterward, the silence only being broken by the crackle of fire or moans and screams of wounded men. Once we were sure it was over, we slowly stood up and looked out of the trench.

I stood and glanced around, taking in the damage. The attack left several halftracks and jeeps in burning wrecks where they were stopped. Several AT guns were blown to pieces, their crews scattered about the sections of twisted steel. Dead and wounded troopers lay about over the ground, many unmoving. Those that were alive moaned and cried out in pain as medics dashed out to help them. Officers began issuing orders and reorganizing to troops.

"Joe, head out with Swanson, Lipton, and the two new kids and help. I'll stay here with Dike and Allen to guard the line," Sergeant Patrick ordered.

"You heard him, let's go," Sergeant Joseph grunted, brushing sand off his uniform. I picked up my rifle and climbed out of the trench, following Vic. Together, we walked down the line looking to help anyway we could. Vic and I found an MG team digging out a collapsed foxhole.

"Want a hand?" I asked one of the soldiers. He turned to me and tossed up two spare shovels.

"If you're not busy," he said, returning to his digging. I slung my rifle over my shoulder and began digging. Working hard, we dug out the loose sand that now filled up the foxhole. The four of us managed to dig out most of the new sand, but lots of it kept falling back it.

Eventually, we discovered where the original foxhole stopped. We unearthed a buried.30cal machinegun with several boxes of ammo, all now clogged with sand.

"Thanks for the help," one of the gunners said, opening up the breach of the machine gun.

"No problem," I said back, walking away with Vic.

"Wonder where the squad is?" he asked as we walked around the line.

"They'll probably find us somehow," I answered. We passed by a halftrack mounted with an AT cannon, dug in behind a wall of sandbags. The track and her crew had avoided any damage, but the track next to them was now a burnt our crater. Past them, we spotted another set of trenches. We jumped in and bumped into Nate.

"What the hell happened to you?" he asked, seeing us for the first time in several days.

"Had a fight with a few German tanks," Vic grunted, passing by him to see the rest of the squad.

"We won," I answered for him, shaking Nate's hand. "What'd we miss?"

Nate shrugged and said, "The Germans have been attacking us in full force for days. We've lost of lot of men and are running low on supplies. If we don't get relief soon, we'll lose the pass."

I looked past him at the rest of the squad sitting in the trenches. "We lose anyone?" I asked.

"Thankfully, no, Captain Hiller's been keeping an eye on us," Nate explained. There was a series of small explosions out in the desert that drew everyone's attention. Captain Hiller appeared and scanned the area with his field glasses.

"Defensive positions!" he shouted. "They're coming back." Everyone grabbed their weapons and ran to the firing lip of the trench, standing up to shoot out. I stood next to Nate and readied my rifle. In front of our lines, the Germans were amassing for an attack.

We could see tanks of varying models lining up for a blitz attack on our lines. Halftracks and infantry lined up behind the, loading up last bits of ammunition and fuel. Then, they were ready and began the attack. The first line of tanks and skirmisher infantry advanced forward on our position, moving slowly to act as a rolling cover. Both of our forces were out of range, creating an uneasy silence.

As the seconds ticked away, everyone could hear and feel the tension in the air. The soldiers around us tensed up as the gripped their weapons, fingers hovering over their triggers. Officers carefully watched their troopers, reassuring those who were too jumpy. Captain Hiller walked down the trench, placing a hand on a shoulder or two to ease worried troopers. I held my rifle tight as he passed, keeping my eyes frozen to my iron sights. Hiller placed a hand on my shoulder.

"Keeping steady, Bolger," he said calmly.

"Yes, sir, I am," I said dryly, tensing my shoulders slightly.

"Remember to aim a little low when shooting and don't waste ammo on tanks." After giving his advice, he walked back down the trench. I glanced next to me and saw Nate tapping his fingers on the barrel of his rifle. He looked nervous, but kept his composure. He looked at me and nodded his head, helmet slipping a little. I nodded back and turned to face the Germans.

They were soon in range of our heavy guns, which were several portable mortars called knee mortars. The mortars fired a barrage of a dozen or so shells into the air that arched up and then zoomed back down to the ground. The high volatile shells exploded as they hit the hard packed ground. Explosions ripped across the enemy formation, killing dozens of the advancing German infantry. Several halftracks were blown to shrapnel in the process while the tanks kept on coming, unfazed by the loss of their comrades or the mortars.

"Well, that was a waste," Nate grunted, seeing the rolling tanks.

They continued on as they came into range. The tanks aimed their main cannons towards us and fired. A salvo of heavy tank shells screamed towards us, exploding in random spots across our lines. The shells were poorly aimed, but every time they exploded, I flinched. They continued firing as they sped towards us, sending shell after shell our way. Still, all soldiers on our end held fire, knowing it would be useless. When the tanks were in range of our track mounted guns, they opened up in a carefully aimed salvo. Our AT fire slammed into the lead tanks, landing accurately on their treads instead of their frontal armor.

The explosions knocked the treads off several tanks. Crippled, the wounded tanks stalled out and stood motionless on the field. Our AT guns blasted them away in seconds, before turning back to other tanks. Despite the fast and accurate firing, the Germans closed the gap between them and our lines in seconds. The skirmishers out front rushed our lines, firing blindly. At once, our line erupted, in a burst of gun fire, as everyone opened fire. I lined up the nearest Germans and fired several rounds. A tan uniformed soldier dropped, both his legs shot out from underneath him. The others were cut down in seconds beneath the relentless fire of our .30cal machine guns and rifle fire.

The German infantry managed to get close to our front defenses and mixed in our foxholes and trenches. As they fought hand to hand, we picked off those that we could. I could here the high cracks of Jay's Springfield Rifle firing mixed with the hard cracks of Vic's BAR. I fired as accurately as I could. Once eight rounds were fired, I quickly reloaded and returned shooting. While I only killed two or three soldiers, I sent a lot of lead down range when the tanks arrived.

Panzer IVs rushed our lines firing at pointblank range. Their heavy machineguns ripped up the crews of unprotected AT cannons, chewing up the helpless men. Their tank shells gutted our light halftracks in seconds, ripping our defenses to shreds. One tank fired at our trench from several feet away. I jumped down and covered my head as an explosion sent dirt showering down on my helmet. Once it past, I stood back, only to have Nate pull me down. I lay at the bottom of the trench as a German tank drove right over the trench.

"We're being overrun!" Jay yelled.

"Keep fighting!" Hiller yelled, standing back up as the tank passed. I stood back up and scanned for targets when a screaming German jumped into our trench. He threw himself at me, knocking away my rifle. I fought back and pulled out my knife. The German threw his hands around my neck and attempted to strangle me. I caught him in the chest with my knee and stabbed right into his ribcage, most likely puncturing a lung. His grip slacked as he drew back in pain. I pushed the attacker and brought the knife in under his chin, jamming it in as far as the hilt. With a gargled scream, the German dropped, unmoving.

"Watch it!" Nate screamed. I whirled around to see another German charging me, bayonet on the barrel of his rifle. Nate fired and caught the German in the center of his chest, propelling the dead man back. I pulled my rifle from the bottom of the trench and tucked my knife away.

"Thanks," I said to Nate, shaking sand from my rifle.

"Any time," he said, returning to the fighting.

We stood up and began firing again. By now, the enemy forces were mixed in with our forces, fighting in deadly hand to hand combat. Soldiers desperately fought with anything and everything at hand, from knifes, shovels, helmets, and their fists. We tried our best to pick off the Germans tangling with our men, but one missed shot and we could kill one of our own. I ducked down to reload when I saw a Panzer stalled out in shell crater. It was billowing smoke from its engine, but the turret was firing away.

"Captain!" I yelled, pointing to the tank. Captain Hiller looked over and nodded.

"Smart thinking, Bolger!" he yelled, running over to me. He pulled a pair of grenades from his webbing and gave one to me. "Squad, cover Bolger and me!"

"Yes, sir!" Vic yelled, firing his BAR. Captain Hiller reloaded his Thompson and peeked over the edge of the trench.

"Stay on my ass," he grunted to me, pulling himself over the wall of the trench.

"Yes, sir." I pulled myself up after him and rolled in the dirt as I came over the trench. Captain Hiller was up and running, firing at anything wearing a tan uniform. I pulled myself t to my feet and followed. Several bullets whooshed past my head and missed by inches. I jumped as more bullets impacted around my feet, sending up small plumes of sand. I ran after the Captain, firing blindly now and again. I saw the tank turret spin towards us and the Captain slid next to the tank by the treads. I dove forward and rolled next to him, gasping for air.

"Pop the hatch and I'll spray the inside. When I pull back, toss in your grenade, close the hatch and jump clear, got it?" Captain Hiller said and I nodded my head. "'Alright, on three." He glanced up at the tank and back at me. "Three!" He screamed.

Together, we clamored up the side of the tank and stumbled onto the top. I could hear bullets ricocheting off the armor next to us. I fought off the urge to run and grabbed the hatch handle. Hiller pressed the muzzle of his Thompson to the edge of the hatch as I yanked it open. As the hatch spun on rusty hinges, Hiller opened up with a barrage of.45 caliber bullets inside the hatch, pulling back as his clip was empty. I ripped the pin from my grenade and rolled it inside. Hiller tossed in his, as I kicked the hatch shut. Together, we jumped off the top and hugged the sand.

BOOM! The grenade detonated in a low thud inside the tank. What created the big boom was the ammunition inside, cooking off. The hatch was blown off as smoke plumed from the opened gap and the muzzle of the cannon. Hiller grabbed the back of my uniform and pulled me to my feet, throwing me forward. I regained my balance and ran back to the trench. I jumped in with Hiller, breathing heavily.

"That's our Corr," Jay said, looking down at me. Captain Hiller looked over at me and nodded his head before jumping to his feet.

"Look!" someone yelled. Everyone looked up to see a red flare shoot into the day sky. "Fuck, "Captain Hiller spat. "Alright, pull back to phase line Delaware! Move!"

Everyone began pulling back through the trenches to the next defensive line. I followed the rest of the squad through the winding trenches until we reached the end. From there, we had to run across open ground to the next line's dug with AT emplacements. Enemy tanks were mopping up the remainder of our first line troopers while their infantry regrouped. Captain Hiller watched until the tanks were distracted and ordered us to run.

I climbed out of the trench and began running. I took off for the defensive line, running as fast as I could. My gear slowed me down, as it did everyone else. Captain Hiller had no problem whatsoever, running as if he wasn't carrying a thing. I pushed myself harder as more bullets whizzed past me, one nicking my pack. When the sandbag emplacements from the line grew close enough, I jumped up and over them, landing on my chest.

I scrambled back to my knees and dropped behind the sandbags. As I did, the AT guns began firing on the German tanks. These guns were 75mm field guns, made to kill tanks. The crews targeted the side armor of the Panzers and blasted away with extreme accuracy. Peering over the edge of the sandbag wall, I saw three Panzers burst into flames under the hail of anti tank shells. Several others were crippled, trying to crawl away only to be blown to bits. This hail of fire was short lived though, for the gunners were running out of munitions.

The Germans noticed the drop in fire and pushed back. MG teams killed dozens of German infantry, but barely scratched the paint on the Panzers. They fired back with amazing speed and blew away MG and AT positions at random, tearing our lines to shreds. In a matter of minutes, they would plow through this line and grab the Pass. That was something Captain Hiller would not allow and neither would we. Adam snatched a bazooka from a fallen soldier and aimed it at the nearest tank. Nate loaded for him, fumbling with the rocket. He loaded it, tapped Adam's helmet, and backed away. Adam fired the rocket dead on, a whoosh of hot air firing from both ends of the launcher. The rocket streaked away and hit a Panzer right under the turret, knocking out the Panzer's main gun.

"Good hit," I shouted to Adam, reloading my rifle. Adam just nodded as he readied for another shot. Captain Hiller sat behind a sandbag wall next to him, hanging onto his radio. He fumbled with the receiver for a few seconds before screaming into it.

"I don't give a shit what your orders are!" he screamed into the receiver. "You either get me some goddamn tank or arty support up here now, or the Germans will have the pass in an hour!"

Someone responded to him, but it wasn't the response the Captain wanted.

"We won't be here in thirty minutes! Tell those tankers to push it, or we'll be dead!" He tossed the receiver away and returned to his shooting. I knelt down to fire again when a German halftrack crashed through a sandbag wall and began discharging soldiers. I whirled around and began firing at the soldiers jumping out, first killing the gunner manning the MG-42 on top. Then, I pulled a grenade from my belt, pulled the pin, and tossed it into the troop compartment. After a few seconds, the grenade detonated, blowing soldiers out of the halftrack.

"Watch out!" Vic yelled from behind me. I turned to see a Panzer rushing towards me. It barreled through the sandbag wall in front of me, machine guns firing. I dove to the right and hugged the ground as the tank rolled past me. The Panzer blasted another AT gun to scrap and swiveled on its treads, raking the line with machinegun fire. Troopers fell under the torrent of fire, their bodies ripped to shreds.

"Adam, get the bazooka over here!" Vic screamed. Adam leveled the bazooka with the rear of the tank, firing nearly point blank into the engine. The rocket detonated the engine, blowing out the back of the tank. The machinegun fire then stopped as Vic climbed on top and tossed in several grenades.

"Here come some more!" Nate yelled, lobbing a grenade in front of an approaching halftrack. A second line of tanks and tracks rushed our position. This time, they met no AT fire from our line. I was sure we would be overrun. As a Panzer closed on my position, I ducked down as an explosion erupted across the front of the tank, knocking off its treads. I looked up to see a line of Stuart tanks churning up the line in a cloud of dust.

The line of eight little tanks fired furiously as the charged forward. A combination of their weak cannon and mounted.30cal machine guns grabbed the attention of the Germans. The Panzers turned their guns on the new threat, taking the pressure off us. Adam stood up and fired again, knocking out another Panzer. The Stuarts rushed the Panzers, mixing in with their numbers. It was a smart tactic, considering the weak cannon on a Stuart could only damage the treads or rear, integrating with the Germans made them reconsider firing. One Panzer, though, fired at a passing Stuart. Instead of hitting the fast moving tank, the cannon shell hit a nearby Panzer, blowing it to pieces.

"About time!" Jay yelled, watching the Stuarts attack the Panzers.

"It's a band-aide on a friggin' broken leg!" I yelled back, knowing the Panzers would slice the Stuarts up like cheese.

"We've got Lees coming in, hold tight!" the captain ordered. I continued to fire at any Germans that came into sight.

Now and again, I glanced up to watch the Stuarts. The little tanks were crewed by brave men, men who worked furiously to help us. They fought an uphill battle with the Germans, their shells bouncing off the heavy armor of the Panzers. One Stuart took a direct hit, knocking off both treads and splitting the main cannon like a peeled banana. The tank stalled out, propelling black smoke, as the crew attempted to escape. They managed to crawl out the top hatch, only to be blown to bits as the Panzer fired the kill shot.

The Stuart erupted in a ball of fire, consuming the crew in seconds. The victor, a Panzer IV with several kill markers on its turret, turned away and pursued another Stuart. Again, it found his mark on another one of our tanks, cutting off the turret with a single shot. Now, only three of the valiant little tanks lived. Two were circling around to attack the Panzers from the rear while the third sat stalled in a crater. It didn't last long before it was destroyed.

"They're killing us out there," Vic grunted, reloading his BAR.

"Were are those damn Lees?" Adam asked, looking behind, over to the lines. He was back to his rifle now, having dropped the bazooka with no more rockets left.

"There, look!" I yelled, seeing the M4 Lees charging up through the rear of our lines. They were considered medium tanks, mounting a bigger cannon compared to the Stuart. The Lees were not tank killers, but in a pinch they proved effective against light to medium armor. At the time, they were savors to us.

The Lees rushed past our positions and attacked the Germans head on. They fired pointblank, ripping the Panzers apart. The Germans returned the favor, destroying two Lees, but that was their only gain. The Lees quickly destroyed a record seven Panzers, a feat for an infantry support tank. The Panzers turned tail and ran, bugging out in seconds. They took off for the hills, abandoning the attack and leaving the infantry to fend for themselves. They stood no chance alone and were soon gunned down by our MG nests. The Lees mopped up and gave chase to the retreating Panzers.

"Man, that was close," Nate grunted, nudging my shoulder with his. "Right?"

"Close as it comes," Captain Hiller commented, checking his Thompson. "Squad, form up!" Captain Hiller did a quick head count and discovered all of the squad was still alive.

"Orders, sir?" One of the recruits asked, a short dark haired kid with a slight Kentucky accent.

"Stand in incase of a counter. Help the docs if they need it." Captain Hiller said as he glanced around and walked over to a near by tent,which was what was left of our C.P. I slung my rifle over my shoulder and removed my helmet, shaking out the sand from my hair.

"That was fun," Jay said sarcastically, standing next to me.

"I can't wait until the next near death experience." I brushed out the last bits of sand and replaced my helmet. "How did you make out?" I asked.

Jay shrugged, checking the scope on his rifle. "A few bumps and bruises, but alive none the less." He slung his rifle over his shoulder and cracked his knuckles.

"Hey! You two, give me a hand!" We looked over to a nearby foxhole where a medic bent over a wounded trooper. Both of us ran over to his aide, finding a horrific scene.

The medic was kneeling over a trooper with a gushing chest wound. Hands clasped tight, the medic worked hard to hold a bandage down, but the blood soaked through and oozed through his fingers. The trooper laid still, eyes open in shock as blood soaked his uniform. The trooper was young, younger then Jay or me, he couldn't have been more than seventeen.

"Get down here and hold this!" the medic ordered. I dropped down and placed my hands on the bandage, fingers sinking into a collecting pool of blood. I was horrified at the time, getting the sharp feeling I was going to puke. The medic rummaged through his bag and yanked out several sulfur packets and a bandage. He tore the packets open with his teeth and dumped the white powder on the man's wound.

"Hang on, hang on," Jay stammered, helping the medic in opening the bandage.

"Fuck!" the medic yelled as he pressed the new bandage down. The blood continued to ooze out from the edges of the bandage, the trooper coughing up even more blood as he struggled to breathe. The medic furiously fought to save the young soldier, but his coughing stopped and he lay completely still. The medic held the bandage tight, but let go and dropped back on his heels.

"He's dead?" Jay asked.

"Good fucking guess," the medic grunted, yanking off one of the troopers dog tags. He placed the tag in his belt and stood up, rubbing the blood off his hands and onto a rag. "He makes soldier twenty-one I lost today."

As he walked away, I looked down at my now trembling hands. They were still covered with the man's blood, slowly dripping off and onto the sand. I fumbled for a rag in my pocket and began wiping off the blood. I rubbed furiously at the drying blood, getting most of it off. Some clung in between my fingers and under my nails. I pulled out my canteen and washed the rest way with the water.

"Good as new," I said aloud, trying to block everything out. Jay just hung his head and walked away. I looked down at the dead trooper and silently said a prayer. You're not the last, was all I could think.

Part II
Uncommon Heroism

"War's a dirty business to get into, but it's what we're in. Laugh, cry, go quiet, drink, joke, do what you need to find an outlet for your shit." –Corporal Jay Hawkins, US Army

Chapter 6
Gela, Sicily
July 11th, 1943

The fighting for North Africa would slowly dwindle down to the final fights along the Tunisian Coast. Groups of starved and ammo depleted Germans and Italians clung to the small coastal towns for dear life as the steamroller of the Allied armies rolled onward. British and U.S. forces took town after town, slowly cutting down the Germans. After some final, all out fighting, the Germans surrendered on May 1, 1943.

With the fighting in North Africa over, the Big Red One was put on stand down. For the time being, we were sent back to Oran for supplies and training. For the next two months, we trained under the broiling sun, preparing to reenter the war. At the time, we didn't know where or when, but it was a gamble between Sicily and Italy. I bet twenty dollars on Sicily.

Sure enough, we were yanked out of stand down and thrust back into combat. On July 10, 1943, Operation Husky began. The Big Red One was organized into the invasion, tasked with landing at and taking Gela. The Italians, defending the city, surrendered in droves as we came assure, not even bothering to resist. In less than four hours, Gela was ours, but it was too easily won.

"Movement on the road," Jay whispered down to us from his sniper's perch, "thirty to thirty-five Panzers with fifty or so truckloads of troops."

"ETA?" Captain Hiller yelled up to him, standing with us, at the checkpoint guarding the road into Gela.

"Advance teams will hit us in ten minutes," Jay called down.

"Fucking A," the Captain grunted. He scratched his graying hair on the back of his neck and looked around the checkpoint. "Get to your defensive positions. The 16th is coming in an hour or so with arty support. We hold until then."

"Yes, sir!" everyone boomed in unison. Hiller nodded and walked over to his foxhole on the right of the road. I jumped into my foxhole a few feet to the left of the road. Corporal Hank McGee and Private Andrew Dickson sat inside, waiting. We manned a.30cal machine gun that covered the road. Hank, a twenty-two year old farmer from upstate New York, sat manning the gun. Andrew, a nineteen year old textile worker from Delaware, sat next to him cleaning his rifle. I only know this because they mentioned it when I met them. Talk of back home and everyday life is what keeps most soldiers going.

"I heard you two fought in North Africa," Andrew said, brushing sand from his rifle's breach. "See much action?"

Hank glanced over at me, giving a look of 'I'm not taking this for an hour.' I nodded in agreement and answered.

"Yes, we did." I kept the answer short, not wanting a conversation.

"How much?" I rolled my eyes and sighed, rolling onto my back to face him.

"Much, now cut it with the chatter." I growled and rolled back onto my stomach and watched the outlying desert through my binoculars. Andrew was a replacement we received coming to Sicily. He hadn't shut up since we landed.

"What does 'much' mean? Oran, right?" Andrew asked with a nervous excitement.

"Oran, the Pass, Gafsa, and countless skirmishes, so take your pick." I told him and continued to look through my binoculars, observing the advance units of the German convoy.

"Wow, that's a lot of combat. Do you mind…" I held up a hand for silence and cut him off.

"Looks like they have some light arty," Hank commented, squinting his eyes in the harsh sun. "How long before the 16th gets here?"

"Too long, looks like it's your time to see some action," I said to Andrew, switching off the safety on my rifle.

"About time," he said back, fumbling with the safety on his rifle. I sighed, yanked the rifle from his hands, flipped the safety, and tossed it back. "Thanks," he said.

"Hold fire until I say so!" Captain Hiller yelled from his foxhole.

I shouldered my rifle and leaned against it, watching the approaching Germans. I placed my binoculars in my pack and waited. It was eerily quiet as we waited, no one make a sound. Every muscle in my body tensed, arms and legs locking in position. I flexed my fingers, tapping my finger over the trigger guard. I could hear Hank doing the same, thumping his fingers over the ammo belt leading out of the ammo box. Andrew tapped his foot rapidly, tossing up a small cloud of dust.

"Boot!" Hank hissed, shooting an ice cold glance at Andrew. Andrew quieted and retreated back into his thoughts. I glanced at Hank who just shrugged.

I turned back to watch the approaching Germans, noticing they deployed four halftracks with two Panzer IVs. The track stopped halfway down the road and dismounted its infantry attachment. They formed dual lines of two behind the tanks, advancing behind them for cover. The tanks slowly inched forward, vigilant for attacks.

"They're getting smarter," Hank grunted, lining up the lead tank in his sights.

"What are you going to do with an MG?" I asked. "Those things are armored."

"I switched out for AP ammo," he said.

"That'll work on tracks, not tanks." Hank shook his head and snorted.

"Fire!" Captain Hiller yelled. At once, everyone opened fire, pouring down a rain of lead which harmlessly bounced off the tanks. I searched for any shot at the infantry, but they hugged the rear of the tanks for cover. The tanks opened up as they moved, sending two tank shells our way. One smashed into the building Jay was using, two floors under him. The second flew just over our heads, exploding in the sand behind us.

Andrew started to panic, firing blindly at the advancing Panzers. His aim was wide and short, hitting the sand in front of the advancing troops. I still held fire while Hank blasted away with his.30cal, firing controlled bursts of heavy AP ammo. He focused on firing on the armored side skirts of the Panzers, hoping to have the rounds bounce off and hit the German infantry. Farfetched as it was, it was a smart way to think.

"Boot, get up here and feed me more ammo!" Hank yelled to Andrew. Andrew didn't answer, still firing his rifle. "Boot, now!" 'Boot' was an insult, meaning he was fresh out of basic training.

I looked to Hank and saw the ammo belt connected to his MG was nearing its end. I glanced over at Andrew, still frozen his place. I cursed under my breath and jumped to my feet. I shoved Andrew out of my way and knelt next to Hank, opening one of several spare ammo cans at his feet. I pulled the top open and yanked out a section of the ammo belt. Hank continued to fire until the belt was chewed through.

He let go of the trigger and flipped up the breach, knocking the empty ammo can away. I placed the section of belt in its place and locked the ammo can into position,on the side of the MG. Hank slammed the breach back into place and yanked the cocking hammer back. Loaded and ready, he started firing again.

"Andrew!" I yelled, trying to get his attention. Still, he remained frozen and it really pissed me off. I grabbed him by his shirt and pulled him close to me, locking eyes. "Andrew, focus, you need to do your job."

"I…I," he stammered, eyes filled with fear. I repeated my words again, shaking him a little. Still, he was scared and frozen in place. I gave up and pushed him away, returning to my spot.

I dropped to my stomach and shouldered my rifle. I looked down the cross hairs and scanned for a target. By now, the German infantry were still in position behind the tanks. Several had panicked and ran off, quickly they were killed by Jay. The others marched on as the tanks fired repeatedly, unstopping in their torrent of tank shells.

"Adam, get that bazooka up here! Bolger, go with him!" Captain Hiller ordered. I jumped to my feet and looked for Adam, finding him ducking behind the low wall of a nearby house. I ran towards him and hopped over the wall, dropping next to him.

"The bazooka's back in the O.P.," Adam said to me, reloading his rifle. He looked over the wall and ducked back down. "Ready?"

"Just lead the way," I told him.

Adam took several short breaths and darted away from the wall, running across the dirt road to an alley between two stone buildings. I waited until he reached the alley and watched him stand by the edge, waving me to follow. I gripped my rifle in both hands and ran across the road, ducking as bullets shot by me. I quickly sprinted across the road and reached the alley within seconds.

Once in, I stopped to let Adam pass and lead the way. I followed him down the alley as fast as I could, rushing to keep up with him, he was a fast runner. He rounded a corner and left the alley, running down another road. I followed close behind and stayed close to the buildings. Then, the O.P. came into sight.

We had set up our O.P. inside of an abandon building just a block away from the city entrance. It was a small two story building that we shared with a fourth squad, who was currently manning the defenses there. Four men were up on the roof, manning a pair of.30cal machine guns. In the windows, riflemen kept watch, rifles trained on the roads. One trooper carrying a Thompson waved us in.

"What's up, we heard gun fire?" a corporal asked.

"Germans are attacking," I responded, breathing heavily to catch my breath. Adam pushed past the man and ran to a nearby table. He slung his rifle over his shoulder and grabbed a M1 Bazooka sitting on the table. He tossed me a bag that held six rockets.

"I'll need you to load," he said checking the bazooka.

"Hey, we might need that," a rather chubby private argued.

"Well, we do need it, so out of the way, big boy." Adam pushed past him and ran back outside. I lifted the bag onto my back and followed after him, slowed slightly by the extra weight.

We ran back through the alley and emerged at the city entrance. When we arrived, the Germans were yards away, the infantry getting ready to charge. Behind the scouts was the rest of the attack force, now lining up to attack us. Captain Hiller and the rest of the squad we still fighting them off, but to no avail.

Adam and I ducked down behind a low stone wall and readied to fire. Adam shouldered the thin steel tube and lined up the nearest Panzer. I dropped the pack on the ground and pulled out one of the rockets. I held up the small rocket and rammed it into the back of the bazooka, lining the end of the rocket up with the end of the bazooka. I tied a fuse to the rocket and locked into the bazooka. Loaded, I tapped Adam on the helmet and turned away, standing clear.

Adam fired the rocket at the Panzer tank on the left, letting out a gust of air and dual clouds of smoke from both ends of the bazooka. The rocket streaked away and impacted the Panzer on the side, knocking its right tread off. The tank rolled to a stop and began belching smoke from its right side.

"It's still kicking, load again!" Adam ordered, seeing the Panzer firing its main gun. I ducked down and grabbed another rocket, repeating the process. Adam fired again, now impacting on the armor just below the muzzle of the main cannon, sending sparks flying everywhere. The gun then fell silent, the infantry behind her too off running for the other tank. A handful of them were gunned down by Hank and the others.

"One left!" I yelled over the roar of tank fire. The main body of the attack force was now in range and began firing on us. I slumped down to grab a third rocket when I saw the second Panzer aiming towards us. I jumped up and tackled Adam, sending the two of us through the door of a nearby building. We landed inside as the tank fired. There was an echoing explosion as the wall we were behind disintegrated in a cloud of dirt.

"Ah, mind getting off me?" Adam moaned, shaking his head. I rolled over and dropped next to him, shaking dust off my helmet.

"You're welcome, by the way," I said. "Where's the bazooka?" Adam staggered to his feet and searched for the bazooka. He found its remains in the burnt out crater that was once a wall.

"Oops, I dropped it," he said sarcastically.

"Come on," I said, pulling myself to my feet. "Let's get back to the Captain." I looked over and saw several large slabs of stone covering the doorway. "Shit."

"I know," Adam grunted, placing his hand on a slab. "Let's find a back door."

"Hey, get back to the O.P.!" It was Captain Hiller standing on the other side of the doorway directing everyone back. He yelled to us through the debris and we ran back with everyone else.

"Come on," I said, looking for a back door. "Let's get the hell out of here." Adam nodded as we ran to the back of the house. We searched through a makeshift kitchen, but found only wall, no windows, and no doors.

I grunted, filled with anger and annoyance, before grabbing Adam's arm. I suggested heading up stairs, but Adam could not guess why. Instead of explaining, I ran up the stairs to the second floor and searched for a room with a window.

I found an empty room with two windows, both overlooking the roof of the building next door. Hearing more machinegun and cannon fire down the street, I broke the window shutters open with my rifle. As the shutters clattered to the ground, I nodded towards the adjoining roof. Adam looked at roof and at me before getting it.

"You're nuts," Adam said, shaking his head.

"Better than dead," I said back, stepping onto the window frame. I tossed my rifle down to the roof and took a breath. With a small voice in my head saying don't jump, I listened to the other and louder voice that screamed 'jump for your life.' I glanced back at Adam and jumped.

I shot away from the window and soared over the small alley between the two buildings. I passed over the alley and landed on the roof, feeling the shock in my legs and feet as I touched the stone roof. I tucked in and rolled into a ball, rolling sideways and deflecting some of the shock.

I jumped back to my feet and grabbed my rifle, looking up to the window. Adam stood there, still looking unsure. He looked at me and then back inside. There was a volley of machine gun fire as Adam ducked down. I saw some stone splinters fly from the window before Adam stood up. He looked terrified and grabbed the window frame, pulling forward and launching himself out of the building.

He jumped from the window and slammed onto the roof, as I did. He rolled as he hit the roof, gear rattling. Adam came to a stop, as more Germans appeared in the window. I aimed my rifle and fired, causing the Germans to back away. This allowed Adam to get to his feet and run towards me.

"Head to other side and see if it's clear!" I yelled to him.

"On it!" Adam said, collecting himself as he ran past me, heading to other end of the roof. I knelt down on one knee and continued to fire on the window. The Germans stayed in cover as I fired, but popped back up when I reloaded. They fired blindly, hitting the area around me.

"Corr, it's clear! Come on, I'll cover you!" Adam shouted. I finished reloading and ran when I heard him firing. Adam covered me as I ran to his position, stopping when I reached the edge of the roof. Adam continued to fire as I peered over the edge, I saw the alley below was only a few feet down.

"GO!" I yelled, firing on the Germans to cover him. Adam stopped shooting and ran to the edge, jumping into the alley. I finished up the last of my current clip and followed him, landing next to him in the alley.

"Close call," Adam said catching his breath.

"Still not over," I said back as the sounds of machine gun fire and explosions echoed in the city. "Come on, we need to get to the O.P."

"Lead the way," said Adam.

I began walking down the alley towards the O.P., glancing up at the rooftops for Germans now and again while working on collecting my thoughts. I found it easy to think under pressure, thinking on my feet was what my father said I did. It basic training, my squad drill sergeant spotted the talent and recommended I work towards the move to become an officer. That's how I became a corporal, but the fast track to being an officer was never my goal.

"Wait," I said, holding up my left hand.

"What?" Adam stepped closer to me and tapped my shoulder.

"You hear that?" I asked, looking over my shoulder.

Adam listened and just shrugged. "Hear what?"

I listened to the sounds of battle and worked to sort out the distant fighting to the closer ones. I could hear the grinding of tank treads on hard gravel with the hard smacks of jackboots on the ground.

"Down!" Both of us threw our bodies against the right wall of the alley, dropping into a crouch behind and stack of wooden crates that were pushed up against a wall.

"Stay quiet," I hissed, holding my rifle tighter. "Germans."

As the word came out, a group of four Germans walked into view of the alley on the street, rifles held at the waist in a casual way. The four walked out of view and were soon followed by a Panzer IV, a group of seven or eight more Germans sitting on top. The tank was also escorted by six more Germans on foot, three to one side of the tank and three on the other.

I held my breath as the tank rolled by, clenching my teeth. The tank rolled on its way with out slowing, disappearing from view in seconds. The trailing six Germans soon came into view and were about to pass when the last two stopped right in front of the alley. The two began conversing in German, one shifting his legs uncomfortably.

"What are they saying?" Adam whispered in my ear. I listened closely to the conversation and cursed under my breath.

"He's go to piss and is coming this way," I said and rested my rifle on the wall next to me and drew my sidearm and knife.

I watched as one German began walking down the alley, casually looking back and forth as he walked. The soldier, a young man maybe my age, walked only halfway in, stopping a few feet from our hiding place. He peered down the alley and shrugged as he turned his back to us and placed his rifle against the left wall. He faced the wall and unzipped his pants and did his business. I looked down to the other trooper, seeing he wasn't even looking in our direction.

I looked to Adam and nodded towards the German in the alley. He understood and readied his rifle. I held my knife in my right hand and my pistol in my left, looking at the German at the entrance to the alley. When I was sure he was not looking, I readied to strike the other, legs tensing as I crouched.

I was prepared to strike, knife ready, when Adam gabbed my shoulder. I looked at him, who pointed down the alley. I looked and saw the other German turning around. I dropped back against the wall as he turned to face us and began shouting. I feared we were spotted, but he was telling his friend to hurry.

The trooper finished up and ran back down the alley, meeting the other trooper. After exchanging some insults, the two walked out of sight. Once I was sure they were gone, I let out a sigh of relief. I holstered my sidearm and placed my knife away, grabbing my rifle in turn.

"Now that was close!," Adam said, voice shaky.

"So far, but the day's not over." I told him and stood up to gesture to Adam to follow as I slowly walked to the entrance of the alley, hugging the right wall. I stepped carefully to the street and peered around the corner. I pulled back as soon as I saw a German troop truck coming our way.

"Shit, more of them," I whispered, dropping to my stomach and ducking by the edge of the alley.

Staying in the shadows, we watched as the troop truck, loaded with only four soldiers, rolled by with a Pak 38 cannon hooked behind it. The truck rolled by with another behind it, this one carrying a supply cart loaded with artillery shells.

"I think we're behind enemy lines," Adam whispered, seeing even more enemy troopers moving up the street.

"Perfect," I spit.

"Where do we go from here?" Adam asked.

"I'm thinking," was all I could say. We were sitting in the basement of a bombed out building right next to the city square. We found the building by traversing the back alleys of the city, avoiding the Germans while looking for any friendly forces. Adam and I hunkered down in the basement for the time being, having a perfect view of the German staging area set up in the square.

"Well, you better hurry up. I think we only have a few minutes before they find us," Adam reminded me.

"Thank you for that, but I already figured that out," I said.

"Just checking." Adam stood by the front window of the basement, watching the Germans. I sat on an old chair on the other side of the room, looking at a map of the city. The map outlined the entire city and colored in blue was Allied territory, but that was is. It marked no positions in the city, no defensive lines, and no central C.P.

"There are two ideas that are obvious," I grunted, folding up the map.

"And they would be?" He asked.

"Surrender, that's the easier one, but I'd rather kiss Hitler's ass instead." That got a chuckle from Adam. "Or we wait it out here and pray the 16th reaches us in time. That's all I got, you?" I said.

"Well, we could bug out and run, but we might find more Germans. Option two is we fight our way out, killing as many of them as we can, but we'll most likely die," Adam suggested.

"Let's avoid options leading to death or capture, shall we?" I said. Adam nodded his head and returned to his watch. I stood up and walked to him, looking over his shoulder.

The Germans had set up their C.P. in the city center, using the town hall as forward C&C. German troops patrolled the area while others marched into the city. Panzers rolled along with them, moving in one unbreakable line of steel.

"Makes you lose hope, doesn't it?" Adam snorted, shaking his head.

"Hope is never gone, or so I've been told. Personally I think if I'm gonna die, it'll be with my hands around the throat of a Nazi." I snorted.

"You're sounding like Vic," Adam said.

"Yeah well, I'm not giving up," I said, and jumped down to check my rifle.

"So, what's the plan?" Adam asked, as he stepped away from the window and checked his own rifle.

"I think I have a plan, but it's not…complete." I told him. Adam raised his eyebrows and tilted his head.

"Not complete? What the fuck does that mean?" He asked.

"Well, I considered fighting our way out, but that is stupid. I thought of the next best thing instead." I led him back to the window and pointed out at supply truck. "That is loaded with oil barrels and is a ticking time bomb. We sneak over and cut open one of the barrels. We put a rag in said hole and light one end with a lighter and keep it away from the fuel. Said rag burns and reaches the fuel, causing one big bang," I said, quite pleased with myself.

"Clever, but how do we avoid detection?" Adam asked apprehensively.

"Simple," I said grinning.

"Simple?" Adam whispered, trying to get himself out of the basement window.

"Yes," I said, helping to pull him out. "By climbing through the basements, we avoid detection." Adam squeezed through the small window frame and pulled himself up from the ground.

"I don't remember agreeing to this," he moaned, dusting some sand off his pants.

"Corporal," I said pointing to my sleeve. "Private," I tapped his sleeve. "That's all the agreement I need." I told him.

"Of course," Adam sighed,

We walked down the alley to the square, and hid behind a wooden cart loaded with ammo boxes. Adam kept watch while I pulled out a small rag from my pocket along with my lighter. Checking for Germans, I crept over to the truck loaded with dozens of oil barrels. I stepped over to the one closest to the back, drew my knife, and slammed it into the top of the barrel.

I pulled out the knife as a steady stream of clear gasoline poured out. I unfolded the rag and slid one end into the cut, leaving the other to rest on the top of the barrel. The smell, from the gas, was making me light headed. As the rag slowly became soaked, I lit the top half of the rag and ran like hell.

I ran past the ammo cart and shoved Adam forward. We both ran along the front of several stores when two German soldiers appeared from nowhere. Not slowing, we barreled through them and ran into the joining street. I heard several voices scream out in German when the oil barrel detonated.

The supply truck erupted in an echoing explosion and fireball. Oil barrels shot out from the truck like rockets, arching away in all directions. They slammed into nearby supply crates and trucks, exploding when the gas inside reach its flashpoint. More secondary explosions erupted around the town center as fires sprung up everywhere and German soldiers ran for cover. Adam and I kept running as well, diving through the broken window of a stone building. We landed in a clatter inside of a bombed out building. Both of us jumped to our feet and hugged the walls for cover, listening to the explosions in the distance.

"Okay, it was a good plan," Adam said after several seconds. We heard a loud whistling in the distance and looked outside, to see truck door with a German swastika on it, land onto the road; it was on fire.

"Ah, that was a good plan, who'd a thunk it?" I joked.

"You didn't think it would've worked?" Adam asked, looking shocked.

I shrugged my shoulders. "Not really, no."

"You're a piece of work, Corr," he said.

"So I hear, wait, quiet!" I hissed, hearing voices moving closer to us. I listen closely as I could hear men arguing in German, coming closer and closer.

"Fuck, they sent a patrol after us." Adam said as he peered out the window. He jumped back, as a bullet impacted the wall behind them. "I think they spotted us."

I leaned out the window and fired blindly at the Germans, emptying my clip in seconds. I pulled back in and reloaded my rifle as Adam began returning fire. The Germans spread out along the road and began firing at us. Adam and I fired back as best we could, working to kill as many Germans as possible. They had numbers and fire power on us, but we would go down swinging.

"They're setting up an MG42!" Adam yelled.

I leaned out again and fired several more times, seeing a group of three Germans setting up the bipod of an MG42. I pulled in and took a breath before leaning back. I lined up one of the three man crew and fired my entire clip, killing one and wounding the other in the arm.

"Get back!" I screamed, seeing they managed to get the gun set up. We jumped back, just in time, as the gunner opened up with the 42. The air filled with the chilling cracks of an MG42, sounding just like a buzz saw.

Machine gun bullets smashed into the stone walls of the building, throwing up a hail storm of stone chips and shattered lead splinters. Adam dropped to the floor and held his helmet down tight. I turned toward the wall, to shield my face. Stone shards and bullets exploded into the building, pinning us down.

"Adam, are you okay?" I yelled over to him, not being able to turn and face him.

"Fucking peachy, Corr!" he shouted back. "I think they're moving up!"

I turned slightly and tried to get a glimpse outside. I was able to look for a fraction of a second before pulling back. "You're right, they're moving to flank us!" I said.

"We need to get out of here!" Adam tired moving, but stopped as more bullets ripped up the area around him.

"Hang on." I pulled a grenade from my webbing and pulled the pin, letting the spoon fall free. I counted to five and tossed out the grenade, feeling several sharp stabs to my arm. I pulled back to see several stone shards had cut up a section of my right arm. I was halfway through tying on a bandage when the grenade exploded. There were a series of screams and shouts of pain, but the 42 was relentless, keeping a steady torrent of machinegun bullets flying our way.

"This is not good!" Adam cried.

"Fuck, really, I know God damn idiot!" I shouted and finished with my bandage, picked up my rifle, fumbled to reload it.

"Grenade!" Adam shrieked.

A single stick grenade tumbled through the window and bounced along the wooden floor. I dove right for it, grabbing the grenade and tossing it back out the window. It exploded just as it cleared.

Adam screamed out in pain as it exploded, clutching his left arm with blood oozing from in between his fingers. I crawled over to his body and pulled his hand away, revealing a very deep shrapnel wound in his forearm. Blood also began to pool around his legs when I saw a large piece of shrapnel sticking out of his stomach.

"Hang on, Adam!" I shouted, throwing down my rifle and pulling my sidearm. I fired several times out the window, killing a single German who tried to rush the building. I lowered the pistol and began pulling out two more bandages from my pack.

"It's bad, isn't it?" Adam grunted, his face sweating heavily and skin pale.

"Not the worst I've seen. Hold in your guts." I managed a small grin to act like I was just joking. I pulled his hand from his arm and pressed it to his stomach wound. I tied off his arm and began working his stomach. Now and again, I had to stop to fire out the window, showing the Germans we could still fight.

"You have no idea how much this hurts," he gasped.

I pressed the bandage to his stomach wound, forcing Adam to yelp out in pain.

"Sorry, bro," I blurted out, pressing the bandage tighter. Still, the blood soaked through, pouring out over the floor.

"I bet." Adam grabbed my .45 and began firing out the window randomly as I did my best to treat to him. He was loosing a shit load of blood and was the color in his face grew paler. He was breathing heavily and kept blinking as if it was getting hard to see.

"Hang on, Adam. Did anyone give you orders to die?" I screamed.

"Fuck if I know, Corr. Have you seen the Cap?" Adam asked.

"Nope, so you have no orders to die!" I said.

Outside, the Germans were still relentless with their fire, not slowing at all. I could hear an officer shouting orders, moving his men in to storm the building. I figured everything would end in a mater of minutes or seconds. Adam was going to die and I was going with him or get captured.

"Tanks," Adam moaned lowly, dropping his head in chest. Outside, I could hear tank treads grinding towards us. Any second, a Panzer would incinerate us and in a heartbeat it would be over. I was nineteen and that was going to be it. I could picture Matt and Frank getting the news as well as my parents, all of them crying, asking why.

There was a rumble of thunder and an echoing explosion that shook me back to reality. I closed my eyes and waited, but nothing happened. More explosions and machine gun fire echoed outside, as the Germans began shouting orders of retreat. More tanks could be heard with the rumble of their cannons and cracks of heavy machine guns.

A lumbering tank passed by the window, kicking up a cloud of dirt and sand. I grabbed my pistol as several figures ran by, but I held my fire. A dozen or so more ran by when two stopped in the doorway across from us. I raised my pistol to fire, but it clicked empty, the chamber sliding back.

"Drop it!" one of the soldiers yelled in English.

"Hold your fire, we're with the First!" I yelled, holstering my pistol. "I need a medic!" I begged.

"Ones coming," the other soldier said, walking inside. "Oh, shit."

Both men were American soldiers, the patches of the 16th on their shoulders. I stood up and grabbed Adam, holding him up with my arms.

"Give me a hand," I said, struggling to carry him. Both troopers came over and took Adam, carrying him outside. I grabbed both our rifles and followed them. They placed Adam in the back of a jeep, outside as a medic came running up. He hopped in the back of the jeep and began dressing Adam's wounds.

"Doc, how is?" I asked.

"Alive, thanks to you," he grunted, pressing a fresh bandage onto Adam's stomach. "Let's get him back to the aide station!"

"On it!" Anther trooper hopped behind the wheel of the jeep as I tossed in his rifle as he drove off. I stood in the wake of dust both stunned and lost. In an instant I figured it was over, but we were rescued. Adam was just taken away and I had no idea if he would live our die. Thus, the life of a soldier.

"You okay, Corporal?" one of the troopers asked.

"Ah, yeah, thanks guys," I answered, as I put on my helmet and walked to the front of the building. A column of Sherman tanks and infantry were marching by, all from the 16th. They moved into the city and began removing the Germans. I noticed a few soldiers from the First mixed in with them, but not my squad.

"You lost?" the other trooper, a sergeant, asked.

"Yeah, I need to get to the First C.P." I told him.

"That's back that a ways," the Sergeant pointed down the road. "Connors, get him a jeep to take him back."

"You got it, Sarge." Connors waved down one of the jeeps in the column and had it pull over.

"Take him to the C.P., private," he ordered.

"Yes, sergeant," the driver answered in a southern drawl. "Hop in."

"Thanks," I mumbled, sitting in the passenger's seat.

The private pulled the jeep into and alley and backed out, driving down a side road to escape traffic. I kept quiet and retreated back into my own world, blocking out the fighting going on around me. I was tired and felt completely, as whatever adrenaline that was in blood, washed out. My hands were shaking again, Adam's blood stained them. I began rubbing the blood off, trying so hard I nearly rubbed off a layer of skin.

"You okay?" the driver asked. I looked over at him and nodded my head.

"Fine, just fine," I mumbled, clasping my hands together to stop the shaking.

"Sorry we were late to the party, but better late than never, right?" He joked.

I didn't answer him, hanging my head in my chest.

"So Adam's in a hospital?" Nate asked for the fifteenth time since I found the squad.

"Yes, he's in a field hospital," I answered again, grabbing some spare ammo clips from the C.P.

"The Captain nearly bought it here," Jay said to me, running his fingers over several bullets several bullets holes in the wall. "Dove on a grenade, but the thing was a dud."

"Like you, Hawkins," Captain Hiller grunted, walking over to us. "How you holding up, Bolger?"

"Fine sir, my hand is better."

"Good. Alright, listen up everyone. The 16th is taking over garrison duty here, so we are moving out. Command is moving the First up to Ponte Olivo airport so we can secure another supply route. We'll be attacking at midnight to catch the Germans off guard, so gathering what kit you need now." Hiller glanced at his watch. "You've got six hours before night fall when we roll. Use it wisely." Captain Hiller gave a head nod and strolled outside to see Sergeant Hanes waiting for him. When he was out of earshot, Hank whispered to us," Is it just me or is he…disappointed at us?"

Vic shrugged as he cleaned his BAR at a nearby table. "He's pissed."

"Care to explain?" Nate asked.

"Could be he's pissed he nearly died for us," Private Phelps offered.

"No, it's the whole near death experience," I said. "Think about it. Hiller's been through the Great War and is back fighting the second one. He knows his number could be up any day, but it never really bothered him. He buried it in his mind a long time ago, but it's come to the forefront again."

"Can we change the subject?" Hank asked. "We came very close to death again and I'd rather not talk about it. I want Adam back with us, but I don't want to talk about him. No disrespect, but let's try something else."

"Fine with me," I said, sitting down across from Vic.

"Anyone got a smoke?" Andrew asked. Everyone's eyes fell to the kid, looking at him in disbelief.

"Come again, junior?" Hank asked. Andrew walked over to us and repeated his question.

"You even old enough to smoke?" I inquired. It sounded odd to ask, but most of us were nineteen or twenty and he seemed too young, at eighteen. He still had the carefree youthful look we lost back in North Africa.

"Here," Vic tossed him a pack from his pocket and returned to his weapon cleaning. I placed my rifle on the table and began to disassemble it. I cleared the ammo clip inside and began to strip the rifle to its bare parts, and cleaned out the breach and barrel with my tooth brush, brushing out clumps of sand and dirt.

"I hear the Brits are making progress in their beach heads," Nate said, fiddling with the squad radio.

"That's because the Italians and French love surrendering. Honestly, it's like what they're made to do," Hank chirped.

"Not all Italians are like that," Vic grunted, snapping his BAR back together. "Want to test my theory?"

"No thanks, Mr. Missing Link," I chuckled.

"Anyone get mail?" Jay asked, looking out the window.

"Nope," I answered, snapping my rifle back together. "We're in the military, so mail is not top priority."

"Amen to that," Phelps said, cutting open a can of C rations. "I got a letter from my sis two weeks ago saying she had her first kid. From the date she wrote, the kid was born two months before we landed in North Africa."

"Now that is slow," Andrew grunted, coughing as he in hailed a mouth full of smoke. He coughed several more times as he blew out the smoke before taking another hit.

"Smooth, eh?" Vic snorted, laughing as he said it.

Everyone began laughing at Andrew, whose face turned red. He flicked the cigarette and stomped it out. I laughed slightly and finished assembling my rifle. I reloaded it and kept it in front of me on the table. Vic finished with his BAR and drew his knife, sharpening it against the side of an armor plate with a German swastika on it.

I leaned back in my chair, tilting it back against the wall behind me. I propped my feet up on the table and crossed my hands behind my hand, sighing slightly. I was still in shock from the attack, not really believing everything that happened minutes ago and feeling as if it occurred days ago.

"Anyone for a hand of poker?" Jay asked, pulling a worn pack of cards from his shirt pocket.

"Five dollar betting limit?" Vic asked, pulling out his wallet.

"Sure, why not? I'm in," Phelps grunted in between bites.

"What the hell, I'm in too," I leaned forward and walked over to, who pulled over a small table. He placed a neatly stacked deck of cards in front of us and began shuffling them. Vic pulled his chair closer and sat across from him, along with Nate, Phelps, and Corporals Mangon and Ramos.

"Simple five card draw, one dollar to get in, and five dollar max on betting," Jay said, as he dealt each of us five cards; we each tossed a dollar into the center of the table. I picked up my set of cards and studied them. With a five, six, seven, eight, and a two, I had a good hand.

"Raise two," Phelps first raised, tossing in two dollars.

"Check," Mangon tossed in another two dollars.

"See two and raise two more." Vic tossed in four dollars.

"You cannot bluff for shit, *mi hermano*." Ramos checked.

"You're both bad liars. Check." I tossed in another five and glanced at their faces as they each dropped and took new cards. I dropped one card and received a four in place of a two. When the last round of betting came, I raised another two dollars.

"Check." Phelps folded along with Mangon. Vic showed a pair of tens as Nate showed a pair of aces. I dropped my baby straight as Jay revealed a hand of garbage.

Ramos cursed in Spanish under his breath as I took the pot. "I'm watching you," he said, pointing his finger at me.

I just smiled and waited for the next hand.

The poker playing went on for several more hours before everyone, except Nate and I, dropped out. The pot between us was up to two hundred dollars, both of us breaking the betting limit. Ramos was holding his hand close to his face, a small amount of sweat collecting under his eyes. I sat across from him, trying to keep cool and keeping my face blank.

"Well, raise or check, *hermano*," I prodded, eyeing up my hand and the pot.

"Take it easy, Corr. What, is there a war you need to get to?" Ramos asked, shuffling his cards.

"Yes, actually, but it can wait. Now, raise or check before I die of old frigging age" I said.

Ramos shook his head and looked down at the last two dollars in his wallet. He picked up the two and moved to place them in the pot, but decided to keep them.

"Check," He smirked, and dropped his hand, to revealed a full house, two fours and three sixes.

"Good, but…" I grinned and showed my hand, a royal flush. "I do believe this is better."

Ramos's mouth dropped, his cards falling from his hands. "What the fuck?" he gasped.

"*Mira, hermano*," I said as I hugged the winnings, in my arms. "My father was a Marine and I had two brothers growing up, cards were embedded into my brain, like the ability to walk."

"But this…ah fuck it," Ramos stood up and shook his hand firmly, grinning slightly. "Good job, Corr. See me when we get paid, okay?" Ramos said.

"Why not? I like getting money from the first national bank of Ramos." I snickered and pocketed one large wad of money, shoving the overflow into my wallet, in my pack.

"Ten-hut!" Shouted a deep voice. Everyone leapt to their feet at once, standing at attention where they jumped. I dropped my pack on my chair and was up in a flash, standing like a towering statute of steel. Captain Hiller walked into the building with Sergeant Hanes at his side. Hiller stood next to me and looked at the cards and money on the table. He grinned widely.

"Now how many times must I tell you," he bellowed. "Gambling of any type is not permitted at all. Anyone caught gambling is subject to arrest on sight, but next time, please let me join in."

Everyone smiled and laughed. "Next time, Cap," Ramos said.

"Ah, I bet, Ramos," the Captain said, sarcastically. " Listen up, we're rolling in ten, so pack your shit and get outside for transport. Oh, here." He tossed me a bundle of letters. "Mail finally came through." As Hiller strolled out, I dropped the bundle on the table, knowing I would be trampled standing between them and their mail.

Everyone rushed over and fought like a pack of jackals over a freshly dead body. They rummaged through the letters looking for their names, shoving one another to get a better view. Eventually, the crowd subsided and Nate tossed me a letter.

"Just one?" I asked, grabbing my pack and rifle.

"Sorry, I got three," he said, beaming a broad smile.

"From the ladies back home?" I asked.

Nate rolled his eyes and cracked open one of the letters. I looked down at my letter, seeing it was from my younger brother Frank. I tore open the envelope and read eagerly.

> Dear Corr,
>
> It's a another day here in this lovely little island in the Pacific. Gods knows where I am, the name of the island is in Japanese, but I'm doing fine. It's really hot out here and the nights are very humid. It's not the best weather I can ask for, but who cares, I'm a Marine!
>
> Things have been hectic for the last few days. Everyone is still talking about Doolittle and the Tokyo Raid; it's a great morale boost. When we landed here a few days ago, everyone was in high spirits, ready to go and kill some Japs. I killed two, when we landed, and my hands are still shaking, but I'm alive.
>
> I really miss everyone back home, especially Daisy; you think she's still waiting for me? I do, I remember when I last saw her, and she was so impressed by my uniform. She writes me nearly every day, but since mail is slow I get a big bundle of mail every few weeks or so. It's great to hear from her, it makes things bearable. Well,

the Japs are a calling. Best of luck fighting the Nazis and be sure to liberate some nice 'spoils' for me.

Love,
Your brother,
Private Franklin Bolger
28th Marine Infantry

I was so happy to hear from Frank again. I worried about him more than Matt. Both faced great risks, but Matt was a good pilot and spent his days in England while Frank was storming islands. He was young and reckless and sometimes stupid.

"Let's go, let's go!" Sergeant Hanes yelled aloud. I folded my letter and placed it in my shirt pocket. I slipped my pack onto my back and slid my helmet on, grabbing my rifle at the same time. I started walking to the door, but stopped when Nate didn't.

"Nate?" I yelled to him, no response. "Nate, let's go."

"What?" Nate was engrossed in his letter, his face dropping into a look of depression. "Oh." He folded his letter and grabbed his rifle. "I'm coming." He shuffled over to the door, passing by me without a word. I decided not to push him with a mission coming, so I stalked silently behind him, climbing into a waiting truck outside.

I sat last in line of the bench, right next to the rear of the truck. Nate sat across from me, head hanging low. Jay sat next to me and nudged my shoulder, nodding towards Nate. I shrugged, not knowing. Captain Hiller walked to the end of the truck and faced us.

"No lights or noise while on the road, clear?" he said. Everyone responded with a yes sir. Hiller walked to the cab of the truck and sat in the passenger's seat. Once everyone was loaded, the truck pulled into a line of several others before rumbling down a darkened road out of town.

Everyone obeyed orders and was quiet on the drive, no words spoken save for the occasional 'what time is it?' I sat with my head leaning back against the wooden boards running along the truck bed, my face turned skyward. I studied the vast sky of stars, trying to get the directions for north, south, east, and west using some tricks I learned from my father.

My father wasn't the woodsmen type, but he'd taken my brothers and me camping on many occasions. He taught us dozens of different tricks for locating landmarks, reading the stars for directions, learning to see animal signs and such. I never really enjoyed it much, but it made dad happy so I pretended to enjoy it for his sake. It's ironic I live through the thing I hate the most every day.

"Ever wonder if you made the right choice joining up?" Nate asked, saying the first thing in several hours.

"What do you mean?" I asked, sitting forward and looking him in his eyes.

"This," he held up the letter. "You know what this is?"

"Dear John letter?" I joked.

"Ha, I wish," Nate snorted, holding the letter tightly with both hands. "No, this is a letter from my baby sister, Lisa. She's sixteen and…"

"Nate?" I asked as he trailed off, dropping his gaze back to the letter.

"Pregnant, Corr. My baby sister is back home and on her own, and now she's pregnant. Our mom's dead and dad's paralyzed below the waist from an accident. Lisa took care of dad and worked a job at diner after school to help pay the bills and everything. I send home most, if not all, of my pay for her and now….she needs me more than ever."

"Nate, no, don't even think it." I sat up and placed a hand on his shoulder. "Think about this, going AWOL is just going to get you arrested or killed. Besides, how the hell do figure you get back home?" I reminded him.

Nate shook off my hand. "I'll swim if I fucking have to. You'd do the same if something happened with your brothers."

"Being thrown in jail or getting killed will not help her," I insisted.

"Doing nothing isn't helping." His voice was lower now and he dropped his head into his hands. "The money I send her isn't enough, Corr. What's gonna happen when the money runs low, huh? The

Army isn't going to help, that's for sure. The baby's father? Ha, like he's ever going to show his face again."

"Nate…" I said, placing my hand on his shoulder.

"What, Corr, what? He asked, impatiently. "Besides sending money home and going AWOL, what else is there?"

"Everyone out, move!" Captain Hiller yelled as the convoy rolled to a stop. Sergeant Hanes was already out, waving everyone to follow.

"We'll talk latter, Nate," I said, hopping out behind Jay.

"Sure," Nate snorted, jumping out behind me.

"Fan out!" Hiller ordered. "First squad, move up through the gully on the left! Second, follow them through and rush the two hangers on the edge of the runway. The rest of you, with me!"

I checked my rifle and followed behind the Captain, charging across the road to the hills overlooking the airport. The Captain led us to the top and scanned the area. I looked out and saw the lights of the airport burning brightly in the night. The runway and surrounding area was well light by portable lights and patrolled by several German fire squads. A pair of snipers were perched atop the control tower, both watching the area near the northern road of the airfield while we were moving in from the west.

"Jay, the low light going to be a problem?" Hiller grunted.

"Not as long as there's light in the airfield, no sir," Jay answered.

"Okay, Jay, sniper cover from this spot, cover our approach to the control tower by picking off those snipers. We're going to use that dried up creek bed to advance forward. When we reach the perimeter fence, rush the control tower and secure it at all cost," ordered Captain Hiller.

"The airport is still unaware," Hanes pointed out.

"Even better," Hiller tucked away his binoculars. "Ramos, how's the radio?"

"Ready, sir," Ramos answered, kneeling next to the Captain and handing him the receiver.

"Longbow, this sword, over," Hiller grunted into the receiver.

"Longbow, here, go ahead sword," we heard the radio squawk.

"Longbow, is our arty ready?" Hiller asked.

"Copy, sword, arty is ready and awaiting your go ahead. Coordinates stand at Oscar 33, Charlie 11, copy?" Answered the voice on the radio.

"Sword copies and will call if needed. Sword out." Hiller handed back the receiver and checked his rifle. "Ready to roll? Good, on me, move!" He ordered.

Hiller leapt to his feet and was running down the hill to the creek bed. Hanes rushed after him with the rest of us, gear rattling. I held my rifle close and sprinted behind the Captain as he led the way. It was pitch black in the creek bed, the only light was coming from the airport. Several times someone nearly stumbled over rocks on the ground or bumped into the man in front of him.

"Shermans coming up on the right flank," Hanes hissed, glancing over his shoulder. I turned to see a group of ten Sherman tanks grinding across the desert land, barreling towards the airport.

"Fuck, they're going to give us away," Vic grunted, BAR swinging in his arms.

Up ahead, there was an echoing whistle followed by shouts in German. Then, a dozen or so spotlights snapped to life followed by a high pitched klaxon. The Germans were alerted and they jumped to life.

"Heads down!" Hiller yelled.

The buzz saw sounding of several MG42s clicked to life. Bullets spewed from several MG nests across the edge of the runways along with two in the control tower. Spotlights dashed over the black desert, searching for anyone to cut down. One light washed over us, nearly blinding me.

"Down!" I yelled. Everyone dove to the dirt as the tower MG42s opened up, sending a hailstorm of lead our way. Bullets peppered the dirt around us, ripping up everything they touched. I heard a scream from behind me, followed by something warm spraying the back of my neck. I turned onto my back in time to see Corporal Mitchell Evans, who stood no more than several inches from me, clutching his throat. Blood shot for between his fingers and soaked his uniform before he dropped to his knees and fell face forward into the dirt.

"Medic!" I screamed, eyes locked on Evan's body. "Medic!"

Doc shot out from the darkness. He leapt over to Evans, clutching his medical bag. Doc dropped next to him and pulled his body to the edge of the creek bed, using it as a shield. Working with skill and speed, Doc checked the gushing neck wound, packing down bandages over the exposed vein or artery. Evans clutched at his throat in horror.

"Bolger! Bolger, snap the fuck out of it!" Hiller grabbed my pack and pulled me around, shoving me into the dirt. "Bolger, fucking focus!"

"Sir…" I squeaked, eyes still wide in shock. "Yes sir, I'm here, sir!"

"Fucking A, when those crews are out, we run to that hanger!" He pointed to the hanger right to the left of the control tower. "Stay right on my ass, clear?"

"Yes, sir!" I shouted, yelling to clear my head.

"The rest of you get it? Fucking A!" Hiller screeched.

We hunkered down as the Sherman tanks rolled on, using their machine guns as to prevent any 'unneeded' damage to the airfield. Jay still sat on the hill and picked off the MG teams until the last tower nest fell silent.

"Go! Go! Go!" Hiller yelled.

Everyone jumped back to their feet and ran. Hiller was out front, Tommy gun spitting out bullets at any hapless German that stuck his head out. Hanes was right on his flank, firing his Garand off the hip. Vic and Ramos ran next to me, all of us breathing heavily. Ramos fired his rifle randomly and emptied his clip in seconds.

I didn't fire, my mind still lingered on the image of Evan's body lying in the creek bed, eyes wide open in a vacant stare. My legs continue to throw me forward, running by simple reflex. I had no real clue on what was happening. Bullets shot by, soldiers fell, explosions roared, men screamed, and time blurred on. Everything returned back to 'normal' when we reached the hanger or rather, when I hit it.

With a rattle and a thud, I slammed into the side of the hanger, pressing my back to it. Hiller slammed his back into the wall near the edge, peering out as everyone stumbled over. This area was well lit with spot and work lights set up around the hangers. Hiller shot out several near us, cursing when the Germans started shooting again.

"Let's clear the tower," he ordered, reloading his Thompson. "Ramos, on the door with me. Ready? Go!"

Hiller shot out from behind the hanger and darted across a dirt road running between the hanger and the control tower. A single German ran out of the control tower, shoving the door open. Hiller and Ramos fired a volley and knocked the German back, sending his body back in with the door slamming shut. They then stood on opposite side of the door as the rest of us lined up behind Hiller on the left.

"On three?" Ramos asked, pulling out a grenade.

"Now!" Hiller shoved his boot into the door just under the handle, sending the door inward. Ramos tossed in the grenade and backed away. The grenade detonated, sending out a plume of smoke and wooden splinters. Hiller ran in as the dust rose, Thompson spraying the room. Empty shell casings fell to the floor, creating a carpet of lead as I stormed in, pulling to the left and pushing my back to the wall.

My eyes scanned the room, looking for anyone in a German uniform. Three Germans wielding MP40s rushed in from the stairwell at the opposite end of the room. I fired at point blank range, sending three bullets into the lead German's chest and face. He tumbled backwards as the other two rushed forward, weapons firing.

I ducked down, diving behind an overturned table. Bullets tore into the wall behind me as I dropped, impacting just where I was. Captain Hiller killed one of the two while the other fell to Ramos. The room then went quiet as the roar of fighting continued around the rest of the airport. I picked myself back up and ran to Ramos's side as he moved to the stairwell. Captain Hiller charged ahead of us and blocked our path.

"Wait!" he ordered, peeking out into the stairwell. "Move slow and stay alert, they might drop grenades on our heads."

"Yes, sir," Ramos answered, looking out himself. There was a roar and explosion somewhere outside. Everyone froze as the lights flickered and died. Sergeant Hanes stepped in from outside.

"The tankers just blew the field generator," he reported.

"Perfect." Hiller snorted, removing his helmet to wipe his forehead. "Slow and easy, Ramos."

"On it, sir," Ramos said.

Ramos looked up the stairs and nodded forward. I nodded and followed behind, walking up the first flight of darkened stairs. The metal steps creaked under our boots as we slowly walked up the stairwell, now pitch black. I had to hold onto the handrail with one hand while balancing my rifle in the other. I could barely see my out hands and I did not want to trip and fall down the stairs.

Ramos led the way, eyes searching the darkness. He stepped slowly and lightly, checking for movement or sound. Outside, the battle for the rest of the airfield raged on. It was getting harder and harder to distinguish sounds from inside from out. Captain Hiller followed close to Ramos and me, moving without sound.

Up ahead, there was the creak of a door opening. Everyone froze, looking up ahead. I scanned the upper stairs, but I couldn't see a thing. Captain Hiller stepped in front of Ramos and ordered us to wait while he scouted ahead. Following orders, everyone stepped to the sides of the stairs, clearing the way just in case. I stood on one of the landings, maybe halfway up the tower. I leaned back against the wall and crouched down, wiping some sweat away from my eyes.

Everyone waited in silence and darkness as Captain Hiller crept up the last bit of stairs. He moved silently, stalking an unseen target. I glanced around, looking at those around me. I could only see Ramos and Nate, both crouching next to me. Ramos waited with his rifle at the ready, bayonet locked onto the barrel. Nate was quiet and tense, fingers silently drumming against the side of his rifle. Vic stood several steps down, though I could only see the bare outline of his BAR.

"They're gone!" Captain Hiller yelled from above, breaking the silence, causing me to jump. "Bolger, get up here and bring Ramos and the fucking radio. Hanes, get the rest of the squad back outside and set up a perimeter around the tower."

"On it, sir!" Hanes rallied the squad and marched them back down the stairs. Ramos, Nate, and I marched up the rest of the stairs to the top of the control tower. We passed through a single door at the top. Captain Hiller stood at one end, leaning over a control panel and looking out at the rest of the airport, Thompson slung over his shoulder. The rest of the room was dark, some slight illumination coming from the fires burning outside. I stepped in and nearly stumbled over two dead Germans, both with half their heads missing.

"That Jay is not bad with the rifle," Hiller grunted, turning back to us. "The radio working?"

"Yes, sir." Nate walked over to the Captain and handed him the receiver.

"Sword to Armory, Sword to Armory, we've got the control tower under our control," Captain Hiller said.

"Copy that, standby for further orders," said a crackled voice, from the radio.

Hiller handed the receiver back and returned to look over the airport. I walked over and looked out with him. We were facing the runways and the hangers. The Sherman tanks were grinding across the runways, providing mobile cover for the infantry. They moved from hanger to hanger, clearing out the Germans.

"This was quick," Hiller snorted, watching a group of Germans being escorted out of a hanger by several troopers. "Seems…strange."

"Sir?" I asked, looking over at him.

Hiller shrugged. "The Germans are tough fuckers, they don't give so easily. I sure as hell saw it back in the trenches."

"Saw what?" Ramos asked, sitting down in an empty chair.

"The Germans only gave way if they were all dead or if they had another plan in the works. Only time will tell us what happened here." Hiller pushed away from the railing and began walking back down to the ground. "Clean up this place and get an O.P. ready," he said.

"Yes, sir, on it, sir," we said.

Captain Hiller stalked back down the stairs. Once he was out of ear shot, Ramos sighed and removed his helmet.

"This has been amazing," he joked. "Any idea on how to get some light up here?"

"Here," Nate picked up several oil lamps from a crate on the ground. He placed them on top of the tables that ringed the room and lit them with his lighter. Soon, we had enough light to see. I knelt down and checked the bodies of the dead Germans. It was sickening work, sorting through their pockets, it made me feel like I was grave robbing. It took some strength not to vomit.

"Not what the recruiter said you'd be doing, eh?" Ramos snorted, leaning back in his chair and propping his feet up on a table.

"No," I said with little emotion. I riffled through one dead soldier's pockets and found some folded area maps along with some spare rifle clips and a wallet. In the wallet, I found a dozen German marks along with several photos. They were of the dead German with his friends and one of his wife or girlfriend with him, in his dress uniform. They were standing in front of the Reichstag, in Berlin, both looking so happy. I wondered what that woman would say to me if I ever met her.

"Picking his pocket?" Nate said, dropping the radio off his back and onto a table.

"Look," I whispered, fumbling with the picture in my hand. "You think she'll ever smile like that again?" I asked, already knowing the answer.

Ramos looked over my shoulder and said, "too bad she's a Nazi lover, she's a pretty good looking dame. Such a waste."

I shot Ramos a cold look and slipped the small picture into my pocket. I wasn't sure why, but I kept it. I returned the wallet to the dead German and stood up, closing my eyes and sighing.

"Fuck," I grunted, wondering how many more women are waiting back home on both sides for soldiers that would never come home. My head hurt and my stomach rumbled with hunger. I slipped into a chair and leaned my head back, and pulled my helmet off.

"Maybe I'll visit some of these widows when we storm Berlin," Ramos snickered.

"Shut the fuck up, Ramos," I said coldly.

Ramos threw his hands up, in a defensive way. "Whoa, take a breath, *hermano*. Shit, I'm just joking," he said, jumping backwards.

"Just make sure you don't go over the line," Nate added.

"Christ, will you two lighten up for a minute?" Ramos said.

Nate and I glanced at each other and rolled our eyes. I dropped my gaze back to the runways, seeing groups of Germans being herded to waiting transport. For them, the war over, but for us, it was just starting. I dropped my head into my chest and closed my eyes. In my mind, I just asked one question, what the hell did I get myself into?

The fighting in Sicily changed since we took Ponte Olivo, the balance tipping for us. The First stormed across Sicily, meeting success after success, though we slowed as we approached the center of Sicily. This area was mostly, if not all, mountains and hills. Fighting up hill in terrible the heat took its toll on us. Our forces, already weakened from heavy fighting, we were crippled by malaria and the Germans were putting up stiffer resistance. Several times I came close to death, as well as many of my fellow soldiers, but we fought on.

By the end of July, we'd nearly taken the entire island. The last fight was to grab the city of Troina. Troina was one of the last major German controlled cities in Sicily, providing the last hold for the Germans. Intel said the Germans were on their last legs and that we would take the city in a day or two. By the fifth day of fighting, we'd didn't even get into the city. Somehow, Intel missed four German divisions sitting in the city.

"Keep alert," Hiller hissed at us, as we sat in our foxholes a few miles from Troina. For nearly a week we fought to grab the city, but German arty pounded us to a stalemate. The next day, we would advance into the city under our own arty cover.

"Yes sir," Ramos answered, sitting with me in our foxhole.

As Hiller walked off, I turned back to watch the city. "This is such a waste," I grunted.

"Sitting here?" Ramos asked.

"Yeah, it's better to attack at night so we have cover," I explained.

"The last night attack failed," Ramos pointed out. "Didn't a sniper nearly kill you?"

I removed my helmet and looked at the dime size hole on the side of my helmet, above my right ear. A sniper's bullet nearly blew my brains out during the last night attack, but the bullet passed through some wooden fence and lost enough velocity and didn't kill me.

"I'm still here, aren't I?" I joked.

"Are you?" Ramos grabbed his binoculars and scanned the night. "Wonder what the Germans are doing?"

"Laughing at us for fucking up so much." I took a drink from my canteen. "I wonder if the attack tomorrow will work."

"So long as Intel doesn't drop another 'mistake' on us, right? I mean, how smart do you need to be to spot four Kraut divisions, huh?" Ramos asked.

"It was military intelligence, after all," I said.

"Now that's a fucking paradox," Ramos said, sounding surprised by his choice of words.

"Big word, Ramos," I joked, slapping his back.

"What, we poor Mexicans can't read and use big white people words?" Ramos was grinning ear to ear, but soon turned serious. "You hear that?"

I listened carefully and heard the roar of engines in the night. I turned and looked to the line of Sherman tanks sitting behind our lines. The four nearest us sat quietly, engines off as the crews fueled them and loaded in fresh ammo. I turned back to the city in the distance, watching it through the binoculars.

It was difficult to make out much in the night. Little light came from the city, only pinpoints of light coming from campfires or lanterns. I could see vehicles moving about, mostly supply trucks loaded to capacity. They drove through the dirt streets in long columns, but they were moving away from the front as well as lines of German troops.

"What the fuck?" I shouted.

"You're seeing this too?" Ramos watched the Germans drive away. "What are they doing?"

"I….running, the Germans are retreating." I dropped my binoculars and grabbed my rifle, slinging it over my shoulder. "Wait here."

"Where are you going?" he asked

"I'm going to get the Captain," I said.

I pulled myself out of the foxhole and jogged towards the C.P. I ran behind the front lines, passing by the waiting Sherman tanks and halftracks. The C.P. was situated a few yards behind the lines, set up in an abandoned farm house. I ran over to the bombed out house, the guards at the front stopping me. When I told them I had urgent information for the Captain, they let me through.

"What the hell is wrong, Bolger?" Captain Hiller asked, standing over and area map with Major Irving.

"I think the Germans are retreating," I spat out, breath short.

"What?" Major Irving asked, stepping away from the map.

"Ramos and I heard engines running and we scanned the city. We spotted convoys of troops and supply trucks moving away from the front. They were pulling as much stuff as they could away from us."

"We should send out a recon…" Captain Hiller was stopped with a wave of the Major's hand.

"And?" I stood silent. "So you spotted them moving supplies. They're probably setting up a fallback position for when we take the town. If anything, we should meet lighter resistance when we attack tomorrow," said Major Irving.

"Sir, I don't think…" I tried to explain.

"Corporal, enough, return to your post," the Major ordered/

"But, sir…" I started.

"Corporal!" The Major pointed to the door. "Get back to your post before I have you written up for dereliction of duty."

"I'll handle it, sir." Captain Hiller ushered me outside and to the side of the house. "What the hell did you think you were doing?" Hiller asked.

"Sir, we should check this out. If the Germans are running they can pull out a big chunk of their forces before we attack, sir," I said.

"Easy there, Bolger." Hiller placed a hand on my shoulder. "Don't give the bastard a reason to screw you over. I'll work on getting a patrol out, so head back to the line and hang tight, okay?"

"Yes, sir," I said reluctantly, lowering my head in defeat.

"Hey, being a good soldier means sometimes doing and following orders that you know are fucked up."

"I know, Captain. Good night, sir." I saluted and walked away, head still hung in defeat.

"Night, Bolger." I stalked back to my foxhole feeling like I was seven years old again and my father yelled at me for breaking a window with a baseball. The same feeling of belittlement and inferiority hung in my chest. This time, however, I realized that those leading us into battle have no real clue what to do. They only listen to what another officer has to say instead of what some grunt has to say. What does he know about strategy and planning?

"How'd it go?" Ramos asked as I dropped next to him.

"How do you fucking think it went?" I shot back, lashing out because he was the first person I met.

"Relax, *mi hermano*, relax," Ramos said, pulling out a pack of cigarettes. "Smoke?"

"No, sorry about that." I leaned back in the dirt and removed my helmet.

"Hey, brass can do that to you, fuckers give me indigestion, 'cept the Cap, of course." Ramos yanked out a single smoke and placed it in his mouth, lighting it with a lucky strike match. He took a deep breath and then let out a long cloud of smoke.

"Wonder who said commanders had to be halfwit jackasses?" Ramos asked, removing the smoke.

"Have you forgotten the Soldier's Creed? It is not our place to ask why, but to do and die," I reminded him.

"All too right." Ramos took another hit from his smoke and sighed deeply. "Simple pleasures, eh?" He grinned and took a final hit of the smoke before dropping it into the dirt and squashing it out with the heel of his boot. I just shook my head and stretched out, crossing my feet and propping my boots up on the lip of the foxhole.

"I believe it's your turn to take watch?" I said, crossing my arms over my chest and closing my eyes.

"You know it is." Ramos rolled to his stomach and faced the town, picking up his binoculars. "Sweet dreams."

I yawned and simply rested until I could drift into some well needed sleep, which would be the first in ten days.

"Bolger, get up," Ramos whispered, tugging on my shoulder. I opened my eyes, but shot my hand up to block out the blinding sunlight of day time.

"What time is it?" I asked, stretching my legs and sitting up.

"Fucked if I know, my watch has been for shit since I got here. Never did understand how this time zone works," Ramos said.

The ground shook under me as a column of twelve Sherman tanks rumbled by, soldiers sitting atop the turrets. More soldiers marched behind them in two columns on opposite sides of the dirt road. Above us, P-38 Lightings streaked by, shooting off towards Troina.

"What's going on?"

"We're attacking," Captain Hiller said, stepping to the lip of the foxhole. "You planning on sleeping through it?

"No, sir!" I jumped to my feet and collected my equipment. I tossed on my pack and helmet, grabbing my rifle in the process. In seconds, I was back up and fully loaded with all my equipment.

"Move it squad, mount up!" The Captain yelled.

Everyone crawled form their foxholes and climbed aboard a pair of Sherman tanks waiting on the side of the column. Ramos jumped onto the first tank and found a seat next to the main cannon. I climbed up and dropped behind the turret, sitting across from the mounted .50cal machine gun, next to the commander's hatch. Captain Hiller sat across from Ramos and tapped the top of the turret.

"Ready to go, Cap?" the tank commander asked, popping up through the hatch.

"Move this tin can," Hiller ordered.

"Let's get her rolling," the commander radioed to his crew. The troop laden Sherman leapt forward and squeezed into the stretching line of men and machines. We rumbled into the growing dust storm the column of machines churned up, pushing towards Troina.

Arty boomed in the distance, followed by echoing explosions as arty shells rained down on the city. Fighter bombers shot by overhead, dropping bombs onto the city as well, adding to the deafening explosions the engulfed the town. Steadily, the column raced on, cutting though the barren wastes that surrounded the town.

The burnt out husks that once were Sherman and Stuart tanks littered the ground, a reminder of the failed attempts to take the city, as we moved on. I looked down at them from the Sherman, seeing the remains of their crews and infantry. It was an omen of sorts, making all of us feel like death was impending. My stomach flipped when I saw the vultures feeding on the bodies.

"Poor bastards," Vic said, observing the grizzly scene.

"All Intel's fault," Jay snorted. "They missed four fucking divisions, but they won't loose a minute of sleep. Sometimes, I just what to bring one of those pencil necks out here and show them what their mistakes cause."

"Never place faith in Intel," Captain Hiller said over the rumble of the tank engine. "They always screw up."

"Plus, they ignore shit," Hanes added. "I was a clerk with Intel before we met in basic. They had info on Japanese fleet movements that pointed to something heading to Hawaii, but they ignored it, fuckers."

"Seriously?" Ramos asked.

"Like a fucking heart attack," he shot out. Phelps and Mangon glanced at one another and then at me. I just shrugged, looking back at the battlefield.

"So, how long before we take Sicily, do you think?" Phelps asked.

"Too long," Captain Hiller grunted.

"We'll take it…eventually," Mangon answered.

"Yeah, then what, we take Italy?" Jay asked.

"In a matter of fucking days," Vic said.

"Planning on visiting your folks?" Ramos asked.

"Yeah, I'll pay my respects before I slit Mussolini's throat," Vic said, moving his finger across his neck in a slicing motion.

Ramos turned to face Vic and dropped his voice. "You mean they're…"

"Dead," Vic said coldly. "Been dead since Jun 21, 1940 when Mussolini had my father killed for not supporting him. My mom died of a heart attack when they dragged my father away. I wasn't there with them, my parents sent me to live with my uncle, Vito, in the states when I was about 13. I left my younger brother, Henry, there too." Vic explained.

"Vic, I'm sorry, I didn't…" Ramos tried.

"Drop it." Vic looked away and lowered his head, helmet dropping over his eyes. Ramos looked to me, but I shook my head, knowing about his family since training. Ramos nodded and looked towards the town, everyone on the tank was now quiet. We sat like that until the tanks approached the edge of the town. All troops were ordered off the tanks and to form two lines on opposite sides of the road.

I jumped off and landed on my feet, dropping into a crouch on the side of the road. Nate and Ramos landed next to me as the tanks rumbled on a head of us, leaving my fellow soldiers and myself standing in a choking cloud of dust and sand. My throat burned and my eyes began to tear, along with everyone else, save for Hiller, who raised a bandana over his face to cover his nose. Private Donald Malks, a man who used to be an engineer before transferring to the infantry, dropped a pair of goggles over his eyes and raised a bandana over his face, getting a series of dirty looks.

"Smart bastard," Ramos grunted, wiping away tears.

"Move it," Hiller ordered, strolling off into the dust like we were walking through some park. I stood up and began to walk close to the Captain, fighting to not lose him in the growing dust cloud, as more tanks rumbled by.

The sides of the road were clogged with infantry marching towards the city. Dust thrown into the air cut visibility to nothing even though the sun burned brightly in the sky. The sounds of coughs and gagging troopers filled the air as I followed the Captain down the road; the booms of explosions grew as we approached.

"Stay focused, and stay with me!" Captain Hiller yelled to us, not turning or breaking stride.

I kept walking in silence, knowing opening my mouth meant getting a gulp of sand. Instead, I fought hard to prevent myself from vomiting. The dust, smells of unwashed soldiers, and fumes of rolling metal crates created a unique collection of smells and sensations. The dust and oil fumes felt gritty and rough against my hands and face while the smells were something unknown by me until that time.

The column of Sherman tanks soon passed us, the clouds of sand and exhaust fading. The town came back into view, the smoke from fires rising up out it. Fighter bombers flew in on steep strafing runs, machine guns chattering, and bombs falling. Tanks fired, and cannons booming alongside the explosions of 250lb and 500lb bombs. Surprisingly though, I could hear no rifle or machine gun fire coming from any ground troops.

"Here we go, follow me!" The Captain yelled.

The entrance to the city was only feet away, the road blocked, by a pile of debris. The rest of the infantry rushed forward, charging over the debris and running down the streets. Captain Hiller led us over the pile and to the right, to a side street near several bombed out buildings. The remains of the German garrison, some discarded helmets and rifle clips, were scattered about abandoned sandbags and MG nests.

"Where are they?" Vic asked as we stood near the buildings. "These positions have been abandoned without a fight."

"Brilliant observation," Nate grunted.

"These positions are undamaged," Hiller said, looking into one of the MG nests. "Wonder what the tanks were shooting at?"

"Must be jumpy crews," Vic commented.

"No," Hiller stood up and looked down the street at the other empty positions. "They're gone."

"Sir? I asked.

"The Germans, they abandoned the fucking town. I saw it back in the first war when the Germans slunk away from a small hamlet in the night before we attacked. Bastards pulled that shit again."

"Then what are the tanks firing at?"

"Empty fucking buildings, what else? This whole shit hole of a town is empty, follow me," the Captain ordered.

The Captain led us back to the town center. Around us, the tanks blasted away at buildings that still had empty enemy firing positions, ripping many to the ground. Soldiers rushed, others clearing them out as if anyone was in them. Captain Hiller just strolled down the street, giving looks of anger at the other officers, most of which were much younger.

"Waste really pisses me off," he grunted as we entered the town the square. "All the supplies, the troops, the time, this city…all fucking wasted for nothing."

"No such thing as an efficient war," I whispered, not to mock the Captain, but simply repeating words I would need to hear for the rest of the war.

"I think that's the town hall," Sergeant Hanes said, pointing to largest building in the square.

"Right, let's secure it," I said.

The town hall may have been a large building, but that was about it. It was constructed of brick and stone with a simple entrance of two wooden doors which had been blown away. It was three stories high, but a huge section of all three floors in one corner of the building was gutted by bombs. We could see the innards of the building, mostly hallways clogged with debris piles or simply missing sections of flooring.

Walking up a half destroyed stairway, we entered the building. Upon entering the lobby, we found the place devoid of life. Overturned chairs and desks, with forgotten equipment and papers scattered about. Broken glass covered the floor, alongside burned papers and books.

"Fan out," Hiller ordered.

I tapped Vic on the shoulder and we walked up the nearby set of stairs to the second floor. We carefully crept down a long corridor that ran the length of the building. Dozens of offices and side hallways jutted off to the main hallway, but we kept on walking until the floor ended into a wide crater. We turned down the first corridor and ran into the mayor's office.

Stepping in carefully, we cleared the two offices, one being a waiting room and the other, the mayor's real office. The German commander must have set up shop here, as images of Hitler hung from the walls alongside Nazi flags. The fireplace inside the main office was filled with ash and burned papers as well on the simple wooden desk in the center of the office.

"Germans sure do love Hitler," Vic snorted, knocking one of the Hitler photos off the wall.

"And burning shit," I added, poking the piles of burnt papers in the fireplace with the blade of my knife.

Vic riffled through the suitcases lying on the floor and grunted as he tossed the books he found onto the floor. "All pro-Nazi fucking bullshit."

I said nothing and began searching through the desk, pulling out drawers and emptying them on the desk. After finding useless papers and office supplies, I found a small book that was heavier then it looked. I flipped it open and found it was hollowed out, a 9mm Luger found inside.

"Hmm, I found something interesting," I whispered, weighing the Luger in my hand, gripping it tightly.

"Nice," Vic said, seeing the Lugar. "Any ammo for it?"

"Ah," I flipped through the desk and book again. "Nope."

"Too bad, it's a great keepsake though." Vic continued to scavenge through the office while I slipped the Luger into my pack.

"Find anything else?" I asked Vic, seeing him eyeing something in his hand.

"What? Oh, no, just some requisition papers for supplies," he answered, handing the torn papers to me. I took them and examined the closely.

"You know, this could be worth something," I said, seeing they were numbers for supply levels, mostly fuel and medical supplies. "Might tell us how much the Germans had when they bugged out."

Vic shrugged and stood back up, dusting himself off. "Let's tell the Captain," he said.

I nodded and we walked back into the hallway, tracing our steps all the way back to the main entrance. We found Captain Hiller speaking with the Major near the door. Behind them, more soldiers poured inside, most carrying in supplies to set up a command center.

"My man warned you the Germans might pull this shit, sir," Captain Hiller was saying, fighting hard to control his own rage and utter contempt for the Major.

"And? We now have the town and we took it with no losses and when moved in today. I say that's a win, don't you agree, Lieutenant?" The Major asked.

"Yes, sir," Lieutenant Price, the Major's assistant and teacher's pet, responded.

"Well, nearly four German divisions were here last night and now they're gone. Any idea where a force that large can go now that it has such a large head start on us, sir?" Captain Hiller asked.

"I don't like your tone, Captain," The Major said.

Captain Hiller remained in control of his emotions and saluted. "Sorry sir," the word "sir" coming out like an insult. The Major returned the salute and Hiller marched off, eyes filled with rage.

"Sir," Vic and I said with a salute.

"Find anything?" he asked, returning the salute.

"These sir," I handed him the papers. "It's a supply listing for the German forces here."

"Hmm," Captain Hiller took the papers and looked them over closely. He studied every page and word, analyzing each one like he was readying his own will or something. "You know what this tells me?"

"I'm not sure, Captain," I admitted.

"This tells me the German's had a shit load of supplies here and that it took a lot of trucks to haul out of here," he said.

"Sir?" Vic said, tilting his head in confusion.

"Shit load of supplies, shit load of trucks, only a few hours head start; what does it mean?" Captain Hiller was pointing something out, but I didn't get it. Then it hit me.

"They need open road to move everything quickly so they can get away," I said.

Hiller grinned. "Right, and since the areas around here are all hills and rough terrain, the options of open roads are limited." Captain Hiller led us over to an empty table and pulled out a map from his jacket, unfolding it on the table. He began tracing different roads displayed on the map, grunting to himself.

"Any thoughts?" he asked, still looking down at the map.

"Ah," I leaned over his shoulder and studied the map myself, eyes running up down the nearby roads. "Here," I pointed to a road labeled 'Causeway 72.'

"Why 72?" Vic asked.

"Causeway 72 is connected to the road leading right out of town. From the connection, 72 is mostly strait roadway that cuts through the hills and mountains and exits close to the northern part of the island, where the German held ports are. If the Germans wanted to haul hundreds of tons of supplies alongside hundreds of troops, armor, and mechanized forces fast enough to avoid us, then it's the best shot. All the other roads are too rough," I explained.

"Smart thinking Bolger, I agree. Now we just need to convince the royal ass of a commander to let us see if they're there." Hiller folded the map so the town and surrounding roads were on top. He led us back to the Major and outlined what we thought. Again, he was reluctant to listen.

"I can't waste my needed troops to scout a maybe, a guess," he said. "We're too thinly stretched as it…"

"Major!" Yelled the Captain.

Everyone quieted as General Cruz, commander of the First troops in the area, entered the lobby. Standing somewhere near six feet tall and weighing 300lbs. 300lbs of pure muscle, Cruz was one to intimidate just by being. The Major realized this and drew back as he stood at attention.

"General, sir…" the Major stammered, fumbling to salute. The Captain grinned slightly and stood as he was, not snapping to attention or saluting, just nodding his head.

"Is there a problem here, Major?" the General bellowed, removing his cover and running his hand over his short cut hair.

"I, ah…no, sir. Captain Hiller was just…" the Major stammered.

"Hiller, holy shit you're still alive!" The General said. The two shook hands and patted shoulders.

"Do you see me dead?" Hiller joked.

"Fuck no, but the Major on the other hand…" he looked to the Major and flashed a look of disgust. "What's troubling you?" The General asked, annoyed.

"Corporal Bolger here might have just located the escape route the Nazis took last night, and they still may be there," Captain Hiller said.

"And you're still here because…." the General said, turning his head towards the Captain.

"The Major says it's too much of a stretch and we don't have the troops needed," Captain Hiller replied.

The General's eyes drifted over to the Major, though he still spoke to us. "Hiller, you have an able bodied squad, so why not head out?"

"The Major has not cleared me, General," Captain Hiller answered.

The Major broke out into a waterfall of sweat. "I….I, you're clear to perform the recon of the route," he stammered, voice cracking with fear and anxiety.

"Wonderful Captain, do what you feel is right and report your findings to me. Should you find the Germans, well, give them a warm going away party," the General joked.

Hiller grinned like a little kid who just got away with stealing a bottle of pop. "The warmest the Big Red One can give."

The General returned the grin and shook hands. "Best of luck and smart thinking, Corporal…Bolger, was it?"

"Yes sir," I squeaked, still feeling a bit unnerved.

"Well, smart thinking, Bolger. Keep it up and we may have an officer with some intelligence in this military. Now let's talk, Major…" The General said as he glanced over to the Major.

As the General walked off with the Major, Hiller sighed and looked at me.

"Shame he's the only commander with a fucking brain," Hiller said, gray eyes boring into me. "Be sure to keep using yours."

"Of course, sir," I snapped, standing strait and snapping my rifle to my leg.

Hiller chuckled. "Now, let's get the others."

The two of us waited in the lobby until the squad returned from the building search. Captain Hiller laid out the plan as simply as possible to us, providing a basic outline. No one raised any questions when the Captain finished talking; they silently followed outside.

We exited the city hall, and were told to hang back and wait. Captain Hiller took Sergeant Hanes and disappeared into the growing collection of soldiers pooling together. As we waited, I found Nate sitting near the edge of the hall stairs, head low and eyes locked on his boots.

"See something interesting?" I joked, sitting down next to him.

"Just that I might need a new pair in the near future," he responded, not looking up.

I nodded my head as both sat silently for several minutes. "How are you holding up, Nate?"

He didn't respond right away, still looking at his boots. "I don't know," he said several seconds later.

"Are you thinking about your sister?" I asked, watching as he raised his head back up.

"Our father emptied his bank account and paid the rent for the next three months, giving the rest to Lisa. He bought some time for my sister to save up more money from her job, and I'm sending them my entire pay," Nate said.

"So they're getting by," I said, trying to sound upbeat.

Nate nodded slowly. "Just barely, but I still have no clue what to do next. If you have any ideas, I'd like to hear them."

I shrugged slightly. "The Army might have some type of compensation…thing you could use."

"Like what?" Nate shot back, sounding slightly annoyed.

"I don't know, ask the Cap. He's been in the service for a while and might know," I said.

"Okay, that's one thing I could do, but if I do find something like that, I bet it'll take a while to work," Nate replied.

I gave Nate a caring look. "I'll back you all I can."

Nate nodded and placed a hand on my shoulder for a second. "Thanks, I owe you a lot."

"Cash only," I joked, grinning slightly.

"Can I work out some sort of installment plan?" He asked.

Chapter 7

Our timing had to be perfect; the stars had aligned just right for us. The day heat had tapered off. A light wind had started up, creating a slight cool breeze, while not picking up and throwing sand. The German convoy of men and machines sat stalled out in the only steep section of the canyons along their chosen route of escape, just before everything evened out on flat plans.

I lay on my stomach alongside Captain Hiller and Jay, at the edge of the ridge overlooking the convoy. Propped up on elbows, Hiller and I watched the enemy through our binoculars, Jay using the scope on his Springfield rifle. Looking carefully, a German Panzer IV stalled out in front of the long convoy of idle armor and transports.

"Bastards can't even fix a tank," Jay grunted, watching a group of engineers fumble about the engine block of the tank.

"Yea, but they'll get it fixed eventually," Hiller replied.

"Or shove it out of the way," I added, eyeing up the Panzer behind it.

"Then we best hurry up with our ambush while they're bottlenecked in that canyon." Hiller rolled slightly onto his back and signaled Nate. Nate slowly crawled over to our position and readied the radio.

"Sir," he said, handing him the receiver.

Hiller passed it back. "Are the others in position?"

"Easy is in position, but Kilo hasn't reported in," Nate said.

Hiller sighed, eyes rolling in anger. Easy and Kilo squads were attached to our unit under the Captain's command, to help with the ambush. Easy was headed by Lieutenant Rogers, a leveled headed soldier that Hiller liked for his ability to turn a situation around to his advantage.

Kilo was headed by Lieutenant Vance, the complete opposite of Rogers. The man was an idiotic fool that was too much of a fuck up in the Captain's eyes. He wasn't the least bit pleased when he was given control of Kilo.

"Fuck," the Captain grunted, "wait three more minutes. If they don't report in, contact Easy and tell them to begin the attack."

"Yes, sir," Nate responded, glancing down at his watch.

I looked back at him and shrugged my shoulders slightly. Nate titled his head slightly and sat quietly. Behind, the rest of the squad sat, ducking down in a small creek bed. Everyone sat with weapons in hand and heads down. Andrew sat in the center of the group, looking nervous and high strung. Chances were he'd lose it all when the attacks began.

"Don't trust him?" Captain Hiller whispered.

I turned back and picked up my binoculars. "I'm not sure. We've all adjusted to the fighting."

"You and the others were lucking, you kept cool and collected when the first German bullets started flying. Andrew might need more time," the Captain said.

"Or he doesn't adjust at all," I snapped. My body jolted when the words came out, not believing someone, as new to combat as myself, said them.

Hiller caught the slip. "Easy Bolger, you've got the makings of a good soldier, juts ease back on the rookie."

"Sorry sir," I responded.

"Don't apologize too much, makes you look weak," he said.

I simply nodded, and turned back to watch the stalled convoy.

"Any response from Kilo?" Hiller asked.

"No, not…wait." Nate raised the receiver to his ear and listened to someone speaking. "Kilo's ready, sir."

"Tell both squads to attack in one minute." Hiller turned to the rest of the squad. "Hanes, take the men down the slope and grab cover behind the rocks. Wait for the others to attack and then give it to'em."

"Yes, sir!" Hanes responded, quickly moving everyone out.

Hiller turned to me and Jay. "Jay, cover us from up here. Bolger? You're with me. Let's go."

Hiller and I began crawling forward together, quickly edging close to the steep slope of the canyon. Hiller crouched down by a jutting boulder and checked his Thompson. I checked my rifle to be sure it was clear and loaded, tucking the butt into my shoulder. I glanced over the boulder and watched as the squad crept into position on the side of the canyon, seeing Hanes leading the way.

On the opposite side of the canyon, I could just see the men of Kilo squad moving into position as well. Three men sat up a machine gun while a bazooka crew moved in. At the other end of the canyon, Baker moved into position, finishing up the last bits of prepping for the ambush. I glanced at my watch and counted off. Thirty seconds.

All hell broke loose at once. Kilo squad jumped the gun and attacked thirty seconds too early. Their machine gun crew cut loose on the open top transports, lighting up the fuel and ammo stored inside. Explosions erupted across the transports, engulfing nearby troops and tanks. The bazooka crew blew away the stalled tank.

"God damn it!" Hiller yelled, firing his Thompson.

"Sir?" I started firing myself.

"Vance attack too early and blew the fuel and ammo trucks!" Hiller shouted. He was pissed.

"But it was going to happen..." I said.

"No! The security detail was going to pass by them, so the explosions would take them out. Now they've got the chance to fight back!" He yelled back.

More bullets slammed into the rocks and dirt around us, all coming too close for comfort. Baker squad fought hard at the end of the convoy, destroying the rear guard, blocking the convoy from retreating. So far, they remained hidden in the canyon walls, taking carefully aimed shots at the Germans. Kilo, on the other hand, was unorganized.

Their machine gun and bazooka teams blasted away at the Germans without any coordination. The Germans ducked for cover and returned fire more accurately, spotting the machine gun crew and gunning them down.

Our squad tried to help cover Kilo, but to no avail. Vic hammered away with his BAR and Hank was setting up his machine gun, but the Germans put up stiff resistance, firing just above our position to shake rocks loose, which rolled down onto us.

Captain Hiller and I moved down the canyon quickly, jumping from rock to rock. I fired my rifle as I went, sending rounds in all directions as my hands bounced with every jump. I spotted Ramos ducking in a small enclave in the canyon wall, hanging back with Andrew. I ran towards them when a *panzerfaust* rocket shot over my head, impacting on the rocks above me.

Shards of rock and dirt rained down on me, bouncing off my helmet. Shrapnel fell amid the rock, sizzling in the air as it past. I cursed loudly, as it burned my skin; I leapt forward and slammed into the dirt next to Ramos.

"Man can't fly on his own," Ramos joked, dragging me behind the boulders for cover.

"So I've learned," I grunted, struggling to get back to my feet. I could feel the metal shrapnel burning through my uniform and onto my skin. Quickly, I brushed the tiny pieces of steel off me and dropped next to Ramos.

"Who jumped early?" Ramos asked, clearing a jam from his rifle.

"Kilo, who else?" I snorted, lining up a shot with my rifle. I sighted a German lieutenant preparing another *panzerfaust* for firing. Finger squeezing the trigger, the man's head jerked back in a fine mist of pink.

"It's their Lieutenant," Ramos realized. "Man's a nervous son of a bitch."

Kilo's bazooka team blasted another supply truck, this one packed with demolition charges. All at once, a few hundred pounds of high grade TNT exploded with a deafening roar and blinding explosion that sent Ramos and me tumbling backwards.

I landed several feet back, my head violently snapping back against the hard rock. My head throbbed with god awful pain, my vision blurred and the vomit was rising in my throat.

"Ramos!" I yelled, my hearing hampered by a loud ringing.

"Uh…" Ramos moaned, laying several feet to my right.

"Ramos?" I struggled back to my feet and crawled over to his side. Seeing he was on his side, I gently rolled over Ramos's body and removed his helmet, seeing blood running across his black hair.

"Uh, Corr?" he asked, blinking as he looked up at me. "Shit, when did I get drunk?"

"You slammed your head into the rocks," I said, finding a large gash running on the back of his neck and scalp. A nice sized bump jutted out from the back of his head, just where his helmet did not cover.

"Really, I thought I downed another case of tequila." His hand went to his head. "Oh, that's one hell of a bump."

"You guys okay?" Andrew squeaked from the lip of the enclave.

"Wonderful, idiota," Ramos hissed.

"Are you good?" I asked, handing Ramos his canteen from his belt.

"I'm fine…I think," he stammered.

"Ya think? Hang on." I grabbed my rifle and placed my helmet back on my head and ran over to Andrew. "You bleeding?"

Andrew kept eyes locked down on the battle still unfolding in the canyon below. I couldn't see any blood or opened wounds, but he could've had a concussion or something.

"They won't give up," Andrew said in a monotone voice.

"What?" I asked, looking back to Ramos.

"The Germans, they just…they're coming!" He screamed.

I turned back and saw several German soldiers creeping up the side of the canyon, weapons at the ready. I shouldered my rifle and aimed for the nearest German, firing three times. All three shots missed, but forced the Germans to duck for cover.

"Ramos!" I yelled.

Stumbling slowly, Ramos moved to my side, rifle in hand. "I'm here."

"They're coming back, can you shoot?" I asked.

Ramos leaned against a boulder and tried to aim his rifle. "Are there three or six?"

"That would be a 'no', he's not alright to shoot," I said to myself, ducking down as a volley of machine gun fire stitched the area. I turned to Andrew and was about to repeat my question when I saw him staring down at his feet. Following his gaze, I spotted his M1 on the ground, the stock and breach shattered by shrapnel.

"Sorry," he mumbled.

"Don't be," I snapped. Ramos tossed his rifle to Andrew and drew his .45.

Out of the corner of my eye, I spotted the Germans trying to move up. Whirling back to face them, I fired off three more shots, forcing the enemy back to cover. One soldier stuck his head up and I blew away most of it. His comrades held firm and returned fire, un-phased by the death of the soldier.

I tucked down and fumbled for one of the grenades on my belt. I held the small 'pineapple' in my hand, pulling out the pin while still holding the spoon down. When the Germans ducked for cover to reload, I lightened the grip on the grenade and let the spool spring free. The fuse hissed slightly as it quickly burned down the explosive charge. Counting to three, I sent the grenade over the boulder.

It bounced across the hard rock several time, tumbling end over end towards the Germans. The grenade exploded no more than a heartbeat later, blowing chunks of rock into the air amid a cloud of shrapnel. Several screams rose from the echo of explosions and two Germans tumbled down the side of the canyon.

"Get clear!" I heard Andrew scream from behind. I turned my head to see Ramos fling himself over the boulders down to the outcropping below. Andrew tackled me and threw the two of us down the canyon wall.

I cursed loudly as my body slammed against the hard rocks, each impact reverberating through my skull. I had no clue why Andrew tackled me, but seconds after we cleared the enclave, it erupted in a ball of fire and smoke. The boom of tank fire soon echoed through my ears as we landed on the rock.

"Thanks," I mumbled. My was really back sore. Andrew rolled off me and rested on his knees. I took several deep breaths and rolled to my stomach, pushing myself up to my heels. "Ramos?"

He didn't answer, so I called out again. "Ramos!"

"God, I need a drink," he moaned, rolling to his back.

"Shit, don't do that," I said to him, moving to his side. "I thought you were dead."

"Fuck, I felt dead." Ramos struggled to his feet, retrieving his.45 from the dirt.

More machine gun fire peppered our position, tossing all three of us to our stomachs. I held my rifle tight to my chest and inched forward to the edge of the rock surface. Reaching the lip of the rock, I looked down on the German forces.

The convoy was in flames, most, if not all, the supply trucks burning. The halftracks and Panzers were gutted by rocket fire, though several were still on the attack. Easy squad was holding the Germans in the kill zone, preventing anyone from retreating down the canyon. Our squad fired from the canyon wall, killing the enemy left and right. Kilo was holding tight near the exit of the canyon, but their bazooka and machine gun teams were dead.

The last surviving Panzer burst into flames, as a man from Easy squad calmly fired his bazooka. The steady stream of machine gun fire soon died down, the pop of rifle fire echoing sporadically. I reloaded my rifle and watched the burning convoy, eyes searching for any Germans. Ramos lay next to me, blood now running down the left side of his face. Andrew sat behind us, quiet, in shock, with Ramos's rifle in his lap.

"That was quick," Ramos observed,.45 at the ready.

"It's not over yet." I craned my head around and scanned Hiller's position. He was too far away to see clearly without binoculars, but I could just make his hand signals. I pulled myself to my feet and told Ramos to follow.

"What?" he asked.

"We need to move down there and check for anyone alive, come on," I ordered.

Ramos shrugged and nodded at Andrew. "Coming kid?"

At first, he did not answer, eyes down. Andrew seemed to be in a trance, but then he snapped out of it all of a sudden. "Yes," he mumbled, moving to his feet.

Ramos and I could only sigh, knowing Andrew could freeze up on us at any moment. I led the three of us cautiously down the rest of the canyon wall, eyes on the convoy. At first, everything was quiet, a low roar from the flames providing an eerie background noise. I ignored it and moved on, pressing against a shot up halftrack.

The dead were everywhere and anywhere. Many were lying in unnatural positions, their bodies mutilated by bullets and shrapnel. The smell of burnt meat soon filled my nostrils, nearly forcing me to gag. I blocked out the God awful smell and moved on, slowly walking alongside the convoy.

I kept alert, my eyes moving from one body to another. Most were dead without a doubt, the missing limbs was a giveaway. Still, I nudged each body with the tip of my boots, looking for movement of any type. Ramos followed behind me, checking any vehicle that wasn't incinerated in the ambush. Andrew trailed behind, watching as Kilo moved in from their positions.

"Poor fuckers," Ramos mumbled as he passed a German with both legs blown off.

"Wait," I said, hearing a low moan over the crackle of the fire of a nearby truck, "you hear that?"

Ramos froze. "Sounds like a live one."

I looked across the ground and tried placing the moan to one of the bodies. The moan grew louder as I approached a nearby Panzer that was charred black. The turret hatch was open and the moan echoed from inside. I signaled Ramos and we climbed aboard the ruined tank, stopping by the edge of the top hatch.

I slung my rifle over my shoulder and drew my.45, flicking off the safety. Slowly, I peeked over the edge of the hatch, staring down into the turret. I recoiled in a split second, bile creeping up my throat. Inside the crew had been cooked from the tank's fuel spilling inside and catching fire. What was a four man crew mere minutes ago was now four cooked hunks of blackened flesh.

"What do ya got?" I turned and saw Hiller running over to the tank.

"I…God, I don't know," I admitted, choking back vomit.

Hiller leaned in and looked for himself, his expression turning to one of pity. "One's still alive, doc."

Doc ran up to the tank and looked in, sighing at the sight of the charred German. "I can't believe he's still alive after bathing in fuel," he said, running a hand over his mouth. "There's no way he's gonna make it."

Hiller nodded. "I figured as much." He stood over the hatch and shouldered his Thompson, aiming into the tank. Without hesitating, he fired a quick four round burst, causing Andrew to jump.

"What the hell, you just killed him!" he yelled in surprise and disgust.

Hiller jumped off the tank and shook his head. "He wasn't gonna live and was in a world of pain. Mercy may not pretty sometimes, but it's mercy nonetheless."

I hung my head and had to agree, knowing Hiller saved the wounded German from more agony. Ramos agreed as well, sighing lightly and returning to his search. I hopped off the tank and looked at Andrew.

"You okay, Andrew?" I asked, seeing him staring at Hiller's back as he walked away.

"He just shot him," he said in a flat, bleak tone.

"That German was cooked alive, Andrew. Death was the only thing we could do to ease his pain. It's not like he was shot or something, in that case we would provide medical attention," I tried to explain.

Andrew still remained doubtful. I shook my head and walked away, seeing talking wasn't helping. I figured he needed some time and space. He was acting very strange, but he was still alert.

"Grenade!" Andrew screamed as I pasted another halftrack. I spun around to identify the threat and spotted a potato masher stick grenade a few feet from me. Andrew bolted forward and flung himself on the grenade as I dove for cover. An explosion erupted, sending dirt and shrapnel flying into the air. Something hot slammed into my helmet, sizzling as it knocked me to my ass.

"Medic!" someone screamed over and over again. "MEDIC!"

I tried pulling myself to my feet, but my vision was blurred again. I tried to blink away the shaking vision, my head echoing with an incessant ringing. Everything seemed to flip as a sense of vertigo overcame me.

"Hang on," Doc said, suddenly appearing over me. "Just breathe."

"Where's….where's Andrew," I asked, struggling to stand.

"Relax, Corr, I need to treat you." Doc pressed me back to ground, using a little force.

"Damn it, Doc!" I yelled in the strongest voice I could muster, which was a low grunt.

"Corr…he's dead. He dove on the grenade, now stop struggling," Doc said.

The words hit like a baseball bat to the head, my mind bursting in a furry of thought, cycling through hundreds of thoughts, but my body froze in shock. I felt my stomach knot up and a mass of bile crept up my throat. I swallowed hard and let Doc treat me.

"He…" I mumbled, "he can't be dead. You've got to help him, not me."

Doc shook his head as he plucked shrapnel from my left arm. "He's gone, Corr. I wish I could've done more, but…" Doc's words trailed off.

I shook my head in disbelief, wishing I could get up and see Andrew. Doc kept my on my back and worked hard to patch me up. Captain Hiller stood behind him, speaking with Sergeant Hanes. After talking to Lieutenant Vance, a pair of soldiers from Kilo squad brought over a stretcher. Doc helped me to my feet and led me to the side of the road.

I sat on a boulder and watched as the two men gently lifted Andrew's body, or what was left of it, onto the stretcher. A blanket was placed over the dead child and taken back down the road. Hiller finished speaking with the squad commanders and walked over to me.

"How are you?" he asked, holding his Thompson by the barrel in one hand.

"I…I'm fine, sir," I lied, sighing and averting my gaze to the dirt.

"Don't lie if you can't get away with it," Hiller said, looking down at me. "Can you fight?"

The question was directed to Doc. "Physically, he's good beside some cuts. Mentally…" Doc said.

"I can fight sir," I answered, rising to my feet.

Hiller nodded, and tossed my riffle into my hands.

"Check your shit then, son," he said to me, "this fight isn't over yet."

"Yes sir." I rose to my feet and checked my rifle, pulling back the breach cover slightly to check the loaded clip. "Ready and able."

Hiller nodded and signaled the rest of the squad with a wave of his hand. Everyone fell in besides us, readying to follow the next set of orders. Ramos and Nate moved next to me with Jay and Vic, Both Ramos and Vic sporting bandaged heads.

"Listen up," Hiller bellowed, "the sun's still burning and we got shit to do before it sets. First, good work on the ambush, all of you. We lost Andrew in the attack, but we can grieve later." Hiller turned and pointed towards the open desert past the canyons. "We still got members of this damn convoy who passed through the ambush before we got into position. Some of the flyboys are doing recon runs for us to find out just what got through. Until the update, we're moving to a small hamlet three miles down the road."

"Sir," Nate said with a slightly raised hand, "are we going it alone?"

"Yep, Kilo and Easy are holding here to make sure no one else tries to slip through. We take the hamlet and set up a forward O.P. Now, if there are no more questions, let's move," Hiller yelled.

No one raised a hand as Hiller and Hanes began walking down the road. The squad fell in silence, eyes fixed straight ahead.

"Hey buddy, you okay?" Ramos asked, running up alongside me.

"Fine," I answered, shaking my head and clearing my thoughts.

"Man, a second or two more and we could've bought it too," Ramos said, as he stared right through me.

"Fate's funny that way," I snorted, shaking off the stare. "It's, not easy, but less complicated to kill the guy gunning for you, but to see your friend die…"

"To think I figured him for a coward greeny," Ramos huffed.

I held back another growing lump of bile in my throat. "Me too, I wish he proved me wrong another way."

"Isn't it called an uncommon virtue?" Ramos said, not expecting an answer.

We exited the canyon and moved into two columns on both sides of the road. Ramos stuck behind me, removing his helmet to wipe away sweat from his hair. I felt sweat trickle down my neck like warm rain, the sun heating the already warm water. I wiped it away with my left hand quickly, keeping my right holding the rifle steady.

Captain Hiller marched a few feet away, seeming unaware to the steadily rising heat level. Vic, on the other hand, was nearly drowning in his own sweat. His face was slick with a shiny coating, and he was breathing heavily with each step, the heavy BAR held tight to his chest. I shook my head and looked out over the vast desert.

Flat, empty land stretched out for miles in all directions, save for the canyons we exited from. There appeared to be nothing around us, just the ripples of heat dancing over the hard packed road. A light wind picked up here and there, tossing sand around that scrapped against our skin like sandpaper. Several men grumbled to themselves about the heat and sand, but I was lost in my mind, body on auto pilot.

Thoughts were of home for the most part, Frank and Matthew. I envied Matt for being a pilot, being able to fight the war for several hours a day and return to good food and a real bed at the end of the day. The cool days of England and beautiful women filled his life while I toiled in some burning desert. Of course, I did not hate him for it. Frank was getting it worse.

News, actually civilian news, not military Stars and Stripes, was hard to come by. What we did manage to get painted a rather grim view of the war in the Pacific. For days at a time, every head line was detailing the Japanese snatching more land from us or the Brits.

Japanese ground troops cut a swath through China while their fleets craved up the Pacific like a samurai sword through a water melon.

Frank's letters told of his jungle fighting against a cunning, merciless enemy. Piss poor weather, disease carrying bugs, supply shortages, the deaths of friends, all filled Frank's life. Things were no better for Matt and myself in the deaths of friends department, but Frank had the worst of it. I feared for his life more than my own, seeing death coming for him before me, the worst case scenario.

The overhead drone of aircraft engines soon brought me back to reality. Keeping to protocol, I kept my eyes forward and didn't look up. Instead, I waited until they pasted overhead and could be seen in the sky in front of me.

Four greenish-tan RAF Spitfires zoomed overhead, cutting through the sky with ease. They hung in a loose box formation, each fighter separated with several feet of empty sky. The old looking crates buzzed the hamlet we were moving towards, swooping down like vultures to take recon photos. Nate walked alongside Captain Hiller, radio in hand, with a signal to the recon fighters.

"Well, Queen Eight?" Hiller asked, walking with his eyes on the hamlet. For several seconds he walked in silence, nodding to himself. "What does 'possible armor' mean?" he mocked, followed by more silence. "Well, shit, Queen Eight! Tell me if there's armor or not in that damn town."

More silence as the planes dove at the hamlet.

"Copy, Queen Eight, finish your run and pull out." Hiller handed the receiver back to Nate and ordered us to halt with a raised fist. "Listen up, recon says Kraut armor may be hiding in the hamlet alongside possible tracks.

"Since we have no anti-armor to take on Panzers, we go in quiet." Hiller pointed to the low rising hills to the west side of the village. "Sergeant Hanes will take half of you through the hills and infiltrate the west side of the hamlet. I'll take the other half and use that farm, to the east, as cover.

"Take it slow and easy as you approach. I want to clear this hamlet before nightfall, but I don't want to run into Kraut tanks. If you spot a track or armor, spike the thing as fast as possible. Sweep the area for armor and regroup….in the center of town. Questions?" No one spoke. "Move out," Hiller ordered.

Captain Hiller took Ramos, Phelps, and myself east, through the small farm. We approached along a dirt road leading behind the farmhouse. Everyone moved in a half crouch to keep as low profile as possible. I moved quickly behind Hiller as we drew near, eyes on the farmhouse. The farmhouse was only several yards down the road, standing two stories tall with a large hole blown in the roof. No movement could be seen as we came within reach, Hiller stopping us at a low stone wall several feet from the house front door.

"See anything?" Ramos whispered

I carefully edged towards the wooden gate in the wall, leaning out to see.

"The front door is open," I whispered back, seeing the door ajar.

"Ramos, Phelps, check around the rear," Hiller ordered.

Ramos and Phelps flanked around to the rear while Hiller moved to the door. I vaulted over the wall and ran at full speed to meet him, slamming my back into the hard wall just to the right of it. Hiller stopped to the left and shouldered his Thompson. I readied my rifle and pressed it to the center of the wooden door.

Slowly and cautiously, I pushed it open, hinges creaking slightly. The door swung open and Hiller and I rushed in, moving to the far corners of the room. My eyes moved through the empty room with speed, looking for anyone hiding. Seeing only a table and several chairs scattered about, the room was clear.

Hiller and I moved to what used to be the kitchen, finding it empty and dust filled. The small room had a single wooden table with two chairs, both splintered and covered with mold. Hiller glanced at them and up at the bare cupboards, shaking his head. He waved me on to move to the doorway leading to a staircase. I quickly crossed the room and pressed myself against the doorframe. Hiller moved alongside me and patted my shoulder.

I took the signal and spun out, moving onto the stairs. I scanned the steps and landing above for enemies, finding the area clear for the time being. Hiller moved ahead of me and slowly ascended the stairs, pressing himself to the far right wall. I moved behind him with slow, determined steps to avoid the wooden steps from creaking. Captain Hiller moved with the same slow steps, Thompson held tight and at the ready.

When we reached the top of the stairs, a long hallway extended down to a single closed door. Captain Hiller nodded forward and continued on, pushing to one side of the wall while I took the other. The walls were bare, the paint chipping and dull colored. Marks shown where old pictures hung, but were now long gone. The floorboards creaked under our boots with each step, causing Hiller to cringe slightly. He shook off the sounds and stopped at the door, looking to me for a second.

I moved to the opposite side of the door and checked my rifle. Hiller held up a hand and slowly edged the door open, looking through the crack between the door and its frame. I stood by impatiently, the adrenaline urging me to rush in. I held tight, though, letting Hiller take precautions. Hiller kept focused as he pushed the door open just a bit more, but stopped suddenly. He waved me back and shoved himself closer to the wall.

A volley of machine gun fire ripped through the door, splintering the wood. The shots blew by us within inches, showering us with wooden splinters. Hiller raised his Thompson and waited for the shots to cease. After several seconds of sustained fire, the machine gun fire stopped and Hiller moved into the doorway, emptying his twenty round clip through the gaping hole in the door. As Hiller reloaded, he kicked what was left of the door open, rushing in with me right behind him.

A dead German lay on the floor, an MP40 SMG on the ground next to him. Hiller kicked the weapon away and bent over to look for a pulse. I moved past him to a window. A bolt action Mauser rifle leaned against the window sill, a makeshift sniper scope bolted on. Looking out, through the window, was a decent view of the hamlet and the road approach.

"Captain Hiller, he was a sniper and a scout," I said, putting two and two together, "looks like he was waiting for anyone coming to the hamlet on the road."

"Well, he's dead now." Hiller removed the firing pin from the MP40 and threw it out the window. "I guess this means the Germans are in the town."

"Yes sir," I responded, looking towards the hamlet.

"This is gonna be one interesting day," Hiller sighed and shook his head. "Come on, let's get back and see what Ramos found."

"Yes sir," I answered, stepping over the dead German.

Hiller led me back through the house and to the road where the squad was waiting. Ramos and Phelps were back, speaking with Hanes. Captain Hiller walked over to the three and asked for a sit-rep. I slowed and dropped next to Jay, sitting on the sand next to the road.

"We heard shots," Jay said, drinking from his canteen, "and thought you were in trouble."

"I can see that," I joked, nodding at the canteen. "Worried so much that it made you thirsty."

Jay shrugged and placed the canteen on his belt. "It's the sun, but a little bit of worry mixed in somewhere."

"We found a German sniper positioned up there, and Hiller took him out. He figures that the Germans are holding up in the hamlet."

"I hope we just call in arty or air support and dust the town." Jay looked down at his boots and sighed. "I really don't want to lose anyone else."

I nodded my head, tugging at my dog tags. "It's hard to believe he's gone, but when I realized I was alive, I was happy."

"Happy it wasn't you?" He asked.

I nodded. "My dad said it's called survivor's guilt when the feeling of being happy it was him and not me makes you feel like such a bastard."

"Listen up," Hiller said once he collected his thoughts, "the Germans are in town and we have to assume they know we're coming. We need to clear them out, we'll hit the flanks. Sergeant Hanes will flank right while I flank left taking the usual fire teams. Once we flank, we clear the surrounding buildings until we meet at the main road."

"There are only a dozen or so structures in the town," Hanes added, talking over for the Captain, "so it shouldn't take long to clear out. This place is just a waypoint along the road, so there's a supply building adjacent to the road that's probably loaded with fuel, food, ammo and the like, that the Germans didn't get out in time. Let's watch our fire around this building just to be safe."

"Questions?" Hiller asked, arms folded over his chest. No one spoke. "Alright, break up into the fire teams and let's get this rolling."

I pushed myself off the ground and readied my rifle. Jay checked his sniper rifle and nodded to me as Hiller moved across the road. Along with Vic, Nate, Ramos, and Phelps, we proceeded back around the farmhouse and across the barren fields. Dead plants clung to the remains of wire fencing as our boots threw up dirt and sand with every step. Captain Hiller charged ahead of us, taking the lead as always. He led us past the fields to another dirt road leading the eastern side of the hamlet. Everyone moved in a low crouch to help compensate for the lack of cover along the open road.

The humid air was still as we approached, only the thin whisper of the wind and our grunts breaking the even silence. I was breathing heavily from the run mixed with the heat, humidity, and the weight of my equipment. The others around me were breathing just as heavily, sweat collecting on our faces and necks. The heat was stifling, the sun's rays slowly, but surely, eating away at our exposed flesh. My sleeves were rolled to the elbow, a rag lined the inside of my helmet and my hands were caked with sand like everyone else, all methods to combat heat and sweat.

Captain Hiller kept his sleeves rolled up, but he never appeared bothered by the heat. Being in his late thirties or early forties, he moved at the same rate, if not quicker, then the men half his age. Very little sweat ran down his cheeks or forehead while the rest of us were practically drowning in it. Hiller's physical prowess was very peculiar and a topic of discussion when he wasn't around. Many of us debated if Hiller aged like everyone else or is he aged at all. While stupid to think, he was healthier than most of us, had the features of a twenty year old, and finely sharpened senses. If It wasn't for the short cut salt and pepper hair and his service in the Great War, most pegged his age between twenty-two or twenty-five.

Hiller's hand shot up in a fist as we approached the buildings on the edge of the road. Signaling the stop, everyone dropped down to the dirt, and held position with no sound. I glanced over at Jay as he scanned the buildings through the scope on his rifle. I turned towards the buildings and looked for movement, but spotted Hiller signaling us to get back up.

I jumped back to my feet and moved up the road, stopping alongside a two story building to the left of the road. Hiller knelt near the edge of the building and leaned out slightly, scanning the road beyond. He pulled back after several seconds and issued a series of orders through hand signals. Nate and Phelps moved up behind Hiller while I moved with Ramos and Vic around the back of the building. I led the two through an alley around the back and moved around a building several yards down.

As we approached the adjoining alley, I stopped when I heard to the low murmur of voices. I first thought the voices were in English, but I recognized German words and gave a quick signal to halt. Vic spun around and covered the rear as Ramos moved to the opposite side of the alley. I edged closer to the turn in the alley and listened. I could make out three different voices talking about women and booze in German. Judging from the volume and echo of the voices, I guessed they were at the opposite side of the alley, so I risked a quick glance.

I saw four German soldiers at the end of the alley next to a compact anti-tank cannon. Three were talking while the forth sat against the canon, face buried in a book. The other three joked about the forth, calling him 'professor' in a mocking tone. On the opposite side of the hamlet machine gun and rifle fire boomed. The distinct cracks of M1 Garand Rifles and Thompson submachine guns mixed with the buzz saw cracks of MG42 machine guns. Sergeant Hanes and his group made contact and we began firing on the Germans.

The group of four were startled by the eruption of gun fire and jumped. The three speaking moved for the weapons and rushed out into the street while the fourth waited with the cannon. When the three were out of sight, he grabbed his rifle and helmet, tucking the book into his uniform. Expecting him to join the others, I waited until he ran out to move, but the man started running towards us. Confused, I pulled back and signaled the others. Ramos took aim and waited, but I signaled him not to fire. Something wasn't right and I wanted to figure out what.

I leaned back against the wall and listened to the footsteps of the soldier. As the echo drew louder and closer, I slung my rifle over my shoulder and drew my.45. Holding the sidearm tight in my right hand, I extended my right arm out. The soldier ran straight into my outstretched hand and tumbled to the ground. Feeling a slight sting in my arm, I spun out and aimed the pistol dead center at the man's face.

"No, don't!" he screamed in German, throwing his hands up. "I surrender, I surrender!"

"*Auf Ihrem Rücken, jetzt!*" I barked, it meant 'get on your back, now' in German. The soldier complied and rolled over, hands stretched over his head. "Ramos, cover the front."

"You're covered," he responded, moving into position.

"*Verletzen Sie mich bitte nicht,*" the soldier yelled, face in the sand. That translates into 'Please, don't hurt me!'

"*Verschlossen!*" 'shut up' I yelled back, patting him down. I removed a Luger from his waist holster and small pocket knife, tossing them to the side. Once I was sure he was clear, I rolled him over, fishing out a wallet from his uniform pocket.

"*Bitte, ich…*" 'Please, I..' the German begged.

"Surrender? I know." I opened the wallet and read the name aloud. "Private Henry… Vineti?"

"What?" Vic grunted, moving to my side and grabbing the ID. He studied the soldier on the ground and the ID for several seconds. "Henny?'"

"Vincent?" the man stammered, eyes filled with hope instead of fear.

"Holy shit, this…this is my brother Henry," Vic responded, suddenly dump founded.

"Brother?" Ramos repeated, looking over at us. "When the hell did you say anything about a brother?"

"Henny," he said, kneeling over the soldier, "what the hell are you doing in that uniform?"

"They conscripted me after dad died," Henry answered in Italian. "They dragged me off and said I could take a bullet in the brain or be conscripted. Mom was still alive and I thought they'd leave her alone if I went along. I've been trying to escape since they dropped me here in Sicily."

Vic stood silent, appearing to contemplate his next words. Instead, the emotional black hole that was Vic bear hugged his brother, tears welling in his eyes. Ramos looked over to me in a look of confusion and shock, as I shrugged my shoulders.

"Vic, let's get back to the Captain," I said, listening to the gun fire increase. "We shouldn't be standing around."

"Yeah,' Vic finally said, moving back from his brother. "Let's go."

"Ramos, watch him and let's go," I whispered, just to play it safe.

Ramos nodded and the four of us moved down the alley, towards the street. I moved on ahead, leaving Vic and his brother to follow with Ramos behind them. I was unsure if I could trust Vic's brother, wondering just how much he'd fallen to German propaganda and their brainwashing techniques. While I trusted Vic with my life, his judgment could be clouded and that might threaten the rest of the squad.

I slowed my pace as I came to the end of the alley, stopping a few feet from the street. I leaned out to check the street and pulled back as a group of three started creeping up the street. Jerking back too quickly, I couldn't tell if they were German or American. Ramos moved over to opposite wall and dropped to one knee, leaning back against the building. He leaned forward slightly, trying to see into the street without exposing himself. He squinted his eyes slightly and sighed in relieve.

"It's the Captain," he sighed, moving back to his feet.

"Come on," I said, moving out to the street, "Vic, keep his hands on top of his head."

"Hands up, Henny," Vic admonished, keeping his voice soft. His brother complied and placed his hands behind his head, interlocking his fingers.

I nodded and carefully moved into the street, hugging the nearby building to prevent the Captain and the others from being spooked. Captain Hiller spotted me instantly and lowered his Thompson slightly, holding the weapon ready, but not pointing it towards us.

"Who the hell is he?" he asked once he was few feet away.

"Ah…Vic?" I didn't try to explain and just handed it over to Vic.

"He's my brother," Vic answered flatly. "He surrendered to us when we moved through the alley."

Hiller switched his gaze from Vic to his brother, eyes moving to size up the man. "He really is your brother?"

"Why the hell would I say otherwise…sir," Vic declared.

Hiller sighed and rubbed the bridge of his nose. "This is gonna need to wait until we secure this place. Make sure he's got nothing on him and find a place to hold him. Once he's stashed, we need to finish securing-"

Machine gun fire erupted from the end of the street, sending all of us running for cover. I dove to the dirt and rolled to face the direction the fire was coming from. Hiller was already down on one knee, firing his Thompson in controlled bursts. I lay on my stomach and leveled my rifle, firing towards the group of Germans that ambushed us. A halftrack rolled out to the street and swung around to face us. The MG42 mounted above the cab swung around under the hands of its gunner, the buzz saw echo filling the air.

"Get back!" Hiller yelled, throwing his body through the door of the closest building. "Get out of the street!"

I jumped to my feet and moved for the door, leaping through as bullets peppered the building's stone walls. Hiller moved back out and grabbed Ramos by his pack, throwing him, with one hand, inside. Vic shoved his brother through next, jumping in after. Phelps and

Nate moved in the building across the street, just making it, as their position was raked with machine gun fire.

"Where they hell did they come from?" Ramos yelled in anger, holding his bleeding arm.

"You hit?" I asked, moving to his side and take the arm in my hands.

"No, I think it's just stone fragments," Ramos announced.

Ramos gritted his teeth, as I pulled back his ripped sleeve, seeing several stone shards sticking up from the exposed flesh. I grabbed my medical kit and removed a bandage and sulfur power, dumping the powder over the wound.

"We need to flank that track and take out the crew." Hiller said and moved to the rear of the room,to look for an exit, as I tied up Ramos's arm with a bandage. "Come on, this way."

Hiller led us out the back way of the building, into an empty side street. He and I checked the area first and signaled the others to follow. I moved quickly down the road, eyes darting from window to window for any German looking to ambush us. My body was tensed up like a knot, every muscle locked into place, as if readying to strike at something. Pushing pass the pain, I kept up with Hiller until he stopped at the end of the street, ordering a halt, as the machine gun fire intensified.

Around the corner was the enemy halftrack and supporting troops. The mounted MG fired away in steady, long bursts, producing a deafening echoing for several yards around. Captain Hiller studied the soldiers guarding the halftrack and quickly developed an attack plan. Using hand signals, he sent Vic and me to the opposite side of the street while he stayed with Ramos and Henny. Once in position, he ordered Vic to open fire.

Not hesitating, Vic squeezed the trigger on his heavy BAR, the weapon emitting a low pitched crack with every shot. The heavy bullets ripped through several German soldiers standing closest to the halftrack, blowing off limbs. I aimed for the gunner and killed him with a well-placed shot to the head as Hiller inched forward, Thompson chattering away. Vic kept up the suppressing fire as the enemy scrambled for cover. Once he emptied his twenty round clip, I continued to fire while he reloaded. Hiller sent a frag grenade flying behind the Germans, ducking by the halftrack for cover. Resulting in a shrapnel filled explosion,killing them and the last of the resistance.

"Move in," Hiller barked, as he walked forward with his weapon aimed at the bodies.

Vic and I moved from our position and crouched by the halftrack, scanning for more targets. Captain Hiller moved to the end of the track, firing a quick burst into the troop bay, in case any Germans were still alive. Satisfied, he moved from body to body checking for any signs of life. Once the area was clear, he called out to Nate and Phelps, who appeared from their hiding spot down the street.

"Captain!" Ramos suddenly yelled out, moving to raise his rifle. I spun around in time to see a German sneak up on Hiller with a combat knife in hand. Captain Hiller spun to meet the attack, but a shot rang out and the German dropped. Everyone followed the shot back to Henny, standing with a German Luger in hand. Captain Hiller locked eyes with the young Italian and shrugged his shoulders slightly.

"Nice shot, bro," Vic said, moving to slap Henny on the back.

"Who's the Kraut?" Phelps asked as he returned with Nate.

"Vic's brother," I answered, moving to Captain Hiller's position.

"Long story," Hiller grunted, moving down the street. "Let's go and regroup with Sergeant Hanes. Vic, give your brother a weapon and dump the Kraut uniform before someone shoots him."

"You sure that's smart, sir?" Nate asked, shooting the Captain a questioning glare.

"You doubting my decision trooper?" Hiller asked over his shoulder, not turning around.

"Come on," I urged Nate, moving after Hiller.

Nate shook his head and eyed Henny cautiously, keeping watch as he moved with Vic. I gave him a reassuring slap on the back and fell in behind Vic. Ramos moved with Nate and Phelps, the three of them sticking close to the buildings.

The roar of the nearby firefight intensified as we moved down the dirt street, to the intersection, at the center of the hamlet. The quick shots of Garand rifles mixed with the single, hard shots of German Mauser bolt action rifle, drowning out the rattle of SMG fire the popped up now and again. My heart rate quickened again as we closed in on the ensuing fight, the sight of tracer fire dancing in the air, getting closer. Soon, I could see the German shoulders ducking down at one end of the center road and Sergeant Hanes and the rest of the squad at the other.

The Germans dug in, firing from fortified buildings and foxholes while Hanes and the others hid behind anything in the street for cover. Two MG42 nests poured fire down on our guys from the building, believed to be a supply storehouse. Captain Hiller moved Vic to the front of a nearby house and established a base of fire on the German's right flank. Henny trailed behind his brother as Ramos and Nate moved to flank through the back alleys, hoping to hit the German rear. I moved with Phelps and the Captain, running up the street to come out at the intersection.

Sparse cover was available as we moved up, though the Germans had not spotted us yet. Captain Hiller rushed to the far left of the road and dropped behind an overturned wooden cart. I dove to the dirt behind the remains of a low stone wall, rolling towards a gap in the stone. Phelps jumped into a crater at the edge of the road and hugged the dirt for cover.

"Shift fire right!" I could hear Sergeant Hanes order from a few yards away. Moving to the gap in the wall, I leaned out slightly, bringing my rifle to my shoulder. I sighted the first German that came into view and fired three times, hitting the German at least once. He dropped down as I swung left, aiming for a soldier reloading an MP40. Two quick shots to the back quickly dispatched him, as one of the 42s swung around, gunning for me.

I fell down as the heavy bullets pelted the tiny stone wall, ripping off huge chunks of stone. The chunks rained down on me like hail, pelting my helmet and back. The hard pounding of bullets against the wall soon overtook my hearing, dulling the sense. I cursed under my breath and held my rifle even tighter, perspiration making my palms slick. The machine gun fire relented slightly and I popped back up, firing off the rest of my clip before dropping back down. The shooting picked up again as I fumbled to reload with a fresh clip, spilling the small bundle, as my hands shook.

The heavy thumps of Vic's BAR soon kicked up, spraying the MG position. The gunner swung around to target the new threat and exposed himself through the window. Jay, unseen in a nearby building, picked him off with a single, well placed shot. Hiller took the opportunity and tossed several grenades behind the German defensives, the tiny explosives shredding a group of Germans with shrapnel.

"Phelps, move up!" he ordered, rising to his feet and running for a burnt staff car, closer to the center road. "Bolger, cover him!"

I knelt up and aimed in the direction of the German position. Out of the corner of my eye, I spotted Hiller and Phelps running for their new position. I moved my rifle from left to right over the enemy positions and fired at anyone aiming in their general direction. When my last round was fired and the clip ejected, I quickly shoved a fresh one in and was shooting in less than a second. Hiller and Phelps were halfway to the car when the second MG nest targeted them, ripping up the ground around them. I fired in quick shots at the nest, but they impacted on the wooden planks covering their position. Captain Hiller knew the impending fire would cut him and Phelps down, so he leapt forward like an attacking lion and tackled Phelps, landing behind the staff car as bullets punctured the car.

Vic focused his fire on the second MG as I vaulted over the wall and ran towards Mangon's position, several yards away, in a building doorway. I ran at full speed across the gauntlet of machine gun fire, both friendly and enemy alike, aiming for the doorway. Not slowing, I ran passed Mangon and charged inside the building. Arms out, I ran to a wall and stopped, leaning over as my breaths came in ragged intervals.

"That's pretty fucking ballsy!" Mangon yelled, clearing a jam from his rifle.

"More like stupid," I mumbled, moving to the doorway.

I moved alongside Mangon and crouched low in the doorway, leaning against the stone frame. Mangon stood above me and we leaned out, maneuvering to get off clear shots at the German positions. Nate and Ramos took up positions in a building to the rear of the German lines, raining grenades down on their heads. Suddenly attacked from behind, the Germans shifted their base of fire to cover the new threat. This shift in attention allowed Captain Hiller and Sergeant Hanes to move up closer with the rest of the squad, breaching the German positions at the storehouse.

Mangon and I moved from the doorway as Sergeant Hanes rushed up the street, leading his group with him. Captain Hiller moved up as well, signaling Vic to set up a new firing position. I followed Hanes to the far storehouse, stopping near the large loading dock. The massive wooden doors, covering the bay, were wide open as the Germans fired from behind crates, boxes, and sandbag emplacements.

I moved around to a side entrance to the far right of the loading bay, heading for an unguarded door. Hank ran behind me with Sergeant Hanes, Mangon, and Sanders, rushing through the door and flanking the German emplacements. Sergeant Hanes stayed with Mangon by the door and fired on the Germans, drawing their fire, allowing Hank, Sanders, and myself to run down the side loading platform. Sanders moved to a ladder leading to the upper catwalks with Hank standing by, to cover him. I moved behind a large shipping pallet stacked high with oil barrels, to the far right of the ladder.

Sneaking around the massive stacks of barrels, I edged over to a second room behind the main loading area. Finding the small office empty, I moved through silently, quickly running to the second door that exited to the central loading platform and hid behind the German sandbag emplacements. The heavy rattle of the German machine guns and loud cracks of rifle fire hid any noise I made as I crept to the doorway, pulling a grenade from one of my webbing pouches. Yanking out the thin, metal pin, I let the spoon spring free and listened as the fuse began to burn, hissing softly. Counting down four seconds, I gently tossed the grenade onto the loading platform.

Holding my rifle at the ready, I waited the remaining seconds for the inevitable explosion. Soon, the fuse burned down and the explosion erupted several feet away, throwing wooden splinters and metal shards back through the doorway. Before the dust cleared, I swung out and emptied my entire clip into the Germans, firing at anyone moving. The machine gun fire died down suddenly and the dust began to settle, as the storehouse fell silent.

"Clear!" I yelled, reloading my rifle as my eyes were on the dead Germans.

"Clear up top!" Sanders yelled down from above.

"Good work," Captain Hiller answered, "Let's fan out and make sure this hamlet is secure. Get it done by night and set up a perimeter, CP here in the storehouse."

The rest of the hamlet was easily secured before nightfall, the last of the German defenders going down in the storehouse firefight. No prisoners were taken besides Vic's brother, Henny, who was not treated as most prisoners were. We allowed him to move about freely; Sergeant Hanes kept close tabs on him. Captain Hiller trusted Vic to make sure nothing happened with his brother, but Hiller never left his bases uncovered.

It was coming close to sunset, as I sat in the wide open room above the storehouse loading area. Leaning back in a rickety old chair, feet propped up on the wooden windowsill of one the windows facing the western side of the town, I watched the sky turn its light orange to purple as the sun slowly set. Coming down from the adrenaline rush of the day, my nerves were fried and muscles exhausted beyond belief. My hands shook slightly from gripping my rifle too tightly and were clammy from all the sweat. Trying to relax, I sat by myself and watched the sunset.

Shifting slightly, I picked up the half eaten can of Spam from the tiny footstool next to my chair. Shoveling another mouthful of the overly salty meat into my mouth, I dropped my gaze from the horizon to the others in the room.

Ramos slept deeply from his tiny corner of the massive room, snoring loudly as the drugs Doc had given him eased his sleep. Vic sat with his brother near a stack of crates across the room, both catching up since their separation. For the first time, Vic was actually smiling and laughing at something more than killing German soldiers, the two speaking of some childhood event. Jay leaned against another window a few feet to my left, head leaning against his Springfield sniper rifle. He yawned and sighed lightly, moving back from the rifle and rubbing his eyes.

"Tired?" I asked, washing down the overly salted meat with some warm canteen water.

"Just need to rest my eyes," he mumbled, slipping to the floor and leaning his rifle over his pack. "It's been one hell of a day."

"That's an understatement," I yawned, offering the can of Spam to my friend as he walked over to me.

"No thanks," he declined, waving off the food. "Isn't Spam just ham that didn't make it?"

I chuckled and agreed, setting the can back down. "It beats starving."

"Barely," Jay snorted, pulling a worn pack of cigarettes from his uniform pocket.

"They'll kill you," I stated, watching him pull out one smoke and raise it to his lips.

"Ah, fuck it." He returned the smoke to the pack and returned it to his pocket. "I quiet now and start up when this war ends. Oh, before I forget, I need a favor."

"Sure," I answered, looking over to Jay.

"I been working to get my hands on a pair of Colt.45 pistols for any close quarter fighting. You always had a knack for getting your hands on all kinds of stuff during basic and I wonder if you still have your…contacts."

I grinned and grabbed my pack, rummaging around one of my half melted candy bars. "I'll see what I can do when we meet back up with the rest of the division."

"Thanks, bro, I'll figure out a way to pay you pack when I can," he said.

I waved my hand at the thought. "A few Kraut weapons I can scavenge from the field, but why two?" I asked.

"Dad was a cop and gave me two of his underarm holsters before I left home. I'd carry the two.45s under my arms in case they get too close to get with my rifle," Jay answered.

"I'll get them for you, may take some time, though." I found the melted bar at the bottom of my pack and held it up, seeing the chocolate seeping through the edges of the paper. "Such a frigging waste," I said, disgusted.

"Thanks," Jay said, pulling the bar from my hand. "Well, better get back to watch."

Jay got up and moved back to his post, munching down on the liquid candy bar. I turned back to the sunset and closed my eyes, pinching the bridge of my nose to focus my thoughts. Andrew's death played over and over again in the back of my mind, the sight of his twisted body clear as day. When I enlisted, my father and grandfather both told me that soldiers were always going to die during war. It was the immutable law of war and could never be changed. All you could do was keep moving forward and bring the fight to the enemy, the real way to avenge your fallen comrades. Flying into a blinding rage over the death of your friend was a sure fire way to get you killed, as my grandfather realized while fighting in the Spanish-American War.

My father, Jonathan Bolger, experienced it as well during the Great War. An underage recruit with the Marines, he lost four friends during the fighting in Belleau Wood. Driven to the edge from the horrors of trench warfare and the sudden loss of four friends, he flew into a blind rage. For weeks to follow, he took any, and all, dangerous assignments that gave him the chance to kill more Germans. After nearly losing his life from leaping into a German filled trench, he realized he had to control his feelings.

So far, I managed to keep things in check, both after Donny's death and those at the docks as well as Andrew's death. In check as they may be, I still felt the urge for revenge, to kill an equal number of Germans for those I've lost. Knowing it wouldn't bring them back, I suppressed the urges, but still had them.

"Bolger," Captain Hiller grunted from behind me.

"Sir?" I responded, jumping from my seat and standing at attention.

"Easy there," Hiller said, holding out his hand in a calming gesture. "I'm just checking in on everyone."

"Oh, I'm doing alright, sir," I answered, slacking back my shoulders slightly. "Just tired from everything."

Hiller nodded his head, understanding. "I'm here if you want to talk, son."

"I know, sir. Thank you, sir," I said.

"Ease back on the sirs and get some sleep," he said.

"Yes…, ah, Captain Hiller," I stumbled.

Sicily was deemed 'secure' on August 17, 1943, another win chalked up to the Allies. In truth, it was more of halfhearted win, we gained a launch off point for the looming invasion of Italy, but a large amount of Germans jumped across the Strait of Messina to Italy before we could stop them. Now, the Big Red One was on temporary stand down while the big wigs at Allied Command planed their next big move.

During our stand down, we were ordered to a large military ceremony in full dress uniforms, the whole nine yards to hear a worthless speech from Old Blood and Guts himself, Patton. One of his all encouraging speeches ruined a good day as we sat under the broiling sun to hear about killing more Germans and kick the bastards back to Berlin. In truth, many of us could careless, preferring the Germans to up and surrender, then we could go home. Weeks later, we discovered the entire thing was an 'apology' speech for the arrogant general's slapping of a mentally stressed soldier in a field hospital.

Captain Hiller personally despised Patton more than any other man in our squad. He told us the man looked like something out of western movie; the ivory handled revolvers, the polished riding boots, the overly shiny helmet, all coming ashore at Gela was a joke to him. 'All that bullshit,' he used to say, 'the whole blood and guts thing is absolute crap. His blood and our guts is what is.'

Near the end of October, the division request, to head stateside for a cushy training position, was granted, in a way. Herded aboard rusted transports sitting off the Sicilian Coast, the Big Red One was redeployed to England after an unpleasant ten day sea trip. From the sunny, humid weather of Africa and Sicily, we were greeted by gray, overcast skies of Liverpool, England. Cold, gray, and wet, I began to want the ungodly heat of the desert again. Once the ship came into port, however, my feelings changed when I realized that England was a cushy posting considering the invasion of Italy was underway. Decent food, warm beds, average weather, women, and booze awaited us beyond the bleak Liverpool docks. Matt was somewhere on an airbase and I considered paying him a visit, as our squad was hustled down the ship gangway, bulging packs on our backs and rifles over shoulders.

The idea was quickly suppressed when I remembered the security precautions in place. For some reason, we were not to wear the Big Red One patches on our uniforms when we arrived, nor were we allowed to say we were with the First. Captain Hiller never did tell us why this was, but most of us figured that it was to prevent the Germans from getting a good number of how many of us were here in England. I pushed the thought out of my mind as I walked off the gangway and was herded down the docks to a nearby train station.

"Lovely weather the Brits have here," Ramos joked, looking up at the gray clouds.

"My brother told me the weather here can change in minutes," I reassured Ramos. "Though, rain is their most common weather pattern."

"As long as I can still meet some British *bonitas* and down booze in the pubs, I'm good."

I grinned and patted the overly loaded pack hanging over his shoulders. "Well, when it does get sunny here, Matt said it's very beautiful and the dames love to walk in the countryside."

"I guess the ladies have had to go with the flyboys since the start of the war," Ramos mumbled. "I think they'll like the changeover to us war hardened ground pounders."

"What bullshit is that?" Phelps asked, walking ahead of us. "Them dames will get one look at your greasy, slick back hair and run to me."

"Hey, the ladies will love this amazing *Mexicano* and not some drunk Irish bastard, no offensive, Corr," Ramos joked.

"None taken," I grinned.

Sanders appeared from behind and smacked the back of Ramos's head and then Phelps. "Hey, not all us Irish are drunks," he said, sounding harsh but with a light, joking intension. He slapped Phelps next. "And cut the greasy shit, I am part Spanish."

"Sorry Sans," Phelps responded and in a fake, wounded tone. "I'll be building international bridges with our multi ethnic soldiers."

"Yeah, then I'll burn 'em," Malks snorted, enjoying the fact he was an expert with explosives. Everyone burst out laughing, drawing funny looks from the other squads. If there was one thing that bonded us closer, it was the fact we could insult one another openly, on any level. To an outsider it sounded like we were seconds away from a fist fight, but in truth it was just a few seconds until someone caved and bought the next round of drinks.

"Okay, ease of the racial cracks," Captain Hiller ordered in a low tone. "No telling what uptight officers we might meet on the train ride."

Moving with the flow of the crowd, we were hustled aboard a quickly filling passenger train and told grab a seat. Moving through the cars filled with jabbering soldiers, the squad filled in the seats of one of the half full cars. Plopping down on the old, faded red seats in the center of the car, I dropped my pack between my legs next to my rifle. Ramos pushed in next to me, nearly shoving me against the glass window. Jay and Vic slid in the seats right across from us, all for over loaded packs and weapons leaving no room for our legs or feet to move.

"Ah," Jay sighed, resting his rifle against his shoulder, "Nice and snug."

"I hope they feed us on this ride," Vic grunted next to him, BAR leaning against his thigh.

"Always food or booze with you, eh?" I asked, hoping to keep his mind off Henny, who was being moved to a POW camp stateside.

"What else is there?" he asked. "Henny's getting the royal treatment out in Nevada, so I can relax."

"So that's where the POW camps are?" Jay asked.

"Seems the logical place to put the camps," I commented. "Miles of barren desert in all directions dissuades any escape attempts and I bet the treatment is better than they get in the German military."

The car quickly filled up with even more soldiers as the minutes dragged on. Before too long, the car filled to and beyond capacity, with more men from the First. Once the car was filled, the conductor on the platform moved the remaining groups of soldiers back from the train and steam shot out from the rails and the breaks were released. The car jostling slightly, the sharp whistle blew and the car lurched forward, slowly pulling out of the station.

"Any idea where we're heading?" Jay asked, watching as the train started to move away from the port and into the countryside.

"We're going southwest," Captain Hiller said from across the aisle. "Just get off when I tell you to."

"Yes, sir." Jay turned to me and tapped my boot with his to get my attention. "You think we're going to Europe?"

"Yeah," Ramos answered sarcastically, "The train's gonna take us across the Channel and drop us off in Berlin."

"I'd prefer to enjoy England for a little bit first," Vic said, leaning his head back against the seat. "But first, a nap."

"Sleep, eat, drink, and kill," Jay mocked, "That's all the man knows."

"Not in that order," Vic grunted, crossing his arms over his chest. "And ya forgot sex."

"Speaking of eating, do they feed us on this train ride?" Ramos asked.

Jay tossed him a candy bar from his pocket. "Just don't start complaining about food."

Ramos grinned as he tore open the paper wrapper and bit down on the thick chocolate brick. I shrugged slightly and turned, moving to look out the window. If there was one thing England had, it was rolling countryside. Fields of endless green grass filled the valleys and hills surrounding Liverpool, as we rapidly lost the city behind us. Small, dirt roads rarely appeared, connecting the tiny hamlets and sparse farms and homes. The only signs of technology were the few fighter patrols roaming the skies, the British pilots well versed in flying in poor weather.

The overcast skies soon opened up as we snaked over way through the countryside, rain suddenly pelting the side of the train, in near solid sheets. The wind picked up as well, its strong howl soon rivaling the hard clacks of the train running over the rails. I enjoyed the rain, listening to the drops hitting against the ground was always comforting and relaxing. The constant, steady grinding sound of Vic's snoring soon brought me back from a daydream.

Vic was snoring the paint of the walls with Ramos asleep across from him, head leaning back at an uncomfortable angle. Jay was awake, scribbling down his thoughts in a letter for his family back home. The rest of the men in the car were quiet, most asleep as we moved into the third hour of our train ride. There was an underlying murmur of chatter that was just audible over the clatter of the train moving over the rails. Looking across the way, Sergeant Hanes was fast asleep as well, while Captain Hiller was awake, writing a letter of his own.

"Can I get you something?" a young British woman asked. I looked up at the tall attendant pushing a small cart loaded with containers of coffee and plain doughnuts through the isle.

"Coffee, thanks," I said, holding up the empty metal can from my mess kit. The woman poured the hot liquid into the cup and offered me a doughnut. I politely declined. "No, thanks, ma'am."

She smiled graciously and nodded her head. "You're very welcome," she said before moving on to the next set of seats.

I smiled again and held the cup in both hands, enjoying the heat and smell of the coffee. While I enjoyed the rain, I'd prefer summer rain over anything else. Being the start of November, the rain and wind dragged in a piercing cold that went straight to the bones. Each bit of warmth brought by each gulp of the strong liquid was a welcome relief.

"That actually smells good," Jay mumbled, looking up from his letter.

"It's a godsend," I said, enjoying the strong taste. "You should've got one."

Jay shook his head and folded up his letter. "Ah, I'm good. Hey, any idea on how far we're out from…where ever we're going?"

I shrugged, glancing back out the window. "We've been passing more and more small hamlets, so we must be getting close."

"Attention," a British Army sergeant announced in a tired tone, appearing at the head of the car. "All men in units Able through Item are to de-train at our next stop. Please collect your equipment and be ready to move when we stop, we are on a tight schedule."

I looked to Jay as I reached down to grab my pack. "Closer than I thought."

"Yeah," Jay sighed, leaning over and shoving Vic's shoulder.

With a few grunts, he awoke and angrily looked at Jay. "What?"

"Grab your stuff, we're getting off soon," I answered, waking Ramos as well.

"About time," he moaned, stretching out his arms. We reached down to the floor and collected our equipment and weapons. The train began to slow in a few minutes as the rest of the men shuffled about, filling the small isle as the station came into view. Captain Hiller stood and elbowed his way to the front of the car, moving for the door as the train stopped with a low screech.

With a wave from the British sergeant, everyone moved forward. I followed behind Phelps as we moved down the aisle and out of the train car. The rain had lightened up a bit, moving from a solid sheet to a light drizzle. The platform was filling with dozens of soldiers shouldering their large packs. I moved ahead of the crowd and searched for the Captain, finding him moving off the platform towards the small town.

"Where are we?" Ramos asked, following the rest of the squad.

"The tiny town of Ellis," Sergeant Hanes responded, walking alongside us. "It's a barely noticeable hamlet a few miles east of Dartmouth. The Division is split up all up and down the coast from here all the way up to Portsmouth to confuse the Germans. For the time being, this is gonna be home."

"So, we're living in the town?" Jay asked as we plodded down the dirt road leading from the station.

"No," Captain Hiller said over his shoulder. "The Army set up a tent base just on the edge of the town."

"I hope we get to spend time off base," Ramos said eagerly as we turned onto another road, the camp just at the end.

"You will, but remember we are soldiers and have a war to fight," Captain Hiller stated sternly.

I heard a few groans and moans arise from the squad, but they quickly died out. I kept silent, I'm not one to openly complain too much. Instead, I began to wonder about how life would be different now that we're in a safe area. Despite the German bombing raids, England was far safer from Africa and Sicily. I was looking forward to enjoying the vacation time, though it would be mostly military training during the day and nights on the town. Either way, repetitive training regiments was something to look forward to.

The military base, Camp Baker, was larger than Sergeant Hanes described it to be. Instead of being a collection of tents, the base was rather immense, holding dozens of prefab buildings ranging in sizes, alongside dozens of tents. Walking through the main entrance, a large command center could be seen dominating the center of the base. What once was a large mansion was now the CP and the surrounding farmland made up the base. From the brief trip from the gate to the center of the base, a motor pool, armory, mess hall, and supply station could be seen. Before we were allowed to see the rest of the base, a welcome speech was given by the base CO.

"Welcome to Camp Baker," the Major bellowed from a top the mansions steps, looking down on the large group of soldiers. "I'm Major Philips and I'll be your acting CO for your time here in England. Standard military procedures and rules are in effect here regarding your behavior and such. Daily training will be handled by your squad commanders, while weekly training will be as a company. Reveille is before day break and you will train the majority of your time here.

"Now, the town of Ellis in just down the road, with Portsmouth and several other cities nearby. You are permitted to leave base and enjoy yourselves in town, but bear in mind you are soldiers of the United States Army and will behave as such. Unless otherwise instructed, you are allowed off base after training, but must be back before midnight when you have training the next day. Exceptions are made when you are given passes; your squad commanders can better explain. To wrap this all up, be good soldiers, don't miss training, and for the love of God, be nice to the locals. That is all, dismissed."

Everyone snapped to attention and saluted the Major until he returned to the mansion. Once he was gone, the base sergeants handed out the barrack listings to the squad commanders. Our squad was housed in one of the prefab buildings. With ten double bunks on each side of the long building, we were housed with Bravo Squad. I quickly grabbed a bunk a few feet from the door to the right.

Dropping my pack and rifle to my bunk, I sat down and removed my uniform shirt, feeling relieved in my olive drab t-shirt. Jay grabbed the bunk on my left with Ramos taking the one to my right. I began unpacking my things and quickly filled up the footlocker at the foot of my bunk. Packing away my spare clothing and personal effects, I slid the large travel pack under my bunk alongside my field pack. Once everything was secured, I then moved with Jay to the base armory.

The armory, held in another prefab building with reinforced walls and several MP patrols, was located a few yards away. We checked in with the MP guard unit and moved inside, stepping into a long line of soldiers. Per standard orders, we had to check in our weapons. I gave in all my rifle, any explosives, and all rifle ammo, receiving a small ticket stub with a letter and number on it. From then on, whenever I needed my weapons, I would first need to check them out. I was only permitted to carry my Colt.45 and combat knife. Jay reluctantly gave up his sniper rifle and we returned to the barracks.

Captain Hiller was waiting for us and soon gave everyone the full rundown of new rules. Filling in for the missed information the Major forgot, Captain Hiller stressed how much security matter the most. At no point were we to say what division we're with, nor that we fought in Africa or Sicily. We were only allowed to go off base with passes and were restricted to base all other times, despite the Major's claims.

He stressed even more the penalties for breaking security protocols, informing us that demotion and prison time would be handed down for any type of breach.

"Any questions?" Captain Hiller asked after his little speech.

"Ah, what do we do now, sir?" Phelps asked.

"Day's nearly shot, so tour the base and get some rest. Tomorrow, we start training nice and early," said Captain Hiller.

I took a self-tour of the base which took up an hour. I went over every inch of the compound, trying to memorize the location of every building and tent. Walking the base four times, I soon had the layout memorized from the CP mansion, down to the location of each oil barrel. Occupying once what was a large estate, the base was evenly spread out across a couple dozen acres. The majority of the base was clustered around the mansion and the surrounding fields, stopping at the road to the west and the tree line to the north, south, and east. A large shooting range was set up on the northern part of the base with an obstacle course running through the eastern woods.

It was nearly five in the morning when Captain Hiller rousted us from the first real sleep we got since before landing in Sicily. Quickly, everyone dressed in full battle rattle, loaded packs and leg bags, full gear webbing, heavy all weather jackets and pants, water sealed boots, and helmet. Once dressed, we retrieved our weapons and ammo from the armory. Taking five minutes, everyone was assembled in neat, five rows of ten in front of the barracks.

"Good morning," Captain Hiller greeted, seeming to not feel the chill in the air. "Today we start a long, near endless routine of training. We will rise before the sun and go for a little predawn jog to loosen us up from the daily routines. To keep us on our toes, we'll eat when we get back. Now, keep together and let's go!"

Captain Hiller along with the junior squad commanders led the large group of soldiers through the center of the base and out of the main gate. Turning off to the paved road, we began jogging alongside the base, following the road. The sky was still gray from the previous day, only a little light appearing from the slowly rising sun. The road and rolling grass fields were covered in a fine layer of dew and water left from the rain, making footing easy to lose if not focused.

I jogged next to Jay in the center of the group, keeping a steady breathing rate. I personally enjoyed jogging, having a daily routine to go running before and after school to relax and unwind. Now, the enjoyment was slowly depleting with the heavy equipment weighing me down. I worked harder to keep a steady rhythm of breathing, feeling the to urge to breathe harder as my lungs began to burn when we pasted the mile and half mark. We kept to the road for the majority of the run, using the nearby farms as distance markers. Once we passed three miles, Hiller led us off the pave road to a muddied side path that cut through a large section of woodland.

"I hope we get to do combat training through here," Jay grunted, holding his rifle a few inches from his chest. "This place is perfect for sniping and hunting."

"People?" I asked, voice a bit hoarse.

"What else is there?" Jay joked, grinning as we moved.

We continued along the muddied road, boots dredging though the soup that was the ground. Despite being 'water resistant' boots, I could feel mud soaking through and it add weight with every step. Several men stumbled ahead of us, nearly falling face first into the soggy, wet earth. Captain Hiller, a man who's handled the conditions of trench warfare, easily compensated for the hard pull of the muddy muck, not slowing one bit. I struggled to continue, sweat starting to streak down my cheeks in the cool morning.

Ahead of us, we closed in on another farm, the road suddenly sinking down by its gate, the heavy rain from the day before filled the dip in the road with water, creating one large puddle. Captain Hiller did not even look down as he ran though the stagnant water. I didn't hesitate and pushed forward, slogging through the filth as it rose to my knees, soaking my pants and filling my boots. Jay cursed to himself, but didn't slow either.

"Keep moving!" Hiller yelled over his shoulder, urging on anyone slowing or hesitating. "Mud is fucking spring water compared to the shit you'll be slogging through!"

"What's he talking about?" Ramos mumbled from behind us.

"You'd be amazed what a mixture of blood, mud, oil, and shit can make!" Captain suddenly yelled, hearing Ramos.

The group moved on down the country road until we crossed another paved road, turning onto it and moving back towards Ellis. The sun was now rising in the sky, melting away the dull gray sky. Foot traffic on the roadway was picking up with people heading to Ellis or Portsmouth by foot or car. Many people passed us on bicycles, giving us strange looks. At one point, we passed a large group of children and several, walking to the small school in Ellis.

The young children looked on in awe at the large, burley American soldiers running by. Many pointed and chattered to one another as we passed, eyes moving to the rifles and submachine guns we carried. Several cowered by the adults, stunned by fear when they saw us. The weapons, bulky equipment, and mud stained uniforms terrified some, but fascinated others.

"Morning ma'am!" Hanes yelled to the woman leading the group.

"Morning Yanks!" the woman yelled back, smiling at the Sergeant and Captain Hiller. The other adults and the majority of the kids waved as we passed, some yelling words of encouragement.

"And to think we rebelled against them," I joked, nodding to the smiling Brits.

Jay laughed as we moved on, drawing closer to the edge of the town. A group of British soldiers were sitting on the grass near the road, they were resting from their morning run. Naturally, no one could let the moment go and we exchanged insults and stupid jokes between each other. The Brits yelled insults about American sports and threw in a few accusations of stealing their women. We yelled back with much vigor, calling them tea drinking Tommies that couldn't hold onto their women. Both groups were filled with laughter which drew a slight grin from the Captain.

"Okay, okay," he said, holding in a few chuckles, "let's play nice with the Tommies."

Captain Hiller led us around the edge of the town, sticking close to the muddied dirt roads over the paved ones. Soon, we rounded the town and were on the final stretch back to the base. My legs were sore and my lungs ached with every breath, but I kept going as the base entrance drew closer and closer. The MPs at the gate let us pass through, Captain Hiller brining us to a stop behind the barracks. Everyone broke up and looked for a spot to sit or lean and catch their breath.

"Whoa, whoa," Captain Hiller said, turning to us. "The day's just getting started. On your feet and let's get to the firing range, I need to see how bad your skills rusted since the last fight."

Hiller led us past the barracks to the northern edge of the base. The open fields were filled with a myriad of targets, ranging from paper cutouts tied to stacks of hay to old vehicles. We were divided up into groups based on our current armament; rifles, submachine guns, heavy weapons, and explosives. I was placed alongside the majority of the men who carried the M1 Garand Rifle, while Jay worked with a small group of snipers, and Vic was with the heavy weapons team.

"Let's keep this simple," Sergeant Hanes said, taking charge of my rifle group. "Out in the field are a variety of targets to hit, at ever extending distances. Now, each man will load two rounds into their rifles." He held up two fingers and pointed down the field. "At the fence are forty tin cans. Now, with your two rounds you need to knock off at least one, but two is preferred. Phelps, you're up first."

"Yeah, Sarge," Phelps said, moving up to the low wooden wall that acted as a firing line. He pulled two rounds from the eight round clip and loaded his rifle, bringing the butt up to his shoulder. Aiming, he fired once, the round slamming into the dirt behind the fence, which was one hundred yards away.

"That's one miss," Hanes muttered, shaking his head. Phelps sighed to himself and took a tighter grip on his rifle. A second shot rang out and one can suddenly shot off the fence.

"That's a hit," Phelps said with a bit of pride.

"Yeah, but you should have hit both," Hanes scolded. "If the cans were Germans, offing one, out of two, isn't that great when you only have two bullets. Bolger, you're up next."

Taking a breath, I moved up to the firing line as Phelps moved away. I loaded my rifle with only two bullets and leveled it, maneuvering the iron sights on the first can I saw. Taking in another breath and holding it, I wrapped my finger over the trigger, slowly squeezing as I adjusted for wind and bullet drop. The rifle cracked and jumped slightly as the round shot across the field in the blink of an eye. One of the cans suddenly shot into the air and fell back to the ground.

"Hit," Hanes stated, tone suggesting it was luck.

I leveled the rifle again, switching aim over to the next can on the wooden fence. The crosshairs fell on the center of the metal can and I squeezed the trigger for the second time, a second can flying off the fence.

"Two for two, good work," Hanes said in an approving tone.

I grinned slightly and slung my rifle over my shoulder, returning to the group of soldiers. The rest of the group stood up to the firing line one by one, each firing their two rounds. At the end, Sergeant Hanes was a bit flustered to say the least. Besides me, Ramos, Malks, Nate, Adam, and Sanders hit both cans. The rest of the men either hit one or nothing. Thankfully, the men that we went to Africa and Sicily with managed to hit at least one can. The new recruits, however, missed completely. Hanes gave them a nice chewing out for their 'piss poor marksmanship' as he called it.

"Baring another...display," Hanes muttered once everyone was done, "Form up on the firing line and let's see you hit the targets spread out along the range. Each of you empty one clip, eight rounds."

We stepped up to the wooden wall and loaded our rifles with a fresh clip. I stood shoulder to shoulder with Ramos and Nate, the three of us near the center of the line. One Hanes's order, everyone fired together, independently picking targets across the line. The training run was to see how well we could handle a weapon jam, should one occur, and to accompany the new recruits with the sound of heavy gun fire. Accuracy would come later.

"We ready? Aim and fire!" Ordered Hanes.

The line erupted in a volley of rifle fire as everyone fired together. I blocked out the loud cracks of the rifles around me and jumped my crosshairs from one paper cutout to the next. Quickly, I cycled through eight targets, firing all eight rounds with eight hits. Soon, rifles began to click empty as the men finished the practice. I lowered my rifle and looked across the line, seeing several men dealing with jammed rifles. Most of them quickly cleared the jams, but two or three had trouble. Sergeant Hanes moved up the line, checking each rifle to make sure they were emptied. For those who had jams, he threw out a few curses and cleared the weapons, forcefully throwing them back to their owners.

"Okay, this has taught me two things." Hanes bellowed. "One, my vets know what they're doing and two, you recruits can't shoot for shit. Vets from my squad, report to the Captain for cross training. The rest of you will keep drilling with me."

Ramos looked to Phelps and me, but we shrugged. Following orders, we took our equipment and walked down the line to where the Captain was. He stood at the edge of the next field, a table of Thompson submachine guns spread out in front of him.

"Listen up," he ordered, as we assembled. "The veteran troopers will be cross trained in the use of multiple light and heavy weapons while the new recruits handle the basic stuff first. Now, I need to see how well each of you handles the Thompson. Pick one up, load, and step up to the firing line."

For the remainder of the day, we continued down the line, testing our skills with the variety of weapons the armory supplied. At first, we fired each weapon as a test to see where we showed a degree of skill, mainly to tell what we would specialize in. I used an M1 Garand, Thompson SMG, bazooka, BAR, 30.cal light MG, and Springfield Sniper rifle. The Captain determined I could easily handle each weapon, but my area of training would be built around the Garand, Thompson, and BAR. I handled the three with the most ease and best accuracy and was to train the most with the three weapons.

From that day, our routine was set. Each day, the squad went on our runs every morning, then moving to the firing range, then the obstacle course, and lastly, to the prefab classrooms where we were taught map reading skills, navigation skills, procedures on field cleaning our weapons and equipment, combat first aide, and such. If we made it through the days without screw ups, the Captain would hand out weekend passes. After the first full week of nonstop training, I went down to Ellis with the guys.

Ramos, Nate, Adam, Jay, Vic, and myself went into town for the first time after training on Saturday, heading for the closest pub. *The Den* was the only pub in the tiny town of Ellis and was packed with soldiers when we arrived. Nearly half the base was jammed into the pub, all enjoying their first weekend passes. Jay and I elbowed our way to the bar while Ramos and the others fought for a table.

"Busy night, eh?" I said to the bartender as he quickly moved, filling glass after glass.

"You Yanks love to drink," the bartender huffed. "And I sure do love your money."

"Don't we all," Jay said, pulling out his wallet. " Round of drinks for me and my friends, six in all." He scanned the bar and found Ramos sitting at our table. "Table in back."

"Ah, with the tall soldier, short black hair?" The bartender asked.

"Yep," Jay answered, handing the man fifty dollars, more than enough to pay for the drinks.

"I think I'll like you Yanks," the bartender said with a grin, pocketing the money.

"They'll be by in a minute."

"Thanks, my good man," I said, pulling away with Jay.

The two of us maneuvered through the sea of olive drab soldiers, struggling to reach our table. With some rather hard pushes and some elbowing, we stumbled back to the table and grabbed a seat just as Ramos was starting to tell one of his world renowned stories.

"So, back before I shipped out for training," he started out, setting his hands out in front of him. " I was enjoying the company of one fine woman when she turned to me and said…"

Phelps jumped in ahead of Ramos. "'Ramos, dear, I'm a man."

Everyone burst out laughing except Ramos, who sat defiantly with his arms crossed. Nate started shaking his hands and mouthed his own comment.

"No, wait," he said, trying to control his laughter, "she said your hour was up and the next was gonna cost more money."

"Wait, I got it," Jay announced, "She said she felt sorry for you and was giving you a refund for your time!"

"Fuck all of you," Ramos mumbled, rolling his eyes.

I reached over and patted his shoulder. "Easy, Ramos," I assured, "No need to be mad at the truth." My grin broke through as he started cursing in Spanish, insulting each of us.

"Anyway, let's hear something that's not a bunch of bullshit," Adam suggested, rubbing the thick bandage wrapped around his left arm.

"Okay," Nate said once the laughter died down. "You meet any… nice nurses while in the hospital?"

Adam thought back and a grin broke across his face. "Well, when I arrived here, I was in this hospital up in London. I swear there is no way they sell shirts big enough to…cover her completely. I mean, you talk about being out of uniform, but…"

"London you say?" Ramos said, suddenly excited.

"She's seeing a pilot in the 95th Bomber Wing," Adam explained. "She told me and every other guy in the recovery ward so."

"So unlucky," I joked as a waitress brought over a set of drinks. She set down the tray and handed each of us a pint of warm, British beer. Before she left, I placed a generous tip on the tray and provided a polite smile and head nod.

"Finally," she said as she walked away, "a Yank with manners, not used to seeing that around ere."

"Bastard's a charmer," Phelps laughed, watching the waitress walk away.

I rolled my eyes, grabbing the large class of warm British beer. Eyeing the cream colored liquid, I brought the edge of the glass to my mouth and took a large gulp. The second the liquid touched my tongue, I cringed and fought the urge to spit it out. The stuff was sour and bitter to taste, the fact it was warm was not helping. Forcing down the alcohol, I placed the mug back on the table.

"Nasty," I mumbled, now getting the after taste.

"I'll take that," Vic grunted, reaching out and snatching the mug for himself.

"That is some horrible shit," Ramos agreed, handing off his drink to Jay. "I'm gonna see if they got tequila." Ramos stood up and walked towards to bar while everyone at the table started to laugh and threw some insults at him and me.

"Choke on it fuckers," I snorted, leaning back in my chair. "Show up to drill tomorrow hung over and see what the Cap does to you."

"I'd pay to see you hung over in front of Hiller," Jay said, passing him Ramos's untouched beer. "Drink up."

The two broke out into a halfhearted argument between each other while I sat back and I watched, laughing to myself when Nate and Adam were suddenly dragged in. I kept quiet and simply watched the four fire insult after insult at one another until all the alcohol on the table was gone. Vic was plastered while the other three were a bit hammered. Things intensified as the night dragged on, coming to a point when a group of pilots somehow became involved.

When the five of us were in a heated cursing match with ten pilots, I slowly backed away as a blind person could see the ensuing fight. One of the pilots got into Vic's face and insulted him as an Italian, which sent Vic into a psychotic rage. One second, the pilot's screaming at Vic and the next he's on the floor, blood flowing from a newly broken nose. The pilot's friends suddenly jump in and Vic takes a blow to the jaw, reeling back slightly.

Nate rushed in and smashed his half-filled mug into anther pilot's head, shattering the glass and drenching them man in alcohol. Two more pilots rush Nate, as Adam and Jay jumped in, grappling with the two. Cursing under my breathe, I rushed into the fray and worked to pry my friends away as the bar irrupted into a fighting ring. The MPs had to be on the way and I didn't want to spend my first day in England in prison.

"Jay, we need to get the fuck out of here!" I yelled, pulling a pilot off his back.

"Ah, right," he stammered, blood trickling down from the side of his mouth. "Get Nate and Adam, I'll grab Vic and Ramos."

"Just get them and meet me near the road leading to the camp," I yelled.

"Yeah, good luck!" He said.

Jay ran off into the mob of drunken soldiers as I moved to grab Nate, who was fending off another soldier. I leapt in between the two and pushed Nate back, swinging my left arm back with my elbow out. The hard blow broke the man's nose and sent him tumbling to the floor.

"Come on!" Nate protested, "I had him!"

"Sure, but the MPs are gonna hand you your ass."

The mention of MPs grabbed Nate's focus. "MPs? Shit, where the fuck are they?" He worried.

"Almost here, now let's go!" I grabbed Nate by the arm and pulled him to the door. Along the way, I scooped up a semi-conscious Adam from the floor and made it outside without trouble.

Hearing the screech of tires around the corner, I tossed Adam over my shoulders and ran in the opposite direction with Nate. We ran down the street and ducked into a side alley, letting Adam drop to the ground. Breathing heavily, the three of us sat in the darkness as the shouts and yells of the MPs echoed down from the bar. After waiting several minutes, we figured we weren't spotted.

"That was fun," Nate grunted, backhanding sweat from his forehead.

"Amazing," I huffed, taking a second more to collect myself. "Come on, we need to see if the others got out. Adam, you awake?"

"Barely," he hiccupped, rolling his head from side to side. "What happened?"

Rolling my eyes, I reached down and helped the drunk to his feet. "You just went ten rounds with Patton," I said sarcastically.

"Really?" Adam moaned, barely standing on his own. "Who won?"

"You did, soldier boy," Nate answered, helping me carry Adam onto the street.

"I did? Shit, I should get a….what do you call it? You know, when they give you those shiny metal things," Adam fumbled.

"Medals, Adam?" I sighed, shouldering half of his weight as we dragged him down the barren street to meeting spot.

"Yeah," the drunk blurted out, suddenly amazed. "And…and a promotion too."

"Sure, Adam," Nate responded, speaking in a tired tone. "Just tell the Captain all about it."

"You g…guys might need to tell 'em, though. I don't remember shit…" Adam mumbled.

Nate sighed as we rounded the corner and spotted the base down the road. "What are we gonna say when we get back?" he asked. "It's gonna be hard to explain all this."

"We'll burn that bridge when we get to it," I grunted, seeing Jay standing by the side of the road with Vic and Ramos. "I see you made it."

Jay shrugged. "We ran through the back, as the MPs burst in. They nearly got us, but we snuck through a back alley before they got a good look at us."

"I could've taken them," Vic grunted, holding a bloodied rag to his nose.

"Would that be before or after that flyboy fucked up your nose?" Ramos asked in a mocking tone.

"Ah, fuck you…"Vic snarled.

"Enough," I said firmly. "You've got a broken nose and Adam's plastered. That and the fact we just started a bar brawl are gonna be hard to explain to the Captain."

"Wonder what he'll do to us?" Jay thought aloud.

"Who knows, but I think we should tell 'em flat out and take our shit now then have the Captain find out on his own."

"Corr's right," Nate agreed. "We tell that Cap and we won't end up in prison."

Everyone silently agreed and we began to slowly walk back to the base. Vic's nose stopped bleeding and he cursed under his breath as he tried cleaning the blood from his uniform. Adam was struggling to stay up and leaned on Nate for support while Ramos cursed his luck.

Jay and I walked silently, dreading the moment we would have to tell the Captain.

"Ten bucks says he goes ballistic on us," Jay wagered as we approached the gate.

"Twenty says I lose a stripe," I countered, picturing the loss of being a corporal and becoming a private again.

Captain Hiller was returning from the latrine, to his barracks, when we stumbled back to ours. Seeing Vic's blood encrusted uniform and Adam's drunken stumble, he began to laugh to himself, shaking his head slightly. He walked up to me and crossed his arms over his chest.

"Had a fun night I see," he said calmly.

"Amazing, sir!" Adam yelled, receiving a slap to the back of the head from Ramos.

"We…ah…got into some trouble," I stammered, not really sure what to say.

"One man is drunk, out of his skull, another has a broken nose, and I bet there is a bar in shambles somewhere out there," Hiller sighed and shook his head. "But you managed to get everyone home un-arrested."

"Ah, yes, sir," I said.

"I allow one minor fuck up with the squad, remember I told you guys this in training." I nodded and listen to him talk. "This doesn't even rate minor screw up, let alone fuck up. Now, I have a selective memory thing, so this will be let go for now. Granted, our new routine will stay in effect tomorrow, so sober up fast because," he looked to his watch, "you got six hours till morning run. Good night men."

Early morning drill arrived quicker than usual; Sergeant Hanes rousting all of us from a sound sleep induced by far too much alcohol.

"Wake up, kiddies!" Hanes yelled as he barreled through the barrack door. "Get up and get dressed in PT gear!"

"Ugh," Ramos grunted from his bunk, fighting to open his eyes.

"Come on, we're burning moonlight!" Hanes yelled as he walked down the barracks, clapping his hands loudly.

I rolled out of my bunk blinking my eyes several times to make the change over from sleep to awake. My head buzzed with a slight headache and my muscles were soar from the work out the day before, the sudden exertion coming back and biting me in the ass. Rubbing my aching legs, I pulled a pair of black running shorts and a white t-shirt from my footlocker and quickly dressed.

"Did I eat a tennis ball last night?" Ramos asked, rubbing his jaw.

"That would be the tequila," I said, grinning at the fact I abstained from drinking any of it.

"Really, because I swear I got the skin of tennis ball on my tongue." I only shook my head as he fumbled trying to put on his t-shirt. Vic was having similar difficulties with trying to don his shorts and keep out the noise of the others moving about. Hanes knew about the drinking last night and used the squad hangover for full effect.

"Come on, let's go, let's go!" he bellowed, clapping his hands even louder and louder. "You people act like you got a hangover!"

"Do you think he enjoys being a bastard?" Jay asked in a hush tone, moving with me to the door.

"Oh, I very much do!" Hanes yelled, smiling at Jay.

"Oh, fuck," Jay mumbled, looking back at the Sergeant.

Outside, it was still dark, the sun only showing a small trickle of light beyond the eastern hills and tree line. The portable lights set up around the base burned brightly, illuminating the flow of soldiers rising for their early morning training. Captain Hanes stood in front of the barracks, looking us over as we fell in for the morning run.

"I see the first night in England has treated you well," Hiller commented, observing several men were clearly hung over. "I'm sure a nice, long run will just burn that…pub sickness right out of you. Let's go!"

"Ah, this is gonna suck," Ramos moaned, struggling to get a rhythm with his jogging.

"You see why I never drink," I joked, smiling arrogantly at him.

Ramos gave me a dirty looked and began to curse under his breath as we moved out of the base and down the road. I kept up quite easily with the Captain, the burn in my legs slowly ebbed with each step and I felt my headache throb to an end. The cool morning air was a very good stress relief, each deep breath bringing me more energy and focus. The smell of the morning air soon brought me back to the time of my childhood. For so many summers, I spent time with my brothers on my grandfather's farm, listing to his old war stories and playing tricks, on our little brother, Frank. When our grandfather died before the war started, I inherited his farm, but I left it to my father when I enlisted.

"Why the hell are you so damn happy?" Vic grunted from behind me.

I realized I was smiling. "Oh, you'll see," I said, switching over from the memories to my father's advice about drinking.

"See wh…" Vic was cut off when he snapped his mouth shut. A sheet of sweat suddenly appeared on his forehead and his cheeks puffed out, turning a bright red. Adam was running next to him and turned in time to see Vic suddenly and violently vomit, covering his shorts and shirt with putrid smelling vomit.

"That's why," I pointed out, turning back and focusing on my running.

"Trouble back there?" Hiller called from the front of the group as we turned onto the dirt road.

"Just peachy, Cap!" I yelled back, resisting the urge to laugh.

"Then we can speed up a bit. Sprint for thirty. Troopers, count it off!"

Everyone lashed out at full speed, pounding down the hard packed road. We cried out the numbers from one to thirty in order, voices echoing across the empty countryside. A slight burning in my lungs picked up as I sprinted down the road, my voice still loud and clear as I counted up to thirty.

When we reached thirty, we were back on the paved roadway and breathing heavily. Hiller dropped back into a jog and kept everyone moving forward. I worked to control my breathing and take deep, easy breaths to prevent over exertion and giving way to heat exhaustion, as the sun began to rise, the temperature along with it. Sweat began to soak my shirt and raced down my forehead and cheeks. Thankfully, we quickly made it back to the base in a few minutes.

"Okay, take a minute to catch your breath," Hiller said, backhanding some sweat from his forehead. "Good? Okay, now spread out because we're going to do some conditioning. First, you do two pushups and then one sit up. Next, you do four pushups and two sit ups, working your way up to twenty pushups and ten sit ups. Once you reach that, you work your way back down till zero."

Without complaining, I dropped down to the ground and started the pushups, doing two in quick successions. I switched to the sit up and worked on, keeping count in my head. From two one to twenty to ten and back down, I fought through the burn of my muscles and completed the routine, sitting on the ground and breathing heavily.

"You're quick," Hiller said, giving me a head nod.

"Thank…you…sir," I panted, working hard to regain control of my breathing.

"Come on, all of you. It's time to hit the books."

Ramos tapped my shoulder. "Books?" he asked.

"Yes, books, Ramos. You see, a soldier needs a sharp mind and a strong body to get to Berlin," Hiller remarked.

Hiller took us to a set of buildings near the entrance of the base. These buildings were used as classrooms for us, where we were taught any skills that couldn't be taught in the field. From then on, we learned what it took to be soldier besides how to handle a weapon. The classes taught us the best way to read maps, draw maps from memory, use the stars for direction, tell the difference between German uniforms of the regular army, the paratroopers, and that of the SS. We were also offered language classes in French, German, and Russian. I took German and French, studying the languages with great interest.

From the classroom, we kept up with the hard work of physical training. We ran the base obstacle course, trained in close quarter combat with everything from knives to our bodies, and spent countless hours honing the skills with our weapons. Now and again, we would meet with other companies from the division and have mock combat drills across the English countryside, learning how to properly fight across heavily wooded and civilian areas. Now and again Captain

Hiller would train us alongside the Army Air Corps, teaching us how to call in fire support.

The training was tough and grueling, some days I felt close to passing out from exhaustion. Just like the men in the squad, I soldiered on and fought the pain and exhaustion. Soon, winter passed us by and spring arrived and our training turned to amphibious operation training. We were kept in the dark about just what we were training for, but rumors were that the Allies were going to invade France, open up a second front and divide the attention of the Germans.

Our training was mostly spread out across the English countryside and involved, working with the other squads in the companies while learning to better fight alongside armor support. Now and again we'd work with the Air Force and on coordinating air strikes, though it was all with smoke shells and paint bombs that a few division engineers created. All in all they were war games, though we did scare the shit out of some of the locals.

As April drew to a close and May began, security tightened. Our training intensified even more, with more and more focus on assaulting on beaches and grabbing vital targets inland, with a limited window of time. I was enjoying the training, taking pride in myself as I mastered French and German while I learned better ways to fight with a wide variety of weapons and explosives. I could kill a man with my bare hands in at least a dozen ways and was adept in the ways of fighting with my combat knife. The confidence soon turned to eagerness and I began to want go and fight. The feelings stopped when I was called to the Major's office in the middle of May.

"Corporal Bolger," Major Philips said, sitting from behind his massive oak desk. "Please, have a seat."

"Yes sir," I said, grabbing one of the two seats, in front of the desk.

Major Philips folded his hands on the desk, resting them on an envelope. "Corporal, I have some news for you and I'm not sure how to give it to you."

I tilted my head sideways. "Sir?"

The Major sighed. "Well, you're being promoted to first sergeant to fill the gap since Lieutenant Hanes was promoted. Under the recommendation of Captain Hiller, you are now the squad sergeant."

"Thank you, sir," I said, resisting the urge to smile. Instead, I thanked him and took the pair of sergeant stripes off his desk.

"Now, you do have two brothers, correct?" He asked.

The question caught me off guard. "Ah, yes sir."

He sighed again, this time more heavily. "You're younger brother, Frank Bolger, is a Marine serving in the Pacific with the 28th Infantry Division?"

Oh, god, no. "Sir, what's this about?" I panicked.

He handed me the folded letter, which was from Frank addressed to me. "I'm sorry to tell you this son, but your brother is dead. He was reported KIA by the Marines four days ago. This letter was found, in his pocket, with a note asking it be delivered to you upon his death. I thought I should tell you instead of letting you find out after your daily training. I'm sorry, son."

The news hit me like a gunshot. At first, I could not, or would not believe what the Major told me. I didn't know what to think as I looked down at the letter and opened it, reading the contents without hesitating.

> *Dear Corr,*
>
> *Hey, I guess you might already know what happened by the time you read this, though with the military you might get this a few years after the fact. In any case, I'm gone, killed out in the Pacific somewhere on some island. I know this is gonna hit you and Matt hard, but I'm worried about mom and dad more than anything else. I'm sorry I never got see you guys again after I shipped out, but I love you, bro. I love you, Matt, mom, and dad so much. In this letter should be the silver Celtic cross and cover necklace granddad gave me. You remember his stories about the thing coming over from Ireland, staying with him, then dad, and me. Well,*

I want you to have it as something to remember me by.
I'm gonna miss you, Corr.

Love,
Your baby brother, Frank

The shock was now hitting me as I removed the necklace from the letter. The silver cross and clover rested in my hand as I looked down on it. The cross was bent and scratched with bits of sand and dried blood still clinging to it. Without thinking, I slipped the necklace over my head and let it lay on the outside of my uniform.

"Now, Sergeant, you've already been though the mission briefings of your objectives and you've been told where the landings will be. Now, you are capable with your skills to go through, but I can understand if you feel you should…"Said the Major.

"No," I said, cutting him off. "Frank would want me to continue on."

"In that case, we're moving your squad down to the docks at Portsmouth, where you'll be confined to the military camps for the time being. It's no longer a secret that the invasion is looming, but this is your last chance. Do you want to continue?" The Major asked.

I didn't hesitate as I fought back the tears. "Yes, I want to rejoin my squad." I said.

"You are dismissed, Sergeant," the Major said, placing his hand on my shoulder.

The next few days were unbearable for me. The entire company was confined to the large tent base at the Portsmouth docks. Security tightened even more, all trips into town were off, letters going out were stopped, and we were cut off from the rest of the world. The only thing we could do as the weather turned to rain was go through our equipment and review the area maps of Omaha Beach, our landing area on the Normandy Coast.

I spent my time in the map building, which contained a scale model of the entire beach area, all made from recon photos. The building housing the maps and displays was massive and under tight security. I stayed there for hours on end, reviewing the maps, but more enjoying the solitude at the far corner of the room. I kept to myself and worked to sort out my thoughts and emotions on my own. Ramos, Jay and the others tried to help, but I turned them away and preferred to work alone.

As May turned to early June, I managed to keep things under control and pushed the issue, of Frank, to the back of my mind. I would face things later when I had the chance, not when I was about to participate in the largest invasion of the entire war. I kept my thoughts and emotion controlled and to myself, finding I needed to keep a control even more that I was the squad sergeant. There would be a time to grieve for Frank, but I had to be a soldier first.

"Hey, Sarge," Jay greeted, stepping up behind me.

"Jay," I responded, eyes down on the amazingly detailed display. "They did good work."

"Yeah, they really built this thing to scale," Jay commented, looking across the display and eyeing the bunkers on the bluff. "It looks well defended."

"The Navy's gonna pound the shit out the bunkers alongside the flyboys before we land. With any luck, some bunkers should be knocked out."

Jay nodded and crossed his arms over his chest. "We've trained so hard for the past months; I think we can do it."

"We can do it, Jay. Hiller and Hanes know what to do and haven't failed us yet," I stated, shifting my gaze over to a group of soldiers at the other end of the display.

"You won't fail us either, Corr," Jay reassured, looking over at me.

I looked to him and shook my head. "Don't try to comfort me, Jay. I know you mean well, but I'll handle all this later on, after the squad is out of harm's way."

"Corr, it's not smart to bottle everything up, it'll come back to bite you in the ass one day," he said.

I laughed with no humor to be found. "Did you get a degree in psychology when I wasn't looking?" I asked.

Jay grinned and placed a hand on my shoulder. "Got in a box of Cracker Jacks, but it's all legal."

I couldn't help but smile and nodded. "Look, I'll talk once we take Omaha from the Germans. Is that good enough for you?"

Jay sighed and shrugged. "I guess that's the best I'm gonna get from you, so I'll take it…for now."

"Thanks, Jay," I said.

"Any time, bro." The large metal door to the warehouse squeaked open on rusty hinges and a Captain walked in, clearing his throat to grab everyone's attention.

"This is it," he bellowed, "you are to report back to your squads and move to your selected troop ships. Get on the move, the shit's started."

Jay looked to me and I nodded, moving for the open door. The two of us passed the MPs standing outside and returned to our tents. It was raining in sheets as we walked, the rain unrelenting for the past several days. The camp was crowded and packed with dozens of rifle squads and companies, the constant foot and vehicle traffic carving up the muddied ground. Jay and I had to work hard to not have our boots pulled off by the mud as we walked, struggling to move quickly to our tent.

When we reached the tent, the squad was already collecting their equipment and weapons, Captain Hiller was geared up. I moved to my bunk and began to dress in my equipment. First came the heavy tactical vest that was stitched with dozens of multi sized pockets. Each pocket was filled to the brim with needed equipment as well as a full pack and ammunition belt. Spare ammo clips, fragmentation grenades, smoke grenades, entrenching tool, combat and utility knifes, rope, gasmask, two medical kits, a few bricks of C4 explosive, spare uniforms, a shaving kit, packs of C rations, combat light, Lucky Strike matches, and such were all packed away in dozens of pockets and on my back. Next was the life belt that went around my waist to help should I fall overboard, then my new belt holster for my Colt.45, followed by my newly issued Thompson SMG, and then my steel helmet. Altogether, I had roughly my body weight in equipment and gear.

Everyone else was loaded down similarly with Malks carrying extra explosives as our engineer, Vic carried his heavy BAR, Jay with his sniper rifle, and Adam with his field radio. We all trained day in and day out on how to move quickly under the heavy weight, both on land and water. It was difficult to slog through the water with all the heavy kit, but we would do it.

"Let's move it!" Hiller ordered, ushering us out into the rain. "Follow me aboard the HMS Charles and stick together."

I moved at the rear of the group and kept everyone form losing one another in the massive crowds of soldiers all moving to the dozens of troop ships docked in port. Hiller led us through crowds to one of the dozen troopships, all waiting at port and towering over us. Rain pelted us mercilessly as we marched up the narrow gangway, the wind forcing the wooden bridge to sway above the gray, churning seas.

Once onboard, the squad moved to the port side of the ship, we were told to find shelter under a set of tarps stretched over a few stacks of supply crates. I huddled under the edge of the tarp and was given a momentary relief from the rain, as did dozens of other soldiers. I was cold, soaking wet, on the verge of getting the flu or worse, and suddenly exhausted from the weight of my equipment, but I showed no wavering or weakness.

"Do you think they'll let us go below decks?" Ramos asked over the howling winds and chatter of hundreds of soldiers.

"What's the matter, Ramos?" mocked Vic, shoulder his BAR. "The rain bothering you?"

"No, just your face, Vic." A few of the guys chuckled.

"You should go for a swim," Vic snorted, sniffling from the cold.

"Easy," I ordered, not putting too much force, "save it for the Germans."

The two exchanged dirty looks before turning away. I ignored the two and looked over the deck of the ship which was becoming more and more packed with soldiers. Each of us wore the bright red patch of the First Infantry Division, the need to keep us hidden gone with the invasion close at hand. Everyone shared the same expression on their face; a mix of fear, determination, and uncertainty. I sighed to myself. I'm twenty and about to use what instinct has repeatedly told me not to; run towards the shooting and not away.

"Listen up!" Hiller ordered, suddenly reappearing from below deck. "The Brits over counted and it's too late to go back, so we bunk down on the deck."

Several men grunted in annoyance, but accepted the order without outright complaining, they were better than that. Jay turned to me and tapped my shoulder.

"So, how long do we stay on the ship?" he asked, nose red and skin pale from the cold.

I shrugged. "Till we reach France." It was June 3rd, 1944.

For the next two days we huddled above deck under the tarp awning, fighting to keep warm. The rain had not relented one bit and the fleet remained at anchor. The Brass had called off the invasion twice already and we were rounding day three, June 5th, 1944 when the order came through.

The skies were still overcast with a mix of dark gray and black clouds, though the rain and wind subsided to light drizzle. The port erupted into a hornet's nest of furry, every single ship moving to leave port and form up into the invasion fleet. Our troop ship began to plow through the shallow water of the dock and soon entered the Channel, following a large group of other troop ships to the fleet rally point.

Ponderous battleships, destroyers, frigates, cruisers, tugs, mine sweepers, and support ships of all types filled the ocean in all directions as the fleet came together. For as far as the eye could see, the massive fleet stretched out in the churning waters of the English Channel, each ship moving into proper position. Overhead, American and British bombers and fighters of all types filled the overcast skies, the drone of their engines producing a thunderous roar. They were the advance elements, to bomb and strafe the beaches with everything they had to soften up the Germans. Behind them were the C-47 transport planes, carrying the brave men of the 101st and 82nd Airborne Divisions.

The massive fleet churned on through the choppy seas of the Channel, tossing and turning under the waves. Many men were sea sick, throwing up constantly over the railing of the ship. I managed to keep my breakfast of C Rations down, the Spam churning in my gut nonetheless. Waves crashed over the sides of the ship, soaking anything that wasn't already drowned by the rain. The burden, a body's weight worth of equipment, was increased by a good twenty pounds of soaking wet clothing. I was so drained of energy; I wondered if I would be able to make it ashore.

Thankfully, I managed to grab a few hours of sleep as night fell, though one could not sleep for long. The parade of aircraft over head never relented; planes raced towards France in one direction while others raced back to England in the other. The bombing raids would continue hour after hour up until ten minutes before we were to land. The fleet, on the other hand, would pound the beach ruthlessly, in the early morning hours before the landing.

My last bits of sleep ended, as the massive guns of the fleet opened up on the beaches, a little before sunrise. The immense capital turrets of the battleships started off the hellish thunder, sending salvo after salvo of steel overhead and crashing down on the beach. Smoke and flame rose into the sky off in the distance as we were herded to the port side of the ship, moving in a long line to get into our Higgins Boats.

The process to enter the tiny boats was rather simple, yet deadly. You needed to climb down the rain slick cargo netting over the side of the ship and get into the Higgins Boat. All occurred as the ship and the Higgins Boat bobbed and pitched widely in the water and you descend the ropes with so much weight on your back. One wrong move and you fell to the unforgiving sea, your gear pulling you under and keeping you under.

I watched as Higgins Boats began to fill with men one after the other. By the time it was my turn, no one had fallen in yet. I took a deep breath and slung my Thompson over my shoulder and onto my back, grabbing the rail with both hands and throwing my legs over the side. The ship bounced widely as I grabbed the rain slick cargo netting and began my slow and careful descent. My back, arms, and legs ached from the weight and stress as I climbed down, my hands losing all feeling from the ice cold water. I began to come close to the Higgins Boat when the sea tossed the tiny boat into the side of the troop ship. My left hand slipped and I fell back, my right hand coming free as well.

I fell backwards and moved away from the netting. My mind began to race as I fell, the thought of drowning filling my mind. Time seemed to slow as I fell and tried to reach out, but to no avail. *I'm gonna drown before I reach the damn beach!*

Suddenly, I felt a sharp pain in my back as I came to a sudden stop, landing in the Higgins Boat. It took a few second for my brain to catch up, but I realized how damn lucky I was, hitting the boat and not bouncing into the sea. Captain Hiller held out a hand and pulled me to my feet.

"That was a close one," he said, grinning at me.

"Way too close," I sighed in relief, stunned.

"Hey, focus, Corr," Hiller said, shaking my shoulder. "Day's just starting."

I nodded and moved towards the front of the boat, just near the forward ramp. Ramos was standing by and looking in awe, as the fleet pounded the shore. It seemed every ship was firing on the beach and none of us believed any Germans would escape the hellish torrent of steel.

"Shit," Ramos cursed under his breath, "The Navy's gonna kill all of them before we can."

"So?" Nate asked once he entered the boat. "It'll be easier to march ashore and liberate some of that fancy French wine."

Adam stood silent behind Nate, drumming his fingers against his rifle. I un slung my Thompson and turned to him.

"Nervous?" I asked.

"Panicked," he answered in a shaking tone.

"Just stay close," I reassured, "You'll be fine."

The boat suddenly lurched forward as the last of the squad entered. Captain Hiller did a quick head count and moved to the forward ramp, leaning against it. The boat pulled into formation with the rest of the boats readying to rush forward and drop the first wave of soldiers onto the beach. The bombardment was tapering off as we sat and waited for the go ahead. Nearly an hour after entering the boat, the fleet silenced their guns and a whistle blew over the wind. The Higgins lurched forward again and we raced straight into hell.

Part III
Into the Breach

"Why do soldiers die in war? Civilians say it's for the ambitions of government, the government says it's for what's right or just, but it's all bullshit. As a soldier, you fight for the man lying in the dirt next to you."
–Sergeant Corrigan Bolger, US Army

Chapter 8
Normandy, France
Omaha Beach
June 6th, 1944

The first few minutes on our trek to the beach were an eerie quiet. Nervous glances were exchanged as we faced no opposition from the defenders, but they were alive and well. Out of nowhere, machine gun fire erupted from the bunkers on the beach, cutting into the approaching Higgins Boats. Mortar fire screeched overhead and slammed into the sea, sending up huge sprays of water. Bullets showered down into the water and bounced off the ramp of our boat. Several Higgins Boats were tossed into the air by mortar and arty hits, throwing the men inside around like rag dolls.

The Higgins Boat next to us took a direct hit from one of the shore batteries and was ripped from the water, throwing the men inside into the air. Helpless, we watched the men fall back to earth, splashing down in the water as several slammed into our boat, bouncing off the sides. We could do nothing as the survivors were pulled under the water by their equipment, other then watch and pray it wouldn't happen to us.

"Keep your heads down!" Captain Hiller screamed as MG fire barely passed over our heads.

"Sixty seconds!" the Higgins driver yelled, as we approached the landing area.

"Get to the sea wall no matter what!" Hiller ordered. "Keep your heads down and move from cover to cover all the way to the wall. Look for me, Hanes, or Bolger!"

My stomach lurched as the Higgins Boat jumped to one side, at a near miss of mortar shell. Nate couldn't hold back and threw up all over the bottom of the boat, splashing the contents of his stomach over our boots. I turned away and gripped my Thompson even tighter, bringing the weapon up to my chest.

"Thirty seconds!" The driver counted down.

"Run, just keep running when the ramp drops. Run to the wall and don't stop." Hiller yelled.

"Ten seconds! Good luck and God be with you!" Said the driver.

The Higgins Boat suddenly slammed into something hard and came to a sudden stop. The boat driver hit the ramp release and the forward ramp suddenly dropped down, crashing into the water. Captain Hiller didn't even flinch, as he leapt across the ramp and splashed down into the water. I cursed under my breath and ran after him, vaulting over the ramp and landing into the freezing water.

My body screamed, as the water rushed up to my chest, before my boots touched sand. I held my Thompson just above the top of my chest and began to wade ashore, fighting hard against the rolling waves. Machine gun fire pelted the water all around us, ripping the other squads to shreds, as they dismounted from their transports. Several were blown to pieces, as the fearsome Flack 88 Anti-Tank guns on the ridge opened fire. The 88's targeted the transports depositing men on the beach, blowing dozens to hell left and right. MG fire suppressed those that made it ashore long enough for the 88s to zero in on them.

"Get to cover, get to cover!" I yelled as the water began to drop down to my knees.

I spotted a large crater left over from the bombardment near the edge of the water line and ran for it, throwing myself to my stomach once I past the lip of the crater. MG fire peppered the edges of the crater as Nate, Jay, and Vic jumped in alongside me. Jay crawled up to the lip of the crater and began targeting the gunners in the bunkers, but had to pull back when he was targeted by German snipers.

"C'mon!" I urged them, running out of the crater.

I moved up the beach towards a set of large Belgian Gates, which were very large tank traps. Captain Hiller was already lying prone at the base of the massive gate, a pair of binoculars in his hands. Adam was next to him, radio receiver in one hand and a map in the other. I ran across the distance of open beach and dove to their side, getting a mouth full of sand in the process.

"God damn it!" Hiller yelled, as he studied the ridge. "I can't get a clear view of the bunkers, the fucking smoke is too thick!"

"Why not walk the arty up the ridge?" Adam suggested.

"No, we might drop shells on our boys." Hiller turned and studied the five us. "Okay, we need to get to the sea wall, call in the arty, and blow a gap in the perimeter wire. Adam, stay on my ass the entire way and keep the radio ready. Bolger and Nate get up on the wall and set your C4 charges to blow a gap. Jay and Vic, cover them both."

Bullets stitched the top of the fence and sent us all even lower, in the wet sand. Hiller cursed aloud and ordered everyone to move. I picked myself up and scanned the beach for the next piece of cover, spotting a cluster of hedgehog tank traps. The metal clusters looked like giant jacks, but when bunched together; they provided cover from the unwavering MG fire.

I took another breath and rose to my feet, running at full speed across the dozen or so yards of open beach. MG fire plunged into the sand around me, impacting mere inches from my body. I kept running as fast as possible with my head down and body pressed into a low crouch. Men around me charged forward in the same manner, but many were dropped as MG rounds tore into their flesh, without mercy. Snipers picked off the others at random intervals, killing soldiers without warning.

I continued on and dropped at the base of the tank traps, slamming my back into the hard metal. Nate, Vic, and Jay crouched with me along with several soldiers from the other squads. Vic rested his BAR on the edge of the trap and squeezed the trigger, hitting the bunkers, in a vain attempt, to suppress them. I rolled on my chest to the far right of the trap and crouched by a private from Kilo Squad.

"There's no cover from here to the wall!" he yelled over the cracks of the heavy 88s.

"The wind is blowing in the wrong direction to pop smoke," I noticed, feeling the wind blowing on my soaking wet uniform.

"Then…" The man's, well, teenager's, helmet ruptured out, metal snapping with a gush of blood. Despite what the movies display, there's no glory in death, no final movements to fight back, no last acts to lash out or anything. It's more like a marionette that has its strings cut. Everything loses control and just falls. One second the trooper was speaking and the next his muscles go limp and his body falls to the sand, blood trickling from a new hole in his helmet and coloring the sand pink.

"Down!" I yelled out, throwing myself back.

"I got him!" Jay yelled, aiming his rifle towards the bluff. His rifle cracked once and he gave the thumbs up.

"Okay, I want everyone to follow me and run for the seawall. Jay, hang back and cover us until we stop. Once we're there, Vic, you'll cover Jay's run up. Good?" No one spoke, just nodded. "Jay, call it out," I shouted.

I checked my Thompson and turned to Jay. He leveled his rifle and aimed at the nearest bunker. Once he lined up the scope on his rifle with a German gunner, he gave me a slight head nod.

"Advance!" I screamed, suddenly jumping to me feet and bolting out into the open.

The sandy seawall was about twenty to thirty yards away from the tank traps, with no cover at all, no tank traps, no craters, nothing. I didn't stop for anything and ran, swiveling by upper body around to face the bunkers. I didn't shoulder my weapon, but fired from the hip as I ran, sending quick bursts of submachine gun fire their way. The gunners swung around and began firing on us, but Jay still had our back. Two gunners, in the far bunker to our right, were silenced for the time being, offering us some breathing room.

A group of engineers from another squad pushed up along with us, carrying their heavy packs loaded with equipment. The men were slowed by the heavy equipment and struggled to cover the open ground. The Germans targeted them first, gunning down the group of soldiers. The engineers were torn to shreds under the unmerciful MG fire, the entire group of seven falling dead to the sand. I kept running, not even looking back in their direction. The others followed close behind, knowing stopping to help would only kill them as well.

Mortar rounds streaked down from above, crashing into the sand with thunderous roars followed by the fizzling hiss of flying shrapnel. I continued running against the incoming hail of bullets and mortars, eyes now locked on the seawall and the men huddled behind it. The man running in front of me was suddenly thrown into the air by a violent explosion from under his feet.

"Fuck, mines!" He yelled.

I dropped my eyes to the sand, quickly passing under me, scanning for any footprints to follow in, to avoid the mines. With all the shells landing, the MG fire, and the rush of men up the beach, it was near impossible to find a set of prints that didn't end suddenly. When the seawall was a few feet away, I threw myself forward and landed hard on the sandy seawall. I rolled to my back and looked behind, as the others dropped to the seawall. Once everyone was accounted for, I looked back to the bunkers and shouldered my Thompson.

"Covering fire!" I ordered, sitting up on my knees and targeting the nearest bunker. Vic and Nate aimed at the bunker and opened up with their weapons, several other troopers nearby added their firepower to the fight. Jay saw the signal and ran from his position, weaving as he ran towards us.

Jay was the quickest son of a bitch I ever knew. The man was fast, nimble, accurate, and a hell of a shot, the makings of a good sniper. He weaved across the sand without trouble and dodged the incoming MG fire better than the troopers around him. While it took us a minute to cover the open land, Jay was at the seawall in seconds.

"What?" He asked, breathing heavily as he dropped to the seawall.

"Nothing," I grunted, dropping back down to reload.

"Bolger!" Captain Hiller yelled, appearing with Adam a few feet down the wall. "Bolger, where the hell is Malks?"

"Not sure, sir," I responded, slapping a fresh clip into my Thompson. "Last I saw him he was on the Higgins."

"Do you have your C4 satchel?" Hiller asked.

My left hand reached down to the large pocket over the lower section of my ribcage and felt the bulge of the satchel charge. "Yes, sir!" I answered.

"Good, I want a hole blown in the wire…there!" He said and pointed to a section of barbed wire a few feet away. "Clear us a way off this beach!"

I nodded my head and tapped Nate on the shoulder, gesturing for him to follow me. He nodded and picked himself up, following close behind as I ducked behind the seawall. I ran the few feet to the section of wire where there were no troops taking cover. I dropped to my knees and pulled my entrenching tool off my pack, snapping the folding shovel into position.

"Cover me!" I yelled, ramming the tool into the soft sand.

"Got your back!" Nate yelled back, rifle firing.

I quickly shoveled as much sand as possible from under the barbed wire, working hard to create a nice sized hole to place my satchel charge. MG fire pelted all around me as I worked, ducking low to avoid the incoming volleys of bullets. The constant ducking of MG fire made the simple task become complicated, taking me a few minutes to clear a hole. Once enough sand was moved, I pulled the satchel from my pocket and stuffed it into the hole.

"Nate, I need your charge!" I yelled, seeing the single explosion would not clear a big enough gap.

"Yeah, here," he said, tossing me his satchel. I stuffed it in alongside mine. Quickly, I calculated the size of the blast and pulled the cords on each satchel, the fuses burning with a hiss.

"Go, get to cover!" I yelled running back down the wall. "Fire in the hole!"

I dove to the ground several feet away and buried my face in the sand, covering my head with my hands and holding my helmet down tight. The fuses quickly burned down and an earsplitting explosion echoed over the roar of the artillery. The fountain of sand thrown into the air rained down on me, pelting my back and legs like hail.

"Go, go, go!" Captain Hiller yelled as my ears rang.

I picked myself up and turned back, seeing the large gap in the barbed wire. The smoke was still settling as Captain Hiller lead every nearby solider through the breach, rushing ahead. I quickly ran after the squad, jumping through the gap and looking for cover. The nearby bunker was the only area to duck behind and everyone ran for it as the other bunkers turned their fire on us. They tried drowning the area in MG fire to close the gap, but two to three squads' worth of men made it through. All of us huddled in the shadow of the bunker, our only port in the storm.

"Charlie and Lima Squad!" Hiller ordered, "Take the bunker on the left. My squad on me, we're gonna take the one on the right!"

Hiller began scanning his map and grabbed Adam, taking the radio receiver from him. As he called in artillery support, he looked out at the bunker we were to take. The concrete bunker was a few yards away from the one we hid behind, a stretch of mined sand in between. The hill, the bunkers were built into, was dotted with dozens of smaller MG and sniper nests as well as several 88's and two Flack 38 AA cannons. Crossing the open area would be a death sentence, the open ground providing a perfect kill zone.

"I need the support right on top of them, exactly at the coordinates," Hiller was yelling into the receiver. "Smoke the fuckers!"

One of the many ships out in the sea rotated its heavy main cannons towards the coast, raising or lowering to hit the area. The big guns boomed and sent a vicious twelve shell salvo onto the Germans, pounding the hillside mercilessly. The MG nests and light cannon emplacements were burned to hell by the torrent of explosive shells. The remnants of the positions tumbled down the hill alongside loose sand and twisted barbed wire.

"Follow me and keep your heads down! Jay, stay here and cover our asses!" I yelled.

Jay moved to the edge of the bunker and knelt down, checking his rifle. Captain Hiller knelt next to him and held his hand up in a halt signal. As the arty barrage tapered off, he waved forward and jumped up, running out into the open. Jay swung out and searched for targets as I ran out after Hiller, following in his footsteps.

The area was still clogged with smoke and ash, making it difficult to keep track of the Captain. The smell of cordite still hung heavy in the air, my breaths coming in hard, uneven intervals. The muscles in my legs burned with pain with every step, but the adrenaline in my blood and the fear of death blocked out the pain for the time being. I kept my eyes locked on the Captain's back. as MG fire rained down on the area around me, and mortar rounds exploded in every direction.

An incoming mortar round screeched overhead and crashed into the sand, several feet in front of me. The shockwave hit me like a hammer, but I kept on moving, leaping over the small crater it created. My uniform was speckled with sizzling shrapnel and I could smell the chemical coated cloth beginning to burn. I paid no mind to the sound and kept running, the opposite bunker seeming to get no closer. It felt like I was running on and on for miles, not getting an inch closer. Reality hit me when Hiller grabbed my arm, yanking me behind the concrete bunker.

"Hold here!" he ordered as everyone ran across the open ground and piled in behind the bunker. I stopped and pressed my back to the bunker, head dropping to my chest, as I fought to control my breathing.

"Captain," Hanes called, "there's a battery of four Flack 88s on the ridge hammering our reinforcements coming ashore. We're losing boats left and right."

"Hanes, take Bolger and a few others to knock out those guns. The rest of you, with me and let's clear this bunker."

"Right, Nate, Ramos, Sanders, Phelps, with me," the Lieutenant called, gesturing towards a set of trenches leading up the hill. "Bolger, stick close."

I nodded and followed the group, jumping into the trenches running parallel to the bunker. Hanes took the lead followed close by me and we snaked our way through the muddy trenches. Everyone kept in a low crouch, staying low to maintain some level of surprise. The section of trenches we were in was empty at the lower sections, the Germans manning the defenses at the top near the 88s.

The four cannons were in a neat line set in shallow cement bases just behind the trench line. Several MG42s were set up in the trenches covering the frontal approach, but the side trench we weaved through was on their right flank and was not under their guard. The German soldiers had their attention on keeping the MG42s and 88s supplied with ammunition. Lieutenant Hanes led us through the trench, to the firing line.

"Okay, I'm gonna clear the trench with Ramos and Sanders. Bolger, go with Phelps and Nate and take out the 88s. Stay low and spike the guns with your C4 bundles. Once they're cleared, regroup with us at the end of the trench. Ready? Let's go!" The Lieutenant ordered.

I crept across the trench connection and grabbed a handhold on the wooden planks lining the walls of the trench. Quickly, I pulled myself out of the trench and rolled across the sand. Phelps and Nate were barely over the wall when Hanes attacked the Germans with Ramos and Sanders. Machine gun and rifle fire filled the trench, grabbing the German's attention. I took advantage and rose to one knee, aiming towards the closest 88.

The crew was still working hard to blow as many Higgins Boats out of the water as possible. I squeezed the trigger and emptied the entire clip on the tight cluster of men manning the gun. The five men fell to the barrage without offering resistance; the three of us were at the gun in seconds before they hit the ground. Phelps pulled one of the C4 bundles from his vest and yanked the safety cord, tossing the bundle down the barrel.

I was reloading when the charge detonated, ripping open the barrel. Nate moved to the next gun and tossed a grenade into their laps, killing the crew in the single blast. I moved up and tossed a C4 bundle into the barrel and ran for the next 88, glancing over my shoulder to check on Hanes. The three of them were halfway down the trench and cleared out two of the MG nests. Hanes was moving against the torrent of German fire and taking no prisoners.

The two other 88s fell silent as the crews realized we took out the other two cannons and ran for cover. Rifle fire pounded our position, forcing us down to our stomachs at the lip of the emplacement. I held my Thompson close against my shoulder and fired in short, controlled bursts at the Germans. The gun crews managed to grab an MG42 and set it up on a stack of crates, setting up its tripod and loading up an ammunition belt.

"Take out the gunner!" I yelled, moving my iron sights onto the MG team.

Nate and Phelps shifted fire to take out the crew, but they managed to set up the MG42. The gunner shouldered the lightweight weapon and gripped the handle, swinging the weapon around to face our position. He squeezed the trigger, but suddenly jerked right, MG swinging off target and firing into the sky. Lieutenant Hanes hit the German's flank after he cleared the trench line, creating crossfire. I grabbed a grenade from my webbing and pulled the pin, tossing the grenade overhead. It sailed through the air and landed in front of the 88, detonating and spewing shrapnel all around. Several Germans fell to the blast while the remaining crew pulled back and retreated to one of the concrete bunkers.

"Spike that 88!" Hanes called, moving to the fourth gun. "I got the last one!"

I ran to the 88 and placed my last C4 charge in the barrel. Once the gun was spiked and Hanes finished with his, we moved on to the closest bunker. Captain Hiller and the rest of the squad were clearing the bunker to our rear, so we moved up and readied to rush the other bunker.

"This might be a problem," Ramos whistled, seeing the reinforced steel door, at the bunker's entrance.

"Didn't Malks say the right amount of explosives could solve anything?" I said, thinking aloud.

"Nate, blow the door!" Hanes ordered, moving to left side of the bunker entrance.

Nate nodded and moved to the door, removing a satchel charge. He wrapped the fabric strap of the satchel to the metal handle of the door and placed the charge just right to blow open the door. Once he yanked the primer, everyone ducked behind the side of the bunker, waiting for the blast. The satchel detonated with an echoing bang and the steel door fell inward with a loud, metallic clang.

Hanes was first inside, Thompson up and spraying the room. I was behind him and covered the right side of the room as he covered the left, Ramos and Nate right on our heels. The two, three man gunner groups were stunned by the blast, dropping their weapons. Hanes and I quickly killed the group with several bursts from our weapons, the sound of machine gun fire echoing loudly in the concrete room.

"Clear!" I yelled, as the last man fell to the ground.

"Pull out and mark this bunker!" Hanes ordered, moving back outside.

I pulled a red smoke grenade from my webbing and pulled the pin, dropping it near the edge of the firing position. We pulled out as the smoke billowed, signaling the Navy and Air Force to blow the thing to hell. Hanes pulled us back to the original bunker Hiller was clearing. We moved through the trenches and found the Captain and his half of the squad at the entrance to the bunker, reloading and checking their equipment and weapons.

"Update, Lieutenant," Hiller called when he spotted us.

"The Flack 88s and overlook bunker have been cleared, but our guys are still getting the piss pounded out of them," Hanes reported, backhanding some sweat from his eyes.

"We created a gap in the line here, but we need to secure a foothold if we're going to grab St. Luarent-sur-Mer before the sun sets. Now, let's grab the German OP along Route Baker and clear a way for the tankers to roll in when they hit the beaches.

"Sir," Adam interrupted, holding the radio receiver. "Echo is taking heat from several bunkers covering the entrance to Route Gamma. A group of engineers is pinned in the kill zone and can't clear the path through the tank traps."

"Right, change of plans, we head back down the line and clear the path for the engineers. Let's get going and see what we can do. Adam, call in to Echo and let them know we're on the way."

The next wave of soldiers was coming ashore as we snaked our way through the cleared trenches to Echo's position. The second wave deposited more men onto the beach, but the Germans were still holding tight all around, the rear units fighting to keep the route we cleared open as German reinforcements fought back. Several of the smaller LCVs were rushing to drop off their cargo of tanks and help shore up the gap in the lines, but there were still dozens of bunkers, MG and sniper nests, and AT emplacements lining the Atlantic Wall in the small area that was Omaha Beach.

Echo Squad was pinned down with several other rifle squads at the entrance to Route Gamma, which was no more than a dirt road that led off the beach. The tiny road was critical in getting our armor off the beach quickly so we could push as far inland as possible before the day ended. The Germans knew this and filled the area with extra tank traps that had mines of all types scattered around them. Concrete bunkers lined the ridge and created an overlapping kill zone in a U shape that the engineers fell face first into.

We approached from the right flank of the roadway, approaching on the center most bunkers. Two Flack 88s sat either side of the bunkers, covering the approach with the bunkers, spraying the area with bullets. The group of engineers was pinned down near the center of the kill zone, huddling behind a Belgium Gate and in a shell crater for cover. From what I could see, a dozen of the men lay dead. The rifle squads were thirty yards to the rear, still on the beach with a group of six Sherman Tanks stuck behind rows of Dragons Teeth.

"Get down and shut up!" Hiller hissed, leading us to sunken remains of a blown out bunker near the road.

Everyone ducked down in the ruins and shut their mouths, looking to the Captain. I lay on my stomach under some twisted rebar rods and watched him crawl to the lip of the crater. He looked over the edge and dropped down as two fully loaded German halftracks raced by, heading for the bunkers. Once they past, Hiller laid out the plan.

"Let's keep this simple and easy." He pointed to Hanes. "Hanes will take Ramos, Nate, Malks, and Phelps around the left side of the road and hit the 88s in the rear. As they moved up, I'll hit the center bunker with Adam, Jay, and Vic. Bolger, you take Sanders and the rookies to the bunker on the far left. Once we clear the two bunkers, we take out the third and cover those engineers so they can clear the way for the tanks."

"Why not call in the Air Force or Navy to take out the bunkers?" Sanders asked.

"We do that and we risk dusting the engineers. I'm not gonna take the risk, so we do it the hard way. Do we have problems with that?" No one spoke. "Good, let's move."

I nodded to Sanders and moved to the lip of the trench, first checking for Germans before running out. I didn't bother to check to see if the rookies were following, I knew Sanders was and the rookies followed without question. The five squad rookies were younger than everyone else, eighteen or just under. They could barely shoot strait and this was their first combat operation, so Sanders worked out the plan with me.

"Clear the back trenches and then the bunker?" he suggested.

"Yeah, we'll clear the trenches first. Once they're clear, I'll leave the rookies to cover our rear while we clear the bunker."

"Just dump a couple frags inside?" Asked Sanders.

I nodded, as we darted from cover to cover, quickly moving up the line and stopping several feet from the trenches in a shallow crater. The rookies followed close behind and huddled with us, hands shaking and eyes filled with fear and uncertainty. At the time, two looked like they might turn tail and run for it.

"Look," I said, glancing over my shoulder and spying several Germans in the trench. "Let's keep it basic; we lay down a hail of grenades into the trenches and swoop in to clear the survivors. Once the trenches are clear, you four hang back and cover our rear as we take out the bunker, clear?"

"Yes Sergeant," Private Hackett said, flexing his fingers over his rifle.

"Okay, on my mark." I pulled a grenade from my webbing and watched the rookies pull out their grenades. Everyone had their fingers wrapped around the pins, looking to me. I nodded, yanking the pin out of my grenade. I let the spoon spring free and tossed the grenade into the trench. Sanders tossed his overhead along with the rookies. The five grenades landed in the trench and detonated in rapid succession.

Seconds after the last grenade detonated, I was out of the crater and rushing the trench line. Once I was a few feet from the edge of the trench, I ran parallel to it and covered the area with machine gun fire. My Thompson boomed as I sprayed the trench, Sanders at my side and firing his rifle. The Germans were blindsided and killed in seconds. I hopped down into the trench and rushed for the bunker entrance, swapping my ammo clip for a fresh one. I stopped just at the turn to the bunker and pressed myself against the wooden planks of the trench wall.

"Rookies are looking extra shaky," Sanders grunted, standing behind me.

I looked back and saw three of the four covering their mouths with their hands, holding back vomit at the sight of the mangled German bodies. The fourth looked past the bodies and waited behind Sanders to move.

"Edwards, up here," I said with a nod of my head. The young private moved up and held his rifle firmly against his shoulder, hands steady and eyes focused.

"Yes Sarge," he said, nodding his head slightly.

"We're gonna clear the bunker," I pointed to Sanders and myself. "I want you to hang back and cover our rear once we're inside, staying near the bunker door. We'll clear the area and I want you to watch for any surprises."

"Yes Sarge," he replied, voice full of confidence and courage. "I got your backs."

I gave an approving head nod and tapped Edwards' shoulder. "Stay sharp."

I pulled a frag grenade from one of my pockets, holding it my left hand. Sanders moved to the opposite side of the door and readied himself, giving a nod. I nodded back and pulled the pin from the grenade, letting it cook off for several seconds. Once I reached four, I tossed the grenade underhanded inside. The metal pineapple bounced across the concrete floor to the feet of the German gunners. One had the sense to look back and spotted the grenade, diving towards the right side of the bunker.

The explosion threw a cloud of cement dust outwards as I rushed in first, Thompson up and spraying the confined bunker with bullets. Sanders was right behind me and moved to left side of the room as I did, Edwards dropped into a crouch, at the bunker door.

The dust was choking and blinding me, as my eyes scanned for targets. I spotted a figure moving low at the far edge of the room and leveled my weapon, firing a four round burst at the center mass. A muffled scream broke through the dust, but ended with another two round burst. The figure lay still and I moved on, scanning the pair of MG42s sitting on the bunker firing position. Sanders cleared his side of the room and moved up with me.

Down below, the engineers were still pined behind the gate and in the crater. Captain Hiller silenced the center bunker along with the 88s alongside Lieutenant Hanes. Our bunker was clear, but the last bunker was active and still firing on the hapless engineers below. The two halftracks we spotted were now at the top of the roadway, firing down on our boys while German troops fought to take back Hiller's bunker.

"Looks like Hiller's gonna need a hand," Sanders grunted, taking a second to catch his breath.

"Yeah, but we can't leave this bunker for the Germans to take the second we turn our backs." I looked down to the tanks waiting behind the Dragon's Teeth with the rifle squads then changing my gaze to the third bunker.

"Orders, Sarge?" Edwards asked, as I thought.

"Yeah," I grunted, nodding to myself. I turned to Sanders and Edwards. "Okay, let's get these two MG42s up and firing on that third bunker. Maybe we can grab the attention of third bunker and take the heat off the engineers long enough to get the tanks through. We do that and the tanks can help the Captain."

"Dumb enough to work, Corr," Sanders agreed moving for the first 42.

"Edwards, get one of the others in here and have the other three cover the door."

"On it!" He said.

As Edwards dashed out the door, I turned and grabbed one of the MG42s, Sanders grabbing the second one. I scanned the German weapon and checked the ammo belt, seeing the majority of it was still unfired. Sanders shouldered the second weapon and chambered a new belt. Edwards returned with Private Vegas after a few seconds.

"Edwards, help me and Vegas assist Sanders," I said, gesturing to the ammo cans stacked next to each 42. Edwards understood and crouched down next to me, readying to help load a fresh can. Vegas moved to Sanders side and I readied the 42.

I brought the iron sights of the MG42 down on the opposite bunker, wrapping my finger around the trigger and holding the stock of the MG with my other hand. Bracing for the kick back, I squeezed the trigger, the machine gun jumping, as a long volley machine gun fire streaked away. Sanders opened up alongside me, the two of us pouring bullets onto the German bunker. The echo of the two MG42s dulled my senses as I fired, swinging the weapon slightly from side to side.

The gunners were blindsided by the sudden MG fire from one of their bunkers. At first, they stopped firing and ducked down in confusion, but soon figured things out. They returned to their weapons and opened fire on our position, blasting away at the hard concrete. The tiny shards cut into my exposed hands, cutting my fingers like dull razors. Pain burned through my hands, but I kept my finger squeezing the trigger, emptying the rest of the clip.

As the MG42 clicked empty, Edwards was quick and pulled the empty can free. He pulled a fresh can from the stack and connected it to the MG42, closing the breach cover on the fresh belt of ammo. I returned to firing and continued to hammer at the Germans, watching the engineers out of the corner of my eyes.

The men took the sudden relief as a chance to finish their work. Several of them moved back to the Dragon's Teeth and began placing explosives to clear the way, as the others prepped the charges around the steel barricades near the Belgium Gate. Moving quickly, they detonated the explosives and cleared the tank traps, allowing the Sherman tanks to roll in.

The idle tanks leapt through the cleared path and pounded the third bunker with fire, blowing the bunker walls down one concrete slab at a time. The rifle squads pushed forward and hit the German halftracks, knocking them out quickly and hitting the ground troops as they fought with the Captain. I dropped the 42 and moved for the door.

"Let's get back to the Captain!" I yelled, moving back down the trench line.

I moved quickly, nearly running down the trench to reach Captain Hiller. Sanders moved right behind me while Edwards kept the rookies moving. The remaining Germans were pulling back in droves, leaving their positions empty as we ran through. With no resistance, we quickly found Captain Hiller sitting down by the center bunker with the squad. Everyone was at ease and watching the tanks roll down the road.

"We all clear?" I asked, breathing heavily.

"Yep," Hiller responded, "the route is open and our boys are rolling off the beach. Take a minute to catch your breath; we're rolling out with the tankers in five."

I nodded and slung my Thompson over my shoulder, moving to talk to Jay. He was sitting on a crate next to Vic, taking a drink from his canteen. Vic was smoking a cigarette and watching a group of German prisoners being marched away from the bunkers.

"My hands are shaking," Jay said, watching the canteen shake in his hands.

"Adrenaline withdrawal," Doc said, as we walked over to the Captain. "You'll be like this for a while."

"Uhh…" Vic grunted, entailing another breath of smoke.

"Smoking won't help," Doc said, pointing to the smoke in his hands.

"I think Edwards might have what it takes," I said, leaning against the bunker.

Jay glanced over his shoulder. "Yeah, he was a good shot in training."

I nodded in agreement. "He didn't freeze up back there either."

Jay nodded and took another drink. I sighed to myself as I began to feel the adrenaline in blood thin out and disappear. The pain in my muscles came back with a vengeance, and I slid down into the dirt, sitting back against the concrete bunker. I removed my helmet and shook loose sand from my hair, feeling the sweat drying and sticking to my head. Yawning, I grabbed my canteen and took a drink, sighing at the relief brought by the semi warm liquid.

"Hard to believe it's been a few hours," Nate sighed, dropping down next to me. "It feels like it's been a few minutes since we landed."

"I feel like I ran twenty miles," I admitted, my entire body dull with pain and exhaustion.

"Yeah, well I feel like shit," Vic grunted, dropping his smoke and pulling out another.

"You look like shit," Ramos joked, slapping Vic on the back.

"You are shit," Vic cursed, taking a deep inhale of smoke.

"Enough," I ordered, closing my eyes. While nothing would come of their bickering, our nerves were frayed and words of false bravado could send the two into a fist fight.

"Yeah, Sarge," Ramos mumbled, dropping down next to Jay, propping his rifle against the bunker. "Oh, I've never felt so…wrung out."

"Just think, Ramos," Jay pointed out, "This was just day one, well, half of day one really. We still got a long way to Berlin and Hitler's doorstep."

"Guys," I said, opening my eyes and seeing the sky still gray with rain. "My dad told me to put things in a different light, set smaller goals. We took the beach and now have to grab a nearby village to secure said beach. Let's focus on that for the time being." Jay nodded in agreement as Captain Hiller dispatched new orders.

"Smoking break is over, boys!" he called, swinging his Thompson into his hands. "We got a town to secure before the Germans can get their tanks onto the beach. Check your kit and fall in!"

Sighing, I rose to my feet and waved the squad to get up and follow the Captain. Everyone complied and fell into a two column formation on the dirt road, marching inland. The Air Force was back, fighters zipping overhead and chasing down the retreating German forces as we moved inland. Looking back and seeing our tanks grinding down the road, I believed things might be easier then when we stormed the beaches. The deep labyrinth of the boscage loomed at the end of the road.

Chapter 9

Never trust Army Intel, was another set of my father's values and a bit of his wisdom. Intel has the skill to either have out of date intelligence on an area, or they just don't get it to the right people in time. They told us the hedgerows of Normandy were like the ones in England, short, low to the ground, nothing more than mounds of dirt with some bushes on top. They were wrong, dead wrong.

"Son of a bitch!" Hiller hissed, lowering his Thompson. "The Krauts are living in the hedgerows."

It was the fourth time on the road we encountered a German patrol. So far, we were not engaged as the Germans scattered into the crisscrossing hedgerows, disappearing into the thick woodland. We hadn't mastered the skill yet and were confined to the natural checkpoints on the roads and entrances to the open farming fields. Our tanks tried running through the hedgerows, but the thick roots of the tree growing in them acted like cement, binding the dirt and creating an unmovable wall.

"Okay, stay sharp and let's go," Hiller finally said, eyes still studying the road.

I nodded to the men behind me and rose to my feet, continuing on with the patrol. Our objective was the tiny hamlet of Fitts, situated two miles from the beachhead on a low hill that provided a decent spotting point for artillery. Captain Hiller wanted the hamlet under our control before nightfall, and we never fail the Captain.

If there is such a thing as Hell, then hedgerow country was the path to it. The trees tangled over the road, blocking out the sun and creating hundreds of shadows that tricked the eye. Snipers were everywhere and the thought of the man in front of you suddenly dying with a shot to the head was terrifying. We were only out for two hours, but machine gun fire and artillery explosions could be heard all around. Death was literally one step away.

"Let the tanks lead the way," Hanes suggested, gesturing to the four Sherman tanks following us.

"Okay, the town is just down the road." Hiller turned and waved to the lead tank. "Bolger, tell the tankers to follow up this road to the next crossroads and hold position for my signal."

"Yes sir," I responded, seeing Hiller already had his attack plan forming in his mind.

I turned on my heel and ran down the muddied road, heading for the lead Sherman tank. As the lumbering machine came to a slow stop, I climbed up its armored side, engine still humming like a heartbeat. The tank commander appeared out of the top hatch and turned to me.

"What's going on?" he asked in a Texas drawl.

I filled him in. "Captain Hiller wants you to head up to the next crossroads and wait for his signal to attack the town."

"What's the signal?" He asked.

"Trust me; you'll know it when you see it," I said.

The commander nodded,as I jumped off the tank, landing with a sucking sound, as my boots sunk into the soft ground. Captain Hiller called everyone forward to the side of the road, crouching in the shadow of the six foot high hedgerow. I moved next to Jay and took a knee, listening in.

"Okay," he said, picking up a stick and drawing in the mud. He was like that, preferring to use something he can touch, and manipulate with his hands more than a map. "The town isn't that big, but it has an old church dead center with a bell tower, that more then likely, has a sniper in it. Now, the only approach to the town is along the main road, here," he drew a strait line and then a large rectangle. "But we can cut through the fields here and approach on the southern side. We'll get to the town faster, but we'll be exposed in the open, for the time being, and will be able to hit the German flank."

"We're gonna cross the field and duck behind the stone wall of the church cemetery at the edge of the field, " he continued. "Once everyone is across, we head to the right of the wall and hit the enemy in the church, hopefully securing it as a foothold so we can take the town. The tankers roll in as we attack and grab the German's attention, dividing their forces along the main road. We need to move fast and hard, clearing the church the second the tanks hit the main road. We do it fast enough and we can grab the town in a matter of minutes."

"Do we have air support?" I asked.

Hiller looked to Adam who shook his head. "No, the Air Force is running sorties near Utah Beach to help connect with the 101st and 82nd. "

"The tanks are our support, so kill anyone mounting an AT weapon. If there no questions, let's get to it," The Captain said.

Everyone was silent as Hiller stood up and began walking down the road. I did a quick check on everyone and quickly followed after, eyes darting from tree to tree until we came to the next hedgerow. The church bell tower raised high into the sky over the thick hedges, like a beacon, though it was beacon of death, at the time.

Hiller dropped down next to the towering hedgerow on the south side of the field and began to deeply study the wall of earth and rock. After covering each inch, he pointed to a section low to the ground and moved towards it, pushing away a tangle of bushes which revealed a tiny gap in the roots, most likely an old German scouting post. He looked to us and nodded before crawling through the gap. Once his feet were through, I knelt down and propelled myself through the opening, falling into an irrigation ditch on the other side next to the Captain. Once everyone was through, Hiller left Jay behind to cover us and ordered everyone else to crawl across the field.

With a slow and controlled pace, I began to belly crawl across the field, which was barren except for the hedgerows lining it and the dirt on the ground. There was not an inch of cover from the ditch to the church wall, not to mention we were in the shadow of the bell tower. Cursing to myself, I continued to crawl, hands and knees scrapping against the tiny, yet painful rocks imbedded in the dirt. Edwards crawled to my left, Private Vegas to my right and Hanes behind.

My heart was racing from the second I left the ditch, eyes up and feverously searching the town for any movement. Paranoia began to creep across my mind with each inch of field crossed, threatening to overrun my mental controls. I fought off the thoughts and pushed on, focusing on just reaching the opposite end of the field.

"Oh shit," Vegas hissed, stopping his crawl.

"Vegas, stay down," I ordered, turning to see him trying to sit up. "Keep going," I told Hanes, crawling over to Vegas.

"I'm stuck," he complained, laying flat on his stomach.

"How?" I asked.

"My leg, I think it's caught up on a rock," he said.

I looked down at his leg and spotted his pants caught up on a rock, in the dirt. Ordering him to remain still, I grabbed the tangled fabric and yanked it free from the rocks. With a few rips he was free. Vegas craned his neck around and smiled, mouthing a thank you when his body suddenly went slack. His head rolled to one side, his body following and lying still in the dirt. I dropped low into the dirt when I saw the hole in his helmet and the blood pooling around his face.

The sniper spotted us and opened fire, as the German garrison appeared behind the stone wall of the church, firing at us while an MG42 was set up. Everyone remained low on the ground and returned fire on the Germans. I raised my Thompson and sprayed the top of the wall, killing the German gunner setting up the 42. Another man took his place as another sprayed my position with his MP-40. Hanes dropped him quickly, as Nate crawled forward and opened up with his rifle. German machine gun and rifle fire streaked across the open field as we fought back. Jay was still in the ditch and covering us with his sniper rifle.

As the MG42 was set up, I rolled away from Vegas' lifeless body and crawled for the edge of the field. When I was close to the border hedgerow, I took a knee and leaned against it for cover. Suddenly, a German with a panzerfaust fired towards me, the rocket landing short and blowing a gap in the hedgerow. I quickly rose to my feet and ran through the gap in the hedge and found myself in another ditch between our field and the next one over. The tiny path between the hedgerows was barely wide enough for me to walk, but I kept in a low crouch and ran towards the town, stopping as I spotted the road near the church.

Taking a second to reload, I leaned out slightly and spotted the Germans behind the church wall. The tanks were attacking on the other side of town and there was no one out in front of the church. Carefully, I stepped out and ran for an overturned cart in the road, ducking behind it. Now with some cover, I leveled my Thompson at the Germans behind the wall and emptied my entire clip into their flank, killing three and wounding a forth before several turned on me.

I dropped back down to reload as bullets splintered the wooden cart. Fumbling with a new clip, a German soldier appeared a few feet down the road, shocked to see me. He raised his rifle and fired, but nothing happened. His weapon jammed, so I shoved a new clip into my Thompson, but the German charged me as I came up to fire. He knocked away my Thompson and slashed at me with a knife. I leapt back in time to miss the first swipe of the blade. When he missed a second time, I moved into the attack and grabbed his knife hand, gripping his wrist like a vice. I balled my right hand into a fist and punched him hard below the rip cage in four, upward strokes.

The German howled in pain, but fought back like a wounded animal. I brought my right knee up into his stomach and yanked him downward with both hands, throwing him off center. With a vicious jab of my elbow into his spine, I sent him face first into the cart. I whirled around, drawing my Colt.45 from my side holster. I leveled the sidearm at his back and fired four times and then a fifth in the back of the head to be sure.

With one threat handled, I holstered my.45 and retrieved my Thompson from the ground, pulling back on the cocking hammer on top. Reloaded, I returned fire on the Germans, as the bell in the church suddenly sounded. Out of the corner of my eye, I saw the German sniper crash through the wooden slats of the bell tower windows and fall to the street below. Jay had found him. Now with the sniper dead, I rushed forward to the stone steps of the church, moving around the side to the cemetery. I jumped behind a large, stone cross shaped gravestone.

The grave stone was splattered with rifle fire, but I spun out and shot two German riflemen before pulling back. The squad was close to the wall now and lobbed several grenades over the wall. The resulting explosions finished off the Germans, allowing the squad to get out of the field. Captain Hiller vaulted over the stone wall and ran for me.

"Good work, Bolger," he grunted, nodding his head. "Now let's grab that church."

I nodded and followed behind Hiller as he rushed for the massive wooden doors of the church. Hanes and Nate ran up behind us and readied to rush the church. Hiller approached the wooden doors and edged it open with the tip of the Thompson. The doors squeaked open halfway and Hiller checked inside before flinging the door open completely. He rushed in and dove behind a stone pillar as I moved in with Hanes and Nate, ducking behind a wooden pew. Adam moved in with Ramos and Edwards, heading for the far left side of the church. I looked to Hiller, who shook his head slightly.

"They're hiding, move up," Hiller whispered.

I nodded and tapped Hanes on the shoulder, gesturing for him to move up with me. He nodded, silently moving to the isle to the right of the row of pews. I followed closely behind him with my Thompson held tight against my shoulder. I walked with delicate, careful steps to avoid making excess noise, my head sweeping back and forth. The church was very large and old, the stone sculptors and masonry designed like those seen during the Renaissance Period. A very ornate altar sat in the front of the church, several, just as ornate crosses, on the walls around it. Just to the right, was a stairway that led up to the bell tower.

"Check out the tower," Hiller ordered, pointing to us. "I'll check the basement with Vic and the rookies while Adam clears the rectory. Regroup out front once this church is clear."

"We're on it," Hanes responded, "Let's go."

Hanes led us to the doorway to the stairwell and carefully climbed the wooden steps, each one creaking under our boots. I followed behind him, keeping to the side of the stairs with my Thompson aimed just ahead, on the next landing. The echo of cannon and machine gun fire could still be heard outside, as the tanks engaged the German defenders. Inside, the heavy cracks of Vic's BAR could be heard, as he and the Captain cleared the basement.

Hanes held up a closed fist to signal a halt, as we approached the door to the bell tower. He looked to me and nodded forward to the closed door. I understood and moved up past Hanes, placing one hand on the old metal handle with my Thompson at the ready. With a slow turn, I edged the door open and slowly crept inside. The tiny room was dominated by a massive metal bell with a thin walkway moving around it. Three windows provided a clear view of the town below, but they were covered with wooden planks. One window had the planks broken out, where the sniper fell through.

"We're clear," I responded, lowering my weapon. "Okay, let's get back to the squad."

The rest of the church was cleared with only a few Germans fighting back. The tanks ran the remainder out of town. We were based down in the town square while we set up an OP in the church. Captain Hiller had us sweep the town for anyone, but the entire place was empty, not even bodies, besides the dead Germans, to be found. While strange, chances were the entire town packed up and left when the Navy started their early morning bombardment. Even so, Captain Hiller wanted a scouting patrol of the area. I was dispatched with Ramos and Jay to scout along the northern road leading out of town.

"Well, it's a farmhouse," Jay called down from his position in a tree jutting out from a hedgerow. "But, I can barely see past all the damn hedgerows."

"Alright, get back down here and let's check it out," I said back, looking down the road.

Jay jumped down from the tree and nodded his head. I gestured down the road and began to walk, staying to the far left side of the road. The farmhouse was three fields down, with a single entrance just off the road behind some trees. A barn stood just off the main house with a grain silo. I planned to just check it out and then pull back to the town and report.

The situation changed as we approached the entrance to the farm when a series of screams shot through the still air. I dropped down into a crouch and looked back to Ramos and Jay. Jay held up a hand and scurried up the hedgerow, sitting a top a branch in a tree. He scanned the farm house and looked down at me, mouthing the word 'Germans.'

I nodded and signaled him to stay and cover us. I led Ramos to the main gate and leaned around the hedgerow. I saw a group of five Germans standing in front of the barn with two by the front door of the house. Another German appeared from the house, dragging a young woman, maybe nineteen or twenty; she was kicking and screaming, as they headed towards the barn. The other Germans cheered him as I moved forward behind with Ramos to the low stone wall just past the hedgerow.

"Hiller said to scout and avoid fighting," Ramos whispered, looking to me.

"And what?" I hissed, "Let her be raped? No, that does not happen while I'm still breathing. Open up once she's dragged out of the line of fire."

Ramos nodded and waited until the woman was taken into the barn. Not hesitating, I stood up and fired on the group of Germans by the barn, dropping four before the clip was empty. Ramos leaned out and dropped the forth as Jay killed the two by the house. Hearing the screams again, I reloaded and leapt over the wall, running for the barn. I stopped at the entrance and took a breath before spinning around and appearing in the doorway. I spotted the German standing over the terrified woman, hands raised over his head in surrender.

"*Auf Ihren Knien!*" (On your knees) I yelled in German, aiming for the man's face. He complied and dropped down, clasping his hands behind his head.

"We're clear," Ramos reported, moving to my side. He saw the German and the woman. "Well, shoot him."

"He's our prisoner now," I responded, suppressing the urge to put a bullet in the bastard's head.

"And? You said it yourself that he was gonna rape her. The fucker has it coming to him," he said.

I remained fixed in my position, crosshairs on the German's head. I felt the overwhelming urge to squeeze the trigger and send him to hell, but I couldn't lower myself to his level. This was different from fighting in a war.

"No," I said, lowering my weapon. "Tie his hands up and sit him somewhere for the time being. Get Jay down here and wait for me."

"Yeah," Ramos snorted, moving up the German. Without blinking, he slammed the butt of his rifle into the man's head, sending the German to the ground.

Ignoring him, I slung my Thompson over my shoulder and noticed the woman was gone. Something moved in the far corner of the, and I carefully approached, not wanting to frighten to the woman. Moving forward, I found her huddled behind a stack of crates, a German Luger in her hand and aimed at me. Her hands were shaking, but the Luger remained pointed at my chest.

"Easy now," I said, holding my hands out, palms up. "I'm here to help."

"Who are you?" she asked in French, the weapon still held steady.

I crouched down a few feet in front of her and removed my helmet. In French I said, "I'm an American."

"American?" she repeated in French.

I nodded and patted the American Flag I had sewn on the pocket just above my heart. "I'm not going to hurt you."

The woman studied me with terrified eyes and lowered the Luger slightly. I slowly took a few half steps forward and placed my hands over the barrel of the Luger, gently taking it from her.

"It's okay," I repeated over and over again, keeping my eyes locked with hers and seeing how mesmerizing grey they were. "You're safe now." She nodded her head and let me take the Luger before pulling back and huddling against the wall. I pulled out my canteen and unscrewed the cap, handing it to her.

"Thank you,' she mumbled, drinking the water in small sips. Her eyes suddenly averted over my shoulder, as Ramos walked to my side.

"How is she?" he asked, looking at the young woman.

"Shaken up," I said, still looking her. "I'm going to try to have her come back to town with us so Doc can help her."

"Well, I'm gonna check out the house, Jay is with the German just outside," Ramos said.

I nodded and looked over the woman, looking for any visible wounds I could treat. She was young, maybe eighteen or nineteen, at the most, with dark, almost black brown hair that passed her shoulders. The woman was very attractive, almost shockingly beautiful, the thought of which unnerved me slightly with the situation at hand.

"Here," I said, pulling out my field medical kit, "you have several cuts that should be treated before infection can set it."

She nodded and let me wipe away the blood forming around the cuts across her cheeks and a rather large gash at her hair line. I gently applied some sulfur power to some folded gauze and dapped at the wounds, working to kill any infections. It was all I could do without bandages small enough to cover the wounds.

"My name's Jessica," she mumbled, as I cleaned her cuts.

"Oh, my name's Sergeant Corrigan Bolger, but most people just call me Corr."

Jessica nodded her head. "I'm with the Underground, Sergeant Corrigan."

"You are? Well, that explains how well you aimed this," I held up the Luger and handed it back to her, grip first. "You sure you're okay?"

"Fine, they caught me off guard." Jessica rose to her feet, standing a few inches shorter then me.

"Well, we've got an outpost just down the road in Fitts, with a medic. I would like you to come back with us and be checked out properly."

She thought on it and agreed. "Sure, I'll go with you."

I nodded and led her back outside, finding Jay sitting on a pile of wood with the German at his feet, hands bound behind his back and unconscious.

"Hey, Corr," Jay greeted me, looking over my shoulder at Jessica. "How's the dame ?"

"Fine, but Doc will do a check when we get back." I said, as Ramos returned from the house empty handed.

"It's all clear, Sarge," he reported. "The lace looks long abandoned."

"Corrigan," Jessica whispered, "this farm is abandoned. It's been empty since the Germans invaded."

"What did she say?" Jay asked.

"The place is abandoned, has been for awhile. Okay, let's pack up Mr. Sunshine here and get back to town," I said.

Ramos nodded and picked up the German, hauling the unconscious man over his shoulders. Jay took his rifle and the four of us began walking back to base, not bothering to hide the bodies of the other Germans. It was no big secret we invaded and dead Germans would be very common to find. I walked lead with Jessica at my side, so I tired to speaking with her.

"So, you're with the Underground?" I asked as we walked.

"Yes, I've been part of it since the Germans invaded France," she responded, looking over at me.

Her eyes were amazing. "Not to be intrusive, but how old are you?"

Jessica laughed dryly and managed a smile. "I'm nineteen, how old are you, Corr?"

I smiled slightly. "I'm twenty, been in the military since I was eighteen."

"Ah, so two young people who have no business in the ways of war," she smirked.

I began to laugh. "I see you're one who knows philosophy, but isn't it the rule of war to be started by the old and fought by the young?"

She shrugged. "Okay, so you know some philosophy as well. Strange, I was nearly killed, but yet I'm here making small talk a few minutes later."

"A way of coping with stress, I've done it plenty of times," I said.

"So have I," Jessica agreed, brushing her hands against her worn and faded skirt.

We walked on in silence, from then on, covering the remaining distance to the town in several minutes. Since we were sent out, forward elements from the main body of the Big Red One were arriving in town. Several squads of engineers were setting defenses around the town while columns of tanks and infantry passed through. Captain Hiller was still in the church, speaking with Major Philips and some captains from the other rifle squads, laying out some sort of plan on a large map.

"So, we bring up our armored units along Route Epsilon with our mechanized units bringing up the rear," Hiller was outlying the plans to the Major and the captains. "As they move up, our infantry precede ahead of the force as our scouting element."

"No," Philips said, shaking his head. "We have the infantry move up with the tanks so when we hit the city our forces are consolidated."

The majority of the captains, all young, agreed with him. The older captains looked to Hiller and shook their heads. Hiller nodded and agreed. "Sir, that'll…Bolger, what's going on?" Hiller asked.

"Sir," I said with a salute. "We scouted two miles down the north road and ran across a German patrol at an abandoned farmhouse. We took out the patrol and rescued a civilian who says she's with the Resistance." I stepped aside and gestured to Jessica. "We also have a prisoner."

"A prisoner?" Philips' eyes lit up for a second. "Leave him here. You find anything else?"

"No sir, all quiet on the road," I said.

Philips mumbled something and had two MPs take the German. Hiller stepped away and led us back to the church steps.

"Good work out there," he said. "Does she need medical attention?"

"She says no, but I'll keep an eye on her," I said.

"Okay, the situation around here is getting…hectic. We've secured Omaha and are moving to set up a formal defensive line while we work to link up with Utah and then the Brits and Canadians. For now, we're regrouping and preparing to move out in the morning, to finish securing Route N4 with armor covering our ass. Bunk down for tonight and get ready to roll in the morning."

"What about Jessica, sir?" I asked.

Hiller looked over at her and nodded to himself. "Have here bunk down with us for the time being. If she's underground, I'll have her work with the Intel guys in the morning, but just have Doc check her out. Squad barracks is in that house." I nodded and saluted before leading Jessica towards the barracks.

"That was my commander, Captain Hiller," I told her, "He's got to be the best officer around."

"That's saying a lot for an officer," she responded. I gave her a confusing look. "Oh, my father was a soldier and he used to talk a lot about officers."

I nodded in agreement. "Yeah, my father was a soldier too, just like my grandfather."

"So military service is a family tradition?" Jessica asked as we approached the barracks.

I shrugged, "Yeah, I guess so."

We walked into the house, which was rather large and met Vic at the door, a cigarette in his hand. He gave me a head nod and paid no attention to Jessica, instead focusing on his chain smoking. Inside, Nate and Adam were fast asleep in the open living room, both taking the only two couches. Ramos dropped his pack next to an armchair by the roaring fireplace and sat down, sighing deeply. Jay moved to the kitchen and placed his rifle on the table, removing his cleaning kit to do repairs. I walked through the living room to a small dining room and removed my heavy pack and equipment, setting it all down on the table.

"Are you hungry?" I asked Jessica, placing my helmet next to my pack.

"A little bit, yes," she said.

I nodded and pulled out my C rations, opening a can of Spam and handing it to her. "Taste wasn't a big need when they made these."

Jessica sat down and grabbed on of the metal forks from my mess kit. "It's okay, food is food, right?" She asked.

"Civilian food, yes, but not Army," I said. She carefully scooped up a spoon full of the meat and took a cautious bite. Her face said it all.

"Ah, I understand," she said. "But I don't want to starve."

"Me either," I said, pulling out a metal can filled with stale crackers. "Spam on crackers isn't that bad."

Jessica nodded and took a handful of crackers, using them to eat the unsavory Spam. We ate in silence at first, she seemed to be lost in thought while I fought the urge to stare. Jessica was undeniable beautiful, that was a fact, but I felt thinking about her like that after she was nearly killed seemed…out of place.

"Corr, you're leering," she said.

"What? Oh, sorry, I didn't mean to…"I stammered.

She waved off my apology. "It's alright, I was joking."

I grinned and nodded my head. "Yeah…so you're with the Resistance? That's what, the third time I asked?" Jessica nodded, placing the can of food on the table.

"Since Paris fell," she answered.

"Must be an interesting…way to serve. Sorry, I don't know how to put it. I guess it's different from what I do as a soldier somewhat." I said.

"Sort off," Jessica explained, "I don't handle taking out commanders and such, like some others do. While I'm good with a rifle or pistol, I've always helped in sabotage missions."

I nodded and pulled out my canteen, taking a drink and then offering it to her. "You have family around here?"

She took the canteen. "No, not around here, my mother and sister live farther away. My mother is from around here though, she grew up in Caen," Jessica explained.

Something about her was so familiar, like we've met before. "Have you ever been to the States?" I asked.

"No, never left Europe, why?" Jessica asked.

"Oh, you just look so familiar, like I've met you before," I said, sounding like an idiot.

Jessica shrugged. "I cannot tell you how many airmen have said that me."

I laughed, thinking of Matt for a second. "Yeah, that's definitely an American pickup line."

"So tell me, where are you from, Corr?" She asked.

"I'm from Bayonne, New Jersey; I doubt you've heard of it," I said.

"No, not Bayonne in New Jersey, but I've been to the Bayonne in France. Very nice place, I must say."

I leaned back in my seat and let out an exhausted sigh.

"You look very tired," she said.

"Yeah, it's been one hell of day. I should probably get some sleep," I sighed.

Jessica nodded and stood up. "Get some sleep then, I'm going to see if I can clean up a bit."

I nodded my head and leaned back even more until the chair touched the wall. I propped my feet up on the table and let my head rest against my chest. Exhaustion was slowly creeping up on me and I let it wash over me. Soon, the effects of adrenaline withdrawal took over and I was fast asleep.

"Sarge? Sarge!" Ramos shoved my feet off the table and woke me, my heart suddenly racing.

"Shit," I cursed, looking up at Ramos, "trying to give me a heart attack?"

"Nope, just getting your lazy ass up," he said with a grin. "C'mon, we're rolling out."

"Right," I said, moving to my feet and collecting my gear. "Where's Jessica?"

Ramos shrugged. "Probably changing, the Captain gave her one of his spare uniforms."

I nodded and tossed my heavy pack over my shoulders. The weight pulled at my sore shoulders, but I blocked out the pain as I grabbed my helmet and Thompson. Nate and Adam were collecting their equipment, Jay was checking his rifle. I moved past them and walked outside, the morning sun nearly blinded me. Captain Hiller stood with

Lieutenant Hanes across the street, map in hand and a grim look on his face.

"Problems sir?" I asked, placing on my helmet.

"'Problems' is a mild way to put it," Hanes snorted, shaking his head.

"Philips is an incompetent bastard," Hiller grunted, handing me the map. "We're heading up Route N4 with the tanks to push the line forward and link up with some boys in the 82nd that were way off course during the drops. Right now, they're held up in Surrain and we're going in to relieve them."

"Take a look at Route N4," Hanes insisted, pointing on the map.

I held up the map and studied Route N4 as well as the surrounding area. "It's an open route with fields on both sides of the road with thick tree line behind them," I said, cursing in my mind.

"Yeah and if the Krauts have any sense, they'll hit us on the road," Hiller sighed. "They have perfect positions to hit us on the open road while they're concealed in the tree line."

"Philips may be an idiot, but even he has to see…" I tried.

Hiller stopped me. "With the prisoner to give to the Brass, he's trying to grab as much fame as possible to make general. He hopes that if he reaches the 82nd in Surrain quickly enough, he'll get the eagles to replace the cluster on his uniform."

"Fucker," Ramos whispered under his breath.

"Alright, bitching isn't gonna help, so let's get moving." Hiller nodded towards the column of idle tanks down the road.

I nodded, and stood by the barracks, counting off each member of the squad. Once everyone was accounted for, I waited an extra minute to see Jessica, but I had to get going, so I gave up and began walking towards the tanks, when Jessica appeared from the house.

"Hey, I thought I was going to miss you," I said, working to use the right words in French.

"Sorry, I was trying to change quickly." She said, and was now wearing a pair of olive drab combat pants with an olive t-shirt, her hair pulled back in a tight ponytail.

"It's alright, I just wanted to say goodbye before I left," I said.

Jessica smiled and shook her head. "Goodbye? No, I'll be going to Surrain with you to meet my contact and help with your intelligence gathering."

I tilted my head in confusion. "You're going with us, as in, on the tanks?"

She nodded. "I am a Resistance fighter and your Captain said he'd keep me safe."

"Well, I'll keep you safe too," the words came out rushed and fumbled, making look foolish. Jessica just laughed it off with a grin.

"I feel safer already," she joked, walking towards the tanks. "You coming, Sergeant?"

"Yeah," I said, shrugging off the news. "Right behind you."

"Anyone have the feeling we're being watched?" Ramos asked, as the convoy of tanks snaked its way down Route N4.

"We probably are," Hiller grunted, sitting next to the top turret hatch and the mounted.50cal machine gun.

I silently nodded and looked to Jessica, who sat behind Hiller over the engine compartment. She sat with her head swiveling from one side of the road to the other, a German MP-40 in her lap. I sat on the front of the tank, just near the front hatch with my Thompson in my lap and my eyes watching the forest. We'd been on the road for little under an hour and so far things were quiet. Now and again, I could see movement in the woods, but it was quick and I could never really make out what I was seeing.

The weather was far better then it was on D-Day, the sky was clear and the sun was out. A light breeze blew across the road, that was relaxing to feel, but it was all a smokescreen. The Germans were out there, somewhere in the woods, but it was not smart to stop and investigate. Instead, the convoy rolled on at an even pace, the men on the tanks keeping a vigil watch for the enemy. Overhead, pairs of P-47 Thunderbolts shot by, drifting over the countryside in hunt for anything German on the roads.

"We're walking into a trap," Jessica called from the rear of the tank.

"That's why when I tell you to get off the tank," Hiller said calmly, "you get off the tank. Stick to the ditches on the side of the road and stay clear of the tanks no matter what, they'll turn into bullet magnets."

The hatch next to Hiller popped open, a Lieutenant sticking his head out. "Hey," he complained, "I can here you."

"So you're not deaf, Harrison," Hiller snorted. "Want a medal?"

"No," Harrison answered, "I would like you and your friends off my tank."

"Uncle Sam's tank," Hiller corrected.

"Sure," Harrison paused as he listened to the tank radio. "Lead tank just reported movement in the woods, both sides."

"You know the drill. Good luck, Harrison," Hiller said.

The tanker nodded his head and dropped back in the turret, sealing the hatch. Hiller swung the heavy machine gun around and yanked back on the cocking hammer, creating a metallic ping. I flicked off the safety on my Thompson and looked to Jessica, who held her MP-40 at the ready. I was about to call out when the tank in front of us erupted in a ball of flame, with a roaring explosion. The men onboard were flung into the air like toys, as the tank rolled to a stop.

"Get off the tanks!" Hiller ordered, abandoning the machine gun.

I leapt to the ground from the tank, moving for the gulley, to the left of the road. A second tank was hit and gutted as I dropped into the gulley, moving next to Ramos and Jessica. Machine gun fire soon erupted from both sides of the road, the Germans held up in both tree lines. Tanks up and down the line were gutted by indiscriminate AT fire and the men aboard were gunned down as they ran for cover. I pressed myself to the bottom of the gulley as MG fire shot in from all directions and mortars landed up and down the road. The Sherman Tanks returned fire, but the medium tanks failed to acquire targets in the thick woods. Instead, they struggled to fight back on the open road.

"We need to silence those guns!" Hiller yelled, crouching down with us.

"There are at least twelve Pak 30's in the tree line," Jessica called, gesturing to the woods, to the left of the road. "Maybe more in the other!"

"Not to mention MGs, snipers, and tank hunter-killer squads!" I yelled, my ears ringing.

"Okay, I'm taking Hanes and regrouping the squads to attack the right tree line," Hiller said, looking down the line. "Bolger, take the squad and hit the left line!"

I nodded as Hiller left with Hanes, running to the opposite side of the road. I rolled to my stomach and studied the tree line. The German's were well hidden in the trees, but I could see soldiers moving in between the nearest two guns. The land between them was wide open with no cover and was being watched by snipers.

"Orders Sarge?" Ramos called, waiting alongside the rest of the squad.

"Okay," I said, the plan forming in my mind, "we need to get in the trees and fight the Germans close up. Pop smoke grenades on the open ground and wait for the screen to form. Once the smoke builds, charge across the open ground and hit them hard."

"It'll be tight quarters over there," Jay pointed out, gesturing to the sniper rifle in his hands.

"Hang back and see what you can do with Captain Hiller. Move to the other gulley and provide sniper cover." Jay nodded and ran out of the gulley for the opposite side. As he disappeared behind the Sherman Tank and I turned to the squad, preparing the issue, one of the most difficult orders, to issue.

"Fix bayonets!" I ordered, unflinching in my order.

The squad understood and those armed with rifles pulled out the large combat knifes and slammed them into position one the barrels of their rifles with a click. Once everyone was ready, I pulled out a red smoke grenade and looked to Ramos and Nate. They understood and pulled out red smoke grenades. With a head nod, the three off us pulled the pins and sent the cylinder grenades into the air. They dropped down in the field and began to billow a fine, red smoke.

"Wait for it to build!" I commanded, seeing the rookies' edge towards the edge of the gulley. The smoke from the three grenades began to build into a thick, red screen that the German gunners could see through. Not knowing exactly what to say, I thought back to the old war movies. "Charge!"

I vaulted over the side of the gulley and rushed forward, at full speed, Thompson held tight to my shoulder. At first, I began to worry no one was behind me, that they stayed in the gulley, but I glanced back to see Jessica no more then two feet behind me with Ramos and Nate on her flank. Edwards was on the left with the rookies following him. Adam was brining up the rear with Vic and Doc. Once we passed into the thick envelope of red smoke, visibility was cut down to a few inches around me and I lost sight of the others. It didn't matter, I knew the directions the Germans were in and I knew my squad was around me, nothing else was needed.

Quickly, I approached the edge of the smoke screen, seeing the trees mixed in with the red. Something moved between two trees and I fired, the figure dropping to the ground. Another figured appeared as I spotted the first AT gun. It was set behind several trees with camouflage netting around it, but I could see several Germans manning the gun. I sprayed the rear of the gun with the rest of my clip and stopped behind a tree, dropping the empty clip and slapping a fresh one in place.

A German, screaming some war cry, appeared from the trees and rushed me, bayonet attached to his rifle. I dropped low as he fired, the bullet impacting the tree trunk. Since he carried a bolt action rifle, he had to manually empty the spent cartridge. I took the lapse in fire and dispatched him with a burst to the chest. Another yell from behind forced me to spin around in time to see a German soldier fall to my feet, Jessica a few feet away aiming her MP-40 my way. I nodded my head and rushed towards the next AT gun.

Vic crouched behind a fallen tree and leveled his BAR, firing the heavy weapon on the exposed gun crew. I pressed against a tree and sent a grenade towards the gun, moving past Vic and heading for the next gun. I rounded a stand of trees and spotted Edwards struggling with a German soldier, both fighting over control for Edward's M1

Garand Rifle. I aimed for the German, but the two were violently fighting and thrashing around, that I risked hitting Edwards. Instead, I slung my Thompson over my shoulder and drew my Colt.45, rushing over to Edwards' aid.

I moved up behind the German and grabbed him by the back of his uniform, yanking his head back. I raised my.45 and fired into the side of the German's head, dropping him instantly and freeing Edwards. He gave a thank you nod and retrieved his rifle, moving up for the next gun with alongside me.

The red smoke had hit the wind and was being blown into the woods, soon making it difficult to see. A German suddenly appeared to my right and rushed me, throwing his weight onto me. I whirled around, with my arm out like when you stiff arm a player in football and took the brunt of his weight, turning it against him. I raised my arm up and dropped my head down, the German rolling over my back and falling to the ground. I brought my Thompson and fired into his back.

Edwards rushed ahead and took the third gun on his own, killing the four man crew with one rifle clip. A soldier tried to stab him with a bayonet, but Edwards was quick and parried the block, rushing in with his own rifle and burying the bayonet in the man's stomach. He fell back under Edwards' force, Edwards' drawing out the bayonet and delivering several hard and powerful stabs to the man's chest and a final blow to the throat. When I got to his side, Edwards' was drawing out his bayonet with shaky hands.

"You or him," I said, seeing the horror and disgust in his eyes.

He nodded slowly and reloaded his rifle. "I'm gonna see my sister again."

"Then you have something to fight for, c'mon," I said.

The remaining four guns were farther down the road, near the front of the convoy. The rifle squads with the lead tanks were already clearing them out, so I had the squad double back and make sure each gun was spiked and see that every German was either dead or surrendering. I moved past the guns and scanned the woods, seeing a large hedgerow at the opposite end of the tree line. Several Germans were running for the field on the opposite side and I considered pursing them, but running into the hedgerows alone meant certain death.

"Don't," Jessica was at my side again, "they'll have men waiting."

I turned to her. "Are you okay?"

"I'm fine," her eyes moved from mine to my shoulder. She suddenly slung her MP-40 over her shoulder and pressed her hands to my left shoulder. "Corr, you've been shot!"

"What," my eyes drifted down to my shoulder when I saw the dark stain. My hand moved over hers and I felt a sudden stab of pain, my fingers now covered in my crimson blood. "Oh, shit, I really…did not feel that."

Jessica shook her head as I handed her my medical kit. "You mean to tell me you didn't feel this?" She asked.

"I…nope," I admitted, not remembering or feeling the shot. "All that adrenaline in my blood must have blocked it out."

"Well, you're blood's spilling out," she said, pressing a thick bandage to the wound.

I took the bandage from her hands and held it tight. "C'mon, let's get back to the squad."

I held my Thompson in my left hand, my right, holding the bandage against my wounded shoulder. The red smoke had blown away, the last bits of the screen slowly drifting away in the wind, revealing the remnants of the tank column. The red smoke was swapped out by the black smoke of burning fuel, the bright morning sky seeming to get darker. Dozens of tanks were sitting on the road with flame burning all around, the turrets and sides ripped open with the men riding aboard dead around them. Several Sherman Tanks managed to survive the attack, but most were paralyzed on the sides of the road. I spotted Captain Hiller near one of the remaining tanks with Adam, the two working on the field radio. Doc was a few feet away treating wounded men, so I walked over to him and sat down on the grass.

"I see you got a paper cut," Doc snorted, tying off the bandage on a soldier's wrist.

"A German threw some papers in my face," I said, pulling back the bloodied bandage.

"Ah, looks like a shallow wound," Doc said, peering into the bullet wound. "The bullet's a few inches in, but I can get it out." He pulled a pair of forceps from his medical bag and washed it with a tiny bottle of alcohol. "Now, this might feel…unpleasant."

"Unpleasant?" I asked as he placed the forceps into my shoulder. Pain shot out like lighting, forcing my left arm to go rigid. With a twist and a wet pop, the flattened pistol round was pulled free.

"Okay, now let's clean this up and slap a band aide on." He pulled out a sulfur packet, tore it open with his teeth, and dumped the powder on my wound. Next, he pulled out a clean bandage and placed it over the wound, tying it on under my uniform shirt.

"Do I need to head to a aide station?" I asked, feeling the pain.

"Well, the wound's small, so it'll heal on its own, but some stitches will help it heal faster," Doc said.

"Then I guess it's the slow healing process," I sighed, moving back to my feet and taking my Thompson in my right hand.

"Then get going, I've got patients to see." Doc had his hands full with dozens of soldiers stumbling over to him, the section of the gully suddenly turning into an aide station.

"Corr, I'm going to help with the wounded," Jessica said, moving to assist Doc.

I nodded. "Okay, I need to check in." I turned and walked towards Captain Hiller standing by the tank, seeing a look of controlled anger on his face. It didn't take any though to figure out way.

"This is just fucking perfect," he cursed, looking down the road full of destroyed tanks and dead GIs. "What's the count?"

"Eighteen of the thirty tanks are knocked out," Hanes reported, voice low and almost shameful. "Of the remaining twelve tanks, seven are crippled and need repairs. Charlie Squad is gone and Gamma is down to eight men. I took a head count and our squad is all a counted for. Easy is down four and Lima is down one man."

Hiller swore under his breath and rubbed the bridge of his nose. "Have we made contact with the 82nd?"

"No, sir," Adam responded, shaking his head slightly. "I can't get anything from the 82nd or even our boys back in Fitts."

"So we're isolated on this road with heavy casualties with no contact with Division or the 82nd," Hiller summarized. "Okay Hanes, talk with Doc and let's get the wounded into the tree line just encase the Germans come back. Adam, keep trying the radio and let me know if can get through. Bolger, take two guys and scout the road up ahead to see if you find any Kraut armor or scouts from the 82nd."

"Yes sir," I responded, already knowing who I would take. I turned on my heel and grabbed Ramos and Jay, both standing by the gully on the side of the road. I filled them in and led them down the road, walking just off the road to avoid the gasoline that had spilled and was still burning. Dead soldiers lay alongside the burning tanks, the bodies peppered with shrapnel and bullets. The pungent smell of charred flesh and gasoline hung heavy in the air alongside cordite and burning metal.

"The Germans took one big bite out of us," Ramos commented, looking over the remains of the lead tank. "All in what, five, ten minutes?"

"All we need is to get out of the hedgerows," I said. "Once we clear this hell hole, we'll kick the Germans back across the Rhine."

"And then cross over and take Berlin," Jay snorted.

I nodded and led the way down the clear roadway. The road was wide open for another mile or so before the hedgerows returned. The road to Surrain was just off the main route, weaving through the hedgerows all the way to the town. The three of us turned off the main road and began to cautiously scout out the dirt road, moving on a single file line by the hedgerow, with a three meter spread. I took the lead with Jay behind me and Ramos taking up the rear.

The air was still and silent as we walked, the overlapping canopy of trees now blocking out the majority of the sunlight. I could hear my heart pulsing in my chest, the throbbing in my shoulder matching it beat for beat. The pain was still there as the muscles in my shoulder stiffened from the trauma, but I fought it by constantly flexing the muscles to prevent them from locking up completely. It hurt like hell, but I had gotten off lucky when compared to the men that lay dead in the fields. A rustle of leaves ahead suddenly grabbed my attention and I dropped into a crouch, my left hand held up to signal a stop.

Jay and Ramos dropped down quickly at the signal, weapons up and scanning for targets. I kept my Thompson down at my hip and scanned the winding road until it came to a T intersection, a dozen,or so, yards down. The light rustle of leaves could be heard nearby mixed in with the low hum of voices. They were very close, based on the noise, and I soon realized they might even be on the opposite side of the hedgerow. I turned to Jay and Ramos and signaled them to stay put. I slid my Thompson over my shoulder, turning to face the hedgerow. Slowly and carefully, I began to scale the solid mount of dirt, rock, and grass until I was near the top. I stopped a mere two inches from the top and strained to listen for more noise.

I could here voices on the opposite side, though I could not make out words or even if they were German or American. After some personal arguing, I swung my Thompson off my shoulder and into my right hand. Pulling with my left, I vaulted over the top of the hedgerow and came crashing down on the men on the opposite side. I landed on two men, the three of us struggling to bring our weapons to bear. When I heard cursing in English, I pushed away and rolled on the grass, moving to get a better view of the soldiers.

"Hold your fire!" one of the men ordered, lowering his M1.

"Christ," another said, cursing under his breath, "What kind of shit move was that?"

"All balls, no brains," I said, lifting myself to my feet. I looked at the group of four soldiers, who wearing the double A patch of the 82nd Airborne Division.

"Fucking infantry," a lance corporal spat, shaking his head.

"Shut it, Franklin," the sergeant commanded, helping me to my feet. "Sergeant Jeffery Smith, 82nd Airborne."

"Sergeant Corrigan Bolger, First Infantry," I said, shaking Smith's hand. "Jay, Ramos, get over here." Jay and Ramos quickly scaled the hedgerow and dropped down on opposite side.

Smith looked them over and turned back to me. "So, you boys must be the link up force?"

"We are, but our combat group was ambushed on the road and now we're scrambling to get reorganized," I said.

"Fuck," Lance Corporal Franklin moaned, shaking his head.

"What Franklin means," Smith explained, "is that the Germans have a group of Tiger Tanks in the area with Fallschirmjager support, maybe four squads. They're heavily armed and well trained sons of bitches that have been trying to retake Surrain since last night. We only have two full sticks of soldiers, with a few stragglers to hold the line, and we need tank support."

"Well, we were coming to link up with thirty tanks, but the Germans ambushed us on the road. Most of the tanks were knocked, with two of our rifle squads, and the group it stalled out on the road."

"Wonderful," Smith sighed and looked back to his three men. "Where is your squad?"

"Stalled out on Route 3," I answered.

"The Tigers are going to attack them once the ambush force reports or fails to report in." Smith turned and said something to his men. They nodded and quickly ran back down the hedgerow until they crossed onto the road.

"What's the plan?" I asked.

"I sent them back to prepare the rest of the boys to brace for the next attack. While Major Spencer would like to send help, we're barely holding off the Krauts. You're best hope is to get back to your squad and warn them," he said.

"Well, our captain moved everyone off the road, but we need to warn them. You mind coming with us to brief our commander?" I asked.

Smith nodded. "Lead the…wait," he held up a hand. "You hear that?"

I nodded, dropping to the ground as the sound of tank treads grinding against the dirt echoed through the hedgerows. The four of us hugged the hedgerow and listened to the sound, the tanks were getting closer. Smith looked to me and gestured to the top of the hedgerow. I nodded and climbed up alongside him, taking the risk to peer over the side.

The sight sent a chill down my spine. Six of the massive, heavily armored Tiger Tanks crawled down the road, just inches from our position. Several squads of the elite *Fallschirmjager*, or German paratroopers, marched with them. The troopers were highly trained, well armed, and had skilled officers that were veterans from the Eastern Front. During our briefings we were warned about them, being told that a single rifle squad carried several light and heavy machine guns with a variety of anti tank weapons. Compared to the Wehrmacht units, they were the elite of the German infantry, next to the Waffen SS.

The squads were smart, walking the wake of the Tigers with one squad taking the lead ahead of the tanks. They stayed spread out to avoid high losses from an arty attack, but still stayed close to the tanks for cover. These men were carrying a dozen or so MG42s with six 8mm mortars, eight panzerfaust, and a dozen MP-40s and FG42s. Alongside the massive Tigers, they were a force to be feared.

Smith and I carefully climbed down and began to move parallel to the road behind the hedgerow, moving silently to avoid detection. The deep rumble of the Tiger engines muffled out our light footfalls, but we moved with caution, not to take the risk of being detected. I hadn't figured out what the plan was, but we would shadow the force until we reached the edge of the hedgerow. From there it would be a matter of field hopping until we regrouped with the convoy, hopefully before the Germans reached them.

As I came up to the end of the hedgerow, there was a small opening onto the road, just large enough to fit one man at a time. I stopped near the opening and dropped to one knee, listening to the rumble of the engines when I heard a low, hard pop. The Tigers came to a stop with a metallic grunt, the infantry stopping alongside.

"We've blown a fan belt!" someone yelled in German.

"God damn it!" another man yelled in German. "Fix the thing and be quick, you've stalled the entire group! Grits, take first squad and secure the crossing up head. The rest of you, fan out and set up a security screen!"

I turned back to Smith and moved within inches of his ear, voice in a low whisper. "They're stalled out, now's our chance."

Smith nodded and pointed to the hedgerow, across from ours, gesturing to climb over it. I nodded and the four of us quickly ran and climbed over, dropping onto the soft road. From there, we proceeded down the road until we came back, to the turn off to the main road. I led us back to the remains of our tank convoy and moved for the tree line where Captain Hiller waited. He'd moved everyone into the trees with the tanks rolling as far back in as possible.

"Bolger, I see you made contact," he said, nodding towards Sergeant Smith.

"I did sir," I responded, "but the news isn't good."

Hiller cursed under his breath. "Fill me in."

"The Germans have Tigers," Smith said, stepping forward. "Along with Fallschirmjager support, they have one hell of a fighting force. We've been struggling to keep Surrain with the constant attacks and we can't send any groups out to meet a link up force. Hell, they can barely afford to send me and two men out, but we needed to make contact. We're low on ammo and supplies with the Germans breathing down out necks. It's just a matter of time till the Germans knock us out of the town."

Hanes cursed and looked over his shoulder. "We've got five working tanks and two rifle squads; maybe we should form up in a group and rush to Surrain."

"The Germans are advancing on the route," I said, shaking my head. "If we go to Surrain, they'll pick us off before we reach the outskirts."

"Well if we sit here, they'll get us," Hiller pointed out, reaching for the folded map in his jacket. "Let's hope there's an alternative route."

"Nothing big enough to fit tanks," Smith pointed out.

"That's not entirely true," Jessica said in French, appearing from behind Hiller.

"What'd she say?" Smith asked, tilting his head slightly.

"I know of an irrigation ditch that runs through the hedgerows," she explained, gesturing to the map in Hiller's hands.

"Jessica knows of another route to get to Surrain," I interpreted.

Hiller handed her the map. "Where?" he asked.

Jessica took the map and quickly studied it. "Here is the irrigation ditch that runs parallel to the road with thick hedgerows on either side which provide cover from the road. If you move your tanks through here, you'll reach Surrain without running into the Germans.

I translated to the Captain and then repeated his questions. "How do you know the Germans haven't found the route?"

"The Underground has used the route to help commando units move without hitting German patrols before the landings. The Germans hadn't found it last time we used it, maybe two-three days ago," Jessica said.

I translated again, this time putting in my thoughts. "It seems like the only option, sir," I said.

"It's a long shot," Smith pointed out, "but that's what the 82nd works on, long shots."

Hiller nodded. "Well, a risk is better then sitting here. Hanes, pack everyone up and get those Sherman tanks rolling. Bolger, take Jessica and lead the group down the path once everyone is ready. Smith, you'll need to get me to your CO once we reach Surrain."

"Yes sir," the three of us responded before Hanes and I moved to carry out our orders. I led Jessica back to the road and unfolded the map, spreading it out on the side of a burnt out tank.

"Okay," I said, peering at the map. "Show me where we enter the ditch."

"Well, the entrance is just past the tree line here," she pointed to the tree line two miles down the road. "You'll have to leave the main road here and then continue on through a gap in the trees. Just follow the gap and it opens up to the ditch. The ditch runs all the way to the small creek, south of Surrain." Jessica explained.

"And you're sure we'll get by the Germans?" I asked.

"If we reach the ditch before they hit the main road, yes," She said.," The ditch runs between the hedgerows with the nearest road a half a mile away, so we won't hit a German patrol."

I nodded to myself and refolded the map. "Good, all that's left is to get underway before the Tigers arrive."

Lieutenant Hanes quickly organized the tanks and rifle squads, forming a new combat group. The wounded were placed aboard the working five tanks with the rifle squads walking close by for support. The crippled tanks were abandoned, their crews given weapons and ammo from the dead before joining the rifle squads. The abandoned tanks were cleaned of spare ammo, passed on to the five running Sherman tanks, with the gas siphoned off and loaded into jerry cans. Once they were picked clean, engineers sabotaged the engines. This would prevent the enemy from using them, but they could still be picked up by the engineers and refitted for combat duty.

Once everyone and everything was sorted, Hiller dispatched new orders. The orders were simple, get to the ditch before the Germans arrived, reach Surrain in time, and then hold out for the rest of the First to catch up. No one had questions and we were quickly underway, moving down the road as quick as we could on foot. I marched alongside the lead tank with the Captain, Smith, and Jessica.

"Strange how we didn't see this route," Smith said as we walked, map in hand.

I translated this to Jessica.

"Well, the trees in the hedgcrows overlap, blocking out overhead view," Jessica explained, MP-40 held tight in her hands. "It's a natural cammo netting your recon photos can miss, which is why the Germans never found it."

"Well, the Luftwaffe isn't what it used to be," Ramos said, beaming with pride.

"Yes, God bless the flyboys…for once," Nate snorted, suppressing a grin.

"Do they mean the *Jabos*?" Jessica asked, using the German slang.

"*Jabos*?" I repeated, struggling to figure out the correct German word. "Oh, you mean Jager Bomber."

"Hey, mind speaking English?" Ramos asked, overhearing the two of us.

"She's asking if we mean the Jabos, which is German slang for hunter-bomber. I'm guessing she means the Thunderbolts."

"*Jabos?*" Ramos repeated, testing the new word. "Hmm, seems to fit. *Jabos,* I like it."

"The turn off is up ahead," Hiller announced, studying the route Jessica pointed out. "A few more yards."

Jessica scanned the road ahead and pointed off to the right, near a section of trees that looked like any other stand of trees. Hiller turned the tanks off the road and we proceed to the trees, still not seeing this irrigation ditch. When we approached the trees, Jessica moved ahead of us and began pulling on the tree branches, tossing them aside. Soon, a wide open passage appeared in the trees, revealing a shallow ditch that ran in between two dominating hedgerows.

"Now that's interesting," Nate sighed, seeing the hidden route.

"Well, let's keep going, move out!" Hiller waved us in, sending our squad in first with the tanks rolling behind us, the other squads in a single file line. Once everyone was in, Jessica covered the path up and the entrance was gone, the view of the road obscured.

"Spooky," Adam grunted as we started down the ditch, the wet soil squishing under our boots.

"Feels like we're walking in liquid shit," Vic grunted in a low tone.

"Thanks for the visual," Ramos responded.

"Everyone," Hiller hissed, "keep it down."

I walked on silently with my Thompson held close to my chest. Very little light drifted down from the thick jumble of overhead trees. The massive trees reach up and over the sunken road, the branches interlocking like fingers. The air was thick with water vapor, a thin fog could be seen just a few inches over the mud. The lumbering Sherman Tanks slowly churned through mud with the rumble of their engines creating a deep, grumbling hum.

I kept ready and alert, eyes darting from the tops of the hedgerows to the road beyond, senses scanning for anything out of the ordinary. The smell of cordite was heavy in the air, the odor of some battle nearby, though I heard no weapon or artillery fire. Smith picked up on the odor and shook his head.

"I think they're hitting Surrain again," he said, taking in a deep breath. "Definitely using Tigers."

"How can you be sure?" Ramos asked.

"You can smell cordite in the air, right?" Smith asked, glancing over his shoulder.

"Yeah, it's very sulfur like," he said.

Smith nodded "Well, the Tigers use a high explosive charge in their shells when engaging infantry in cover. When the stuff it fires leaves a very copper like smell behind that is hard to pick up, but once you've been under long shelling by them, you pick it up."

"How have you managed to hold back Tigers?" I asked knowing paratroopers jumped with light equipment.

"Well, when we landed, we'd lost most of our equipment. A few guys managed to find one of our supply drops that held two recoilless rifles with a bazooka. Since Surrain has tight roads, we held off the Tigers through knocking out two by trapping them and hitting with the rifles from the rear.

"After the first two were popped, the Germans bombarded us from the countryside. We held off the infantry attacks, but the tanks have pounded us around the clock. It's down to a game of who can take the most shit without breaking. Hopefully, the Shermans can help," Smith explained.

"The exit is just up ahead," Jessica pointed out, grabbing my arm.

"Captain," I called, "the road's up ahead."

Hiller nodded. "Head up there and scout the road, make sure it's clear."

"Yes sir." I quickly jogged ahead of the main group, moving towards the turn onto the road.

It was quiet and still as I approached the roadway. The irrigation ditch ran under a small, stone bridge that passed alongside the hedgerows. I approached carefully with my Thompson at the ready, moving to the left side of the bridge. Slowly, I climbed up the short dirt embankment to the road, crouching down by the hedgerows to check the road in both directions. Finding it clear, I returned to the ditch and waved the rest of the group forward.

Captain Hiller moved on with the tanks to the bridge, checking the road for himself, just to make sure everything was clear. Satisfied, he watched as the Sherman tanks barely squeezed between the hedgerow and the bridge. Once the column was on the road, Smith took the lead and led us to Surrain.

Surrain was a bombed out shell when we arrived, the German artillery attacks nearly gutting the small town. The men of the 82nd turned that shell into a solid defensive position, establishing dug in fighting positions along the edges of the town, the paratroopers using the confined roads and hedgerows to their advantage. MG nests were built into the buildings lining the main roads, AT emplacements of captured German Pak 38s were hidden in burnt out buildings, and destroyed tanks and building debris clogged the major roadways.

"Oh, look who decided to show up!" one of the sentries called from behind a sandbag wall, seeing Smith leading our group.

"Hey, I brought friends," Smith called back, walking up the sentries.

"About time, Major Spencer is waiting in the church. Have the tanks head in with you guys, but they'll have to snake their way through the debris field," said the sentry.

"Hanes, take the tanks in with the squad. Bolger, come with me to the CP, bring Jessica with you," Hiller ordered, moving ahead of the tanks.

"C'mon," I said to Jessica, shrugging my shoulders towards the Captain. She nodded and the two of us followed close behind him, as the tanks and the squad made their way to the center of town.

The streets of Surrain were barren as we walked, not one French civilian to be seen. Paratroopers patrolled the streets now and again, moving from building to building, shuffling supplies. Outside, the streets were quiet and empty, shell craters and hollowed out buildings were the only reminder of what occurred no more then a day ago. The church was a different story.

Captain Hiller pulled open one of the massive wooden doors and moved inside with Jessica and myself following. Inside, the small church was converted into a CP and a field hospital for the men of the

82nd. The area around the doors was the newly built aide station, the pews filled with wounded men with medics tending to them. Ten dead soldiers lay against one of the far walls under a stone cross, the bodies covered with blankets.

"There were more," Smith pointed out, looking down at the fallen men. "We lost a transport plane belonging to our company during the drop to AA and then six or seven more taking Surrain. I'm not sure about losses since the last attack."

The church priest preformed last rights for the fallen before offering whatever aide he could to the wounded. Medics worked to keep the wounded alive, many working hard to make dwindling medical supplies last as long as possible

"Bolger," Hiller called, as we walked to the altar, "when we finish here, see if the squad can spare any medical supplies for the paratroopers."

"Just thinking the same, sir," I responded, pulling out one of my spare medical kits. It wasn't much, but medics had a knack making the most out of everything, so I handed it to one of the medics as we passed.

Major Spencer stood at the front of the church with his senior officers, all huddled around maps spread out on the altar. The Major was young, maybe a year or two older then me, but a West Point grad who knew to listen to the veteran men in his squad. He was reading the maps and shaking his head as we approached.

"So they'll overrun us by nightfall?" he asked, looking to his group of NCOs.

"If the landing forces don't linkup with us or air cover arrives, then yes," explained a Staff Sergeant.

"How are we on ammo and medical?" The Major asked.

"Roughly down to five or six shells between the captured guns," a sergeant reported. "The.30cals are almost dry and the captured 42's crapped out on us during the last attack. The recoilless rifles are all out and we have four Kraut launchers left. Medical's no better, Doc's says we're nearly out of bandages and the morphine is gone," Said the Staff Sergeant.

"Sir," Smith intervened, snapping a salute.

"About time you're back, Smith," Spencer growled. "Wait, are these the linkup forces?"

"The forward scouting elements," Hiller answered, saluting the Major. "Captain Hiller, First Army Division."

The Major nodded. "Damn good to see you, Hiller. Please tell me you've brought me support."

"We were sent out with a thirty tank column to make the linkup, but the Germans ambushed us on the way in. We're down to five working tanks and two and half rifle squads" Hiller said.

"Well, it's a lot better then what we had in the jump." He turned to the staff sergeant. "Reilly, get those tanks into defensive positions along the main roadway," The Major ordered.

"On it, sir," Reilly responded, collecting his gear and moving for the door.

The Major turned to Captain Hiller and said, "Captain, I'll need what ever supplies you can spare to help bolster the defenses and to have your men assist in fortifying our positions, no telling when the Germans will be back."

"Yes, sir," Hiller agreed. "Just tell us where."

"Ah," he looked over the maps, "Okay, we've secured the town for the most part. The last attack hit us hard along southern edge of town along a line of open fields. I've only got several foxholes and MG nests covering the area, so get your men there."

"Any idea when the next attack will be?" Smith asked.

"Not a clue, but I'm sure they'll hit us the hardest in the next strike. The Germans need this town back before the linkup can be made so they can form a defensive line. We hold the line and we hold open a route into the enemy lines."

Chapter 10

"You sure these will work?" Smith asked, watching me closely.

"Well," I grunted, struggling with the metal disk slightly, "these will slow the infantry in their tracks for sure. Our engineer says they have a good chance of knocking off tank treads too."

Smith shrugged and wiped some sweat from his forehead. "Is this the last one?"

"Yep," I answered, pushing some dirt over the mine. "C'mon, let's get back to the line."

Smith nodded and the two of us carefully maneuvered through the newly laid minefield, walking in our own footprints to reach the safety of our foxhole, at the edge of the field near the outlying buildings. Malks had already set down four other minefields around the town with the help of the remaining engineers, who have managed to survive the jump with some of their equipment. We had no anti-tank mines, but anything was better than nothing.

"So, what's left?" Smith asked, as we dropped into our foxhole.

"That's it," I answered, rolling onto my stomach. "We set the minefield, dug a few dozen foxholes, and helped shuffle ammo to the MG nests, we're done for now."

"Great, now we wait," I said, with a sarcastic grin.

I raised my binoculars to my eyes and scanned the open fields, down to the tree line. Lieutenant Hanes was out by the road with several of the men from the 82nd, working on building some simple tank traps. They built up low walls of stacked brick and stone from the building debris and lined them with our smaller mines. German troops would duck for cover behind them and set off the mines, or the tanks would rush over the mines detonating inside the treads.

"So, where are you from?" Smith asked, cleaning his carbine.

"Jersey," I responded, lowering the binoculars. "You?"

"The only place worse than Jersey, Iowa," Smith laughed.

I rolled to my back. "You're from Iowa?"

Smith grinned and nodded his head. "Yep, from a tiny farm in the middle of central nowhere. Dad wanted me to be a farmer, but I said hell no to that life. Instead, I became a paratrooper for the extra fifty dollars in pay, though money isn't a priority with me."

"Me either. Military service is a family thing, so I enlisted with my brothers," I said, as I thought about my brother, Frank.

"You married?" Smith asked, resembling his weapon.

"No, but I plan to. You married?" I asked.

Smith held up his right hand. "Going on two years next week, been married since I was nineteen. I'm guessing that nice French girl you came in with is…"

"She's not, I've only known her for less than a day," I said, trying to sound like I wasn't interested in Jessica.

Smith tilted his head. "You look at her like I look at my wife, kiddo. You'll figure it out soon enough."

I laughed. "Who the hell are you calling kiddo? You're a year older than me."

"Germans on approach!" Lieutenant Hanes yelled, running across the field and back to his foxhole. "Line of tanks and infantry coming up the road!"

I rolled back to my stomach and rose into a low crouch, Thompson held firm to my shoulder. Smith crouched next to me, carbine resting on the lip of the foxhole as he lined up grenades within easy reach for both of us. The other men, on our side of the line, began to do final checks on their equipment, as the rumble of Tiger Tanks began to echo down the dirt road.

"You ever face a Tiger?" Smith asked, picking up his carbine.

"No, but I've faced Panzers in Africa and Sicily," I said.

"They're pushovers compared to these behemoths. Side and rear armor is pretty thick, but a weak point, should you be manning a tank. Shoulder mounted rockets bounce off the thing like baseballs, even the treads are covered. The only thing is the Tiger is slow and prone to breakdowns, so if one gets close, go for the hatches, engine compartment, or the main gun. Grenades work fine, but be quick. The other tanks will hose down each other with MG fire if they spot you," Smith explained.

"An expert, huh?" I joked.

"Got to be, it's how we held during the night," Smith said, smugly.

The ground seemed to shake, as the tanks rumbled towards us, the loose dirt falling back into our foxhole. I remained in a low crouch, legs and arms locked into position, in both fear and courage, as the first tank appeared from the hedgerows. All steel and death, the massive Tiger followed the road and maneuvered to face us, the German paratroopers following behind the rolling cover.

The machine gun stationed, in the upper window of a nearby building, opened on the advancing group. Bullets streamed down from the rest of the men, all aiming for the lumbering tank, only to have the rounds bounce off the tank, like rain on a rock. I held firm, trigger finger resting against the guard, as I held fire not wanting to waste ammo. Smith did the same, laying prone in the dirt.

German MG fire peppered out position, as German paratroopers took potshots at us, from behind their Tiger. The Tiger's forward mounted MGs opened as well, covering, as the massive 88mm main gun pivoted in our direction. With a massive boom the 88 fired, blowing a huge chunk of the building behind us to dust, the MG team with it. One of the captured 38s fired on the Tiger's side armor, the anti-tank shell bouncing off the side plating.

Our minefield stood between the Germans and our positions, still undiscovered. Enemy paratroopers ran to the stone tank traps for cover, as the booby traps detonated, killing several. The remaining troopers stayed behind the single Tiger, as it ran over several mines, all detonating together and knocking off one of the treads.

"Pour it on!" Hanes screamed, seeing the tank roll to a stop.

I lowered my Thompson and grabbed one of the grenades Smith had set out, yanking out the pin and sending it over the tank. Smith and I laid down a barrage of grenades behind the tank, catching the

Germans under an impromptu mortar barrage. They scattered for cover, from our attack, one ran straight into our awaiting minefield. The unlucky men detonated our mines, explosions of heat and shrapnel lopping off feet and legs, as bodies were flung into the air like a children's' toys.

"Panthers bringing up the rear!" I yelled, seeing two of the slant armored tanks crawl up the road.

"They'll run past us and get into the town," Smith hissed, ducking, as tank shells screeched overhead.

"What?" I asked, not understanding.

"The Panthers!" Smith yelled. "They're running past us and are leaving the infantry to wipe up!"

German screaming brought me back to real time, seeing several enemy paratroopers rush our foxhole. Smith and I quickly dispatched them with controlled shots, when a Panther rushed our way. Its machine gun peppered our position as it closed in. Seeing it would not stop, I grabbed Smith by his webbing and threw him to the bottom of the foxhole, lying next to him. The massive Panther drove right over our foxhole without slowing; its metal bottom passing mere inches from our bodies.

"Where are your tanks?" Smith demanded after the Panther passed.

I turned to look for one of our Sherman tanks when one suddenly dashed out from an alley behind our position. The medium tank fired point-blank into the Panther, with the shell bouncing off the frontal armor. The Panther fired back as the Sherman shot by, missing the shell by a fraction of second. Undeterred, our Sherman circled around and fired into the Panther's engine compartment. With one lucky shot, the engine exploded in a ball of fire, lighting off the fuel and stored ammo, which promptly blew the turret from the tank.

Seeing the other Panther and Tiger, the little Sherman darted back down a side street for cover. The remaining Panther gave chase to the running Sherman and turned down the tiny street, rushing forward without realizing the road quickly narrowed. Oversized and bulky, the Panther wedged itself in place against the sides of the buildings, stone and brink tumbling onto it,as the crew struggled to back up.

Our Sherman reappeared, swinging around to blast the Panther in its engine compartment. This time, however, the Sherman fired two shots before the Tiger split the tank in half with a single, 88mm shell. In a flash, the tank and her crew were incinerated, its shattered remains suddenly stopping and burning with ferocious flame.

"Now's our chance!" Smith yelled, yanking me up. "Cover me!"

I nodded and fired clip after clip of ammo at the Germans while Smith leapt from our foxhole and rushed for the trapped Panther tank, a satchel of C4 swinging under his arm. With the courage and devotion seen, not only in the 82nd, but in all soldiers, Smith ran through a hail of bullets and shrapnel to reach the enemy tank. Dodging the hellish firestorm, he leapt onto the smoking rear of the tank, climbing onto of the turret.

With his pistol in hand and the satchel in the other, he yanked open the turret hatch and fired several rounds before throwing in the satchel, its fuse burning. Quickly, smith slammed the hatch close and threw himself to the ground, landing on his feet, as he raced back to our foxhole. Soon, the satchel charge detonated, blowing the top section of the turret into the air, killing the metal monster.

"Ballsy move," I said with a grin, dropping down to reload.

"All in, balls out," Smith grunted, swinging around his carbine, "the only way to live."

"Well, we got one Tiger left." Smith studied the field, grabbing another satchel charge and a smoke grenade.

"This one is all you, okay?" Smith said.

I nodded, taking the satchel. "Try not to shoot me."

"Just run like hell when I pop smoke. Ready?" He yelled.

I nodded, swinging the satchel over my shoulder. Smith griped the grenade, yanking out the pin and tossing it overhand, in front of the tank. I watched the smoke build until a sudden burst of energy, in my legs, propelled me forward.

Without realizing it, I was running at full speed across the field, skirting the minefield and running in a curved path to the Tiger. The thick, white smoke from the grenade swelling in the air, provided a protective screen from enemy fire. Still, I could see the boxy outline of the Tiger Tank in the road.

Heart pumping and pulse racing, I slid to the side of the massive tank, using a blind spot in the gunner's field of vision to prime the C4 charge. With the hiss of the fuse, I had twelve seconds, give or take, to plant it before it blew me to hell. Forcefully, I climbed aboard the tank and ducked behind the turret, placing it between me and the German infantry. I threw open the metal turret hatch, while still holding my Thompson, tossing in the satchel with my other hand. I slammed the hatch back into place and threw myself off the tank.

I landed in the dirt on my chest, the air rushing from my lungs. I gulped for air and rose back to my feet, running on pure adrenaline and fear. Bullets bombarded the dirt,at my feet, and zipped through the air, passing me by mere inches. Smith waved me back to the foxhole, still providing covering fire. I launched myself through the air and came crashing down in the foxhole as the satchel detonated.

I rolled onto my back just in time to see the Tiger Tank's turret rupture outward, the steel plates bending like tree branches in the wind. Smoke and flame shot out, as the ammo and fuel kicked off, the explosions were a death rattle, from the deadly behemoth. The German infantry, now without tank support, began tactically retreating, disappearing into the woods and hedgerows like phantoms.

"Shit, that was fucking stupid," Smith grunted, looking down at me, sprawled at the bottom of the foxhole.

"Then I'm fucking stupid," I mumbled, Smith pulling me to my feet.

Smith grinned when I saw a private from the 82nd running towards our foxhole, face flushed white. "We got wounded!" he yelled, grunting in exhaustion. "I need men to bring them to the church!"

The two of us didn't hesitate. "Where?" we asked together.

The solider shrugged his shoulders. "Look around."

I climbed out of the foxhole and scanned the line, looking for the nearest man I could help. Smith and I didn't have to look far, the wounded littered the field and foxholes, those that could, moaning in pain and agony, for help. The two medics, with our part of the line, were moving frantically, hoping from man to man, to provide what aide they could before moving on.

I spotted two men in the next foxhole over, barely moving, one waving his hand to get someone's attention. Smith and I ran to their aide, finding my stomach tighten and burn at the sight; the two men were laying in pools of their own blood, one with his left arm completely torn off and the other with his stomach ripped open. Both were barely alive, the man with the missing arm fought us.

"Take…care," the Lieutenant struggled to say, "of Gavin…first."

"We're taking care of both of you," I said, grabbing my aid kit.

"Gavin's a kid, help him!" the Lieutenant argued, holding the bloody stump of an arm with his right hand.

"Take the kid," Smith ordered, "I'll help Herb." He turned to the Lieutenant. "You're not gonna give me shit are ya?"

"Just because I have one arm? No fucking way," Herb grunted through clenched teeth.

I turned to the other wounded trooper and did my best to treat his wounds in some way. The mash of intestine, stomach, and blood was horrifying to see, and I came close to throwing up, as I struggled to place a thick bandage over the wound, trying to figure out the best way to stop the bleeding,or at least, hold his torn stomach in his body.

"Just press tight," Smith said tying Herb's arm off with a pressure bandage.

I mumbled a 'yeah' to myself and pressed the bandage into the bloodied mess that was the man's stomach, the blood quickly soaking through the bandage and covering my hands. Cursing, I tied the bandage down and retrieved a second one along with a sulfur pack. I coated the wound in the white powder and tied on the second bandage, but the solider moaned in pain and started breathing in short, shallow breaths.

"We need to get these two back to the church," Smith called out, looking for a medic. "I need a stretcher over here!"

Out of nowhere, one of the medics appeared with a pair of troopers carrying a stretcher. The medic, another man from the 82nd, quickly checked the two wounded men and turned the stretcher over to us, taking his two men to the next foxhole. Smith grabbed the Gavin by the legs, while I lifted his chest, the two of us placing him on the stretcher.

"Go," Herb grunted, rising to his feet, "I'll follow."

Smith nodded and picked up the front of the stretcher as I lifted the back, taking Gavin's weight, which had to be next to nothing. Smith quickly took off, setting the fast pace to reach the church quickly through the empty streets. Herb kept up with us, not slowed at all by the loss of his entire left arm. Instead, he cursed constantly at the pain, seeming to use it to drive him.

The wounded Gavin continued to struggle to breathe, as we ran to the church, hurrying to save the young man. Much like Herb, he was in terrible pain, but we had no morphine in our kits to give them for a moment of relief. Instead, the two toughed it out as best as possible, Gavin soon passing out from the pain as we climbed the steps of the church.

Struggling, Herb held the door open for us to get Gavin inside. One of the troopers inside directed us to place Gavin on a pair of crates near a group of even more stretchers filled with wounded. Several medics moved through the stacks of wounded, struggling to stem the tide of dying men. Judging from the moans and cries of pain, and for help, they were slowly failing to stop the losses.

A staff sergeant came to our aide, first checking on Herb, and then turning his attention to Gavin. Peeling back the bandages, he cursed to himself and yelled for help. Jessica appeared, at his side, acting as a nurse to help where she could.

"Keep pressure until we can slow this bleeding," the medic growled in French, grabbing something from his medical bag.

Jessica pressed her hands onto the bandages, applying force to slow the flow of the man's blood. The medic dumped more sulfur onto the wound and replaced the bandages with new ones, which appeared to be no more then cloth cut from linen or clothing. He then jabbed the man in the arm with a morphine needle before scribbling an "M" on his forehead, with a pencil.

"His pulse is fading," Jessica reported, checking Gavin's wrist.

"Do we have any more of the blood?" The medic asked.

"No, the last vials were used up and we can't get anymore from the donors," Jessica yelled.

The medic cursed and looked to us. "What's your blood types?"

"A positive," Smith responded.

"AB negative," I responded.

The medic glanced at Gavin's dog tags. "Maybe there is a god, he's AB neg too. Get over here." I nodded and moved to the medic's side. "You give blood yet or have a disease of any kind?"

"No to both," I answered, already rolling up the sleeve on my left arm.

"Set up a direct transfusion from him to him," the medic told Jessica, handing her a pair of needles and a length of rubber tubing.

"Try holding still," Jessica whispered, quickly finding a vein in my arm.

I nodded and watched as she slid the needle into my arm, a flash of blood appearing as she left the needle in, securing one of the ends of the tubing to the waiting needle. She then set up Gavin's arm and quickly attached the other end of the tubing, to his waiting arm.

"Keep flexing your arm," the medic ordered, struggling to bandage Gavin's stomach.

I nodded and began to flex my arm, the blood flow in the tubing turning from a slow trickle to a steady flow. My mind was struggling to slow down from the fight, but I managed to form one thought. Just how dangerous is this? It actually made me laugh internally, a quick smile flashing across my face. Jessica flashed me a dirty look, for the smile. Cursing myself, I tried to explain, but she was called to help another medic.

"Stay with him," the medic suddenly said, tying down the new bandages. "Try to not to move too much, you might pass out."

"Wait, I can't stay tapped to him for too long," I said, knowing I could bleed to death.

"He's lost a lot of blood. You got enough to spare long, enough for him to not bleed to death. Don't worry, I'll be back to check on you," the medic yelled, as he took off to help another solider.

Smith walked over to me and patted my shoulder. "Noble thing, kiddo."

"Noble?" I repeated. "Just wanted to have a blood brother."

Smith laughed. "Keep that sense of humor, it'll keep you sane during this giant shit storm we call war."

I looked over the church filled with dead and dying men. "It's the easiest thing to do."

Smith looked me in the eyes. "Hang on to it. The worst thing that can happen to you is that you let this," he gestured to the church and the men around us, "get to you and shatter what little sanity you have. A sense of humor is the best tool to keep you sane, trust me."

I nodded and silently agreed, what Smith said made a lot of sense, but seemed so wrong. Since Oran, I made jokes to cope or made sarcastic and smart remarks, but I always wondered where the limit was, where it became wrong to joke. Going by Smith and what Hiller had told me, I had to use my own digression to find the limit. The limit, however, could only be found by going over it.

Chapter 11

The fight in Surrain ended, with me sitting beside Gavin in the cramped, hot church, with my blood flowing in his veins, while the 82nd repelled another counterattack. The rest of the linkup forces rolled into town just before dark, driving back the rest of the Germans and evacuating the wounded. Twelve of the 82nd died in the church waiting for the link up, along with several men from the rifle squads, though our squad came through without a scratch.

The sun was setting on Surrain as my squad prepared to move on, though I didn't know where we were going. Instead of inquiring, I sat on the steps of a bombed out building across from the church, slowly easing my body through the transition from being adrenaline fueled to running on nearly no food and very little water or sleep. My hands still shook, and my stomach was tight, but I was ready to roll when the order came.

I watched, as the convoy of tanks and halftracks from our division rolled through town, moving deeper inland in the hopes of keeping the landing momentum going. Smith and his squad were pulled back to the rear, with the rest of the boys from the 82nd, to regroup and get new troops to fill the ranks. Our rifle squad was readying to move out that night, but Hiller hadn't given us new orders.

"Hey, Corr." I turned to see Jessica walking over. She sat next to me, sighing with exhaustion.

I simply nodded, unsure of what to say. "You mad at me?" I asked.

"Why did you smile?" she asked, looking at me with tired eyes. "That man was laying there with his stomach ripped open and bleeding to dead."

"I wasn't smiling because of that, I'm not a nut job," I protested, trying to watch my tone and choice of words.

"I know that, but why?" She pleaded.

"I'm standing there, feeding him my blood and thinking of the health risks involved with directly giving blood. The smile was from thinking I survived the landings only to be killed by some disease," I said.

Jessica began to smile and shake her head before laughing herself. "That's not funny."

"And yet we're laughing," I said, smiling myself. "So, where are you going from here?"

"With you," she responded. "I have lots of knowledge on the area and will be helping you as best as I can."

I nodded my head and removed my helmet, leaning back against the charred remains of the building's front door. "You tired?"

"Very," she responded with a yawn.

"Sergeant!" Hanes yelled from the church steps. I shot back to my feet and ran to the steps, taking my gear with me.

"Sir?" I reported with a salute.

"Get your stuff together, we're rolling out," he ordered.

"Yes, sir" I said, not wanting to leave yet. "Where are we moving to next?"

"New orders are to secure a farm several miles down the road, that sits at a critical crossroads. We're moving out now so we can hit the place and have it secured before dawn," Hanes said.

"Yes, sir," I acknowledged.

Hanes returned my salute and walked back into the church. I turned around and saw four jeeps parked at the far edge of the front steps, the squads packing up their equipment for the operation. I glanced over to Jessica and nodded towards the waiting jeeps. She quickly darted across the street and walked with me.

"Hey," I said to Ramos, seeing him in the passenger seat.

"*Hermano*," he sighed, rubbing his tired eyes. "Spending time with your woman?"

"Keep talking," I joked, shoving his legs off the dashboard of the jeep.

"Oh, I will." Ramos propped his feet back up and closed his eyes.

"I guess this is good bye for now," Jessica said, averting her gaze from me slightly.

"You're staying back here?" I asked.

"For now to help with the movement of forces in the region, I may rejoin you later on," she answered.

"So then its good bye," I sighed, drumming my finger against my Thompson.

"For now, at least," she said, as she tried to look brave. "Stay safe out there, Corrigan

"Thanks, you try and stay safe too," I said.

"Corr, we're moving," Jay called out, placing his rifle in the rear of the jeep.

"Yeah, I'm coming," I responded, saying my goodbyes. Reluctantly, I finished up the goodbyes and hopped into the back of the jeep.

"Let's get going," Captain Hiller called, sitting behind the wheel of the lead jeep. "Stay close and keep the headlights off."

The squad finished preparing their gear and started up their jeeps, engines humming to life. I stood up and grabbed the mounted .30cal machine gun, grabbing the weapon with both hands, to keep steady. Jay pulled in behind Captain Hiller as he drove off with Adam and Hanes, driving past the line of tanks and turning onto the barren road leading westward.

The sun was nearly gone from the sky, darkness slowly creeping over the hedgerows. Captain Hiller drove quickly down the empty roadways, sticking to the smaller side roads to avoid German armor which now moved only at night thanks to the Jabos flying during the day.

"She was a good lookin' dame," Ramos mumbled, as we drove through the night.

"I didn't even get her last name," I admitted, looking down at him.

"Tough luck, maybe we'll see her again," Jay suggested.

I nodded to myself and sighed, leaning up against the .30cal. Still, exhaustion clawed away at my body and mind, slowly eroding away my will to fight. I needed sleep, but chances were good that sleep would be far off and a last priority when we found the Germans. It was amazing how the most basic things, such as sleep, matter so much once they are gone.

"The Captain's signaling to pull over," Jay reported, seeing the Captain slowly turn onto the side of the road.

Jay followed close behind, as the small four jeep convoy rolled to a stop, next to one of the massive hedgerows. I took in a deep breath and stood up straighter, tightening my grip on the .30cal as I readied for anything. Captain Hiller jumped out from his jeep and walked back to the second jeep, gesturing for everyone to gather around the vehicle's hood. Ramos tapped my leg and stood up to mount the .30cal, so I could listen to the Captain.

With his flashlight out and the red filter on, Hiller spread out an area map on the jeep's hood. Glancing down at his portable compass, he quickly checked his bearings and formulated a plan for something.

"Listen up," he ordered in a low tone, "We need to grab the farm here," he jabbed the map with his finger. "The surrounding area is all open farmland with hedgerows on the outer boundaries. This is rare to find, but it's the opening we need to exploit.

"The crossroads helps link up the First with the majority of the 82nd, who have LZs all up and down the countryside. Our job is, as strait forward is it gets; grab the farm and hold the crossroads by sunrise, so the tankers can roll through and cut off the German forces in the area. This crossroad runs dead center down the German lines and if we have it, we split the bastards in half, cutting the supply line to Cherbourg."

"Any idea on defenses?" I asked Thompson slung over my shoulder.

"The farmhouse is just off the crossroads, here. A grain silo is several yards away next to a barn and a small stable. Recon photos put the farmhouse as the German OP with an MG set up on the porch, to cover the western road. Two Pak 38s are dug into shallow fighting pits in the southeast field and have full arcs of fire on all approaches.

You can bet a sniper or two are in the grain silo and the barn and stable house light armored vehicles, probably tracks and armored cars."

"The plan off attack is simple," Hanes stated, taking over the briefing. "We'll form three combat groups, attacking the flanks in unison, while the third element moves up the center once we have their attention. Our left flank force will clear the barn and stables, while the right hits the silo and Pak 38s center clears the farmhouse."

"Sunrise is in," Hiller glanced at his watch, "eight hours, but bear in mind that taking the farm house is not or only goal. Once we take it, we'll need to hold out till morning. The second the OP is hit, you can be sure the Krauts will send troops to take it back. So let's do this hard and fast. I want that farmhouse under our control in two hours' time. Let's get to it."

The night air was still and quiet, even peaceful, had I not known a hellish firefight was going to occur. The night sky was clear and bright with stars and the moon, providing decent light as we skulked across the open wheat field, Thompson held firmly in my ever steady hands. Each step was slow and careful as to not make noise and alert the enemy to our presence. Adrenaline again flowed through my veins, heart racing in preparation for the hell storm that was soon to be released on the sleeping Germans.

Vic, Ramos, Edwards, and Parker moved silently alongside me, heads low and rifles held ready. Each of them breathed in controlled intervals, as to not cough or grunt, and risk exposure. The lit stables came into view as we crept forward, seeing a pair of unmanned halftracks sitting inside. Three German soldiers stood by, one smoking under the flickering lantern light, while the other two tinkered with one of the tracks top mounted MG42s.

I held up a raised fist, signaling a stop, as I dropped into a low crouch. Studying the area for any more German soldiers, I signaled my group to move, behind the stables, to catch the enemy off guard. Watching the smoking German, we began to creep forward inch by inch, sneaking around the rear of the wooden stables without making a sound.

With pinpricks of light leaking out between the wooden boards of the stables, we crept to the far side of the building, stopping at the very edge of the stables. I slung my Thompson over my shoulder and drew my trench knife, the steel blade reflecting some of the light. Vic and Ramos drew theirs as well while Parker and Edwards covered our backs. Silent and determined, the three of us crept around the side of the sables and hid behind the first half track. Ramos and Vic snuck around the rear of the track and moved to get the two men repairing the MG, while I moved for the smoking German.

The man had his back to me, attention all on his smoking and the clear night. He wasn't even armed, his bolt action rifle leaning against the front of the track. The strong odor of tobacco filled my nostrils as I crept up behind him, trench knife held firm in my right hand. My body was tense, knowing what grizzly act I was about to commit, my mind numb to the fact I was about to slit this man's throat, with a quick slice of my blade.

Mere inches from the man, I could see the matted green uniform of a German paratrooper, or *Fallschirmjäger,* that reeked of dirt, mud, and sweat. Smoke from his cigarette plumed into the air as he exhaled, sighing slightly to himself as I moved even closer. Silently, I asked God for forgiveness for what I was going to do, but I remembered my duty as a soldier, the trench knife in my hand feeling even heavier.

Moving with speed and grace, I leapt forward with my legs, left hand griping down on the man's mouth like a vice, as my right moved across his throat, the blade not cutting yet. With full force, I pressed the blade under his Adam's apple and drew back, the blade sliced open his throat, like it was the skin of an apple. Warm blood rushed out over the knife, as I drew it back for a second, final blow into the gap between his shoulder and the base of his throat. The man went slack, as I pressed the blade down to the hilt, and yanked it out.

It took only seconds, but the man fell in my arms, all muscles suddenly useless. Carefully, I dragged his lifeless body behind the halftrack and placed it on the ground. Vic and Ramos were placing the other two Germans down, as the shooting started near the grain silo.

The stealth approach did not work for Lieutenant Hanes, as rifle and machine gun fire shattered the serene night.

I slid the knife back into its sheath as I swung my Thompson around, the weapon slipping into my hands, I yanked back on the cocking hammer and rushed out the stables, moving for the barn no more than a yard or two away. Parker and Edwards were already waiting for us near the front entrance, as I returned with Vic and Ramos. I took Edwards with me and ran to the rear entrance, as Vic, Ramos, and Parker tossed in several grenades, to clear the interior.

Edwards and I came to the rear entrance, as the grenades detonated. I rushed in right away, Thompson up and firing, at the first German I saw. Edwards covered my side, as we moved in, the two of us scanning for targets. The bulky metal rear of a Panther Tank suddenly filled my vision, the massive steel animal dominating the center of the barn. A German mechanic appeared from the turret with a Luger in hand. Edwards and I fired together, tossing the man to the barn floor. Vic, Ramos, and Parker rushed in seconds later, killing the other two mechanics working on the Panther.

"Clear!" Parker yelled, seeing Edwards and me.

"Clear!" Edwards yelled, reloading his M1.

"All clear!" I responded, moving to the front entrance.

"Whoa!" Ramos yelled, placing his hand on the deadly Panther Tank. "This thing is fearsome!"

"No fucking shit," Vic grunted spitting on the Panther's armored side.

"Make sure it's clear," I ordered, pointing to the open turret.

"On it!" Edwards climbed aboard the tank and stuck his head into the open turret hatch. "All clear, sir! Looks like the fuel tanks are empty."

"No wonder it's not on the road." I reloaded my Thompson and rushed back outside, as the two Pak 38s fell to Hanes and his group.

The hard cracks of a sniper's rifle could be heard above the chatter of MG fire. I ran to the side of the farmhouse and looked out at the silo, seeing the German sniper still perched atop, on a makeshift firing platform. I shouldered my Thompson and took aim at the enemy solider, firing a quick burst that threw the sniper from his perch. A sudden burst of MG fire, inches from my face, forced me to my stomach, as a German officer firing an MP-40 rushed from the farmhouse.

Edwards was close behind me and killed the officer before he could aim his weapon at me. Nodding in approval, I jumped back to my feet and proceeded to the front of the farmhouse, as Captain Hiller and his team approached. Edwards and I cleared out the MG team on the porch and held back as the Captain arrived with his team. Following orders, I held outside and covered the perimeter as the others rushed in to clear the farmhouse.

More weapons fire echoed inside, as Hiller rushed in first with Adam right behind him. I had the strong urge to rush and aide the Captain, as more gun fire echoed, but I held my post and watched for anyone trying to get inside who wasn't in an American uniform. Lieutenant Hanes and his men secured the right flank and were in the process of doing a final sweep when several German halftracks shot down the northern road, MGs firing at our position.

Instinctively, I dove to the dirt and kept my head down, as MG fire showered the front porch, splintering the wood and creating a hailstorm of shrapnel. Edwards dropped next to me and rolled to get a view of the approaching Germans, in order to fire. I crawled to the edge of the porch and readied my Thompson, as one of the Pak 38s fired, the lead halftrack taking the hit in its side before slamming into a ditch on the side of the road.

The MG fire turned towards Hanes, as he readied the Pak 38s, to fire again, giving Edwards and me a chance to reposition. The next two halftracks were blown to shrapnel,as the 38s fired again, knocking out the light armored tracks with only signal hits. The last track suddenly charged off the road and into the nearby field, in an attempt to evade the anti-tank guns. Panicked, the track driver tried to cut across the field, only to be promptly destroyed halfway across. Everything soon went silent, both in the farmhouse and the surrounding fields.

"You hit?" I asked Edwards, seeing him still laying prone.

"No, I'm good," he answered, climbing back to his feet. "Are you okay?"

"Peachy," I responded, seeing several wooden splinters lodged into my left hand, blood spots around them. "Fucking peachy."

"Clear inside!" Adam yelled, moving through the front door.

"Fields are clear," Nate added, walking up to the porch with Hanes.

"Good work," Captain Hiller grunted, walking back outside with his Thompson held in his left hand. "Any wounded?"

"No sir," Hanes reported.

"Some scratches, sir," I responded, feeling the pain from my hand starting to radiate. "That's it."

"Good, now let's set up a perimeter and get some defenses in place. Hanes, see to the Pak 38s and round up as much MG ammo you can find."

"Sir," I said, interrupting.

"Yeah?" The Captain glared.

"We found a working Panther Tank in the barn, I think it just needs gas."

Hiller exchanged glances with Hanes. "A Panther Tank?"

"I'll show you, sir," I said.

"Malks, come with me." Hiller ordered. "Hanes, work on the defenses and get the men reorganized. C'mon, Bolger, lead the way."

I nodded my head and lead the two around the farmhouse and to the barn. I grabbed one of the gas lanterns from the stables and showed them the massive Panther Tank sitting in the barn, the light from the lantern throwing eerie shadows across the space.

"I never did want to get this close to one of these things," Malks sighed, looking in awe on the German war machine.

"This could come in handy," Hiller mumbled, rubbing his mouth for a second. "Malks, see if this thing can run if we get it fuel and if it has any ammo left. Bolger, give him a hand anyway you can, and report to me the second this thing is running."

"Yes, sir," I responded with a salute.

Hiller returned the salute and left for the farmhouse, as Malks scurried aboard the slumbering Panther. The Panther Tank was a fearsome war machine to face, well rounded in armor, speed, and weaponry which provided a good stand in for a Tiger. The only draw back to it, as well as the Tiger and the large *Jagdpanther*, was it sucked down gas like water and was prone to engine breakdown. This made them easy pray for the Jabos and the agile Sherman Tank, provided the Sherman avoided the unbelievable range of their main guns.

"Does it work?" I called out to Malks, who was hidden in the turret.

Malks suddenly appeared from the lower driver's hatch. "I think so. Some gas, a little love, and an oil change, and I think I can bring this beast to life."

"I'm here to help," I told him, "if you need it."

Malks grinned. "As in my helper?"

I reminded him," you don't order me around, if it doesn't involve reviving this tank."

He shrugged. "Well, I'll need the help." Malks climbed out the hatch and walked to the rear of the tank. "C'mon, let's check out the engine."

I walked around the side of the tank and noticed the kill markers painted under the turret. Twelve silver stars were painted, meaning the crew destroyed twelve Allied tanks. Shaking my head, I climbed aboard the rear of the tank and stood over Malks as he pried open the cover to the engine.

"Look at this," Malks moaned in a wounded tone. "They let this poor baby go to shit." He dropped to his stomach and reached into the innards of the engine. "Light, if you don't mind."

I held the lantern above the engine. Malks' hands danced over the massive engine with grace and speed, checking for oddities that I'd never see if I had it in my hand. The man new his cars and was an expert on engines, having the ability to fix just about anything, or blow it up.

After some tinkering, he looked to me. "These Germans, they really have no skill."

"Why is that?" I asked.

Malks reached in an opening in the engine and drew back his hand, a large chunk of blackened oil sludge in his grasp. "Look at this engine sludge crammed in here. Christ, it's a wonder the clogging didn't blow the entire engine to shit."

"So, no easy fix?" I wondered aloud.

He dropped the sludge to the ground, with a smack. "Easy, yes, but very time consuming. Anyway, we need fuel for this beast and ammo; otherwise it'll be worth shit, other than a large bullet magnet."

I nodded and jumped on the tank, starting to scavenge through the barn in search of any fuel or ammo the Germans may have been storing. Even with a twelve minute search, I turned up the cache of a dozen 75mm shells for the tank and a few boxes of ammo for the mounted MG42s, but not a single drop of gas. Remembering the two halftracks, I returned to the stables and grabbed four half-filled jerry cans, the gas sloshing about, as I brought them back to Malks.

"How'd you do?" he asked, sleeves rolled up and arms slick with oil and grease.

"One crate of shells, four boxes of MG ammo, and," I held up one of the jerry cans, "four of these half filled with gas, so roughly fifteen gallons."

Malks sighed. "These gas guzzlers suck up ten gallons just starting up. Fifteen will get us twelve feet out of the barn before it shuts down."

"Does that mean the engine works?" I asked, placing the collected supplies near the side of the tank.

"In a manner of speaking." Malks gestured to the open engine. "Fan belt is chewed down to a threat, spark plugs are nearly fired, oil sludge is backed up in the fuel valves, and the engine block is popped full of holes from a *Jabo* attack."

"So….yes, no?" I asked not really having a great deal of information on engines.

"It could go either way; if I can make the repairs with what I got to work with." He scrounged through one of the German tool kits and sighed to himself. "This is going to take a while."

"What can I do to help?" I asked.

"Nothing unless you can strip down and rebuild an engine blindfolded," he joked.

"Ah, then I'll leave ya to it," I answered.

Malks grunted to himself, as I walked outside, the air still and quiet now that the fighting was over. The squad was moving about the fields, to set up new fighting positions, to hold the crossroads until morning, when the linkup was set to arrive. The captured Pak 38s, *Panzerschrecks*, MG42s, and hopefully the Panther, were to be used in our defense. We had a sturdy armament to work with, but it was nothing if groups of Tigers and Panthers thundered down the road.

Lieutenant Hanes was overseeing the defense construction in the fields with the squad redeploying the captured munitions. I strolled down to the farmhouse, as Jay climbed up to the silo to take up position in the sniper's perch. Captain Hiller was setting up the CP in the farmhouse with Phelps standing by the door, acting as a guard.

I walked past him and stepped inside, nearly stumbling over the body of a dead German in the doorway. Body torn by gun fire, Sanders was in the process of clearing the bodies from the farmhouse, with one of the replacements. I looked away from the ripped up corpse and walked into the living room. It was wide open, with a fireplace, a couch, and several stairs, the living room was being set up as the forward CP. Captain Hiller stood by a coffee table near the fireplace,with several maps spread out.

"Contact the division," Hiller was ordering Adam. "Let them know the crossroads are now under our control, and we are setting up defensive positions."

"Yes, sir," Adam responded with a head nod, holding the radio receiver to his ear.

"How's the Panther looking?" Hiller asked, glancing in my direction.

"Corporal Malks thinks he can get it rolling with some engine repairs. We have ammo and fuel should it get rolling," I reported, removing my helmet.

"That's good to hear." Hiller pulled a folded map from his pocket, a German insignia near the key. "This is a German area map we found."

I took the map and studied it. "Sir?"

"The Germans have a mechanized force six miles west of here based in the hedgerows. An infantry force of unknown strength is even closer, about two miles south of here is not engaged in combat. Our biggest risk is the mechanized force, if they realize we took the crossroads," Hiller explained.

"We should barricade the southern and northern approaches," I recommended. "It'll slow enemy advances and give us a chance to concentrate on our forces."

Hiller thought on it. "But do we have anything to barricade the roads with?"

"There're two halftracks in the stables around back. I took the fuel from them to give to Malks for the Panther," I said.

"Okay, once we set up the AT pieces take a detail and get those tracks on the southern and northern approaches," Hiller commanded.

"Yes…" The high pitched whine of artillery cut me off as the sound echoed through the air.

"Incoming!" Phelps yelled from the doorway.

Captain Hiller yelled for everyone to get to cover, as the first shells began to land. I turned to run outside, as two shells exploded out front, just from the porch. A third and fourth shell slammed into the roof of the farmhouse, with ear shattering roars. The windows blew out, as the roof support beams blew inward, the wood splintering and raining down on us. I ran for the doors as the concussion wave slammed into me, tossing me across the room and into a wooden chair in the corner, the chair splintering under me. My vision began to fade, as I looked up to see the wooden ceiling rapidly falling down onto us, before everything stopped.

The ringing, that reverberated in my skull, was the first sign that I was, somehow, alive. My vision was still black, but slowly grayed until things started to come into focus around me. My eyes burned from the thick smoke and my lungs ached from the sudden loss of oxygen. I rolled my head from side to side to clear my vision, when I realized a heavy wooden support beam was pressing down on my chest.

Having difficulty breathing, I reached out to the heavy beam and pushed, hoping to roll the thing off me. The heavy beam wouldn't budge, as I put every ounce of effort into getting it off me, my breathing becoming slower and slower ; I struggled to take in air. I screamed at myself, to force the timber off me, but my muscles stung with pain, and I could feel the pinpricks of heat brushing against my legs. I began to realize that my luck of dodging death had run out.

"Let's not give up!" I heard Captain Hiller yell. I turned my head to see Hiller pushing through the burning debris with blood running down his forehead.

"I…" I struggled to speak with the little air still in my lungs, but failed.

"Don't die on me, otherwise I'll take back those stripes," Hiller bellowed as he grabbed the beam with both hands. I placed my hands on the underside and pushed, as Hiller yanked the beam off my body and rolled it to the side and away from me.

Still struggling to breathe, Hiller pulled me to my feet and pushed me towards the door, as the farmhouse continued to burn and crumble around us. He shoved me out first and followed as the rest of the house caved in on itself, the flames consuming the remains of the building. Artillery still rained from the skies as I stumbled out and fell to the cool grass, breathing deeply, of the night air, in between fits of coughing.

"C'mon, still got a war to fight." Hiller helped me to my feet and shoved my Thompson and helmet into my hands.

"Thank…you, sir," I mumbled, placing my helmet onto my head and griping my weapon.

"Thank me later," Hiller grunted, as MG fire shot through the air.

I turned to see a group of halftracks and armored cars race up the southern road, MGs and auto cannons firing. The two Pak 38s were destroyed in the artillery attack, and the vehicles approached without slowing, even as the squad fired back with the light MGs we had, and their weapons.

I dropped into a low crouch and took aim with my Thompson, firing at the MG42 gunner in the lead halftrack. Vic's BAR sprayed the armored cars alongside two of the captured MG42s, but the tracks rushed into the open fields and dropped off their troops while the armored cars worked to suppress us.

"See if Malks has that Panther running!" Hiller ordered, reloading his Thompson. "Go!"

I jumped to my feet and ran around the side of the farmhouse, as the squad moved into position, to cover the crossroads. Jay was still atop the grain silo with his sniper rifle, picking off the German troops, as fast as he could. Phelps was shuffling ammo cans from the German store area to the forward MGs, while Adam furiously worked to reach division for any type of support. I ran for the barn with bullets whizzing through the air and more artillery rounds landing around the burning farmhouse.

Several shells destroyed the stables, as I rounded the farmhouse, the barn still standing undamaged. I could see the light from the gas lantern flickering through the barn door as I approached, Malks nowhere in sight, as I entered. I circled the Panther Tank and could not find him, even as I shouted his name.

"Malks!" I yelled, climbing on top of the tank. "Damn it, Malks, where the fuck are you?"

"Getting this thing running!" he yelled from inside the turret.

I climbed to the open hatch and looked inside. "What?"

"I nearly got her running again," he explained, working with the controls of the tank. "Engine is fixed, but it won't run for long. I've put in all the gas I could find and loaded up the two 42s and the main gun."

"So it'll run?" I asked, as more heavy MG fire echoed outside.

"Get me someone to load the gun and yes," he said.

Cursing under my breath, I climbed through the hatch, into the cramped inside of the tank. Malks squirmed out of the way and sat down in the driver's seat, activating the massive engine with a low rumble. I reached up and slammed the hatch closed, switching the lock into place. I dropped into the gunner's seat and looked to Malks.

"Ah, this works like an 88, right?" I asked, eyeing the breach of the cannon.

"Actually it's a 75, but yeah. Grab a round from the holder to your left, shove it in, close the hatch, and then step on that peddle. Open the breach up and repeat as many times as needed," Malks explained.

"Is it that simple?" I asked, very unsure of my skill to operate a tank.

"What?" Malks mocked, as he pulled the tank out of the barn. "You think ya need an IQ of a thousand to use a tank? Shit, most tankers are dumber then dirt!"

I sighed to myself and looked out one of the forward sights located on the side of the main cannon. The view was greatly restricted; I was only able to see what was in front of the tank. Peripheral vision was next to nothing, but I guess it didn't matter when the only real threat to a Panther came from the Jabos in the clouds.

Malks drove the tank as fast it would go, maybe five miles an hour, onto the field and around the brightly burning farmhouse. As he turned to face the crossroads, I spotted even more halftracks spread out in the fields. There were at least ten tracks and eight armored cars firing on the squad with several infantry platoons mixed in with them. Captain Hiller and the squad where barely holding on by their teeth, as we arrived. The sight of the deadly Panther created a loud chorus of cheers to rise from the Germans, believing that we were one of them.

"Targets left and right!" Malks yelled from his seat. "Best knock those fuckers down a peg or two."

Not believing I was operating the main gun of a German Panther, I grabbed one of the large tank shells and rammed it into the breach of the main cannon. Slamming the breach closed and locking the cover into position, I gripped the cannon joy stick and looked through the forward sights. Using the turret controls, I swiveled the main gun to face the nearest halftrack still dropping off troops. Hands sweating, I pressed down on the pedal and felt the massive concussion in my entire body, as the cannon fired with an awe inspiring boom.

The massive cannon exploded, with a burst of flame and super-heated air, the cannon shell propelled through the air and slammed into the loaded halftrack. With one amazing explosion, the track disintegrated in a fireball, consuming the crew and the troops around it, which halted all cheering from the Germans.

The recoil of the cannon shoved the breach back several feet into the turret and rolled back into position. I opened the breach cover and let the spent shell roll free, still hissing with searing heat. I shoved a new shell in and closed the breach, reaching for the controls once it was secure. Again, I moved the turret to the next track and fired, destroying it and the track next to it in a large fireball. The armored cars seized firing on the squad, and fired on us. Just like with our Sherman and Churchill tanks, the rounds bounced off the tank, with a skull shaking ping, that rattled the brain and created a God awful migraine.

"Ah, bad news, Sarge," Malks called from the driver's seat.

"What now!" I yelled, firing the third round and taking out a pair of armored cars.

"Ah, the engine just crapped out on me, so we're stalled out," Malks said.

The sudden odor of exhaust grabbed my attention and I yelled, "We're stuck?"

"The turret and MGs still work," Malks explained, "but this thing won't move without an engine overhaul."

"Ugh, then grab one of the MGs and hit the infantry!" I ordered.

Malks nodded and crawled back to the driver's compartment, grabbing the handle for the forward mounted MG42. The high pitched buzz saw screech of the 42 echoed through the tank, as I continued to fire, rolling the turret down the line of tracks and armored cars in the fields. The squad now had the advantage with our Panther in the fight, but the Germans still fought on with unshaken confidence. Were we not at war, I'd buy most of those brave bastards a drink.

A sudden, hard crack against the turret armor startled me. I looked through the forward sights and scanned the attacking Germans, spotting the bright muzzle flashes in the night, for the distinctive flash of a German bazooka, what we called a 'stove pipe' because of its shape and frontal armor plate.

"Stove pipe, center field near the over turned tracks!" I yelled to Malks, as I destroyed another armored car.

"Got him!" Malks yelled as, saw MG fire rip up their position.

With the AT threat silenced, I swung the turret around and fired on the last armored car, ripping the small turret off the top and gutting the thing, like a cow in a slaughter house. What was left of the infantry detachment began to pull back into the fields, moving for the safety of the thick hedgerows, like back in Surrain. Malks continued to fire, while I let the main gun fall silent. Using the cannon against infantry was ineffective and wasted ammo, so I took a count of the last shells we had, only two were left.

"The Germans are retreating," Malks called from the lower compartment.

"Stay with the tank, I'll talk to the Captain," I told him, unlocking the top hatch and climbing through with my Thompson over my shoulder.

The open, clear air of the night was a relief from the cramped, exhaust filled turret of the Panther. Mixed with the ringing in my ears and the hard thumping in my heart from the concussions, I felt even more pity for the courageous bastards that were the tankers. I jumped off the turret and ran for Hiller's position near the farmhouse.

"Always cutting it close," Hiller grunted, standing up from grass. "No doubt they'll be back, though."

"Well, the Panther engine is a chunk of steel now," I explained. "It gave out and the tank isn't going anywhere."

"Well, I think it bought us time. The Germans think we have one of their fearsome Panthers under our control and have seen it still works. They won't be back until they can scrounge up more AT weapons, or find a Tiger or Panther to help."

"Anyone hit?" I asked.

"Not sure, I sent Phelps to do a head count. Are you okay?" Hiller asked.

I shrugged, still fighting to block all my fatigue and pain from my mind.

"I need a medic!" someone yelled from the eastern road.

I turned to see Lieutenant Hanes stumbled down the dirt road with Jay under his arm. I couldn't make out their wounds, but Jay's uniform was stained with blood and something was off with his walk. I ran to their aide with Doc and the Captain, the three of us helping two of our wounded brothers, as best we could.

Jay was slipping in and out of consciousness,with a nasty head wound, and a thick laceration running across his left cheek. Hanes seemed to be better off, with only minor shrapnel wounds to the thigh and a shallow bullet wound to the left hand. Doc quickly looked to Jay, assessing his wounds and working feverously to keep Jay alive. Captain Hiller worked with Doc to help Jay and I helped Hanes, using my medical kit.

"Ah, I'm getting too old of this shit," Hanes cursed as I checked the bullet wound to his hand.

"Aren't we all, sir?" I joked, dumping a sulfur packet onto the wound.

"How's Hawkins? I found him near the silo, looks like an AT hit destroyed the firing position."

"He'll pull through," I said, working to convince myself more than Hanes. "He always does, sir."

"Knock of the 'sir' bull…" Hanes trailed off and rolled onto his back, his body going slack and falling to the grass.

"Lieutenant?" I asked, grabbing his arm. "Hanes? Doc!"

Doc looked over at Hanes and swore under his breath, jumping to Hanes's side with his medical bag. Doc scanned his eyes with his flashlight and took a pulse before looking to his wounds. He cut open Hanes's pant leg and exposed the shrapnel wounds, more blood pooling in the dirt. It was then I realized Hanes took the hit in the critical artery in his leg, one, that if cut, could lead to death within minutes.

"Damn," Doc cursed as he opened up Hanes's wounded leg. Without hesitating, Doc shoved his hand into Hanes's ripped open leg, as he fought to grab the artery with his hand. He didn't worry or care about infections, by shoving his hand into the open wound; they were all a moot point if the man died from his wounds. Doc struggled to grab the severed artery, his face twisted in anger and frustration.

The color in Hanes's face was quickly draining and his eyes were shut. Sweat no longer poured down his face and his hands dropped from fists, to relaxed, at his side. More and more blood pooled in the dirt, but Doc never gave up, never stopped fighting to save Hanes from the cold grip of death. I stood with Hiller looking on helpless as Hanes died before our eyes. He stopped breathing and didn't move at all, but Doc cursed louder and still fought to grab the artery.

"It's over, Doc," Hiller said in a low tone, placing a hand on Doc's shoulder. "It's over."

"No!" Doc snapped, shrugging off Hiller's hand. "It's not over!"

"You need to help Jay," I reminded him, putting some force behind my words.

Doc suddenly stopped his feverous work and went still, eyes locked on Hanes's lifeless body. Without a word, he moved back to Jay's side and finished dressing his wounds. Captain Hiller left him to his work, crouching down over Hanes and gently removing one of his dog tags. For a man not prone to showing emotion, Hiller had trouble removing the tags and looking away from his fallen friend. We all have our breaking points, but you never what it is until you get to it.

"Bolger," Hiller grunted, standing back up and stuffing the tags into his uniform pocket. "Check with Phelps and see if anyone has been hit."

"Yes, sir," I responded, my body still numb.

"Then send out a detachment to scavenge the dead for supplies and see if Adam has reached division," Hiller yelled, trying to get his emotions in check.

I nodded my head and took a last look at Jay before walking back to the farmhouse. The squad was already assembled, the guys spread out around the house in fighting positions from the battle. Many had sullen looks on their faces, others simply looked away, as if focusing on a target that wasn't there. Phelps was standing by one of the Mgs,with his arms crossed over his chest, eyes looking at his boots.

"Anyone else hit?" I asked.

"Everyone's good," he curtly responded, not even looking up.

"Take three men and search the Germans for what supplies we can use," I ordered, finding it difficult to form the words.

"Yes, Sarge," Phelps said, taking Nate, Ramos, and Vic to do the grizzly work.

"Adam, you reach division yet?" I called out.

"Yeah," he sighed, looking down at his radio. "They'll be here by dawn."

I nodded, understanding the mood of the men. I wanted to feel just like them, to stop and grieve for Hanes, but I was the second in command of the squad, and I had to remain strong and give them a reason to keep fighting.

"We'll get them," was all I could think to say. The words were hollow and empty, the drive of vengeance one that got good men killed. Each of us wanted to…do something for Hanes, find some way to make the feeling of sickness and helplessness go away.

Only time would heal the wound, but it was not what I wanted to hear. I looked away from the squad and walked to the side of the farmhouse. Out of sight and earshot, I leaned against the smoldering side of the building and sighed deeply. Everything was overwhelming, overwhelming to the point where I just didn't know what to do. I was numb, my nerves and body stressed to the point where it didn't matter what you did, it didn't help. I was on the verge of breaking, when Hiller did what he did best: grab you by your belt and yank you back from the edge of desperation and set you straight.

"Bolger!" Hiller grunted with strength and power.

"Sir," I croaked with a salute.

"Since day one I knew you had what it takes to be a soldier, to be a leader. You have the courage, conviction, and common sense to be the best the nation has to offer." Hiller fished something from his jacket and held it out. "You've more then earned it."

I looked down to see two gold bars in Hiller's callused hand. They were lieutenant's bars, Hanes's lieutenant's bars.

"Sir, I can't take these," I protested, shaking my head.

"Don't give me that shit," Hiller responded. "Hanes would be proud to see you where the bars. You've done more shit in this war and seen more then anyone should have to and it's going to keep occurring till it's over. What you need to do is not let it get to you, to keep your sanity. It's harder then fuck, I know, but keep being yourself, it'll be more then enough."

I took the bars and held them in my hand for a second,as Hiller walked off. The bars weighted heavy in my hands, almost too heavy to hold. They were blotched with Hanes's blood, the crimson liquid now coagulated across the gold colored steel. Sighing deeply again, I closed my hand into a fist and held the bars thinking about the man that wore them. Feeling that I was not betraying him, I pinned the bars onto the collar of my uniform shirt.

Chapter 12

The fighting in the thick hedgerows of Normandy nearly lost the fight for the Allies. German forces well versed in fighting among the merciless hedgerows. it gave our advance a bloodied nose, but it was just a stalling battle. Allied air power owned the skies while we grabbed town after town, city after city, slowly kicking the Germans back across, to Normandy. Losses were high, but we pushed on and on without pause, as June turned to July and July to August. St. Lo fell after merciless bombing and infantry attacks, Caen was held by the Brits, and Cherbourg was ours, its ports under repair, so it can fuel the war effort.

The last remainders of the German Seventh and Fifth Panzer armies were being encircled all around; the Brits, Poles, and French in the north and northeast, and the U.S. in the south and southeast. Allied command was working to cut off the two armies and crush all resistance, so the liberation of Paris could begin. The fighting was tough and fierce, but our squad was pulled out of combat and sent to the town of Mortain for RR after nearly two months of strait fighting in the hedges. We believed we would be left out of the attack.

The sun was setting over Hill 314, on the edge of Mortain, and night was fast approaching. What was once a fully equipped and supplied rifle squad, was now under supplied and three men short of a full squad. After the fighting at crossroads 121, we lost two of the replacements grabbing St. Lo. Now, we were based at an OP near Hill 314 for some RR while we waited for resupply,before moving back into combat.

"How much ammo do you have left?" I asked Jay as, we sat in the trenches at the lip of the OP.

"Four clips, twenty rounds and two clips, fourteen rounds," Jay responded cleaning his sniper rifle and pistol. "You?"

I shrugged, working on removing my quickly growing beard, with my small shaving kit. "Three clips for the Thompson and one for the pistol. That's with two grenades and nearly no ration kits."

"When's the resupply coming?" Jay asked.

"Don't know." I flinched slightly as the razor nicked a bit of my cheek, though no blood bled through the skin. "It should be soon, if they want us back in the fight."

"Hey, Corr," Jessica called in,somewhat clear, English. "I bring meal."

I grinned. "Still need to practice the English more, but good try."

"I will…learn," she added, handing Jay and me a box of K rations.

"You two," Jay sighed, grinning at the two of us. "So close since St. Lo."

"Jealous the French girls don't like you," I mocked, still regaining my sense of humor since the fall of St. Lo. "You gotta be smooth, like Boggy."

"Haven't met the right one yet, and I'm smoother than Boggy," Jay joked.

I shook my head and opened the small box of rations, tossing some of the sealed cans to Jay and Jessica. Jessica accepted the food with a polite smile. The two of us had become a lot closer since D-Day, having spent a lot of time working together since Operation Neptune was launched.

"You know, I like you with a bit of beard," Jessica said in French. "Gives you a, what do Americans call it, a 'rugged look?'"

I still worked with the blade and removed the stubble. "I prefer the clean shaven look." "

"The rugged look works for Jay?" Jessica asked, jokingly.

"What?" Jay asked, hearing his name. "C'mon, you know it's not polite to talk about me in French."

"She says you should shave too," I joked.

Jay rubbed his chin. "Nah, I like it, gives me an edge."

Sighing, I finished up shaving and washed away the loose hair and shaving cream, with the little water I had. I kept my canteens filled, using rainwater that filled our helmets the night before. Supplies were very scarce for our unit, the four rifle squads, besides ours, were undersupplied with little or no more ammo left.

"Anything out there?" Ramos asked, waking up from his fifth nap of the day.

"Nope," I said, picking up a pair of binoculars and scanning the surrounding terrain. "All quiet for now."

"Resupply get here yet?" he asked, being one of the men with no more rifle ammo.

"No, it's still taking its sweet ass time," Jay grunted, cleaning down his rifle. "Food's here, though."

"God be praised, stale K rations," Ramos complained, grabbing a can of beans from the box. "I wonder if this will give me the shits again."

"Yeah, the one time you were laughing out the other side of your mouth," Phelps snickered, jumping into the trench.

"Laughing out the other side of his mouth?" Jessica asked.

I laughed slightly and tried to explain. "Let's just say he would've sold his soul for a bathroom at the time."

"Oh," she said, with a confused look on her face.

"Hey, have any of you spoken with Hiller?" Ramos asked, cracking open his can of beans.

"No," Phelps said with a head shake.

"Only when he's giving orders," Jay responded.

"He doesn't talk much now," I explained. "He's one tough old bastard, but with Hanes and all…" I looked to the lieutenant's bars on my uniform for a second. "Just give him time."

Phelps shook his head and tired to turn around the mood. "So, I was gonna start up a card game, anyone care to join?"

Jay sighed. "What the hell, I'm in."

"Me too," Ramos chimed in.

"L.T.?" Phelps asked me.

I shrugged. "No, I'll cover watch tonight."

"I'll take watch," Ramos offered. "I'm broke anyways."

"Guys, it's alright," I protested. "I caught up on my sleep and I quit gambling."

"Corr, c'mon and relax for a bit," Jay insisted.

"You should relax," Jessica whispered in French. "You've been really stressed since…Surrain."

"Look, take the time to relax, I'll play the next game," I said and started to walk away.

Phelps shrugged his shoulders and walked into the small dugout built into the trench line. The place was small, but acted as a bunker during mortar attacks. Ramos and Jay followed him inside and began to set up their card game while I returned to the firing line of the trench.

"How are you doing, Corr?" Jessica asked, standing next to me with her captured MP-40.

"I really don't know," I admitted, watching the rolling landscape.

"Corrigan," Jessica said more firmly.

"What? I'm in a permanent state of exhaustion and I'm always tired regardless how long I sleep," I snapped.

"Sounds like battle fatigue," Jessica suggested.

I laughed. "I think I just aged a few years, made a jump from twenty to forty in a few days."

"You look good for your age then," Jessica said with a smile.

I smiled and sighed. "Yeah, I'm secretly hundred."

I turned back to my watch and scanned the rolling hills for anything unusual. Things were quiet across the line, most of the squads in the trenches, sitting back and relaxing, instead of being on watch. Many were out of ammo and the Germans were believed to be miles away, so it didn't matter how vigilant they were. I still kept a constant watch, knowing never to let my guard down until I made it back stateside.

Something stirred in the tree line two miles down the hill, near the last line of hedgerows. I zeroed in on the area with my binoculars and searched for any anomalies when I spotted the unmistakable box shape of a Tiger tank. My heart skipped a beat as several more Tigers and Panthers appeared in the tree line. I lowered the binoculars and was about to yell out when the artillery started falling.

The rolling artillery barrage pounded the line with a single, deadly volley which was soon followed by another and another. I grabbed Jessica, wrapping her in my arms, and throwing the two us to the bottom of the trench, as the shells dropped around our position. The noise was incredible, as we landed in the ground, geysers of dirt shooting into the air before failing back and pelting us in a dirt shower. Once I felt the dirt stop pelting my back, I released Jessica and helped her to her feet.

"Get to the bunker!" I yelled over the barrage of arty shells.

Jessica understood and ran for the dugout, as fast as she could. I ran behind her as shells exploded all up and down the line, the ground shaking under my boots. I stopped near the dugout entrance and looked down the trench for anyone still caught out in the open. Seeing no one with all the dust and smoke filling the air, I dove inside and moved away from the entrance, as the shells washed over the line, like rain drops in a hurricane.

"You okay?" Jay yelled over the explosions.

"My ears are ringing!" I responded, rubbing my ears with my hands. "I'm fine, though!"

I looked over the group as the shells detonated over and over again. Dirt fell from the ceiling and the wooden support beams lining the walls shook. Everyone was a bit shaken up and unnerved, but alive nonetheless.

"What do we do now?" Ramos asked.

"The Germans are coming behind the barrage, I saw the Panzers," I shouted.

"We barely have any ammo left and nothing to stop tanks," Jay reported.

"I know, I know." I cursed under my breath as my headache intensified. My hearing was still returning, the ringing still echoing like church bells. "Who has no ammo at all?"

"I got nothing," Ramos said, looking a bit defeated.

"One clip," Phelps reported.

"So roughly nothing between the four of us besides what Jay and I have," I rubbed the bridge of my nose as the artillery outside intensified. "Okay Ramos, when the shelling stops find the Captain and report our situation. The rest of us will hold out here, with what we have, until we get relief."

"What can we do against tanks?" Phelps asked.

"Nothing now, we can only engage infantry, with what supplies we have left." I looked out the bunker entrance as the artillery barrage quickly tapered off and stopped. "C'mon, back to the trenches!"

We rushed back outside to find the trench line ripped apart by the arty fire. Sections of the line were collapsed, bunkers were gutted, and fighting positions were cratered up and down the line. Many of the survivors stumbled out from their shelters and worked to get reorganized. I moved to the lip of the trench and scanned the terrain looking for the advancing German Panzers and troops.

"Oh…" was all I could say, with a staggering twelve Tiger and eight Panther tanks rolling up the hillside towards our position, no more then fifty yards away and closing.

"That's a lot of German steel," Jay mumbled.

"Fan out and prepare to hold the line!" I yelled, dropping the binoculars and swinging my Thompson into my hands. "Ramos, get back to the Captain!"

Ramos quickly darted down the line, to the CP, while the rest of us lined the edge of the trench, near empty weapons held at the ready. My heart raced and adrenaline flooded my system, as the imposing tanks rolled forward in a steady, unwavering line of steel. Infantry followed behind them, using the rolling monsters as cover, our MG positions were all but destroyed in the attack.

"Stay steady!" I called out, feeling my own fear and the urge to run grow. "We lose this position and the Krauts can flank Hill 314 and hit the men in Mortain."

"We're not going to run," Jay whispered, head resting on the stock of his Springfield rifle.

"You're not thinking it?" I asked, fingers drumming against my Thompson.

"I'm screaming to myself to run, but I rather marry Hitler," Jay said.

I grinned slightly, but my fear crept into my mind and I could feel the urge to run grow and grow. Shaking my head, I suppressed the urge and clenched my jaw, the muscles tightening, to the point where my teeth might shatter from the pressure. It worked to hold back the fear, but it was still there, in the darker parts of my mind.

The line of approaching Panthers and Tigers opened up with their 75 and 88mm guns, pounding the line with heavy cannon fire. Several shells detonated around our positions, causing me to flinch now and again. Still, my body locked up and my legs shut down to prevent me from running. Death was once again minutes away, but I refused to budge, refused to give in to my fear.

"Target the infantry!" I ordered, seeing the German troops separating from the tanks as they approached the line.

Jay opened fire with his rifle, as I squeezed the trigger on my Thompson, a three round burst firing out. I steadied my weapon, as best as possible, moving the sights from target to target, until I had a clear shot. The German soldiers returned fire on our positions in much larger volume then we could put back, the enemy achieving fire superiority without any real effort.

Bullets smashed into the dirt inches from my face, causing me to drop down for cover. A German 'potato masher' grenade tumbled into the trench behind us, rolling to stop inches from our backs. I dove forward, gabbing the grenade in one hand and throwing it back down the hillside. I quickly moved back to the firing line and stood up, as the hail of enemy gun fire continued.

"I'm out!" Phelps yelled as his rifle clicked empty.

"Down to two rounds!" Jay added, clearing a spent round from his rifle.

I stood, up in time to see four Germans rushing the trench line. Raising my Thompson, I emptied the clip into the advancing soldiers, cutting the four down with one, long burst. Ejecting the clip, I loaded a second, taking note of the last two in the ammo pouch hanging from my waist. Again, I fired on the advancing Germans, trying to control my ammo usage, but the Germans just kept coming and coming. I was down to my last clip in minutes.

My last clip ran dry in an instant as the Germans made it into the trenches. Phelps charged the German officer that jumped in first, launching himself into the soldier with full force. The two fell to the dirt as Phelps drew his trench knife and rammed it into the German's chest, the blade most likely puncturing a lung. Another German appeared behind him, MP-40 aimed to fire into Phelps's head. I whirled around and killed the soldier with the last of my bullets.

Thompson dry, I slung it over my back and drew my Colt.45 sidearm, left hand yanking back on the slide. I fired at the nearest German at point blank range, putting two rounds into his head just under his helmet. Three more men appeared from my left, as I dropped to one knee, and aimed for the soldiers. Again, I squeezed the trigger and killed two, hitting the third in the right thigh. Adjusting my aim, I hit him in the heart and dropped him to the dirt. I turned to face the trench line, expecting to see more German infantry, when I saw the armored hull of a Tiger tank climb over the trench.

"Pull back, pull back!" I ordered, seeing the situation was hopeless.

German soldiers poured into the trenches, like water through a sieve. The Tigers and Panthers climbed over the trenches and circled around, to hit us in the rear. I ordered everyone back up the trench, to the secondary line, at the top of the ridge. I covered the others as they pulled back, moving with them once we reached the connecting trench.

"Jessica, get back!" I yelled, reloading my.45. "Get back to the line, we'll cover you!"

"I'm not leaving you!" she argued, MP-40 hanging empty at her side.

"I will not let you be captured, go!" I ordered as the Germans approached the connection trench. I pulled out the area map from my jacket pocket and handed it to her. "Tell Hiller the Germans have overrun phase line Dakota and are pushing to phase line Washington with heavy tank support!"

"Corr, I can't…won't leave you," she cried.

"Just go, we'll be going too. Just run!" I barked.

Jessica hesitated, but took the map and ran up the connecting trench, as the Germans moved in. I stood with Phelps and Jay, as our weapons ran dry, the last bits of ammo being fired. My pistol clicked empty and Jay was down to his trench knife, as the Germans encircled our at the mouth of the trench. They stood around us, weapons aimed to fire, but a German officer stopped them.

"Lower your weapons and surrender!" he barked in perfect English, Luger pistol held at his side.

"What do we do, Corr?" Phelps asked, holding a captured Mauser rifle.

As officer in charge, the safety and wellbeing of my men came first and for most above all, I would not let them be slaughtered. "Lower'em," I ordered, flipping around my empty.45 and holding it by the barrel. "We surrender."

The German officer took my.45. "Take their weapons and ammo."

The German soldiers obeyed and striped us of our empty weapons and supplies. We turned over packs and equipment without resisting, the Germans taking everything besides our helmets. One German reached for the silver cross around my neck and tried to take it, but the German officer intervened.

"Don't even touch it!" he screamed in German. "Anyone looting these men or any prisoners under my command will be shot." He handed me back my empty sidearm. "Take them back to base."

The German soldiers took us back down the hill. We were led past the advancing German forces that pushed up the hill with heavy armor support. Seeing so many Panzers and Panthers rush up the hill with supporting infantry and arty booming in the distance, my heart sank and a feeling of dread set in.

"Now what?" Jay whispered as we walked.

"Let's just survive, for now," I responded, eyes darting between the Germans leading us back to their forward staging area. "And keep your eyes open."

Jay and Phelps nodded as the German guards took us to the mud road at the base of the hill, where the German forces were gathering at the edge of the hedgerows. It was a marvel to see how an army prepared itself for battle and maintained itself during the fighting. Engineers built up the forward command and observation posts while defenses were established and supplies brought up. Medics established forward aide stations to treat wounded, supply officers stored and readied ammo and fuel, to be brought to the advancing soldiers, and intelligent units established forward communications between supply, the medical corps, artillery and air support, and armored or mechanized command.

Security came in two forms, at the staging areas: tight or lax. MPs stood watch over critical areas like the CP and supply areas, but everything was open mostly because so many soldiers were passing through. When it came down to it, a commander wants more men in the fight then he does pulling guard duty that isn't protecting him. The exception is with prisoners, who are moved to holding area behind the lines.

"Sit!" one of the guards suddenly grunted in fractured English.

The three of us sat down on the soft ground near the side of the road, between two halftracks. Two soldiers stood watch over us while the others wandered off somewhere. The guards watching us, paid more attention to the battle in the distance then us.

"Got a plan yet?" Jay whispered, keeping his head down to avoid detection.

I folded my hands together and held them by my mouth. "We have an opportunity here."

"What?" Phelps asked, voice cracking with surprise.

"Lower your fucking voice," I hissed, looking at the guards. They still watched the fighting in Mortain. "Look, we're in the enemy camp right now seeing everything."

"But they'll take us to a POW camp," Phelps sighed.

"No, I don't think they will." I glanced up at the guards and rested my chin against my chest. "Think about it, they need to take Mortain and breakout before we encircle them. Right now, they won't waist fuel and men to transport us. Chances are they'll keep us here until the fighting is over. Let's use the time wisely."

Jay and Phelps both nodded in agreement. A sudden rise of voices drew my attention to the road, as the guards returned. They argued, in German, with one another, before speaking to the guards, in front of us. After some more arguing the group left, leaving one man standing watch.

"What was that about?" Jay asked.

"I was right, they're gonna hold us here until the fighting is over. They can only spare one man to watch us," I said.

"So, we escape?" Phelps asked, looking jittery.

"Not yet," I said, "we need to help out the boys in town."

"How?" They asked.

"Ah, still working on that. For now, let's just hang tight and stay calm," I told them.

Jay nodded, but Phelps just shook his head and watched the German guard, in front of, us pace back and forth between the halftracks. Phelps was very nervous and tapped his fingers against his knees in a steady, quick beat. Both from fear and eagerness, Phelps couldn't sit still and it unnerved me; the risks of such an unstable soldier threatened both Jay and me.

I diverted my attention from Phelps, trying to come up with a way to somehow sabotage the Germans from their camp, before we were taken to a POW camp, or Mortain fell. There were plenty of targets to hit; ammo and fuel stores, the forward CP, artillery positions and the like. The only trouble was we had no weapons of any type, it was three of us against hundreds of German soldiers, and we had no way to contact for support.Overhead, three P-47s buzzed the rally area, strafing several tanks, which were still on the road. German soldiers started cursing the *Jabos,* when I figured out what to do next.

"I think I have something," I whispered, as the *Jabos* made a second pass.

"I'm listening," Jay responded, leaning towards me.

"The *Jabos*, we need to get a signal to them." I glanced over my shoulder for a second. "The Germans have their artillery in the hedges, covered from the P-47s. We set off a signal to alert the *Jabos* and take out the artillery, cutting off some of the German support."

I quickly shut up as a group of German soldiers walked towards our position, two negro troopers in the center of the group. Amid insults and profanities, they shoved the two men to the ground next to us and left the single guard to watch us. I looked at the two new soldiers, who sat next to us, and acknowledge the two with a head nod.

"Welcome to our little home," I grunted, trying not to attract too much attention.

"Nice place," one man responded, a fresh cut running across his chin. "You have a bit of a pest problem, though."

I looked to the Germans and shrugged. "We're working on way to handle it."

The two new troopers picked up on the comment. "Anything we can help with," the second man mumbled.

"We need a plan," Jay explained. "So far, we got shit."

I nodded in agreement as a P-47 shot overhead, eight.50cal machine guns pounding a group of Panzers crossing the roadway. The German guard, in front of us, looked up in amazement at the *Jabo*, gawking at the fighter bomber as it blasted a tank with rocket fire. A second and third P-47 soon followed the first, strafing the road where we were. The German guard didn't see them in time, as heavy.50cal bullets tore through his body, and splattered the dirt roadway, with his blood.

I didn't have any escape plan, as I dove forward and grabbed the German's body, dragging him back in between the two halftracks. Quickly, Jay and I stripped the dead soldier of his rifle, sidearm, trench knife, and every bit of ammo he carried. Phelps and the two other soldiers dumped the body behind one of the halftracks between the track and the hedgerow.

""Now what?" Phelps asked as I shouldered the bolt-action rifle.

I looked around and saw no one noticed the missing guard. "Well, the air strikes are keeping them off balance and they won't notice us…yet."

"Then what do we do?" Jay asked, taking the Luger for himself.

"Running, like hell, is not very smart." I glanced behind the tracks. "Let's sneak behind the halftracks and see what we find."

"Anything beats sitting here. I'm Drake, by the way." The scarred trooper said, shaking my hand.

"Allan," the second soldier said, nodding his head.

"Nice to meet both of you. Now, let's get the fuck out here," I spat, with no time for pleasantries.

I moved behind one of the halftracks and squeezed into the space, between the armored side of the track and the hedgerow. There wasn't much space, but it was enough to squeeze through and thankfully there was a line of halftracks stretching along the road. One could only guess why the tracks were just sitting there, but I was told never look a free horse in the mouth, or something along those lines.

I led the group with Phelps, Allan, and Drake behind me, while Jay trailed behind last. We could still here the loud drone of the *Jabos* overhead, followed by the hard cracks and thumps of.50cal machine gun fire and rocket attacks. Now and again, there was the roar of an explosion, as a German vehicle was destroyed in a strafing attack.

"Sounds like we're giving it to'em," Allan grunted as we stalked down the hedgerow.

Phelps was about to respond when the hard, echoing blasts of Flack 88s filled the air. Judging from the times, in between each boom, there were at least seven 88s. Our hearts sunk the second we heard the screech of metal and the death rattle of a dying aircraft engine, which was closely followed by a reverberating rumble of earth, as a *Jabo* fell from the sky.

"That's what we need to do," Jay hissed as we came to the end of the line of halftracks.

"How?" I asked.

"How what?" Allen asked, not understanding what Jay and I were saying.

"Before we leave this place, we need to do something to help the boys in Mortain. Destroying those 88s will help our air cover pop the Panzers, Panthers, and Tigers."

Drake and Allen nodded. "We'll help anyway we can."

I silently thanked the two and turned to scan the area beyond the hedges. There was a T intersection several yards away where the hedgerow ended and opened up into the roaming fields around Mortain, that had no hedges to offer cover. It was in the field just off the intersection which held seven German guns, all arranged in two rows, three 88s in front, four in the rear. A dozen or so troopers were nearby, besides the crew brining in ammo, for the gunners. A single halftrack sat opposite the field, by a stand of trees.

"Okay, we have a rifle, Luger, and a trench knife," I said, outlining our situation. "They have…a shit load more than that, plus, armored support and a few thousand times more men," I said.

"Long odds," Phelps grunted.

"We just need to stop the guns somehow," Jay said, holding the Luger tight in his right hand.

"We screw their ammo up," Drake suggested. "Back when we were running supplies in the Express, the arty shells needed to be watched over, to prevent damage to the timing fuses. If we alter them then the shells don't explode into flack."

"Too many shells," I grunted.

"Or we can blow them to hell," Allan stated mater-of-factly.

"Who doesn't like a good fireball?" Jay joked. "We just need explosives."

"That's easy." Allen pointed to the stacks of artillery shells. "Get me one and I can rig the fuse to blow. Sort of like a large grenade."

I looked to Jay and Phelps, who nodded. "Okay, we set off the ammo stores to take out the 88s. The *Jabos* can have free roam of the area, while we sneak away in the confusion."

Everyone nodded in approval of the plan, mostly because it was the only plan we had. It had its faults and was half assed, at best, but it beat sitting around listing to our friends die in Mortain.

Jay was the quickest among us and volunteered to head out and grab an arty shell, from a stack of several dozen. Allan turned him down, running out from cover before anyone could object. He quickly darted from behind the halftrack and ducked behind a stack of supply crates, mere feet away from a rolling line of Panzers. Not evening hesitating, he ran from the crates to the ammo stores, grabbing an 88 shell and jumping into a ditch alongside the road.

We closely watched as the young soldier unscrewed the tip of the shell and tinkered with its innards, doing something to the firing pin. It only took a minute or two for him to sabotage the shell. Once Allan was done, he placed the shell back within the stack and ran back to us, still, unseen by the hundreds of Germans around us.

"Now we just wait," Allan grunted, crouching next to me and breathing heavily.

"Good work," was all I could say, amazed by the trooper's act of bravery and courage. "How long?"

Allan shrugged, dropping down to sit in the dirt. "Can't say for sure, but it'll only take a few minutes before the-" Allan was cut off as a massive explosion erupted from the stored ammo pile, tossing our destroyed debris in all directions.

We looked on as the fireball expanded and lit several nearby ammo crates, which in turn, spread to the 88s. All eight popped like fire crackers, on the Forth of July, just a few thousand times bigger. The guns, their crews, and surrounding forces were consumed by the explosions, which threw of us to the dirt. It wasn't long before the roar of the *Jabos* filled the sky.

"Now where do we run?" Phelps asked.

"We need to hide, for now," I said. "It's not right to sit out and watch, but dying pointlessly will not help. I think we wait this shit storm out. We helped the *Jabos* deal with the 88s, now we wait."

Allan nodded with Jay. "We can't stay here," Phelps said.

"Then we need…" Shouting and yelling, in German, grabbed my attention. Even though there was a lot of yelling, I could tell some was about us. The following shots at our position explained why.

"We've been made!" Phelps yelled in terror.

"Then go down fighting!" Jay yelled, standing up and firing his Luger at the Germans.

Swearing under my breath, I stood up and leaned around the end of the track, rifle tucked into my shoulder. At least four squads of German paratroopers stood along the road, all firing our way. I lined up a shot on the nearest solider and fired, the man dropping, as blood erupted from his chest.

I pulled back in and cleared the chamber of the rifle, again cursing the German bolt-action rifle. Bullets pinged off the metal side of the track and grenades detonated around us. Drake fell to the dirt clutching his throat, as blood gushed out from a pierced jugular. He lay still, only after a handful off moments, passing out before the massive blood loss killed him.

Allan tried to tend to his wounded friend, as I spun out to fire again. In rapid fire, with a bolt-action rifle, I fired the last four rounds, killing two more Germans. Pulling back, I reloaded, as a grenade detonated under the halftrack. Phelps went down as shrapnel tore into his legs.

I reloaded and was about to hand the rifle to Allan,while I tended to Phelps, when something slammed into the side of my head. A searing hot pain shot through my head as blood splattered across my face, and I fell to the soft earth, my body suddenly unable to move. As everything faded I believed I was dead, with a bullet in my head.

Chapter 13

I always wonder what death would be like, how everything would end for me. My life never flashed before my eyes, I didn't see a white light or anything, I didn't even think of Jessica or my family. Instead, I felt nothing as the world spun and went dark. It was the pounding head ache, that throbbed in my skull, afterwards, the first evidence I was alive.

It felt, as if something heavy was pressing on my head, as the world slowly returned to me. At first, I believed I had died, but I was always told there was no pain in death. Slowly and carefully, I opened my eyes with some trouble, my blood having formed a thin crust over my eyelids.

With a little effort, I was rewarded with a view of the orange sky, the sun slowly being smothered by night. I moved a hand to my head and felt a thick bandaged taped to the left side of my head, freshly crusted blood running along its edges. It was then I remembered being shot, or hit with shrapnel, during the fighting around Mortain.

Cursing, as pain shot up my spine, I propped myself up on my elbows and saw I was lying on the side of the road, near an overturned troop truck. I saw it was a German troop truck, when I spotted two German soldiers lying on the road, both dead by the looks of them. I stood up and wiped coagulated blood from my cheeks, as pain radiated from my head and through my body.

Looking around, I realized I was on an empty road running through an open field, the tree line far off in the distance. Several halftracks and troop trucks littered the road, all burning or smoldering. Dead Germans laid about them. The heavy drone of *Jabos* echoed in the sky when I realized the convoy was strafed by the *Jabos*.

A low groan from the troop truck grabbed my attention. I looked to see Jay lying in the dirt, blood crusted across his uniform shirt. I rushed to his side and felt for a pulse in his neck, finding a very weak one. He was alive, but with several deep gashes on the front of his head and a large bump on the back of his head, most likely from a rifle butt.

Seeing his wounds, I slowly pieced things together. I was wounded, knocked unconscious, grabbed by the Germans, and thrown into a convoy probably heading for a POW camp. The *Jabos* strafed the convoy and killed the Germans, saving my life and Jay's. We'd be POWs if it weren't for Allan and his work at sabotaging the German 88s.

"Corr?" Jay moaned, rolling his head from side to side, before opening his eyes. "Man, you look like shit."

"You look handsome too, you son of a bitch," I sighed, looking around for Phelps or Allan.

I spotted Phelps a few feet away near a crater created by a rocket blast. He was slowly coming to and struggled to walk over to us, dropping down in the dirt on his back.

"Am I dead?" he asked, voice low and horsed.

"Nope," I grunted, speaking too loud that my head hurt even more. "We're alive."

"They…they killed Allan," Jay struggled to say. "I saw it. They overran us after you got hit. They dragged you, Allan, and Phelps off since you were all wounded. They smacked me in the back of the head with a rifle butt, which put me out. Before I passed out, I saw an SS officer put a bullet into Allan's head."

"Fuckers," I spat, feeling more pain from the news. "I hope the Kraut bastard was killed when the *Jabos* attacked."

Jay and Phelps grunted in agreement, as the low roar of burning fires drifted down the barren road. None of us had the energy to move about, so we stayed where we were, slowly regaining our strength. I could feel my muscles were past their breaking point, as my arms and legs, were more or less, numb.

"What are we going to do?" Jay croaked.

I shook my head. "Get back to our lines before night falls."

"Is Mortain even ours anymore?" Phelps asked, still lying on his back.

Struggling, I forced myself to my feet and leaned against the troop truck. "C'mon, we need to get walking anyway," I ordered.

I reached out and helped Jay to his feet, fighting to stay balanced while taking the majority of his weight. Jay grunted and stood up on shaky legs, pressing his body against the troop truck for support. I helped Phelps up, finding several deep shrapnel wounds running up his legs, some poorly bandaged by the Germans.

Once they were back up, I scavenged the dead Germans for rifles and ammo, giving Jay and Phelps their own rifles, with several ammo clips. The two were not in fighting shape, Phelps using the rifle as a crutch, while Jay struggled to keep the weapons in his hands. I was the most fit of the two, but my vision was blurry and I could hardly keep the rifle steady in my hands.

"C'mon, let's go," I urged, treading across the grassy field parallel to the road.

Fires crackled and ammo stores popped with energy from the strafed convoys. Dead Germans lay sprawled out across the field and roadway, many torn to bloodied shreds, by MG fire and shrapnel. The sun was setting and night began to fall, the fires illuminating the stretch of road.

Jay and Phelps limped along behind me, both struggling to walk in a straight line, without falling to the dirt. I stopped now and again to help the two, but it took us nearly an hour, to walk from the front of the convoy to the rear. Night had fallen and we were near the last few halftracks of the convoy.

"This isn't going work," I said, gesturing for the two to stop. "We've only covered ten yards, in under an hour."

"Sorry, but it's a bitch to walk," Phelps grunted, sitting on the ground and sighing.

"It is, but we can't stop now," Jay stated, sweat running down his cheeks. "I'll help you walk."

"No," Phelps waved away Jay and stood back up. "I can keep going."

"Let's just make it to the tree line," I encouraged, setting a goal to keep them focused.

"Right," they agreed.

Phelps and Jay were dead tired and near the edge of total exhaustion. I was close to the breaking point, my head throbbing and muscles burning, like an inferno was raging under my skin. I continued to grit my teeth and forced myself to walk forward, sweat dripping into my eyes and dried blood sticking to my skin. Everything hurt, but I pushed everything out of my mind, just focusing on reaching the trees and nothing else.

Grunting in exhaustion, I passed into the tree line and shuffled towards a small clearing on the ground. Jay dropped down and leaned against a fallen tree, resting his rifle across his chest. Phelps eased himself down and propped himself up against a tree. I sat across from the two and found a comfortable seat, leaning against a smooth boulder.

"Get some sleep," I suggested, laying my rifle across my lap. "I'll keep watch."

Phelps was fast asleep the second he touched the ground, but Jay was awake. "You sure?" he asked.

I nodded. "Get some sleep, I'll be fine."

Jay sighed and leaned back, closing his eyes. "Wake me when you want to change guard."

I silently nodded and kept watch, eyes still on the roadway, which was a dozen or so yards away. Things were still and quiet, the burning convoy now smoldered out and blackened. My mind switched over to Allan and Drake, the two negro servicemen that gave their lives for ours. Drake died waiting for his chance to fight, while Allan was murdered most likely because he was colored. Nazi bastards.

What 'master race' gets its ass kicked across France and into Germany while the Russians kick their teeth in on the Eastern Front?

I felt a wave of sadness smack into me, as I remembered Frank and Matt. Frank was gone, gone for good, from our lives. The realization was hard to accept in England, where I expected a letter to come in from Frank saying it was another of his stupid jokes, but no letter came. It took four days, but I grasped the entire meaning of Frank's death. I took time, to cry alone, in the barracks before drowning my sorrow with every drop of booze I could afford at the pub. The liquor hit me hard, as I'm not a drinker. The next morning I snapped myself out of the self-pity trance and returned to my duties, as squad sergeant.

Matt was dealing with his own troubles, after Frank's death. They weren't because of Frank's death, but of something with his girlfriend. Knowing how strong Matt was, it was something big to rattle him. Just like when we were growing up, we shared everything. Then we shared our own personal hells. It wouldn't be the last time, however.

The drone of aircraft engines brought me back from my thoughts. I craned my head skywards and caught a glimpse of two *Jabos* returning to base, from a full day of flying. For a second I pondered on whether or not to signal them, but it would do no good, provided I had something to signal them with.

As the drone tapered off into the distance, I sighed and dropped my head, chin resting against my chest. My breathing slowed as I began to fall asleep, but I caught myself and snapped my head back up. The woods were still quiet and calm, the local wildlife driven off by the fighting.

Jay stirred slightly and nudged my foot. "Ready to change the guard?" he croaked.

I glanced at my watch, but realized it was gone. "Fine," I grunted, resting my rifle on the ground next to me. Sighing, I rolled to my side and drifted off to sleep in seconds.

"Medic!" There was another volley of MG fire followed my several grenade detonations. "I need a medic!"

The words seemed to be falling on deaf ears as Hackett ceased to breathe. More rifle fire cracked in the distance along with MG fire that seemed to go on for eternity. It took a few seconds to realize that I was shaking, my hands slick with Private Hackett's blood. Captain Hiller appeared above me and helped me to my feet.

"C'mon!" he yelled as another platoon of German troops rushed our position. "They're herding us into a murder hole!"

I responded without thinking. I was back on my feet and running, Thompson held firm in my hands, as the still shook. Rifle fire cracked from behind us, bullets zipping past us in close enough proximity I could hear them cutting through the air. Hiller grunted and cursed as we retreated into a house that overlooked one of St. Lo's gutted parks.

"Get down!" he yelled as an armored car shot down the ruble strewn streets.

We fell to the wooden floor of the home, as auto cannon fire punched through the building walls, exploding sections of cement and brick on contact. The hard rain pelted our backs, as the soft *whomp* of a bazooka rose above the cannon fire. An echoing explosion silenced the armored car.

I picked myself up and moved to the front window, ducking behind an overturned couch. Bullets shot through the shattered window, as the Germans advanced on our position. I sprayed the advancing group with my Thompson, killing at least four Germans, as a Sherman tank rounded the corner.

The coaxial and turret machine guns chattered along with its main cannon, shredding the Germans in the street. I watched as six men were incinerated by one of the tank's new, white phosphorus rounds, the deadly chemical flash frying the soldiers. A German AT gunner fired one of his compact *panzerfaust* rockets at the Sherman and blew a gaping hole in the turret armor. Another shot blew the stored ammo, killing the tank crew.

"Out the back!" Hiller snarled, gesturing to the hole in the back wall.

I obeyed and ran, hurling myself through the massive hole. I tucked in my head, as I hit the ground, rolling to a stop, as Hiller landed next to me. Grunting, I rose to my feet, as four German soldiers burst into the yard, weapons spraying our position. Something hot grazed my arm, as they closed in, one heading for me.

I realized I'd dropped my Thompson, as the German leveled his rifle with my face. I stared down the barrel, a clap of thunder echoed through my ears. The German tumbled backwards a volley of shots slammed into his body, the force flinging him backwards. I rolled to see Jessica charge the other Germans with Ramos and Phelps in toe.

A second clap of thunder echoed as another searing pain shot up my back. Driven by the force, my face fell to the dirt, as the shattered remains of St. Lo faded away.

"Corr," Jay hissed, driving away the nightmare that was the fight for St. Lo. "Corr, we've got company."

My eyes shot open and I rolled to my stomach, hands reaching to my rifle. "What?" I croaked, voice cracking from my dry throat.

"Someone is coming down the road," Jay reported, lying prone, next to Phelps.

"Ours or theirs?" I asked, crawling next to the two.

"Can't tell," Phelps grunted. "They're too far down the road to tell for sure."

I squinted my eyes, realizing it was a little before dawn. At least twelve soldiers were walking up the road towards our position. It was too dark to make out their uniforms and we couldn't sneak around to get a closer look.

"I can get…three of them," Jay mumbled, resting his cheek against the German rifle. "They'll scatter after that."

"I'll be lucky to get two," I hissed, my eye sight better than before but not back to normal. 'But they'll get us without a doubt."

"So die here or die running," Phelps snorted. "What a fucking choice."

I cursed my blurry vision as I pressed the butt of my rifle into my shoulder. My mind raced over any and all options we had, but came up with three: fight, run, or hide. All three were death sentences, as the soldiers drew closer and closer.

"They could be ours," Jay pointed out.

"Or it could be another group of SS storm troopers," Phelps added, the words mumbled and hushed.

"Think positive." The words seemed hollow, but a little optimism never hurt. "They could be ours since we helped the *Jabos* take down the German tanks. Prepare for the worst, hope for the best, and expect the unexpected."

The advancing soldiers were a dozen or so yards down the road from our position, in the tree line. No talking could be heard, and they walked silently, taking a cautious but quick pace.

"I got the lead man," Jay whispered, eyes fixed down the iron sights of the rifle.

"I got the second," Phelps added, rifle moving to follow the man.

My sights fell on the third in the line, finger shifting from the rifle's trigger guard to the trigger. I began to do a quick calculation, guessing on how long I had to live from the second I fired, to the second they found our position. Three minutes. My finger slowly compressed around the trigger when something caught my eye.

"Stop!" I ordered, hand pulling away from the trigger. "Hold fire!"

Jay and Phelps looked to me in puzzlement. "What?"

"It's the squad," I hissed, lowering my rifle.

"How can you tell?" Jay inquired.

"I can see that frigging 'E' Malks wrote on his helmet in orange paint," I explained. "To think I criticized the bastard for it."

Jay and Phelps let out sighs of relief, as the squad walked a few yards away from us. Not risking spooking them, I let out a sharp whistle while still hugging the ground. True to their skill, everyone dropped to the ground and scanned the area for the source of the whistle.

Again I whistled, grabbing Captain Hiller's attention. I saw him at the front of the formation, his head turning our way. I raised my hand into the air and whistled a third time. Hiller spotted me and raised his Thompson, barking out, 'halt order in' German.

"Wrong person!" I yelled out, still hugging the soft earth. "Hold your fire!"

"Out, now!" Hiller barked, unmoving. "Hands on your heads!"

I signaled to Jay and Phelps, telling them to stand up slowly with their hands on their heads. The three of us slowly rose up, Phelps still having trouble with the shrapnel still in his legs. The look on Hiller's face expressed no surprise as he saw us.

"We got a little lost!" I called out, helping Jay shuffle Phelps to the road.

"Son of a bitch!" Parker yelled out. "You fuckers are alive."

I grinned, as Doc ran out to take Phelps. "Barely, but yes."

Hiller shook his head and walked over to the three of us. "What the hell are you doing out here?"

"One long story, sir," I stated, spotting Jessica among the squad.

"Care to explain?" he asked.

I looked to the Jay and filled Hiller in, from the time the attack on Mortain started to the few seconds before I spotted Malks. Hiller sighed and wiped some sweat from his forehead before responding.

"I had a feeling you had something to do with silencing those 88s," he finally said.

"It was more of Allan's doing, sir." I silently cursed myself for not getting his last name or Drake's.

"We all of you helped us on the hill. With no AA, the flyboys pounded the Germans with everything they had. Their attack faltered by nightfall and we shoved them back." Hiller said.

A pair of *Jabos* shot by overhead, passing by and shooting towards the horizon. After a short break, four more shot by with rockets and bombs hanging from under their wings.

"Where are the Germans now?" Jay asked.

Hiller jerked a thumb down the road. "About twelve miles east, heading for the Falasie Gap, before it's closed. Our orders were to keep following them and take as many of the bastards down before they escape. Of course, we were on the watch for you three. I couldn't, no wouldn't, write you all off as missing in action, without doing something.

"Sanders, take these three back to the aide station in Mortain." Hiller ordered. "We've got a patrol to finish, but I want you checked out first. Get some rest and I'll be back later."

I managed a week salute. "Yes, sir."

Hiller nodded, as Sanders and Jessica appeared. Jessica said something to Hiller, but I who shrugged.

"My God, you look terrible!" gasped Jessica, as she moved to my side, shouldering some of my weight.

I managed a feeble smile. "Thanks, you look wonderful too."

Jessica smiled back, but I could see the fear and worry in her eyes. "Don't do this again." She moved closer to my ear, as we began to walk back down the road to Mortain. "I thought this might be like St. Lo again."

I didn't say anything, both from exhaustion and from not knowing what to say. The terror that Jessica experienced, the fear and worry when I came within an inch of my life, buried under a collapsed building, was back again. Seeing it again tugged at my heart and knotted my stomach.

The aide stations of Mortain were packed with wounded soldiers, most critical and near death. Many young men lay on stretchers, in and around an aide station, set up in the town hall, bodies broken and bloodied, by the hellish German attack. What medics and doctors that were in the city, raced about the wounded, offering any aide they could. Many were dead and dying, as more and more men were brought in.

I was laid down on a stretcher in the back of the main area of the town hall, which was a wide open reception area under a rotunda ceiling, like the Capitol Building. Hundreds of wounded soldiers were laid alongside me, stretchers everywhere, forming disorganized rows of torn and bloodied men.

I lay on the stretcher, with a fresh bandage on my head, and a second on my arm, for a wound I did not notice at all. The medics refused to let me leave, saying that I could drop any second from my exhaustion and fatigue. I believed it was all bullshit, but I couldn't be fighting with my vision blurred.

The air was hot and stale with every breath, like the air had been breathed a dozen times before, being pumped into the room. Wounded men groaned, moaned, and cried out in pain and agony, while medics rushed about. The trooper next to me was dead, having died minutes after he was brought in while another lay silent and still, alive but unresponsive to the world around him. The fact that he was missing both legs below the knees explained why.

"Tully hasn't said a word since the attack," a trooper sitting on a stretcher near me said, "He's off in his own world. Lucky bastard."

"How old is he?" I asked.

"Nineteen," the trooper replied. He scratched at a thick bandage over his shoulder, his right arm in a sling. "I think, he didn't say much when he arrived yesterday."

"A replacement," I sighed, looking away from the unmoving soldier. "You hit bad?"

The trooper shook his head. "Some shrapnel in the arm, with a bullet in my shoulder; nothing serious. You?"

"Head wound," I responded, seeing a set of Sergeant stripes on the trooper's uniform. I extended a hand. "Corr."

"Arthur," he answered, shaking my hand with his bad hand. "Where you from, Corr?"

"Jersey, you?" I answered.

"South Carolina, outside of Charleston," he said, grinning.

Two soldiers passed by, with a wounded man on a stretcher, between them. The poor kid was missing his right arm and had a large stomach wound. Judging by his silence, he was either dead or unconscious.

Arthur sighed and shook his head, as the men passed. "That kid was another replacement from my squad. Crossing him off the list, only four other guys made it back. I think I'm the only one that's gonna see tomorrow."

Crap, I thought to myself. "How many men did you have?"

Arthur shrugged. "I had fifteen up until last night. I lost four in the artillery barrage, another three when the Germans attacked, four during the retreat, and then one just now. Tully and I are what's left. You an only child now?"

"No, all of my guys made it through." I said, as I looked around. "We were right in the thick of the shit, but I told them to pull back since we didn't have much ammo to start."

"None of us did, it's a miracle that we weren't overrun. What really helped was the flyboys after someone knocked out the German 88s," Arthur said.

So, our loss meant something. I said, trying to justify, it in my mind. "Good bunch of troopers, eh?"

Arthur shrugged and tugged at his bandages. "Ya know, I've only been a Sergeant for all of two days. Two fucking days and I lose my entire squad."

I didn't reply; there was nothing that could really be said. It wasn't easy being the last man standing from your squad. You survived while your brothers, men you train, fought, ate, lived, and died with, didn't. It made you question why, but there is never a real answer, just what you need to stay sane.

There was a low rumbling off in the distance, a steady *thump-thump-thump* of hollow echoes. The air was still as the thumps echoed, my mind dismissing it, as the fighting continued, securing the northern section of Hill 314,or one of the skirmishes along the countryside, but there was something off. The sudden whistle of artillery shells overhead signaled the barrage.

"Incoming!" a Lieutenant yelled,standing atop the main staircase.

"Down, down!" I yelled, flinging myself off the stretcher to the floor.

Artillery shells landed across the city with a ferocious thunder that shook the earth. Echoing explosions ripped across the city as everyone in the field hospital scurried for cover. I rolled myself under the stretcher and Arthur dropped under his. Men screamed and yelled. Several arty shells tore into the building, sections of roof off were blown in, under a hail of stone, dust, and shrapnel.

Outside, shells pummeled the front stairs, tearing apart the wounded caught outside. Explosions shattered windows and flung glass shards through the air like thousands of flying daggers. More screams and a section of the building was blown to rubble, and a dozen, or so, wounded men were consumed in a flash of fire and steel.

"Help the wounded!" medics were yelling, as people struggled to get to cover.

Arthur and I were back on our feet as the barrage tapered off, the hospital and town were in a shambles. We grabbed a still and quiet Tully off his cot and placed him under his stretcher. Once he was safe, we moved to the next stretcher in the row, and helped another wounded trooper to the floor. The barrage continued, as we moved to help others.

It was the thump-thump-thump of artillery again, but with the God awful screech and scream of rockets. Called 'Screaming Mimi's' by most who've been hit by them, they were portable German rocket launchers that fired six incendiary rockets in one barrage. The unique scream of the rockets was the only warning, of the hell they were bringing.

The first rockets slammed into the building's roof, blowing huge junks of stone into the air. The next barrage slammed through the shattered remains of the roof and exploded in the crowded aide station. Fireballs consumed dozens and dozens of wounded, as fires began to spread, and smoke clogged the air.

"C'mon, we need to get out!" Arthur yelled to me.

I nodded towards Tully, grabbing the wounded trooper and lifting him over my shoulders. Arthur grabbed a dazed trooper nearby, who could walk, and pulled him with his good arm towards a newly formed hole in the wall. Struggling, I held Tully firm on my shoulders and raced for the open air, as more explosions rocked the building. Arthur was right behind me with the dazed trooper hanging on his arm.

Jabos shot overhead, just as we emerged outside onto the front lawn of the building. The *Jabos* shot over the town and went hunting for the German artillery. It didn't take long before the fighter bombers hunted down the German artillery positions and took them out through several strafing runs.

The echoing booms, of the artillery, died down, as soldiers ran to the field hospital, to help with the wounded. I led Arthur down to the base of the stairs and set Tully down next to the wounded trooper Arthur pulled out. Breathing heavily, I stopped for a second to catch my breath while soldiers converged on the field hospital.

"Never a moment's rest," Arthur sighed, pressing down on his wounded shoulder. Several of his stitches broke and his wound began to bleed again.

"You okay?" I asked,, my head throbbing with a migraine.

"It's nothing, just a popped stitch," he said.

"Corr!" someone yelled behind me. I turned, as Jay ran up to me, face covered in dust and sweat.

"You hurt?" I asked, as we shook hands.

"Nope, I got lucky," he explained. "I was out back taking a leak when they attacked."

More wounded were being brought back as several jeeps pulled up in front of the hospital. Medics were swamped, as they struggled to treat the incoming wounded, while they had to tend to those wounded in the hospital. Judging by the influx of wounded, the fighting was getting worse.

Jay and I helped with the wounded, all through the night, until the next morning, when the squad returned. Captain Hiller gave us new sets of weapons and equipment, before taking us to the field. I hadn't slept for more than a few minutes since the first wave of the attack, on Mortain, but I kept going once I geared up. Captain Hiller told us we were heading west to a small town just off the main German escape route, to scout out a group of Panzers believed to be hiding out there until nightfall.

"How come the flyboys can't do a few recon flights?" Nate asked as we were walking down the road.

"Cause, the Krauts are hiding in the town and have disguised themselves from the recon planes," Adam explained shrugging his shoulders with the squad radio on his back.

"Disguised?" Sanders mocked. "I think the flyboys are smart enough to realize that no cow is that big."

A ripple of laugher spread across the squad. Captain Hiller grinned slightly, as he marched at the front of the group. I walked a few feet to his right, along the edge of the road, Thompson resting in the crook of my arm. It was another clear day with the sun slowly rising into the sky, as it approached 10:00 AM. So far things were quiet, aside from the occasional Thunderbolt or Mustang flying overhead.

"You think they'd give us some jeeps to use," Jay sighed, resting his Springfield over his shoulders.

"Jeeps are for the recon units," Vic grunted, bringing up the rear of the column.

"And what the fuck are we doing?" Jay asked.

"A recon run," I answered. "We're a rifle squad doing some recon, so no jeeps."

"What the fuck kind logic is that?" He demanded, his temper about to be lost.

"You got an 'R' chalked on your helmet?" Malks asked.

Vic grunted to himself. "No."

"Then you ain't recon and ain't getting' no jeeps," Malks said, hoping to put an end to this discussion.

Hiller held up a hand to signal silence and to stop. Everyone crouched down, as Hiller drew his binoculars, to scan down the road. Everyone was still and silent, as I drew my own binoculars. Pressing to my eyes, I peered the outer parts of the town.

A handful of old, graying buildings were in sight on opposite sides of the road into town. No German forces could be seen and there was no movement besides the flowing laundry drying in the air, in several yards. Only two people were in sight, a young woman collecting laundry off a clothing line and a young boy helping, maybe her son.

"They don't seemed worried," I said watching them move without any real care to anything else. "You think she'd be doing that if the Germans were there?"

Hiller grunted to himself. "Could be a trap." Hiller lowered his binoculars. "Jessica, up front," he hissed in French.

"Yes?" Jessica responded crouching next to Hiller, in a faded infantry uniform.

"You know anything about this town?" Hiller asked.

"I have some contacts based here, but I've never been here myself," she said.

Hiller handed her his binoculars. "See anything out of the ordinary?"

Jessica took a look. "Where I've been, most women wouldn't be out if the Germans were around. They defiantly wouldn't have their children out."

"So the Germans aren't there," I mumbled. "I'll take Jay and scout it out."

"Right, we'll hang back and watch your six. Signal us if it's clear, but hightail it back here if the Germans are there."

"No problem." I waved over to Jay. "C'mon, let's scout this out."

Jay nodded and we ran off the road, into the open field, off the road. We had a few dozen yards of open ground to cross before we reached the outer buildings. So far, things looked clear, but Jay and I laid still on the ground for a few seconds. Still, things remained clear.

"Take it in on a dead run?" Jay suggested, as he watched the town through his sniper scope.

"No, let's do it in sections." I did a quick calculation in my head. "We run eight yards, then drop down. After a quick check, we run to that shed near the first building on the left. From there, we move in and scout it out."

"Right," Jay agreed. "Just say when."

"Now." Jay and I shot to our feet and quickly ran across the field. Gear rattled as we sprinted across eight, or so, yards before dropping to the ground. Jay checked the area for anything to signal, it was clear. Grunting, I jumped up and ran to the wooden shed, a few feet from the first stone building.

Jay and I hugged the wooden shed for cover, as we took a second to catch our breath. Moving slowly, I edged my way to the side of the shed and took a peek around the corner. The town streets were made of cobblestone, starting near the first building, on the edge of town, where the street turned to dirt. Before the stone started I could see tank tread tracks, several sets of them. I nudged Jay's shoulder and nodded towards the tracks.

"You see any in town?" he asked crouching next to me.

"Nope," I sighed, seeing nothing on the road.

"Hey! Hey!" a strange voice called.

Jay and I turned, to see an old man, standing near the house across from us. He was waving his hands, while Jay and I kept our weapons trained on him. The man didn't waver, as we kept our weapons aimed, instead he waved again and yelled out in French.

"What the hell is he saying?" Jay asked as he kept his Springfield aimed.

"He's saying the Germans are gone," I translated. "Well, he's saying 'gone.' I can't tell what else, he's talking too fast."

"So Germans 'gone' or us 'gone' as in leave?" Jay asked.

"Who…" I spun around, as the woman and child we saw, walked out from their house. I lowered my Thompson slightly, as the woman called out 'liberators' to us.

"What do we do?" Jay asked.

I lowered my Thompson and the old man drew a small, crumpled French flag from his jacket pocket and began to wave it. "Lower your weapon." I held my Thompson one handed and waved back to the Hiller, signaling the squad to move up.

"Smart move, Lieutenant," a French man called out emerging from an alley.

I turned and saw him with a French flag tied around one arm, an MP-40 slung over the other. He was wearing a brown leisure suite with black, slick back hair.

"French *Résistance*?" I said more then asked.

The man nodded. "Reynard Hask, formerly Capitaine Hask, French Infantry."

We shook hands. "Former infantry officer? Guess a lot of the Underground is former military."

"Those, of us, who were left behind at Dunkirk had nowhere else to turn," Hask explained.

"This town secure?" Jay asked, still holding his rifle at his waist.

"The Germans retreated, in the night, on foot." He jerked a thumb towards the center of the town. "They ran out of gas and left their Panzers and Panthers to sit across the town."

Captain Hiller appeared behind us, as he ran with the squad following him. The squad quickly fanned out, as Hiller approached Reynard, with Jessica.

"Captain Hiller, 1st Infantry Division," Hiller introduced himself with a handshake.

"Nice to meet you, Capitaine." Reynard turned to Jessica and hugged her. "I thought I lost you," he whispered to her in French.

I felt a sudden hit of jealousy, in my gut, as the two hugged and kissed.

"He's getting your girl," Ramos whispered as he stood at my side. "Want me to handle him?"

I shook my head and shrugged it off. "She's not my girl, *amadán*."

"*Amadán*?" Ramos repeated "What the fuck is that?"

"Gaelic, Ramos," I said ignoring Reynard. "The language of the Irish."

"What does it mean? Ramos demanded.

I laughed to myself and slung my Thompson over my shoulder. "Something you, and every man in command are."

Captain Hiller had us do a check of the town, to be sure the information was reliable, and it wasn't a trap. Sure enough, we found a dozen, or so, Panzers and Panthers abandoned within the wide alleys and in a few barns, left abandoned without gas. Several Panthers were left in the center of the town. Probably because they were out of gas and ammo.

Once things were secure, Hiller called back to Mortain and reported in the village was secure. About an hour later, an advance column of Sherman tanks and jeeps thundered up the road and into town. The sight of so many tanks and soldiers had the towns people throw a huge party for them. Nearly the entire town was out, as the tankers rolled in, many clapping and cheering on the sidewalk. People were happy and grateful, most waving American and French flags, or tossing food and wine to us, as a thank you.

"Fucking tankers," Vic snorted, as we walked down the streets, to the OP, set up in the center of town. "They get all the fucking praise."

Ramos laughed, as he was stuffing his pockets with bread and wine bottles the locals gave him. "Hey, they love us too! Look at all this."

I grinned, as I shuffled through the dense crowds of people cheering to the tankers, as they rolled by. Several women were riding aboard the tanks, alongside their crews, while others hugged and kissed every soldier who walked by. In the five minutes it took me to reach the center of town, nearly a dozen women kissed me on the cheeks, while every man wanted to shake my hand. After a while, I gave up on saying thank you, over and over again.

"You'd think we won the war or something," Jay called out,as we stepped into the store, being used as the CP.

"We did for these people," I said standing in the doorway. I laughed to myself, as I saw a group of kids climbing all over the abandoned Panthers and hanging flags off their cannons. "Now that we're here, the Germans won't be back."

Jay shrugged. More kids began to crowd around the Shermans and soldiers on foot. A group of six or seven kids came up to Jay and me, all looking up in awe at us, or at least, our weapons. I smiled, as I fished out several chocolate bars from my pack. That was the way to win over the kids, give them some chocolate and gum, and they were instantly your friends. The kids happily accepted our chocolate with smiles and laughs, before running back into the crowd.

"I think I can get used to this," Jay said, as we watched the kids run off.

"Yeah, it's a nice change from everything else," I admitted.

"Hey guys," Malks called out, passing through the crowd to reach us. His helmet was off and dangling from his belt, with his hands full of bottles of French wine.

"See, you've been making friends," I said gesturing to the wine.

"Hey, I just liberated these bottles." Malks handed a bottle to Jay and me. "Stuff's from 1904."

"Good year," Jay sighed, as we placed the bottles in our packs.

"Don't you just love all this? I already ran out of candy and gum," I said, with a smile.

Malks was all smiles with the kids. He was one of the only guys in the squad, with a wife and child back home. Malks always showed how good of a father he is. He always spoke so lovingly of his wife and daughter.

Malks sighed to himself and shook his head. "Hope I can be like this with Kayla when I get back."

"You know you will be," I said.

Malks nodded. "Yeah and I hope the rest of the war goes like this." He gestured to the crowds of cheering people. "At this rate, I'll be back home for Kayla's third birthday."

Malks was depressed when November rolled around. Kayla was born just as we touched down in North Africa, but Malks didn't find out until January.

"Bolger," Hiller called, as he stood near a map spread out on the bakery counter. "Come here for a second."

"Sir?" I asked and I stepped over to the counter.

"The Germans have a hidden airstrip set up in the woods, to the northwest of here," he pointed to a stand of trees on the map. "So far, the flyboys haven't found it yet and probably won't."

"The Germans went to great care to cover the airfield from your planes." I felt a bit of annoyance, as Reynard spoke. He seemed like such an arrogant bastard. "We haven't had a chance to see what is there, but it is an airfield."

"Division wants us to secure that airstrip," Hiller explained. "The Germans are believed to be working on jet powered aircraft, much like how they've built the V-1 and V-2 rockets. Ike is very interested in any information concerning jet powered aircraft, of any type, and had deemed the securing of such information top priority, while we have the Germans on the run."

I nodded. "When do we move out?"

"Two hours," Reynard answered. "It won't be long before the forces, at the airstrip, decide to retreat, as well. When they do that, they'll destroy whatever they cannot take with them. It's best we strike now, while they're still there."

"I'll make sure everyone is ready to go in time, sir." I made sure to look only at Hiller, when I said sir.

"And we'll be doing this on our own, Bolger," Hiller added. "The tankers will be pushing east, to pursue the Germans. The airstrip is too far off the path for them to traverse. Air cover is a no go, as well, since they can't see the base."

I raised an eyebrow. "What about the other squads?"

"All heading east. We'll be working with members of the Underground from the town. *Capitaine* Reynard will be leading an eight man group of fighters."

"Yes, sir." I saluted Hiller and left the bakery, where Jay and Malks were still waiting. Malks had already cracked open one of the bottles of wine and was sucking down the bottle's contents.

"So, now what?" Jay asked, leaning his rifle against his hip.

"We're rolling out,to secure an airstrip, in two hours," I said, switching my gaze to Malks. "That better be grape juice, trooper."

Malks laughed as shoved the cork into the bottle. "Of course, sir, it's juice, or it was in 1904."

I suppressed a grin. "Just cut back on it till later."

Malks continued, laughs were drowned out, as three *Jabos* flew over the town, in a loose formation, full payloads of rockets and bombs clinging to their underside rails. More tanks were passing by, at a snail's pace, to wiggle through the crowds of civilians. Several Sherman tanks grumbled by with a pair of Sherman Fireflies following them, the Fireflies, crewed by men from one of the British tank corps in the area. All of them were burdened down with sandbags, logs, and spare tank treads, to add a tiny bit of extra armor, in an attempt to stop the heavy shells fired from Panthers and Tigers.

Following the tanks, were several jeeps loaded down with a recon squad from the 16th. All of them were fresh recruits, strait from state side, faces young and energetic, with clean and undamaged uniforms. They were the far opposite of us, uniforms torn, burned, and patches that were faded and caked with dirt, grit, and mud.

"We moving out again?" Nate called out, as he crossed in the wake of dust, from the passing tanks.

"Yup," I answered, "going on a little sortie, up north."

"Sounds, oh, so wonderful," Nate snorted, his newly 'acquired' M1A1 carbine, greatly favored by paratroopers, hanging from his shoulder.

As Nate began to walk away, I lightly grabbed his shoulder. "How's your sister doing?" I asked in a low whisper.

Nate glanced over his shoulder. "Better, now that I'm sending her all of my pay. I spoke to the Cap like you said, and he arranged it so my pay goes directly her instead of, to me, and then her. Don't know how, but Hiller even got me a small boost in my hazard, pay to go to her."

I nodded. "If you ever need a little extra now and again…"

Nate laughed dryly. "Hey, I'll just take what I need when we play cards."

I forced a small grin. "You can try."

Nate managed a small grin, before wondering off in the crowd of people. I crossed the cobblestone street, to the town hotel, which was now being used as a barracks to house men passing through the town. Several men from Dog Company were standing out front, speaking with members of the local Résistance group, the soldiers sharing their supply of smokes.

"Sir," one of the Dog Company troopers said, with a head nod. He held up a torn, white pack of cigarettes. "Smoke?"

I waved it away. "They'll kill ya," I said.

The trooper laughed. "Better this then the Germans right, sir?"

"Good point," I chuckled.

Stepping into the motel, the harsh glare of the sun was cut off, offering a small relief. Within the lobby, stood several more troopers from Dog Company, with Vic and Sanders near the reception desk, speaking to the motel owner. The two were trying to get a room, but the language barrier just frustrated Sanders, while Vic watched in amusement.

"A room," Sanders was arguing, expressing the word 'room' slowly and gesturing with his hands. "You know? The place this frigging hotel is full of?"

"I'm no idiot," the innkeeper remarked in French, enjoying Sander's plea for a room, just as much as Vic.

"What?" Sanders asked shaking his head. "Damn it; just give me a room key!" Sanders pointed to the wall of hooks behind the counter, keys dangling from most of the hooks. "C'mon, how hard is this?"

"As hard as you make it," snorted the innkeeper in French.

Shaking my head, I intervened and got between the two. "Sanders, just shut the fuck up for a sec, would ya?" I asked in a sarcastic tone with a smile. "We won't be here long enough for you to need a room."

"What, we're moving out?" Sanders asked.

"In two hours." I turned to the innkeeper and waved off Sanders. "Please excuse my friend here," I said in French. "The man means well, but isn't the best at public relations."

The man laughed. "So I've noticed. I've been told to hold the rooms until all officers have been given one."

"Don't worry, we're moving out with the bulk of the forces." I turned and gestured for Vic to follow. He nodded, as I walked after Sanders, who stood outside, puffing on a cigarette near the door.

"Thought you didn't smoke," Vic said as, we walked out.

"New habit," Sanders replied before inhaling deeply.

"No bitching or complaining," I told Sanders in a helpful tone.

"Right," he slurred.

I ignored Sanders' insubordinate tone, letting it slip, without a second thought. Vic laughed to himself, as he watched Sanders angrily inhale two more cigarettes, before he ran out. I turned away from the two and walked down the street, in search of the rest of the squad when I spotted Jessica. She stood by herself, near a still column of tanks, her MP-40 still slung over her shoulder.

"Hey," I said, as I drew close to her.

"Hello," she responded with a warm smile. "How are you doing?"

"Good. We'll be moving out in two hours, so don't get too relaxed," I said, sarcastically.

Jessica nodded. "I still practice English, as you say." Her English was still broken, but she was picking up the language, at a very quick pace.

I smiled and nodded. "You're getting it, just takes time. Tell ya what, when you master English I'll teach you Gaelic."

She tilted her head slightly. "Gaelic?"

"The language of Ireland," I explained. "My dad and grandfather taught me to speak it when I was young,." I looked off for a second to think. "The first word my grandfather taught me was *saighdiúir*."

"That word sounds familiar," she said.

I nodded. "It means soldier. He also taught me *gaiscíoch,* which means warrior or hero."

Jessica tested the words. "*Saighdiúir* and *gaiscíoch*. Hmm, sounds very strange to me. It makes English seem that much easier."

"Try learning it when you're eight." I said, remembering how difficult I found it, at first.

The two of us laughed, as a sudden thudding in the distance, grabbed our attention. Our eyes turned towards the east in the hopes of seeing something, but the thud-thud-thud was very familiar.

"Incoming!" A tanker yelled out, from atop his Sherman.

"Down!" I yelled, grabbing Jessica. I pulled her away from the column of tanks and led her away from the cluster of people and soldiers, nearly shoving her into the doorway of a nearby building. "Follow me!"

Jessica tried to argue, as the first shells began to land, several explosions erupting across the small town. I ran with her, as knots of people still crowded the streets. Just like the rest of the soldiers still in the town. We worked to disperse the civilians and get them to safety. Where safety was, in the middle of artillery barrage, meant a hole in the ground or a basement or anywhere away from the explosions.

"Get to cover, get to cover!" Jay was yelling, as he stood in front of the CP, directly people away from the town square.

"Jay!" I yelled, running to him with Jessica. "Jay, where's the Captain?"

"Inside!" He jerked his head towards the CP.

I raced past him, into the bakery we used as our CP. Hiller stood with Adam near the maps, spread out on the counter, with several officers from the other rifle squads. Hiller worked between issuing orders to the squad Lieutenants and shouting into the radio.

"Preston, take your squad and clear out the town square!" Hiller ordered one of the Lieutenants. "Make sure the civilians get to safety and away from the bulk of our forces passing through the town. Mason, take second platoon and head to the northern edge of the town, to set up defensive positions. Wex, take third and sure up the checkpoint on the eastern road, out of town. Make sure things are secured, incase the Germans are using the barrage as cover for an advance. Go!"

"Sir," I said, as the Lieutenants ran out to their men, "waiting for orders."

"Round up the squad and get to the northern road for regroup." Hiller glanced at his watch. "I sent out the Résistance cell, to scout the area around the airfield, a few minutes ago." More artillery exploded outside, as civilians screamed in horror, when a Sherman was consumed in a ball of flame. "You'll need to take the airfield once you reach the RV."

"Sir?" I asked.

"I'm the only ranking officer here and need to keep things from falling to shit. I trust you to take the squad and secure the airfield. Can you handle it?" Hiller said.

"Yes, sir," I said, "We'll have it under our control."

"Good. Get going, Bolger and report back in when you've captured the airfield,: he grunted.

I nodded and turned to Jay. "Squad's already assembled," he said nodding towards to the front of the building.

"Good, let's get to the RV along the northern road," I yelled.

The three of us left the CP and collected the squad before dispatching our orders. Once everyone was readied, we made our way across the town center, to the road leading north. We ran, as more and more artillery shells slammed into the town, the ground shaking under our boots. Buildings erupted in clouds of flame and shrapnel, as shells tore into them. Civilians ran for cover and soldiers moved to their positions, in preparation for a counter attack.

The attack had started, no more than two minutes ago, but the damage was catastrophic and mounting. Several tanks were blown apart, while several were buried under debris, as the buildings around them crumbled. Bodies littered the cobblestone street, more civilian then military. It took all my willpower, to not stop, at the sight of dead children, the urge to help was nearly overwhelming.

"Through the alleys!" I yelled, as we crossed the square and approached the buildings along the northern edge.

The roads were targeted by the German artillery, as tanks crowded them, the alleys were safer. While very cramped, we ran in single file, to squeeze through without slowing. I was at the front of the group, with Jay close behind. An artillery shell slammed into one of the buildings lining the alley, its roof exploded in a cloud of debris. Wooden splinters and ash rained down, as the concussion wave thumped in our chests.

The alley soon widened and it opened up into several yards along the edge of the town. The yards were separated by several low stone walls, with a handful of wooden sheds. I emerged first and vaulted over one of the low walls, as several shells exploded across the yards. I fell face first, into the dirt, as a shell exploded several feet away, inside one of the wooden sheds. I held a hand to my helmet, dirt and wooden splinters peppered my back.

"You hit?" Doc asked, as he helped me to my feet.

"No, I'm good."

I stood up and led everyone across the yards, to the northern road leading out of the town. Near the road, was a shallow gully, that intersected it and ran towards the tree line. I ordered everyone to duck down inside for cover, as we waited for the Résistance fighters to return.

I jumped down, into the shallow gully first, my boots splashing into the shallow water, at the bottom. The squad split up on reaction, several covering the front and back edges of the gulley, the rest took cover.

"Hold fire, unless I give the order," I announced, crawling on my chest, to the top of the gully. Slipping my Thompson over my shoulder,

I took out my binoculars and held them to my eyes. I quickly scanned the northern approach and the tree line before Edwards called out.

"Sir, I've got movement on the right," he said lying prone, on the opposite side of the gulley.

I moved to his side and looked out. "Hold fire," I whispered, seeing the approaching men. "It's them."

Reynard, and two of his seven fighters, darted across the open ground from the tree line, towards our position. Everyone was silent, as they approached, several rifles still trained on them, just to be safe. I waved slightly, to signal them,and crouched at the bottom of the gulley, as they dropped in.

"We heard the barrage," Reynard grunted, as the artillery still echoed in town. "How bad is it?"

"Not sure," I answered, fumbling for the map tucked into my jacket. "We had to bug out quick, but a few of our tanks were hit and there were civilian losses, not high, but some nonetheless."

"The artillery is near the airstrip," Reynard explained, as he saw me take out my map. He shuffled over to me and outlined the area where the Germans were. "The airstrip is half a mile away to the north, but it's deep in the woods and not easily reached by any means, other than on foot."

"We don't have any armor support anyway," I added, as he traced out the area on the map.

"Well, the only way in is a small footpath running south to north. I have the rest of my men waiting by the path, they're watching enemy movements. The hangers are on the far edge of the airstrip, under cammo netting; there's four in all. Two barracks are located right next to it, housing pilots and soldiers. A single command building is located opposite the hangers, with the artillery close by," he explained.

"How many men we looking at?" I asked.

"Thirty to thirty-eight armed soldiers, with a dozen, or so, pilots that we know of. There are six artillery emplacements, four 8cm mortars and two 8cm model 42's. There's nothing heavier than that besides three MG42s, but they're not deployed in entrenched fighting positions.

I nodded. "What's our best way to go in?"

"We split your forces into three groups. One moves up the footpath, to hit the German front and draw fire, while one attacks the hangers, and the other hits the artillery positions. My men will go for the command building and secure it, while the rest of the base falls."

"Okay," I said, as I placed the map back into my jacket. "We split into three groups to take the airfield. Edwards, head with Sanders, Nate, and Vic to hit the mortars. Jay, take Ramos, Mangon, and Phelps to head up the center and distract the Germans. I'll take Hank, Malks, Doc, and Jessica to secure the hangers. Reynard and his men will hit the German C.P. as we strike, so watch your fire out there. We'll split up when we reach Reynard's men, on the edge of the airstrip. Once you've secured your objective, hold your position and wait for my all clear. Questions?" Everyone was silent. "Good, let's get going. Reynard, lead the way."

Reynard nodded and climbed back out of the gulley, running at full speed, for the tree line. I climbed out of the gulley right behind him, as the squad followed. Quickly, we ran for the trees behind Reynard and his men. They moved with speed and ease through the dense woods, as we stumbled along and tried to keep up. I swore under my breath each time I stumbled over a tree branch or rock, noticing Reynard seemed to grin each time one of us stumbled or fell.

"Cheeky wanker," Nate mocked in his best British accent.

"Arrogant fucker," Vic grunted, in translation, as he carried his heavy BAR.

It took us half an hour to reach the small dirt path leading to the airstrip. True to Reynard's words, it was expertly hidden, to preserve secrecy, right to the moment where you're on the path itself. Slightly overgrown with plants, we moved much quicker over the path, until we found Reynard's men waiting for us several dozen yards away from the airstrip.

"Okay, this is where we split up," I said, as I knelt down. "Jay, wait here with your group until Edwards and I can move into position." I glanced down at my wrist watch. "Wait six minutes for us and then open up on the Germans."

"Six minutes," Jay repeated, as he checked his watch. "Got it, boss."

"The second Jay and his team open up, we move in." I looked to Edwards, a newly made corporal. "Make sure the artillery is silenced before the crews can pull out. The less armed Germans we face, the better."

Edwards nodded. "No problem, sir."

"We're ready when you are, Lieutenant," Reynard reported as he checked his StG 44, a new and rare find only carried by veteran SS and paratroopers.

I looked to Jessica who nodded slightly. "Move out."

Everyone quickly broke off into their groups and disappeared into the woods. I took my men and moved through the woods to the far edge of the airstrip, where the hangers were located. We moved quickly, without the risk of detection, as the constant thump-thump-thump of mortar fire muffled out all sound. I found it strange the mortars would be firing from the airstrip, since any German artillery was quickly silenced from the air minutes after opening up. As we approached the edge of the airstrip, I found out why no one had spotted the base.

Stopping several yards from the hangers, we waited a few minutes for the attack to begin. I studied the airstrip through my binoculars and found the Germans had done one hell of a job camouflaging the airstrip. The hangers were low, rectangle concrete bunkers covered in bushes and overgrown plant life with cammo netting stretched over them. The airstrip, itself, was covered by massive wooden carts, which were full of patches of grass and bushes, that were wheeled into position, to completely cover the concrete runway. It also appeared to be longer than most runways. It was perfect cover to hide from recon flights.

"You think there're any jet planes or whatever here?" Hank asked.

"Well," I said, as I lowered my binoculars, "the entire area is heavy camouflaged, even for an airstrip. The hangers are concrete bunkers that are made to stop rockets and bombs with even more cammo paint and netting. If it's not jets, it's something worth hiding."

"I think the jets are here," Malks chimed in, as he cradled his World War One era combat shotgun. "The runway is longer, like you said, and I can see burn marks where the backwash from where jet engines started up."

"Think they're still here?" Jessica asked.

I shrugged. "Possibly, but if not we may get lucky and find diagrams and design specs for the engines. We might even find an intact engine or two."

"So look for papers and jet engines?" Hank asked. "What does a jet engine even look like?"

"Ah, my brother wrote me about them a little before the invasion. He said it looks like one of the underside drop tanks on a P-51, a long cylinder with openings at both ends, with the rear end having black scorch marks from the heat of the jet," I explained.

Hank and Malks exchanged unsure looks, while Doc shook his head slightly, and Jessica took in the information. I glanced at my watch and signaled for everyone to move. We had less then a minute as I began to edge forward, to the closest hanger. Hank and I reached the edge of the tree line, several yards away from the first hanger, when machine gun and rifle fire split the thud of the mortars.

The guards began to return fire towards the base entrance, as my group emerged from the woods. Several soldiers ran from the hanger, spotting us, as we approached.. Hank and I raised our weapons and quickly killed the group of soldiers. I pressed myself against the side of the hanger and waved the others forward. Quickly, Malks, Jessica, and Doc ran from the cover of trees, to the hanger, as several grenades exploded on the opposite side of the runway.

I glanced towards the mortar pits, as Edwards and his group moved in. Edwards was the only replacement to survive since D-Day and had earned his corporal stripes in St. Lo. He was no longer a 'replacement,' but a member of the squad and a veteran soldier. Edwards still had more to learn, but he made great progress in the two months since D-Day.

"Our only way in is through the hanger doors," I whispered, as I looked at the two steel doors blocking our view inside. There was a slight part in the center where the guards emerged from and was still open. "Stay close."

Hank nodded, as I moved around the corner and edged forward, to the split in the hanger doors. Raising my Thompson into my shoulder, I approached the door with Hank and Malks covering me. They stopped and hugged the hanger doors on either side of the opening, while I approached from the right near Hank.

Moving with a quick burst of speed, I rushed in and did a quick check of the area, in front on me, before shuffling to my left, as I scanned the interior of the hanger again. Hank and Malks rushed in right behind me and moved right while Jessica and Doc covered the doors. I slowly crept to the small mechanic's repair station, on the left side of the hanger, near the doors, as I spotted a pair of pilots ducking behind several barrels, near the workstation.

Several shots from a Luger rang out; and I dropped to one knee and fired. Bullets pinged against the metal doors above me, as my volley took one of the pilots in the chest, tossing the man's body to the oil slick ground. The second pilot jumped up and sprayed my position with bullets, as he squeezed the trigger on his MP-40, I threw myself forward onto my chest and fired another burst. The pilot yelled, in pain, as several shots tore into his leg and grazed his left arm.

"Drop it!" Hank yelled suddenly appearing over the German with his M1 leveled at his face. "I said dropt it!"

"Don't think he speaks English," Malks snorted, as he walked over, shouldering his Trench Gun.

"Get up and place your hands on your head," I barked in German as I climbed back to my feet. The German glared at me defiantly, swearing at me in German. "Get up!"

I grabbed him by the arm and pulled the wounded pilot to his feet, shoving him against the oil barrels. Quickly, I removed his Luger pistol from his hip holster and handed it to Hank. "Yours to keep."

"Always wanted one," Hank sighed, as he slipped the German pistol into his jacket pocket.

"There a light switch in this place?" Malks asked.

I noticed only the area around the mechanic's station was illuminated by a single hanging light. "Oh, wait," Malks found a black box bolted to the wall with a faded, yellow lighting bolt painted on it. With a slight metallic squeal, he pulled on the lever on the box and the hanger was illuminated by several bright lights, hanging from the ceiling.

My eyes went wide with shock and amazement as the small hanger was fully visible, ten Me 262 jet planes parked in two, neat rows of five, now visible. The sleek, cylinder shaped fuselages painted in an olive green, sat silently with a pair of the new jet engines bolted under their wings, long fuel drop tanks. The double 'z' shape of the Nazi Swastika was clearly painted on the nose of each jet, just behind their armament of four 30mm cannons.

"Those are jets?" Hank asked, as he shoved the wounded German pilot to the floor and rested the barrel of his M1 atop the man's head.

"I've never seen one before," Jessica sighed, as she brushed her hand against the side of one of the engines. "I wonder what they fly like."

"Fast, very fast," Malks said, as he glanced at some technical drawings on the mechanic's table. "From the look of these designs, they put out a lot of energy to reach speeds around 500 miles per hour, maybe even higher."

"That's a lot faster then our planes," Doc pointed out.

"Matt tells me they're fast, but aren't very maneuverable." I loaded a fresh clip into my Thompson, as I began to walk for the hanger doors. "Let's go and secure the rest."

"What about him?" Hank asked, tapping the barrel of his M1 on the man's head.

"Tie his hands around the landing gear," I said, pointing to the closest 262. "He won't escape with that kind of wound right, Doc?"

"No way is he walking out of here," Doc remarked, as he checked his M1. Medics weren't allowed to carry weapons, they were to save lives only, but most Germans couldn't care less. Doc once told us that he'd rather die with a rifle in hand then be weaponless and dead.

"Tie him off and follow me," I ordered.

Malks collected some rope from the mechanic's station and tied the wounded pilot to the landing gear of a 262, the German screaming at us the entire time. Jessica soon became even more pissed and kicked the man in the groin, which put an end to his yelling.

"Now let's go," I said, with a, as Malks and Hank laughed.

I moved back to the hanger doors and did a quick check outside. I quickly spotted Edwards and his men securing the mortar pits across the airstrip from our position. Reynard was still working to breach the C.P. building several yards away, but the Germans had barricaded themselves inside and were using three MG42s to keep Reynard's men away.

"Looks like things are playing out as planned, so we'll move to the next hanger, do a quick sweep, and move on."

Hank nodded. "I would think the Germans are more focused around the CP and arty pits, so the other hangers might be empty. Why not split up and take two at a time before regrouping for the last?"

I thought it over. "Too much of a risk if ether groups runs into a dozen, or so, pilots or soldiers. Let's just stay together and secure each hanger. Hang back and cover us."

Hank nodded again, as I signaled Malks, Doc, and Jessica. Checking again, I ran out first and hugged the hanger doors for cover, as I moved. Doc was right behind me with Jessica, followed by Malks. Hank still stood in the hanger and fired on the Germans retreating from the mortar pits. Edwards had secured more then half of the position, as the remaining mortar crews abandoned their positions. They decided to run for the hangers and us.

Doc fired first at several Germans crossing the runway and reached the second hanger before us. I fired a short burst, as the German returned fire. Several bullets whizzed past my head and slammed into the hanger doors, with an ear shattering ping. My heart began to race, as I ran and fired, my shots missing their marks and flying wide. The Germans ducked behind several barrels and crates, near the second hanger and had the element of cover and fire superiority, with ten soldiers, to my five.

"Down, down!" I yelled. I ran past the edge of the first hanger.

More bullets shot by, as I spotted a large generator, sitting between the two hangers, which offered some degree of protection. Jessica ducked down with Doc, Malks and I dove to the cement runway, laying prone for cover. I struggled to aim with my Thompson lying prone, the magazine smacking against the ground. Malks had no trouble aiming and firing his pump action shotgun, keeping up a steady rate of fire.

"Having trouble?" Malks asked, as he shoved his face to the ground, to reload.

"The Brits got it right with the clips on the side of the fucking weapon," I responded, shoving the Thompson into my shoulder and moving into a low crouch.

Several shots slammed into the, in front of me, with an explosion of cement shards. I returned fire with better accuracy, draining several clips in a matter of seconds. Two Germans fell from the broadside while Malks dropped another, nearly taking off the soldier's leg with a single blast of twelve gauge buckshot.

"Grenade out!" Hank yelled, as he tossed a grenade overhead. A hollow thump echoed, three more Germans fell to the ground. The remaining four pulled back into the hanger and gave us a chance to regroup.

I waved Hank, motioning to the move up, as Malks jumped up and ran for the hanger doors, which were opened wide enough for one person to pass through at a time. I ran up behind him and held up a hand, to single everyone to stop.

"Anyone hit?" I asked, quickly patting myself down for wounds. Adrenaline was a great thing to dull pain and push away exhaustion, but when running on an adrenaline high, I had been hit and didn't know it. I nearly bled to death during the fight for St. Lo because I didn't feel a rifle round lodged in my thigh, that clipped an artery.

"All good," Doc answered checking the breach on his rifle.

Several shots pelted the hanger doors from the inside. "How many grenades do we have left?"

"All out," Malks answered, firing several times through the door. The shots were rewarded with a muffled cry and a hollow thump. "Though I think we have three left to handle."

"Two left," Hank answered, patting his last two grenades hanging from his webbing.

Doc snorted to himself. "The rifle was a frigging bitch to get, grenades were impossible."

"One," Jessica said, while I just shook my head with nothing left.

"Hank, toss your two in when I say to." I turned back to Malks. "I'll head in first and you'll follow, since we have the best weapons for close quarter fighting." Jessica loudly cleared her throat, tapping her MP-40. "I need you to cover our backs with Doc. Hank will follow us in with his M1 and help clear the hanger. Once we call out the entrance is clear, you'll come in."

Jessica silently nodded, appearing to be able to see what I was thinking. Personal feelings clouding your judgment, Corr. Can't happen when you're in combat, I thought.

"Ready when you are," Hank suddenly said, standing by the entrance.

"Do it." Hank pulled the pin from one grenade and tossed it through the open hanger doors, his hands moving quickly, to toss the second grenade.

I pushed away everything around me, from my mind, as the two grenades bounced across the hanger floor. MG and rifle fire still popped from inside, as both grenades boomed into a cloud of razor sharp shrapnel. Once the explosions boomed, I was I rushing in, firing away with my Thompson. The hanger was dark, with the lights out, as the flashes of my Thompson flared to life. I shuffled to my left, with my back brushing against the hanger doors. Several muzzles flashed opposite the hanger doors, as a dozen armed Germans appeared behind several crates and barrels.

Malks' shotgun roared to life, in a steady beat of hard cracks and metallic clicks, as he fired and chambered a new round. The air was suddenly thick with cordite and smoke, as I dropped an empty clip for a fresh one, my breathing suddenly labored, in the smoke laden air. A sudden stab of pain shot up my leg, as a bullet tore through the air and sliced open a top layer of skin.

I dropped down, into a crouch, to level my Thompson, as a light ripple of pain continued to flow into my chest. A German pilot dropped at my feet, as several rounds tore open his throat and upper chest. Hank was inside now, the metallic clacks of his Garand, audible over the single cracks of Kar98k and Gewehr 41 rifles. I looked back to check on Malks, but there was not enough light to see.

"Grenade!" Hank suddenly yelled. appearing to my right. I threw myself to he ground and Hank picked up the German stick grenade, tossing it back into the darkness. A bright flash erupted alongside an ear shattering, as several soldiers dropped to the ground.

I shuffled back to my feet as to German pilots appeared over me, one armed with a Luger, the other a Walther P38 pistol. They fired first, but we were far enough apart, that the shots missed my chest by inches. I brought my Thompson up, to fire, and squeezed the trigger, to have the weapon click empty.

"Shit," I grunted, taking the Thompson in my left hand, while my right dropped to the.45 hanging in its holster. The hard boom, of Malks' trench gun, echoed twice as both pilots were tossed back, geysers of blood erupting from their chests.

"Can't let ya die now, Corr," Malks said, as he fired at an unseen target.

"Why's that?" I asked reloading before jumping back to my feet.

"I got a feeling Jessica might gut me alive if I did," he joked.

Another grenade detonated several yards away, though I did not see who threw it. More soldiers fell, the volume of rifle and MG fire tapered off. I moved forward, at a slow pace as several shots range out before being answered by a single shot from Malks. A muffle thud could be heard, and the hanger fell silent. With a slight crackle of energy, Hank shoved the handle to the power box up and flooded the hanger with light.

"Clear!" he called out, as the results of the firefight could be seen. Fourteen Germans lay dead, on the now blood slicked hanger floor. All, but four, were soldiers, the others pilots.

"Clear!" I responded, seeing the death laying about eight Me 262s. Doc and Jessica rushed in with weapons raised, as I called clear. The two lowered their weapons as they saw the battle's aftermath.

"Got a live one here!" Malks called, as he shoved a German soldier into the open. The man had been hiding under a worktable during the fighting and didn't have a mark on him.

"Don't shoot!" he pleaded in German. "Don't shoot."

"Sure, Fritz," Malks snorted, and he thrust the man with the barrel of his trench gun.

"Please, I'll tell you everything you want to know!" The soldier was a flight mechanic, judging by his oil smeared jumpsuit.

"Two in one day," Hank commented, "what luck!"

I nodded and told Malks to tie up the prisoner, but my words didn't get far when a massive explosion erupted from outside. The blast was huge, and the concussion wave shuttered the ground beneath our boots. I stumbled a bit, but held my balance, before rushing to the hanger doors. I peered outside, to see the last hanger was now a burning shell, of what it once was, a large amount of aviation fuel stoking the flames. I spun around, as footsteps echoed.

"You okay?" It was Jay.

"Yeah, the base secure?" I asked.

"Yeah, arty is taken out and the OP is ours," he said.

I nodded. "Both hanger are secured and I got two POWs. One's tied up in the first hanger, and I got one in here. Have the squad set up a perimeter, and get me a link back to command. Also, get Reynard up here."

Jay nodded and ran across the runway to dispatch the orders. I turned back inside and approached the German mechanic, who sat on the floor with Malks standing guard.

"What the hell was that?" Malks asked.

"Last hanger just blew up," I said. "Most have been rigged by the Krauts." I turned to the mechanic and switched to German. "So you'll talk?"

He nodded vigorously. "Ya, just ask!"

"What was in the other hanger? More jets?" I questioned.

"Yes, but not like these. The last hanger held much larger ones, that required a lot more repairs."

"Bigger?" I repeated. "Bigger, as in, bombers?"

The mechanic shrugged. "Not like I've seen before, and I've been to lots of airbases. These things were larger and bulkier, with larger engines then on the 262s."

"What'd he say?" Hank asked, standing behind me.

"They may have had jet bombers in the other hanger." I scratched my chin and sighed. "What ever is left of them is gone now."

"We still have all the blueprints and schematics," Malks said. "That's better then nothing."

I nodded. "Okay, take this guy to the CP with our other prisoner and keep an eye on them."

"Yes, sir." Malks reached down and pulled the German to his feet, before moving him out of the hanger. I followed after the two with Hank, Doc, and Jessica already waiting outside. Reynard was among them, speaking to Jessica with an arm draped over her shoulder.

I cleared my throat loudly, to get his attention. "Your men secure the CP?"

Reynard dropped the arm back to his side. "Yes, but the Germans fought to the death and we have no prisoners."

"Don't worry; I've got two for command to talk with."

Reynard seemed a bit hesitant before speaking. "Good, and the two hangers of jet fighters will go nicely with your commanders."

I shrugged, nodding towards the burning hanger. "We couldn't reach the last hanger before the Germans destroyed it. From what the mechanic we captured, told me, there might have been jet bombers inside, but I guess logistics will need to sift through the ashes."

"Corr!" Jay yelled from the CP across the runway. "Radio is up!"

I waved back and ran across the runway, spotting several of Reynard's men rifling through the bodies of the dead Germans. The term 'grave robbing' didn't seem to apply since the war started, as the Germans carried some of the best equipment around and every GI wanted something to take home.

The CP was a small wooden building several yards away, from the now empty, mortar pits. The front door had been blown in, with all the windows shattered, and the walls marked by bullet holes. Inside, a dozen, or so, dead enemy soldiers lay across the floor behind over turned tables and cabinets used, as makeshift cover. Maps, files, and papers were strewn about, alongside pools of blood, spent shell casings, and shattered weapons.

"Reynard and his boys really did a number on 'em," Vic commented, as he stood by the front door, BAR in hand.

"Ever heard of overkill," Jay sighed, examining a dead officer.

I picked up a fist full of burnt papers and dropped them. "Anything useful left?"

"Radio works," Jay jerked a thumb over a large radio set in the far corner of the room. "I managed to get a direct line back to Captain Hiller. in town."

Sidestepping over the dead, I made my way to the radio and sat down in front of the radio receiver.

"Captain Hiller," I called. as I held the receiver to my mouth. "Lieutenant Bolger reporting on the airstrip."

"Is it clear?" Hiller asked, the radio crackling with bursts of static.

"Yes, sir, the airstrip has been secured. We've got two prisoners, a handful of intact jet fighters, and multiple diagrams, and technical data on the planes."

"Fine work, Bolger. Any casualties?" He asked.

I glanced at Jay, who shook his head. "All alive and accounted for, including Reynard and his men."

"Really fine work you did. Hold the airstrip until I get another squad up there to relieve you." Hiller paused, as I heard a second voice on the radio. "Bolger, command is dispatching a logistical group to comb over every inch of the airstrip. Hold until they arrive, and then report back to town."

"How long until they arrive, sir?" I asked.

Hiller grunted to himself, a sign of annoyance. "Command is giving me bullshit information. Don't expect to see them for a few hours.

I'd recommend you hunker down, in preparation to hold through the night."

I nodded to myself. "Yes, sir, I'll report in when the relief force arrives."

"Good luck." The line faded into static as I switched off the radio to conserve its dwindling battery life.

"I'm guessing we're staying the night?" Jay asked, leaning against the wall.

I sighed and stood up, feeling the ammo pouches hanging from my webbing, were a little light. "Yeah, so we need to get a check on ammo levels and see if we have enough to hold out."

"Expecting trouble?" Vic asked.

"I'm guessing 262s don't come cheap and they're may not be that many built. Not only do we have the plane designs, we have the planes themselves and the Germans won't let that go." I walked back to the front door and looked out over the airstrip. "If they have any real sense, they'll be back."

"It'd make more sense for them to launch a counter strike at night," Jay concluded. He looked down at his watch. "We have about five more hours before the sun sets and another hour before it get's dark."

"Jay, we need to get the squad set up in defensive positions before nightfall and set up a defensive perimeter. The only thing is that there's more space then we can effectively cover."

"We'll need to defend what's important," Vic pointed out.

"The hangers would be most logical. They're armored bunkers with limited access ways and hold the jets. Best move would be to pack up everything important we found and split them in the two hangers." I looked to the two remaining hangers. "That'll limit our fields of fire and visibility to anyone approaching from the northern edge of the runway."

"So we're undermanned, low on ammo, and boxed into a corner." Vic was always blunt. "So that makes us shit out of luck and jolly well fucked."

Chapter 14

"The news isn't the best," Jay always took it upon himself to deliver bad news, even if it had nothing to do with him.

I sighed to myself, watching the sky darken. "Give it to me straight," I said, with my hand rubbing my chin, a thin layer of stubble scratching my fingers.

Jay looked down at his worn note pad. "Ammo levels are low, but stretchable for everyone. Clips for M1s were in good supply, but we've got enough for maybe five minutes of nonstop firing. Thompson ammo is running up short, as you and Edwards only carry them, and Vic's down to eight clips for the BAR. Nate's on his own, with his carbine, while we only have twelve grenades collectively, which includes the ones we scavenged from the Germans."

"Jolly well fucked." I sneered. "What if we used German weapons?"

"Still low, the Krauts had little to start with, and they used up a lot in the fight. The mortars are a bust because Edwards spiked each tube, but we got two 42s and roughly several hundred rounds per gun. Outside of that, there's nothing left unless someone can fly a 262."

A low grunt escaped from my throat, as I thought. Jay stood silently across from me, near the shattered remains of the CP's front door. Reynard was standing by, with one of his men, who we only knew as, Luke, and appeared to be Reynard's second in command. The two had remained silent during Nate's report on the layout of our defenses and remained the same as Jay finished.

"Is there anything else?" I finally said, looking up at Jay.

"Edwards was out scouting with Sanders a few hours ago and reported seeing three German scouts around the eastern edge of the woods. They avoided detection and returned, to base, observing the scouts turn and move east."

"They'll be more," it was Reynard who finally spoke. "I've seen this before."

"The Krauts have changed tactics, now that they're running," Malks pointed out, as he worked on the radio. The piece of crap had died a few minutes after I reported to Hiller.

"They will not abandon such valuable aircraft in our hands," Reynard's voice had a harder edge to it. It may have been our frayed nerves, but I didn't take kindly to those talking down to my men. "Only someone, overly blinded by arrogance, would think such advanced technology would be left, in the hands of the enemy."

"Who the fuck you calling arrogant, Frenchy?" Malks replied, voice filled with venom.

"Both of you," I hissed, keeping Reynard from responding, "do us all a favor and shut the hell up." A migraine began to blossom in my head, as I felt pressure in my sinuses.

"Let's save the anger bullshit for the Nazis," Jay grunted and he rested his hands on his dual .45s. Everyone thought he looked foolish when he found the second Colt .45 in St. Lo, but they worked. More then once he'd relied on the two pistols to save his neck when the enemy was too close to handle with his Springfield.

"I want everyone to their posts," I said, standing up from the table, where several maps spread out. "Let's hope things stay quiet, but if they don't, stay smart. I hate to be the downer, but we have our backs to the wall here. It'll be over when the ammo runs dry."

"We'll make every shot count," Jay reassured.

"My men and I will not fail," Reynard assured, as he and Luke left first. Malks and Jay stayed behind and waited until the two had crossed the runway.

"He gives me a weird feeling," Malks stated, deadpan.

"My gut says watch him," I admitted, "but it might be my heart fucking with me."

"You're not one to fall into jealously," Jay said, in an even tone.

"I'm human, Jay." I said, "that means I can and do fuck up."

"But never when it counts." Jay complimented.

"What does that mean?" I asked.

"Fuck ups never happen when our lives are on the line," Malks explained.

I laughed off the thought, moving for the door. "There's always a first time for everything."

Night was quickly approaching, the sun was all but covered, by the trees to the west. The sky had gone from orange and yellow to the dark blue and black of night with a light wind picking up. The tiny airstrip was still alive with activity; the squad continued their work on establishing effective fighting positions, to repel a German counter attack, which everyone no longer asked if, but rather, when it'll come.

Fighting positions were dug in around the two remaining hangers, to cover the main doors. There were no rear exits or secondary entrances, beside the hanger doors, which limited where we could dig in. Our final plan had a wall of logs and sandbags arranged in front of the hanger doors, that offered us a 180 degree arc of fire. From the hangers, we covered the southern approach with a decent view of the east and the solid protection of the hangers, to protect the north. The west covered by our own forces, still moving to secure the area around Mortain, from the last German attack.

"How are we looking?" I called out to Hank, near the first hanger.

"Ammo levels aren't the best, but it'll do," he answered assembling an MG42.

"Controlled bursts only," I remarked, climbing over the low, makeshift firing line. "Be as cheap as possible with your rounds."

Hank grunted, as I walked to the hanger doors, the light from inside spilling out. Sanders passed by with Edwards, the two carrying a crate of captured MG ammo, out to Hank. Inside, Jessica was talking with Phelps. They tallied up all the information we discovered and the best place to store everything, without risking them in the attack.

"We could roll out a jet and use her cannons to help," Nate called out, sitting within the cockpit of one of the 262s.

"No way do we risk the planes," I argued. "Each one of these babies is needed intact and with a flawless paint job."

"Just saying," Nate sighed, as he climbed out and jumped off the jet. I shook my head and walked, looking for a quiet corner of the hanger.

My head still throbbed in pain, and I felt tremendous pressure slowly pressing down on my temples. Sighing, I removed my helmet and ran a hand through my hair, a thin layer of sweat covering my scalp. I was slowly getting sick with something that preyed on my body, some germ taking advantage of my poor diet and lack of sleep to drain what little energy I had left. Taking a breath to fight back a wave of nausea, I returned to the firing line out front, making a mental note to have Doc give me a checkup, when it was over.

Reynard and his men held the second hanger, while the squad held the first. It was Reynard's request, though he made it sound like an order, that helped quell the distain my men had for his. I had an abstract annoyance towards Reynard, that the squad had picked up on. Now they listed Reynard and his men as 'pain in the ass fuck offs,' as Ramos put it.

"Everything is just about in place," Jay reported, as he returned to his position on the firing line. "Reynard said his men are ready."

"You trust them?" I asked, without looking at Jay.

"I'm glad they're on their own," he admitted. "I prefer it that way, then have one fighting next to me, watching my back."

"Why?" I asked.

"Just a feeling, Corr," he said.

I nodded, sat down and leaned against the firing line, propping my Thompson up next to me. Jay kept his rifle at his side, while he scanned the woods through a pair of binoculars, sighing to himself every few minutes. I closed my eyes, as the last bits of sunlight faded away and night descended. The airstrip fell silent just as I fell asleep.

"German counter attack!" Jay's voice and the hard cracks of machine gun fire, filled my mind, as I slept. At first, I believed I was dreaming of the horrors of St. Lo and the shattered graveyard that city became, but reality flooded back and adrenaline surged through my veins.

"Watch your aim and conserve ammo!" I shouted as I awoke, groping for my weapon.

"Targets to the left!" Hank yelled, his MG chattered to life, green tracers shooting into the air.

MG and rifle fire leapt through the air, as I jumped up to fire. The moon was covered by clouds and no light, to aid in my targeting, as visibility was extremely low in the night. I locked my eyes down the iron sights of my Thompson and searched for the muzzle flashes in the trees. There were plenty to be seen and the trees were thick with German soldiers, all firing at us.

"It's got to be a whole frigging company out there!" Jay yelled, as his rifle cracked with another shot. "No telling what they have to use against us."

A German AT rocket shrieked in the distance, the warhead burning a bright red, before slamming into the hanger doors, behind us. Steel splinters rained down on our backs, from the explosion; I fired towards the soldiers moving to set up an MG42 near the abandoned CP building. One of the gunners dropped, my rounds rippled across his chest. The second gunner dropped to the ground, his helmet was torn off his head, a shot from Jay's rifle zipping.

"Flanking fire on the right!" Edwards yelled out, as two rifle squads emerged from the woods on our right flank.

"Shift fire, shift fire!" I yelled, leaping from my position, to the far right side of the firing line.

I ran in a low crouch, rounds exploded in the ground around me in plumes of dirt and cement. I slammed my back into the low, log wall. Nate dropped down to reload. He glanced over at me and tapped his rifle, with a shake of his head, signaling, he was running low on ammo.

"Tighten your aim," I grunted, with a hint of sarcasm.

Nate rolled his eyes, reloaded,and returned firing. I crouched next to him, as the two squads of German soldiers rushed our lines, one squad hanging back to cover the other. I fired in short bursts, and a dozen soldiers advanced on our positions, most armed with MP40s and FG42s, in place of bolt action rifles. Their weapons would tear us apart if they broke the firing line, but we held the advantage, of cover and rifle fire.

A grenade detonated in the center of the advancing Germans, killing three and wounding five. The squad dropped to the ground for cover, as another fell dead. Nate lined up his shots with deadly control and moved across the German squad, picking off those who still fought. I gave specific orders that any wounded Germans that were not firing back were not to be targeted.

"Think we got them suppressed!" Edwards yelled over the roar of the battle, his voice a low whisper, within the explosive cracks of rifles and machine guns.

"Watch the second squad!" I yelled, reloading and readied to return to the front of the firing line.

"Got it-" Edwards was thrown back, as several rounds ripped across his chest and arms. Blood splattered over his uniform, as he fell to the ground, with a yelp of pain.

"Doc!" I yelled, running to Edwards' aide.

I slung my Thompson over my shoulder and worked to treat Edwards' wounds, but he clutched at this throat, hands locked in place like a vice. Even in the low light I could tell his throat wound was life threatening, the wounds to his chest and arms superficial, the bullets were not deep into the flesh.

"Relax," I said, as calmly as possible, over and over again. "Try to breathe."

Edwards tried to speak, but his voice was garbled, blood poured down his throat. I swore under my breath and pried his hands away from his throat, pressing a bandage to the wound. Doc ran to my side; I held the bandage firmly against the wound, but light enough to allow Edwards to breathe.

"I go this," Doc grunted in my ear, taking over.

Looking down into Edwards' terrified eyes, I told him he would be alright, before returning to Jay. An explosion erupted in front of the firing line and sent a shower of cement into our faces which sent Jay diving for cover alongside Hank. I dropped down next to him, as four German soldiers tried climbing over the firing line.

The first German was over the wall and too close; he slammed into me. I fell back, as the soldier struggled to grab his holstered Luger, the two of us fighting one another. Ramming the muzzle of my weapon into his chest, I squeezed the trigger and tore open it open, rolling his dead body off me. A second German vaulted over the wall, but fell back, as if he ran into a brick wall, Jay standing behind me with a.45 in hand.

"Push them back!" Hank yelled, slamming his trench knife into the spine of an enemy soldier.

I pushed myself back up and gripped my Thompson in time, to kill another soldier rushing across the runway. Jay was behind me and firing away with his pistols, another German fell and then another. Hank's MG42 hammered away at the tree line, in a hail of green tracer fire, that ripped apart whatever was in its path. I dropped the empty clip from my weapon when a soldier threw himself into me.

I fell down, with him on top of me, the two of us fighting over control of his knife, which was held ready to strike. Grunting, I slammed a knee into his ribs and then shoved my head into his face, a snap of bone echoing, as my steel helmet made contact. A gurgled cry filled my ears. I forced the German off me, tossing him to the ground. I rolled over and drew my.45, firing two rounds into his chest.

With the immediate threat handled, I holstered my weapon and picked up my Thompson, quickly reloading a fresh clip and yanking back on the cocking hammer. I was back up with my weapon at the ready, and I noticed the Germans, who crossed our lines, were pulling back, the attack tapering off. MG fire from the tree line slowly stopped, and the last of the surviving soldiers retreated into the night.

Quiet fell; I could hear the pounding of my heart in my chest, blood and adrenaline pulsing through my veins. I was breathing heavily and felt my hands shaking, clenching my Thompson. With the sounds of battle gone, it took me a moment to sort everything out, before Jay placed a hand on my shoulder.

"We broke the attack," he reported, as he holstered his pistol. "They're pulling back into the woods."

Taking a deep breath, I lowered my weapon and nodded. "They're regrouping for another attack. Keep everyone, at the line, awake and alert."

"No problem." Jay moved up and down the firing line to check on the squad, while I moved to find Doc. He'd set up a makeshift aide station in the hanger and was tending to Edwards, as I walked in. Edwards was laying on a stretcher, with a thick bandage wrapped around his throat; Doc patched up the other, less serious wounds on his chest and arms.

"How is he?" I asked, standing just behind Doc.

"Stable and unconscious," he responded, as he packed a bullet wound. "He's not out of the woods yet, but I'm pretty sure he'll make it to morning. He won't last longer then another day if we can't get him to a proper aide station, though."

"Do your best," was all I said, I left and went outside.

The squad still remained at their positions, Jay checking on them. Everyone was checking ammo and weapons before patting themselves down for wounds that might not have been felt. No one else had been wounded, besides Edwards, from my men except for minor cuts and burns, from grenade and shape charge attacks. The ground was littered with spent shell casings and empty ammo clips, showing the little skirmish had clawed at our dwindling ammo supply.

"Everyone is running low," Jay said, as he finished his rounds. "Most of the men are next to tapped out and we're out of grenades. Heavy MG ammo is holding, but another strike, like this, will dry it out."

I nodded towards the body strewn runway. "Send out two man teams to scrounge for Kraut weapons, ammo and anything else we can use from the dead. I'm going to check in on Reynard and his men."

"Didn't see much fighting over there," Jay snorted, walking away. I shook my head and walked over to the second hanger, where Reynard was, with his men. I did notice that there were not that many German dead around the firing line compared to ours.

"Anyone hit?" I called out, seeing Reynard speaking with one of his men. He glanced over his shoulder at me and waved off his man, before turning to face me.

"A minor shoulder wound, but nothing more," he responded, nodding towards Luke, who stood with a bandaged arm.

"Ammo levels?" I asked.

"Holding, we just started to scavenge the dead for spare supplies," he said.

I nodded. "Just stay close to the hanger, no telling when they'll be back."

Reynard waved me off and returned to his work, not even letting me inspect his men on my own. Something felt off even more now, but I dismissed the feeling and returned back to my hanger. I was approaching the firing line when I spotted Jessica standing near the hanger doors, face flushed. I quickly hopped over the line and moved to her side.

"Hey," I said, as I approached, "you feeling okay?"

"I…" Her eyes were red rimmed from crying.

I moved closer and placed a hand on her arm. "Jessica, what's wrong?"

"It's Jonathan," she sobbed.

Reality slammed into me. No, not again. "Did Edwards die?"

"No, God no, it's just when I saw him…he's so young and to be in that way…" she sobbed.

I gently squeezed her arm. "He'll be fine for tonight, and I'll make sure we get him to an aide station."

Jessica nodded and said something, but I did not hear the words. The first explosion erupted atop our hanger, the solid construction of the building shrugging off the impact. Another explosion sparked off, to our left, with a skull shattering crack that sent out a concussion wave, slamming into me and sending me flying forward, into the hanger.

My back slammed into the concrete hanger, with a hard crack of bone and cartilage, the metallic taste of blood suddenly filling my mouth. Everything seemed to be moving in slow motion, as I slipped down to the ground, a sensation of warm liquid now flowing over my mouth. My body slumped to the ground and my senses began to fade, I felt the strong breath of heat brushing against the back of my neck.

The world around me was slowly come back into focus, sometime after the attack. It was just a jumble of voices, which brought me back to reality, before I could see anything. A grunt, hard voice was speaking to someone, who responded in a low, tired tone. The hard voice was that of Captain Hiller, and the second was Doc's.

"Don't tell me I trekked all the way out here only to find my Lieutenant dead," Hiller grunted somewhere close by.

"He's not dead," Doc snorted, equally far away. "The LT was thrown into the wall and knocked unconscious. Look past the blood, from the broken nose, and he's fine."

"And Edwards?" Hiller inquired.

"Alive and breathing, but we need to get him back to an aide station," Doc said.

I felt feeling beginning to return. "It'll be another four hours until the relief team moves out at dawn. They'll take time to get here; I was nearly lost stumbling around in the dark."

Moaning slightly, I opened my eyes and saw the ceiling of the bunker above me. The stretcher under me began to vibrate for a few seconds and I thought I was feeling nausea, but it was a tremor from an artillery strike.

"He's awake," Doc said, standing over me with Hiller.

"Captain," I sighed, as I carefully sat up, my nose and jaw sore. "What are you doing here?"

"We could hear the fighting back in town," Hiller explained. "Orders were to stay in town, to facilitate supplies and troops, heading to Chambois, but the fighting captured my attention. You're one hell of a commander, but I decided to come out with a few men and extra ammo."

Easing myself off the stretcher, I steadied myself and heard the constant shutter of artillery strikes. "Things aren't going well?"

Hiller shrugged. "I brought eight men from a recon team with me and sent them to help Reynard. We brought in a small amount of ammo, that'll last till morning, but we're now stuck in the hangers. German Hummels have been pounding us, for about an hour now, and I haven't spoken with Reynard's bunker."

"The hangers are solid bunkers," Malks chimed, standing near the hanger doors. "We'll be safe, as long as the ceiling isn't breached."

"Then we stop the Hummels," I grunted, as Doc handed me my Thompson and helmet. "They can't be that far away."

"They aren't," Sanders called out. "When Edwards and I went out scouting, we saw tracks on a path leading north. We thought they were from tanks, but it could be the arty."

I looked to Hiller. "I'll head out there and scout it out, sir. You're the ranking officer now."

Hiller sighed to himself, as another shell slammed into our hanger, shaking the ground with a muffled boom. "I don't like the idea of sending men out in the dark, especially now with a few squads of Germans still out there."

"I'm willing to go out, sir," I said, deadpan.

"Me too, sir," Sanders added.

"I'll go," Ramos added. "It beats sitting in here…sir."

Vic simply grunted with a head nod.

Hiller shook his head, but agreed. "Okay, the four of you will head out and try to silence the artillery. Don't take any stupid risks out there and be as careful as possible." He nodded towards Adam, who sat with his radio near several crates of ammunition. "Take spare ammo and get going."

"Yes, sir," I replied. "We won't fail."

"Just don't die," Hiller ordered.

Hiller and I saluted one another, before I walked over to Adam. He sat at the mechanic's bench, with the radio in front him, hands fiddling with the internal wiring. That damn radio was always breaking down on us, regardless of how much Adam tinkered with it. He gave me a slight head nod towards the ammo crates, before returning to his work.

"Take what you can carry," I said, filling my empty ammo pouches with fresh ammo clips.

"You remember where the path was?" Ramos asked Sanders.

Sanders nodded, as he stuffed rifle clips into the ammo pouches on his belt and webbing. "It's about half a mile east, from the end of the runway."

"So is the rest of the German Seventh Army," Vic snorted.

"Relax," I grunted, trying to finish up with the supplies. "The Germans move their tanks and supplies, at night, to dodge fighter patrols. If we come across any tanks, we'll hear them before they see us."

"Provided the arty doesn't blow us back to England," Ramos sighed, as we finished gathering ammo.

"Let's go," I commanded.

I led the three to the center of the hanger doors, which were open, just a little. Hank stood by with Malks, who pulled the doors open a little bit wider, for the four of us to squeeze through. I went first, shuffling through the opening sideways and pressing myself against the doors, as I exited.

The artillery bombardment was still pounding the airstrip without mercy, the runway now cratered and was no longer useable. An arty shell had flattened the CP building at the start of the attack, and now was nothing more then a smoldering crater. The ground shook each time a shell landed, the ground shaking ever few seconds. I moved in terror, trying to make my way out to the rear of the hanger, as shell exploded in orange fireballs up and down the runway, mere yards and feet from us.

No more then a minute outside, and my ears were ringing from the deafening explosions, and my chest ached from the concussion waves. Ramos moved close behind me and flinched, at every shell that landed a few feet from us. I could just hear the hiss of shrapnel following the explosions, and I felt my heart pound in my chest.

As I approached the edge of the hanger, I broke into a full run. The four of us ran down the small space between the hangers, to the shelter of the woods at the end of the hangers. The German gunners were focused on the runway and hangers, but were not firing into the trees. When we crossed into the shade of the trees, we were safe from artillery fire.

"Lead the way," I grunted to Sanders, as the moonlight was cut off by the thick tree canopy.

"Right," Sanders replied, looking around. "Okay, the runway runs west to east, and east is that way." He pointed to our right. "We walk on hugging the runway and then continue on for half a mile."

Shouldering his rifle, Sanders began to lead our group eastward, with Ramos and I following, while Vic brought up the rear. All of us moved silently, with each step carefully placed, to prevent any loud noises. The echoing explosions of the artillery blocked out most sound, but we erred on the side of caution.

The dark, eerie feeling of the woods was all too familiar to me, it reminded me of my father taking my brothers and me out camping, at least four times each summer. It was fun and enjoyable most times, but the very first time I went camping at the age of ten, I got lost. My father and brothers were working on setting up a camp before nightfall, while I was sent out to gather firewood. I was told a few dozen times not to wander off too far from camp, but I had no clue what 'too far' meant and soon found myself alone, and lost.

Everything was quiet and still, but I was terrified and imaging things. I wanted my father and brothers, as I stumbled through the dark and endless woods, but walked on in the hopes of finding them. I didn't know which way led where, but I walked on and on in one direction. My heart raced in chest and adrenaline flowed. I kept walking, falling a few times and scraping up my arms and legs. It would be another hour until my father found me.

"Corr, I found the path," Sanders reported, breaking my concentration.

"Ah, you see the tracks?" I responded, remembering where I was.

"Yeah," he pointed down to the ground, "just look."

The path cut through the thick woods running north to south and was well worn. Thick, wide spaced tracks could be seen pressed into the soft earth, a clear marker of tanks or any type of tracked vehicle, such as Hummels. I scanned the path and listened to the constant thud of artillery, slowly, it tapered off. Arty barrages didn't last forever, though it felt like it, when under one. Ammo levels ran low, barrels overheated, and the like quieted the Hummels and offered me a chance to think.

"They're a mile to the southeast," I said, as I made the calculations. "Let's stick to the woods and hug the path."

We walked back into the woods and proceeded to head south, staying within visual of the path. I constantly looked back, towards the path, to make sure we were heading in the right direction, as everything around me looked the same at night. It wouldn't take more then one bad step to send you heading in the wrong direction.

Soft dirt and fallen leaves, crunched under our boots, with muffled cracks and pops. Everyone was on edge and was a bit jumpy, Sanders constantly stopping at every sound,while Ramos froze whenever he saw movement. I kept my wits about me and kept the group moving, my nerves barely in check. About halfway to the artillery, we froze at the sound of running engines. Holding up a hand to single a stop, we crouched down low and sat silently.

The path was several yards away from us, a handful of German halftracks and light Panzer IV tanks rumbled past. Several trucks, loaded down with soldiers, rolled by with them heading south towards the Hummels and our objective. They quickly passed by. The sounds of the engines died off, into the night.

"Not good," Vic whispered, when silence returned.

"Think they're heading out to reinforce the Hummels?" Sanders asked.

I slowly exhaled, licking my lips slightly. "Chances are they're heading to Chambois, but they'll pass by anyway. Let's keep going and see what's with the Hummels. If it's doable, we take out the arty and head back."

"Just how many Germans are too many for us?" Vic asked.

I snorted to myself, and we began to continue on. "I won't face a company on our own."

Our trek through the woods continued for several more minutes, with nerve racking silence. We spotted no German patrols out along the path, since the small convoy of tanks and troop trucks earlier on, but as we came closer to the Hummels we could hear the metallic grumble of engines. Another artillery barrage started up marking we were close to their positions.

"Sounds like two to three of them," Sanders whispered, as we crouched near the path, a split leading off to the left several yards ahead of us.

"Let's assume four total, with one down from repair trouble," I responded. "That'll give us twenty-four soldiers, at six, to a Hummel." I nervously clicked my teeth, thinking about what needed to be done next. "Since Hummels carry only eighteen or so shells, they'll be ammo wagons with them, so that adds more soldiers."

"We're outmanned just by one arty piece," Ramos pointed out.

"It's dark and noisy out here and we're the element of surprise." I did a quick pat down of my ammo pouches and checked my grenades. "Follow my lead."

I darted across the path, to the opposite side and crouched down, glancing down both ways of the path. Seeing everything was clear, I waved Ramos, Sanders, and Vic over in short increments. Once they were across, we began to creep forward towards the position of the artillery pieces. Pushing through several yards of trees, we came to a stop at the edge of a small clearing, alongside a dried stream.

Laying prone, I scanned the area and mapped out a route of attack. I was right with my assumption, as there were three Hummels sitting in the clearing, firing into the sky. There was no forth, but there were three supply wagons nearby. They were built on the Panzer tank's chassis, with an armor configuration, the same as the Hummel's, but they did not mount a howitzer. Instead, they carried a single MG42, for protection, while the space was used to carry spare ammo.

The ammo wagons were stationed behind an assigned Hummel, each of their crews feeding shells to the arty crews. A dozen soldiers stood watch, German Wehrmacht, judging by their field gray uniforms, in loose formation in the dry stream. The stream offered good cover, but was on the far side of our positions which put the Hummels between us and them and open to attack.

I moved Vic into position, a few yards to the right, near the clearing, to set up his BAR. I then sent Sanders and Ramos to the closest Hummel, while its crew was handling shells and calibrating the howitzer. They crept over to the side of the arty piece and stayed out of sight, from the four men near the ammo cart. As they moved up, I skulked over to the second Hummel.

The second barrage had ended with the arty crews working to cool down the howitzers and more shells were stacked for the next attack. I crouched near the rear of the second Hummel and pulled a grenade from my webbing. I waited until the crew was manning their howitzer and then tossed the grenade into the open crew compartment. There was a soft metal clank, as the grenade settled on the bottom of the crew compartment, followed by a shuffle of boots.

I readied my Thompson, whilst someone realized there was a grenade at their feet, but it was too late. An explosion of shrapnel killed the Hummel's crew and wounded one of the men, from the ammo cart. A second boomed, Ramos and Sanders were taking out the first Hummel, and I rushed around to the second cart. Three dazed soldiers scrambled for their weapons, as I came around, my Thompson chattering.

Rifle fire cracked throughout the night. The first gun fell, and the Germans moved to retaliate. Ramos and Sanders rushed to my position, and Vic opened fire from the tree line, to suppress the soldiers in the dry stream. The third Hummel opened up on us, with its single MG42 and pelted the second Hummel with MG fire. I dropped to the ground; Sanders tossed another grenade overhead.

The MG42 fell silent. The grenade killed the most of the Hummel's crew and offered us a chance to move up. Sanders ran out first and killed the last of the men loading ammo, as Ramos moved to the front of the machine. I followed him and grabbed his shoulder.

"We need to break off and pull back," I called out. The soldiers, in the stream, were firing back. "They'll out number us."

"Orders?" Sanders called out, while finishing off the last of the crew.

"Fall back to the tree line!" I yelled, waving at Vic's position, in the woods. Vic was still firing when machine gun fire crackled in the woods, muzzle flashes pointing to four or five people firing at Vic. "Shift fire!"

The three of us opened up on the tree line to Vic's left. A flanking force silenced our BAR cover. Vic turned to face his new attackers, and the fire intensified, on his position. I could not see the attackers, but I could see Vic, as he abandoned his position and moved back into the woods, moving farther away from us and taking the flanking force with him. Ramos ran out first, but I grabbed him by his webbing and pulled him back.

"You'll both end up dead!" I yelled,as he struggled to break free.

"So, we leave him?" Ramos pleaded.

"No." I let Ramos go and signaled Sanders. "We go in and get him back, together. Sanders, go with him and I'll cover."

Sanders nodded and reloaded his M1. I moved towards the front edge, of the Hummel, and glanced back, at the two. "Covering fire!" I yelled, opening fire on the Germans still ducking down, in the dry stream.

Sanders and Ramos rushed back to the trees, whilst I covered them, emptying several clips into the German's positions. I couldn't achieve fire superiority over the dozen, or so, German soldiers, with just my Thompson, but I allowed Sanders and Ramos to pull back, to help Vic. Once they were back in the woods, I tossed a grenade towards the Germans and ran for the thick trees myself.

I propelled myself forward, at top speed, bullets were streaking through the air and tore up the area around me. An MG42 growled,to life, and spat green tracer fire over my head, as I approached the trees, the heavy rounds splintering the branches, in the trees. A figure appeared, in the trees ahead me, but they were not wearing the olive uniform, of an American solider, and I fired without thinking. The figure fell back, as I rushed past and continue on, running on instinct, feeling my way, trying to navigate in the darkness.

Light MG and rifle fire popped around me, and voices yelled out in both English and German. I could hear Vic's BAR still firing with its hard, low pitched cracks, while two M1s popped and cracked alongside it. I rushed towards the familiar sounds, spotting our attackers, far to my right. Muzzle flashes marked five confirmed soldiers, in the woods.

I slowed and pressed myself against a tree, in an attempt to gather my thoughts. My heart pounded in my chest. I edged around, to face the Germans, finding it difficult to focus with so much adrenaline surging through my body. Shouldering my Thompson, I moved to a fallen tree that was closer to the soldiers and readied to fire when I noticed movement to my left.

I dropped down into a low crouch and scanned the area for any other soldiers, when I caught a glimpse of two trying to flank towards the left. I fired on the closest figure and caught him in the face, the figure dropped to the ground, with a wet thud. The second fired with an MP-40 and peppered my position, forcing me to scramble for cover.

Hands shaking slightly, I reloaded my weapon and moved back to my feet. Another burst of fire hit my old position as I crept forward to catch the solider off guard. He continued to fire at my old position, and I edged closer, stopping a few feet to his right. Taking a breath, I spun out and squeezed the trigger, only to hear a metallic clack.

My eyes widened, both the German I realized my weapon had jammed. I quickly reached for my sidearm. The German threw himself forward at me, using his weight to force me to the ground. His hands groped for my throat, while I fumbled for my.45, the German grabbing my wrist, as my hand wrapped around the pistol grip. I rammed a knee into his side and forced him off me. I rolled on top of him, and drew my pistol. I froze. The soldier swore at me, in French, his voice very high pitched for a man.

The slight hesitation allowed the solider to grab my helmet, which fell off in the fight, and slammed it into the side of my head. My vision blurred, and I fell back to the ground, whacking my head against a rock. I struggled to move, and the soldier grabbed my.45, shoving it, into my ribs.

"Do it!" I yelled without even thinking, not really understanding why I said such a thing.

"Corrigan?" the figure asked.

Confusion consumed me. I began to realized the figure was dressed in an olive uniform, like mine. "What?"

The figure drew the pistol back. "Corr, it is you?"

"Jessica?" I said, recognizing her voice. She immediately shuffled off me and gently helped me up, brushing a hand over where the helmet hit me.

"Oh, God, I'm so sorry," she gasped, while she hugged me. "What are you doing out here?"

"Silencing the artillery," I responded, standing up and collecting my gear. "Why are you here?"

"Reynard took me with him, and his men, to take out the artillery, too. He said we'd do it while you waited," she said.

"What-" I pushed away the thought, for a second, to clear the jam in my weapon. Yanking on the cocking hammer a few times, a new round was chambered, the jam finally clearing. The Germans were still firing on Vic, and the others soon turned towards us and began firing our way. I jumped back to my feet and began returning the fire.

"Stop!" Jessica hissed, shoving my Thompson down. "It's Reynard!"

"He's still firing on my men!" I protested, wondering for a second, who it was that I killed before. "Tell him to stop."

"Come with me." She grabbed me by the arm and led me away from the shooting, nearly shoving me behind another fallen tree. "Stay here until I call for you."

I objected, but she ran off, into the woods, before another volley of fire showered my position. Again, I dropped down, as I groped at my Thompson and resisted the urge to stand up and fire back. Instead, I gritted my teeth and kept low while Reynard and my men fought off one another, most likely both groups didn't know who they were really shooting at.

I thought about that first man I killed when I entered the area. Then there was the man Jessica was with, most likely one of Reynard's men. It was possible the first was also a Résistance fighter, but I could not know for sure. Chances were good he was, but why were they out there in the first place? Captain Hiller didn't say anything about Reynard and his men moving out, with us. He shouldn't have been our there at all, Reynard's duty was to hold the second hanger.

The sudden silence caught my attention, all gunfire ceased. I still held my weapon firm, as I moved to my knees and peered over the fallen tree. The woods were still and silent, with no sign of my men, or Reynard's. My heart raced. I took a breath and emerged from my cover, edging myself forward, at a slow pace. A sudden crunch of leaves behind me forced me to spin around, Thompson aimed and ready to fire. I swore under my breath and lowered my weapon.

"I told you to wait," Jessica sighed.

I let my weapon drop down to my waist. "Silence makes me jumpy."

Jessica shook her head and led me towards Reynard's position. He was with five, of his eight men, hiding behind several fallen trees, within a small dip in the forest floor. A body lay several feet away, Reynard's sixth man killed in the firefight. Vic, Sanders, and Ramos crossed over and stood by, all three unharmed.

"What the hell was that?" I demanded, as Reynard stood up to meet me.

"What were you doing out here?" Reynard countered.

I felt the rage burning, in my chest. "Us? We're out here to stop the German artillery before they flatten the hangers. I told, no, I ordered you to stay in the second hanger and hold it until morning. Why the hell are you out here with your men?"

"Doing what you were doing! I thought you died during the barrage and decided to head out. Your men are watching the hanger," Reynard spat.

"My men? You mean the recon team the Captain brought in?" I let out an angry grunt. "Jesus, why did you attack my men? Judging by where we found you, you had ample opportunity, to see us hitting the Germans. What made you believe we were Germans?" Reynard didn't say a word, as he brought up his MP-40, aiming at me. His men trained their weapons on Vic, Sanders, and Ramos, without hesitation.

"Drop your weapons!" He barked.

"What the hell?" I gasped.

Towards the clearing came the murmur of boots trampling through the woods. Reynard told one of his men to get the advancing Germans and tell them they had prisoners.

"You're a fucking spy!" Vic spat, unwavering, holding his BAR.

"Reynard…" Jessica whispered. She tried to push the barrel of the his MP-40 away from my chest. He shrugged her off and kept the weapon level.

"You were trying to regroup with the Germans and help them take back the hangers," I figured it out. "You couldn't let such advanced technology fall into Allied hands."

"Smart, for an America, but you are too slow," He laughed.

I glanced over at Jessica, her face showing her shock, while her eyes filled with rage.

I still held my Thompson at my waist, as did my men. We refused to drop our weapons, as ordered, prompting Reynard to threaten us. He didn't get a chance to yell the fire command. Jessica grabbed the barrel of the MP-40 and shoved it up and into Reynard's face. I dropped back, gunfire erupted and Reynard fired on me, his shots going wide. Luckily, for me, the arrogant bastard was a lousy shot.

I fired at point blank range, ripping open Reynard's chest with a short volley. Vic's BAR tore open two other of the fighters, and Ramos slammed his rifle's butt into another's head. Sanders shoved the barrel of his M1 into the third's chest and fired twice, the two rounds punching through his back. I rolled and jumped back, in time to drop the last man, as the quick firefight ended. I ran over to Jessica and helped her, she was unharmed in the fight.

"C'mon, we have to go," I said, loud enough for the others to hear.

I stood up and checked, to see if any of Reynard's men were still alive. All were dead except Reynard, who lay semiconscious in the dirt with blood oozing out through the bullet wounds. He couldn't speak, the only sounds being wet grunts and muted gurgles. Instead of putting a bullet in his face, I moved away and signaled everyone to pull back to the hanger. Jessica spit on the body and followed me without a word.

The German soldiers were yelling and shouting orders. We ran, a bad decision to make, when stumbling around in the dark. I was constantly stumbling and falling on rocks and tree roots, but I kept moving and urging the others on. German voices still echoed throughout the night, the pursing soldiers fumbling around, while they searched. No shots were fired. They were out of range, but we still ran to keep some distance between us and them.

Vic swore to himself, as he tripped in front of me, falling to the soft earth. I didn't break stride. Reaching down, I pulled him back up. It was approaching two in the morning, and we crossed over the dirt path and ran for the airstrip, moving away from the path, instead of hugging it. It would make it harder for the Germans to follow after us and slow them down a bit. That hope was shattered. A rifle shot cracked from behind, the bullet exploding, into a tree ahead of Ramos.

I spun around, stopping behind a tree. "Keep going and let Hiller know about Reynard," I ordered, when the others stopped running.

"What are you doing?" Ramos grunted. Several more shots echoed.

"They'll catch up on us," I replied, shouldering my Thompson. "I'll slow them down, so you can get back."

"Bullshit, I'll stay," Vic volunteered. "I can hold them off longer."

"All of you are to head back, now! That's an order," I screamed.

"You can't do this, Corr," Jessica pleaded.

"Get going!" I ordered, again. "If I don't stall them, they'll kill us all. GO!"

Ramos and Sanders exchanged nervous glances, but agreed. Vic had to pull Jessica with him, but the four turn and continued on running. I turned back to face the advancing soldiers and leaned against the tree for support. They were close, close enough for me to hear the shouts of orders and even the clicks of rifles.

The first German appeared to my right, stumbling over tree roots while holding his bolt action rifle in one hand. I squeezed the trigger and took the German down with a blow to the chest. Two rifles cracked to my left, as two bullets slammed into my tree. I spun around, firing towards the soldiers crouched behind some bushes. There was a muffle scream. One was hit, and the other took off running. He fell to the ground with three shots to the back.

I pulled back and swapped out for a fresh clip, more soldiers rushed towards my position. I tossed two grenades ahead of me, to catch the advancing soldiers, the explosions only getting three of them. More rifle shots, aided with fire from an MP-40, pounded the tree I used for cover and forced me to crouch down lower. A sudden snap of twigs caused me to turn around, just in time, to see a figure raise a rifle, in my direction. A four round burst shaved off the top of his skull, in an instant.

More bullets bombarded my position, with at least ten to twelve more soldiers lurking in the trees. I decided I had allowed the others enough time to pull back and began to move back myself. It was a careful process, silently moving to the airstrip by jumping from cover to cover while fighting back. A fighting retreat offered me better protection compared to running and leaving myself exposed, to a shot in the back.

There was a lull. The soldiers reloaded their weapons and I made my move. Silently, I ran back to a tree several yards away, stopping, as the shooting picked up again. They still fired on my first position, so I arched a grenade overhead and had it landed nearby. I ran again, once the explosive detonated, and moved back ten yards and stopped, when I noticed another soldier following me far to my left.

I dropped down into a crouch and fired towards him. The rounds slammed into the trees around him, forcing the soldiers to drop for cover. Once he was down, I jumped back up and continued on without stopping for another fifteen yards. I glanced back to make sure no one was following and continued, again running a longer distance. I repeated the process over and over again until I found the edge of the concrete runway, in the distance.

Sighing in relief to myself, I did one last check before sprinting forward. My heart pounded in my chest, as I approached the edge of the tree line, when something heavy slammed into my back. I fell forward and lost my Thompson, when I realized another soldier was on top of me. I rolled over and slammed a fist into the attacker's jaw, a reassuring crack echoing upon contact. A counter hit shot pain up my side, as we struggled, both of us swinging at one another, while trying to gain control.

I elbowed the attacker in the cheek and gained enough movement to reach my knife. The trench knife was held in a pocket, on the side of my pack, but I had left it back in the hanger. Instead, I pulled out the knife my father gave me, which was tucked in a sheath, on my belt. I withdrew the blade and cleanly slashed the attacker's throat with a single strike. Warm blood washed over my uniform, as I forced the stunned soldier off me. I struggled, to get back on my feet, and gathered my Thompson before running to the hanger.

The runway was crated completely, from one end to the other, but both hangers were still intact. I noticed several members of the squad moving about out front, near both hangers, but I could not tell who. Only Jessica stood out with her long hair and Captain Hiller, with him being taller the rest of us. Stumbling, I made it to the hanger doors and dropped from exhaustion.

The sudden noise drew everyone's attention, Ramos turning with Sanders and training their weapons on me, but lowered them, as Doc rushed forward. He crouched next to me, a grim look on his face when he saw the blood.

"Relax," I groaned, forcing myself to stand, "I'm not hit."

"And the blood?" Doc asked.

I jerked a thumb back towards the trees. "You'll find his body back there."

"He's dead?" Hiller asked without saying anything else.

"I dropped him myself, sir," I answered. "He's dead."

Hiller nodded in approval. "Get some rest, son. Intel will be here in the morning and we'll be moving out." He glanced over at nervous Jessica, who stood back with Jay. "Might want to change or clean your uniform."

Hiller dismissed me and returned to his work. Jessica ran over to me and we hugged, she squeezed me a little too hard, my muscles were still sore, but I didn't mind one bit. The warmth of her body was more than welcomed.

"You need to stop taking those damn risks," she demanded in French. "You're not invincible, after all."

I let a low chuckle escape. "Hey, I plan to live old enough to see my great grandkids get married. "

Jessica looked up at me with her calming gray eyes. "You don't seem to act like it."

I shrugged off the thought. "We're soldiers, do we ever?"

Chapter 15

I managed five hours of sleep, which didn't cover the few hundreds of hours I missed since the landings, when the replacement force arrived. Since no vehicles could get closer than the dirt path, all of the replacements arrived, an hour after dawn, carrying their equipment. The second they arrived, the eggheads from Intel tossed us out of the hangers and gathered up every scrap of paper we collected. After they spoke to each of us, about what we found, they locked themselves inside the hangers.

Major Philips even arrived, somehow getting his jeep through the woods and onto the runway. He spoke with Captain Hiller, with a very pleasant attitude, patting his shoulder and nodding his head in approval. Once he was through, Captain Hiller met with us near the path leading back through the woods.

"How'd the Major like it, sir?" Phelps asked when he returned.

"Unnerved when I told him about that puke Reynard and his men," Hiller answered. "That changed when I handed over twenty Me 262s in prime condition with technical specs and schematics. He's very happy with our work here and passes along his thanks to whomever silenced the Hummels, they were pounding the town too." Hiller fished out a handful of chevrons from his pocket.

"Demotion, sir?" Sanders remarked.

"Nope," he tossed the stripes to Vic, Ramos, and Sanders. "You three are here by promoted to the rank of corporal, for your acts in removing the artillery."

"And the LT?" Ramos asked, as he admired his new rank.

"Bolger, he's putting you up for a medal for taking out Reynard and the arty. Don't know which medal, but one nonetheless," Hiller said, with a smile.

Jay patted my shoulder. "Not a bad job, Corr."

"Ah, thank you, sir," I responded. "Where to now?"

Hiller pulled out his folded map and held it for us to see. "A little town called Chambois."

Chambois was the last town needed to be taken and held, in order to encircle the shattered remains, of the German Seventh Army, the very defenders of Normandy. Since their attack on Mortain had failed, they were in full retreat, hoping to escape the grasp of Allied forces. They were also trying to regroup with the bulk of the Germany forces farther west. Our next objective was to head into Chambois and help with the defenses, while our forces linked up with the Brits, Polish, and Canadian forces, to the north, in Trun.

"Make sure we've got plenty of ammo for the AT weapons!" I called from the forth floor, of an abandoned apartment building. Hank was down in the street with Phelps helping an anti tank crew set up an old model 75mm antitank gun, behind a sandbag wall.

"Got eighty rounds!" Hank yelled back. He spoke with the crew chief for a second. "Should get another fifty stacked in ten-twelve minutes!"

I waved back and pulled inside. An MG team was setting a .30cal machine gun in one of the nearby windows facing east, the barrel had a shaped water cooling jacket attached. Captain Hiller was given the command of two 75mm AT guns, three light MG teams, four M19 mortars, and three bazooka teams, to hold the eastern road, into town. We were to hold back the Germans, for as long as possible, before pulling back to the next defensive line.

"Just about set up here, sir," one of the gunners reported. His three man crew had finished attaching the MG to its tripod.

"You have enough ammo?" I asked.

The private, from Florida, shrugged. "How much is ever enough? We got eight boxes of ammo, which is 'bout few hundred rounds. No AP, though, that's been tapped out for some time now."

I nodded. "Try and make them count."

He tipped his helmet, in salute. "We can try, sir."

I walked down the barren corridor until I came to a gap in the cement ceiling, a mortar strike. "Jay, you set up?" I yelled up to him.

Jay appeared overhead and looked down to me. "All set up here, Corr. Got enough ammo and have a nice little sniper's nest set up."

"Keep watch up there and call out if ya see anything," I said.

"Gotcha, boss," Jay yelled.

Jay returned to his post, and I walked to the corner stairwell. I quickly walked down, to the bottom floor, and emerged into the street. The two AT guns were set up on opposite sides, of the main road, behind sandbagged walls, covered with logs and any bricks salvaged from the rubble. A second MG team was set up in the opposite building with the third dug into a ditch, that ran in front of the buildings, and under the roadway.

"Mortar teams set up and ready," Phelps reported emerging from an open courtyard behind Jay's building. "Got the road and nearby fields zeroed in."

I waved back to him, as Ramos worked with Malks and Vic, to build up a sandbag wall, for a firing line behind the AT guns. At the same time, a group of engineers from the 16th were building tank traps and roadblocks, on the main road, covering some distance ahead of us.

"Bolger!" Hiller called waving me over to the makeshift CP, inside an abandoned storefront.

"Sir?" I responded, as I ran over and stepped inside.

He nodded towards Adam with his radio and several area maps. "How are the defenses coming?" He asked.

"Just about there, sir," I reported. "MGs and mortar teams are deployed, with the AT emplacements just about there. The firing line is almost done, and the engineers are finishing up with the tank traps."

"Mines?" He inquired.

I shook my head. "None left, to use, sir."

Hiller shrugged it off. "Well, I've got some heavy arty to cover us, incase of retreat. Several 105s are set up to saturate our position with shells, should we need to retreat. Two batteries will be on standby, to provide support during the fighting."

"Any track or armor support?" I asked.

"We're seeing," he nodded at Adam. He was glued to the radio and scribbling notes.

"Copy, Swordsmen out," he said, as he placed the receiver down. "First Polish Armored is still resupplying, but they have several Fireflies rolling our way. Two M10 Hellcats will be deployed to cover us, and they will be here in thirty minutes, after a refueling."

"Better than nothing." Hiller studied the area map of Chambois and made a few grunts. "If we play this right, I think we can bloody a few noses."

"Sirs, we've got movement!" Doc yelled to us, as he appeared in the store.

Both Hiller and I ran out to see everyone moving in overdrive, as they moved to their fighting positions. "Jay, what do ya got?" I yelled up to our sniper.

"'Couple of Panzers and Tigers heading along the road." He took another looked through his binoculars. "Maybe a mile out or so!"

"Keep watch and get ready!" Hiller ordered. "This is it! Let's knock out a German Army, shall we?"

The men shouted back in approval and raced to finish their work and get to their stations. Extra crates of ammo were rushed up the sandbag emplacements, while the AT crews stacked shell, for rapid firing. I ran to the forward sandbag line, in the street, between the two AT guns, and stuffed a few extra ammo clips into my jacket and pockets. One of the bazooka crews stood next to me, preparing a live rocket for firing, with Vic on my opposite side, with his BAR.

"Just how many Krauts are we looking at?" He asked, resting his BAR on the sandbags, he'd tossed the weapons bipod before the landings, it added unneeded weight.

"Whatever is left of the Seventh Army," I responded. "Should be about 15 divisions, so about 150,000 men."

Vic tossed me a sideways glance. "Shit, I'm gonna need some more ammo for that then."

The two of us laughed, as we stacked spare ammo clips. It was a practice Hiller taught us about fighting defensively. You stack spare ammo clips, on the cover, in front of you, and use those first. It would allow me to use up six clips, that I couldn't carry, so I'd have a full load to carry later.

"Jerry tanks on approach!" Jay suddenly called out. "They're in range!"

I looked to the AT crews who nodded in agreement. I waved my hand forward and signaled them they were weapons free. The crews quickly sighted the approaching tank column on the road. The engineers pulled back, to our position. The fire command was yelled out and two armor piercing shells shot from the 75s and slammed into the leading Panzer. An encouraging fireball forced the tank off the road.

The mortar crews sent shells flying, in a long barrage, that rained down on the roadway. German Tigers, Panthers, Panzers, and the strange looking *Jagdpanthers* rolled on, through the barrage, and broke off into separate groups, to pour down the road and surrounding fields. It didn't take them long to fling shells our way, to knock out the AT guns.

German infantry was close behind and advanced with their tanks ahead. Our MGs opened up first, red tracer rounds zipping through the air and bouncing off the tank armor. Jay did his best to pick off soldiers carrying AT weapons, or mortars, and soon the rest of us opened up. Rifles and machine guns chattered, as we let loose a broadside attack on the advancing forces.

Enemy soldiers began to out run their tank cover and advanced ahead while the heavy Tigers worked, to blow away our tank traps. I opened fire on the Germans snaking their way through the tank traps and across the small bridge over the ditch. Everyone was pouring fire into the kill zone. Germans fell left and right, an effective wall of steel, holding back the enemy advance.

I pulled an empty clip from my Thompson and moved to reload. A tank shell slammed into the building, to my left. The shell tore open a section of the second floor and blew concrete and dust onto us. I fought off the chocking dust and continued to fire, whilst the bazooka next to me fired, with a whoosh of heated air, that danced across my back, like the heat radiating, from a hot oven.

Eight Panzers and three Panthers were burning across the battlefield, with dead Germans around them. Our AT crews made each shot count, as a slant armor *Jagdpanther* rolled forward and fired. The tank killer blew apart the AT gun, to my right, the crew killed, in an instant, while the gun was tossed back a few feet. I ducked down and several AT rockets shot overhead and spun into the nearby buildings. I stood back. Another rocket exploded, into the dirt, several feet, in front of us, with a shower of black dirt. Vic swore a several pieces of shrapnel ripped into his right shoulder, but he blocked out the pain and continued firing.

"Shift fire!" I yelled to Vic, waving towards the left edge of the ditch.

He nodded and sprayed the area. The Germans tried to push through and rush Jay's building. Jay and the MG team, inside, halted the flanking force, while a pair of Tigers moved up. Both fired into the building with HE rounds, that resulted in massive explosions, blowing out huge chunks of the buildings. The MG team fell silent, as I looked up. Jay didn't appear near the edge of the roof.

"Bolger," Hiller yelled, standing near the CP. I turned to face him, "concentrate AT fire on those Tigers!"

I nodded and told the nearby bazooka team to target the Tigers. As they shifted fire, I ran out to the remaining AT gun and repeated the orders before running to the other two bazooka teams. The AT teams shifted fire, to hit both of the closest Tiger tanks. Their combined fire had little effect on the thick Tiger armor, but they managed to knock the treads off, one of the two, paralyzing the Tiger.

I returned back to the sandbag line, and another Panzer tried to cross the bridge. The bazooka team, closest to me, fired on the Panzer and knocked off its left tread, stopping the tank, on the bridge, as it billowed smoke. The turret was still active and fired on us, blowing away the MG team,set up in the ditch. Its hull mounted MG42 fired my way and killed the two man bazooka team. Vic and I dropped behind the sandbags for cover.

Vic yelled something to me, but I couldn't hear, the Panzer was suddenly blown apart, the turret blown off, as well. I looked back, to see our two Hellcats rolling down the street, side by side, Polish flags painted on the front turret armor, next to the main gun. The two tank hunters rolled to a stop behind the sandbag line and quickly silenced the two Tigers threatening to overrun our lines.

"'bout time they showed up!" Vic yelled, standing up, to fire.

I climbed aboard the closest Hellcat and stood behind the open turret. The crew inside worked to reload their main cannon. Their commander looked up at me, his face covered by a thick coating of grease and sweat.

"Thanks for showing up," I said.

"We had to drive all the way down from the Mace to get here," the Polish Lieutenant responded, shaking my hand. "Don't worry, we'll make up for it."

"Take on the Panthers and Tigers, we'll handle the Panzers," I said.

The commander waved a gloved hand at me, in acknowledgment, as I hopped back off the tank and ran for the sandbags. Vic was the only one left standing, the bazooka teams and the last AT crew were dead. The rest of the squad was taking cover in the ditch and fighting back, while Vic and I stood alone.

The Hellcats blunted the armor attack, while we managed to slow the infantry, but they were unrelenting. Enemy mortar halftracks had set up just outside of range of ours and began to pound our position. A lucky hit landed in the open turret compartment, of one of the two Hellcats, and knocked it out, no more than a minute, after it arrived. I fired with my Thompson into the advancing horde of Germans and ran through twelve, twenty round clips in fifteen minutes. Vic was running low, as he slowed his rate of fire, the dozens of empty ammo clips, at his feet, adding more proof.

"Polish armor is tied up in the city center," Captain Hiller grunted, running up besides me. "Orders are to pull back to the school and hold out till armor arrives."

"Yes, sir," I responded. "Vic is covering fire."

He nodded and picked up the rate of fire. I ran for the men ducking down in the ditch. Working my way from trooper to trooper, I issued the retreat orders. Everyone understood what to do,and they pulled back from the ditch, to the sandbags. Once everyone was clear of the ditch, I pulled back and ran into Jay, who stumbled out of his building.

"What's going on?" he asked,still clutching his rifle.

"Pulling back, c'mon!" I responded, shoving him forward. The two of us returned to the sandbags, and Captain Hiller told the Hellcat to pull back.

"Full retreat, boys," Hiller said, as the tank hunter flew back in reverse. "Arty line will turn this place to dust. Pull back!"

Enemy MG and rifle fire followed us. We ran back through the street, hugging the sides. A fighting retreat would not work. The artillery barrage was inbound and we needed to lure the Germans in. Sure enough, tanks and infantry rushed over our old positions and rushed into the city. We were a block away, when the first shell landed.

White phosphorous rained down on them, in burning clouds, that swept over the street. The ground shook with each strike, as we rounded the corner to the second defensive line, at a small school,two blocks away. The Hellcat maneuvered its way into the front courtyard and slid into an already prepared fighting position. Two squads of Polish riflemen were bunkered down inside and gratefully welcomed us; their artillery stalled the Germans.

"Fan out and put a rifle to a window," Hiller barked, when we entered through the old wooden doors, to the school.

"Captain Hiller," a Polish Captain greeted Hiller, with a courtesy salute.

"Captain Lewinski," Hiller acknowledged, with a handshake. "Hope you boys are ready."

"MGs and AT weapons, all set up." He glanced out front. "Ah, poor Henry didn't make it?"

"German mortar," I explained for the missing Hellcat.

Lewinski nodded sadly, but composed himself. "Let's get you set up to prepare a proper Polish greeting, for our German friends. You'll find ammo stored inside a classroom, just through the doors behind me. Our medic is in the nurse's station and barracks in the cafeteria."

"Captain," a Polish soldier called out, with a radio, on his back. He reported something, in Polish,to the Captain and returned to his radio.

"It would seem we have Fireflies coming to aide us," Lewinski said.

Hiller nodded. "Bolger, find a spot to fight and get ready. I'll handle everything else."

I saluted. "Yes, sir."

Hiller dismissed me, before returning to speak with Lewinski. Jay and I walked up to the top floor of the three floor school, and found an open window facing the street. We dropped our packs to the ground and checked over our supplies.

"You okay?" I asked Jay, as he cleared his rifle.

He shrugged. "Had a close call, but nothing major."

I eyed Jay with suspicion. "Are you sure?"

Jay slammed his rifle's breach close with a hard click. "Without a doubt."

I shrugged my shoulders and leaned against the wall, resting my Thompson in my lap. There were a handful of other soldiers around the floor, with two others, in the same hallway, with us. Both were speaking to each other in their language while assembling a Lee Enfield Rifle. The one working on the rifle looked over at me and Jay. He said something to his friend and the two walked over to us, with the rifle.

"Sergeant Martin Obrinski," the older of the two, greeted. "This is my brother, Mitchell."

We shook hands. "Pleasure to meet you. I'm Corr and this is Jay."

"Sniper?" Mitchell asked, nodding at Jay's Springfield.

"Yeah, best shot in the First," Jay said, with pride.

"Uh-huh," was the response. "Don't think you can hold up with me and my Enfield."

Jay laughed. "This is a born sniper tool, while that is an Enfield, with a bolt on scope."

"Germans on approach!" Someone yelled, from below, in English, and then, in Polish.

"Let's see who does better," Mitchell grunted, as he and his brother ran back to their window.

Jay took up the challenge with a head nod and stood up to aim out the window. I moved to the window a few feet away and broke the last bits of glass still stuck to the frame. Orders were shouted in Polish below, as the men ran to their positions, in the courtyard below. Several heavy machine guns were set up by the Hellcat and in the building, with a handful of snipers.

The Poles were equipped with British made weapons and equipment that, while reliable, was not the better in comparison, to us, or the Germans. Lee Enfield rifles were accurate and could reach out and hit someone, but they were still bolt action. They lacked the rate of fire put out by our Garand rifles, or the German *Gewehr* 41. Still, the Poles made good use of their weapons, such as the anti tank rockets, called the *PIAT*.

"Targets up," Jay mumbled to himself.

The skirmish force appeared at the end of the block, advancing forward with a Panzer IV following close by.

Jay's rifle cracked first, before the others, a single German trooper falling, to the debris strewn ground. Several Enfield rifles followed, with a volley of cracks, more Germans fell. The others ran for cover, while the Panzer rolled up and raked the school with MG fire. A fireball consumed the tank, with a single shot of the Hellcat, the armor piercing round ripping open the driver's compartment and front of the turret. A second shot spilt the turret in half.

I still held my fire on the enemy; they were just out of range and the snipers were easily picking off the stragglers. Sighing, I pulled back from the window and listened, sniper rifles cracked and German rounds randomly thwacked against the building. Jay's rifle cracked for a third, and final time.

"All clear," he announced, clearing his rifle, "they're dead."

The first sign of trouble was a low whistle off in the distance, that was barely audible, over the claps of artillery near the northern edge of the town. I instinctively looked outside and craned my head skyward, in the hopes of seeing something. Nothing was to be seen, as the whistle grew louder, and then it hit me.

"Incoming!" I shouted, as I ducked down, and moved away from the window.

The first mortar slammed into the roof of the school and broke through to top floor, exploding on the opposite side of the floor. The blast was more muffled then normal, and the building shuttered slightly, more shells hit. My nostrils filled with the thick odor of smoke and burning wood.

I scrambled to the edge of the hallway and looked down towards the area of the blast. Black smoke billowed out tendrils of flames that leapt out from an empty room. The strange, metallic smell of an incendiary chemical soon mixed with the smoke, as I realized what was happening. I rushed back to my position and grabbed Jay and the two Polish soldiers.

"We need to get out now!" I ordered. "They're using incendiary rounds to burn down the building."

"Fire has broken out?" Mitchell asked.

I didn't answer; a shell slammed into the floor below us and blew out a chunk of the outer of wall. Flames quickly enveloped a section of the lower floor, and the incendiary chemicals sparked a quickly growing fire. The four of us rushed for the nearest stairwell at the opposite end of the hallway, with the fire growing underneath our boots. More shells exploded,and the fire spread from floor to floor, fires even sparking out into the courtyard.

The strategy was perfect for the Germans; burn out the defenders from their fortification and advance on them while they are confused and disorganized. I could hear the crack and pop of machine gun fire outside. We raced down, to the stairs, to get outside. Our Hellcat was still firing along, with the troops on the first floor, where the fire had not spread, yet.

"Keep up the fire!" Hiller was yelling, as we exited to the ground floor. Both he, and Captain Lewinski, were fighting back while, encouraging the soldiers to fight harder.

"Find a spot to be useful," I growled, while running up to an empty window, in the entrance lobby.

Jay ran to a sandbag emplacement, next to the Hellcat, with Mitchell while Martin stayed with me. He stood to the right side of the window, while I crouch by the left, the two of us having ample room to fire out. I stayed low and squeezed the trigger, while keeping the sights down range. I didn't see if my shots stopped or hit anything, but I kept firing round after round.

A Tiger tank had snaked its way up the road and shoved the dead Panzer off the street, forcing the smoking hulk into a bombed out building, and moved into firing position. Four different *PIATs* opened fire, from multiple parts of the building, catapulting several two pound warheads, at the iron beast. Each warhead exploded upon contact and killed several nearby soldiers, with razor sharp shrapnel. The Tiger rolled on unharmed.

"Jam!" Martin yelled angrily pulling back in. I glanced up to see he was struggling to clear the chamber of the Enfield.

"Gotcha covered," I responded, picking up my rate of fire. I sprayed the advancing forces with bullets, that bounced off the Tiger, or slammed into the ground.

The hull, of the MG42, of the Tiger, opened up and sent a broadside of heavy MG fire our way. Rounds tore up the stone masonry of the building, like a buzz saw cutting through a sheet of plywood. Sandbags were ripped up along, with the Polish soldiers ducking behind them. Cannon fire boomed and took chunks of building away, in fiery explosions. That tank was taking the building apart, brick by brick, and soldier by soldier.

"We need something heavier!" I yelled out to Captain Lewinski, who was dragging a wounded tanker inside. The Hellcat was gone.

"Fireflies are coming!" he yelled back, in a thick accent. "Keep doing what ya can!"

I turned back to reload, as did Martin. He fumbled with his rifle and shoved two, five round clips, into the breach, of his weapon. With a slap of his hand, the bolt slid into place and locked. He glanced down at me with a grin, happy to have cleared his weapon. I looked back down, struggling to shove the new clip into my Thompson. I swore, as something warm and sticky splashed over the back of my neck. I reached out to wipe it away, and a large amount of weight suddenly fell, on top of me.

"Martin!" I yelled, realizing, he was on top me.

I dropped my Thompson and rolled his body off me and helped him to the floor. Blood soaked the lower part of his uniform, near the bottom of his ribcage, several bullets now lodged inside him. Martin groaned with pain, pressing down on the wound and clenching his teeth.

"Fuck!" he swore in Polish. That's as far as my Polish went, besides a few other insults.

"Hang on," I grunted, while pressing one hand over his and fumbling for my aid kit, with the other. "Keep pressure on the wound."

"Medic!" he called out, in both English and Polish. "Medic!"

I dumped a sulfur packet over his bleeding stomach and pressed a white bandage down, forcing Martin to yelp in pain. He sucked in another breath of air and locked his jaw in place, to fight the pain. I kept the bandage firmly pressed to the wound and looked around for Doc. The Polish medic, a stocky looking kid with sweat soaked black hair and the name Kaploski written on his uniform, appeared from nowhere and took over.

"Thanks," Martin grunted. I backed away to give the medic room to work.

I groped for my Thompson and returned to the window. Struggling, I clear the jammed weapon and reloaded, in time, to see the Tiger grind to a halt near the crumbled courtyard wall. Its main 88mm gun swung around to face the upper floors. Another boom echoed and shook the ground, as a shell tore open another part of the third floor. I crouched down, two explosions blossomed along the Tiger's side armor.

Cheers and cries of joy soon rose, as a pair of Sherman Fireflies rolled alongside the school and opened fire on the Tiger. Another three appeared off to the left and blasted away at a Panther trying to cover the Tiger. The Fireflies were born tank hunters, enhanced Sherman tanks fitted with a British 17 ponder anti tank cannon, to penetrate tank armor. It only took several side armor hits, to knock out both the Tiger and Panther.

Fifty caliber machine guns rattled from atop each Firefly, manned by the tank commanders. German infantry were torn apart by the heavy weapons and began to pull back, as their tank cover was burning before them. Watching the tanks crush the enemy attack, I held fire and stood silent, while the last of the soldiers were routed.

"Cease fire! Cease fire!" both captains yelled, the tanks halted their assault.

"We do it?" Martin croaked, as the medic finished dressing his wounds.

I turned back to him and nodded. "Yeah, we did it."

"Everyone pull out now!" Hiller ordered with Lewinski, repeating the orders in Polish.

I then remembered the building was still burning, from the mortar attack, and began to direct people to get outside. Everyone heard the orders and proceeded outside without panicking or rushing. I reached down and helped Martin to his feet, letting him lean on me, as I led him outside.

"Where to now, sir?" Vic asked, helping to carry out another wounded Pole.

"Next defensive line," Hiller answered, after speaking on the radio. "We need to get setup before the next attack."

"So, we stop the Germans, only to retreat when they do?" Martin whispered.

I laughed, shouldering most of his weight. "I had no idea the Polish were so philosophical."

Martin nodded with a grin. "Shhh, it's a guarded secret we use to win over the ladies."

Aside from the loss of the Hellcat, all of the Polish forces had survived with the most severe wound being Martin's. Our squad had taken no losses, with no wounded, aside from scratches and minor burns, nothing that a bandage and a little water couldn't fix. Ammo wouldn't be a problem; each defensive line was stocked with ammo in preparation for attack. Same went for food, the defensive line was the last one before the command post set up the town church.

Defensive line Texas was set up along a large housing complex, two blocks from the school, and was more heavily fortified. A dozen Fireflies were spread out inside streets and allies, to create ambushes, while AT guns were set up on the only roads not blocked by debris. The housing complex, which stood six floors high and spanned five blocks, was heavily fortified with a dozen MG, sniper nests, bazookas and mortar teams. Best of all, there was food and room to sleep indoors.

"Aide station is set up in the northern basement," a rifleman from the First said, standing out front, behind a sandbag wall. "Armory is rooms A4 to A6 and you're free to sleep wherever you can find a place."

"Who's in charge?" Hiller asked, watching our squad march inside.

"Major Philips is," the trooper answered. His accent was strait out of the bowery, in New York, with a slight hint of Irish.

"What of Major Nesco?" Lewinski asked.

The trooper shrugged. "The Poles are keeping command, of all armor, while Philips is regulating infantry. Don't know where Polish infantry fit in, though."

Lewinski shrugged. "A rifle to a window is where?" He continued inside, with his men, without another word.

The Polish medic took Martin from me. "Thanks for letting me fall on you," Martin said, with a grin, flinching from the pain in his side.

"Not to mention bleeding on me," I added.

"Bolger," Hiller called, "get the squad inside and let them get some sleep."

I finally noticed the sun was beginning to set. "No problem, sir."

Hiller nodded, sticking to his persona of keeping the talking short. None of us knew very much about the captain even though we've been together since basic training, before the landing in Oran. Hiller never spoke too much, about himself to us, or anyone else, for that matter, besides Hanes. What we knew of him came from rumor and the little Hiller did say.

Captain John Hiller served, as a rifleman, with the Army during the Great War, though we never knew how old he was when he started, some say twenty others say sixteen. After the war ended he remained in the service, as one of the first men, in the First Infantry Division. When Germany and Japan declared war on us, the squad came together, in training, under his command. He wore a gold webbing band, but he never spoke of a wife, ex-wife, or kids to us. Hiller was a man shrouded in mystery, but an expert soldier, nonetheless, that everyone in the squad respected and, in one way or another, loved like a father.

"I'm gonna take a leak," Vic grunted, before wandering inside. He was another man of little words that came off as cold and grim to most people. I only knew he was from some nowhere town in South Carolina, smoked or chewed tobacco, to pass time and loved to take apart and assemble his BAR.

"Want to borrow my glasses to help you find it?" Adam snickered patting his breast pocket, where he kept his reading glasses.

Vic responded, by spitting some chewing tobacco at Adam, from the doorway, and then walked inside. A few of the guys laughed before leaving Adam to wipe the sticky goo from his boots, a look of annoyance crossing his face. I shrugged off the little scene and walked inside the housing complex, yawning, the sun was slowly dropping behind the buildings of Chambois. It had been one hell of a day, but it was just one, out the few hundreds I would live through, in Europe.

"Shift fire, left flank!" The Germans were hitting us with endless waves of armor and infantry, to keep us busy, while they fought for the Mace, some miles away.

"My MG ain't gonna scratch the paint on that fucking Panther!" Hank responded, swinging his light MG to face a new line of German tanks and infantry.

"Where's our air support?" Hiller yelled to Adam, as another tank shell exploded feet from our position.

"Air Corps is sending it our way!" Adam yelled back. He tried to listen to the radio receiver, while blocking out the noise of battle. "ETA is thirty, maybe forty minutes!"

"Armor?" Hiller asked.

Lewinski was removing the dog tags, from one of his dead men. "Nothing for us, they're trying to route the Germans attacking our brothers at the Mace."

"Ain't that the Canuck's job?" Vic asked, now down to using a scavenged Sten machine gun, his BAR dry and slung over his back.

"Would you do no less, if they were Americans?" Lewinski asked, as he returned shooting.

Several Panzers were approaching from the wooded area, just across the road on the northern edge of the city. They easily tore into us, our position, now inside and in front of an empty house. We abandoned the housing complex four days earlier when the Germans shoved through the north and ran for the Mace. Their vanguard force was hitting us, and it was hard to keep the gap open.

I was running low on ammo, only four spare clips left, in the holders, over my chest. German troops still pushed, on our position, with armor support, and had killed nearly all of Lewinski's squad. Only four, of a fifteen man rifle squad, was left with Lewinski, Martin, Mitchell, and a Bren gunner, whose name I didn't catch.

The four men were ducking behind a low stone wall, for cover, to my right, with my squad spread out, to my left, and behind me. We poured, as much fire, onto the advancing enemy, as we could, but to no avail. Our bullets bounced off tank armor or harmlessly slammed into the ground. It was nearly impossible to get off accurate shots, while avoiding tank fire.

"Get down!' I yelled, jumping away from my position in the wall.

A German Panzer crashed through the stone wall and into the house we were using for cover. The front end of the tank slammed through the building wall and stopped, while the crew tried to spin the turret around. I lay a few feet away and watched, as the main cannon slammed into a support beam, and became stuck, the hydraulic motors of the turret whining in protest.

"Sticky bombs!" I ordered, as I scrambled back to my feet.

Malks rushed past me holding one of the premade sticky bombs. The simple weapons were a brick, or two, of C4 or TNT, wrapped in a sock, and coated with tar to make sure it stuck to the side of a tank. Lighting the fuse, Malks tossed the sticky bomb against the turret and pulled back. The fuse burned down and ignited the packet of C4, blowing a large chunk of the frontal armor off and opening a gap in the armor. Nate rushed in and tossed a grenade inside, the following blast killing the crew.

"We're almost out of them," Malks reported.

"Down to four," Nate added.

MG fire whacked into the ground around us.

"Orders, Captain?" I asked.

Hiller was emptying his Thompson and then pulled back to reload. "We keep holding until air cover arrives," he responded, with a grunt.

"Grenade!" Adam suddenly shouted, from behind us.

I didn't glance back, as I threw myself in the opposite direction and crouched behind an overturned table. I braced myself for the blast, but instead heard a low hissing sound. When no blast came after several seconds, I peered over the table and spotted the grenade several feet away from me, white smoke billowing out.

"It's a smoke grenade!" I yelled out, realizing what was happening. I rushed back to the window, white smoke began to fill the house and cut visibility. Outside, it was the same with dozens of smoke grenades pumping smoke across out lines. The strategy was savage. The smoke cut visibility for both forces, but the attacker rushed into the smoke and hit the defenders, in the fumbling confusion.

"Eyes peeled!" Hiller yelled out. The machine gun fire suddenly died down.

I shouldered my Thompson and walked over to the side door leading out to the stone wall outside. I could make out Mangon's back at the wall, but nothing more. Everything was enveloped by smoke. It was suddenly and unusually quiet for a battlefield, the only noise coming from the distant thud of explosions. My heart pounded in my chest, the fast beating felt like my heart would rip through my chest.

Something moved to my left in the fog, a slight, dark shadow against the white. I spun in time to see a German soldier rush at me, with a bayonet fixed to the barrel of his rifle. I dropped down to one knee, and fired into the attacker's chest, stopping him in his tracks. The machine gun and rifle fire suddenly picked up, and the German troops crossed our lines.

Fumbling through the smoke screen, I heard the cries and grunts of men fighting hand to hand against one another. Rifles cracked, now and again. I rushed to the wall in, search of enemy soldiers, when I bumped into Lewinski, who was wounded, a bullet in his left shoulder. He was struggling with a German soldier, the two struggling over control of Lewinski's revolver.

"Get over here!" Lewinski cried, as the German brought a boot down on his bleeding shoulder. Face fixed in a snarl, Lewinski shoved the soldier back clear enough for me to fire. I fired several times into the man's back and head; Lewinski rolled free and put two rounds into the German's chest, for good measure.

"Could you be any slower?" Lewinski remarked.

"Could you be any weaker?" I countered, watching for any other surprises.

He snorted. "Good point."

A grenade detonated several feet from us and tossed a body our way, the man rolled, to a stop, on the blood stained grass, near the wall. Lewinski rushed over, to check him, while I followed and kept watch.

"One of us?" I asked not looking down.

"Polish uniform," he responded, voice dry, "but his face is a mess. I can't tell who he is."

I spared a quick glance at the man behind me. He did wear a kaki colored uniform worn by Polish soldiers, but a tangled mess of blood, bone, and flesh covered what was once his face. My stomach lurched in disgust at the sight. I fought back the urge to vomit.

"Ah, fuck," Lewinski sighed, retrieving the man's dog tags. "It's Mitchell."

I shook my head, in disgust. Lewinski slipped the tags into his pocket and stood back up, tapping my shoulder to signal to move on. The two of us continued past Mitchell's mutilated corpse and ran to the edge of the stone wall, near the street, which was the regroup point, in case of a line breach.

As we approached the edge of the wall and the smoke screen, four Germans were waiting for us, standing over the body of the Polish soldier, who carried a Bren machine gun. Lewinski cried out, at the sight, and killed one of the soldiers, with a shot to his head, under the helmet. I sprayed one with my Thompson and emptied half a clip, into his body, while the third circled around.

I wasn't quick enough,to see him in the fog, as he charged with his bayonet fixed. Pain tore through my side as the bayonet tore into me, the blade cutting through the skin, just above my waist. A muffled cry of pain escaped my throat. I dropped to my knees and turned to fire as another stab sliced into my left shoulder, the driving force shoving me to my back, on the ground. I shoved my Thompson into the attacker's chest and emptied the rest of the clip, the man fell back and withdrew the blade.

"Hang on!" Lewinski cried out. He finished the fourth trooper off. Pain flashed over my body, and I felt warm blood trickle down from my side and shoulder. I dropped my empty Thompson and drew my Colt.45, with my right hand, while my left lay at my side, blood pooling in my open palm.

I looked up and saw Lewinski rushing to my side, calling out for a medic. The pain was dulled somewhat by the rush adrenaline in my blood, but everything was dulled, and I realized I was loosing too much blood. Lewinski pressed firmly down on my side wound, the shoulder wound more superficial, in comparison. I felt suddenly tired, all the exhaustion and mental stress suddenly rushing over my mental controls and washing over my body.

"Eyes open, Lieutenant," Lewinski said, his voice suddenly low and sounding faraway.

"Tired," I managed to grunt, I felt the strong urge to sleep.

"Uh-huh, but fight it off." He looked around, in the confusion, for the medics.

My eyelids seemed to get heavier and heavier, as I blinked constantly to fight off sleep. It wasn't sleep that would occur if I closed my eyes, instead I'd pass out and probably die from blood loss. Knowing that simple fact, didn't help.

"Hang on, Corr," a second voice called out. I managed to turn my head enough to see Doc rushing over, his medical bag in hand.

"Better hurry it up," I sighed, as Lewinski moved away to let Doc work.

Doc was one of the best medics around, working with quick and expert hands to clean and cover my wounds, but he could only do so much with his equipment. A field hospital or aide station would get me patched up. There would be no ignoring the pain and soldiering on when you just came close to being gutted.

"You'll need to get him to an aide station," Doc said, to Lewinski. "I need to stay here, but he can't."

Lewinski rubbed his wounded shoulder. "I'll get him there."

Doc nodded and packed up his kit. "And get yourself checked out, too."

As Doc ran off to another cry for medic, Lewinski holstered his revolver and reloaded my Thompson for me. He lifted me back to my feet, shouldering my weight by walking to my left and handing me my Thompson. I could still shoot while Lewinski helped me walk, though it was more him dragging me, with my left leg cramping up from the pain, in my side.

"You Yanks are pretty damn heavy," Lewinski grunted. We shuffled down a ruined street towards the city church and away from the battle.

"It's all that muscle I have," I responded as I struggled to keep my Thompson from slipping from my grip.

Lewinski just grunted, while we struggled to move forward. He shouldered my weight, even though he had a wounded shoulder. The majority of the fighting was going on at the edges of the city, mostly to the west and north, but German forces were fighting skirmishes through many of the streets. The sudden drone of engines drove our gaze skyward, to see a pair of silver Thunderbolts streak by, rockets and bombs held under their wings.

"Is that our air cover?" Lewinski asked.

"There should be more," I said. "They might be the forward scouts to check for enemy AA emplacements."

"How do you know?" He asked.

"My brother's a pilot," I answered, thinking about Matt for a second.

Lewinski nodded. "So was mine, back in Poland, but he was killed just after the Germans invaded."

I solemnly nodded. "My younger brother was killed in the Pacific, back in May."

"Takes some time to feel real, right?" He said.

"Yeah, it does," I nodded.

Lewinski nodded to himself. "Navy?"

I shook my head. "Marines."

The church was just another two blocks away. We cut through a side alley, to get around the remains of a bombed out building, that clogged a street. We could see the church steeple, in the distance, over the rooftops, a pair of artillery spotters sitting, at the top, twenty-four seven. The pair would be having a field day, with so much enemy infantry and armor swarming over the countryside.

Another pair of *Jabos* shot overhead flying towards our positions, on the northern edge, rockets leaping from the underside launchers and heavy machine guns spitting out fifty caliber chunks of American steel, at our Nazi enemies. Matt may have been in love with his beautiful P-51, that dominated the skies, and swatted down anything flying the Nazi emblem, the *Jabos* hunted down anything bigger then a bicycle on the roads and were the saviors of the infantry.

"You think your brother is on the Mace can hold out until the Canadians arrive?" I asked Lewinski, who had originally been slated to have his squad up there.

He laughed dryly. "As you can imagine, we Polish aren't going to give up anything, to the Nazis, without it being paid for, in blood. I know I wouldn't give up, not just because I'm a Pole, but because I'm also a Jew."

"A double reason for you to be killed on sight," I sighed having known other Jewish soldiers, who'd never surrender, to an enemy soldier, or officer.

"Triple actually; I am an Allied soldier after all," he smirked.

The two of us briefly laughed, as we exited the alley, but quickly sobered up when we came to the church. Out front were dozens of stretchers bearing bloodied and torn men, all waiting to be tended to, by the medics. Jessica was one of them, as she was attached to the undermanned medical detachment in the church, choosing to work on preserving life, rather than taking it. Just like most of us, she was a fierce and capable soldier, but would choose to save a life then take it, if the option was available. Unfortunately, the option is near none existent during war.

"Is that your girl there?" Lewinski asked, as we approached, nodding towards someone.

I looked and, sure enough, Jessica was kneeling over a wounded man, changing a dressing. "That's her."

Lewinski gave his own nod of approval. "More than a looker?"

"A whole lot more is there besides looks, Louie," I said, calling Lewinski by the nickname his squad gave him.

"Well, let's get you a seat and find a medic," Louie said.

Carefully, Lewinski lowered me to the steps of the church, as some of my muscles tensed from the pain. I gritted my teeth. I leaned back slightly, on the stone steps, a hand going to my side, out of instinct. Lewinski wandered off to find a medic and left me alone, to fight the pain, and ignore that urge to sleep. More wounded men were beginning to pile up along the steps, all flowing in regular intervals from the fighting. It was a sea of bloodied olive and khaki colored uniforms, that threatened to drown the medics, in blood and bodies.

"The Captain tells me you are a bit of a cut up, sir," a medic joked, as he appeared with Lewinski.

Great, I thought, he finds the one medic whose a comedian.

"Just sew me up and get me some blood and I'll be good," I answered.

The medic laughed. "You're just in luck, sir. You see my mother was a seamstress and taught me a few things about a needle and thread."

I winced, as he pulled the bandage from my side. "Anything sliced and diced?"

He shook his head. "Looks like it was a clean cut through and through," he explained, waving over another medic. "The blade went in a little under the skin and passed out the other side, slicing up some fat tissue, but it's nothing to fret over."

"You sure?" I asked.

The medic snorted. "Another thing mother pushed me into was medicine. I was in medical school just as Jerry rolled over the border." The second medic appeared. "Let's give the Lieutenant a local for his wounds and sew them shut. Then give him what blood we can spare, and find him a place to rest, where he won't be in the way."

"Can I head back?" Lewinski asked.

The medic glanced back at him. "Let me fix the shoulder and then you can go."

Despite his young appearance, the medic was very skilled and as adept as any stateside surgeon or doctor. The only pain came from the two jabs of a needle that delivered a low strength pain killer to my shoulder and side. I only felt minor tugs of my skin, while the wounds were stitched closed.

From the stitches came one more needle prick. The second medic set up a blood transfusion to help fill the gap left from the wounds. Only a little more then half a liter could be spared, as the increasing wounded were cutting through the medical supplies, like a wild fire. Once the liter was emptied, I was hustled off to a nearby building, that was being used as a holding area, for stable wounded, that didn't need constant care, but weren't cleared for combat.

What used to be a shoe shop was now the recovery ward, of the aide station, for the stable. A dozen, or so, cots were neatly arranged, in four rows of four, with all the beds full. The next two top floors were set up the same way, but with the second floor being a former home, three to four cots were set up in separate rooms, to house men that had fallen to sickness, instead of bullets. Diarrhea didn't kill a trooper, it was the dehydration brought on by it.

The third floor was once a storage area, or attic, with the room wide open and big enough to fit thirty cots, fifteen on each side of the room, with an isle in between. There were a handful of a dozen, or so, nurses working with the men inside, all of them, local girls, who volunteered, to help out. A handful of them were nuns, though most were average women, the medically trained nuns were at the church.

"Just lay back and try to relax, sir," the medic, whose name I learned was Peter, said.

"That'll be hard," I admitted, wanting to be back with my men.

"Well you can't be up and running with blood loss," Peter explained. "You'll pass out pretty quick, but lucky for you red blood cells replace themselves fairly quickly now that the half liter of that stuff was replaced."

I nodded and sat down on one of the empty bunks. "Where are the other wounded?"

Peter nodded towards the window. "Across the street, in a clothing shop, or something. It has a lot of tables and store room to fit a hundred, or so, critically wounded, with others in the basement and rectory of the church."

With that, Peter quickly left to continue with his duties. I lay back in the cot and looked around, at the other men, around me. Most were American riflemen and Polish tankers. A dozen riflemen were stuck in bed with bandages covering arms, legs, stomachs, and chests. All will be back within the fighting, at one point, while the tankers were not as lucky.

Being a tanker, was a hard life, with its own risks. Many men died horrible deaths being trapped insides their tanks while they burned, the metal war machine suddenly becoming an incinerator. The handful of Polish tankers were horribly burned and scared from fire, some worse off, as they had been covered with burning fuel.

The nurses were kind and caring towards all the wounded. Five were working on this floor and attended to each wounded man, as if they were their own children, working to make sure each of them was comfortable. They changed bandages, cleaned and drained wounds, applied medication, and talked in loving and compassionate tones, to the wounded. They even managed to hold back tears and feelings of disgust, treating the disfigured tankers, who were all young kids.

"Can I get you something, Lieutenant?" one of the younger women asked. She was somewhere around twenty or twenty-one, with light brown hair, and a relaxing smile.

I remembered I still had my gear. "Ah, this might sound strange, but…"

She smiled and giggled. "I can help, Lieutenant."

Carefully, I managed to sit up enough for the young woman to help be remove my pack and webbing. Once the webbing was off, I manage to wiggle out of my ammo pouch, slinging it over my ribs and then my jacket. As my kit was removed, the nurse neatly stacked everything under my cot, including my Thompson and pistol.

"Would you like some water?" she asked.

"No thanks, ma'am," I answered, trying to lie down, I just wanted to sleep. She politely nodded and returned to the other wounded men; I did my best to relax.

Through the two small windows in the attic, both open to let in fresh air, I could clearly hear the sounds of the fighting. Muffled explosions and MG fire were constant now that our air support finally arrived and were hunting down German armor support. Our main objective was not so much to hold the city, but to keep the Germans occupied for the Mace to be reinforced and the Brits to linkup from Trun.

Allied forces inside the city, were a mix of rifle squads from the 90th and the First, along with tanks and armor from the Polish 1st Armored Division, that had developed a working relationship. Since tanks were in short supply with the Poles, splitting their forces between Chambois and their besieged brothers at the Mace, our Polish infantry would protect them. Rifles fought off the infantry and let the armor handle the enemy tanks and then the rifles covered the tanks, as they drew back after.

"Hey, Lieutenant, sir," a trooper,from a few bunks down, called.

I sat up and looked over. "Yes?" I answered, propping myself up on my elbows.

"You just came in off the line, right?" he asked

I nodded.

"Did the Krauts overrun the northern perimeter yet?" He asked.

I shrugged. "Not sure, I was taken back hear while the fighting was still occurring. My squad is still there and trying to hold back the Germans."

"Do you know if Fox squad is okay?" He asked, hopeful.

I thought back for a second. Fox was another American rifle squad that was holding the northern perimeter, when my squad arrived. The entire squad was dead the second day after we arrived, the building they were taking cover in brought down around their ears.

"Not sure, sorry," I lied, I didn't have the heart to tell him the truth. The trooper shook his head and returned back to his own world. I did the same, mentally noting I would be out of the fighting for several days. They would be uneventful aside from the removal and adding of the other wounded, while I sat back and did nothing, my men still fighting without rest.

Four days of bed rest, blood transfusions, and then the removal of the stitches, had me back up and ready to fight. I was loaded up with all my equipment and gear, somewhat eager to be back in the fight, only to learn that the Germans were routed. On August 21st the Falaise Gap was closed and the fate of the Seventh Army sealed when Allied forces linked up near Hill 262. Any remaining German forces, who didn't run to cross the Seine River, were either dead or captured. Operation Overload ended two days later, on the 25th, when Allied forces liberated Paris from the Nazis.

The squad had come through the fighting intact, all unharmed from any major injury. I was the only one wounded, as we stood waiting outside of the newly established replacement depot in Chambois. As usual, Captain Hiller was off speaking with Major Philips, getting our next set of orders.

"Anyone got a smoke?" Vic asked, watching steady lines of infantry marching eastward, a line of German infantry marching several feet away, in the opposite direction.

"Take the pack," Nate replied handing over his last pack of cigarettes. "I don't smoke."

Vic happily took the unopened back and quickly tore it open, a fresh smoke in his mouth within seconds. The others watched the parade of infantry before them.

"How many Krauts we take?" Ramos asked.

I shrugged. "Last count I heard was over thirty thousand and climbing."

Jay let out a low whistle. "That's a shit load of POWs to handle. Where do they send them all?"

"Arizona, Nevada, Utah," Malks answered. "Any place back stateside where you can find wide areas of empty desert."

I sat down on an old and worn wooden chair left near a bombed out building. My side was mostly healed, but the pain was still there.

"Feeling any better?" Jessica asked, as she pulled over an empty crate to sit on across from me.

I shrugged. "I've done worse while shaving," I joked with a smile.

Jessica shook her head, gently touching the white bandage over my shoulder, which stuck out from under my jacket. She, thankfully, had remained unhurt during the fighting, tending wounded at the church. Lewinski had told her about me while I was stuck in recovery and she'd been with me as much as her duties would allow.

"I have some bad news to tell you," she said in a low whisper.

My stomach muscle tightened. "What?"

Jessica bit her lip and pulled a piece of paper from her pocket, handing to me. On it was the name of the division HQ with some colonel's name along with hers, the title of logistical staff written before it.

"What's this?" I asked.

"I've been attached to the division headquarters, as part of a logistics group, to aide with the proper dispersing of food, medical supplies, and the like to displaced civilians, as the Allies move into

Germany. Since I can speak French, German, Dutch, and, with your help, English, they want me to help."

I folded the paper and placed it in my pocket. "So if I write you, I put this down as the address?"

"If you write?" she asked in English.

"Sorry, when I write, and I will, every spare moment I get, I'll send it to the division HQ," I said. My heart was aching.

She nodded. "Don't worry about me finding you, the command staff keeps an updated location on all rifle squads."

I forced a smile, as I saw Captain Hiller returning, map in hand, now that the new orders were in. It was obvious we'd be moving out soon. "So, this is goodbye." It was more of a statement then a question.

"For now, at least," Jessica said.

Hiller waved me over to rejoin the squad. The two of us stood up and hugged. Tears were already running down her cheeks. "I'll be back after this ends, I promise," I told her.

Jessica could only nod. "Try not to keep a girl waiting."

"Bolger, hurry it up!" Hiller called out.

We kissed for a handful of seconds before I had to pull away, my men waiting for me. Jessica was about to turn and leave when I lightly grabbed her shoulder. Fumbling with tired hands, I removed the silver cross from my neck and handed it to her.

"Keep it safe," was the last thing I said before leaving for the squad.

"She dump you?" Ramos asked, when I returned. I didn't respond, choosing to shoot him an icy glare.

"Sorry, sir," I mumbled to Hiller, but he waved it off and turned back to the squad.

"Orders just came in, from the higher ups," he announced. "Now that Overlord is over and Paris is free, the next move is to push into Germany and drive for Berlin. The First is to continue the drive east and head for the German city of Achen and the Siegfried Line, which is the German border. It'll be a difficult trek, but we are to take Achen and open a route into Germany.

"This is gonna be it, boys. By October or November, we'll be fighting the Nazis on their own land, their homes. None of us want to hear this," Hiller continued, "but France was foreign soil to the Nazis and not home to their families. Now, we'll be fighting a force working to keep their homes and families safe. It's gonna be a long, mine ridden road to Berlin."

Chapter 16

"How close are we?" Jay's voice was a low whisper, barely audible, over the roar of tank fire, in the streets below us.

"The theater is two blocks away," I answered, my hands gripping my Thompson. The cold had long numbed my fingers and I couldn't feel my palms digging into the grip.

"Just two?" Sanders asked from his position, in a boarded up window. "Why aren't we moving then?"

"Do you not see the shit blocking the road?" Malks snapped. "It isn't easy to just clear away two dead Tiger tanks from a road, that can't even fit one." We'd been in Achen for nineteen days already, the Germans putting up stiff resistance.

"This place is a damn fortress," I grunted. "All these damn buildings are so old they're built like bunkers."

The squad just sat by, in cold silence, whilst we waited for the move order. We were hold up in the second floor a building, overlooking a thin road, connecting to the city theater, the German CP. We'd move in once the road was clear, to cover the tanks and Long Tom artillery, as they moved to the German CP. The theater was so well built, that only an attack of Long Tom artillery, at point blank range, could rattle the Germans.

"Any word on Edwards?" Nate asked, to break the new lull of silence.

"Still in England recovering," Hiller answered, unseen in the darkness of our hiding spot. "He'll back by December."

"Is it true he's supposed to make sergeant?" Adam asked. One rumor floating around was that Edwards would be promoted, to sergeant, after Jay made staff sergeant. He was a good soldier and had the qualities of a good leader, that was what others believed made him deserving of the new rank.

"Philips hasn't told me anything," Hiller responded.

Again we fell silent. The engineers toiled in the street. Six Sherman tanks sat idling behind them, with a pair of M12 Long Tom artillery pieces behind them, the crews shivering, as a cold wind blew through the open troop compartment. They were our responsibility, to safe guard until they reached the theater. Command made it clear the arty was to not be touched by enemy fire, while the Shermans were expendable.

Adam's radio crackled with static, as a message came through. "Swordsman, here," he answered in a hushed tone. Someone spoke to him and then ended the connection. "Engineers say they're ready to blow the wrecks."

Hiller nodded. "Let's get down there."

Everyone collected their equipment and marched back outside to take up positions for advancement. The wind was unrelenting. I stepped outside and it bit through my uniform. The thin fabric was the same I wore when I landed in Normandy and was not made for cold weather. Proper winter gear had yet to be delivered to us even as snow was beginning to coat the ground. My boots were falling apart, as well, though a multitude of patches had kept them together and held out a decent amount of water.

"Move up on the right flank," Hiller ordered. The squad split up, into two groups, to cover the tanks. "Stay behind them for cover, and stop any AT infantry from getting close."

"Yes, sir," I answered, moving up the rear of the lead Sherman.

A group of ten engineers was putting the finishing touches up on the roadblock. They worked with packed TNT and C4 charges, to blow away as much of the Tigers, as possible and weaken the remaining steel enough for our tanks to push through. It wasn't the cleanest way through the streets, but it was quicker then tugging the wrecks away.

"Fire in the hole!" the lead engineer cried, as his men ran back to the tanks.

"Heads down!" I yelled, ducking behind the Sherman and bracing for the blast.

It only took several seconds for the timer to count down to zero. A massive explosion erupted a few yards from my position and blew open a clearing through the burned Tigers. The blast wave rattled my teeth. Dust clouds enveloped the area.

On queue, the Shermans shuttered, whilst they began to roll forward. I moved away from the lead Sherman and stayed near the buildings. It rolled forward and forced its way through the wrecks. Sparks flew, metal grinding against metal,as the tank shoved aside the burning hulks and proceeded down the street. I moved up and climbed over the debris to keep with the line of tanks.

The winding street squeezed in between the ancient stone buildings for thirty yards, before connecting to a small intersection, which led to another road, connecting to the front of the theater. There was no more debris to be seen, no German soldiers in sight. I kept my Thompson tucked into my shoulder and watched the many windows in the buildings for any Germans lurking, in wait, to spring an ambush.

The sky was gray and overcast, the threat of another snowfall looming ever closer. We didn't have air support because of the bad weather, with all planes grounded at their bases. Artillery support was available for use, but our 105s didn't do much damage to the stone buildings of Aachen, which stood up to direct tank and rocket fire. German troops were using this to their advantage, to make us pay for every street we ever took.

"Follow me," I whispered, to Nate. "The intersection is a good ambush spot."

Nate and I ran ahead of the column, to the end of the street. We still kept close to the buildings, for cover, and stumbled through the shell craters. I ordered Nate to hang back a little bit; I slowly crept forward, to the corner of the street. A wall, from a house at the corner, had collapsed into the street and offered me some cover, which was helpful during my check.

The intersection was big enough to hold a park, at its center, with the street looping around it, in a square pattern. What was once a park, its center was turned in a cratered wreck of mud and dead trees, that appeared to be clear enough for the tanks to roll through without trouble. A large number of houses and stores offered clear fields of fire,onto the park, creating a perfect kill zone, for an ambush.

Keeping low behind the small pile of fallen bricks and mortar, I scanned the rooftops and windows for any movement through my binoculars. Good cover and concealment would be a problem for anyone moving through the park, to reach the opposite road, but there was no other way to turn.

Rolling to my back, I waved the tank column forward, but signaled to move slowly, drawing closer, to the open square. There had to be an ambush waiting to great us, the Germans took full advantage of such kill zones, wherever they could be found. I had no way of really checking for a hidden enemy from my position, instead, I could just wait and try to ride out the storm of flying steel.

The leading Sherman, named Party Girl, by her crew, rolled through the cover of the buildings and into the open without any trouble. Nate and I kept down behind cover, following five tanks that rolled along, the Captain ordering the Long Toms to wait, in the cover, of the side street.

"I can't believe we're walking into this," Nate grunted, as the column rolled through the dead park.

I tried to respond, when the trap was sprung. Heavy machine gun fire erupted from every rooftop and window. The Germans started the attack on the enticing targets, that were our M4s. Antitank rocket fire screamed down on the medium tanks from unseen gunners, in the buildings. Two tanks, in the center were hit, in the first broadside and knocked both out, with kill shots to their turrets. Several rockets missed the lead and rear tanks, a blessing that prevented the tanks from being bottled up in the open.

The squad opened up on what targets could be seen, they were everywhere. Nate and I lay prone, in the debris, and concentrated on the nearest building, where I could see an MG42 set up in a top floor window. Nate had better aim with his rifle, than I did with my close quarter SMG, so I tossed a few grenades their way. I managed to get one into the window, where the crew was, resulting in an explosion, taking out the MG team.

"There's no way to take them all out!" Nate yelled,as the tanks opened fire.

I agreed and tried to think of some way to get us out of the kill zone. MG and AT fire were taking apart our tank cover and pinned down the squad. If we didn't move soon, all of us would be gunned down within a few minutes. I jumped to my feet and ran for the closest tank, for cover, several yards ahead of me. Captain Hiller was close by, with Adam, inside a shell crater.

Taking a controlling breath, I ran out into the merciless hail of machine gun fire, for Hiller's position. It felt like Normandy all over again. I ran over the barren battlefield, German troops all around occupying the high ground. The tank column had stalled out dead center, of the kill zone, with all enemy fire concentrating on them. I glance over my shoulder and was relieved to see the Long Toms were still safe and untouched.

"Call it in on the buildings!" Hiller was yelling to Adam, while still firing.

"This is Swordsman to any one-oh-five batteries outside of Aachen," Adam called out, over the radio. "I repeat, this Swordsman to any one-oh-five batteries outside Aachen, we need fire support!"

"Sir, we need to pull out now!" I reported, to Hiller, as a 42 stitched our position with heavy MG fire.

"The only way is forward!" he yelled. "We need to get the tanks rolling forward!"

"I'll see what I can do!" I yelled back.

Again, I picked myself up and rushed back into the firefight. Pure strength of will kept me running, bullets tore through the cordite laden air and some how missed me. Adrenaline washed away the exhaustion and the fear, my body running without any real thought to why. Three Shermans were dead from the center of the column, while the lead and rear tanks were still functional and fighting.

I ran to the lead tank and dropped down in a crouch behind the engine compartment, bullets still bouncing off the armor. Without delay, I scrambled up the side of the tank and over to the commander's hatch, in the turret. I banged on the turret with my Thompson, to get the commander's attention inside. I was exposed and an excellent target for even the most inept sniper or gunner.

"What the hell are you doing?" the commander asked.

"You need to get moving!" I ordered. Another explosion boomed. The rear tank was blown apart, from concentrated AT fire.

"Get off the tank!" The commander slammed the turret hatch shut, and his tank began to roll forward.

I turned and was about to jump off when a rocket slammed into the opposite side of the turret, with tremendous force. A blast of heated air exploded against my back. The concussion blast tossed me from the tank. I flew a few feet, from the now burning tank, and landed face first into the muddied ground, with a wet slosh. My Thompson was ripped from my hands, so I pressed down on my helmet and kept down for cover, shrapnel bounced across my back.

My ears were ringing, as someone rolled me over to my back, and patted me down. I blinked away the mud and dirt covering my eyes to see Mangon standing over me, reaching out to help.

"You hit?" he asked, handing me back my Thompson.

"My ears are ringing!" I yelled, my own voice sounding low and muffled.

Mangon pulled me back to my feet. "Our tanks are gone. The Toms are still safe, but we have no armor."

The two of us dropped down into a shell crater. "Adam reach the arty yet?"

He shrugged. "Don't know."

I crawled out of the crater and made my way back to Hiller's position, near the middle of the destroyed column. It was down to our squad, to fight off the ambush, with that we had, which was down to rifles and submachine guns. Artillery would not be the best thing to use against such properly constructed buildings, but it would level the fight.

"Anything yet?" Hiller asked, crouching next to Adam.

"I'm connected!" Adam responded. Hiller took out his folded map.

"Call this in, danger close." He held up the map and read off the coordinates. "Fire reference grids 2-4, 2-5, 1-4, 1-5; enemy infantry inside fortified positions."

"Fire reference grids 2-4, 2-5, 1-4, 1-5; enemy infantry inside fortified positions. Fire is danger close, over!" Adam repeated and listened. "Support on the way!"

"Get down!" Hiller yelled. "Get down!"

I pressed myself deeper into the dirt, at the bottom of the crater. Adam and Hiller did the same. Time seem to slow down between the time the barrage was fired, to the time it arrived on scene, no more than a dozen, or so, seconds later. The noise was ear shattering; the salvo of explosive 105mm shells bore into the buildings around me. It felt like rain. Dirt and mud pelted my back, the backwash of the explosions.

Someone was screaming, either one of us or, a German. It could have been me, but I couldn't tell, as I clutched my chest. The concussion waves felt like hard punches rolling over me, the force nearly crushing my chest. I risked a glance over the lip of the crater, at the buildings, and saw what horror the Germans created. Each of the buildings was being tore down, brick by brick, with each explosion of a shell. Bodies flew out of windows and off roofs, soldiers screamed out in fear and horror; all the while, I lay still in the crater, praying for it to end soon.

Several salvos of artillery fire raked both sides of the square and hammered the Germans into submission. Slowly, the barrage tapered off and silence covered the area. No one moved from their positions, all remained still, unsure of what still remained alive in the shelled buildings. Captain Hiller crawled back to the lip of the crater and did a quick area check, before waving to me. I crawled over to him, my heart pounded in my chest.

"See anything?" Hiller whispered, laying prone.

Plenty of bodies and pieces. "Nothing alive, sir," I grunted.

Hiller and I climbed back to our feet. "Let's get a head count first and check on the Toms."

I nodded and began to walk alongside the column of dead tanks, checking up on everyone to make sure they were still alive. There were plenty of body parts strewn about, covered in both gray and olive uniforms. To my relief, everyone had come through alive and unharmed, though some were shaken up by the barrage. The Long Toms and their crews were alive, having been shielded between the buildings.

"All accounted for, sir," I reported, once the headcount was done.

"Damn lucky," Hiller grunted, to himself.

"Think we should continue?" Jay asked. He'd became the senior NCO and third in command.

I glanced at my wrist watch. "The other squads will be in position, to hit the theater, in an hour, sir."

"And they need the arty to breach that damn fortress. We continue on and get to the rally point," Hiller said.

Jay and I nodded and collected the squad. We had one block to the theater, but the roads were blocked by debris, making out route longer. It would be slow going, since we were the only defense for the artillery and had to be extra careful with no more tank support, to cover us.

"Let's set up a scouting unit to move ahead of us," Hiller ordered, once the Toms were across the square.

"I'll go out with Mangon and Phelps," I said, taking the risk.

"Move ahead only a few dozen yards and keep in sight, to contact us with hand signals."

"Yes, sir," I replied.

Hiller spread the squad out to cover the front and rear of the two artillery pieces. He kept to the front of the short column, while Mangon, Phelps, and I ran ahead in the ruin filled street. The three of us moved in a loose skirmish formation up the street, on the lookout for enemy forces. I was out ahead with Phelps behind me and Mangon moving up on the opposite side of the road.

Since the main route to the theater was blocked by debris, we had to detour around by heading another block over, to a clear street that would let the artillery pass through. Between us, was an open courtyard

area of a bank, that sat opposite the intersection of the streets. From .
the bank, a defending force had clear fields of fire over the street we
were advancing on and the street we needed to reach.

As we advanced on the opening to the intersection, I held up a
hand, to signal a stop, and ducked into a blown storefront. Phelps and
Mangon crouched down inside to wait for my orders, as I dropped to
my stomach and crawled over to the wall of the building facing the
bank. Several, large sections of the wall were missing and offered me
a point to lookout at the bank, without exposing myself.

The bank was larger than the surrounding buildings, with massive
wooden doors in the entrance. A dozen, or so, windows faced out at
the street and offered good positions for MGs to be set up. Looking
closer, I could see a line of trenches dug into the front courtyard of
the building, several German soldiers visible along with to MG42s.

"They're dug in deep," I whispered to Phelps and Mangon,
"trenches and MG nests out front and probably more in the bank."

Mangon sighed. "Sounds encouraging."

"Let's report back and see what we can think up to get through,"
I said.

I crawled away from the wall and climbed back to my feet. The
three of us marched back to the Captain, who was waiting with the
artillery, near the turn in the street. Hiller opted to keep the tracks safe
behind the buildings, incase an 88 was waiting for us.

"This isn't good," Hiller sighed, once I reported in. "We've got
nothing to really handle the trenches with. The bank is another
fortress, but the Toms can fire a round or two at it for us."

"Sir," I said, "we found a good position, to hit the trenches, in a
store near the bank. It'll get us close enough while still keeping the
element of surprise."

"Then I got a plan." Hiller dropped down to one knee and picked
up a rock. He began to scrape the rock against a low wall, drawing out
a plan. "Bolger, you'll head back to the store and assault the trenches.
You will begin your attack once I roll one of the Toms into position,
and have it fire two rounds into the bank. Take the trenches after the
first shot."

"Are there any good sniper spots?" Jay asked me.

"Top floor, for the store, just follow me," I explained.

Again, Hiller glanced at his watch. "Alright, let's get this rolling. We've only got forty minutes before the attack starts. Get this done fast, but don't take stupid risks."

"Yes, sir," Jay and I answered in unison.

Hiller returned to the artillery while I took five men from the squad to hit the trenches. Mangon, Jay, Phelps, Nate, and Malks moved with me, back up the street, to the store at the end of the block. When we arrived the Germans were still unaware of our presence, giving us a chance to attack, with the element of surprise. Jay stalked up to the second floor of the building to find a good sniping spot, while the rest of us waited for the artillery strike.

"Keep low and get to the trenches," I whispered, while we waited. "Stay in the trenches unless the Captain or I say different."

The low, metallic grinding of tank treads emanated from down the street, as the lead Long Tom rolled into firing position. Several Germans,in the trenches, spotted the bulky American artillery pieces moving towards them. I readied to run, as orders were yelled in German, and the Tom came to a stop several yards away.

A single 155mm shell broke through the silence and slammed, into the front of the bank, above the doors, tearing open a gaping hole in the wall. The five of us rushed out, into the street, and moved for the trenches, at a dead run. Nate and I dropped in first, landing just feet from three Germans, who were tossed to the bottom of the trench, by the explosion. Nate and I opened fire and killed the three before they could get back up or even reach their weapons.

Malks jumped in ahead of me and raced forward, with Phelps trailing him. The two would hit the far left side of the trenches, while I covered the right with Mangon and Nate. There were a few dozen enemy soldiers manning the trenches, most running for underground dugouts, thinking the 155mm strike was a full on artillery strike. Two officers rushed forward, to man an MG nest, when the spotted us. Both carried MP-40s and sprayed our position.

The three of us split up and hugged the walls of the trench, for cover. I raised my Thompson and fired back, as Nate tossed a grenade forward. The grenade blast killed both officers and cleared the way for us to move up. Another explosion boomed. The second shot, from the Tom, was fired. The resulting blast, as the round exploded, was much louder than before. I looked up at the bank and watched, in amazement, it was collapsing, falling in on itself. All of Aachen's buildings were built with solid stone, but the constant pounding of artillery had taken a toll on some. Two shells knocked the last of the bank's supports out, and it fell in a plume of dust.

I rounded a corner, in the trench, and ran into four soldiers struggling, to upright an overturned MG42. They didn't have their weapons ready and quickly fell from a broadside of machine gun fire. Malks suddenly appeared. I reloaded, he and Phelps just cleared the trenches.

"All clear, sir," he reported, shoving more shells into his trench gun.

"That Tom did a number on the bank," Nate commented. Enemy fire had stopped.

"Follow me," I said, walking back to the front of the trench line.

With the sudden stop of enemy fire and the collapse of the bank, Captain Hiller began to move the artillery up the street towards my position. I climbed back out of the trench and waved at Jay, to signal him to regroup with the column. I looked down at my watch, seeing it was twenty-seven minutes to the attack.

"All clear!" I called out to Hiller.

"Regroup!" he yelled, as the artillery rolled on.

Quickly, I reorganized the squad back into a defensive formation around the armored column, rolling past the bank and down the cleared street. I moved with Hiller, at the front of the column, alongside Mangon and Doc, following at our flanks. We moved at double pace now that the rally point was in view, at the end of the block, another rifle squad already waiting for us. Hiller and I ran out head, to speak with the squad commander, while the rest of the squad stayed with the artillery.

"Good to see you, Captain," the squad's CO greeted. "The attack is about to start, so get the Long Toms into position."

The main German headquarters was established inside Aachen's largest theater, near the center of the city. Just like all of the city's buildings, the theater was a protective fortress that stood up to all our attempts, to dislodge them. Surrounding streets were blocked off and cratered from earlier artillery strikes, while barbed wire and sandbag fortifications covered the theater.

Our attack plan revolved around the two Long Tom artillery pieces. While designed for indirect fire support, the 155mm cannons could provide direct fire support on hardened targets, with enjoyable results. Similar strategies were used during the start of the battle, where buildings were torn, brick by brick, by 155mm attacks and it was now used to end the fighting. The Long Toms would be positioned to the right of the theater's main entrance, with a diagonal line of fire to cover more area. On command, they would open fire on the main entrance and hammer the Germans into submission. Our rifle squad, along with five others would converge on the building, once the entrance was clear and then purge the Germans from the area, soldier by soldier.

"We're going in first," Hiller told us, as we waited near the artillery. "Fox and Able will be right behind us with Dog and Bravo bringing up the rear."

"We going right for the German commander?" Jay asked.

"We'll clear out the main hall, at the center of the building, which is their communication center. Fox and Able will take a supply store on the second floor, while Dog and Bravo go for the enemy commander, on the third floor."

"We should get the commander," Vic argued. "We did haul the artillery up here for the damn attack."

"You have a problem with your orders?" Hiller asked, in a harsh tone.

"No, sir," Vic responded in a lower tone, "sorry, sir."

Hiller finished up the briefing. The artillery rolled into position and locked down, in preparation to fire. Both 155mm cannons rolled down, to bring a firing solution onto the main entrance, the gun crews stacking and loading shells. German machine gun crews were firing on the artillery, while snipers took potshots at the crews. Jay returned counter sniper fire, and the rest of us crouched behind an abandoned German MG nest.

"Firing!" The artillery commander suddenly shouted.

The words still lingered in the air, the two 155mm Long Toms fired with a ground shaking boom, flames leaping from the barrels, as the shells were flung at the theater. Twin explosions rippled across the stone steps and walls of the buildings, the weaker MG nests nearby being atomized, in the blast. Enemy fire had suddenly gone silent, as the Toms were reloaded. Two more shots were fired, ripping a stone pillar near the entrance to the street in a cloud of gray dust.

My ears were ringing. The third salvo was fired, more of the theater being ripped, in plumes of dust and fire. The squad lay still behind the sandbag wall, another volley was readied. Three more volleys would be fired before the Toms went silent and we would rush in. I silently prayed the German commander would see reason before the barrage halted and surrender to us, with no more loss of life. It would not be. The final volley fired, and the artillery fell silent.

Captain Hiller hesitated, before ordering us forward, he to looking for the German surrender. None came, we rushed across the open street, to the shattered entrance, enemy MG and sniper fire was not seen or heard. I ran to the front of the group and reached the broken steps first, Able and Fox squads converging, on the right and left sides, of the entrance way.

The massive wooden doors had been ripped clear off the entrance and thrown into the main reception area, having been reduced to splinters and ashes. We used hand signals to communicate, as the squad carefully moved inward, the building all too quiet. The main lobby of the building was a wide open room, which connected to the main hall through a set of doors under a walkway, which led to the private boxes in the hall. A pair, of elegantly built staircases linked the two floors together, with a shattered chandelier resting on the floor.

Vic and I moved,up to the glass chandelier, for cover, and scanned for hidden targets. Still, no German soldiers were about, not even bodies were left behind. Fox and Able squads rushed past us and up the stairs, as our squad moved to the main doors to the center hall. The wooden doors were closed. I moved to one side with Vic on the other.

Captain Hiller moved up first and kicked open the heavy doors, with a muffled grunt, as his boot made contact. Both doors swing open as Vic and I rushed in first to the hall. A dozen, or so, German soldiers were waiting inside, the group groping for weapons, charging up the center aisle. The two of us opened fire first and drained our clips into the tight group of soldiers, killing maybe half before we dove behind the last row of seats.

Unseen, enemy troops, opened fire, as the rest of the squad piled inside, weapons chattering. I dropped down behind the rear of row seats and scrambled to see the other enemy soldiers firing on us. The center hall was immense, a high chandelier filled the ceiling above us, with a dozen private viewing boxes, on the second level. Thousands of chairs filled the main area, while an impressive stage lined the opposite wall.

An MG42 had been set up on the stage, behind a sandbag wall, and was firing into the seats, at us. The red velvet covered seats were chewed up by the heavy fire, and our cover was quickly disappearing before our eyes. I ran in a low crouch behind the row of seats, to the far right aisle, at one end of the hall along with Vic and Sanders.

We made our way down the aisle, to the stage, in attempt, to flank the German troops, at the front of the rows of seats. They were firing on us from reinforced positions, near a wide array of radios and communication gear set up, where an orchestra might have played before the theater was defiled by war. If it wasn't for the fighting, I thought I might have enjoyed seeing a play or show in the theater, but those thoughts lasted only seconds. An AT rocket blew away a huge section of seats a few yards away from us.

"Surprising fire!" I yelled,as we approached the enemy positions. The three of us opened fire together, in a full broadside attack on the German's left flank, that caught them off guard.

Several soldiers were caught in the attack and were quickly killed in the salvo of steel before they could turn, to face us. The 42, on the stage, swung around to hit us, but we were just outside his arc of fire, as the rounds slammed into the wall several feet behind us. I felt plaster and wooden splinters rain down on my back. I tossed a grenade towards the Germans, while Vic moved down a little more, to get a clearer line of fire.

As my grenade exploded, consuming four men in a flash of fire, I spotted Captain Hiller moving with Nate, Adam, and Phelps down the far aisle opposite us. Our two groups hit the German flanks, while the rest of the squad still hit their front. A sudden near miss that splintered the chair in front of me, revealed a hidden sniper in one of the viewing boxes, across the center of the hall.

"Sniper!" I yelled out and dropped to my ass, crawling to a new position. Jay was already on it, silencing the sniper, with a single shot before checking the other boxes.

"You hit?" Vic called out when he spotted me crawling.

"I'm good," I answered and scrambled back to my feet, to return fire.

I rushed down to the edge of the aisle and worked to find a good position, to hit the MG42. Sanders followed behind me while, Vic stayed put to provide covering fire. Sanders and I stopped at the first row of seats and opened fire on the Germans, just in front of the stage, as they were the closest threat to handle.

Out of a ten man squad, eight Germans were dead on the floor, with the other two wounded, one of which, was still shooting. Sanders and I finished him off, but left the other wounded man alive. Hiller and his group closed in from the left. I turned to the MG42 gunner and finished him with a short burst that tore open his chest and tossed him to the ground. Sanders and I moved in closer, checking the stage for any other enemies before turning our weapons on the wounded German.

"Hands up!" I ordered in German, as I approached, my Thompson leveled with his chest.

"Don't shoot!" he yelled back raising one hand, while the other clasped his wounded leg. "I surrender!"

"Doc!" I yelled out while I kicked a dropped rifle away from the soldier.

Doc ran up, Sanders still kept his weapon trained on the soldier. I lowered mine and ran over to Hiller. He moved to examine the German radio equipment.

"Keep the radios intact," Hiller ordered, noting the surviving equipment. "The engineers might be able to cannibalize them for parts."

"We're clear, sir," I reported. "Got one prisoner."

"Good job, hand off the POW to our boys outside. Once he's handled, we'll begin to clear out the rest of the building."

"Yes, sir," I turned, to face the squad, as they regrouped near the stage. "Doc, get him patched up and then move him to the rest of the troops outside. Once that's taken care of, we'll start to clear out the rest of the theater."

"He can be moved," Doc answered lifting the German to his feet.

"Nate, let's get him outside."

Nate nodded and helped the wounded soldier limp out of the theater, with me following, as a guard. We made our way back through the lobby and to the main entrance, where the wounded, from the other squads, were being taken back to the aid station. Several soldiers stood guard and with some complaints, two took our prisoner from us.

The two of us turned back to walk inside, when we spotted the men from Dog Company walking our way. Nate and I stood back and watched, as several German officers, high ranking ones at that, were marched outside under the guard of several soldiers. Judging by the looks on the faces of the officers, they had surrendered to us, and then it was confirmed, by our soldiers.

"Kraut fuckers surrendered without a fight," a private announced, in enjoyment, as they marched by.

"Just them?" Nate asked.

An exhausted sergeant answered. "Nope, they surrendered the entire city to us, the second they saw us. Not sure if it's official with us, but it will be when we get them back to HQ."

Nate and I couldn't help but smile. "A surrendering German," Nate commented, "a gift, indeed."

Chapter 17

Dear Jessica,

How's life behind the lines, working as a clerk? Things have been the same with me and the squad since Chambois, everyone's still safe. We did something big a few days ago, that I'm sure you've already heard about, but we took Aachen from the Germans. I already saw it in the papers. *The First German City to Fall*, which sounds a little over dramatic for me.

Things have been tough for us since then, mostly with the weather turning against us, and the lack of cold weather gear. The squad and I have pushed on anyway and finished clearing out the last bits of Aachen, for the past few days. It was pretty hard to do, even with the surrender, since many Germans didn't receive the order and they wouldn't believe us.

We've left the city about a day and a half ago and we're just about to launch another attack, so far, the go order hasn't come down. I can't say what we're doing, but I guess you would know anyway. I'm a little on edge, waiting, but the feeling goes away when the fighting starts. I need to get moving soon, so I need to wrap this up. In response to your letter, I'm keeping safe and not taking too many risks. I'll write, once I have another chance to. I miss you every day, but your letters really help. Keep writing, as much as you can,so I don't go nuts.

Lovingly,
LT Corrigan Bolger
1st Infantry Div

"We're getting ready to move," Captain Hiller announced, watching the German positions.

"Pack your gear and check weapons," I ordered, folding up my letter and slipping it, into my pocket, for safe keeping.

A chill ran through my body, as I stretched my arms and legs, keeping in a low crouch to not make a target for a sniper. The squad was taking cover behind a stack of logs just off the main road near a newly captured German outpost. Just over the small ridge, we waited on the German border defenses, known as the *Siegfried* Line. In a few minutes we would began our attack. A light snow continued to fall and the winds picked up, stirring a chilling breeze.

"They sure went all out," Vic commented, watching the German fortifications, with interest. "How long is the line anyway?"

Malks shrugged, cradling his shotgun. "About 390 miles, give or take a foot or two."

I crawled to the edge of the ridge, next to Captain Hiller, and scanned the line through my binoculars. Even with the winds and snow, it was near impossible to miss the sheer girth of the *Siegfried* Line. As Malks said, it stretched for 390 miles across Germany's western border, forming another defensive line, just like the Atlantic Wall. Thousands of concrete bunkers and pillboxes ran along the line, with rows of Dragon's Teeth tank traps, barbed wire, all sorts of mines, trenches, and artillery emplacements, all arranged to funnel attackers into kill zones, if they rely on tank support.

"Think we can do it?" Hiller asked without turning my way.

"I know we can, sir," I answered, eyeing up the six guard towers in the area.

Hiller grunted to himself. "The Nazis believe tanks and air power dominate the battlefield,with infantry, as support, and it's reflected here. You can see that they have more tank traps and anti-tank mines than anything else because they believe infantry cannot function properly without, tank support.

"While true, in most cases, tanks will just be a hindrance now, so we will do this with armor, acting as a rear guard. We will move in amongst the Dragon's Teeth, to avoid MG fire, and cross the line, to get around the bunkers. Once we reach the opposite side, we move up and clear the two bunkers, overlooking the roadway. After they are silenced, the engineers can clear the road, for armor to move up."

"They must have 88s watching the road too," I said.

Hiller nodded. "Just behind the main trenches, under camo netting, but they are watching for our air cover before they look for tanks. After the bunkers are clear, it'll be a long task, to clear out the trenches and silence any AT weapons, waiting for us.

"Our main objective is the bridge over the Saar River, which is past the trenches. We need to be quick and grab both sides before it can be blown by their sappers. Remember that control, of the opposite side, is where we stop. Secure the bridge and then we wait and let the armor move up."

I nodded silently, as the squad stirred behind us. Hiller and I pulled back. Jay moved up to the ridge, to set up for sniper cover. Major Phelps was waiting for us near the road, a group of Sherman tanks rolling by, several other rifle squads moving with them.

"Your men ready?" Philips asked, voice a bit deeper, with a harder edge then a few weeks earlier.

"They are, sir," Hiller answered. He stood, watching his squad finish preparing their gear.

Philips nodded, looking at his watch. "Then it's time to get rolling. Move your men into position, Captain."

Hiller tucked away his binoculars. "Squad, move out!"

Everyone moved to their feet and marched down the muddied road, to the launch position, near the main road that crossed the Line in our sector. Six other rifle squads would be attacking with us, all with others to breach the line and clear a route for the armor, to rush through, and reach the river. Artillery had already pounded the line where we would attack, as well as, several other random spots to keep the Germans off balance, while air cover picked at targets of opportunity, across the border.

"Move through the breaches in the wire," I said.

We moved to the launch position, a dozen yards down the road from the edge of the German line.

"Is it true we're on our own, Cap?" Ramos asked, watching the tanks stopped even farther down the road than us.

"Tanks are just bullet magnets," Hiller answered. "We'll be fine moving on our own through the fields of tank traps. Besides, it's better to rely on each other then the tankers."

The squad moved into the tree line overlooking the road and marched towards the German lines. We moved to the edge of the trees, to where a thin stretch of snow covered ground, acting like a small divider between the trees and the barbed wire edge of the *Siegfried* Line. Everyone dropped down behind a tree, for cover and waited, eyes glued to the bunkers and towers a few yards away from them.

"Watch each other's backs," I said to calm them a bit, "out there and we'll be fine."

The others grunted in response, each of them having been in combat long enough to know that it didn't pay to worry about death. They didn't need inspiring words to rush into combat,without hesitation, each man found their own reasons for doing so. My drive was first, pure survival, but after Jessica and I met, I had something better waiting for me.

The air was still. A shrill whistle cut through the silence. There was no hesitation, no wavering, as I propelled myself forward, running at full speed towards the German fortifications. Up and down the line, waves of soldiers flung themselves at the Germans, as our air support shot overhead and strafed the enemy, with MG and rocket attacks.

We were out a few feet from the trees, when the air around us exploded with MG and rifle fire, from the defenders, no more than two dozen yards in front of us. Men fell left and right. I moved through the smashed barbed wire defenses and into the triangular shaped Dragon's Teeth. I ran through the maze of concrete blocks, with bullets smacking into the dirt, and the tank traps going off.

"Keep moving!" I yelled, without thinking about it. I saw men from other squads dropping for cover only to be pinned down. Stopping would mean death, in this kill zone.

A concrete bunker was directly in front of me, across the tank traps, a pair of MG42s flashing orange, pumping out bullets, at an amazing rate. I didn't know if anyone in the squad had been hit, my eyes only looking forward. Some had been cut down by snipers. German mortars and 88s soon opened up, as we crossed halfway through the defenses.

It felt just like Omaha Beach again; men were ripped apart by bullets and shrapnel, others mangled, by mortar blasts. Bullets showered the ground around me and mortar exploded off to my left, the blast wave shoving me. to the snow covered ground. I felt the icy touch of snow smack my face, scrambling back to my feet and crouching behind a tank trap. I leaned out and fired, on the bunker, to draw their fire, while Adam, Hiller, Doc, and Sanders rushed ahead, to cross the sudden gap in firing.

I pulled back. The MG team, in the bunker, pumped more rounds my way, the concrete of the tank trap being chipped away with each strike. I dropped down to my stomach and rolled over to the next trap and rushed back to my feet, running forward again. I caught sight of Vic and Phelps rushing ahead of me, stopping just short of the German lines, as sniper fire pinned them.

A pair of *Jabos* strafed the sniper's nest and the nearby guard tower, in a single pass, silencing the sniper and an MG crew. I rushed up to them and reached the barbed wire emplacements, at the German side of the *Siegfried* Line. The sudden destruction of the guard tower blew open a gap in the line, clearing the wire for me. I waved the squad on and rushed across first, dropping down, at the edge of a bunker.

"First one across," Vic grunted, quickly moving up behind me with Phelps.

"So, get me a medal," I remarked, turning back, to do a head count. I watched each man cross the German border and counted them off, until each man was across. Hiller brought up the rear with Adam; they were the last, of the squad, to cross. Everyone was accounted for and alive.

"Grab the bunkers first then the trenches," Hiller ordered as we moved up the small ridge to the German bunker.

We moved up the side of the ridge, to the first German bunker, overlooking the main road. A small trench extended out from the bunker door, that connected with the rest of the trench system, while a steel door sealed off the bunker. Malks moved up first and jumped into the trench, to blow open the bunker door, while the squad split to cover Malks. Meanwhile, the other group hit the second bunker.

I led the attack on the first bunker with Malks, Ramos, Nate, and Vic, while Hiller took the rest of the squad, for the second bunker. Working with a C4 satchel charge, Malks set the charge and jumped, out of the trench, as the fuse burned down. I stood on top of the trench with my group, waiting for the explosion, with weapons aimed at the door.

The charge exploded, in a flash of light, that ripped open the bunker door. There was a loud metallic clang. The dust was still flying as we opened fire and sprayed the inside of the bunker with rifle and machine gun fire. Our bullets shredded any soldiers inside, within seconds, only a few muffled cries reaching out, before they were silenced. I jumped down into the trench and checked the bunker for any surviving soldiers, only finding the bodies of five German soldiers on the ground, in pools of blood.

"Clear!" I called out, once I saw the bodies.

"Counter attack!" someone called out, as I left the bunker.

The squad returned fire, a reinforcing German force moved up through the rear trenches, to take back their bunkers. Vic dropped down in the snow and opened fire on the group of twenty soldiers, while they rushed down the trenches. Nate and I moved through the trench and met the attacking forces approaching. I squeezed the trigger and fired all twenty rounds from my clip into the Germans, as they crowded together.

Ramos and Malks approached by walking along the trenches, firing down on the Germans from the sides, creating a cross fire. A dozen, or so, of the attackers were killed in the brief attack, with the rest pulling back to better fighting positions. Vic, Ramos, Malks, and Nate continued the attack while I pulled back, to the bunkers to check on Captain Hiller.

"We're clear!" Hiller called out, moving up to the trenches. "Engineers are moving up to clear a path for the tanks!"

I waved Hiller forward and returned back to the fighting. The bulk of the German defenders quickly organized themselves and readied a counter attack, from their trenches. The squad regrouped and returned fire on the handful of smaller bunkers dotting the trench line, as the other squads soon began to move up and assist on the attack.

"Adam, call in air support on those bunkers!" Hiller ordered, as enemy MG fire picked up.

"Yes, sir!" Adam responded, dropping down behind cover, to work the radio. "Hammer, this is Swordsman requesting air support, over." I listened to Adam call out the firing order on the bunkers and enemy trenches. "Mark targets west of red smoke."

Adam tossed one of his red smoke grenades, into the snow, behind us, to mark our position for the air support. The circling P-47s soon pounced on the air support call, a pair of the silver *Jabos* dropping from the sky, no more than a minute after the call went out. The twin fighters dropped low and passed over the enemy trench line, sixteen.50cal machines guns tearing at the Germans, with rockets leaping from their wing mounted launchers. Several bunkers were blown open, by rocket hits, while bullets tore through the infantry.

"Move up!" Hiller yelled, as the *Jabos* peeled off from their strafing run.

I reloaded before moving and then followed Captain Hiller into the enemy positions. I could still hear the drone of aircraft engines, as an unseen battery of 88mm AA and several 38mm flack cannons opened fire, filling the sky with black clouds of flack and streams of tracers. A wing of five P-47s were passing overhead and were caught in the attack, one of the planes, taking a hit in its engine, which pulled the plane from the sky, in flames. Two others were hit and trailing smoke, while the fighters broke off and ran from the AA positions.

"Sir, air support is requesting we silence the enemy AA before they can be back on station!" Adam called out, passing a gutted bunker.

"Bolger, take Vic, Ramos, and Mangon to clear out the 88s, while we finish off with the trenches," Hiller commanded. "We regroup at the bridge."

"On it, sir," I answered. "Guys, follow me."

A line of four 88mm cannons sat behind the trenches, along a ridge above the Saar River, with two of the four barreled 35mm, on either end of the firing line. Side trenches ran along the edge of the main trenches, which opened up to the AA positions, allowing to us flank around and avoid the main bulk of the German troops.

We moved feverishly, in a skirmish formation, through the trenches, avoiding any fighting with enemy troops already tied up with the rest of the squad and the other two rifle squads, that had crossed into our area of operations. Our tank support had not yet arrived, as they were still lagging behind with the engineers, still working on clearing a path.

"Target the 88 crews with grenades, while they are still on the guns," I ordered. We had come to the end of the trench line. "Vic, I want suppressing fire on the crews once the grenades go off, while Mangon and I hit guys manning the '38. Ramos, hang back a little and watch for anyone trying to hit us in the back. Also," I pointed to the area just in front of the 88s, "stop anyone who tries to get to the trenches when we attack."

"Ready to go," Vic grunted, once he checked his BAR.

I nodded and waved my small group forward. We moved quickly and quietly, keeping low, to avoid detection and catch the gunners by surprise. The first emplacement we'd reach was a 38mm Flakvierling, a four barreled antiaircraft gun manned by a three man crew. With the constant blasts from the 88s and artillery, we easily silenced the crew, with quick bursts of machine gun fire, that hadn't alerted anyone.

Vic moved up to the silenced gun and lay prone facing the 88s, a clear line of fire set up for his BAR. Ramos remained in the side trench, while Mangon and I moved around to the rear of the 88s. We approached along the edge of the ridge, the risk of falling into the icy river below suddenly appearing. Mangon and I took the risk, to hit the exposed rear of the 88s, stopping a few yards from the first 88s, to ready our grenades.

Silently counting to three, the two of us tossed several grenades overhead, throwing two to each gun. The crews were occupied with firing their weapons and didn't notice the grenades until they exploded. Most of the crews were killed in the blast, several being thrown into the river, as Vic opened fire. Mangon and I opened with him and caught the remaining crew in a cross fire, which killed off the remaining men. Two, or, three, managed to escape the attack, only to be cut down by Ramos, before they reached the trench.

"Spike the guns," I ordered, as we moved over, to the silent guns. Mangon and I spiked each of the 88s by setting off thermite grenades inside each of the breaches, to weld the weapon's loading mechanism shut. For the '38s, we placed satchel charges at their bases, and waited until the packed charges rendered the guns useless.

"We clear?" Ramos called out.

"Regroup!" I yelled, waving Vic and Ramos over to our position. The two fell back in, air support returned to the skies, now that the AA was silenced. Captain Hiller was finishing up with the trenches and was advancing towards the steel bridge, over the Saar River. "Let's get to the bridge," I ordered, once we were reassembled.

The bridge, over the river, was a few dozen yards away and crawling with German troops. Two MG nests sat at both sides of the road, while snipers crept along the upper arc of the bridge. A German Panzer IV sat in the roadway, on our side of the river, with another two on the opposite. Looking closely, I could see soldiers on the underside of the bridge working with explosives, to drop the bridge into the water.

"We need to stop those sappers from knocking out the bridge!" I yelled. "Let's move!"

The five of us ran down the ridge towards the bridge, to a small outcropping several dozen yards from the bridge, that jutted out from the ridge. The small foothold was large enough for two people to stand or crouch side by side and offered a clear line of fire, on the enemy troops moving on the bridge. Mangon and Nate took up the position, carrying rifles, which would cross the distance far better than Vic's BAR, or my Thompson.

"Hit the ones on the underside catwalks first!" I ordered, pointing to the exposed sappers, as they worked. "Vic, get ready to suppress anyone, who tries to shoot back."

Mangon and Nate opened fire with their rifles first, catching four of the enemy soldiers with solid hits to the chest and stomach, before they returned fire. Vic blasted away with his automatic rifle, as several soldiers returned sporadic rifle fire. Two soldiers tumbled to the icy waters of the Saar River, as they were hit by our fire, only one of the two, dead before they hit the water.

A chill went up my spine, at the sight of the bodies hitting the frozen water near the banks, a sickening crack of bone and ice somehow rising above the roar of combat. Still, I added my weapon's fire to the deadly salvo, to help in suppression, my men with the rifles making any real hits out of us. Another German fell over the edge, his body splashing into the clear water and staining the area around him, with shades of pink and red. I still fired, as bile churned in my stomach, still fought on, as my humanity pleaded for it to stop.

"Let's move to the regroup!" I ordered, watching the last of the enemy sappers fall dead on the catwalks.

I reloaded and ran along the ridge, my eyes drifting down to the river. Eight men were dead down there, eight men who suffered horrible deaths by my hands, eight men I didn't know. How can you let yourself do this? My mind screamed, and I moved forward. What the hell kind of person does this to another? I tried to the shrug off the thoughts, but they kept coming back. I fought on, for Berlin. Killing tore at me at first, but I suppressed the feelings, as the death of my enemy meant the survival of my men and me. That day on the *Siegfried* Line, it haunted me, I couldn't shake the thought.

Captain Hiller was with the squad, on our side of the bridge, with another rifle squad. I quickly saw the squad had come through unharmed, while others didn't. American soldiers lay dead in the road. I do this because the Germans; no the Nazis, are the enemy. They're evil and wrong, in every way possible. They had to be, why else would I kill them? These thoughts plagued me, day in, day out.

"Enemy AA silenced, sir" I reported to Hiller. "We also took out some sappers trying to blow the bridge."

Hiller leaned out, from cover, to fire a quick burst of his Thompson. "Damn fine work," he said, pulling back. "Air cover is back and you may have bought us some more time to cross this damn river. Adam, call it on that damn tank."

"Yes, sir!" Adam answered. "Already did, sir!" Adam had become a natural radio man. He called in all forms of support on target, without fail from the start, and could spot targets before the Captain could. "Sir, our armor is finally rolling up!"

"Then let's have them force their way across. Bolger, we're moving up behind the tanks and use them for cover," Hiller yelled.

I nodded yes, and kept still behind the sandbag wall of the destroyed MG nest. Even with my adrenaline pumping and my mind focused on the fighting, my body was still aching because I hadn't slept for more than thirty minutes, at a time, since the wait before the attack on Aachen. Eating was another rarity, as was being warm, or clean. The only food left, for me to eat, was C rations, most of which were on the edge of being spoiled, while I still wore the same uniform since D-Day, which was filthy, soiled, and not meant for fighting in cold weather.

I glance at the other guys in my squad, they were in the same condition. No one complained about the conditions, aside from the occasional moans and groans shared during our down time, which was a few minutes, at the most. They were all toughing it out, pretending that the problems were minor, which they were when compared to the risk of death, every second of everyday, but they chipped away at us. A fighting spirit and good attitude could only get a GI so far.

"Tanks moving up!" Adam shouted, as the first two Sherman tanks appeared from the rows of tank traps beyond the ridge.

"Fall in behind them!" Hiller ordered.

I moved to my feet, as the two tanks rolled by, main cannons and machine guns pounding away at the Germans. As the second tank rolled onto the bridge, we moved up behind them and marched on in double lines, using the tanks for cover. Machine gun fire bounced off the tank armor, while the enemy Panzer sat smoldering, to one side of the bridge, after being split open by a *Jabo's* rockets.

Our lead Sherman was equipped with a bull dozer blade, mounted on the front, to clear through debris for the engineers. Dropping the blade into position, the Sherman rammed into the burning Panzer and shoved the smoldering hulk off the bridge. Water splashed into the air, as the massive hunk of steel dropped to the bottom of the Saar River.

"Watch for snipers!" I called out, as I spotted the men stalking the upper catwalks of the bridge.

I opened fire on the men above us, picking off the men around me. Several men from Dog Company, who moved with us, were cut down from behind the tanks, the snipers easily avoiding our fire. Jay was moving with us, having regrouped after we crossed the line, and was providing counter sniper fire. It was bizarre and sickening to see the German snipers die and fall from the catwalks. Instead of falling to the river, over the ground, they were stopped in the air by safety harnesses that kept them dangling under the catwalks.

I was moving behind the lead tank with most of the men from the squad, Dog Company, while my squad was behind the rear tank. Machine gunners, on the opposite side of the bridge, were still hitting us and killing the troopers around me. Repressing the urge to puke, I worked with squad's Lieutenant, to roll the dead bodies to the side of the road, to prevent our tanks from rolling over them. It was all we could do for the dead.

A pair of Panthers appeared from the woods, rolling into position, to knock out our advance. The small guns of our Shermans fired, in a vain attempt of self defense, as they split up from the column, trying to cross the bridge and flank the enemy armor. As if on cue, a pair of *Jabos* dropped down from the sky and wiped away the Panthers, in a salvo of rockets.

"Fan out!" I yelled, as the tanks rolled to the opposite bank of the river. "Clear out those pillboxes!"

Four MG nests were built into a short trench line near the bridge, two nests to a side. German troops had fired on us from the trenches, but no machine gun fire had come from any of the pillboxes. I approached the trenches, to the right side of the bridge, and was about to jump in when the urge to puke suddenly broke through my control. I had to turn away and empty, what little food, was in my stomach, at the sight.

Inside the trench, was a reddish gray soup of blood, bone, and organ. A *Jabo* on a strafing run pumped the trench full of heavy MG fire, that had literally pulverized the soldiers inside. It was impossible to tell how many men were inside at the time, as the bloody mess was all that was left. I then understood why the MG nests were quiet, as their crews, like the men in the trenches, were killed by the strafing run.

"Clear!" I called out, once I composed myself.

"Clear!" Hiller called, as the squads poured across the bridge with the rest of the tank cover. "Squad, fall in!"

I rallied the squad, and Hiller moved back to the bridge, removing the folded map from his jacket. I sighed with relief, once the squad was all together again. No one was dead or wounded, which was more then what the other squads had to deal with.

"All accounted for, sir," I told Hiller.

"We have our route into Germany and the heart of the Reich," Hiller announced. "We are to hold position until the bulk of our armor can move up, while the rest of the division finishes up with their sectors. All of you did a hell of a job today! You just broke Germany's defenses. From now on, we'll be fighting on German soil."

Part IV
The Bulge

"Being a hero isn't what you're here to do. Your job is quiet simple, really. Keep the man next to you breathing and prevent war from reaching the people you love back home and you'll be what really matters, a soldier."
–LT Corrigan Bolger, US Army

Chapter 18
1st Infantry defensive line
North of Elsenborn, Belgium
December 15th, 1944

"You know what I miss the most, Corr?" Jay asked, as we walked to the edge of the forest, in front of our defensive line.

"Warm clothes?" I answered, rubbing my hands together. We'd been stationed on the front defensive line while the advance halted, but no winter gear had been given to us. I was wearing both of my uniforms, my thin jacket, an olive colored wool cap, a very thin pair of gloves, and three pairs of socks, with a scarf wrapped around my neck, tucked under my jacket.

"Nope," Jay laughed, as a fine mist of his breath trailed from his mouth. "What I really miss is a Christmas Tree. Remember how Christmas was back home?"

I laughed at the memories. "Our dads would go all out with decorations to see who could do it better. I spent so many freezing nights outside helping to put up decorations, that my hands were numb for days."

"Then our moms would stand off to the side, arms crossed and giving our dads their disapproving looks for using their sons, to help in the petty rivalry." Jay looked down at the town of Trad, which sat in the shallow valley before us, separating two sections of the forest, one for us, the other for the Germans.

"Remember when Matt lit my front lawn on fire?" I said, laughing again. "We never did find out why he did it, just that he could never be trusted with a match."

Since the beginning of December, the lines had stabilized and things quieted after the failed attacks in Holland, as part of Operation Market Garden. As winter rolled in, the advances seemed to slow and then stop, as new orders were to dig in and wait. No winter gear had arrived to us yet, while we sat in the snow and watched time pass by. The only bits of happiness came from letters from home and the people of Trad.

Trad, a town so small it didn't appear on any of the maps we had, was in the middle of the war. The town was found when we arrived to set up defenses in the trees, overlooking the town. Men from Able Company were set up in the town, near the eastern edge. Things were very quiet considering the Germans were a mile or so away.

"You get any letters from home?" Jay asked,as we finished up our short patrol.

"A few from the last supply run. Since my dad served, he sent Christmas letters and birthday cards, ahead of time so I'd get it around the day. You?" I asked.

"Yes, I got a letter from my parents. When's the next supply drop coming?"

I shrugged, as the sound of an engine rumbled through the cold winter air. Jay and I walked through the trees, over to the approaching jeep, which carried a few mail bags, some boxes of supplies, and a soldier in the passenger's seat. The two of us stood by as the jeep rolled to a stop near Captain Hiller's foxhole, and the driver and passenger got out.

"Resupply sir," the driver said, removing the crates and mail bags. "No winter gear this time, though. Just mail, food, and some ammo."

Jay and I helped were helping with the supplies, when I recognized the trooper near the jeep. "Edwards?" I asked.

The trooper removed his helmet. "Reporting for duty, sir," Edwards answered.

"Welcome back," Jay said, shaking his hand. "How ya feeling?"

Edwards shrugged. "Much better and ready to fight." Edwards had been sent to England after the airfield attack, to heal from his wounds. "All healed up, too."

"Find him a spot to stay," Hiller said, as he looked through the supplies. "I'll get all this sorted out. Jay, head out to the forward CP and relieve Sanders."

"Yes, sir." He turned to Edwards before walking off. "Good to have you back, kid."

"C'mon," I said, tapping Edwards on the shoulder, "you can stay in my foxhole. It'll take you too long to dig one out yourself, ground's like cement."

The two of us walked back to my foxhole near the center of the defensive line, along the edge of the trees. I dug the foxhole close enough,to the edge of the woods, to get a clear view of the area beyond, while still remaining hidden in the trees.

"How was England?" I asked, while we walked.

"I didn't get to see much outside of the hospital." He still had fresh scars over his throat, which could be seen under his scarf. "My sister spent nearly all her time with me, when I was there. I even met the pilot she's dating, one of those flyboys that protect bombers and the like. How's the squad doing?" He asked.

I shrugged. "Everyone's still here and breathing. Jay made sergeant and I was wounded again fighting in Chambois. Nothing really special besides that." I spotted my foxhole and jumped in first. "Here it is, home sweet home."

I dropped down and stretched out in the dirt. Luckily, I dug the foxhole wide enough and long enough for me to stretch out and deep enough for me to crouch down, with protection up to my face. Edwards sat down across from me, with his back to the valley. He looked like a replacement, with his clean and pressed uniform, when compared to the rest of us.

"I read about the fighting in Aachen," Edwards said, as he crossed his arms to stay warm. "Was the squad there too?"

I nodded. "All of the First was there. It was a tough place to take, but we did it. After that, it was the *Siegfried* Line, and then we ended up here. News is pretty slow here, but is what happened in Holland, as bad as we hear?"

"A lot of wounded guys were brought back from Market Garden. The Germans took out a British paratrooper, in Arnhem, killed a whole lot of soldiers, and took the rest prisoners."

I snorted to myself. "Guess we won't be home for Christmas. Thank you, General Montgomery."

"Hey guys," Ramos sighed, as he walked up to our foxhole, with a bundle of letters in hand.

"Playing mailman?" I asked, as he shuffled through the letters.

"Hiller caught me napping," Ramos explained, and handed two letters. "This is my penance."

"I told you to stop sleeping, when you're alone in a foxhole."

Ramos rolled his eyes and walked off in the direction of the nearest foxhole. Hands shaking from the cold, I looked down at the letters and saw one was from, the other from Jessica. Feeling a little bit of warmth in my chest, I slipped Matt's letter into my pack and opened Jessica's first.

"Is that from the dame from D-Day?" Edwards asked.

"Yea, she's attached with division HQ now." Without looking up, I could feel Edwards was fidgeting nervously, as he drummed his fingers against his rifle. "There a problem?"

"Ah…can I ask your advice on something, sir?" Edwards asked, lowering his head.

I smiled, reading the last few lines of the letter, finding a small picture tucked into the envelope. It was of Jessica, wearing some type of light summer dress, with her hair down. She stood beside a flowing river. Her flawless and loving smile shone through and made me grin. As I flipped the picture over, I noticed there was some writing on back.

"A little something to remind you of who's waiting eagerly for your return," it read in black ink. "Stay safe and come back to me." On the lower corner the date was written, June 2nd, 1942. I slipped the picture into my breast pocket and tucked the letter into my jacket.

"Sure, what's on your mind?" I asked Edwards.

Edwards looked nervous as he spoke. "Ah, have you…"

I tilted my head in confusion. "Have I…what? Wait, are you blushing?"

"Ah…" Edward's face was turning red, though the cold did that to all of us. "I'm not sure how to ask this, sir."

I nodded and made a guess. "Women troubles I'm guessing?"

"Yeah, it is. There was this girl I met in England, a clerk from the airbase my sister's boyfriend is stationed, and we hit it off. Things were going great with us until I was getting ready to ship out. She invited me to her place and…"He blushed again.

"Are you telling me you're a father?" I asked.

A look of shame crept over his face. "No, I got really nervous and left. I'm worried she got the wrong, since she didn't see me off the next day. When we were together…I've never….you know…with a girl and didn't know what to do. Well, I know what to do, just not…"

I held up a hand. "Relax, take a breath, okay? Don't be ashamed of yourself for anything. You're nineteen, right?" He nodded. "You're young and entitled to mess up the first time. Write to her and try to explain as best you can, she'll understand if she cares about you."

"Have you…" Edwards stumbled.

I sighed. "Nope, and I'm twenty, so relax. I've never really got the chance since I enlisted right after I graduated from high school. I had a girlfriend then, but it wasn't right between us."

Edwards relaxed a bit. "Thanks, sir."

"Stop calling me 'sir' and that's why I'm here," I said.

"Lieutenant!" Mangon called out from the road, that cut through the trees just south of our position and linked us to Trad. "LT, Able command wants you and the Captain, in town for a briefing."

"Briefing?" I wondered to myself, as I climbed from the foxhole. "I'm coming! Edwards, keep watch here and make sure no one uses my foxhole as a latrine."

Edwards nodded. I collected my Thompson and helmet. The squad from Able Company was led by a Lieutenant Vargas, a freshly made Lieutenant, just out of training, sent over to help bolster support, now that our offensive has stalled somewhat. Captain Hiller wasn't too fond of having such a fresh officer leading combat troops, even more so with fifth squad having only a handful of vets left. The majority of them were replacements. It was better to have a fresh squad, with an experienced officer to maintain effective control, then have a fresh officer sending good men to their deaths.

"What's the briefing for?" I asked Mangon, whilst we plodded across the muddy, snow slicked road.

"I just got back from a scouting run with a few of the greener guys from Able. It was more to test out the kids, than a recon run, but we did find some strange stuff."

"Strange? What do you mean by strange," I asked.

He shrugged. "There's only supposed to be infantry in our area, right?"

"Or so Intel had told us. I think it's a few light infantry units, maybe two under strength companies and an engineering unit." I thought back to the area Intel handed out to us a few weeks earlier. "Did you see a larger force?"

"I saw tank tracks in the snow," he admitted. "I did some checking and they were not from halftracks, but larger armor like Panthers or Tigers."

I felt the hairs on the back of my neck stand up. "Panthers and Tigers? Fuck, are you sure?"

"It could have been something smaller like a Panzer, but it was armor for sure," he said.

I sighed to myself, and we continued down the road, to the town. We were only given a small bit of information on the area, upon arriving at the start of December, which told us to expect light German forces in the area. They were supposed to be under strength, light infantry units, that would be more focused on collecting themselves, than fighting. The appearance of enemy armor was very unnerving, since the majority of our forces in the area were weary infantry units filled with replacements and armed with, next to nothing, to stop armor.

Trad wasn't very large or populated, with a population a little fewer than four hundred people, most of which lived in the countryside, on farms and private land. Roughly 310 people lived in the handful of houses in town. Besides a small bar, an old stone church, three stores, and a small graveyard, the city was empty. The men from Able set up defensive positions along the western edge of the town, near the graveyard, behind the church and the surrounding fields with a CP in the church.

It was just after noon, and most of the townspeople were out on the streets. Most, if not all, of the people had no problem with us being in town, some even giving what little food they had to us, while we were in the field. The head of the church, Father Theo, was very friendly with us,as were the other priest, Father Web, and the four nuns who worked with them.

"After you, sir," Mangon said, holding open one of the wooden doors to the church.

"When did you get manners?" I joked, as I walked in first.

I felt the heat from inside wash over me, as I stepped inside, a slight shiver running up my spine. Taking off my helmet, I walked towards Captain Hiller and Lieutenant Vargas, who stood over a table near the front of the pews, just by the altar.

"Good day, Lieutenant Bolger," Father Theo greeted. He was sitting with one of the men from Able, in the pews. For some reason, everyone had to have at least ten minutes to speak with one of the priests.

"Father," I said with a head nod and polite smile. "Cold weather lately, eh?"

"Just another beautiful day, Lieutenant," Father Theo said.

I laughed lightly and shrugged in agreement,, as I passed him by and walked on. The two squad commanders stood speaking with a pair of soldiers who'd been out on patrol along with Mangon, a map on the table between them.

"You called for me, sir?" I reported with a salute.

"Our last recon run has found some unnerving information," Hiller sighed, moving his hand across the map.

"I still don't think we have enough proof, sir," Vargas said, arms crossed.

Hiller dismissed the two scouts. "You'd take the risk?"

"I can't act on something that may not be there," said Vargas.

"'May not' doesn't mean that we don't have German armor out there," I said. "We can't risk an attack on us." I didn't have a problem with the young officer, aside from him being naïve, every trooper was at one point or another.

Hiller nodded in agreement. "As you said about proof, I need something solid that German armor is not lurking around out there. I'm sure you know that neither of our squads have anything to stop anything bigger then a halftrack."

"Send out another patrol," I told Vargas. "Send out two of your more experienced guys, with one of mine to check."

Vargas looked to Hiller, who just nodded. "I'll send them out now, sir." He quickly marched off with Mangon to set up the patrol, Hiller speaking once he was gone.

"What does your gut say?" Hiller asked.

I shrugged, looking over the map. "From what I've heard from some of the other squads to the south, German supplies are running thin, gas is almost gone. Look what's behind our lines," I pointed to the map, "some of the largest supply dumps in the entire theater, short of the ports in Antwerp and Cherbourg. Antwerp is close by with those dumps and would provide more than enough to fuel attacking tank groups."

"German high command wouldn't shuffle tanks if the fuel was nearly gone," Hiller pointed out. "If they do, it'll be for a push on our lines and the timing would be nice in the next few weeks."

"Sir?" I asked.

"Weather reports say snow storms and overcast will be all we see in the next few weeks. That means our air cover will be grounded for the time being, which was our trump card since every unit up the line is waiting to be resupplied," Hiller explained.

I nodded. "An attack would hit us while we're weak, undersupplied, and without air cover."

"I'm gonna check in with some of the other units in the area, to see if there are any other reports on this. Head back to the line and get the squad alerted just incase some of this pans out," Hiller ordered.

I saluted. "I'll get right on it, sir."

Hiller returned the salute and dismissed me. Quickly, I left the church and returned to our positions. A quick glance at the sky showed the sun still shining brightly through a light cloud cover, but the weather wasn't looking too encouraging off to the north. Any heavy overcast would ground our air support until it blew over, leaving ground forces to fend for ourselves.

The powerful military force, that smashed the Atlantic Wall and freed France, was worn down by the constant fighting, with many new replacements flooding the ranks. With the majority of the supplies having been sent north, to the failure in Holland, the push east had stopped and defensive lines were set up in the hopes of regrouping Allied forces and then continuing to Berlin. In truth, many units had stopped, dug in, and worked to recuperate under the false belief the Germans were now on the defensive.

"Listen up!" I yelled, as reached the tree line. "For the next few days, or until the Captain or I say otherwise, we're to be on alert for enemy movement across the line. German forces in the area may be trying something and we don't need to be caught with our pants down."

"They attacking or something?" Nate asked.

"No, but just keep alert, guys. Things may be slow now, but the German military is still a functioning force. Now this means no exposed lights, of any kind. after dark as well as keeping the noise down. I'll also need a full account of what ammo is like for each of you. I'll be checking over the line, so let me know of any problems." I looked at my watch. "Nightfall is in about six hours, so let's get it done before then."

Temperatures were low during the day, but at night the thermometer dropped twenty to thirty degrees, sometimes even more when the wind picked up. Everyone was huddled up in their foxholes, clutching at what little clothes we had to stay warm. Wearing two sets of clothes wasn't as helpful as a single set of winter gear.

I was freezing, walking up the line during my night patrol. My face red and numb from the constant pounding of the icy cold winds, but I managed to keep my mind off the cold. Thompson slung over my shoulder, I kept my gloved hands in my jacket pockets, with my head down to help fight the wind. I kept the feeling in my ears with a thin, wool winter hat I wore under my helmet, the olive colored hats in high demand among the troops.

The night sky was still crystal clear, with the moon illuminating the sky with dozens of stars. Trad was quiet in the distance, as the streets were empty and the people were sealed off in their homes to keep warm. The squad wasn't that lucky. They sat in foxholes, huddling together for warmth,while trying to keep a vigilant watch. A slight flicker of light caught my eye from a nearby trench.

Walking closer, I saw Vic and Phelps huddled together in their foxhole around a portable heater, the bare flame heating a metal cup sitting above it on a holder. Both men held their trembling hands close to the flame for warmth.

"Lights out guys," I said, my breath freezing in the air.

"Ah, c'mon, Corr," Phelps responded, as he took the cup from the flame. "We can't keep alive without heat."

Sighing, I dropped down in the foxhole with them to regain some strength for a minute or two. "That coffee?" I asked. I held my hands near the fire, trying to steal some heat.

Vic nodded, and handed me a cup. "Best we can make."

I took the cup in both hands, taking a second to enjoy the warmth running through my hands. Still shivering, I took a sip of the warm liquid and handed it back. "Taste like gasoline," I commented.

Phelps shrugged and too a sip, before handing it to Vic. "Better then ice water, sir. God knows we got enough of the stuff."

"Well, you need to cut this off." I nodded towards the fire, which I had to pry myself away from. I stood up and climbed out of the foxhole. "Stay warm."

The two grumbled, as the fire went out, and I resumed my patrol down the line. A dozen foxholes ran under the trees to the road and then continued, with Fourth Squad covering the right flank. We had only a few machine guns set up to cover the line, with one manned by Hank, on our side and another with Fourth Squad. We had no AT weapons of any kind and ammo was running low for the MGs.

"Cold tonight, eh sir?" Nate grunted, as I passed his foxhole. He was paired with Malks, who was fast asleep, wrapped up in a thin blanket.

"Cold?" I asked. "I can't tell since all feeling left my body about an hour ago."

Nate laughed. "If only I were so lucky, sir."

I continued on with my patrol. The winds picked up even more, the loose snow easily jumping into the air and pelting anything in its way. Tiny flakes of snow slapped me in the face, with icy hands that sent chills through me. Sniffling, I suppressed the urge to sneeze, as my body continued to fight off a cold. Or maybe the flu, I thought, no telling what shit is messing with me in this frozen hell.

As I approached the road near the split in the trees, something caught my eye in the German lines across the town and open fields of snow. I stopped and took out my binoculars, to scan the enemy tree line for any movement, but didn't see a thing. Shaking my head to clear my thoughts, I began to wonder just how much my lack of sleep was affecting my judgment, when I heard a low, distant rumble like thunder.

Not thunder! My mind registered the fact too slow, as the first shell slammed into our position a few yards off to my right. The explosion threw up snow and dirt, more began to fall around me. Instinct kicked in, and I ran for my foxhole towards the center of the line, yelling out orders over the roar of the artillery.

"Get to cover, get to cover!" I yelled out to anyone outside of their foxholes. "Keep your heads down!"

With my adrenaline pumping, time seemed to slow enough for me to think, as I spotted my foxhole yards away. I looked out at the town and saw they were being spared from the artillery, for the time being, while they saturated our lines. Diving head first into the foxhole I landed on Edwards. He pressed himself into the dirt, at the bottom. I rolled off him and we both lay prone; the explosions continued.

Lying as still as can be in the dirt, I laughed to myself about the simple idea of a foxhole. Such a basic idea of digging a hole in the ground, to avoid bullets and shrapnel worked, but it was more for comfort during an artillery strike, as even a deep foxhole didn't protect against a direct hit from a shell. I was grateful for my dirt hole, the trees around us exploded from shell hits, spewing shrapnel and splinters through the air in a hailstorm.

Edwards grabbed my shoulder, bringing us face to face. "Captain Hiller isn't back yet!" he screamed, though his voice was still hard to hear, even with him inches from my face.

"Can't do anything!" I yelled back. "We need to ride this out!"

I was always awed by the display of explosives in an artillery strike, more so when I wasn't on the receiving end of it. It seemed like the entire world was ripped apart by fire, as I watched from my foxhole, my mind not quite wrapping around the thought of death being only inches from me until that one shell found its mark.

Then it all stopped five minutes after its start, the night becoming silent again. Body trembling, I gently edged myself out of the trench and looked around the line. Dozens of trees had fallen, while others were shattered and were now standing toothpicks. Shell craters ran across the snow blanketed ground, and no one moved from their foxholes. I was the first one out.

"Keep down!" I called out in a muffled voice. "They might be trying to get us in the open." I moved across the line to do a check on everyone in their foxholes. Everyone had checked out fine, as they stayed in cover and avoided the shrapnel from the blasts. I nearly had a heart attack after I spotted Ramos and Doc together in their trench, a sizzling artillery round lay at their feet.

"Dud," was all Doc could sigh, as we looked at the unexploded shell, sticking out from the snow.

"Get out slowly and find another foxhole," I said. They pulled away from the shell. "Malks, you may need to get over here."

Ramos and Doc shuffled away from the foxhole, while Malks approached, unaware of what we had seen,. I didn't need to explain, he spotted the unexploded shell, his eyes going wide in fear and surprise.

"Oh," was all he managed to gasp, at the sight.

I nodded towards the shell. "Anyway, can you defuse this thing?" I asked.

Malks shrugged, and he dropped down next to the shell. "I think I can remove the charge or firing pin, but it's best if you keep your distance."

"Yea, good luck," I said.

I left our engineer to work his magic on the unexploded ordinance and continued checking on the others. Captain Hiller was not in his foxhole, as he had been doing a check in town just before the arty strike had come in, though he was due back. Adam hadn't gone with him and was sitting with Jay, at the forward observation post set up on our left flank on a low hill, that was covered in trees, but had a good line of sight over the entire area.

"See anything?" I asked, approaching the branch covered trench.

"Yea," Jay answered as he scanned the enemy lines through his sniper's scope. "Infantry, armor, mech, we've seen it all."

"Armor types?"

Adam looked down at his note pad. "Large groups of Panzers supporting Panthers with handfuls of Tigers. All of this is backed by a large infantry force."

"Did you contact division? I asked as the night quiet remained.

"Radio crapped out on me about thirty minutes ago." He held up the large radio by its straps. "The thing generates enough heat to melt the snow which then seeps inside, water logging the thing."

"I got enemy armor and infantry advancing from the German lines!" Jay called out. Adam and I raced to grab our binoculars so we could see the town, but we heard the fighting first.

Peering through my binoculars I watched a skirmish formation of light tanks and infantry advancing on the eastern edge of Trad. Vargas and his men opened fire on the attackers with the weapons he had,which was a collection of his squad's riflemen and two light machine guns. Positioned under Captain Hiller's orders, the riflemen and machine gunners easily took down the advancing infantry, but could not stop the armor. No antitank weapons were with any of the squads, several bazookas promised to be in the resupply scheduled for a week later.

"They'll roll right over us," Adam gasped.

I climbed out of the OP. "Adam, keep trying to reach division and tell them we need anti armor support or else we'll lose Trad. Jay, keep an eye for any other fighting across the line."

I didn't wait for a response. I ran back down the line to our defensive positions. Machine gun and tank fire echoed through the night air as I ran, Vargas's squad were still holding out, as the tanks began to slow. We then realized their infantry had been killed. The momentary lapse in command was quickly corrected and the tanks sped up and continued on, to the town. The only defense against the enemy armor was the small streets of the town, which forced the tanks to move in single file.

"Orders, sir?" Vic called out, as he and the rest of squad remained in their foxholes. All of them looked to me, before turning back to the fighting.

"Hold positions!" I ordered. I felt the urge to rush into combat to help the other squad. "We can't do anything with rifles and light MGs to stop armor."

"We're just leaving them?" Sanders called out.

"What the hell can we do?" I asked.

Everyone was silent, and the fighting raged through Trad. Two enemy Panzers were knocked out, when several riflemen were able to climb on top of them and drop grenades into the turrets. Six Panzers were still active and another wave of armor and infantry prepared to attacked from the German lines. A feeling of dread grew in my stomach, as I watched enemy forces attack with unrelenting force. The hard, metallic noise of tank treads, steel on rock, cut above all else and seemed to come from all around me.

I heard shouting between the squad from their foxholes. The sounds of grinding tank treads grew louder from behind. Not sure of what was happening, I rolled to my back and looked to our rear. On the road that cut through the trees, was a column of tanks, the outlines of their turrets visible first.

"Ours?" Edwards asked.

"There nearest armored unit is a dozen miles to the south," I answered, watching the tanks draw closer. They were just close enough for me to see some markings on the turrets. I smiled, as I saw a white star painted on the side of the turret. " It's ours!"

I climbed out of the foxhole and ran to the roads, the first tank approaching. Standing by, I spotted five more tanks behind the first. There were two Sherman tanks and four M-10 tank destroyers, a smaller version of the Hellcat built with the same open turret configuration. The lead Sherman rolled to a stop near me, with the commander standing through the top turret hatch.

"Where the hell are we?" the commander called out, noticing the fighting.

"Trad," I answered. "I don't care why your here, but we need those tanks of yours to stop the German attack."

The commander peered through a pair of binoculars towards the town. "Thin shit Panzers," he spat, reaching for his radio. "We'll handle the bastards, Lieutenant."

He dropped back inside his tank and led his column through our lines and towards the town. I returned to my foxhole and pulled out my binoculars to watch the fighting. Being a spectator, when fellow soldiers were dying, wasn't what I wanted, but only armor could stop Panzers. The squad was silent. Our armor rolled into the clearing and opened up on the Germans.

The tank commander deployed his tank destroyers, in two groups of two, to flank the city and hit the enemy tanks from behind, while his Shermans hit them head on. Our Shermans were quick and agile, giving them an advantage to move through the streets and flank the Panzers. The tank destroyers blew apart the second wave of enemy armor, while Vargas and his men handled the infantry. The pair of Shermans worked through Trad with a slow pace to take out each and every Panzer.

The fight was quick with the enemy armor knocked out before any infantry could reach the town. From my position, I watched as the German troops pulled back to the trees to regroup while our armor halted their attack and then pulled back to our lines. Stunned, I ran out to meet the tank commanders, as his column rolled by.

"What the hell are you doing?" I demanded as he stopped.

"Panzers as easy for us," he explained nodding towards the burning tanks, "but not Panthers or Tigers. At least fifteen Panthers are lurking about for another attack and I won't have my men slaughtered. I'll keep my men here, but we won't fight heavies in the open."

I realized what needed to happen. "Move your tanks across the tree line and get ready for covering fire. You carry any smoke shells?"

The commander held up a hand, as he stuck his head in the turret. "Four left."

"When I give the order use the shells to cover the retreating forces from the town, while the other tanks hit the Germans in the tree line.'"

The commander nodded, and pulled away, the soldier yelling orders into his radio to the rest of his men. I gripped my Thompson and checked the clip before walking to the edge of the tree line on the muddy road. Rifle and machine gun fire still popped and cracked, as the men in town fired on the German line, to discourage another attack, while tanks could be seen and heard moving about. Our tanks were unable to go toe to toe with Panthers and Tigers on the open fields around the city and couldn't be effectively used in the town.

"What are we doing?" Edwards asked, standing beside me.

I sighed. "We can't defend the town and still hold our lines. We'll last longer by concentrating our defenses in the trees and using the cover to protect our armor." I nodded towards the town. "C'mon, follow me."

The two of us ran down the muddy road towards Trad and crossed into the snow covered fields. There was no cover between the town and the trees, aside from a handful of haystacks and an old wooden shed that marked the remains of a dead farm. We jumped, from haystack to haystack, for cover until we reached the edge of the town. The moving between cover took several minutes, but we arrived, as the soldiers from Vargas's squad were reorganizing.

"Where's your Lieutenant?" I asked a solider running by, carrying ammo cans.

"Still at the church," he answered before running off with his duties.

Edwards and I ran for the church, chaos filled the streets, the local civilians running about to stop several fires that had engulfed two houses during the fighting. Three knocked out Panzers sat smoldering at the center of the town, with a forth near the church. The two of us rushed inside, as Captain Hiller was leaving.

"Bolger?" He shouted with surprise. "What the hell are you doing here?"

"Sir," I answered as I caught my breath, "a group of tanks have arrived to help us, but we can't use them here. Enemy Tigers and Panthers are rallying for another attack and we need to pull back to the tree line."

"You ordered the squad not to help the civilians?" He asked.

I felt my face burn in shame. "Staying here would lose us the armor support and our defensive line."

Hiller managed a small smile. "Smart thinking and I've already ordered the retreat. The only way we can hold the line is to give up the town. I want to help the civilians escape, but we don't have enough time. The rest of Vargas's men have already gathered what they can take are readying to pull back."

"The tanks will cover us, sir. We just need to signal them…" I said.

The two of us craned our necks skyward, as a hissing sound rose above the gunfire. Glowing a bright red, a flare shot up from the German lines and arced into the sky, illuminating the battlefield. Our tank crews mistook the enemy flares as my signal and fired their smoke shells into the fields.

"Time to move!" Hiller yelled. "Pull back!"

Edwards and I retraced our steps and raced out of the town, with the men from Able Company, who now had twenty soldiers instead of the thirty-five that were sent out weeks earlier. The survivors moved with us through the fields. White smoke billowed from the tank shells and covered our retreat. It was quick and uneventful, as the Germans didn't attack, they were too focused on regrouping to take the town.

We merged with the trees and the hard winds blew away the last bits of our smoke screen.

"Fan out and take up defensive positions!" I ordered to Vargas's men, as they entered our lines. "Fill in where you can for now!"

"Corr!" someone called out. Working to ready the defenses, I turned, to see Jay and Adam running towards me.

"What's going on?" I asked.

"Germans zeroed in on our positions," Jay explained, "and rushed us with armor. We managed to pull out in time before a Tiger incinerated the OP, but I managed to get some halfwit officer sitting on the turret."

I nodded. "Find a spot to set up a sniper nest and get ready for the next attack. Adam, please tell me the radio is working."

He shook his head. "I had a minute, maybe less, to connect with division and sent out a report on this, along with a request for support. I'm not sure what got through, but I'll keep trying."

"Better than nothing," Hiller admitted. "Keep working at it and calling support when you can. Bolger, Vargas is dead and no one is in charge of his squad. I'll handle them since most are replacements, so you'll take command of the squad for the time being. Now, the Germans will take and secure Trad before they hit us again, so do what you can to fix what we have."

"I'll get it done, sir," I responded.

Hiller nodded before leaving to organize Vargas's men, while I had to command the squad. Our defenses were only foxholes, a handful of covered MG nests, and now a handful of tanks which could only work for so long. The German artillery barrage had helped a bit in defense building, the fallen trees and branches would be used to fortify the foxholes, while the shell craters offered starting points for new foxholes.

I issued the orders to the squad quickly and had half of them working while the others kept watch. It was arduous work, as we collected tree branches, of all sizes, and dragged them back to the foxholes. The branches and tree trunks were cut up with our trench knives and a handful of hatchets turning them into building supplies to create low walls for the foxholes. Bundled together and stacked properly, the branches acted as sandbags, covering foxholes and MG nests.

Next came our major support, the four tank destroyers and two Shermans, which were spread out across the tree line. The tank crews dug out wide fighting positions that would drop the tanks lower into the ground and cover the frontal armor up the turret, with an earthen wall. Branches were then placed around the turrets to add a layer of camouflage. Spare ammo cans and tank shells were stacked for easy reach, while the tank crews handed us what little rifle ammo they had from their personal weapons.

"The Germans have taken the town," Edwards reported, as I returned to my foxhole a little after two in the morning. It may have taken four hours, but we managed to build up our defenses enough to hold back an attack of infantry and medium armor.

"They set up defenses?" I asked, dropping down next to him, my back brushing against the stacked logs around our foxhole.

Edwards shrugged. "Looks like infantry have occupied the town and are setting light defenses while their armor hangs back."

I nodded, as I accepted a cup of coffee. We were covered by the branches enough to have an open flame at the bottom of the foxhole for a few minutes. "We won't see an attack until the Germans can pinpoint where our armor is. It'll be a stalemate for a bit before they push against our lines," I said.

I sighed deeply and drank from the metal cup, the heated liquid rushing down to my stomach and heating me from my core. The momentary relief help cut away some fatigue and, very briefly, the unrelenting cold. I had to cut away the finger tips of my gloves to allow me to better and handle my weapon. My fingers were numb with cold, and I hoped frostbite hadn't settled in, yet.

Edwards sneezed and I noticed how much his hands shook. "How you holding up?" I asked, as I handed him the warm coffee.

Missing England very much," he answered with a small smile, taking the cup. "Uh, to think I loved snow as a kid," I laughed, laid down my Thompson, and crossed my arms. "What did you do for Christmas back home?"

Edwards shrugged, still drinking the coffee. "My sister and I lived with our family on Long Island, when we were kids, before moving to Albany. When we were little, dad would take us out to the woods a few miles from our home and we'd cut down a pine tree for our Christmas tree. Stephanie and I argued over which tree to get and then would fight, to death, on who would decorate it and put the star on. Of course, dad would cave in and let Stephanie do it, picking her up so she could reach."

I laughed. "Sounds like me and my brothers. Our dad went all out for Christmas and used us to put up thousands of decorations, to outdo the other houses on our block. My older brother, Matt, didn't like working out in the cold, so he'd force us to do most of the heavy lifting."

"Sir, you have a brother named Matthew?" Edwards asked. I nodded as it started to snow again. "Is he in the service?"

"Yea," I said nodding again, "Matt's a fighter pilot over in England. He's been flying since 1940, when he was a volunteer for the RAF. Now's he with the 8th Air Force running bomber escort and whatever fighter pilots do."

"So he's Captain Matthew Bolger, head of Echo Flight out of Higgins Air Force Base with the 212th?"

I gave him a sideways glance. "How'd you know?"

He laughed. "I, ah, think he's dating my sister. When I was in the hospital before, he was with my sister, some of the times she visited. They never said anything about being involved, but the way he was around Stephanie said it all. Is he like you?"

I suppressed a laugh. "Matt's like me in most ways. Hmm, he did mention a girl in his letters, but just by first name."

Edwards nodded. "Then I guess he's an alright guy if he's like you. I wasn't really in a position to do anything in England."

The two of us laughed before having to stop from coughing too much. Both of us were sick with flu or something along those lines, as was most of the squad. Doc had done his best to keep us healthy with the slowly dwindling supply of meds he had left, penicillin being the wonder drug to cure, but only when a soldier was really sick. Vic was saved at the start of December, by penicillin, when he contracted a powerful flu strain.

"Hmm, is it ironic or funny that we're surrounded by pine trees during Christmas, but can't decorate a single tree?"

I shrugged. "We just need candles or something to put on one."

The two of us lapsed into silence, as the hard metal on rock grinding noise of tank treads cut above the howling winds. I edged to the top of our position and looked down at Trad, to see a pair of light Panzers escorting a column of halftracks into the town. Inside the tracks were ammo, supplies, and dismantled artillery pieces looking like two 88s and a Pak 38.

"Keep watch," I told Edwards before climbing out of the foxhole.

Jay was ever vigilant for enemy snipers from his position, having killed at least four in the last two hours, but I kept low just to be safe. The tank commander, Lieutenant Harold Gram, was sitting behind his Sherman several yards away from my foxhole, with one of his men watching the enemy armor moving around.

"It'll be easy to take them out from here," Sergeant Donovan, Gram's gunner, was saying. "So long as we each pick separate targets," Gram agreed as he moved back to the tank. I approached before he could climb aboard.

"Don't do anything," I ordered, placing a firm hand on his shoulder. "They may be easy targets, but that's how they want it. The Germans are sending supplies to reinforce the town, but they have no trouble losing them it if means marking where," I patted the side of the tank, "our only support is."

Sergeant Donovan looked crushed, but Gram agreed. "Yea, good point. Don, send the word to the other crews to hold fire unless I say so."

"Yes, sir," Donovan replied, climbing inside the Sherman.

Gram nodded towards the dirt wall and we walked over, standing back far enough to see Trad. "How long do we stay here, sir?" he asked.

I shrugged. "Until we can push them back and the advance continues. For now, we hold position and prevent any more breaches through our lines."

"Well," Gram sighed, as he rubbed his blood shot eyes, "I'm not sure what help we'll be. I was leading this group to a supply depot south of here when we got lost and stumbled on this little firefight. Ammo and fuel are running very low and won't last more than a day of constant fighting."

"Now, we can conserve fuel since we have these defenses. Chances are we won't be doing any moving in the next few days, which runs the risk of letting our engines freeze over. That can be avoided by running the engines for a few hours every day, but that'll burn through our fuel,"

"Let it happen," I said, and stood back to watch the German engineers begin building defenses around the town. "German armor will kill your crews in the open, so the tanks are now artillery."

Gram agreed. "Yea, we can't take on Tigers or Panthers. Still, ammo is another concern as we only have so much to use. AP rounds are almost gone, but I've got plenty of HE and phosphorus, which will blunt an infantry attack."

"Then let's use what we got in moderation," I said.

"Supplies aside, the weather is another issue," Gram said.

I looked over at him. "We won't need the engines."

Gram shook his head. "That's only part of it. I took a piss before and the stuff was freezing before it hit the ground. With the temperature so damn low, I run the risk of having the turret and machine guns lock up. Hydraulic fluid that powers the turret will harden up enough to lock down the turret while the oil in the guns will do the same. It won't freeze like ice, we'd be dead by that time, but it'll cause jams more and more often."

"Do what you can," I decided, "just no open flames at night, or around the tanks."

Gram snorted to himself. "Like this metal coffin has a heater." He laughed in a tired tone before saying goodnight and climbing back inside.

Sleep, I thought as I walked back to my foxhole, that sounds like a good idea.

"Sir," something tapped my shoulder, "sir, it's time to get up."

"Uh-huh," I managed to grunt, opening my eyes and stretching out my legs. "What time is it?"

Edwards was sitting across from me with his portable heater. "Little after dawn, sir."

Grunting, I pulled a thin blanket off me and sat up. My back was sore from sleeping on the hard ground and every muscle was ached. Sleep still did very little to help regain some strength. It that it was just a way to past time and prevent total exhaustion.

"Please tell me that's food," I sighed, looking over to Edwards. He was cooking something in his metal cup over the heater.

"Sure is," he answered, stirring the dark orange liquid,with the spoon from his mess kit. "C rations good for you?"

I shrugged, as I pulled out my mess kit and removed the metal cup. "If it's warm, yeah."

Edwards poured out some of the soup into my mess kit and kept the rest for himself. For a few minutes we ate in silence, the soup having no real taste, with nothing in it beside some type of broth. The stuff wasn't the best food I've eaten, but it was hot and filled my stomach enough.

"I'd kill for real food again," Edwards sighed.

I laughed. "A bacon cheese burger, well done, with fries and a Coke," My stomach growled, thinking back to my days in high school. "I'd spent most of money on that."

"I'd give up every cent I have for some real eggs and bacon," Edwards moaned.

The two of us laughed again, as he packed up the small heater and the small amount of rations we had left. I began to worry starvation would kill us before the Germans did, which gave me a weird feeling. No one every worries about food when you need to count bullets and medical supplies, but every soldier needs to eat at some point, so food was a priority

"You okay, sir?" Edwards asked. "You look like something's bothering you."

I forced a smile. "You mean besides all this shit around us?" I joked gesturing to the snow. "Never be an officer, John, it's all headaches and worrying."

"Anything I can help with?" He asked.

I shrugged. "I need to get food, ammo, medical supplies, fuel, winter gear, and a shit load other supplies for the squad while still keeping moral up." Sighing, I ran a hand through my hair as I wondered what was good about being an officer. Edwards glanced at me with a puzzled look. "What?" I asked.

"You've never let us down before as far as I know, sir." He shrugged, as he picked up his Thompson and laid it in his lap. "Why would you start now?"

I laughed, having heard that line before. Am I really that infallible to the others? "Don't put so much faith in me, it'll…"

"Incoming!"

I didn't know who shouted the alert. I placed my helmet on and shoved myself down, into the dirt, the explosions ripped across our lines. The noise was deafening and the air seemed to explode around me, dirt and shrapnel cutting through the air and anything around it. I didn't hear any incoming rounds before and cursed myself, for the lapse in attention.

The pounding, from artillery, forced everyone into their foxholes for cover, but I climbed out. Keeping low, I crawled to the edge of the foxhole and pulled out my binoculars to see what the Germans, in town, were doing. Every bit of instinct and common sense screamed at me to pull back, but I kept still as dirt pelted my back and the ground shook under me.

Down in Trad, I could see three Flack 88s set up near the east side of the town that was firing on us, along with several other batteries, behind the German lines. Enemy troops moved about behind sandbag walls and several Panzers sat idle. Since the tanks were spread out with the infantry moving behind them, it was a sign of an attack.

"What the hell, sir?" Edwards hissed, as he pulled me back into the foxhole. "Got a death wish?"

I pushed him away and climbed up to see if an attack was being prepared. Artillery shells pounded the line still, but that was a cover for their infantry and armor to organize, into an attacking force. From my position, I could just see eight Panzers moving towards us with four dozen, or so, enemy infantry behind them.

"Enemy attack!" I yelled. The enemy's 88s suddenly stopped firing. "Gram, hit those tanks!"

Gram nodded. He and his crew, from their foxhole nearby, and scrambled inside their snow covered Sherman. Edwards crawled forward, and I shouldered my Thompson, to fire. Our two light MGs opened first, with overlapping fields of fire, hitting the flanks of the attacks. Aiming wasn't really needed, with the German infantry rushing us in mass, with a only a few yards between us. Edwards and I kept up a steady pace of firing. Together, our only focus was on swapping out empty clips, for dry ones.

Our Shermans and tank destroyers fired away, in coordinated attacks, that tore apart each Panzer, one at a time. Gram was smart, as he had each tank fire in random intervals, to make it difficult pinning down the location, across the line. Enemy Panzer fire exploded! They slammed into trees leaving splintered shards behind that sliced through anything short of steel plating.

"Medic!" one of the men from Vargas's squad cried out, over the shooting. I glanced over to see Doc run out from his foxhole towards the unseen trooper, Doc ducking enemy fire trying to cross the exposed ground.

"Brave bastard, sir," Edwards said, in awe, while Doc ran,without notice, to the machine gun fire.

I nodded and groped around, for a fresh clip. "He's one of the best."

Two Panzers exploded, off to my left, leaving the infantry following behind them exposed, in the open ground. No mercy was shown. Our left flank MG team zeroed in on the hapless infantry and took them down, in a hail, of bullets, their bodies being torn to shreds, in the firestorm. Four Panzers were left,in the attack, with several rifle squads following behind them, though another tank was stopped in its track, from AT fire.

No sound could be heard, over the battle, as I used hand signals, to issue orders, from my foxhole. Gram was sitting, in the top turret hatch, and directing the fire, of his tanks while manning the.50cal mounted on the turret. Rocket fire streaked, through the air, and slammed into the ground and trees, tossing up dirt plumes while raining wooden shrapnel down. I lost all account of time. Minutes and hours blurred, until the fighting, suddenly stopped.

An uneasy silence drifted,across the line, and another snow storm began kicking up harsh winds. Edwards and I remained still, with our weapons still trained on the open fields before us, unsure if we had stopped the attack. Heart still racing, I crawled forward, to a tree, several feet away and did a scan of the area.

The snow was stained red, dozens of gray clothed soldiers lay unmoving, on the icy fields. Six German Panzers burned brightly amongst the bodies, their fuel leaked out and increased the ferocity, of the fires. I didn't see anything moving, in the fields, as the snow storm increased and cut back visibility enough, to blur Trad, in the distance.

"Clear?" Edwards asked, keeping his Thompson tucked, into his shoulder.

I nodded. I didn't hear any moaning or cries. "All clear."

Keeping low, I moved across the line, to check in, on everyone, and get a head count. The squad survived, without wounded, but had expended a great deal of ammo, in the brief firefight, which had lasted fifteen minutes, from start to end. Captain Hiller was doing the same, with Vargas's men, when he pulled me over, to talk.

"Any losses?" Hiller asked, wiping a fresh cut running, from under his jaw.

"No, the squad's intact," I answered.

Hiller nodded. "I got four dead and two wounded, both critical. Ammo is running very low, after this little sortie, and one, of the medics, was killed."

"Doc can't handle both squads, in a firefight," I said.

Hiller shrugged. "Ramos and Mangon both have some medical training so they'll have to pitch in now and again."

"Sirs!" Adam called out, running over to us, with his radio. "I've reached division HQ in Ellensburg."

I grinned a little bit. "Really good work, Adam," I congratulated and he handed the receiver to Hiller. Adam and I stood by as Hiller spoke, to the radio operator at HQ, listing what we needed, along with an after action report, of sorts.

"Got it working," I whispered. We sat and waited.

Adam nodded. "Damn thing was hit, by some shrapnel, and works like new."

"We need ammo, food, and medical supplies, above all else," Hiller reported, speaking with the division. "No, we can't hold out, for another two days, with what we have. With our current supplies, we'll last a few more hours, a day, at the most. If we're hit again, we'll lose what ammo we have left and will be forced to retreat."

Hiller's expression revealed whomever he spoke to, at HQ, was not listening.

"I can't use what I don't have," Hiller said flatly. "There's no way my men can hold back a determined attack, by armor and infantry. What little tank support I have will not last and we will face enemy armor, with rifles and machine guns only." It was silent, the Captain listened. "Yes, I can see the weather will not permit air cover. What about artillery, or more tank support?"

Adam nudged my shoulder and whispered, "Why not pull back deeper, into the woods, and limit enemy tank activity?"

"We risk getting lost easier and they seem, to be able, to get tanks through the woods," I answered, as Hiller handed the radio receiver back to Adam. "Anything coming our way, sir?"

He shook his head. "This attack is bigger than our sector; it's an all out offensive, across our lines, in the Arden. Similar attacks went off last night south of here, with a lot more power and broke our lines. The Brits and us are still scrambling, to slow the advance, so no support is coming, until the weather clears and the flyboys can get airborne."

Adam and I exchanged glances. "What are your orders, sir?"

"Hold and that's it. We don't have any real strength, to counter attack, so it'll be our only duty, to back the Germans, as long as possible. When the time comes, we pull back Ellensburg."

"Yes, sir." Adam and I couldn't really think of retreating the twenty, or more, miles back to division HQ and letting the Germans through. Retreat or die, I thought coldly, simple enough.

Controlled chaos, that was our situation,on that frigid December night, of the first day, of the German offensive. A frozen Hell surrounded us as we fought back an endless wave, of enemy infantry, a determined and fearless infantry that would not cease attacking. Dead bodies, in gray and white uniforms, stacked up, on crimson snow, before me, like piles of wood, but more and more soldiers rushed up, behind them, paying no attention, to their dead.

Edwards was still next to me, with his Thompson, the two of us now sharing what ammo we had left. He fought, with the cold, focused demeanor of a man whose only goal was the protection of life its self, his life. Nearly all of Vargas's squad was dead as the attack rolled on, to half an hour, in length. All but two of Gram's tanks were burning brightly, in the tress, each one a funeral fire, to the dead crews. Gram was still alive, with his crew, and the other Sherman, but they were running low, on ammo, for their manned guns.

"On the left!" I yelled, as I killed a pair, of German soldiers rushing towards us. Both men were stopped, more hurled themselves at us, in another attack wave, supported by another group of Panzers, with a pair of Tigers following.

"I'm all most out!" Edwards called out. Another empty clip clattered, to the pile, at the bottom, of our foxhole.

My free hand patted the ammo pouches along my ribs, but I found only five clips. Fumbling, I pulled out two clips and handed it to him. "Make each one count!"

A Panzer climbed the hill and rolled, to a stop, just yards, from our foxhole, as its hull and coaxial machine guns flashed. I grabbed Edwards, by his back, and shoved him down, as bullets peppered our position, and chewed away, at our cover. We landed, on our stomachs, as splinters shot up and pelted our backs. We didn't wait long, before jumping back. Gram took out the Panzer.

I jumped back up, to fire. I looked over, to our left flank, but could not see much, with the thick woods, in the way. Bright flashes, of light and fires, marked the pitch fighting hitting out flank. Captain Hiller was right about us not lasting, through the night, as both of our.30cals had run out of ammo minutes earlier and Tiger tanks were backing the enemy assault. It was inevitable when the retreat order finally came. Since voice orders could not be heard, Hiller blew a whistle several times, to signal the retreat.

"Let's go!" I yelled, shoving Edwards, out of the foxhole.

The two of us grabbed our packs and ran, from our foxhole, heading, for the trees lining the road. Captain Hiller planned out the retreat ahead of time, to keep us organized, when the time came, setting up a full escape route for us. When the order was issued, we'd pull back hugging the road, until we hit a small bridge two miles, down the road, over a small stream. The regroup would occur at the bridge, but it was up to each person, to get back under their power.

Machine gun and tank fire still streaked through the air and popped around us as Edwards and I ran, through the trees. The two of us kept close together as we ran to make sure we didn't separate and become lost, in the dense woods, at night. I didn't see anyone else as we ran, my mind more focused on getting away, from the Germans first. The two of us ran a few dozen yards parallel to the road, but still no one was around.

After several minutes of running, the explosions of artillery became a distant echo behind us and it soon became quiet. Edwards and I stopped running and began to walk, to conserve our energy, though we still were breathing heavily. With the low moonlight, I managed to glance at my watch and realized the fighting had gone for an hour before the retreat.

"Want to stop for a sec," I asked as we maneuvered through the trees.

"Sure," he answered, and we stopped.

Edwards sat down, on a fallen tree, to take a few sips from his canteen while I stood watch. Feeling my stomach grumble with hunger, I fished out my last candy bar and broke it in half, handing one part to Edwards.

"Thing's like a brick," I sighed, biting off a small section. The chocolate was ice cold, hard as stone, and very bitter, but food was food.

"Thanks, anyway," Edwards mumbled, devouring the hard chocolate. "How much longer to the RV point?"

I shrugged and looked around. "Should be there, in an hour or two, if we walk on, without stopping."

He nodded, standing back up. "Then let's keep going."

I took a second, to drink from my canteen, before we continued on heading south. I walked out a few feet ahead of Edwards, watching out for any other men, from the squad, or German scouts stalking, through the woods. Our plan was to reach the RV point while avoiding engaging, with German forces, whenever possible, with our low ammo levels. I had just three full clips and one half full loaded, into my Thompson, totaling about seventy rounds of ammunition, along with two pistol clips, of fourteen rounds. Edwards only had one clip left and did not carry a sidearm and he had used up all his grenades.

"Think we're lost?" he asked, as we walked on for another hour, with no sign of the RV, or anyone.

I shrugged and scanned the passing trees. "Well, we're not that lost. This is still Belgium and we're walking away, from the German forces."

Edwards muffled a laugh and took another sip of water. He too was sick like me and just about everyone else, in that frozen hell. Plenty of men were no longer fighting as they were sent back to the rear with paralyzing cases of trench foot, a multitude of stomach viruses, deadly cases of flu, and different degrees of frost bite. If it wasn't the Germans wounding and killing us, it was the damn weather.

Sighing silently to myself, I held my Thompson one handed and slid out Jessica's picture and letter from my jacket, with my free hand. Loneliness was another enemy plaguing each of us, in one way or another, that would slowly erode morale and our will to fight. I read and reread each one of her letters a few dozen times a day, to not only pass time, but to feel, in anyway, closer to her. I'd give anything to have Jessica with me again, but at the same time, it was a happy thought, to know she was behind the lines and out of the immanent dangers of combat.

My mind turned to the future, as I tucked the letter and picture back into my jacket. I often wondered what I would do once the war ended and my tour was over. Marrying Jessica was first and foremost, for my life after the war, but I was terrified. Chances were she'd return home, I didn't really know where it was and wouldn't be staying with HQ long after it all ended. She'd wait for me if I asked, she might wait even if I didn't, but how would we find one another? The future seemed so far away to really think of, but the war would end. Eventually. Hopefully.

"So, what about this girl from England?" I whispered to Edwards. Keeping silent wasn't really a priority, we were in 'friendly' territory and the Germans wouldn't chase us for too long. They were trying to take the main roads, for their tanks. The road, for our RV, was a minor dirt path in comparison to the others that stretched to Ellensburg.

Edwards shrugged. "Rebecca, Lieutenant Rebecca Lawson. She's a clerk with the 212th Fighter Wing."

"Uh-huh, but what's she like?" I asked.

A small smile slipped over his face. "Amazing in just about every way imaginable. She's really into politics and talked a lot about the war with me, we often shared our points of view, on the war, and talked for hours on it. She doesn't like being called Rebecca, just Becca, and is very liberal, for a women, I think that's how she put it. She can drink and swear like a sailor, and she's tough as nails, but she would fall to pieces whenever I had trouble talking or eating or just about anything that happened, from my wounds."

He was rambling a bit, but he was very happy and proud as he spoke. "She makes you happy then?" I grinned.

"Happiest I've ever been, sir," he answered. "But I might have ruined it all…"

"Don't worry about it," I reassured, "just write her and take it slow. You still got plenty of time to figure it out." Something moved up ahead. I held up a hand to stop and waved, Edwards quickly seeing the signal and diving behind a tree.

I dropped down a few feet from him and brought my Thompson, to my shoulder. The forest was very dark, with the branches of the trees blocking out a large amount of the moonlight, which was blocked out even more, by thick cloud cover. A few dozen yards ahead, of our position, something was stirring, in a shallow dip in the ground, most likely a shell crater, from a random missed arty strike. Neither of us could tell who was out there, but it was at least one person.

Using a few hand signals, I waved Edwards to circle around, to the left, while I circled around, to the right, in a pincer movement. I moved slowly and carefully, to cut back the noise, from my boots pressing down on the snow and the rattle of my gear. The trees were thick enough to move without too much exposure, my view of Edwards blocked out as he moved along just a yard or two away, off to my left. I had to stop when I approached the small dip, in the ground, as I did not see if Edwards was in position yet.

He appeared a few seconds later, across from me, and nodded. I waved him forward towards the shallow dip as I began to slowly shuffle forward. I kept my Thompson held up and trained, on the position, but didn't look down the sights. Instead, I approached with my weapon trained, on the area, with my finger resting on the trigger guard. I said nothing as I stopped by the tree right near the position. Taking a calming breath, I quickly spun out and brought my weapon to bear.

"Son of a…" the words escaped my lips. I saw the olive colored uniforms.

"Nice to see you too," Nate answered. He was sitting in the snow with Ramos. Both stood and smiled. "Miss us?"

"For all of a second," Edwards snorted and lowered his weapon. I could see he was breathing heavily, from a sudden rush of adrenaline. "We could've killed you two."

"Glad you didn't," Ramos said. "We were hoping to find someone since we're kind of lost."

I sighed and nodded south. "Just stick with us. How much ammo do you have?"

The two did a quick checked, as we marched on. "Two clips," Nate answered first.

"Five," Ramos answered flatly, checking his rifle.

"Clips?" I asked, looking back at him.

He shook his head. "Sorry, that's five rounds left."

I swore under my breath. "And I'm guessing no grenades." Both shook their heads. "Wonderful, just frigging wonderful."

The four of us lapsed into silence as we continued on, with our cross country march, to the rendezvous point, before morning. We didn't stop at all, pushing on for another hour before I heard the splashing sounds, of running water, off in the trees. It was the small river that marked the RV point, with the bridge crossing nearby. Moving closer, we returned, to the main road, to be greeted by a single Sherman tank sitting on the opposite river bank, along with a handful of soldiers.

"Looks like Malks, Phelps, Vic, and Mangon aren't back yet," I sighed, noticing they were missing from the group.

Captain Hiller was waiting with the rest of the squad. "Good to see you," he greeted us with a small smile. "Did you see anyone else out there?"

"No, sir," I answered.

Gram appear from the tank turret.

"No joy, Captain," he announced, with his headset hanging by his neck. "The radio is crap, without replacement parts."

Hiller sighed, as he rubbed hand over his mouth. "Do you have enough fuel to reach HQ?"

Gram wobbled his hand. "Possible, if I mess with the fuel mixture a bit. I know a few ways to stretch out fuel limits, but it'll do a number on the engine that'll require a full overhaul should it run for too long."

There was the distant rumble of artillery that drew a few nervous glances, from some of the squad. "Sir," Adam called out as he worked the radio, "I still can't reach HQ, but I was able to connect with Kilo for a few minutes."

"And?" Hiller waited.

He looked down at his notepad. "They were attacked late last night as we were, but managed to hold, with several AT weapons they had. Kilo took heavy losses, but repelled several counter attacks since dawn. Renewed attacks have cut down ammo supplies and their position is under constant shelling. Losses are mounting. I lost radio contact just after that."

Hiller looked back in the direction of our old positions, the artillery still firing in the background. "Let's get going back to HQ. The Germans will be pushing up this road by morning and we can't stop or stall them for very long. Form up around the tank and let's move out."

"But, sir," Nate argued, "we won't wait for the others?"

He shook his head. "It's roughly twenty miles to Elsenborn and we have two more hours before sunrise. We just can't wait."

Nate tried to argue again, but I placed a hand on his shoulder to tell him no. Vic, Malks, Phelps, and Mangon were my friends, but I had to think of the squad as a whole. My stomach churned in disgust as we began our march south, the human part of my mind screaming for us to wait a little bit longer, but it couldn't be done.

Everyone was silent and we plodded across the muddy road, the only noise rising from the grumble of the Sherman. Captain Hiller walked out ahead, with me and Jay, all three of us sickened by the thought of having to leave four of our own behind. Hiller, being the solid rock of a man he was, didn't show much as we walked, his face set in stone with a look of determination. Jay fidgeted a little bit, constantly shrugging his shoulders, one of the signs of discomfort for him, and had to stop himself from looking down. I kept as neutral as possible to keep a leveled appearance for the squad, but internally my emotions tore at me, like a virus.

I yearned for Jessica's calming touch, many times her simply holding my hand, relaxing and calming me, in the worst of situations. Just a hug or kiss from her would lift me out of my slowly deepening depression, but I knew such things were impossible. Even if I did manage to find her working with HQ in Elsenborn when we arrived, I wouldn't be able to say or do much. Division would want us back out, to stop the German attack, as soon as possible. Be grateful, I thought, as I marched on, she's safe with division HQ and away from the fighting. So far, at least.

I heard something fall to the ground, with a splash of slushy snow. Turning, I saw Adam struggling to get up from a shallow puddle he fell into. "Hang on," I said, as Doc and I helped him back up.

"Thanks," he responded, looking down, at his uniform. Adam was just about covered head to toe with mud and grime, adding to the misery of being cold and hungry. Still, he managed to laugh it off. "I'm gonna have one hell of cleaning bill for this."

A few of the guys laughed or smiled before going silent, the march continued. Cold, hungry, filthy, tired, and lonely I pushed out as many negative thoughts as I could and focused on reaching the next tree, along the road. From there, it was the next puddle in the road, the next turn, the next hill, the next God damn step.

Three hours of endless marching paid off. The sun began to rise higher, into the air, and Elsenborn appeared, at the end of the road. The Belgian town sat above a small ridge, with a large ring of trenches, and MG nests sitting on the edges, of the town. Forward patrols brought us back, without trouble, as our small group rolled into the center of town and stopped, in front of the Division HQ, set up in a hotel.

"Jay, get the squad resupplied and fed," Hiller ordered, walking towards the hotel. "Meet back here with Bolger and me once things are settled."

The two of us walked, across a small stone path, to the front door of the hotel, two MPs standing guard out front. Both snapped to attention when we entered. We were hit by a burst of warm air. Hiller and I sighed, in relief, the heated building melted away some of the frost, from outside, and warmed us a bit. Clerks and soldiers inside passed us by, without glancing at us, until Lieutenant Hasel, Major Philips aid, spotted us. The short, fair haired soldier waved us over, to a nearby hotel room, converted into an office.

"Major Philips wants to see both of you," the stocky lieutenant huffed as we stepped into the tiny office. A wooden desk sat, where a bed once was, with the wall behind it covered by an area map. Major Philips sat at the desk, behind mounds of paper, rising up around him and a small stove nearby, with a coffee pot sitting atop it.

"Sir!" Hiller and I snapped, with a salute, as we stood before him.

Philips looked up at us and returned the salute. "I'm grateful to see you too," he sighed with sincerity. He stood up and shook our hands, before gesturing to the map behind him. "The Germans really pulled one over on us the other night. They hit us all across the front with heavy tank and infantry attacks and have grabbed a lot of land.

"We've seen our lines disintegrated, all the way from Malmedy, down to the Third Army's lines. The area, in between, is in total disarray, and everyone is struggling to fight back,with such low supplies. The 82nd and 101st have set up defenses around Bastogne as the Germans rush their way in, while we're readying for another assault here. What's going on near Trad?" He asked.

"Enemy forces attacked our positions two nights ago with artillery covered tank attacks," Hiller explained. "Since no forces under my command had antitank weapons, I was forced to pull back to our defensive positions, in the overlooking tree line. To our luck, a group of tanks were lost during the night and arrived, in time to help blunt the first waves of attack. Unfortunately, continued attacks wore down our ammo supply and knocked our armor, forcing our retreat."

Philips angrily sighed, shuffling a few papers. "Supply is still trying to redirect everything, after the fuck up in Holland and left us out in the cold, literally. Now, I'm getting your men resupplied with what we have left and then I want you back, out in the field." He tapped the map behind him, on an area circled, in red. "There is a bridge that crosses the Our River, located west of St. Vith, that needs to be destroyed, to slow the German advance. Troops in St. Vith are currently facing stiff attacks by enemy armor and cannot spare forces, to protect any engineers.

"You and your squad will leave, within the hour, by halftrack. Take a dozen engineers and blow the bridge. Already, German armor has crossed, using several other bridges that force them to hit St. Vith, if they want to control the area. The boys in Vith still contain control of the bridge, for the time being, as several forward units pull back. That bridge needs to be in the river as soon as possible."

"We'll get it done, sir," I assured him.

He nodded. "The two of you haven't let me down before and I'm sure you never will. Report back here, in an hour, and the halftracks will be waiting. The man in charge of the engineers is Lieutenant Morgan Hansen. Good luck out there, dismissed."

Hiller and I saluted before being ushered out of the office by Hasel, who was always in a foul mood, when exhausted. We began to walk outside when I slowed down a bit, to scan the clerks and personal moving about, through the HQ. Jessica would be easy to spot. Since she's the only woman allowed this close to the fighting. My heart sunk when I left with Hiller having not spotted her at all.

"Let's see if we can get Gram to go with us," I suggested and changed my focus back to the mission. "Some tank support would be nice."

"Smart thinking," Hiller said, taking a quick look around for the tank commander. Gram and his crew were across the street from the hotel, unloading an oil drum, from a supply truck.

"Engine works?" I called out. Hoping the answer was what I wanted to hear. We crossed through the traffic of jeeps and supply trucks.

Gram shrugged. "Well, my little fuel mixture didn't hurt the engine too much, so we're loading up with gas and ammo."

"We're moving out to St. Vith, to drop a bridge," I explained, "feel like bringing some armor for us?"

"We'll do it," Sergeant Donovan answered for Gram. "We'll be able to roll soon."

Gram waved the sergeant back to his duties. "I'll have the tank ready in a few minutes."

"Good," Hiller said, nodding in approval. "Stay here and wait for us to return."

A sudden burst of wind hit my face, like a cold slap, and made me shiver. The weather was still awful, with another snowstorm already moving into the area. The temperature was still dropping and things would not get easier. Wherever they were, I hopped our missing men were safe. The sudden blaring of a jeep's horn startled me and broke my thoughts.

"Stop!" someone shouted. I turned to see a jeep roll to a stop a few feet away. Four soldiers were crammed, into the back of the jeep, quickly jumped out. Hiller and I quickly recognized the four men. They were the rest of the squad we were waiting for.

"Got a little lost," Phelps sighed and he saluted.

"Sure. Get yourselves sorted out and grab some ammo, we're moving out in an hour." Artillery barked out, in the distance. "Make that thirty minutes."

Black smoke billowed high, into the sky, with the swirling wind, blowing it over our halftrack. A dozen Sherman tanks lay still and dead, in a field,as we drove on, each one charred black and split open, like gutted animals. No enemy armor sat with them, only spent shell casings and tank tracks marking where several Tiger tanks ambushed the group.

The blackened bodies lying about the battlefield put the engineers on edge, several nervously shaking, as our halftracks had to swerve around a few bodies, on the road. Gram and his tank rolled ahead of the column, with my squad and the engineers, crammed into two halftracks, with a third carrying the engineer's equipment. The group of tracks made a very nice target, crawling across the field and snaking through the, near impassable, forest.

"We'll need some time to rig everything," Hanson explained.

"How long? I don't have the strength to hold back German armor for very long." I explained.

The young engineer shrugged. "I really don't know since I don't know what type of bridge is there."

I shrugged and glanced at Malks, who shrugged to say 'blowing stuff up is hard.' The snowstorm had increased with a merciless furry, in the past hour, the air now clogged with a white fog, of falling snow.

My ears and cheeks were cherry red, growing numb from the cold, my nose running, from time to time.

Captain Hiller sat at the front of the track behind Vic stood up to man the cab mounted .30cal, reading over an area map. Weather, either hellishly hot or icy cold, seemed to not bother the stout Captain, in the least bit. It was a bit scary at times to see Hiller go through hell so many times without flinching.

"When we arrive, I want you to take four of the squad to the opposite side of the river, to cover the engineers." Hiller was speaking to Jay and me. "Jay, there's a ridge on our side that should give you a view of the area and to set up a sniper spot. Hanson, get your men to move quick and rig the bridge."

We just nodded. Hiller always had a plan that rarely, if ever, failed us. The sudden rumbled of artillery, to the north, made several of the engineers jump. I sat still as my mind quickly registered the rumble came from a 105, not a German 88.

The trees soon gave way, to the open ground, around the bridge. Gram rolled his tank, to the side of the road, a few feet from the bridge, allowing us to roll ahead and take up defensive positions. Hiller and I climbed out. Three MPs approached us, from the bridge.

"How can I help you this fine day?" the MP Captain asked. He strolled over, with a Thompson slung over one shoulder.

"We have orders to drop the bridge," Hiller told him.

Hanson and his men began to unpack their gear.

"Oh?" The MP gestured to a dozen men working around the bridge and in the river below. "The engineers arrived a few minutes ago. They're putting down the final touches, as the last forward elements pull back."

I looked past the eight or nine MPs and towards the men moving, about to rig the bridge. Some ran wiring over the top of the bridge while others worked, in rubber boats, to plant explosives on the bridge supports, sticking out of the river. "Hanson, give them a hand anyway, speed up the process," I called out. "That okay with you?"

The MP shrugged. "Hey, I'm just here to guard this hunk of stone." He pointed to one of the engineers overseeing the process. "Talk to the Major over there, he's in charge of the demo work."

Hiller and I approached the officer, who was speaking with one of his engineers. He didn't notice us until several of Hanson's men walked across the bridge. "Hey! What the hell are you doing?"

"Offering some help, sir," Hiller answered.

The Major was not happy. "Help? My men are doing this job and we don't need help. Pack up your men and get out of the area so we can blow the bridge."

"A few extra hands couldn't…" He cut me off.

"No! We're handling a lot of explosives here and I don't need some fool blowing us all to Hell."

Hiller didn't bother to argue. "Hanson, pack it up! We're not needed."

Sighing from the waste of time, Hiller and I walked back to the halftracks and told the squad to pull back. Hanson and his engineers ran back, but Hanson seemed a bit edgy. "Sir, wait a minute," he pleaded, as we walked back.

"What?" Hiller asked.

He glanced back at the other engineers. "Something isn't right, sir."

Hiller and I both stopped. "What's the matter?"

"When I was over there, I noticed they were rigging the explosives the wrong way, on the bridge supports. You see, they ran the det cord from the detonator and it's already connected to the charges. That's a sure fire way to get yourself killed and the charges aren't even placed right. With what they have, the bridge will just be damaged, not destroyed."

I looked over at the engineers on the bridge. They seemed capable enough. "Are you sure?"

"Positive, sir," he assured me.

Hiller sighed and thumbed the safety on his Thompson. "Hanson, get your men into the tracks. Bolger, come with me but stand back a bit when I speak with that Major."

I readied my Thompson and walked behind Hiller as he approached the Major, moving slowly and trying to keep casual. My finger rested against the Thompson's trigger as I held it by my waist.

"Excuses me, Major…," Hiller called out. He approached the officer.

"O'Brien," he answered. "It's Major O'Brien and didn't I order you to leave?"

Hiller nodded. "You did, sir, but my engineers seem to think you've made a few errors, in the placement of your explosives. I'd like my team to check them over just to be safe."

The Major's expression betrayed him. "What? No, I won't have you fumbling around with high explosives and putting my men at risk. Now, get out of here before I put you on report!"

"Just who would you report me to?" Hiller asked.

The Major fumbled to find an answer to the question, the men around him suddenly stopped their work. A sense of dread crept out from my gut and I suddenly felt adrenaline surge into my veins. In a flash, the Major drew his pistol and attempted to fire on the Captain, but Hiller was quicker, slamming his Thompson into the Major's chest and forcing him to the ground.

The engineers were suddenly grabbing weapons, and the squad reacted to the attack. The MPs were shocked to see the engineers turning their weapons on them. Gun fire erupted, and I fired on the closest engineer, knocking the man off the bridge and into the river. Hiller jumped back for cover as rifle fire cracked and two MPs dropped. The half dozen engineers, on the bridge, scattered as they returned fire, the men working in the river firing from their rafts. Gram moved his tank forward and sprayed the bridge with MG fire, killing most of the engineers. Vic finished off the men in the river, and the weapons fire died down. The fight was over within thirty seconds.

"Hold fire!" I yelled, moving back to the road. A dozen dead bodies lay stretched out, across the bridge and riverbank, with some floating down river.

Four MPs were among the dead, though their captain was alive, with the rest of his detail. My squad was spread out behind the tracks and the trees alongside the road, Captain Hiller nowhere to be seen.

"Squad, fall in!" I ordered.

"Just what the hell was all this?" Gram asked, appearing from his tank. "Why they shoot at you?"

I shrugged and walked over to the dead Major. He looked just like any other man, out on the line, in the same dirty, olive drab uniform that all of us wore. I carefully searched through the pockets of the dead man, finding no wallet, but a full set of ID papers that everyone carried to get past checkpoints. The ID papers looked the same as the set I carried, the ID picture even matched the dead man.

"Who are they?" Hiller asked, walking towards over, a bloodied bandage wrapped around his left arm.

I looked at the wound. "You okay, sir?

Hiller shrugged. "Just a flesh wound." He nodded to the dead. "I'm better than they are, whoever they are."

I showed him the papers, even holding out my own to compare. "He's carrying a full set of ID papers that are the same as mine. His name was Andrew O'Brien and is with the 3rd Engineer Brigade which is part of the 16th."

Hiller studied the papers. "If these are real, then why did he attack us. Captain!" The MP Captain stumbled over with one his wounded men. Hiller showed him the papers. "Did you notice anything odd about him and his men?"

The MP shrugged. "Nothing really odd that raised an alarm. They bitched and moaned about the weather and supply just like we were, but went right to work when ordered to. I thought they were working fine, until…well this. I had their ID papers checked when they arrived."

"Wait," I said as compared my papers to the dead man's. "Can I see your papers, both of you?" Captain Hiller and the MP handed over their ID papers and I compared them. It suddenly dawned on me what was wrong. "His are fakes."

"Mine?" The MP asked. Hiller casually reached for his weapon.

"No," I held up the dead major's, "his are. Look at mine and yours compared to his. Do you see what's wrong?"

The two studied the papers. "No," Hiller said.

"Look," I pointed to the top of the paper, "See here, it says 'Not A Pass-For Indentification Only.' If you'll notice, you'll see our papers have an extra 'n' that misspells identification, but not on these. The Major's papers are correctly spelled."

Hiller grunted in astonishment. "He's a German infiltrator. That's why Hanson saw they were rigging the bridge wrong; these bastards were just playing the part. I'm sure once the Germans appeared, they'd kill you and your men."

The MP Captain was confused. "You mean these papers are so expertly forged that it's too perfect then the real thing?"

"Check the other dead and compare their papers to ours," I said. "You'll see theirs are all flawless when compared to ours."

"If these guys are here, then where else could they be?" He asked.

Hiller just shrugged and he looked at the bodies. "Hanson, get this bridge rigged the right way!" he ordered. "Captain, have our men gathering what you can from the dead while my men provide cover."

The MP captain nodded, and the engineers raced about to prep the bridge to blow, using some of the gear still left from the Germans. I stood back, with the Captain, and just watched as the bodies were searched and striped of any useable gear and ID papers before being lined up, in a shallow gully, running alongside the road, on the German side of the bridge. Captain Waters, the MP Officer, made it a point to have someone to write "NAZI SPIES-ANY AND ALL WILL BE SHOT ON SIGHT," on a piece of paper and dangled it from a tree branch, over the bodies, all of which, had a bullet hole in the forehead from some angry MPs.

"They're clever," Hiller grunted, replacing the bandage, on his arm.

I agreed. "Very clever, sir, sneaking their men, into our lines to sabotage us, while making every GI suspicious of one another."

Hiller handed me a small bag holding the falsified papers and dog tags. "We'll need to hand this over to HQ, so hang on to it."

"How's your arm, sir?" I asked, taking the bag and slipping it into my pack.

The Captain held out his arm for inspection. "The bullet went right through the meat, but it's close to the skin. If I moved just a little bit to the right I could've missed it or just be grazed."

Gram's tank sat idly, across the road from us, Gram and his loader Sergeant Murphy sitting through the top hatches. Murphy manned the turret .50cal machine gun while Gram watched the horizon with his binoculars. "Germans approaching!" he suddenly yelled.

Hiller and I jumped into action and the squad reacted. They didn't need orders and quickly moved into cover, to set up defensive positions. The engineers worked on, without care. "How many?" Hiller asked.

"Two Tigers and three dozen infantry," Gram answered, dropping the binoculars. "No way can we stop them with just my Sherman."

"Hanson!" I called out, to the young officer.

"Sir?" he asked as he appeared from the underside of the bridge.

"Are the charges in place yet?" I asked.

Hanson glanced over his shoulder. "Just about, we're setting up the last of the wiring."

"Hurry up and stretch a line to there," I pointed to the low, tree covered ridge just off the bridge. "Get the detonator ready behind some cover."

"We drop the bridge no matter what," Hiller ordered, "but let's try and lure them on the bridge. Gram, move this tank off the road, but let it be seen from the road. Make it look like you're stalled out, so we give the Germans something."

Gram looked crushed. "You want me to give up my girl?"

"One empty Sherman, for a Tiger, is a good trade off," he explained. "Is that a problem?"

He relented. "No, sir, we'll get it done." Gram disappeared back into his tank as it rumbled down the road.

Hiller pointed to the ridge. "Let' go, the Germans won't be too far off."

The engineers moved quickly with the final touches, to the explosives, before running the detonation plunger back, up to the ridge. Captain Hiller and I were trying to get the wounded MPs into the trees as the squad lay in wait before us. The engineers finished their work. Hanson was already connecting the last wires to the plunger and Gram and his tank crew finished setting up their decoy. Ignoring the protests, from the crew, Gram sabotaged the tank's engine to start billowing smoke, a beacon for the enemy Tigers.

"I want everyone in the trees, move!" Hiller ordered. "No one is to open fire until I give the order!"

"Forward scouts on approach!" Jay called out from somewhere in the tree line.

Hiller returned to using hand signals and moved everyone, onto the ridge, and into the trees. Hiller and I were the last two people, on the road, when the Tiger spotted our stalled Sherman. A single shot, from the 88mm gun, turned several tons of American steel into smoldering shrapnel and a blackened crater in the snow.

I dropped down behind a tree and lay prone. A dozen German foot soldiers in grayish-white appeared near the bridge. The group saw they're dead comrades in the ditch and then saw the dead MPs on the road. Hiller had the dead left there to sell the idea of a firefight with our tank damaged and stalled out. Hanson and his men cleverly hid most of their explosives, well enough, that only a close inspection would find them.

An officer shouted orders in German, sending the scouts across the bridge. I lay still and watched the two trailing Tigers crawl up the road, with the rest of the infantry. We still held fire. Another infantry squad crossed over, with the Tigers splitting up. One of the armored monsters rolled to a stop, at the side of the road, while the second began to roll across the stone bridge.

Someone fired from our lines, a single rifle shot that brought hell suddenly to us.

German troops dove for cover and quickly opened up on our lines with unwavering rifle and machine gun fire. Both Tigers swiveled their turrets, to face us, and opened up with their fearsome 88mm main guns. Twin explosions tore apart the area near the plunger the engineers set up. The six or seven engineers huddled nearby were incinerated in a heartbeat.

"Pull back!" Hiller ordered as we returned fire, "Pull back!"

Another tank shell slammed into our lines and brought a towering tree down,with a shower of splinters. Hiller was moving for the plunger just as the tree came down, a sudden explosion of snow washing over him. I jumped up and ran towards his position. Hanson ran for the plunger, to drop the bridge.

"Captain!" I called out. I found the down tree, but not Hiller. "Captain?"

A low groan somehow reached me, over the roar, of the gun fire. "Stuck," Hiller moaned a few feet away.

I approached and found Captain Hiller stuck under the tree, his body pinned under the tree and against a rock. Blood was running down his cheeks and forehead from shrapnel wounds and even more was running from his mouth.

"Medic!" I yelled, dropping down next to him.

Hiller slapped my leg with his free hand. "Won't do any good," he groaned. "My legs are crushed and this tree is doing the same to my chest. The squad's yours, so get them the hell out of here." Hiller yanked off one his dog tags and handed it to me. "Now go, that's an order!"

I wanted to refuse and get him free, but there was just no way of doing that. I didn't linger and I issued the retreat order. Only the squad was left, the MPs dead and Hanson being the last of the engineers. German forces were still fast in moving across the bridge with the first Tiger just about to cross. I looked around for the plunger and spotted Hanson running for it.

The young lieutenant reached the plunger in time, pressing down on the detonator and setting off the explosives. It was quick, as the bridge supports were suddenly blown out from under the Germans, several infantry, near the tank, being tossed into the river. The Tiger tried to continue across, but the bridge just gave way and dragged the monstrous tank into the icy water. Hanson cheered. The crossing was denied to the Germans. Gram's face beamed with pride just as a sniper's bullet ripped through his helmet, just above his right temple.

"Pull back now!" I ordered one last time before taking my own advice.

Tucking Hiller's dog tag into my jacket pocket, I turned and began to run deeper into the trees. The squad was pulling back around me, moving close together as to not get lost or separated. We moved south, to avoid the Germans, my plan to keep going far enough to lose the Germans before turning west to St. Vith. I ran for as long as I could, ordering everyone to stop and regroup. The forest around us was silent.

"Head count," I mumbled to myself and counted each member of the squad. Surprisingly everyone was accounted for included Gram and his tank crew.

"We're missing the Captain," Nate pointed out.

I shook my head. "He's gone," was all I said. Everyone instantly understood and went silent just like when Hanes was killed back in France.

"Orders, sir?" Jay asked.

I looked around and saw everyone was on edge. "Let's take a minute to catch our breath then we'll head to St. Vith."

I dropped down, to the ground, and leaned against a tree, taking a quick sip from my near dry canteen. My throat burned with pain as I gulped down the near frozen liquid. I felt sweat collecting under my helmet and in my hands. My stomach was a knot and I just felt so numb all over.

"Did you get hit?" Doc asked, crouching down in front of me.

"What?" I asked. "No, I'm fine."

Doc sighed. "You're very pale and sweating in single digit temperatures, sir." He removed my helmet and placed the back of his hand to my forehead.

"You my mother know?" I asked.

Doc pulled his hand back. "You're really warm, Corr. Everyone is sick with something out here, but this looks serious. How's your throat feel?"

"Dry and sore," I admitted.

"Uh-huh, and what about headaches and migraines? Do they make you feel dizzy or disorientated?" He asked.

I waved off his concern. "Relax, Doc. I got a little bug or something, you said it yourself that we all got something. I'm sure it's nothing a little sleep and some warm food won't fix."

Doc was less then pleased. "Corr, even the smallest bug out here can kill you."

I stood up and collected myself. "Might, Doc. Alright squad, let's move out!"

I collected the squad together and we began to march south. Adam had given me an area map, and I plotted out a route that would take us another mile south before turning and heading west, for another mile, and half to reach St. Vith. While we could easily make the trip in a few hours, we would be slowed by another snowstorm which was just starting to move in.

Endless marching was what if felt like as soon as the snowstorm hit. Ruthless winds and falling snow had to have dropped the temperature by another six or seven degrees while fatigue added weight to my equipment. A horrible migraine tore at the inside of my skull, with an endless throbbing, as sweat soaked m hair and rolled down my forehead. I had already drained my canteens of water and my throat continued to burn and itch, forcing me to constantly rub my throat every few minutes. I worked hard to dismiss the discomfort, but I slowly began to panic as my vision blurred and the world seemed to spin around me. Suddenly the cold snow rushed from under my boots and washed over my face, turning the world around me white before turning black.

Chapter 19
One week later

It was almost impossible to move, my muscles not really responding to me. I struggled to open my eyes, my vision stilled blurred before clearing up enough for me to see I was looking up at a wooden ceiling. I suddenly realized I was indoors somewhere and warm for once, the bite of the cold air now gone. A heavy wool blanket was wrapped around me as I lay in a comfortable bed. It was a great improvement from sleeping in the dirt.

Sitting up, I took in my surroundings. The room was rather spacious with small, wooden nightstands, on either side of the bed, with candles burning sitting on top. A small glass window colored white by snow was off to the left side of the room with a large wooden stove nearby, the fire burning warmly and heating the room. A small table and chair was pressed against the wall, across from me, with my gear, neatly spread out on it.

There was the sound of movement outside the door. Unsure of just where I was, I crept out of the bed and grabbed the.45 from the stack,of my gear, on the table. Working the side slowly to cut back on noise, I leveled the barrel, at the door, and readied to fire. The door creaked open and a young woman stepped in wearing about several layers of clothes just like every civilian in the area.

She stopped in the doorway as she saw me with my pistol held ready to fire. Swearing under my breath I pulled back the.45 and thumbed the safety, lowering the weapon, to my side. The women looked about twenty, or so, with light brown hair and greenish brown eyes, which didn't go wide with fear when she saw me. She spoke to me in a language I didn't know, but sounded like Belgian.

"Do you speak French?" I asked first, in French.

She nodded, carrying over a tray with a bowl of soup on it. "You shouldn't be out of bed."

"And just who are you and where am I?" I asked still holding my pistol at my side.

"My name is Claudia and this is my home." She placed the tray on a nightstand. "You've been very ill this past week and have been drifting in and out of consciousness. Please sit down and relax, the rest of your men are here…"

Jay appeared in the doorway, hands resting on his dual pistols hanging under his arms. He looked a lot better than I remember, from the day at the bridge. "Good to see you're finally up," he said.

"Where are we?" I asked.

"Somewhere two-three miles east of St. Vith," he answered, as we shook hands. "You passed out when we were still pulling back from the bridge. You have a very bad case of flu. Doc told us you could die if we didn't find shelter, so Nate and I scouted out the area and found Claudia and her daughter living out here. She was more than happy to take us in, while Doc treated you."

I nodded. "And I've been out for a week?"

Jay nodded grimly. "Yeah, you were in and out of it the whole time, but I guess you're past it now."

"Hopefully." I collected my kit and threw on my gear webbing before checking my Thompson. "You'll need to fill me in on everything that's happened, in the last week."

Jay nodded and led me into the hallway outside. It was a short walk, to a flight of stairs, that lead to the ground floor which held a medium sized kitchen, a living room, and some sort of storage area. "I had to carry your dead weight ass all the way here, by the way."

"I'm so grateful," I stated sarcastically. "How's the rest of the squad?"

"Everyone's okay now, Claudia was nice enough to share her food with us and gave us a warm place to sleep. Gram and his tank crew are with us as well, we gave them some Kraut weapons to help out."

We walked into the kitchen where Nate and Adam sat huddled by a large fireplace, Nate fast asleep while Adam was tinkering, with our disassembled radio. Vic was propped up in a chair near the door, BAR held firm across his chest.

"Any word from Philips or any part of division?" I asked.

"Just momentary radio messages come in, but we can't call out." He nodded to Adam. "Adam picked up a few bits on the German advance and it's not good. German forces have pushed a huge bulge, in the line, and have advanced far into our territory. Bastogne has been completely encircled, with the boys in the 101st and 82nd. Besides that, we're blind."

I sat down at the table and picked up my area map. "Have you sent out scouts to recon the area?"

Jay nodded, pointing on the map. "I sent out Ramos and Mangon to check the surrounding area, for about a mile, around us. From what they tell me, this area is behind enemy lines. Kraut patrols are everywhere and it's a wonder they haven't found us yet."

Sighing, I dropped the map. "We can't stay here for much longer; the German's will find this place at some point."

Jay was about to speak as the front door opened with a blast of cold air and a swirl of snow, a tightly bundled up Ramos and Mangon rushing inside. The two quickly rushed over to the fire place and tried to warm up.

"Feeling better, Corr?" Ramos asked. He shivered, trying to fill two metal cups with coffee.

"Just ever so wonderful," I sighed sarcastically. "How'd it go out there?"

Mangon shivered and he sat down. He pulled out his notepad and map. "Not that well at all, sir. Ramos and I barely got a mile out before we stumbled on a German patrol just south of here. We avoided getting spotted, but they were a lot of them." He flipped open the notepad. "It's all SS forces in this area with heavy armor crawling all over the roads. We tried to reach the road leading to St. Vith, but had to pull back as truck loads of infantry and a few billion tons of German steel were passing by."

I shook my head. "They must be trying to take St. Vith with so much firepower. Looks like we can't go back there." I picked the map up again and read over it. "The next city we can reach is Malmedy which is farther away from St. Vith. There is a forward recon post north of here, on the river, that's just two miles away, but there's no way to tell if it's there still."

Artillery fire rumbled off, to the south, causing some dust to fall from the ceiling rafters. The sudden rumble was nothing to us, until the louder rumbled of an engine clattered, in the distance. Everyone was up and reaching for their weapons as the front door flew open and Malks rushed in.

"Two Kraut halftracks on approach!" he yelled.

I grabbed my Thompson. I didn't think, just reacted. "Get the squad out of sight fast and let's keep an eye on the Germans," I ordered, moving to the door. "If they're scavengers or scouts let's just watch them."

"Follow me," Jay said, taking the lead outside.

The snowstorm was still hanging, in the area, and visibility was cut down severely. The large cabin we were in was the only building, in the area, amongst the thick tree cover. I couldn't see anyone else from the squad. Jay took me to his small sniper nest, in the trees, a dozen yards away, from the cabin. The two of us huddled down, in a shallow foxhole, covered by branches and mounds of snow.

"We already planned for this," he explained. "Don't worry, I kept things intact."

"Thanks Jay, I know your one hell of a sergeant," I said like I somehow insulted him.

Jay just laughed and he readied his sniper rifle. "Easy boss."

The two of us lay still, on the ground, as the growl of the halftrack engines grew louder off to the east. It wasn't long before a pair of gray halftracks emerged from the trees, and rolled to a stop in front of the cabin. From my position, I counted a dozen enemy soldiers inside the tracks, all wrapped up in white winter gear, with one officer in a gray uniform and bulky winter coat with black, leather gloves.

"Lined up," Jay whispered. He tracked the officer through his scope.

"Hold fire," I whispered back.

With the winds and our distance away, it was difficult to hear orders the officer was giving, but the soldiers were spreading out, to cover the area. The officer took a pair of soldiers with him, inside the cabin, while the rest patrolled outside. Judging by the way they held their weapons and the way they stood, all of them were not too concerned about running into us.

I couldn't hear anything, in the cabin, and just kept still watching the soldiers outside. I didn't know where any of the squad was spread out, but I was sure they were keeping their weapons trained, on the Germans. Something came from inside the cabin that made my heart stop for a second.

"Was that a scream?" I whispered.

The soldiers outside turned to face the cabin with weapons shouldered as another two marched inside. There was no more noise or movement for several seconds before a child, Claudia's child, ran from the cabin and past the soldiers. One or two tried to grab her, but she just ran straight into the woods.

Phelps will reach her," Jay grunted as I slowly stood up. "What are you doing?"

"Helping Claudia." I said.

I didn't say anything more. I got into a crouch and moved along the edge of the trees. The nearest German was about a dozen yards away and not looking in my direction. I crept closer to the cabin. I had to move slowly and keep behind the trees, to avoid being spotted. The enemy soldiers outside turned back, watching the woods just as I reached the rear of the cabin. There was no back door and all the windows were cover by thick curtains, so the only way in was the front door.

Six men were out front, only two blocked, by the halftracks. The first four would be easy to kill, with a quick burst or two of machine gun fire, but that would alert the others. Two would be easy to stop before they spotted me while the officer and four men inside would have cover and a chance to hit me back.

Hugging the wall of the cabin, I could hear muffled voices inside. I couldn't make out words, but the tone suggested things were about to get less then friendly. I moved to the edge of the cabin and ducked down, the closest soldier a mere four feet away, with his back to me. Across the ground, to the opposite tree line, I spotted Adam and Nate signaling me.

The two were in cover, but we could see one another without being spotted. With a few hand signals, I moved them to the German's left flank, behind the second halftrack, which put them in position to hit the two I couldn't see and cover the cabin door. Jay was still tracking the Germans and was covering the one farthest away from me, without being told to. The bonds between soldiers removed the need to talk to communicate.

A three round burst, to the soldier's back, across from me, tore through his spine and dropped him. Two more turned, to face me, as the third lost half his face to Jay's shot, but they didn't get a chance to fire. My rounds cut across their chests as Adam and Nate killed the remaining two opposite the halftracks. I didn't stop and ran, for the cabin door, as I swapped out clips and fought to control myself, with adrenaline rushing through my body.

Two German soldiers rushed outside just as I stopped off to the right of the door. My finger squeezed the trigger and took one, with a burst, to the face, and the other, with another to the chest. Adam was up, across from me, and glanced inside, quickly pulling back as a volley of shots splintered the door frame. He held up three fingers meaning one officer and two riflemen. A single finger, with his other hand, meant one civilian.

Nate rushed up to the cabin, with Malks following, the two stopped behind me. "Head around back," I whispered to Malks, "and bash in a window to grab their attention. Nate, follow me in once the glass breaks."

Malks rushed off without a word, more gunfire echoed inside. They had at least two semi-automatic rifles and one MP-40 as well as good covering position, on the door. We would have to be quick, to spot and kill, the three before they could do the same to us. Glass shattered and I jumped.

I had both feet inside and forced myself to move, to the right, as I spotted the Germans were using the kitchen table as a barricade. There were two soldiers behind the table, but Claudia and the officer were nowhere to be seen. Nate was right behind me and didn't hesitate to empty an entire rifle clip, into the two Germans. I wasn't aware of the shooting as the two fell and I rushed past towards the small living room.

The officer had tossed Claudia to the ground and was about to turn his MP-40 on her when I entered the room. My eyes locked with the officer's. He spun the MP-40 around to fire at me, but I had my Thompson shouldered already and I fired first. In an instant, an entire twenty round clip was emptied, into the German, and I was standing still, with my finger still pressed down, on the trigger.

"We're clear," I managed to grunt, lowering my weapon.

"You hit?" Nate asked, moving to help Claudia.

"Ah, no." I didn't linger inside and returned, to the front of the cabin, as the squad regrouped. Jay approached me first.

"All clear inside?" he asked.

I nodded. "She's fine, what about her daughter?"

Jay nodded towards the trees as Phelps appeared, with the little girl, in his arms. "Short of being scared, she's fine. What are your orders?"

"Search the dead for anything we can use then get everyone ready to move. We can't stay here for much longer and this patrol will be missed, at some point."

Jay agreed. "Just where do we go from here and what do we do, with Claudia and her daughter?"

"We should take them with us, but can we?" I sighed.

"Well we can't leave them behind." He gestured to the dead soldiers. "What'll happen when more German patrols come looking for them?"

"Do not worry," Claudia was standing in the doorway with Nate, "My daughter and I have avoided the Germans before and we can do it again."

"You'll get whatever supplies we can spare," I said.

Phelps returned her daughter.

"Nate, give them what we can spare and then help, with the dead. Let's move fast, we need to roll, in half an hour."

"Just what the hell have we become, huh?" Adam had become the most vocal of the squad since we left behind that poor woman and her daughter. "We're supposed to help these people, yet we just leave them when it suites us?"

Nate worked to keep him calm. "What could we have done different, Adam? Huh, tell me. Nothing, we could've done, nothing else to help. The Germans are looking for their missing patrol and we couldn't stay there."

"Adam's got a point," Malks agreed. I had kept quiet for the most part as we marched north, my own thoughts just as conflicted as anyone in the squad, but I needed to do something. I was the leader of the squad and had to set things straight.

"Look," I said without breaking stride, "we've been fighting together since, what, Oran? It's all most been three years that we've been fighting and is anything as black and white as we thought? We can't help every single person we come across during this war, it's just not possible."

"Then how do we tell who deserves our help?" Adam snapped.

I kept my anger in check. I hated all of this as much as all of them did. "They all do, Adam. Each and every poor civilian displaced, by this God damn war, deserves and needs our help, but there's only so much help that can be given. Think back to the times when we couldn't help. Have you ever wondered why we couldn't help?"

It was a rhetorical question.

"We stop to help everyone we come across and we can't help ourselves. If we stayed back there, the Germans would've killed each and every one of us and that would have been it. Each of you would be dead and become another number, on a causality list."

"But…" I cut off Adam quickly. Hiller taught me that being a real leader meant keeping our men alive and in line.

"Like it or not, my duty is to get each of you through this war alive and back home. To make sure this happens, we need to stop the Nazis. It doesn't matter how many we help along the way because everyday Hitler leads the Nazis, thousands upon thousands of more people die. You want to help all these people? Then you stop the problem at its source."

Adam went quiet as did the rest of the squad as we marched on. I wanted to help every civilian caught up in the fighting, each of us did, it's just our nature, but rarely was it possible. We needed to have the mentality of getting the job done and our job was to stop the Nazis. But how much of your humanity are you willing to trade away? The words constantly played across my mind, with each day that passed.

Some movement, off to our right, grabbed my attention and snapped me back to reality. I held up a fist, to signal a halt, and dropped down, to one knee. The forest around us was still silent and calm, but nightfall was just beginning and it would be very dangerous, to stumble around, in the dark.

"Do you hear that?" Jay whispered as he pressed himself against a tree.

I removed my helmet to hear better, the only noise coming from the howl of the wind. Closing my eyes, I could just pick up the faint murmur of voices coming from our right and front. I dropped down, to my stomach, and crawled forward, with great care, until the voices became a little bit clearer. I couldn't really make out most of what was being said, but whoever was speaking, was speaking in German.

I rolled, to my back, to face the squad and issued a series of orders, through hand signals. With no real count on how many soldiers we faced, I ordered the squad,to remain low and still, to avoid detection and not to open fire, unless I did. Ammo was still a problem and we would avoid firefights at every point possible.

Gram and his crew were doing really well, for makeshift infantry, but got a little jump as we waited. Sergeant Donovan kept very still, but his eyes darted about and the German rifle shook, in his hands. I looked, at the young sergeant, for a second, to judge his current status, when a rifle fired with a loud, hard crack! It wasn't Donovan who fired, but the single shot was quickly answered by a snarling volley, from my men.

The enemy patrol fired back, with concentrated rifle and machine gun fire, on our position, they having been a lot closer to us than I realized. Bullets harmlessly thwacked, into the hard packed snow and trees, as I fired back, at the muzzle flashes. Private Gold, Gram's driver, suddenly screamed out in pain as a bullet tore into his side, with the wet crunch of bone.

"Medic!" Donovan cried out. He still worked the bolt, on his rifle.

The sudden buzz saw noise, of an MG42, cut through the rifle pops from the German position and tossed green tracers our way. I dropped my head down as the hail storm of bullets ripped, through the air, and shredded whatever they touched. I pushed myself back and rolled to my left, pressing my back, to the trunk of a tree.

I felt the tree shake and shutter with each bullet hit, snow from the branches falling, to the ground. Jay was laying prone several feet away near a low groove, in the dirt, with his Springfield tucked unmoving into his shoulder and his right eye resting against the metal scope. All hell could be rising around that young Sergeant and he would still work his rifle with slow, careful precision, making each and each every shot hit its mark.

"Shift!" I yelled out waving my arm, to the right. Vic quickly moved up and dropped down, with his BAR, on our right flank, the weapon soon firing in short bursts.

Another scream rang out from the battle, this one, from the German position. I rolled out, from the tree, dropping down, to the ground, with my weapon up. Rifle flashes snapped, across the forest and drew my attention, to a group of rifle men. I fired at them or just in their general direction, in the confusion, just to put rounds down range.

"There's another squad out there!" Edwards called out as a dozen or so more German soldiers materialized, to our left.

I swore under my breath and rolled back behind the tree, propping myself up to face the new attackers. The noise level was almost deafening now and I signaled Nate, Phelps, and Mangon, to shift fire to the left to meet the new force. Three rifle men couldn't hold back another squad, but anything, to hold them off was needed.

Jay signaled me from his position, with a wave of his hand. He tapped his rifle and held up his hand, folding his fingers, into a fist five times. He only had twenty five rounds left. I was replying when something grazed the side, of my helmet, with a hard clank. I dropped down lower as a bullet just missed, puncturing my helmet.

"We're being encircled!" Gram yelled out as he lay a few feet away. Private Passwell, the crew's loader, was dead next to him, with the snow around his head, now pink.

I signaled Jay, to get ready, to pull back, and the two of us passed the order down, through the squad. A quick retreat would leave us open, to be hit, in the back and encourage the Germans, to chase after us. At the same time, an unseen attack force could be waiting,to our rear, to hit us. Sitting around and thinking on it wasn't helping as bullets continued to whiz, through the air.

"Orders?" Nate called out as he dropped another empty clip, from his carbine.

I racked my brain for an answer when I suddenly noticed the German rifle and machine gun fire was tapering off, slowly lightening up on us. Bullets still impacted the snow around us, but the torrent that first slammed into us was now gone, replaced, by the slower crack and pop, of single rifle shots.

"Stay down," I whispered, looking towards the German positions ahead of us. "Something's not right here."

I pulled my binoculars from my jacket and scanned the snowy landscape ahead, several German soldiers easily spotted ducking behind trees, but I saw an officer. He was older then the men around him, he was maybe, in his forties, or so with sharp, strong features that just made it clear he was in charge.

"Americans!" the officer suddenly shouted, in accented English. "Surrender and you shall not be harmed!"

Jay and I glanced at one another at the sudden call, unbelieving some officer would stop a battle he would clearly win, to take prisoners. I looked back, to the others, in the squad, our two losses lying still, in the snow. Edwards was several feet away, Thompson cradled close, to his chest, and face set in determination.

"Orders?" he mouthed silently.

"Americans!" It was that officer again. "Will you surrender?"

I looked back to Jay, who already knew what I was thinking. That officer wanted an answer,to if we'd surrender, or not and Jay was going to give it. I rolled back to my chest and slipped my last full clip, into the Thompson as Jay was lining up his rifle, one hand gently adjusting the mounted scope. He didn't need a fire command.

"This is your last chance!" The officer didn't get to finish the cry, Jay's rifle cracked, with a hard snap, and hiss of air. There was no cry of pain, instead a wet thud and crack as the officer's head jerked back and he fell, to the ground.

Rifle and machine gun fire erupted, across the frozen battlefield, more cries rising up, from the German positions. Several grenades were tossed, into the trees, followed by the muffled thumps of explosions and the flying dirt and snow, into the air. Several screams were silenced as wounded men died, a merciful relief as, even with my limited German, I could hear men crying names as they died.

It was absolutely gut wrenching, to hear, when you know you're the one killing people. All across North Africa, Sicily, Normandy, and Belgium I heard the cries. The names were varied, though many were heard over and over again. Lisa! Ann! Emma! Mary! It happened over and over again; dying men calling out, to the one person, they loved the most, in their short lives. And, of course, there was the worst of all, Mama!

"Stay low! Stay low!" I called out as a grenade exploded several feet away from me. My body was protected by a tree and a thick snow drift, though I felt heat prickle, across my face, from passing shrapnel.

There was a screech of pain, off to my left, and then the splatter of something warm against my neck and back. I rolled, to my right, and brought my Thompson up as a German soldier fell, to the snow, inches from me, an unprimed stick grenade in hand. I looked to my right and saw Edwards looking towards me, small curls of smoke rising from the barrel of his Thompson. I just nodded, no real proper way to thank such an act possible.

"Flanking force to the rear!" Sergeant Donavan shouted.

I rolled to my back and fired towards the trees, to our rear, bullets cutting through several Germans crossing open ground. More followed as I drained the rest of my clip, hands fumbling, I yanked out a fresh one, from my pocket, and slammed it home, my hand yanking back, on the bolt. Several rifle shots slammed, into the tree, behind me and I swung around,to face the new threat. They're gonna slaughter us! I squeezed the trigger, several rounds finding theirs marks, in the man's face. Something felt wrong as I targeted another German and I depressed the trigger, only to be answered by the metallic click of a dry weapon. Son of a…

"Boss!" Edwards called out, my eye catching the glimmer of a clip flying through the air. "Got your back!"

I caught the clip one handed and rammed it, into the weapon, the bolt being yanked back again and a round chambered. The next soldier I saw took a belly full of lead, before falling, to the snow. My mind struggled, to accurately count, just how many Germans we had killed as there could not be an endless amount attacking us, though it sure as hell felt like it. Jay had given up with his sniper rifle and was now using his.45s, though he didn't wield both,in his hands, instead using one at a time to conserve ammo. It was relieving to hear Vic's BAR still going loud and proud.

Again my weapon was dry and I drew my.45, the handy sidearm now chewing through my reserve clips. It would be just a matter of minutes or seconds before it would be hand to hand,with knifes and fists. The crazed cries of a charging soldier alerted me in time,to see a steel bayonet, stab for my chest. I was quick, pulling back, with just space to spare, as the blade rammed,into the ground, and I shoved my.45 into the attacker's chest, three rounds punching, through his back.

His sudden dead weight pushed against me and I fell back, to the ground, with him on top of me. I forced the body off me and scrambled, to reload, as more soldiers advanced, on our position. Another man attacked, bayonet fixed to his rifle, and I could not reload so I pulled my knife, from its sheath, and rushed head long into him. I ducked low and pushed up to force the rifle away while brining my right hand to his face. I slammed down with full force, the blade slicing, into the gap, between his neck and shoulders. The soldier shrieked, in pain, as I withdrew the blade and delivered another savage blow that sliced clean across his throat.

Adrenaline kept me moving without fatigue, though pure animal instinct and rage blocked out the horrific sights of the dead and dying by giving me tunnel vision that focused, on the nearest German. I reloaded my.45 and dropped another two soldiers before I threw myself, to the dirt, for cover. Another explosion, more screams, rifle pops, and then silence.

At first, all I could hear was the sound of my breathing, heavy and labored. My heart was beating rapidly, the hard thumping echoing, through my skull. I looked up and saw nothing moved around me, though I did see the squad keeping alert for more attacks. I swallowed hard, my throat sore, and eased back to my feet, one holding my.45 while the other held my Thompson firm slung over my shoulder.

"Who's hit?" I called out, stumbling, to the group of men.

"Two dead," Jay whispered as a few men stirred. "Both from Gram's crew."

I nodded numbly, taking a few a seconds, to compose myself, everything still feeling strange as the adrenaline tapered off. I felt my hands trembling and there was a swagger, to my steps, that would mark a drunk at first glance. Jay moved the same way as he stood up and checked over the squad. I stumbled around and counted the German dead, forty, in all, the snow now colored red and pink.

"Sure had us outnumbered," Vic stated as he stood up, the area around his feet littered, with spent shells, from the BAR.

I glanced around the silent trees. "No telling how many more are out there. Gather up what you can, from the dead, and take anything useful." I looked to Gram. "We can't take the dead with us."

He nodded and agreed somberly, taking the dog tags from the two of his fallen crew. Edwards handed me one of his last two clips, before scavenging grenades, from a dead German. I looked past the dead, part of me not wanting to even look at them. Death was something well known to me, having caused some of it, not proudly, myself. Many times I'd seen smoldering piles, of ash, be all that was left, of what was once a person, a person. Still, you can't look a man in the eye as you took his life without feeling…something.

"How are we going to continue on, sir?" Nate asked, I now realized that the sun was all but gone, from the sky.

"We push on," I answered as I reloaded my Thompson. "Our ammo is almost gone and we need to reach friendly lines, so we keep moving."

No one spoke, no complained, instead choosing to remain silent and we continued to move forward through the trees. We left behind all of the dead and what we couldn't take, where they had fallen, a clear sign of a fight to anyone else, who would stumble across it. Night was fast on us, the temperature again plummeting back down, into the negatives and snow failing like rain. Harsh winds smacked our bodies and blew snow, into our faces, the cold making it hard to even see strait.

I kept my scarf wrapped over my mouth and nose, only my eyes taking the brunt of the cold. My hands were clenched,onto the Thompson, held tucked into my shoulder, all feeling now gone and replaced by empty numbness. Malks and Edwards were close by me, both coughing and sneezing, in irregular intervals, that were muffled by the wind. Still, they showed no signs of slowing down, no complaining, and no bitching of any type.

"We won't last long if this keeps up," Doc whispered, appearing, on my left.

I glanced over, seeing Doc shivering, trying to hold both hands, in his pockets, head down, to block out the wind. "No real place to get out of the cold."

Doc sighed. "Yea, but the elements are as bad as the Germans. We need shelter and time to rest, you need it more than any of us."

"I'm cured, remember?" I shot back, my throat still tingling, with pain.

"Don't fool yourself, sir. Sure we helped you out before, but you're still sick."

God damn it, doc! I kept my thoughts in check, the man doing just what he was trained to do. I just shrugged, finding no way to tell Doc off, without saying it directly, to him. I wouldn't of course, the man deserved all the respect in the world just like the rest of the squad. He was right, of course, we needed shelter, from the weather, at least for one night. Of course anything that could be used as a reasonable shelter would most likely draw any approaching group of soldiers.

The trees were thinning out as we approached one, of a handful, of traversable roads that cut, through the thick forests. I ordered the group to halt and move up ahead with Jay, the two of us belly crawling forward, to a fallen tree, a few dozen yards away from the road. It was dark, the blowing snow, in the air, cutting back even more on the visibility. Still, I pulled out my binoculars and scanned the road while pulling out my map.

"I don't hear anything," he whispered while laying prone, next to me.

The road was empty and barren. "Don't see a thing either." I tucked away the binoculars and took a look at the map. "The outpost is here and we're about here." I ran a cold finger over the map, tapping the paper.

"So this is Route 12?" Jay asked, looking over my shoulder.

I studied the faded paper. "I would think so. If that's right then we need to…" The two of us looked up as engine sputtered to life out in the distance, the muffled thumps and cracks of machine gun fire following.

I pressed myself deeper, into the ground, and aimed towards the roadway, the sounds now getting louder. There was the unique buzz saw sound of MG-42s along with the lower pitched cracks of the.30 and.50cal machine guns, our machine guns. I glanced at Jay as an M8 Greyhound armored car darted, across the road, and rolled to a stop beside the trees. The turret gunner was watching the rear while leaning against the.50cal.

"Ours?" Jay asked.

I remembered the bridge. "Well, they are being shot at."

I nodded forward and rose up into a crouch, moving closer, to the road. More machine gun fire and muffled explosions echoed, to the east, as one of our halftracks thundered down the road. Moving slowly, I stopped by the road and ducked down, in a ditch. The turret gunner didn't see me at my first, so I kept pressed, into the dirt, and raised my Thompson over my head one handed, a signal, to him,to not shoot.

The gunner spotted the raised weapon and swung my way, several bursts, from the mounted.50cal punching, into the ground around me. "Fuck!" I yelled out as the rounds came close to hitting. "Hold fire! Hold fire!"

"Out, to where I can see you!" the gunner ordered, still aiming our way.

"Shit, don't fucking fire at us!" I yelled back, slowly rolling back, to my feet, and carefully climbing out, of the ditch. I held my Thompson over my head and slowly walked forward. The gunner tracked me with the machine gun and kept his fingers hovering over the trigger.

"What the hell are you doing?" that came from another soldier, who was in the halftrack.

I turned, the track's.50cal pointed, at my chest. "My squad got lost after the attack and we need help getting back, to the line."

The soldier laughed. "The damn attack is still going on." Another artillery explosion echoed to add emphasis to the trooper's point. "You get your men then get their asses aboard this echoed to add emphasis to the trooper's point. "You get your men then get their asses aboard this track."

Jay was already back in the trees gathering up the squad, who quickly emerged from the forest. They were more than happy to jump on the first chance, to get, to Allied lines. More explosions echoed,from down the road, with the constant chatter of machine gun fire. I wondered just who was taking on the Germans. I quickly climbed, into the rear of the halftrack, finding four other men inside that were just about covered in bloodied bandages from head to toe.

"This all of your men?" the trooper asked, the remains of Sergeant's stripes on his jacket.

I did a headcount, of the squad, and Gram's crew. "All here, go."

The sergeant ordered the driver forward, the Greyhound pulling ahead of us. I dropped down, onto the bench, behind the sergeant, resting my Thompson across my lap. The squad was tightly packed, into the track, as it bounced across the road and raced away from the fighting. It took maybe twenty minutes of driving, on the barren, before the sounds of battled tapered off.

"So, who are you with?" the Sergeant asked as he looked over his shoulder.

"First Infantry," I answered, "out of Elsenborn."

He grunted. "83rd Mechanized with the 9th. They put us on the southern edge of our division and we got lost, in the fighting. You got a map? We lost ours couple days ago."

I nodded, pulling out my map. "We're on Route 12."

He took the map, studying it closely. A few grunts latter, he handed it back. "At least we're running in the right direction."

I took the map. "Who was left back there?"

The Sergeant sighed, running a hand, over his mouth. "In my combat group, I had eight halftracks, six Greyhounds, five tank destroyers, and two jeeps. What you see here is what's left, of that group. My CO was killed the first night, of the attack, and we've been losing guys just about every day."

I silently nodded, looking at the wounded men, under the sergeant's command. Odds were that other squads would fair far worse than us during all this, during the war for that matter, but it felt…strange, to see it. Sighing, I dropped my head, down to my chest, and stared, at the metal floor.

We were taking back, to division HQ, in Elsenborn by the time morning arrived, the rising sun showing the damage done, to the city. Heavy fighting tore, at the men hold up inside, losses mounting as they fought back German attacks day and night. With no air support, to back them up, German armor could've easily overrun the city days earlier, but there were several artillery batteries set up, on a nearby hill, that held back the tide.

The halftrack rolled, to a stop, near the HQ and let us off. The sergeant, who's name I never caught, didn't say a word before quickly pulling off and disappearing, into the traffic clogging the streets. I took the squad,to the HQ building, and left them, to wait outside, Gram and Jay heading in, with me.

The HQ building had sustained heavy damage during the attacks, a dozen or so officers killed by several mortar hits. Major Philips and his, Lieutenant Hasel were both unharmed, though the two were on edge, from lack of sleep, and the constant attacks. Hasel didn't even flinch when I reported Hiller was KIA, though Philips was more receptive.

"How?" was all Philips asked as he took the dog tag.

"Artillery strike when we were dropping the bridge, sir," I explained. I then told him of the Germans, in American uniforms, and our retreat back, to base afterwards.

"We got a few of those spies here." Philips drank from a mess cup, the coffee inside ice cold. "Patrols spotted a few trying, to cut telephone wires and mine roads. We took four, out of a group, of thirty prisoner, who were wearing our uniforms, MPs and engineers mostly."

"What are our orders, sir?" I asked.

Philips didn't answer right away, instead looking at the map behind his desk. With a heavy sigh, he gestured to our position. "Really, I don't have anything specific besides help hold the line. The Germans have made a huge bulge, in our lines, that starts here and runs south past Bastogne, which is still encircled. Rumors are going around that Patton is driving north to help, but I don't know, for sure."

Philips stopped, suddenly deep in thought.

"Wait, there is something you can do. German forces overran a fuel dump a few miles north, of here, before we could destroy it. SHAEF gave orders that we were to not allow our supplies, fuel especially, to fall, into German hands. If capture was imminent then the supplies are to be destroyed as best as possible.

"Now, the depot was captured several days ago so we have a chance to destroy it before the Germans get too much use from it. The weather is clearing up just enough, to allow the flyboys, to get into the air, for a day or two, at the most, so this is our chance. I want you to take your men, to the depot, and call in the Air Force, to blow it to hell. Don't worry, I'll make sure you'll get top priority, with the planes in our AO."

I nodded. "I'll get right to it, sir."

"And Lieutenant," he was speaking to Gram, "I've got a handful of Shermans, with no crews. You'll stay here, with your remaining crew, and help out with our armor detachment."

Gram stiffened and saluted. "Yes, sir."

"Best of luck to you out there. Oh," he held up a hand and reached, into his desk, "I'm deeply sorry for John's….Captain Hiller's death, but I need experienced officers." He handed me a set of captain's bars, these also worn and scuffed. "From here on, you're now in command of your squad."

Again, a salute. "Thank you, sir." I gushed.

Philips just nodded before turning his attention, to the map on the wall, tired eyes drifting over the newly drawn German positions. I left with Gram and returned to the squad out front waiting for us. I delivered the news to the men, laying out our new objectives and, to a lesser degree, my promotion, to captain.

"We'll need to take as much ammo as possible and then we'll make our way to the fuel depot. Adam, make sure that damn radio is working and we have an open link to the flyboys." I looked to

Gram and Sergeant Donovan, shaking both their hands. "Good luck out there."

Gram nodded his head. "Yea, we're gonna be needing it."

The surviving tank crew departed, for their new assignment, as we moved to the supply depot, to grab some much need ammo, for the operation ahead. I stuffed my empty ammo pouches and pockets, with as many spare ammo clips, as I could before we left. The fuel dump was a two hour walk, to the north, into the German lines, through mostly open ground.

Fuel was what the Germans wanted and needed, desperately. Bombing raids, into the heart of Germany, had destroyed the vast majority, of the country's oil stores, and the means, to pump or synthesize more, their powerful Panzer forces were burning up what reserves they had. It wouldn't take much time, before their tanks were useless hunks of steel, unmoving without gas. The Allies had stored millions, of gallons of gasoline, in Europe, in countless fuel depots, such as the critical port of Antwerp or the build ups from the undersea pipeline known as Operation Pluto. If the Germans managed to get enough fuel, they could stall out advance or even push us back, to the Channel.

"Hmm, seems like such a waste," Jay whispered, an eye pressed the scope of his Springfield.

"It'll be worth it," I said back observing the depot, through my binoculars. "You do see what I see?"

Jay grunted. "Think I'm blind? I see it."

We found the fuel depot, with a little struggle, it was not properly placed, on our maps. German forces, in the area, were relatively light, with mostly infantry, combing over the snowy landscape. We found a nice little surprise, at the depot, one that would normally want to be avoided, but these were special circumstances. Several dozen Panzer IVs, twenty Panthers, eight Tigers, and three King Tigers were inside the depot refueling.

"Jeez, we are some lucky sons a bitches, sir," Nate sighed, in awe, as he looked on with us.

I shrugged, waving Adam up. "Let's just hope they stay here for the time being. Did you reach the forward air observer?"

"On the line now, sir," Adam answered, holding the radio receiver.

I held a small note pad, in my hand, the coordinates scribbled down in pencil. To be safe, I double checked them on my map and then handed Adam the note pad. With a clear, calm voice, Adam relayed the information, to the forward air observer back in Elsenborn. There was a pause as the information was repeated back, for conformation. Adam cleared the coordinates and then we had to wait. We were laying prone, on a low rise, about a hundred yards from the depot, over only cover coming, from a handful of trees, that dotted the ridge. Several ridges circled the base, with better tree cover, but the Germans had scouts running around out there.

I glanced at my watch, the time just past noon. The sky still remained moderately clear, white clouds covering most, of the blue, above us. It took maybe five minutes, before our air support arrived, in the form of a wing of six P-51 Mustangs, each one colored silver, with the black and white invasion stripes, still present. The drone of their engines grabbed the attention of the Germans, at the depot, the infantry running, for cover, as tank crews ran, to their tanks.

German tanks could cut down infantry and crack armor, without trouble, but they stood no chance against our air cover. Swooping down, at steep angles, in pairs, the Mustangs ran strafing runs that tore apart infantry and rattled the tanks. A second pass brought the heavier fire power, of the fighters, barrages of rockets that ripped over the fuel stores like burning arrows. Explosions shook the ground as fires spread and fuel exploded. Barrels flashed over and rolling explosions consumed the German armor.

I felt some pity for the tankers as each Panzer, Panther, Tiger, and Kind Tiger were washed away, by flame and explosions. Several passes, with rocket and MG fire, quickly set off all the fuel, barrels popping like bombs and tanks exploding, as their ammo stores cooked off. In under seven minutes the air was heavy, with the oily smoke of burning fuel, as the entire depot was lost, in smoke and fire.

"Hell of a fireworks display, sir!" Malks cheered as the fighters broke off their attack.

Adam tapped my boot, grabbing my attention. "Flyboys are pulling out, rockets are gone. Major Philips requests confirmation that the depot has been destroyed."

I held out my hand and took the receiver. "Major Philips, sir?"

"Is the depot destroyed?" the Major asked.

I glanced at the fires. "Yes, sir. The fuel is in flames and about thirty, or so, pieces of Kraut armor, with it. We called in the strike as they were refueling."

"Heavy armor? Ah, shit it doesn't matter anyway, Kraut armor is armor. Alright, I have new objectives for you. The Air Force reports major movement, of enemy armor and infantry, making a hard push towards our HQ from the northeast, about two miles away, from your current position. Now they have got artillery covering their advance all the way, to my position, and have been pounding our positions. The Air Force will take out the arty and provide over watch, but cannot move in, at this time.

"Your objectives are as follows: You are to move northeast, to hill one-oh-seven, where the Germans have established their forward artillery. Now don't engage the artillery, instead target the AA positions, in the area, and then call in the flyboys. You've got to move quick here before the advance hits the city as we can't take this pounding for long. Copy?"

I nodded. "Copy that, sir. Swordsman out." The radio clicked off and I handed the receiver back to Adam. "We're heading to hill 107, to the north, we're to take out AA positions, to let the flyboys hit German arty positions. An attack is heading for Elsenborn so we gotta move double quick. Stick close and follow me."

We snaked our way back down the ridge, to level ground, and crossed back, into the trees. German artillery barked off, in the distance of hill 107, which was about a mile away from our position. A roadway, about a football field's length, of open fields, and another ridge lay before hill 107. German patrols still combed over the land, to cover the flank, of the main offensive, the destruction of the depot now a burning signal, to just about anyone,in the area for a few dozen miles. Approaching the roadway, from the trees, I could already hear vehicles moving, in our direction.

Everyone dropped down, to the deck, and scurried, for cover, as a pair of German halftracks rolled by, on the road, a squad of riflemen in each track. Close behind them was a convoy of twelve troop trucks, some carrying supplies, others troops. I was laying several feet, from the edge of the road, my only cover a clump of bushes and a small mound of snow. The ground vibrated under me as they rolled by, a German cigarette falling from one truck and landing, in front of my face.

I relaxed a bit once the convoy passed, slowly edging forward, to check, for anymore German troops coming down the road. The convoy was out of eyesight and the road, in the other direction, was clear so I rose up into a crouch and moved across, to the snow blanked field. There was no cover at all until the rise of the next ridge, a handful of trees and bushes dotting the ridge line. Crawling was the only option, but that would take time, a luxury rarely, if ever, found on a battlefield.

Waving back to the others, I ordered the squad, to cross the field, along with me. Moving in a cohesive group, the squad moved, across the road, and proceeded to traverse the field. I led, at the center of the group, with a three meter spread between each man as they followed,in an evenly spaced wedge formation. Instead of crawling we had to move in a low crouch, to increase our speed. Being spotted was a risk, but there's a slight advantage when you're spotted just as you enter cover instead of being in the middle of an open field.

German artillery was still pounding hard past the ridge line, the thump-thump-thump rhythm rising and falling, in even intervals. Mixed in, were the harder cracks of Flack 88s, the fearsome weapons holding even the craziest, of the flyboys, at bay. I glanced at my watch once we crossed the field and were in cover. We chewed up six minutes getting to the ridge and would need maybe twenty more, to reach the Germans.

"We need to pick up the pace," I grunted, catching my breath. "No telling what damage division HQ is taking from the arty."

"Do we even know what type of resistance is waiting for us?" Vic asked.

I shook my head and pointed, to the top, of the ridge. "Let's keep going and don't open fire, on anything, until I say so. So far the Germans don't seem to know we're here, so let's use the advantage."

I moved up the slanted ridge line, to the top of the hill, dropping down, to my stomach,at the very top with my binoculars out and ready. I took a few seconds, to scan the German positions on ridge line opposite ours, hill 107. Enemy artillery was deeply entrenched, at the center of the ridge, with five 88 batteries protecting them. Three 88s were clustered to the right of the arty and two the left. Our attack would come from the right, clear the first three and then fire, on the other two. We would need to be very quick.

"Alright, looks like two platoons of infantry around five 88s and a few pieces of heavy arty." I pointed, to the thick trees, below us. "Follow me through the trees and up the German's right flank. Those first three guns will be our first target. We'll need to knock them out fast and be ready, to take the last two, as if we don't, the infantry will take us down in seconds."

"How do we take out the second group with the arty between us and them?" Edwards asked.

"I've used 88s in North Africa, so once we get one cannon, I'll use it, to take out the other two, we can't reach. Now since we're out numbered," I looked to Adam, "that air strike will need to be inbound fast. Call in the strike, on sighting, of a red smoke marker."

Adam nodded, calling to the air observer.

"Once the guns are down, each of you will need to stick close and pull back, into the trees. As the flyboys do their thing we regroup here. Jay, hang back here for sniper cover. Questions? Okay, let's move out."

I checked the clip loaded into my Thompson and climbed, down the ridge, into the thick tree line below us. Jay remained on the ridge, with his sniper rifle, the elevation of hill 107 just about the same as ours so he could provide good sniper cover. Edwards assumed second in command of the squad, moving up with me, to quickly reorganize the squad, as needed. He would watch my back as I worked to grab one of the 88s and turn it, on the Germans.

We moved a bit slower as we crossed from the trees to the side of the ridge, German forces no more than a few dozen yards ahead of us. Again I checked my Thompson to be sure, my grip tightening as adrenaline suddenly flooded my blood. I could hear voices as I edged closer to the first 88, its barrel just visible above us. I raised my Thompson and pressed the stock into my shoulder, the pressure aggravating already sore muscles.

Edwards pulled out a grenade and yanked out the pin, his hand still holding the spoon in place. I held up a hand to order a halt and crouched down, nodding towards Vic and Edwards. Edwards let the spoon fall free, holding the grenade for three seconds before tossing it underhand over the lip of the ridge. My hear raced as an explosion echoed and men screamed out in pain.

My legs propelled me forward and up the ridge with the squad moving up behind me. Vic was up first, the heavy BAR peppering the nearest 88. I was over the ridge next, my finger depressing the trigger of the Thompson as I spotted German soldiers running about. The first gun crew was dead, all caught by the grenade blast. I moved up and crouched down by the steel cannon as the squad rushed forward, weapons firing and grenades flying. Guns two and three were silenced in the broadside attack as several soldiers tried to man an MG42. Edwards killed the group and dropped down to reload.

"Malks, now!" I called out swinging my Thompson over my shoulder and jumping for the 88.

Malks rushed up alongside me and the two of us manned the Flack88 and worked, to swing the heavy weapon, to face the other 88s. The German arty batteries were protected, by sandbag walls and MG nests, that were positioned, to cover the slopes of the ridge, though all of it was far back enough to not block the two 88s opposite us. Malks moved fast loading a shell, into the breach, as I sighted the fourth 88.

Machine gun fire bounced off the armor guard, in front of the weapon, sparks flying and rolling over my back. The 88 had a flat trajectory, no lobbing the shells, so I brought the sights to bare, the 88 crew working, to the do the same. I fired first, the cannon recoiling, with a massive blast that sent a shell straight into the Germans. The kill was marked by a burning debris pile as we swung the weapon around, to the last 88.

The last 88 fired before I could sight the weapon, Malks working on loading another shell. The shot went short, exploding the ground, before our cannon. I let out a relieved grunt as we returned fire and knocked out the AA battery. I jumped back from our 88, pulling a smoke grenade, from my webbing.

"Go!" I screamed as I pulled the pin and tossed the grenade. "Pull back! Move!"

Rifle fire peppered my position as I returned a brief burst before turning and running. Edwards was right behind me, firing as I did as we ran. Half the squad was already back, in the trees, the other half providing covering fire, from the lip of the ridge. I waved them back as I heard the drone of aircraft engines. I fought to control my footing as the first P-47 appeared off to the south, on course, for the smoke. Rocket fire screeched and I dropped down, to the trees, the ridge suddenly alive, with fire and explosions.

Out of breath, I picked myself up and continued to run back to our ridge as the air strike rolled in force. Explosions filled the air behind me, each one from a single rocket hit. I didn't look back, instead racing forward and back up the ridge. The squad was right with me, all running back up the ridge and dropping at the top for cover. I was there with Edwards and threw myself to the dirt, as I gasped for air. Struggling, I rolled back to see the strike, on the ridge.

There were cheers as a wing of Thunderbolts pounded the Germans, without mercy, heavy machine guns and rockets easily washing away the artillery. There was no defensive fire, from the Germans.

"Adam," I said still breathless, "tell Philips the German arty has been silenced."

"On it, sir," he answered before reporting in.

"Gotta love fireworks, eh?" Jay asked as he dusted off snow, from his jacket.

I nodded as the planes finished up their runs. "Let's hope we did all that, on time."

"Sir," Adam held out the receiver.

"Sword reporting," I said, into the radio.

There was some static. "Good work out there, Captain. Without that artillery hitting us we can focus on the German attack. You were just in the nick of time too, those flyboys are coming back, to help us out. Get yourself back to HQ ASAP, this fight still isn't over."

"Yes, sir! We're coming back now." I handed the receiver back and nodded, to the south. "We're heading back to HQ to help, with the rest of the defense. The Major sends his regards, so let's get moving."

I began to march back the ridge when Jay tapped my shoulder. "Hey, you know what today is?"

I shrugged. "Nope. Haven't seen a calendar in a long while."

Jay laughed dryly. "It's Christmas Day you know. Guess we won't get that truce like back in 1914, huh?"

Again I shrugged. "Like Philips said, the fight isn't over."

Part V
Why We Fight

"They say that it'll be over soon, that the Nazis will surrender. We lost a lot in lives since its start some five years ago, but only God knows just how much of our humanity is gone."
Master Sergeant Jonathan Edwards, US Army

Chapter 20
Remagen Bridge Head
Remagen, Germany
March 15th, 1945

The soft earth turned to mud and squished under out boots with each step, the hard suction threatening, to yank them off my feet. Water splashed as I continued to rush forward through puddles and deep pools of muddy water formed, from shell craters. MG42 fire still echoed loudly through the air along with the shouts and cries, from soldiers and officers alike. Rifle fire popped, submachine guns crackled, and heavy machines guns chattered away all the while my heart beat thudded, in my ears.

I couldn't see much as I ran down the muddied road, high stone walls, on both flanks, with breaks marking where gates were located. The squad was still facing the enemy head on, the majority of the Germans still held up, in the overly ornate, mansion or estate or whatever the Germans called them.

More voices called, in German, as I approached the first gate on my left. Edwards was right behind me and stopped automatically, pressing himself against the wall as I moved ahead a little bit more. Thompson held into my shoulder, I inched towards the gate when it suddenly burst open, the metal slamming against the stone wall. Four German soldiers bolted out, from the gate, quickly turning east and running like hell. Edwards and I killed the four before they could get far.

"Stay close," I whispered moving, to the gate, and swapping out, for a fresh clip.

"On your six," Edwards replied.

Several MG42s were still firing from the front, of the mansion, all firing towards the front gates where the squad was still held up. The mansion itself was three floors high, with about a dozen different balconies protruding, from the front of the building. German MG teams were dug in deep behind sandbags, in the balconies, along with snipers and riflemen. Even more Germans were spread out, in foxholes, across the front lawn.

I looked to Edwards and signaled him, to ready a grenade, as I slipped one from my gear webbing. Pins were yanked and two grenades were tossed over the stone wall into the nearest foxholes. Men cried in pain as twin explosions silenced an AT team. Two 42's swung, in our direction, and opened up on the gate, the heavy fire forcing us back, into cover.

"Last one, sir?" Edwards asked.

"Yea, that was it." I waved back down the road to a group of waiting tanks, the signal for them to advance, on the mansion.

Taking up the lead was one, of the newest models, of Allied tanks, the M-26 Pershing heavy tank. The Pershing was command's answer, to meet German armor, on the field, a tank designed to take on another tank. On an M-26 thicker armor was added along with a 90mm main gun made, to crack heavy armor. While the fast and agile Sherman was still the main Allied tank, the Pershing had use as our advance drove, into the heart, of the enemy.

Two Pershing tanks rolled up the muddied road, with four Sherman tanks following behind as a rear guard. One Pershing rolled around, to advance through the main gate, while the second rolled forward towards us. Edwards and I moved back down the wall and stopped several feet, from the heavy tank. Engines coughing black smoke, the tank barreled through the stone wall and rolled, onto the front lawn, main turret swinging around to face the mansion.

Machine gun bullets bounced off the armor as the main gun targeted the mansion. With a hard boom, the gun fired and a balcony disappeared, in a cloud of smoke and hail of white stone. More booms as the first Pershing rolled forward with my squad moving behind for cover. I moved with Edwards, through the gap, in the wall, behind the tank.

The Pershing rolled forward and turned, to fully face the mansion, the hull and coaxial machine guns firing away at the soldiers manning machine guns, on the front steps. I kept behind the armored machine as its main gun fired again and another balcony was ripped down, to the ground. Jay lead the rest of the squad forward,behind the other Pershing as it rolled behind ours, both firing away, with their full armaments.

"Keep your head down!" I shouted to Edwards as he moved up next to me. Machine gun bullets were bouncing off the tank's armor while others skimmed by the turret and passed just over our heads.

When the tanks stopped,at the base of the main steps, I ordered everyone forward and inside. I checked my Thompson and rushed around the side of the tank, rushing up the now cratered steps past German bodies, to the main doors. Massive, ornate doors once stood where only splinters littered the ground now, a shattered statue spread out, in front of us. Edwards covered me as Vic moved up and dropped by the doorway, BAR barking fire to cover us.

"Move!" Edwards shouted waving the squad inside.

Bullets still cut through the air as I entered the mansion, a massive foyer before me. A single stair case was opposite me, with a large balcony, that overlooked the entrance. A pair of sandbag MG nests were waiting for us, bright muzzle flashes marking their positions. We ran right into an ambush, my mind forcing my body to drop, to the ground, as the volley of lead flew at us.

"Get down!" I ordered firing back. "Get down! MG42s!"

The air rushed from my lungs as I dropped, to the hard ground. The squad reacted instantly, breaking up and spreading out, for cover, as bullets ripped through the air. I crawled over, to a stone support pillar, for cover as India Squad, our supporting squad, entered right into the teeth of the German positions. I cried out for them to stop and get down, but my voice was drowned out as the heavy machine gun fire cut apart the forward parts of India Squad.

Men dropped under the hailstorm of death, bodies mutilated and torn apart by hot lead. Several men were killed instantly when the spray of MG fire cut across their position at head height. Helmets flew off and blood splattered the ground as they fell. I looked away, suddenly feeling a mass of bile creeping, up my throat, my stomach suddenly twisting into a knot. It wasn't a time, to get sick, and be stunned, by the horror I saw.

"Surprising fire!" I ordered, rising up behind the pillar and firing, at the German positions. Bullets slammed into the stone pillar, with tremendous force, chipping away the white stone and tearing apart my only cover. There was no way to hit the Germans from the front, it was pure suicide to even try, which left three lanes of attack. Flank left, flank right, or hit the rear.

I looked to my right and left, both with no way to flank around, to hit the MGs on their sides, there were no doors in the foyer, that we could reach without being cut down by MG fire in a few heartbeats. Attacking to the rear was next, though the back section of the mansion was unsecured and filled with Germans, meaning more time to clear them out and a drain of ammo.

"Orders, sir?" Edwards asked as he reloaded his weapon.

For Christ sake, you can't stay here! I scanned the foyer and the balcony, looking for something that could help us. Stone pillars ran near both walls and moved down to the staircase, but they were barely enough cover for one man. Glancing up, I spotted that the roof, well, the area above the staircase, was a rather overly ornate glass dome or window or something along those lines. Whatever it was, it was my fifth option.

"Adam!" I called out, waving the radio operator forward.

Adam rushed up and dropped down, to his stomach, next to me. "Yes, sir?"

"Where's that mortar section set up?" I asked.

He looked perplexed, but answered. "Ridge line overlooking the mansion, this side of the river."

"Can see the mansion?" I asked.

He nodded. "The elevation is much higher there then here, so yes, sir."

It was one risky move. "Get me the mortar section commander." I ordered.

Adam worked the radio and handed me the receiver. "Call sign Hydra, sir."

I took the receiver and dropped down, in a crouch. "Hydra, this is Sword."

There was static. "Hydra responding."

"Hydra, can you see the roof of the mansion?" I yelled.

The trooper's tone showed his confusion. "Umm…yes we can, sir. Our elevation is much higher than the area of the mansion."

"Okay, I need you to follow my orders, to the letter. Can you see the section of the roof that's glass?"

More silence. "Umm, yes we can, sir."

"Wonderful, I want you to drop some shells right through there, right through the glass. Can you do that?" I asked.

Again, silence. "We…ah….I'm not sure, sir."

"Yes or no," I said deadpan as another man, from India, fell.

"Yes, sir! Rounds are incoming." Said the voice.

The radio snapped off and I handed back the receiver, dropping even lower,to the ground. We were effectively pinned down, but that could change.

"Heads down, mortar support incoming!" I screamed.

"What?" someone called out over the machine gun fire. "We're inside already!"

I didn't respond as the mortar strike began to drop, rounds exploding against the roof of the mansion, the building itself shaking, with each hit. The first four rounds were spread out, impacting across the roof, with no real effect. A fifth round landed close to the glass section of the ceiling, the vibration shattering the glass and sending down a shower of broken glass, on the Germans. Round six passed through the open gap and landed right on the upper balcony. The explosion knocked out the MG nests and blew away chunks of the balcony.

"Adam, call off the rest of the mortar strike." I ordered.

I leapt back to my feet, but felt a hand grab my shoulder. I whirled around to see Adam holding onto my shoulder, the other hand holding the radio receiver.

"New orders from division, sir!" he shouted handing over the receiver.

"Sword reporting in, we're clearing the mansion now." I yelled.

"Doesn't matter now," Major Philips called back. "German forces are setting up Nebelwerfer batteries just north of your position. Pull out from the mansion and regroup, with your tank detachment. Then move up and take out those rocket batteries, before they can hammer the staging area."

I swore under my breath, looking at the bodies from India Squad. "Copy that, Sword is moving to the artillery." The receiver went back to Adam. "Squad, we got German arty, to take out first. Regroup outside and follow the tanks! Move out!"

I swapped out clips, for my Thompson, and moved back out, to the front of the mansion, already two new squads of infantry moving up, to take up our old objective, while we moved to the arty. Both Pershing tanks were already on the move while the Sherman tanks held back, to watch over the mansion. I rallied the squad; all accounted for and unwounded, and led them behind the tanks.

We moved up the muddied road alongside the mansion, both heavy tanks rolling on ahead, to the fields behind the mansion, where the rocket batteries were being deployed. I choked on engine fumes, in the wake of the war machines, but it didn't matter as the dirt road gave way, to open fields.

The tanks rolled on ahead of us, moving from a single file line, to one, next to one another, while I led the squad, into cover, behind a wooden shack and several haystacks, across from the rocket batteries. There was no need for us, to rush forward, when two armored mammoths could do it, for you.

"Hold here and let's let the tanks handle 'em," I ordered ducking down behind a haystack

A pair of 42s were already set up, to defend the rocket batteries, on their flanks, both opening up on the tanks. Watching the tracers cut through the air and bounce off the tanks it was clear that if we advanced,on our own, it would've been right into a kill zone. The leading Pershing suddenly halted its advance as an explosion blossomed under his hull, its right track breaking, with a metallic snap.

AT fire? I thought, but there was no smoke trail, from an AT rocket, and there were no heavy AT guns set up. Smoke began to billow, from the front, of the Pershing, flames licking, at the base of the turret. The engine was still humming away with power, but the crew was abandoning tank as hatches flew up and men, in oil stained olive colored jump suites, leapt out, in a desperate frenzy, to get away from the furnace that a tank could be. Machine gun fire pounded the tank like water on a rock, the crew had no chance.

Pershing number two met a similar fate a handful of seconds later, the tank halted, with the treads knocked off and fire washing over it. The realization hit too late. "Teller mines!" I screamed.

With the tanks gone, the MG42s turned on us, forcing everyone to drop, into the dirt. I crawled towards Adam and called,for the mortar section,again. The only way, across the field, was an irrigation ditch just to the south, but it was too exposed on its own.

"Mortars on the line!" Adam tossed me the receiver before firing at the Germans.

"Hydra, I need smoke shells, on the irrigation ditch, near my position. Target reference Y21XR13." I said.

The section commander repeated the coordinates back to me before I switched off the radio. Belly crawling forward, I moved towards the ditch and dropped down inside. Water splashed into my face, as I hit the bottom, rising up into a low crouch. Edwards was moving the squad behind when the first of the smoke shells dropped into the field right before the ditch. Rather than exploding, the mortar shells slammed, into the dirt, and began to release white smoke. With six or seven shells billowing the thick smoke and the wind no linger blowing, we had cover.

"Wait," I grunted as I pulled Edwards back from rushing ahead. "Let the smoke build."

Green tracer fire still cut through the smoke, the enemy gunners spraying bullets in a wide pattern into the smoke. They couldn't see anything at all, all incoming fire now sporadic, with a simple spray-and-pray pattern.

I let out a hard whistle. "Advance!"

The muscles in my legs uncoiled, my body springing forward, with a sudden surge of adrenaline. Bullets popped and hissed as they cut through the air, rounds throwing up dirt as they slammed into the ground, with hard, kinetic force. Several men behind me fired off quick rifle shots into the smoke cloud, not so much to hit a target spot on, but to just do something. I held fire, but kept my Thompson tucked firmly into my shoulder, and ready to fire once a target presented itself.

The buzz saw screech of an MG42 and stream of green tracers marked the MG nest on the batteries left flank. They were still not in sight, the smoke still thick around us, but the bullets were close nonetheless. When I reached the edge, of the smoke cover, I was about a dozen, or so, feet from the MG nests, the gunners firing far off to my right. A loader spotted me, mouth opening to shout, as I fired three rounds punching through this chest, with a splatter of blood. I swiveled to my left and fired, sending several longs burst into the rest of the MG crew.

The team was dead as I reloaded and hopped over the small sandbag wall, of the MG nest, landing in a shallow trench on the opposite side. German soldiers were working furiously, to finish loading the Nebelwerfer batteries, with rockets, while a dozen rifle men were moving towards us. Our BAR opened up with a furious broadside that dropped more than half of the advancing Germans. Edwards and I took down the rest before moving on.

Nate moved with Mangon, Malks, Doc, and Phelps, to take out the second MG nest, while I moved ahead,with the rest of the squad, to the rocket batteries. There were three of them, six metal barrels built onto a set of wheels and rotating platform, set up under camo netting, behind the trenches. Each rocket battery was manned by three men, all unarmed while loading.

As a soldier, it was always kill or be killed, hesitation meant death. As a person, you don't want to kill the man that is unarmed, but there were always exceptions. My Thompson fired on the first crew, all three killed at the expense of one twenty round clip. A reload and I was attacking the second, though a grenade finished them off in a heartbeat. Battery three was elevating to fire, the crew raising the barrel, in the direction of Remagen. One of the crew dropped,to the ground, as his helmet flew off, one side of his face gone, in an instant.

"Down!" I just registered Edward's voice as he forced himself on me, the two of us falling, to the dirt. I was about to yell out when I felt the prickle of heat against the back of my neck, the sudden whoosh of air against my face.

The bright red star of an anti-tank rocket passed over us, narrowly clipping Edwards pack. Slamming into the ground a few feet away, dirt rained down on us, Edwards getting back up and helping me. "You hurt, sir?

I shook my head, my ears ringing slightly. "No, thanks."

Edwards nodded and was back on his feet, eyes scanning, for targets. I moved towards the last battery, though the crew was already dead. The squad was fanning out, checking for any remaining Germans, in the area. I took a few breaths, to calm down, lower my heart rate, to try and bring my brain into focus. I patted myself down first, feeling for blood or wounds that may have not been picked up by my brain. Everything was where it should be, no bleeding, no bullet or shrapnel wounds.

"Sir!" Nate hollered as he stood over one of the trenches.

I turned and walked towards him. "Yeah?"

He nodded, into the trench, rifle on his hip. "Got a handful of Krauts prisoners here, sir."

I walked to the lip of the trench, peering down on six German soldiers sitting inside. Two were wounded, one in the shoulder, the other the hand. All were young, too young to be in uniform and carrying a rifle. They were kids really, they should be playing war not living it.

"We'll hand them off when the rest of the division moves up," I said looking away from them. Doc was already walking towards us. "Let Doc take a look at 'em."

Nate nodded, pulling out a pack of cigarettes. He didn't speak a word of German, not needing to as he tossed the pack, to one of the soldiers. He took a smoke and then passed the pack around,to his friends, all mumbling thank you, in German. It was a simple enough act of kindness, from one soldier, to another.

A pair of Thunderbolts passed overhead, wings loaded down with rockets and bombs, moving east towards the German lines. Further above them, passing through the clouds somewhere 5,000ft above us, was a very common sight; a massive wing of B-17 Flying Fortresses, each of the four engine bombers carrying death in their bellies. Berlin or bust. I though, news of bombing runs into Berlin appearing in Stars and Stripes or just passed on, by word of mouth.

"I told Malks to spike the guns," Edwards stated as I dropped my gaze from the skies. "His eyes lit up like I just told him we won a million dollars."

I shrugged, slinging my Thompson over my shoulder. "Man loves his explosives. So long as he doesn't blow us all to Hell, he can do what he wants."

"I never get that freedom," Vic grunted, a cigarette sticking out from the corner of his mouth.

Adam slapped him, across the back. "If we let you go free, half of Europe would still be on fire."

I jerked a thumb over my shoulder, at the field, with our lost Pershing tanks. "Anyone mark that field yet for mines?"

Mangon was already setting up a marker, a simple section of wood from a supply crate with MINE! stenciled on it, all propped up on top of a fence post, next to the field. An engineer section would move up eventually and clear out the Teller mines. Mines were big killers as we crossed Germany, such a wide variety keeping the engineers on edge. Teller mines were made to take out heavy armor, no real risk to infantry, as we didn't weigh enough, to trip them. Shoe mines were worse, the bastards undetectable by mine sweepers while Bouncing Betties leapt into the air, to waist height and exploded. Not meant to kill, it maimed plenty, but was feared,for the fact, no one wanted steel shooting at them below the belt and above the knees.

A new column of tanks began rolling up the road. "Okay, tell the squad to take five," I told Edwards and Jay. "Smoke 'em if you get 'em."

Adam held out the radio receiver. "Major Philips for you, sir."

He was permanently fixed to my side, just like every radio operator to their CO. "Sword reporting in." I said.

"The mansion is secured and we're moving our heavy armor up to keep up this momentum. Air support is being called off, to help cover, that over flight, of bombers that just passed by. Gather up your men and I want you to cut across the fields, on our right flank. German armor is held up in a small hamlet, that's in our path and without air support. We have to take them out with our tank destroyers.

"Flank right and take up position, to the south, of the hamlet. Guard that road and make sure nothing rolls in to hit our tank destroyers. There's a German infantry unit somewhere to our south that is not accounted for so be on alert."

"I copy you, sir. Sword out." Adam took the receiver back, standing aside for orders.

I let out a sharp whistle, grabbing the squad's attention. "Okay, new orders are in. We're to flank through the field there," I pointed them out, to our right, "and are gonna secure a road leading, to a hamlet, to our north. We're to hold, until the tank destroyers clear the hamlet, and prevent German infantry from moving up, to reinforce their friends. Gather up your shit and let's move out."

Edwards and Jay helped gather up the squad, making sure the prisoners were handed off to another group of soldiers moving up the line. Hand off the head ache as it were. There were about a dozen fields dotting the area just near the hamlet, though these were wide open and not sectioned off, with the hellish hedgerows. Instead, fields were marked off by roads or tree lines, leaving them very wide open for tanks and infantry to move.

The fields we needed to cut across were maybe two football fields long and were separated, by a road, down the middle, with trees covering the western edge. Recent, or past bombing raids had passed through this area, before our attack and damage was heavy. The fields, once neat and well cared for, were filled with craters, the earth blacken and scorched from bomb strikes.

Rain had hit the area the day before our launch off of the advance, turning the fields to mud pits and filling the craters. Some were deep pools of filth and muck, rising up to a man's chest, if you stood in one, while others were shallow and hidden, making it easy to trip up a passerby. I kept an eye out for that, not wanting to fall into the cesspools, while I watched for any hidden Germans.

"What do you think they saw?" Sanders asked as we crossed the first field, the mud splashing, across our uniforms.

I glanced back at him. "Who?" I asked.

"Well…the flyboys, sir." He gestured, to the fields. "What was out here that they cratered the area?"

"Don't believe all our propaganda. The flyboys are accurate, but remember they're dropping their loads, in mass, from several thousand feet up. Not exactly dropping a grenade into a bucket," I explained.

I dropped my gaze down for a second, to skirt around one of the more larger craters, the pool of collected filth, dull grayish brown in color. A small flash of light, like sun light off metal, grabbed my attention as I passed the crater. At first I thought it was a piece of shrapnel left over from a bomb or something, but it was too smooth and rounded.

"Everyone freeze!" I hissed, holding up a closed fist, to signal a halt.

Each man in the squad stopped dead in his tracks, all suddenly alert and shouldering weapons. Edwards was about six feet behind me, Adam four feet from him.

"Sir?" Edwards called out, with his Thompson tucked into his shoulder.

"Okay, just no one move, at all, until I say so." Swallowing hard, I slung my Thompson over my shoulder and pulled out my trench knife.

In training you're taught to 'probe' a minefield if you didn't have one of those nice mine sweepers handy. The idea, a simple one, at that, was slow and time consuming. Using a knife or some type of stick or tool, you'd carefully probe the ground for mines. Stick the knife into the ground and feel for resistance. You find a mine, you clear away the dirt and put down some type of marker. Repeat as needed.

Taking slow and easy steps, I approached the flat disk sticking out, of the ground. Keeping a few inches away, I gently reached out and brushed away the loose dirt and mud with my hands. Enough of the mine was exposed, and I could tell that it was a mine, an anti-personal mine. Staying in place, I stood back up.

"I think we're in the middle of a minefield," I said noticing that we had passed, into the center, of the field. Several men swore, others now totally frozen, in their spots, as they looked down, at the muddied ground.

"Back out?" Jay asked, as we just stood there, open and exposed.

I looked over my shoulder, my boot prints still left mud. We had to secure that road and cover the flank, of the advance. Proceeding ahead would mean slowly crawling forward inch by inch checking for mines the hard way. "Look, everyone back out the way we came in. Move slowly, very slowly. Use your boot prints and get back, to the road. We'll cut through the trees."

Moving slowly and cautiously, we turned back around and began walking, out of the minefield, in our boot prints. I had to keep changing my gaze, from the ground, to the surrounding area, the threats now coming, from around, and below me. One missed step and I could lose a foot, a leg, or even my life. It was a slow and steady process, one boot down, into a boot print, and then repeat and repeat. No one spoke, the liquid slosh of mud picking up, in the silence. My heart was thumping hard in m chest, the hard rattle filling my ears.

Part of me was grateful it was March and the weather reasonably fair. Had we wandered into a minefield during winter, simply stepping on a mine, was not the only way to trigger one. When the temperature drops and snow falls, the ground contracts and the shift in pressure can trip a mine. Many engineers were killed clearing minefields because a mine was set off from ground contractions.

I glanced ahead and spotted the thin dirt path that ran, in between the minefield, and the fields, with the German rocket batteries. I kept myself controlled, resisting the urge to rush across the rest of the field to the safety of the dirt path. I gingerly put one foot down and then the other exactly, to fit within the boot prints, working hard I wasn't too high or too low to do something. Part of me was just waiting, for a mine to explode, whether it be under my own feet or someone else's.

The men bringing up the rear, of the squad, were first, to reach the safety of the dirt path, watching out backs and offering what cover they could. It felt like an eternity until I stepped onto the path, the minefield now behind us. A quick head count and everyone was out, some now breathing heavily from fear or frayed nerves. We had no time to rest.

"Move out," I ordered.

Keeping a good amount of distance, from the minefield, we proceeded, down the path, towards the woods. Already I could hear the pops and cracks of rifle fire, the muffled thumps of explosions and hard grumble of tank engines. I moved with a quickened pace, nearly running through the tree line, to reach the southern road. The road was still clear and empty when we arrived, no Germans coming from the south or from the hamlet in the north. A low ditch on either side of the road offered covered while the tree line concealed better.

"Jay, over watch," I grunted without needing to be specific. Jay darted off, into the trees, and set up a sniper's nest, working on his own without trouble. "Vic, set up the BAR behind that fallen tree and watch the southern approach. Edwards, take our rifles and put them across the road, in the trees. Doc, hang back with Adams and me."

Edwards moved the bulk of the squad, into the trees on the opposite side of the road, quickly dispersing them, into concealed fighting positions. Adam dropped down behind a tree, with his rifle, while

Doc held back behind cover. I stood near the side of the road,with my binoculars held up to my eyes.

"Radio division," I called out without looking at Adam. "Tell 'em we have the road and are holding position."

I heard something tapping against metal. "Radio's fucked up again, sir. No way to tell if it's us or them." Adam said.

The road was still clear. "Okay, we hold until I say otherwise." I moved into cover and dropped down behind a tree, taking out my canteen and taking a sip, of the lukewarm liquid. My throat was dry and raw, the water only aggravating the pain as it was like throwing water onto a hot stove.

My nerves were…shaken up a bit with exhaustion adding to the problems. Slipping off my helmet, I looked down into the lining and saw Jessica's picture, photo worn and faded. My stomach knotted,at the image, as I hadn't received any letters from her since January. I still sent many back, though who knew if they ever got to her. If anything hurt more than getting wounded, it was being alone.

"Movement on the road." Someone yelled.

My helmet was back on and Thompson was fully loaded and tucked, into my shoulder. I rose up and moved back, from the road a little more, putting some solid cover between the road and myself. "Hold fire until I order!" I shouted. It was clear an enemy force was moving for us.

A pair of halftracks were thundering down the road towards us, a trailing group of troop trucks close behind. A dust cloud marked their position as I lined up my sights on the gunner, in the leading track, the trooper well out of range, for my SMG. Jay was tracking the same target, waiting for a signal, to open fire. I pulled out a grenade, from my webbing, and moved towards the road.

The leading halftrack was about two dozen yards away and closing as I stood just off the road, my body concealed by a tree. I yanked the pin, from the grenade, but held the spoon in place while I held my Thompson, in my other hand. At about ten yards I released the spoon and spun out, my arm with the grenade coming up. I saw shock on the gunner's face as the grenade tumbled through the air and hit the front of the halftrack. There was one bounce and then an explosion followed the screech of tires as the track careened into a tree.

My attack singled the others, all men now opening up a hail storm off bullets, on the convoy. I put an entire clip into the second track, all my shots focused on the gunner manning the MG42. Bullets bounced against the armor plate attached to the 42, but the gunner's head was exposed enough as a dozen rounds found marks against flesh and steel. I pulled back in as Malks tossed a grenade into the rear of the track, the explosion that followed killed the driver as the track veered off the road and slammed into a tree, overturning, on the road.

The following halftrack swerved, to miss the overturned vehicle, a dozen German soldiers, inside firing back, at us. Jay's rifle cracked and one man tumbled, from the back, a nice sized chunk, of his head and helmet now torn apart. I lined up my sights up on the top of the troop compartment where a handful of German helmets bobbed up and down, behind the steel plated sides of the track. I held the trigger down as the track past and let the entire clip drain, before pulling back, to reload.

"Armored car!" Edwards yelled suddenly.

I moved back to the road as a recon armored car shot down the road, its heavy auto cannon barking away. The heavy cannon spewed explosive shells, across the tree line, trees splintering, with each and every hit. A coaxial MG42 chattered away and forced me to dive down, to the ground for cover. Grenades were tossed at the vehicle, but simple fragmentation grenades could do nothing, to the armored car, except scratch the paint.

"Malks!" I called out looking for our engineer. He was crouching down behind the overturned track to reload his shotgun. "Use your C4!"

Malks nodded, fumbling for a small bundle of C4 explosives, in his pack. It was a very crude way to destroy an armored car and a waste of explosives, but it was our only option. I rolled to my stomach and edged forward, belly crawling, to avoid the cannon and MG fire. The troop trucks had stopped now, depositing German riflemen, into the trees and across the road. M1's still fired away and our BAR was thumping away pumping out enough lead, to hold back the riflemen.

As bullets splattered my position, I waved Malks to move up. He moved into the trees and crept forward, the armored car focusing fire on my position. There was a sudden lull as the main cannon was reloaded, offering Malks precious time to creep forward with a newly made satchel charge in hand. Dodging sporadic gun fire, Malks primed the charge and tossed it on top of the car next to the turret.

Working with a short fuse, the charge detonated with a resounding bang, as half of the top turret was ripped open. A grenade was tossed inside for good measure to finish off the crew. German riflemen were now our focus, only about several dozen left from an attacking force, of maybe sixty men. I rose back to my feet and sprayed rounds across the roadway where ever I saw field gray uniforms.

"Grenade!" Edwards shouted as a German potato masher stick grenade landed a few feet away. I dropped down and dove for the grenade, reaching out to grab it with one hand. I wasn't sure what direction I tossed the grenade just that it was away from everyone else. When I didn't hear an explosion I realized the grenade wasn't even primed, just tossed it with the fuse unlit.

A massive explosion erupted down the road near the German troop trucks. The familiar rattle of a .50cal machine gun and garbled coughs, of a Detroit made engine, brought a smirk to my lips. Main 75mm gun firing with hull, coaxial, and turret MGs pounding away a pair of M4 Sherman tanks raced our way, from the hamlet.

German soldiers were cleared away in the wave of steel, none of them carrying any weapon that could even dent the armor on a Sherman. I returned to the road and fired towards the Germans, moving behind the passing tanks for cover. Edwards and Adam were close by, both now on the road with me. Edward's group of riflemen were advancing out of the trees as the last group of Germans decided to surrender then die.

"Hold fire!" I shouted to the squad as the tanks rolled to a stop, turret gunners watching the dozen or so German POWS stumbling towards us. I moved out ahead of the tanks, Thompson raised and shouted orders, in my heavily accented German, at the soldiers. All complied without hesitation as rifles and SMGs fell to the ground and hands went up. It was easy to tell these were not SS or anything of the more hardened units of the Wehrmacht, they were kids. Boys from the age of fifteen to nineteen, along with old men, even the draft board back home wouldn't take. Conscripts and Hitler Youth were the bulk of the enemy we faced since we cross the Rhine and stepped foot on German soil. Kids and old men fighting for a crazed man's delusion of victory and a German empire.

"Jeez, another bunch of 'em!" one of the turret gunners hollered as I ordered the squad to collect up their weapons. "They sure gave up to us back in the hamlet pretty damn quick. Hell, only got one damn tank kill."

I looked up at the soldier, a corporal. "Quit the bitching, trooper," I grunted as he realized I was a captain.

"I…ah, sorry about that, sir," he said.

I grunted in annoyance, another replacement looking to become a hero before Germany surrenders. No one in squad still held those ideas, the only real heroes were dead, out in a field somewhere, or buried in the dirt. The German soldiers we captured had more logic than to fight, to be heroes, for the Fatherland. Only a few people realized hero equals dead man.

"Let's get them to the hamlet," I ordered, waving with my Thompson to gesture for the POWs to being marching. The squad piled up the captured weapons alongside the road and began to move our short column of prisoners back to the hamlet. I glanced over my shoulder as one of the tanks rolled over the weapons pile, before turning back to lead everyone.

"You know they forced us to be here," a German soldier near me said, in relatively clear English. I looked over at him, the man clearly over the enlistment age of any nation. Age had already told this man that war was not his business.

"It's over now," I responded offering the man my last piece of gum.

He gratefully took it. "That's what I was told back in 1918 after the Great War ended, but here I am again."

"You served back then?" I asked.

"Ja, a simple Sergeant leading school children through the trenches since the start in 1914. I was hit twice, in the left arm, by the Tommies and once, in the leg, by you Yanks." He chewed his piece of gum and sighed with exhaustion. "I figured I'd sit this one out, show the Reich my medals and let the young fight."

I could only shrug, thinking back to my father's time in the Great War. "War to end all wars, right?"

The German laughed. "Maybe that'll be this war. God help our children." We both looked back at the other Germans, most around fifteen to seventeen. That was the inevitable face of war, for as long as there has been war. My grandfather was seventeen, my father seventeen, and I was eighteen when we enlisted and first saw combat. I was now twenty-one and had come a long way in about three years of fighting. I still wondered just how home life would be after the war ended.

Armor was already moving through the hamlet and heading east, our advance still going at full speed while we could. MPs took our group of prisoners from us, without complaint, adding them to a large column of POWs already being marched west. There were easily a hundred POWs being marched away while another column of soldiers and tanks marched opposite them.

"This must be the new strategy for them," Jay grunted as we stopped near an abandoned house. He waved his hand out in an arc. "Slow the Americans by surrendering in droves."

I laughed as I drank from my canteen. "They're not surrendering fast enough for my liking."

Jay shrugged, resting his rifle against his hip. "Shouldn't be much longer if things continue to move at this rate. We've taken how many thousands of prisoners since we broke the advance during the Bulge?"

Another pair of Thunderbolts shot by overhead, these two heading for our lines, with underside weapons racks empty. "I'd prefer if every

German soldier just decided to surrender all at once. Hitler would be on his own then." I declared.

Adam was at my side again, handing me the radio receiver. "Major Philips, sir."

"Sword reporting," I said over the static of the radio.

Philips came back right away. "Are you in the hamlet?"

"Yes, sir." I said.

"Captain, get your men to the rally point, at the western road, and wait for me."

I shrugged. "Yes, sir." A sharp whistle grabbed the squad's attention. "Squad, form up and move to the western rally point."

We skirted around the main column passing through the hamlet, the air chocked with exhaust and dust kicked up by the column of heavy armor and mechanized forces moving through. Handfuls of MPs were directing the flow of troops east while watching prisoners head west. Major Philips was waiting for us near the side of the road, sitting in his jeep with Lieutenant Hasel and several other empty jeeps.

"Reporting, sir," I announced over the grumble of the traffic.

Philips sat in the jeep's passenger seat with Hasel behind him and a private, at the wheel. A map was in his lap and his rifle, a rarely used carbine, rested against his leg. "Mount up,'" he ordered without glancing up.

"Sir?" I asked unsure of what he was saying.

Philips glanced up, eyes blocked by the edge of his helmet. "Load up your squad," he repeated nodding at the empty jeeps behind him.

Curious, I nodded at Jay and Edwards to get the squad mounted up. They quickly complied, taking three jeeps to get everyone mounted. I still stood before the Major, unsure of just what to do.

"Paratroopers have secured a German OP about three miles east of here," he finally said, removing his helmet. "They uncovered an underground bunker complex in the hills, near the OP, that they believe maybe an aircraft manufacturing plant. SHAFE is dying to get a look at one of these places, so we're going there right now." He folded up the map and picked up his carbine. "Have your men follow me to the bunker and I'll issue further orders."

I snapped to attention and saluted. "Yes, sir." I dropped the salute once it was returned and walked back to one of our jeeps. Sanders was at the wheel while Malks, Nate, and Adam sat in the rear, Malks on the.30cal machine gun.

"Orders?" Sanders asked looking at me.

I sat down in the passenger's seat. "Follow the Major."

He nodded starting up the jeep as Major Philips pulled onto the road. Our three jeeps followed right after, moving alongside the ponderous column of tanks and soldiers. The forward elements were only a mile out from the hamlet, moving at a slow pace to cover the open ground and clear out pockets of resistance. Philips raced ahead of the armor support and made us follow, heading down a barren road, into the thick area forests.

"Just where are we going, sir?" Nate asked from behind.

I didn't turn back. "Paratroopers uncovered something big in the hills, an underground bunker network of some kind. Philips thinks it's an aircraft factory and wants to check it out."

Building into the ground was what the Germans did to counter Allied bombing raids. With all of their industry being torn apart from the rain of Allied bombs, Nazi high command had instillations built underground or into hills or mountains. Hollowed out, many hillsides became the home of Vengeance weapon's launch sites or factories. While taking a lot to construct, the facilities were well protected from our bombers and hidden in plain sight.

Our group of jeeps bounced across the dirt roadways, at a steady pace, our speed

somewhere near fifty miles per hour. I kept my eyes on the fields and trees surrounding the road being ever alert for German ambushes. We already passed the remains of destroyed German armor and abandoned supplies strewn every which way. We'd been traveling for over an hour and not one German was seen, well no living German, bodies were common sights.

I felt very unnerved to be passing through such open countryside, in a jeep with no support of any kind. German gunners could've been watching us at that very moment, rifles and machine guns following our jeeps. More and more I was looking over my shoulder and at the tree line for any signs of enemy forces. I kept my Thompson held close by, for some comfort, and kept as alert as I could.

Major Philips was pulling ahead of us once the road evened out and the craters were few and far between. A wide gap opened up on maybe a dozen yards between us, but the squad kept their jeeps evenly spaced at about a few yards from bumper to bumper. I leaned back and was about to tell Adam to radio the Major when an explosion suddenly burst in front of us.

Sanders let out a yelp as he jerked the wheel to the right and forced the jeep off the road. I quickly looked around to see what was happening when our jeep slammed into a burnt out tank. Machine gun and rifle fire ruptured out alongside heavy cannon fire as the other jeeps pulled off the road. Everything seemed to be kicked into high gear as everyone piled out of the jeep and dove for cover.

Bullets pinged off the metal of the jeep as I rolled to my right and dropped to the ground. Sanders climbed over the jeep and dropped down next to me, rifle, in hand, as a red stain ran down his left arm and hand. Adam was laying prone in the grass with Nate and Malks, down by the burnt out tank.

"You're hit!" I shouted to Sanders moving to treat his wound.

"Bastard got me," he replied, rifle in his lap and his hand on the wound. "I don't think it's bad, sir."

I didn't have time to properly dress the wound, only having enough time to apply a pressure bandage to stop the bleeding and keep out dirt. Doc would have to make everything pretty once the fighting was done. Another explosion erupted nearby, taking out one of our jeeps, though it was empty.

Crawling back to the front of the jeep I looked to the tree line for Germany AT emplacements. The tree cover was too thick to spot anything, but the bright muzzle flashes were sign enough. There were two MG42s for sure and possibly a squad or two of riflemen. Already they took out the Major's jeep, which was a burning wreck overturned on the roadway. Philips was most likely dead, no sense in checking while the Germans were still shooting.

"Heads down!" I shouted. "Heads down!"

Bullets thudded into the soft earth all around, others snapping and hissing through the air. Edwards was with the rear jeep, his group about a dozen yards off to my right. I couldn't spot Jay, his face not sticking out amongst the squad sprawled out, on the grassy ground. If he was still able too, Jay would be holding up somewhere picking off Germans, with his Springfield.

Rifle fire popped from several Garands, the hard metical clicks echoing across the battlefield as clips were spent. I worked the bolt on my Thompson and sent a spray of bullets towards the trees, the range was too far to be accurate but it was just an act of anger more than anything. I couldn't do much fighting from my position, had to get closer to effectively use an SMG. Moments like that I still wished I had my old M1 Garand instead of the Thompson.

"I need covering fire!" I looked back, it was Doc. He was waving towards Philips' jeep near the road.

I looked at the jeep and thought on it. Philips was most likely dead, the risk of losing our medic not really worth it. Then again he could be alive and need help. I sure as hell would want Doc to help me in that situation. "Squad, covering fire on Doc!"

Keeping tight aim on a target wasn't needed as everyone unleashed a broadside of lead towards the German positions. Doc didn't hesitate as we started firing, taking off at a dead run for the overturned jeep. The man was just about ignoring the shooting, bullets whizzing by our only medic. He kept his head low and threw himself behind the overturned jeep, crawling out of sight as I rolled over to my back to reload.

"Adam!" I shouted as he lay prone behind me. He belly crawled to my side, radio receiver held out for me. Adam knew enough to have artillery or air support on the line when it was needed.

"105 arty back in town," he said, "call sign Archer one-five."

" Archer one-five, Archer one-five," I radioed as a bullet zoomed through the air and thudded, into the ground, near my right thigh. "This is Sword requesting fire support, over."

Static, then a response. "We read you, Sword. Gird reference?"

I fished out my map and read the faded paper. "Fire support danger close, gird reference Charlie one-seven, Romeo niner-two. Infantry in concealed cover, requesting HE rounds, over."

The numbers were read back to me. "Barrage on the way, shot out!"

I tossed the receiver back, waving out to the squad to signal the incoming barrage. I rolled to my stomach and pressed myself lower, into the dirt, face resting on the side of my Thompson. The high whistle of arty shells filled the air with the incoming barrage. The earth jumped beneath me with each shell strike, a hard series of explosions ripping through the trees. Plumes of dirt were tossed up, trees splintered and were torn from the ground, and men were ripped apart. A handful of Germans abandoned their positions and rushed out, into the open, only to hit a wall of lead that took them down. Twenty shells were fired all together, before silence returned.

"Keep low," I hissed as the air was thick with dust and smoke. Keeping behind my jeep I rose into a crouch and looked towards the Germans. My eyes watered, the air thick with cordite and dust, a heavy haze was blocking out most of the tree line from sight.

No more pops or cracks from rifles or the hard chatter of machine guns. Unsure of if they were all taken out, I decided to stay low and did a check of the squad. I moved down the side of the road, taking a head count as well as checking for injuries. Aside from cuts, scratches, and Sander's wound everyone was fine. I looked over to the jeep overturned on the road, still no sign of Doc or Philips.

"Edwards," I called out, "keep everyone down and watch for stragglers. Malks, come with me."

Malks pulled himself up from the ground and moved to my side as I crossed back, onto the road. The air was still again, no more bullets flying around with shrapnel. Major Philips' jeep was about two dozen yards out from the squad's position. Flames had engulfed the overturned jeep, black oily smoke covering any signs of its riders.

"Think they're alive?" Malks asked as we approached.

I wiped away tears from the smoke. "Who knows."

I moved around the jeep and spotted Doc crouching over a body, his back to us. I couldn't tell who was wounded, though the driver was dead for sure, his body wedged under the jeep with a gaping hole in his chest. Doc was working on another man while a third body was next to him. "Who?" I asked moving to Doc.

He didn't look at me. "Hasel is dead, didn't have a chance," Doc answered, deadpan. "Philips is torn up, but alive." I looked down at Major Philips, his face cut up and a deep gash running from his right shoulder to his heart.

"Can we help?" Malks asked looking over my shoulder.

Doc grunted to himself as he fastened a pressure bandage. "He needs to be taken to an aide station for proper treatment or he will die."

I turned, calling out to the squad. "Adam, radio!"

He quickly picked himself up and ran for my position as the others remained still and in position, eyes still watching the tree line. Malks crouched next down to Hasel and the driver, taking each of their dog tags from the bodies. "Adam, contact command and tell them I need a jeep up here right away, Major Philips is critically wounded and needs to get to an aide station."

"Yes, sir," he answered going right to work to reach division command.

Machine gun fire suddenly erupted behind me, forcing me to dive for cover without thinking. Green tracers cut through the air with zips and hisses, hard thumps coming from where rounds hit dirt. "Down, down!" I shouted struggling to pinpoint where the fire was coming from. Engines could be heard, the hard grinding of steel on rock following. Looking ahead of us I could see a pair of Panzer IV tanks advancing on us, infantry moving in from behind.

"Shift fire, shift fire!" I yelled firing my Thompson. "Targets to the west!"

One Panzer fired, the heavy shell blowing away a chunk of the road in front of us. Machine guns chattered away stitching up our position with lead. Doc dropped down over the Major as a shield, until the barrage subsided just enough for him to drag Philips into a ditch besides the road.

"Cap!" Malks shouted a few feet from me. "Cap, we got a bazooka in the last jeep! Cover me and I'll get it!"

A burst of MG fire forced Malks back down, the rounds ripping up the dirt around us. I rolled to my left in time to miss the bullets from ripping across my body. Thompson up, I returned fire with a quick burst before scrambling into the ditch for cover. Doc was still working on Philips, seeming to block out the fighting around us. Malks crawled back towards the ditch under heavy fire, his pack being literally shot off his back. When he was close enough I crawled out and pulled him into cover.

"We need the bazooka," he grunted, fumbling to load shells into his shotgun.

I looked towards the Germans, the two Panzers now twenty or so yards away. "Keep low and stay in the ditch, you get me?"

He nodded already turning to move towards the last jeep. Adam and I crawled to the lip of the ditch and fired out at the German troops around the Panzers. Adam was able to better aim with his rifle then I could with an SMG, so I lobbed the last of my grenades at them. Explosions forced the infantry to halt their advance and move for cover behind their tanks. Several dropped from bullets, but the Panzers were un phased.

Dropping back down to reload, I glanced towards Malks. Our engineer was already down the ditch to where the jeep was near the road. Bullets smacked into the dirt and jeep itself, but Malks made it the entire way unharmed. He moved quick, pulling the large bazooka from the rear of the jeep and tossing the pack loaded with rockets over his shoulder. Keeping to the ditch, he raced back to us.

A two man team usually operated a bazooka to get maximum efficiently from such a clumsy weapon, but only a handful of us had actually used one and that was in training in England. Malks was well versed in the weapon when compared to the rest of us and I maybe had the next best amount of experience. I used the weapon twice outside of training.

Malks swung the hollow tube over his shoulder and sighted the closest tank. "Load!" he shouted as I picked up the pack of spare rockets,

My mind went back to the routines of training, everything now running on memory. I fumbled slightly getting out one of the rockets and then loading it into the bazooka. Next was hooking up the primer from the rocket to the firing mechanism of the bazooka itself. Everything finished I tapped Malks on the shoulder and turned away, hands over my ears.

A hard, hollow thump echoed with the hard screech and whoosh of air, the heat running across my back. I looked out to see the smoke trail off the rocket as it raced towards one of the Panzers. I didn't follow the rocket or see the impact, just heard it as I was already loading up another rocket. I had to be careful with my hands, bare flesh easily being burned or even fusing to the metal of the bazooka itself.

Another explosion erupted by the tanks, this one louder than a tank firing. I looked over for a quick glance to see what had happened when I saw both Panzers had rolled to a stop and were burning in the field. Rifle and machine gun fire cracked and popped from the far tree line behind the Germans, enemy troops near the burning tanks dropping to the ground. Malks let the bazooka drop off his shoulder as I reached for my Thompson.

"Friendly fire?" Malks asked watching the fighting.

I looked closer at the tree line, no soldier visible just muzzle flashes. I tried to get a better view, reaching for my binoculars only to find them broken, the glass shattered and metal dented. A single smashed bullet, a rifle round, was lodged firmly in the center near the adjusting knob, which rested above the center of my chest. I left them to hang from my neck.

"Sounds like ours," I grunted hearing the reassuring metallic clicks of Garand Rifles. Malks and I watched as the remaining Germans were killed in the cross fire, all soon dead or wounded in a few minutes. Before long, all shooting died down and only the cries and moans of wounded men could be heard.

"Doc, how is he?" I called over my shoulder. Doc was still perched over Philips, hands against the bloodied bandages.

"Barely stable…for now." He glanced at his watch, the glass stained with crimson blood. "He's in no way out of the woods yet, but he shouldn't die in the next ten minutes," Doc said.

I turned back to the field, something stirred in the far tree line. Whoever they were, they used American weapons and just took out two Panzers with their infantry escort. I decided to move out into the open and get their attention. Instead of just standing up and risk getting shot, I crawled down into the ditch near the trees and moved towards the edge of the road. I could all most feel weapons being trained on me as I held up my Thompson over my head, high enough to be seen.

"Infantry?" someone one shouted from across the field inside the tree line.

That voice seemed familiar. "Airborne?" I asked.

A pause. "Depends, what unit are you with?" Said the voice.

"First Infantry, Charlie Company," I responded now feeling that voice was very familiar. I decided to call out again. "Smith?"

An even longer pause after I spoke. "What? Corr, is that you?" The voice asked.

I moved up a little bit to look out. Still no one was in sight, but I crawled out a little more to get a better look. A single soldier appeared by the trees, partially shielded in the thick foliage. Even without my binoculars I could see the khaki colored uniform and the overstuffed pants pockets of a paratrooper. I rose back up into a kneeling position and waved towards them. The trooper waved back, turning to issue orders to his men.

"Malks, get the squad up here," I ordered. Malks nodded and turned back to gather up the squad. Doc was still with Philips tending his wounds, though all he could really do now was keep pressure on the wound and hope that the blood loss won't kill him.

The group of paratroopers moved quickly to our position from the tree line, moving to a wide ditch near the road for cover. I moved to greet the paratrooper in command, a friendly face from the chaos of D-Day.

"Of course I'd meet you in some field in Germany," Smith greeted me, hand reaching out.

I happily shook his hand. "I live to surprise."

Smith nodded. "Live to survive is more like it." He looked over my shoulder at Doc and Philips. "Doc, get up here. There more wounded?"

"Besides the Major one of my men took a round to the shoulder. That's it I think."

My squad moved up the road to our position quickly now that the shooting came to an end. Everyone seemed to be fine at first glance, minor cuts and bruises obvious on some faces and then there was Sanders with a blood encrusted bandage wrapped around his shoulder. Again I cursed myself for not knowing right away, I was in charge of keeping them safe and I should have known. Thank God for men likes Jay and Edwards, who ran the squad as much as I did.

"All counted for and combat ready," Jay reported cradling his sniper rifle. "The jeeps are all write offs, I'm afraid."

I nodded to Sanders. "Your arm?"

He shrugged, flinching a little at the pain. "Just a fleshy wound, boss."

Smith's medic, another medically trained young man named Doc just like ours, ran up to Sanders and checked the bandage. Sucking up the pain like so many soldiers do, Sanders tried shrugging it off, but in the end looked away and bit his lip as a new bandage was applied.

"Any word on that jeep?" I asked Adam.

"The front is continuing to shift our way. Another forward scouting element is heading our way and will take the Major back."

One problem handled I turned back to Smith. "Okay, now how faraway is this aircraft plant?"

Smith hesitated a bit. "It's a mile or more west, but the Germans rigged her up good with lots of explosives. Some poor bastard from Able Company stumbled into a trap and tripped the whole thing. That base is buried under a shit load of rock so I left Charlie Company to keep an eye on the place while we tried to reach our lines."

Mangon came up behind me. "Is it bad?" I asked.

"All I saw was a few tons of rock and dirt come down on the entrance," Mangon said.

Malks suddenly looked very eager, tapping my shoulder. "The charges may have just gummed up the entrance. Get me up there with an engineering section and I'll get the way clear."

"Actually there's some kind of German base or camp about a mile north of here we've been trying to scout out for the past few days. We've been tied up with that aircraft plant so my men have been divided up," Smith said.

I caught on. "You want us to go with you?"

He nodded. "The extra man power would be appreciated."

I looked back to Major Philips, the noise of jeep engines now echoing from down the road. "Technically I'm still under the Major's orders to reach that aircraft plant."

"No way anyone is getting in any time soon and we could really use the extra support."

I looked back as the recon team arrived and quickly loaded Major Philips into one of the jeeps. The Sergeant in charge of the group spoke with Doc before taking his group back down the road. Just like that, Philips was gone.

"Adam, tell command we linked up with the paratroopers and are proceeding to a German camp about a mile north of our current position. We'll check in later.

Our radio operator obeyed, calling into division as I regrouped the squad. Smith was already forming his men up in a skirmish formation before ordering them to start moving north. I moved the squad a few yards off the paratrooper's left flank in a loose formation with a standard three meter spread. Jay and Edwards moved at the edges of the group while I moved at the lead with Smith.

Working with the torn and faded maps both Smith and I carried, we worked out that the enemy base was on the opposite edge of the tree line directly due north. There were no towns or anything of the like within four miles of the camp, or any major roadways that were marked on the map. Smith had no real idea what this camp was used for, a prisoner of war camp possibly or a supply dump were his guesses.

We moved slowly and carefully as both squads passed into the tree line and continued onward. Enemy troops were fighting hard to stall our advance into Germany as much as possible, taking hard defensive stands where they could. Forrest were the most effective cover, the thick trees hid armor and large groups of infantry from the flyboys. I had heard reports of patrols moving through forest areas stumbling upon whole platoons of Germans hiding out.

Marching a mile across rough terrain chewed up time quickly, even with trained troops, who knew how to navigate such ground. A hard push through the trees proved to take nearly half an hour for us before reaching the tree line near the southern edge of the camp. Stopping to survey the area, a small dirt road wrapped around the base and ran off to the west. A wide, open clearing ran between the camp edge and the tree line maybe thirty to forty yards wide.

The camp itself was made of about two dozen wooden buildings and shacks set up in an even grid pattern. A wide open area ran down the camp's center from a main entrance, facing us to another on the far northern side. Four guard towers were placed at the four corners of camp, built inside the high barbed wire fence. All were empty and unmanned as was the guard shack near the main gate. No soldiers patrolled the perimeter or the inside of the camp, which struck me as odd.

"Something missing from this picture?" Smith asked.

"No soldiers or guards," I remarked looking at the unmanned MG42s in the towers. "You think they just abandoned everything and retreated?"

Smith shrugged. "I've seen it before in a small village, but they were all conscripts. Hmm, this doesn't look like any military base I've seen."

Jay appeared at my side. "I've done a quick check of the area and I don't see anyone. The place is empty."

"I'll send out scouts." Smith waved towards the camp and signaled for four men to move up and scout things out. The four moved west in the tree line and then turned north, heading through the western tree line. We would wait for their report before moving out.

"Something feels really wrong," I heard Edwards mumble from behind me. Glancing back I saw several of the others nod in agreement, some speaking their thoughts in low mumbles.

Watching the still and silent camp I worried that this was an ambush waiting to happen. A very inviting target was an abandoned base for some patrol of green to find and try and take for glory or something of the like. I was expecting a platoon or two of German infantry to be hiding somewhere in the trees just waiting to spring the trap. I could already feel the blood in my veins running cold like ice water.

"Did you see that?" Sanders suddenly blurted out, the sudden noise making me jump a little.

I looked across the camp. "See what? What are you talking about?"

He moved up to crouch next to me, pointing out towards one of the wooden buildings past the fence. "There, I could've sworn I saw someone walking around."

Everyone tensed up. "Smith, you see anything?" I asked.

"I...I can't be sure if I saw someone. Something is moving out there, though," Smith said.

As he spoke the four man scouting team returned. I noticed their faces were pale, almost all color drained. One trooper seemed to be in shock, eyes wide and glassy while another's hands shook as he held his rifle.

"Well, what did you see?" Smith asked.

They were silent at first. A corporal spoke up first. "Sarge, I...I don't know what they hell I saw."

This drew very concerned looks from both Smith and me. "Take it slow, Morgan."

Corporal Morgan sank down to the ground, eyes still wide. "We were approaching the western side of the fence and everything was still quiet. I was about to get a closer look when Tim said he smelt something really bad nearby. I thought it was nothing, but I knew that smell, Sarge. It was...death."

Morgan paused as he took a slow breath. "We checked it out, heading deeper into the woods when we found it." Again he stopped, resting his rifle in his lap as his hands pressed together and went to his mouth. Tears were welling in his eyes.

"Morgan, what did you find?" I demanded.

He didn't answer right away, taking time to control his sobbing. "It...it was...a grave I think. Oh my God, Sarge. There were so many...bodies just dumped into this trench. There...there had to be a least fifty of them just left there."

Smith and I exchanged glances. "Were they POWs?" I asked.

Morgan shook his head, the young man barely holding it together. "I don't...I don't think so, Sarge. They weren't wearing uniforms, it was more like some kind of pajamas maybe, but there were..." He trailed off, now consumed by harsh sobbing that gave way to full blown crying. Another paratrooper quickly shuffled to his side and held his brother in arms, letting the corporal cry.

Smith and I still needed answer, but we asked one of the other four. "Dan, what did you see?" I asked.

The private rubbed a hand over his mouth. "There were kids in there. God, there had to be twenty kids in there. All were shot dead by something heavy, a 42 maybe."

My blood ran cold as I spoke. "And inside the camp?"

"People, but not many that I could see. They...they looked like skeletons. Sort of like starved, I think. No Germans though," Dan said.

Smith looked to me and was at a loss for words. I managed to think up orders. "Let's get up there and see what the hell is going on. I'll head up to the main gate with my team while you hold back and watch our rear."

He nodded, grabbing a hold of himself. "Okay, we'll hang back and cover you. Once you reach the gate, we'll be right behind you," Smith said.

I nodded in agreement. Jumping to my feet and moving towards the road, I waved the squad to advance up to the main gate. They still moved in a loose skirmisher formation to keep from bunching up and approached with weapons held at the ready. My mind was still a flurry of thought about what the two scouts had told us. If those were the bodies of children then these people couldn't have been captured soldiers or pilots. They would have to be civilians, or criminals maybe.

Edwards and I approached the main gate of the camp, finding a thick pad lock and chain holding it closed. Up closer now we could see that there were no German soldiers around, the tracks on the ground showing a massive movement of personal and vehicles out of the camp and heading off to the west. With no bolt cutters, Nate slid his rifle in between the chain and the fence, turning the rifle to wrap the rusted chain around it. With a hard shove down once the chain was wrapped, the rusted links popped. He pulled the useless chain away and helped open the wooden gates.

The smell was overpowering as we walked into the camp, the odor of death unmistakable for anything else. Bodies were strewn about the ground, most dead from gunshot wounds while others had no marks at all. Getting closer to what the private had said was true; these people were skeletons or at least looked it. They were starved for sure, a clear view of their bones under very loose skin.

"Stop!" Edwards suddenly shouted when I was looking at a group of bodies. I snapped back around as he stood several feet away with his Thompson raised. "I said stop!"

He was aiming at…at a person standing just feet away. It took my brain time to just sort out what I was seeing, but then I made some sense of it. Whoever this person was, he was dressed in ragged black and white stripped clothes that looked like pajamas or something, a cloth yellow star sewn on his jacket. His skin was a sickly pale color, pulled tightly enough to outline the bones underneath. It was like looking at a corpse.

"Easy," I said to Edwards eyeing this strange person. I glanced behind him, seeing even more, dozens more emerging from the other wooden buildings. The squad just stood still where they were, unsure of what to do. "Do you speak English?"

He didn't speak, simply stared at Edwards until he lowered the Thompson. I switched to my fractured French, but to no effect. Next I spoke my very limited German and got a response.

"They are gone," was the man told me. He was most likely referring to the German soldiers.

I turned to Phelps. "Get Smith up here with his squad right away. Check if he has anyone who speaks German."

"Yes, sir!" Sanders replied before running back to the trees.

"Ah, Cap?" Vic asked watching the prisoners emerge from the huts. "What do we do?"

I had no idea what to do as I didn't know who these people were. It was clear that they were starved and sickly, no threat to any of us. "Okay, let's try to keep these people contained and not let them just wonder out of the camp. Adam, get me a link to division command right now. Doc, I…"

Doc stepped forward, moving close to visual examine the man. "It's obvious starvation, Captain. Disease has to be a huge problem too, so I think its best we be careful with them."

I didn't speak as dozens and dozens more these people were emerging from the huts and buildings, some shuffling towards us while others just dropped to the ground. Smith ran up to my side with another trooper, stopping and looking on in stunned silence like me. "What in God's name…"

"You have a translator?" I asked.

Smith nodded, nodding to the trooper with him. "Corporal Allen knows the language."

I turned to the private. "Ask him his name."

Allen stepped up and asked, the man answering with his name as Francis.

I was unsure of just what to asked. "Umm, ask him what's going on here, what happened to the Germans."

Allen repeated the question in German and spoke a translated answer. "He says the Germans left early the day before, heading east to avoid our advance. The guards didn't have much ammo left, but they tried killing as many of the prisoners as they could. When they ran low on ammo, they just locked the gates and left." Allen paused to listen. "He says the people here are starving and are very sick and need medical help quickly. Many people have died already and many more will follow soon."

I looked at the man, my gaze shifting to the star. "Ask him what the star means, are they criminals or something?"

He asked and listened. "No, they aren't criminals at all. They're... average people, sir. Bankers, teachers, doctors, shop keepers, day laborers, just your everyday kind of people."

"Okay, but why the star? Why are they locked up and treated like this?" I asked, impatiently.

Allen seemed to be unsure of the man's answer. "He...he says they're all here because they're Jewish, sir. All of them are Jews."

That made no sense to me at the time. "What? You mean they're here just because they're Jews?"

Allen nodded. "That's why the star, the Star of David is a Jewish... symbol. I think that's how you'd put it."

I could feel my stomach tighten up, bile climbing up my throat. Adam tapped my shoulder, handing over the radio receiver. Major Hendricks was on the line.

"Major Hendricks, sir," I said fumbling for my words. "We...we found this...well I don't know what you'd call it. You need to see this, sir."

"Just what exactly is this place, sir?" I asked Major Hendricks when he arrived. Hendricks looked out at the camp, eyes seeming to be fixed on the group of medics he brought with him. The Major arrived about ten minutes after I called in, arriving with fifteen or so medics and a full rifle platoon.

"We're still unclear on that, Captain," Hendricks answered with a heavy sigh. "Several camps like this one have turned up already as we press into Germany. Most are filled with Jews, but it's also a collection of other kinds people that the Nazis want to disappear. Some were labor camps of some kind, others just prisons more or less."

"How do we handle something like this?" Edwards asked.

"We need to keep these people contained for now. That's why I brought along another platoon, they'll take over here while we get these people help," I said.

Jay chimed in. "So you're locking them back up?"

Hendricks looked at us directly. "It's not pretty, son, but it's what needs to be done. It's for their own good."

Doc nodded in agreement. "These people are starving so they need to be carefully fed, if not they'll try to get as much food as they can and eat themselves to death. Also, a lot are very sick with a wide range of diseases so we can't risk possible spread of any type of infections."

"What are we to do now, sir?" Jay asked.

"The German garrison here might be in a small hamlet two miles southwest of here. A paratrooper scouting force may have spotted them and I want you to head there to check it out. Get loaded up in the halftracks I brought with me and get there right away, that squad from the 82nd is going with you too."

I looked at Jay and Edwards. "Are we to bring them back, sir?"

"Find whoever was in command at this camp and bring him back." I ordered.

I saluted, knowing just how impossible that might be.

"Yes, sir," They responded.

In less than an hour we reached a quiet, out of the way hamlet two miles southwest of the camp. Removed far from the main roadways, I had the halftracks drop us off half a mile from the hamlet itself. To maintain the element of surprise Smith and I led our squads through the thick forests on foot. Smith moved his squad around to approach from the south while my squad moved in from the north.

The tiny hamlet was no more than two dozen wooden homes built around a tiny church and town square. It was near impossible to find on our area maps, but the Germans troops were there for sure. Keeping to cover on a small ridge to the north of the hamlet I could see a German staff car parked with a single troop truck. About a dozen soldiers milled about the vehicles while eight or so more were by a large house several yards away. Chances were good that's where the commandant or senior officer was.

The squad snuck into the hamlet near a cluster of houses a block to the north of the church, keeping off the main road and crossing through backyards. The houses were silent and still, not a single civilian to be seen or heard. Passing through the yards and not seeing any kind of wash hanging out to dry or any other signs of life, it appeared whoever had lived in the hamlet was long gone.

Hoping over a low stone wall, I shuffled across the dirt road to a small store on the opposite side. Edwards was right behind me with the squad trailing behind him. So far we hadn't run into any German soldiers, but as we got closer to the church we could hear the low murmur of voices. I used hand signals to send five men around the back of the store while the rest of us proceeded up the road. Smith and his squad were in position covering the southern road to prevent any Germans from escaping while we flushed them out.

Coming to the end of the street, I stayed behind an empty house for cover and peered around the corner. Roughly fifteen German soldiers were standing about in the square in front of the church. Most were near a small well in the square or near the troop truck and staff car. Some could've been in the church, but it was small enough that it couldn't offer a good spot for a spotter or sniper. The large house where the rest of the Germans were was a few dozen yards across from the church, our direct view blocked by the troop truck.

I turned back to the squad waved them forward, everyone springing to action at once. I move out from behind the building and proceeded up the street towards the church with my weapon raised. Sanders and Vic were moving up on the opposite side of the street as the first Germans were in range.

Two soldiers were standing a dozen feet away from me, facing away from us. I leveled my sights on one of them and fired, the burst catching the soldier in the small of his back. He fell to the ground as I killed the second and the rest of the squad opened up. The Germans were caught off guard, all scrambling for cover as the shooting started. Vic rushed up to an overturned cart on the edge of the square and sprayed the area with fire from his BAR.

"Grenade!" Phelps shouted as he tossed a grenade overhand at the soldiers near the staff car. Four were killed in the blast as ten soldiers emerged from the large house.

"There's an officer with them!" Jay shouted as he tracked them with his sniper rifle.

"We need him alive!" I shouted back. "Don't kill him!"

I fired on the remaining soldiers that sought cover behind the well or had rushed for the church itself. The five man group who went behind the store had found good firing positions already and cut down anyone running for the church. I ran from my position towards the troop truck as the men by the well were suppressed. Jay was picking off the men guarding the officer while Malks and Nate moved with me.

We ducked down behind the rear of the truck, the group of soldiers moved to the staff car. I fired on them, taking care not to hit the officer with them. The men protecting him were taken down easily as the officer ducked behind the staff car for cover. Malks and Nate moved around to the front of the car, and I moved around the rear, being cautious as the officer was carrying a Luger.

I rounded the car and the officer fired, his first shot going wide. I put one round into his leg, the pain forcing him to drop the pistol. I kept my Thompson trained on the man as I kicked away the Luger. "Don't move," I barked in German.

"That's him?" Nate asked looking down at him. "That's an SS uniform."

I nodded. "Yea. Let's get Doc up here and get Smith to…"

There was a loud roar as Malks fired his shotgun without warning, both Nate and I jumping out of surprise. One second I was looking at the wounded officer and the next a gaping hole was ripped out of his chest. Malks just stood there, shotgun still leveled on the body.

"Son of a bitch, Malks!" I shouted. "I told you we needed to capture him!"

Malks didn't flinch as he lowered the weapon. "You saw what he's responsible for. The bastard deserved worse."

I moved close to him, shoving his shoulder to get his attention. "You killed an unarmed prisoner."

He looked at me, eyes full of rage and sadness. "Martha is Jewish, sir! My wife and my daughter both are! The thought of them being… being…" I moved in closer as he trailed off and dropped to the ground. Both Nate and I jumped to catch Malks before he hit the ground. He was now crying uncontrollably, entire body trembling. Doc had not seen what had happened, rushing over thinking that Malks had been hit. I waved him off with a shake of the head. Malks, just like all of us, had been wounded, just not physically.

Chapter 21

No one spoke about what occurred in that nameless hamlet in Germany after we were pulled from the line. Major Hendricks didn't write up or discipline anyone from the squad or myself, for the death of the nameless SS officer. Instead he just offered some words of understanding before saying that the officer was, in fact, the one in charge of the camp and that, eventually, he would've been executed for war crimes. We, he said to me, had just cut back on the time.

After the a foothold was established outside of Remagen, the Big Red One swung to the south, driving into Czechoslovakia as March turned into April. Our squad however, was not going with the rest of the division into Czechoslovakia to take on the Nazis there. Instead, we were going with Major Philips, who was now out of the hospital and back in command, to Berlin. The Allies were still not there, but we would also not be aiding in the drive there either. Major Philips had held us back to place us on 'special assignment.'

Our 'special assignment' was twofold; first we'd be permanently attached with Philips, who was already promised a posting in Berlin, and second we'd undertake a classified operation of 'extreme importance' for the people in the OSS. With the Allies only miles from Berlin by late April, we were to investigate a small German base two miles southeast of Berlin for sensitive data of some kind. The base, by all accounts, was abandoned.

"Place looks like its seen better days," Jay commented as we both lay on a low ridge east of the German base.

I grunted peering through my binoculars. "I don't see anyone down there. Maybe the place is empty."

Quiet and still, the German base looked completely deserted to me. Nestled at the base of a low ridge, about two dozen wooden buildings were arranged in neat rows, behind a large barbed wire fence. Six empty guard towers sat along the perimeter while two pillboxes were set inside, near two concrete buildings. These two buildings were clearly built to take hard punishment, which they did as the rest of the base was falling apart and ruined by multiple bomb or artillery strikes.

Sanders and Mangon stalked over to us, both breathing heavily. "We checked out the area and nothing, sir," Mangon reported.

"A few knocked out armored cars, but that's it," Sanders added.

I nodded, picking myself up. "Alright let's get in there. Jay, stay here for sniper cover. Everyone else, follow me."

The squad formed back up and proceeded to march down the ridge along a dried creek bed, for cover. There was a scattered amount of trees around to use for concealment, so we kept to the river bed until it veered off to our right, at which point it was all open ground from our position to the base.

Instead of moving everyone at once, I had Vic hang back with Mangon and Nate, to provide cover, while I moved over the open ground with the rest of the squad. Once my group made it across I waved the others to follow as quickly as possible. Together again I led the squad along the perimeter to the main entrance on the north side of the base. Taking it slow and careful, we entered the base and fanned out, moving for cover offered by nearby buildings. I moved to my left, near a bombed out building, pressing myself against its wooden side. Nate moved into the building for a quick check and then returned, signaling it was empty. I nodded and ordered the squad to begin searching each of the buildings for anything that might be of interest to command.

Moving from west to east, the squad and I searched each of the wooden buildings. Many were hollowed out shells, roofs ripped off, walls torn down, and windows shattered. There were no bodies or signs of the German garrison aside from abandoned equipment and weapons scattered about. A few trucks and armored vehicles were lying about all burnt out and gutted. The only things of interest were the concrete buildings and the commander's office. I began a close inspection of the CO's office and would leave the bunkers for last.

"Edwards, post sentries at the main gate to keep a watch for anything. Have the rest of the men fan out in the center compound and set up defensive positions for the time being." Edwards nodded and left to carry out the orders. Adam remained out my side as I combed through the CO's office.

A large oak desk sat center of the room opposite the door, an empty fireplace behind it. Several bookshelves of dust covered books and maps covered one wall with a small table near the room's single window. Pictures of Hitler hung behind the desk on either side of the fireplace, a Nazis flag hanging above it dead center. Adam had lit an old oil lamp for light, the flame casting dancing shadows across the walls.

"I wonder who does their interior decorating," Adam joked as he nodded towards the pictures of Hitler.

I shrugged, standing behind the desk. "They don't have good taste," I commented as I rifled through the drawers. The first four were all empty, a fifth containing some papers. I couldn't make out the words, but I stuffed them in my pocket to give to command.

Adam looked over the books, picking out one or two and thumbing through them before putting them back. "I doubt whoever the German officer was, he didn't read all of these. I can't even understand the language and I know its dry reading." He picked up one book and studied the title. "Hey Captain, can you read this?"

I caught the book as he tossed it, brushing grime off the cover. "Mein Kampf, which means my struggle." I grunted to myself as I saw the author. "Figures Hitler would write a book."

I tossed the book aside and reached down for the last drawer, finding it locked. Testing the lock with a few tugs, I saw it wasn't very tough and with one hard pull it broke with the clatter of shattering metal.

"Find something?" Adam asked looking over his shoulder.

Pulling out the drawer I spotted a silver flask sitting on top of a single manila folder at the bottom. I took out both the flask and folder, tossing the flask to Adam. I looked down at the folder, pulling it open to see a collection of papers inside, the first one bearing the Nazi swastika and eagle emblem. Of course, everything was written out in German, but I looked over the areas marked, in deep red ink, with care. No words I knew stood out to explain why the sections were in red, bold faced ink, but they must have been important.

"Hmm," Adam sighed, as he examined the flask. "I think its scotch. Hey, what are those?"

I could only shrug. "I'm not sure really, but it looks important." I placed the folder and the other papers I collected, into my pack for safe keeping. "C'mon, let's go see what's in those bunkers," I said.

The two of us walked back outside to the rest of the squad as artillery thundered off in the distance. Berlin was just visible from our position, the skyline darkened by near endless clouds of black smoke. The Russians had been going all out to crush the resistance in the city, destroying just about anything in their path. If there was any time to feel bad for the Germans, it was when the Russians were at their door.

"All quiet out here, boss," Edwards reported as he waited out front. "Malks is checking out the bunkers, seems the doors are locked."

I nodded, gesturing towards them. "Let's go and see what's in them. Ramos, come with us."

Ramos nodded and fell in behind as we walked over to the two concrete bunkers. Steel blast doors were sealed shut at the front of each one, a smaller door next to them. Malks was at the bunker on the right, near the smaller steel door. He simply stood their reading a variety of signs near the door.

"What do you got?" I asked, as I approached.

Malks silently shook his head. "I don't read German, but these symbols are simple enough." He pointed to the collection of signs. "In any language that means explosives."

I looked at the signs, knowing one did mean explosive material and other was rather obvious to mean death, with skull and crossbones. Now we had to get inside, but the simple plan of blowing open the door might not be so smart. Malks, however, was thinking two steps ahead and had been working on the tedious task of picking the door lock. It may have taken some time, but it worked and the door slid open with ease.

I moved in first, Thompson up and ready to fire with Malks following right behind me. The bunker was dark, pitch black almost if not for light escaping in from cracks in the hard concrete. It wasn't very large inside, something large was taking up most of the space. I couldn't see much, but I bumped into the steel support struts for something. Ramos brought in an oil lamp from outside and lit it, a small amount of light clearing away some of the darkness.

Slinging my Thompson over my shoulder, I took the lamp and held it up to see what I had bumped into. A large web of support struts were holding up a massive steel cylinder of some kind that was white in color. I walked alongside the massive cylinder until I found some faded markings on the rusted sides. The faded German scribbles were hard to read, but there was the explosive symbol and two words I did recognize in the gibberish.

"Oh fuck," I swore as I took several unconscious steps back and quickly smothered the flame in the lamp. "Everyone out, now!"

Ramos, Adam, Malks, and Edwards all looked at me in confusion as I ushered them all back outside. I slid the steel door back into place with a hollow thud, my heart drumming away in my chest. A fresh wave of anxiety washed over me as I leaned against the bunker and felt a cold sweat creep down my back. Edwards gave me a concerned look as I turned to face him.

"Cap, what's wrong?" he asked as I realized I was panting for air.

I took a breath to steady myself. "Adam, get me a line back to command right away."

Adam, still lost, just nodded and worked to get the radio up and running. Edwards was still watching me. "Sir, what's going on?"

"No one goes inside the bunkers and the doors remain closed," I ordered. "No open flames around these bunkers and no shooting at all."

"I…okay, sir. Just, umm, why?" Edwards said.

"There's a massive container in their full of liquid oxygen. I a got feeling there might be another one in there and God knows what else in the other bunker," I said.

Ramos looked at me as he cradled his rifle. "Uh, just why is that bad, sir?"

Malks answered for me. "Liquid oxygen is very dangerous and unstable to handle. One spark and you get a one hell of an explosion."

I regained my composure, quickly regaining my level headed calmness. Adam was standing by with the radio, an open line to command at the ready. "Sword to Overlord, we've reached the base and it's abandoned. There are two bunkers here that contain large stores of liquid oxygen and who knows what else. I've also recovered a handful of enemy documents that I cannot make out, over."

"Copy on that, Sword," Overlord responded over the intermittent burst of static. "Are there stores of ethyl alcohol there as well?"

"I didn't notice, sir." I held back the fact I just came close to losing my head the second I read the label on the storage tank.

"Hmm, that's interesting enough. Okay, I want you and your men to hold the camp at all costs, those bunkers and papers especially. I'm sending a relief force to secure the base, but it'll be a few hours before they reach you."

I looked at my watch. It would be getting dark in two hours. "Copy, we'll be holding things down. Sword, out."

The radio cut out shortly after, Edwards standing by for further orders. We were literally sitting on an unexploded bomb, for the time being, and I had a single rifle squad to keep the thing safe. With night just a few hours away, it would be a real stretch to cover the base's perimeter with just fifteen men to use. I could have everyone pull back to the bunkers, which were built into a low hill and raised up on a concrete platform by six, or so, feet. The perimeter would be smaller and allow for tighter concentration of fire and setting up of kill zones, but that allowed any attackers to get into the base and make use of the buildings as cover and get closer to us.

On the other hand, I could set up men in the towers to hold the base perimeter, but that would stretch out the squad and lighten up just how much fire could be concentrated on one area. German troops had an easier chance of slipping in through a perimeter gap and getting behind us. I decided the base itself was a ruin and the bunkers were our goal, so I ordered everyone back to set up a defensive line around the bunkers. Chances were if the Germans came back they would be careful about damaging the bunkers.

My squad was lightly armed with only two SMGs and single sniper rifle. The rest were basic Garand rifles, nothing heavier then that aside from a low supply of grenades. Some of the men managed to scavenge two useable MG42s from the towers, with roughly one thousand rounds of ammo for each one, which would go fast in a full on assault. I had the 42s set up in the two flanks of the raised concrete platform while sandbags were taken from across the base and set up around the platform, to create a wall about three feet high. Malks cut up barbed wire from the perimeter fence, to plug up the lone stairway, to the platform as well as a wide slanted driveway used for trucks. Ammo was pooled, grenades readied, weapons were checked and rechecked. The squad moved quickly with their work, getting the majority of the defenses up and ready as night fell.

"I can't see very far, sir," Edwards grunted as he peered through his binoculars scanning the countryside.

I just sighed, my eyes adjusting to the low light as I awoke. "You won't be able to see much, no moon out."

A few feet away Ramos snored lightly as he slept, curled up tightly in his jacket while sleeping on his pack. Only a handful of men were taking time to sleep while the others remained awake, eyes focused on the dark countryside. Distant echoes of artillery and rocket screeches could be heard, off to the east, in Berlin, burning fires illuminating the city. Low rumbles high overhead marked another wing of bombers heading to the besieged city. God help the civilians caught up in this, I thought as the bombers passed.

Edwards gave up his searching and slouched behind the sandbag wall. "It's almost over, isn't it, sir?"

I nodded slightly, taking a swing from my canteen. "It's probably a matter of weeks now, even days maybe."

Edwards looked over at Berlin. "I wonder what it's like." His voice was low and soft.

I looked over at him. "What what's like?"

He shrugged. "To be trapped in the city. There has to be a lot of people still living there, you think so?"

"Yea, there are." I removed my helmet, seeing the picture of Jessica looking up at me. Again another wave of grief washed over me as I still had not got a single letter from her since December and all of my letters had been sent back to me. A clerk had been kind enough to tell me that she wasn't working with division anymore and had left, that was on December 31st.

Edwards lightly nudged my shoulder. "You okay, sir?"

Clenching my jaw to stifle any sobs, I shook my head and managed a smile. "Yea, I'm fine. I'm still not too fond of sitting a few feet from an unstable bomb."

He laughed lightly. "I know the feeling, sir."

"Didn't I tell you to cut out the 'sir' shit?" I said.

Edwards shrugged and cracked his knuckles. "Everything was 'yes, sir, no, sir, I don't know, sir' in training. It's been engraved into me."

"Un-engrave it," Adam remarked as he sat next to me, the radio in his lap. It was rare to not see Adam tinkering with that piece of crap radio of ours. "Well, who cares now? War's coming to an end soon, you can practically feel it."

"Movement on the road!" Sanders suddenly shouted his voice loud and clear.

I leapt to my feet and was next to Sanders in an instant. As I pulled out my binoculars he kept pointing off to the north, though visibility was cut down greatly. I couldn't be sure of the size of the force, but there was a large group of supply trucks and armored cars thundering down to the road towards out position.

"Put out any lights, now!" I hissed thinking that the convoy may not be heading for the base. It could've been a group of soldiers heading west to either fight or surrender. It was very common practice for Germans to flock to US and British lines to surrender instead of facing a vengeful and merciless Red Army.

I hustled everyone into position at the sandbag wall and made sure everyone understood to hold fire until I opened up first. Malks and Sanders took up the two MG42s at our flanks while Jay climbed atop one of the bunkers to set up a sniper's nest. If possible we would lay low and let the convoy pass if it wasn't heading for our position. If they were here into enter the base, I would have to engage.

Edwards crouched down next to me as I picked a stop to fight from. I watched as the lead elements of the German convoy, an armored car and a troop truck followed by a motorcycle, up the road, near the camp and turned to drive to the main gate. The armored car rolled to a stop at the gate as the troop truck continued into the center compound and dropped off fifteen or so soldiers. They were about thirty yards away, but had not seen us.

The soldiers milled about around the truck as two more just like it stopped outside the main gate. As more soldiers piled out, two bulky looking oil trucks grumbled down the road and rolled to halt on the main road. Looking closely at the harsh glare, from the headlights, I could see the two oil trucks were burdened with heavy duty armor plating covering the cab and containers itself. I swore under my breath as there would be no lying low, they were here for the liquid oxygen. My trigger finger stayed on the steel trigger guard as I tracked a group of ten soldiers started to shuffle our way. They walked the main road in the camp straight towards us, still very unaware. When the group was just fifteen yards away I wrapped my finger around the trigger and gave a quick squeeze followed by another and another. Bright muzzle flashes erupted, from our positions, as the squad opened up.

Half of the approaching group was cut down in an instant of the first volley. We began to take return fire as the other Germans scrambled for cover and tried to move the fuel trucks to safety. Both of our 42s sliced through the center of the compound taking out a good twenty soldiers before they scattered. The armored car, a simple scout car only mounting a single MG42, rolled out to face us so the gunner could open fire.

Jay was quick and took out the gunner before he could swing his MG42, to face us and fire. The gunner's head jerked back, with a shattering force, and his body slumped forward over the 42 before dropping down, into the armored car. A grenade went off to my right as I was reloading, the explosion going off just in front of the concrete platform on the ground. Most of the shrapnel and force was blocked, but I felt something incredibly hot smack me in the face and force me back.

I dropped back as my free hand went to my face, the slick feeling of blood running down my cheeks. The pain was not overwhelming, but I could feel just where I was cut. It was nothing life threatening and Doc couldn't do much, so I returned to the firing line. Thankfully, my sight wasn't affected as the Germans began to press their attack.

Flanking groups, of ten to twelve men, were trying to use the buildings for cover and get around to hit our rear. Both MG42s kept them back, but the attack was just renewed down the center. The Germans didn't fling themselves into the hail storm of bullets, instead getting as close as they could to us before finding cover and then fighting back.

A hard screech rang out as an AT rocket was fired, the brightly burning warhead cutting just over our heads. I watched the rocket fling past the bunkers and explode into the hillside, with a shower of dirt. I scanned the sea of German soldiers looking to see who was using the rocket launcher, spotting some young faced trooper, near the rear of the armored car. A volley of.45 caliber slugs put him on the ground.

"On the left!" I heard Adam yell. He was watching the left flank, carbine rifle putting out rounds in a steady pace. A handful of soldiers, maybe eight or nine, were pushing up hard on the left flank with an MG42 crew.

I moved to Malks, who was manning the left 42, and told him to target the enemy gunners. Tracer fire ripped across the approaching group without mercy, men jerking wildly as each round hit its mark. Several men tumbled to the ground as the first broadside caught them in the chest and stomach. The group of machine gunners dropped their heavy weapon and dove for cover between the old buildings. Malks didn't hesitate as he raked the buildings with MG fire, their weak wooden walls easily splintered.

Something metal clanked at our feet, slipping over the concrete platform. Before I could shout grenade, Nate was up fast. He scooped up the grenade in one hand and tossed it back at the Germans. The potato masher grenade exploded as it still pin wheeled through the air with the explosive back lash catching one unlucky soldier in the face. He wasn't screaming for long before a bullet ended his misery.

"Adam, radio!" I shouted as groped for a fresh clip for my Thompson. Adam responded quickly and handed me the radio, returning to firing as I had the receiver. "Sword to Overlord, Swore to Overlord, over!" I could only hear harsh static over the rattle and crack of rifles and machine guns. Again, I repeated the call to command and again there was no response. Static still crackled, but a voice did answer back. "…lord is here. Sword, respond."

"Overlord, this is Sword responding." Another grenade blast nearby forced me to duck down.

"Sword, status update, over," the hard voice belonged to Major Philips. The man was hardened after he was nearly killed, but no one could blame him for that.

"Overlord, heavy enemy force is trying to overrun over position at the enemy base." The hard thud-thud-thud of heavy cannon fire echoed off to the north. I looked out as a short column of heavy armored cars thundered towards us. "Infantry with supporting armored cars. Be advised we have nothing to stop armor, over," I yelled.

"Sword, you are to hold your ground at all cost. Do not let the Germans retake those bunkers. Do not let the Germans retake those bunkers. A relieving force is in route to your location as we speak and will arrive in one hour. Hold until relieved, Overlord out."

I held back a wave of insults as the radio snapped off into harsh static. Suddenly, a full side of rifle fire rose up off to my right. Bullets peppered the ground around Adam and me as four German soldiers managed to get to up the staircase and past the first sections of barbed wire. I turned to fire as several bullets struck the radio. Sparks flew and the force threw Adam to the ground, and the radio began to burn. I dropped the attackers before turning to Adam, who began to panic.

The radio was sparking and burning, hissing harshly as Adam struggled to get the radio off his back. I reached down with my knife and quickly cut the straps that were keeping the radio on his back. Working fast, the straps were cut and I shoved it off him, taking a second to brush bits of burning hot metal off of his jacket. I hauled him back to his feet, dropping the carbine rifle back in his hands.

"You hurt?" I asked as Adam tried to regain himself.

He nodded, eyes no longer wide with fear. "Yea…I'm good, sir."

More grenade blasts erupted around our position and showered us with concrete chips and dirt. The squad was still keeping up suppressive fire as best they could, the ground around my feet nearly covered in spent shell casings and empty clips. Our MG42s were still firing, but they were in short five to seven round bursts to conserve as much ammo as possible.

German soldiers were getting closer and closer to us, jumping from cover to cover. Another group of soldiers, three or four at the most, managed to get under Sander's line of fire and started to climb up the platform. Nate was beside Sanders and spotted the soldiers, taking out one with a round to the face as he appeared over the sandbags. The second took another round to the throat, ripping open his lower jaw.

Two more managed to climb up just off to Nate's right, getting behind him without his notice. Both were clamoring over the sandbag wall and struggling to get their weapons to bear as I poured the rest of my clip into them. Both were killed in the assault and fell back to the muddied ground.

Down!" Edwards shouted as he tackled me to the ground. I crashed into the hard concrete with Edwards on top of me and the air rushing out from my lungs.

The hard thump-thump-thump of heavy cannon fire barked out from the far road as the group of armored cars rolled into position. Concrete chunks pelted my back, the shells hit the bunkers, sparks flying as some pelted the metal doors. I crawled forward as the cars dropped their aim lower and forced everyone to duck for cover. The sandbags wouldn't stand against such heavy fire and we would be slaughtered without a fight.

I moved towards Jay as he lay prone several feet away loading his sniper rifle. I was about to call out to him when the section of platform off to my left violently exploded, in a shower of concrete and shrapnel. The force of the blast picked me up and tossed me off to the right. Pain shot through my body as I slammed into the side of the bunker, dropping back down to the platform.

My ears rang sharply, the sounds of battle now muted. My vision faded in and out as I struggled to roll to my back, my muscles refusing to respond. I struggled to even move my head up. Blood soaked through my jacket and ran down my cheeks. Doc was at my side in an instant, rolling me over and my gaze was no longer on the hard concrete, but now on the burning stars above.

"Hang on, Cap," Doc cried out as he tore open my jacket. Everything was fading and I thought that this was it. My number was up, the war finally taking me. Dead on the last day, just as dead on the first. "Just hang on for me, everything will be fine."

Chapter 22

May 7th, 1945. Nearly six years of war that ravaged Europe had finally come to an end with the surrender of Nazi Germany.

2 weeks later

"How long do you think we'll be here?" Nate asked as we watched a group of German civilians. They toiled away in the rubble chocked street, clearing away the remains of a fallen building.

"As long as they need us to," Jay answered curtly, resting his sniper rifle on his hip. "Don't worry, we'll be home soon enough."

I remained silent, closed up in my own thoughts. There wasn't much else to do as I sat with the squad in the exposed second floor of a bombed out building. There was no wall or ceiling, just a shattered floor that overlooked the checkpoint in the street below. We were to just sit and watch as German civilians worked to clear out rubble from the streets. MPs manned the checkpoint and watched the Russian checkpoint no more than a block away.

"Hey whatever happened to that girl?" Sanders asked sitting on the floor with his legs dangling over the edge. "You know, the one from D-Day?"

Edwards gave him a hard slap to the back of the head. "Don't be asking him that stuff," he scolded.

I looked over at the two, just shaking my head. "She's gone, Sanders," I mumbled looking down at the picture in my helmet. "Moved on with her life, I hope."

The others were silent, some looking down at the street as the civilians worked and military traffic flowed. I turned away from them, gaze dropping back to folded and faded picture stuck inside of my helmet's webbing. I had to accept that she was gone for good, now another civilian displaced by the war. I considered trying to search for her, but the odds were slim and it was only a matter of time before I returned back to the states.

"Sir," Adams spoke first, breaking the silence, "we're scheduled for patrol in five minutes."

I slipped my helmet back on, shaking myself back to reality. "I know. Squad, mount up and let's get going."

Even with my depression, I put my effort into remaining the dedicated officer I was for the squad. I stoop up from the rickety chair I was sitting in and shuffled for the far staircase that led down to the first floor of the bombed out house. Our days in Berlin were all the same, with long patrols during the day along the border streets between the American and Russian sectors and then nights to do, basically, as we pleased.

The MPs at the checkpoint briefly nodded in my direction as I led the squad past the road barricades and barbed wire coils. The streets were jammed up with rubble and were mostly impassible by any type of vehicle and extremely dangerous to traverse on foot. Most buildings were hollowed out husks, steel or masonry skeletons gutted by Allied bombs or artillery. Even with such destruction, the German people still went about with their lives.

Many patrols through the war torn streets led us past civilians, fighting to survive or trying to rebuild. Men, women, and children of all ages were about, working on gathering scraps of food or trying to find some type of shelter. In most cases the people were working on rebuilding their city and, in our areas, trying to avoid Russian soldiers. They may have been a defeated people, but they were as determined as anything to continue on.

That day we were patrolling past a gutted park, keeping to the western edge as the eastern edge was Russian territory. They had patrols out as well, mostly ten man squads picking their way across the ruins for anything of interest, spoils of war in a way. I made sure we steered clear of them while we were allies, they were trouble.

Stories of just what Russian soldiers were doing; raping, murdering, looting, stealing, destroying, were common place and I wanted no part of it.

"It amazes me people still live here," Edwards mumbled as we walked alongside the park.

Malks nodded in agreement. His gaze was on the twisted remains of swing set in the park, the only thing recognizable amongst the shell craters. "So much death," was all he said in a low whisper.

It was a clear day, the sky a light blue blotted with gray and black smoke clouds. Occasional fighter patrols would pass by overhead, buzzing the buildings with low passes. I still remained silent, eyes drifting from one bombed out building to the next. A knocked out halftrack sat near the edge of the block, half resting in a shell crater. We passed by without paying attention to the charred skeletons that were once German soldiers.

We rounded the corner and headed north through a deserted street towards an abandoned warehouse. We were to patrol the warehouse and look for anything out of the ordinary before walking another four blocks and then returning to our sector. I had to lead the squad east one more block before we could continue as the street was blocked by debris and the charred remains of two Tiger Tanks.

Cutting through a side alley, I was first out onto the street. Conditions were slightly better, the street clear of debris, save for a shell crater near a store front. Small groups of civilians moved around paying us no heed as they picked through the rubble of the buildings. They worked tirelessly to clear out the shattered bricks and mortar that marked where something once stood. An old man walked past us pushing a wheelbarrow loaded down with bricks, not even looking in our direction.

We continued on down the street as a Russian patrol approached from the opposite direction. They were a ragged group of soldiers, uniforms torn and caked with dirt, faces smeared with mud. While we walked in silence, they walked on talking on in Russian and joking with one another. The civilians quickly took note of the Red Army soldiers and began to move out of sight. Some shuffled over to our side of the street while others pulled deeper into the rubble piles. The women, young and old alike, quickly put us between them and the Russians.

"Just keep walking," I whispered as they passed by. Allies as they may be, no telling what they'd try to start. Thankfully they just strolled on by without a second glance at us. They were quickly past us and disappeared back around the corner.

I eased up a bit and we walked on, the civilians returning to their work. They toiled day in and day out, rebuilding their ruin of a city even with the Reds lurked about causing hell. At points I absolutely hated the Germans for everything that I'd went through, but when we were driving across Germany, that rage melted away. It wasn't Germans that my rage was at, it was the Nazis. The German people had suffered for putting their hopes in the hands of mad man and were paying for it dearly.

Part of daily patrols took us to a Red Cross aide station in between the US and Russian sectors that were still being officially drawn out. In the gray area of a few city blocks, Red Cross workers set up a hospital in the remains of school that hadn't been completely destroyed. Volunteer workers, from abroad and Germany alike, feverously tried to provide what they could for the civilians. On patrol we'd pass by to make sure things were running as smooth as could be and offering any type of help we could.

Doc was out in front of the squad right away as we approached the school. Groups of civilians in filthy, torn clothing gathered around out front while others stumbled in and out. Several Red Cross workers in dirtied white smocks, with red crosses, on them tended the people out front, handing out rations of food and medical aid. Doc checked in with the head nurse at the school to see what he could while the rest of us milled around outside.

I decided to head inside with Adam and Edwards while the others waited outside. Inside, the school the air was hot and stifling, feeling as if each breath I took had been breathed about a dozen times already. The smell was near suffocating, being a mix of filth, body odor, sweat, blood, and death. Pushing down the urge to vomit, I shuffled off to a classroom that acted as a recovery ward, for the injured.

Walking through row after row of bandaged civilians, many missing arms and legs, I found the man in charge of the small detachment of US soldiers stationed here with the Red Cross. Tall and lanky, Staff Sergeant Mitchell Burke was a hardened medic in command of six riflemen and two other medics, who helped out the Red Cross. Burke was a doctor back before the war, working in New York, but enlisted to help save soldiers.

"Yea, he won't be keeping this arm for long," Burke was saying to one of his medics. "Make sure he's comfortable for now and we'll see what can be done in a day or so."

"Hey, Doc Burke," I greeted once he was finished speaking.

Burke glanced over at me, his eyes and face drawn in exhaustion. "Captain, nice to see you again." He looked down at the patient lying before him. "The infection that's set into his arm is too strong to stop with antibiotics at this point. He'll lose the entire right arm to the shoulder or his blood will be poisoned and death will be…slow."

I could only look on in silence as the patient was a ten year old boy. Just as Doc Burke said an infection had turned his entire left arm a sickly greenish black, the blood in his veins became a poison.

"Doc, we brought some spare medical supplies. It's not a lot, but it's everything we could gather up." I said.

"At least it's something," Doc Burke sighed solemnly. "It's kids, old folks, and women that we handle here. Aside from POWs, I haven't seen one man older then sixteen or younger than fifty." Again he let out a heavy sigh and began to walk for towards a small teacher's room which was their break room, gesturing for me to follow.

"Russians giving you trouble?" I asked as we walked into the small, near empty room. All there was were an old wooden table, two couches and a few dozen pots set over portable heaters.

Doc Burke shook his head. "They don't be a bother once they see my boys. Guess the uniform tells them we aren't a bunch of unarmed relief workers. Coffee?" He held out a metal cup of steaming black liquid.

I waved it off. "We'll be able to stay maybe an hour today, so you have some more hands to help."

Again he shook his head. "That won't really be necessary. I got maybe thirty more volunteers the other day, all local civilians. This one woman seemed to be leading them I guess you could say. It was mostly women, some trained nurses and others were willing to help in anyway. For once we're not totally buried in sick and injured people."

I nodded, noticing Doc Burke looked as if he'd aged a few years in just a day. "How much longer will you be here?" I asked.

He shrugged. "I think my term of enlistment should be up soon. I don't even know for sure, maybe a few more weeks. You?" Doc asked.

"They're rotating the squad back to England in two weeks. It'll be home after that." I sighed as I thought of home. "Two weeks...two weeks."

One of the Red Cross workers appeared in the doorway behind us and called for Doc Burke. He finished off his coffee and moved for the door with me. In the hallway we parted our ways. "Safe travels, Captain Bolger," he said.

I didn't have any words and just offered a handshake with a head nod. Doc Burke disappeared into the school as I turned to walk back outside. Edwards and Adam were waiting by the front entrance handing out candy to the children that clustered around them. Several Red Cross workers stood behind a table, off to the right, helping with getting information on the civilians coming into the building. It was a simple attempt to try and get numbers on how many people they were helping in order to apply for needed medical supplies.

"Doc Burke says things are being handled," I called out to Edwards and Adams. "Let's give up anything we can spare and get moving."

Edwards nodded, heading outside to relay the orders while Adam remained at my side. Doc returned back to the main entrance after handing out whatever medical supplies he could. He gave all he could each time, keeping enough to make sure the squad was covered. I gave him an approving head nod, turning to head back outside myself when I bumped into one of the workers. The young woman was a local civilian volunteer carrying a tray of medical supplies, holding onto the tray even as I nearly knocked her down.

"My apologies, ma'am," I quickly said putting out my hands to catch her. She straightened up and mumbled some type of apology, seeming to be lost in her world. I was about to continue on when something caught my eye, a silver necklace just showing under her shirt collar.

"Excuse me, soldier," she said in accented English, though the accent was French and very familiar.

I gently grabbed her arm to stop her from walking off. She flinched at my touch. "Ma'am, I don't mean to bother you here, but what's your name?"

Now she looked up at me, pushing lose hair out of her face. My heart nearly stopped as I saw her face and she answered me. "Jessica."

My entire body went numb as I stared at this young woman, somewhat unbelieving of who I was seeing. "Jessica…" was all I could mumble as I recognized the gray eyes first and a flood of memories from the past summer swirled in my mind.

"Corrigan?" Jessica said, voice somewhat shaky. The realization hit both of us as we flung our arms around each other and hugged. Jessica was sobbing slightly and I could feel my eyes begin to water. We stood together in the tight embrace for what felt like an eternity, but was just a minute in realty.

pulled back lightly to look at her. "I love you," was the only words I managed to form as Jessica stood there with tears in her eyes.

"I love you too," she whispered. "I'm so happy to see you're safe."

Tears were slowly beginning to slip down my cheeks. "I…I thought I lost you. What happened, where did you go?"

Jessica broke our embrace to wipe tears from her face. "It's a lot to tell, Corr. I have to get back to work here, but…"

"Sir," Adam interrupted from off to the side. "Sir, Major Philips just radioed us. He wants us to return back to the road checkpoint for the rest of the patrol, sir. Another squad will cover out patrol route."

"Here," Jessica had scribbled down an address on a sheet of paper. "I'm staying with my mother and sister at their home. I'll be there tonight after I'm done here."

I took the paper and quickly slipped it into my pocket before tightly hugging her again. Just as painful as the first time, we parted ways as I left to carry on my duties and Jessica with hers.

"Nervous?" Edwards asked as he drove our jeep through recently cleared streets.

I shrugged, pulling on the sleeves of my jacket. "Reminds me of my first date back in high school," I admitted. Edwards gladly volunteered to drive me to her home on the edge of the American Sector.

"One of the most awkward nights of my life so far," Edwards laughed as he swerved around a pair of troop trucks.

I laughed slightly. "You and I will have a lot more to come."

Berlin still remained pitch black at night and it was adding to my anxiety. I was just dressed in my uniform with my jacket, everything else left behind at the apartment the military gave me to live in. Edwards still carried his Thompson next to his seat while I had to rely on my .45 sidearm which remained in its holster at my hip. My biggest worry was running into Russians, on the edge of our sector, or being attacked by any number of thugs that roamed the streets.

"So, just what are two doing anyway?" Edwards asked as he turned down a side road to dodge a column of idle Sherman tanks.

"Meeting her mother and sister," I answered. I reached down and pulled a large duffle bag into my lap. Inside were whatever foodstuffs I could take from the mess hall back at the barracks, a small gift.

Edwards nodded as he turned down Jessica's block. Most of the buildings and homes were blown apart, though a few were still standing in somewhat good shape. Edwards pulled the jeep to a stop out in front of a three story home, in the middle of the block. "I'll be back this way around midnight."

I nodded as I got out and slung the duffle over my shoulder. "I appreciate this a lot, Edwards."

He just grinned and shook his head. "You kids have fun."

I stood out in front of the door of the third floor apartment, heart racing and nerves on edge. The hallway was dark and I could see small bits of light sneaking from underneath the door. Settling my nerves, I lightly knocked on the door and straightened up a bit, nearly standing at attention. From inside I could hear the shuffling of feet on a wooden floor and then someone at the door, quickly undoing locks with a series of metallic clicks. A wide smile spread across my face as the door opened.

"Corr!" Jessica shouted with glee as she flung her arms around me and we hugged tightly. "I'm so happy to see you!"

"I'm overjoyed," I responded, as we parted and I looked at her. She was wearing a nicely fitting dark blue dress, something very simply designed, but nonetheless beautiful on, and it showed her marvelous figure. "You look beautiful tonight. Umm…not that you don't look beautiful all the time." Damn, I thought, stopped being nervous!

Jessica giggled. "Still a charmer, I see. Please, come in."

"Here," I handed over the duffle bag. "This is for and your family."

She took the bag with a smile. "Oh, that's very thoughtful of you. Thank you, so much."

I was ushered inside and brought to a small living room just down a small hallway from the front door. Jessica had me sit down on a small, dust covered couch. Jessica disappeared off into a small kitchen near the living room. I could hear two different voices besides hers speaking in German. My German had somewhat improved over time to where I understood it very well, but could hardly speak it in a coherent manner. I did pick up the other two voices were talking in amazement at this things I had brought over. What were simple rations to us was a full feast for the people of Berlin.

As I removed my jacket, the thing worn and faded, Jessica reappeared. Her bright smile was contagious as I began to smile, and she sat down next to me. "Well, you're still as beautiful as I remember," I said just speaking my mind.

"And you're still very blunt," she joked as our hands interlocked. "I'm so sorry I left without telling you."

I shook my head. "That doesn't matter to me. What matters to me is you." She nodded slightly and looked down at her hands. I took one of my hands and gentle lifted her chin up. Any anxiety I had was gone at that moment as our lips met and we kissed. I could feel a sense of calm washing through my body as we parted.

"I was separated from the HQ," Jessica explained referring back to the fighting in the Ardennes. "They wanted all civilians helping in the headquarters to leave when the Nazis were just outside the city limits. I was caught up in a group of fleeing refugees and moved east without knowing it. After a few days the group I was with past a column of German troops and then I realized I was behind the lines."

She paused to take a breath. I sat quietly listening, still holding her hands. "I decided it wouldn't be safe to try and get back to the Allies, I headed back to Germany. I'm sure you can tell by now that I'm half German on my father's side. That was why I didn't tell you my last name at time, but it's Webber. Having a German last name in France was in no way good.

"Anyway, it was a long trip to reach Berlin. To keep as safe as I could, I traveled with groups of refugees, walking the entire way. I managed to get into Berlin in early April and found my mother and sister. All we could do was hide in the basement here for weeks until the surrender. It was an unbelievable joy to see the first soldiers to pass by our home were Americans. The Russians…well…"

I squeezed her hands lightly. "I know about what they do."

Jessica controlled her sobs. "Once the fighting was over, my sister and I found the Red Cross and began to help out as best we could. Then…then I found you."

We kissed again as another woman walked out from the kitchen. Giggling slightly, Jessica's sister introduced herself to me. While Emma, that was her name, looked so much like Jessica, I felt like I've seen her before. It wasn't her resemblance to her sister, but it was something else I could not remember.

"I…Corrigan," I introduced myself in my terrible German. "Nice meet you."

Again Emma giggled, telling her older sister in German that I was cute. Jessica responded by saying I was handsome and then adding that I understood German a lot better then I spoke it. This made Emma blush before returning to the kitchen.

"I'm sorry, she can be very straight forward sometimes," Jessica told me with a slight laugh.

I shrugged. "A family trait I see."

Jessica nodded, taking my compliment. "It can get annoying after awhile, just giving fair warning." She spoke English incredibly well compared to the last time we spoke.

"So you are French and German then?" I asked out of curiosity and not meaning any disrespect.

She nodded. "My mother is from Caen and my father was from here, Berlin. He served in the Great War with the German Army, but he passed away just after the Invasion of Poland from a heart attack."

There was the creak of footsteps on the floor and I looked up to see Jessica's mother walk in. She was just like other German civilians I've seen, the same look of desperation on her face. I quickly stood up, nearly standing at attention as Jessica introduced her to me and me to her.

"Mother," she said speaking in German, "this is Corrigan. Corrigan, this is my mother, Helen."

"Evening, ma'am," I managed to say clearly in German. "It's a pleasure to meet you."

Mrs. Webber looked me over, her eyes very judging. "How old are you?"

I glanced at Jessica for a second. "Just turned twenty-two, ma'am." I had answered in English and Jessica translated an answer. Mrs. Webber nodded, still looking me over.

"And an officer," she sighed. I was getting nervous all over again as I felt very unwelcome by Mrs. Webber. I hoped this wasn't how the rest of the night would go when she suddenly moved close to me and tightly hugged me, sobbing. "Thank you for keeping my girl safe, thank you so much."

I glanced over at Jessica who spoke to me in English. "I told her all about you when I came home." She gently lifted up my necklace from the collar of her shirt. "I kept it safe, just as you asked."

The evening went extremely well from then on. Mrs. Webber and Emma were full of questions about me and asked all throughout a small meal. It ranged from my life back home, my time in basic training, and then everything from Oran all the way up to when I arrived in Berlin. They were overjoyed when I told them I landed at Normandy; a day they told me gave them hope for an end to Hitler's Germany.

I told them what I could for each question, though I left out those details that were too painful or too gruesome to repeat. I left out everything about St. Lo, those memories still locked away in the darker parts of my mind. Of course I had my own questions to ask, though it was just polite small talk until I asked, very carefully, about Jessica's father. Mrs. Webber, pushing back a few tears, spoke cheerfully and lovingly about Jacob Webber. The man served Germany proudly as an eighteen year old rifleman in the Imperial German Army. He had even won the Iron Cross, Second Class for his acts during the fighting in Belleau Wood, the same place where my father was wounded in the shoulder by a German bullet.

They asked me about my parents, my family, home. Emma was interested in hearing of my brother Matt, though I gently added he was seeing someone. Mrs. Webber asked about my own parents, curious on what they were like. It turned out that she, just like my mother, was a nurse and spent spare time working as a librarian. As the night went on, it made me wonder just how I could've once hated the Germans when they had so much in common with me. Such was the naive nature of a soldier.

As the night was rolling on, I couldn't stop thinking that I knew Emma from somewhere or that she looked so familiar to me. Neither of us have been outside our respective countries and it wasn't from her very close likeness to Jessica. When I noticed a small framed picture of a German soldier on their mantel, the man looking out wasn't Jessica's father.

"Emma, forgive me for being so straight forward, but were you seeing a German soldier?"

Her faced flushed red and I felt terrible for asking. "I…yes, my boyfriend was a soldier. He joined just after Hitler came to power. He…he was killed in Sicily."

Then it hit me. I reached into my back pocket where I kept the picture I picked up from the airport back in Sicily. I didn't know why I felt compelled to hang onto it, but I did. I withdrew the small, worn picture and held it out for Jessica to see. The look on her face said it all.

"Then this…would be yours." I handed over the picture, Emma's face suddenly displaying shock with a mix of happiness and sadness. Everyone was silent for several moments.

"Did you…did you…" I knew what she was trying to ask.

I shook my head. "I don't know if I did, there were two other soldiers with me and we cleared out the room so fast…I don't know."

I half expected her to stand up and slap me across the face. Instead she stood up and flung her arms around me, hugging tightly and sobbing. In between sobs, I could hear he mumble thank you over and over again for the picture. I was at a loss for words, unbelieving this young woman didn't out right hate me.

By the time midnight rolled around and Edwards was waiting outside in the jeep, I felt as if I had known Jessica's family my entire life. After exchanging goodbyes and hugs with Mrs. Webber and Emma, Jessica and I stood just at the front door, standing in each other's arms. I had given her the address of the apartment the military gave me and were saying goodbye and good night. We lingered as we kissed, an energy flowing between us, but Edwards had to call out from the jeep and our moment ended.

The hard rumble of artillery echoed off in the distance, another shower of dust drifting down on us. Ramos and I were laying on the top floor of bombed out building, cautiously watching a group of German troops pass by with a Panzer IV. Off in the far distance, through the haze of smoke and the low light, I could make out the shattered steeple of the cathedral of St. Lo.

Ramos nudged me, moving only slightly to avoid attracting any attention. I glanced over at him and he nodded over at the building across the street, a German OP. I looked down at my watch to see how long we had been laying there and saw it had been two hours since Hiller sent us out scouting. I pulled out my map and scribbled down the location of the post when a piece of rubble came loose from the shutter of artillery. It tumbled down to the ground with a loud clatter that startled the passing Germans.

The group of soldiers looked up at our position as Ramos and I froze, hoping they couldn't see anything. One soldier aimed his rifle our way as if looking for us and then fired. The shot went wide and hit somewhere below our position, but the others suddenly opened up as if under attack. Ramos and I quickly crawled away from the window and made for the doorway when the Panzer fired.

The hard explosion of the tank fire suddenly blossomed into a roaring bomb blast as the world warped to blackness and I shot up from my bed. My heart was racing and sweat soaked my chest and face. I was breathing in ragged intervals as I struggled to collect my breath, another nightmare passing by.

The small bedroom I was in was pitch black, no light coming from the window looking out at the street. Slowly I calmed a bit when I heard something off in the kitchen near the front of the apartment. Quickly, I grabbed my .45 sidearm from its holster on the nightstand next to the bed. Quietly, I slid the slide back and thumbed the safety before reaching for the oil lamp next to it.

I heard footsteps in the hallway outside of the bedroom. I remained in the bed and aimed the .45 at the doorway, keeping my free hand on the oil lamp. Listening closely, I waited until the person was in the doorway to turn up the flame. Light suddenly cut though the dark and I sat up, pistol aimed at the intruder. The second my eyes took to adjust, I lowered the weapon with a heavy sigh.

"Jessica?" I mumbled in confusion.

"Sorry, I didn't mean to startle you," Jessica responded as she walked into the bedroom towards me. She was still wearing that wonderful dress from before with a light jacket over her shoulders.

"What are you doing here? Is something wrong?" I asked placing my pistol back in its holster. It would be a risky trip, traveling as far as she did in Berlin alone, even more so at night.

She sat down on the edge of the bed. I realized I was just wearing a thin pair of Army issue boxers and quickly pulled the blanket over my lap. That got a giggle from Jessica. "Still modest."

I shrugged, now fully awake. "Very," I remarked sarcastically.

"Umm, nothing is wrong, Corr. I…I just wanted to see you. I was hoping to get here before you fell asleep, but you were asleep when I got here," she said.

"I…wait, how'd you get in?" I asked.

Jessica smiled. "Do you not lock doors in America?"

I thought back, realizing that I didn't lock the door. I sat up a little more and slid closer to Jessica. "Well, sleep is very overrated and I won't make you leave."

Jessica looked up at me. "I wanted to just…be with you. I've had trouble sleeping and…well I don't know."

I placed my arm across her shoulders. "Nightmares?"

She nodded. "Do…you have them too?"

"Yea…from time to time I do," I admitted.

Jessica sobbed lightly. "How do you handle it?"

I sighed, thinking of the right words. "It's not so much handling it, but more accepting it. I've had these nightmares since St. Lo, it was just…awful what we saw there. I'm reliving moments from then in the dreams and no words can describe just how horrible it was. I try not to think on about them too much. I try to remember those we lost so they won't be forgotten and then I focus on the future."

Jessica had slowed her sobbing and wiped tears from her cheeks, slipping off her jacket. She was calmer now, regaining her composure. "The future…what are your plans?"

"Going home," I answered, "but I don't want to do it alone."

I felt nervous as Jessica looked up at me, taking in just what I said. "You…you want me to go to America with you?"

I nodded. "Yea, I want you to come back with me, but I wouldn't want to take you from your family."

She waved off thought, tears welling in her eyes. "Corr, my family would want me to leave Germany and start a better life. I can't think of a better life then one with you."

I began to smile, kissing her lightly on the lips. Jessica had the same smile on her face as we kissed again, this time with a much stronger passion. We seemed to meld into each other's arms as the passion between us grew. As the oil in the lamp burned out, Jessica had slipped the dress off her shoulders and let it fall to the floor before the room was dark again.

The squad left Berlin two weeks later during the first week of June, but not before attending my wedding. The ceremony was small and simple, Jessica wearing her best dress which was a light blue summer dress that, even being a little worn and faded, looked just beautiful on her, and me in my olive dress uniform with my handful of medals, something presented to me by Major Philips.

We were married in a small church in Berlin that did not take much damage during the fighting with just a rather small amount of people present. Both Jessica's mother and sister attended along with her grandparents and an uncle from a small suburb outside of the city. My entire squad sat by watching as well, all in dress uniforms with Jay standing as my best man. Major Philips was present as well, a man much hardened by war with Sergeant Smith and the surviving ten men of his squad. Some of the women Jessica had worked with at the hospital sat by as well, all smiles and tears for their friend.

The squad was together one final time as we made the long trip across Europe and then to England. In England each one of us received our discharge papers before being told when we would be taken home by ship. As fate would have it, we would not be heading home together. So on our last night together in England we gathered in pub in London and we spent the night drinking and talking about… well everything from training all the way up to Berlin, making sure to pay respects to those who didn't get to see the end of the war. Then, when the night was nearly over, we exchanged out goodbyes. Some of the men kept a cheerful outlook, though a handful let a few tears slip through. I shared some final words with each member of the squad, shaking hands and giving hugs to the people I just spent nearly five years living, fighting, and bleeding with and had become so tightly bonded with. Lastly, we took one final picture together, Jessica included, as a squad. After that night, the war for us was over. I loved each and every one of them and had done my one true duty as a soldier, I brought my brothers home alive.

Epilogue

"Just what's left for us to do? Just suddenly return home, put the war out of minds, and pick up our lives where we left off? For Christ sake, we've just spent about five years fighting and killing other people. There is no way to just walk away from all that and say it's the 'past.' This war changed the world, changed us. Both were not for the good. God help us.".

Captain Corrigan Bolger, US Army

Major Jasper Philips

Major Philips continued to serve with the First Infantry Division after the war ended, serving in Berlin for the next two years. He was promoted to colonel in 1947 and then served in the Korean War. Philips didn't make it past the rank of colonel when the war ended, instead choosing to accept an honorable discharge from the Army and retiring to a quiet patch of land in Georgia. A quiet and simple life helped wash away some of his horrible memories of war, though he returned to the Army after his wife passed away and the Vietnam War broke out. Philips worked in logistics at the Pentagon, though he became very distained with how the troops were being led in the field. Another honorable discharge in 1973 and Philips returned back to his small Georgia farm and began writing his memoirs. He passed peacefully in his sleep at the age of 79 with his family, one full of soldiers, around him.

Sergeant Jeffery Smith

Smith made the jump into Holland during Operation Market Garden, fighting through the entire operation before being wounded in the thigh by shrapnel while storming a Flack 88. One Purple Heart and two months later, Sergeant Smith fought bravely with the men of the 82nd and 101st Airborne in Bastogne, earning a Silver Star for saving the lives of stranded tank crew. Again, he jumped into combat during Operation Varsity, serving on the front lines until the end of the war. Smith left the military after VJ-Day, returning to Iowa and his loving wife, one of many women overjoyed to have their husbands or sons or brothers return home. Smith moved his family to Delaware and settled down working as a police officer. He would have three sons and a daughter, his sons becoming paratroopers themselves and serving in Vietnam while his daughter became nurse in a veteran's hospital. Smith retired from the police force as a detective and lives his days happily with his wife, the two more then overjoyed, to spend their time fussing over there eight grandchildren.

Lieutenant Harold Gram

L.T. Gram redeployed with the First Armor Division after the Bulge, gaining fifteen more tank kills until March, 1945. While on patrol on March 12th, 1945, his tank was hit by several AT rockets which killed all but Gram and Sergeant Donovan in the process. In the attack, Gram lost two fingers on his left hand and took shrapnel wounds to his chest and back. Gram was discharged several days before the Germans surrendered. While recovering in a hospital in England, Gram met a young British girl, who he would fall in love with and marry several months later. The two found a home near Fort Knox, Kentucky, Gram returning to the Army as a tank instructor. Gram left the Army in 1968 after his son, a US Marine, was killed in fighting in Hue City, Vietnam. Living with many fond memories of their son, Gram lives with his wife peacefully to this day.

Sergeant Ronald Donovan

Sergeant Donovan honorably served alongside L.T. Gram through the rest of the war. Donovan was wounded when his tank was ambushed on March 12th, 1945. While surviving the attack, Sergeant Donovan lost his left hand to the wrist and burned twenty percent of his lungs. After his discharge and a seven month stay in an English hospital, Donovan returned to his home in Kentucky, keeping close ties to his close friend Harold Gram. Despite the loss of one hand and near loss of a lung, Donovan maintains his easy going personality, though the horrors of war still haunt his dreams to this day.

Corporal Doug 'Doc' Tavin

Doc returned to his home in Long Island just before VJ Day in August. With his experience as a medic, in combat, Doc returned to medical school to finish what he left undone when he enlisted. In 1947, Doc worked as an ER surgeon in New York City for twelve years. After leaving the hospital, he moved to Washington D.C. to work at Walter Reed Hospital. Doc later met and married a young nurse during his work and would settle down, having two daughters and a son. Doc would work to save lives until dying of a heart attack at the age of 51.

Corporal Nathanial James

Nate worked to recover the life he had left behind in New York and supported his sister. He spent his first few years back home finding a job as a police officer while he tried to settle back into life away from war. In his second year home, Nate married a school teacher a year younger than himself; his new and wonderful wife smoothing out the rough edges left by the war. The two eventually had a daughter, which gave Nate his rock in the world. He and his wife continue to live in New York

Corporal Adam Sullivan

Adam, our highly skilled radio operator, picked up his small town life in Maine when we arrived back home. His family, having closed down their fishing business due to U-boat attacks, was on the edge of financial collapse. With his full pension from the Army and the U-boat threat gone, Adam restarted the family business in just several months. In a year's time, the family business had developed into a thriving fishing company with a fleet of three dozen boats. Once he secured the business, Adam started his own repair shop for electronics. In 1947, Adam married and would later have three sons and a daughter. All three of his sons would later enlist in the Army and fight in Vietnam. Much to Adam's relief, all three came home unharmed. Still managing his repair business and the family fishing company, he lives peacefully with his wife on the Maine coast.

Sergeant Hank McGee

Hank, still the same restless soul he was before the war, couldn't find peace in civilian life. Just four months back and he was being arrested for assault in relation to bar brawls. Hank was slowly slipping into full alcoholism by 1950…and the Korean War. Desperate to turn himself around and be back in the fight, Hank reenlisted and was made a Lieutenant for his service in World War II. Hank found himself again during the war, being the same dedicated soldier he was back in North Africa, Sicily, France, and Germany. First Lieutenant Hank McGee was killed in action on December 9th, 1952 defending his hill top position from an attack by Chinese armor and infantry. He is posthumously awarded the Silver Star for his actions, reports claiming he managed to wipe out two enemy platoons of infantry before dying.

Corporal Mitch Phelps

Phelps was never able to enjoy the world without war after spending nearly five years to end it. Phelps made it home in early September 1945, and spent the next month living with his parents while saving up for his own home. On January 3rd, 1946, while returning home from working in the Brooklyn Naval Yards, Mitch Phelps was struck and killed by a speeding car. He left behind a young fiancé carrying his son. Phelps never got to see his son, Franklin, grow up and honor his father by enlisting in the Navy at the age of 18.

Sergeant John Mangon

Mangon found work in construction in New York just two weeks after arriving home from Europe. Mangon worked multiple construction jobs across New York, eventually starting his own construction company in 1949. When the Korean War broke out in early in the 1950's, Mangon left his company to his older brother and father before reenlisting in the Army. Instead of being placed back in combat, Mangon would remain stateside during the entire war training members of the Army Corps of Engineers. He would remain in the Army after the war ended, eventually being honorably discharged in 1960 at the rank of Major. Mangon continues to help his brother run the construction company, had married while he was still in the Army. Eventually Mangon left the company to his daughter and her husband, retiring to Pennsylvania with his wife to live the remainder of his life quietly.

Sergeant Jose Ramos

Ramos remained in England when he was discharged, declining the ship ride back to the States. Instead, he reenlisted in the Army and returned to Germany as part of the Garrison Force in Berlin. He would remain in Berlin until 1949, marrying a local girl before his discharge. With tension rising between NATO and the Soviet Union, Ramos left Germany with his wife and returned to the States. Having saved up a large sum of money from his military pension and pay, he bought a large piece of land in Vermont and found work as a state trooper. Ramos found his little piece of Heaven and lived the average life his time in the Army made him crave. Ramos would have two daughters and a son, seeing them off into the world before retiring with his wife, Shelia. Ramos still lives with his wife on their land in Vermont.

Corporal Donald Malks

Malks moved back to his home state of West Virginia after the war, meeting his two year old daughter for the first time. The stern, collected Malks broke down in tears as Kayla called him 'Daddy.' Back home with his loving wife, Audrey, and daughter, Malks found work as a local police officer. As the years past, Malks devoted himself fully to his daughter and wife, making up for lost time tenfold. After twenty years of being a police officer, Malks became Chief of Police of his small town. Donald Malks retired from the police department at the age of 59 and now spends his time with his wife, enjoying a quiet life far from the war we all left behind.

Corporal Abe Sanders

Sanders picked up his small town life in Georgia after the war, obtaining his previous job in his father's textile factory. Working there for the next several years, Sanders would marry a local girl named Margaret and enjoy a loving marriage until the start of the Korean War. In 1951, Sanders left for Korea with the US Army and would fight on through to the end of the war. Just weeks before the Armistice in 1953, Sanders was out on patrol with his squad when a Chinese platoon ambushed them. Staff Sergeant Abe Sanders was killed in action, July 10th, 1953, while defending his squad from Chinese forces just North of the 38th Parallel. He is posthumously awarded the Bronze Star for his action and duty.

Sergeant Jonathan Edwards

Edwards took his discharge from the Army, marrying that young clerk in England the first chance he had. The two moved back to the States and would find a home in Albany, New York where Edwards became an electrician. His wife, Rebecca, worked at a local law firm taking up clerical duties, much like during her time with the Air Force. It wasn't too long before Edwards became a father, his first son being born in the summer of 1946 followed by a daughter in September, 1947. Edwards and I would remain in close contact with one another after the war, meeting every now and again to remain good friends. Edwards still lives a relaxed life in New York with his wife, both his children off in the world; his son a pilot in the Air Force and daughter working in journalism.

Corporal Vincent Lenatie

Vic returned to his middle of nowhere home town in North Carolina after the war. He quickly developed a knack working on cars and found a job as a mechanic, opening his own auto body shop in 1946. Vic, still a hard edged drinker and smoker, remained unmarried as his he opened up another auto body shop in a neighboring town. By 1951, Vic had a success, albeit on a small scale--an auto body chain running through North Carolina and found himself collecting a comfortable amount of money. In 1952, Vic married a young woman from South Carolina, but it would only end in divorce in 1959. Vincent Lenatie would die of a heart attack in 1969; he left behind a single son.

Lieutenant Jay Hawkins

Jay remained in the Army after the war, though not in an active combat role. Instead, he was promoted to a Captain and transferred Fort Benning, Georgia. In 1946, Jay was officially an Army Ranger with the 75th Ranger Battalion. He would never enter front line combat--instead training future Rangers in becoming elite Scout Snipers. While working with the Rangers, Jay met and married his wife, Catherine, a local teacher, in 1949. Until his discharged in 1974, Jay worked tirelessly in training snipers before leaving the military and returning to New Jersey. With his wife, Jay settled in Trenton before retiring. Just like Edwards, we remain in contact with each other and are still friends, forever bonded as brothers from our time in the Army.

Captain Corrigan Bolger

Newly married and honorably discharged from the Army, Jessica and I moved back to the New Jersey, quickly starting the family we both wanted. Together, Jessica and I had two sons, Shawn and Philip. I became a fire fighter and Jessica became involved with nursing, finding a love for helping out children the most. The war was over for us, though the scars were still there, physical and mental alike. St. Lo still haunts my dreams to this day, the graveyard city, one of many horrible memories that never left me. Even still, I had the memories of the squad, my men who became my brothers that fought alongside me for three long years. Jessica helped the wounds heal.

Would you like to see your manuscript become a book?

If you are interested in becoming a PublishAmerica author, please submit your manuscript for possible publication to us at:

acquisitions@publishamerica.com

You may also mail in your manuscript to:

**PublishAmerica
PO Box 151
Frederick, MD 21705**

www.publishamerica.com

CPSIA information can be obtained at www.ICGtesting.com
Printed in the USA
LVOW101020101111

254358LV00001B/242/P